STUDIES IN MODERN BRITISH RELIGIOUS HISTORY

Volume 18

The
Royal Army Chaplains' Department
1796–1953

Clergy under Fire

STUDIES IN MODERN BRITISH RELIGIOUS HISTORY

ISSN: 1464–6625

This series aims to differentiate 'religious history' from the narrow confines of church history, investigating not only the social and cultural history of religion, but also theological, political and institutional themes, while remaining sensitive to the wider historical context; it thus advances an understanding of the importance of religion for the history of modern Britain, covering all periods of British history since the Reformation.

Previously published volumes in this series are listed at the back of this volume.

The
Royal Army Chaplains' Department
1796–1953

Clergy under Fire

MICHAEL SNAPE

with a foreword by Richard Holmes

THE BOYDELL PRESS

First published 2008
The Boydell Press, Woodbridge

ISBN 978–1–84383–346–8

The Boydell Press is an imprint of Boydell & Brewer Ltd
PO Box 9, Woodbridge, Suffolk IP12 3DF, UK
and of Boydell & Brewer Inc.
Mt Hope Avenue, Rochester, NY 14620, USA
website: www.boydellandbrewer.com

A CIP catalogue record for this book is available from the British Library

This publication is printed on acid-free paper

Typeset by Pru Harrison, Hacheston, Suffolk
Printed in Great Britain by
Antony Rowe Ltd, Chippenham, Wiltshire

Contents

Illustrations

(Between pages 270 and 271)

This book is dedicated to Hugh McLeod
for two decades of his inspiration and friendship

Foreword

Throughout my working life the British army chaplain – the padre, in that time-honoured term – has been a familiar figure. As a Territorial infantry officer for thirty-six years I served alongside all sorts and conditions of padres. I still have affectionate memories of the padre of the battalion I commanded, who dispensed wise counsel and generous hospitality in equal measure, but who never quite let me forget that not all his business was of this world. As an academic I have often found myself speaking at conferences or study days organised by chaplains in Germany or Britain, for my work on what we now call the moral component of fighting power emphasises that there is a strong spiritual thread running through the soldier's psyche.

Lastly, for a historian with a particular interest in the British army, the padre has never been very far away. At the moment I am working on the Duke of Marlborough, one of whose senior chaplains (Francis Hare according to some, but Josiah Sandby in the opinion of others) kept a useful journal of the duke's campaigns. On the eve of the battle of Blenheim he wrote: 'No body can express the courage and joy which both officers and soldiers showed, when they thought they should come to an engagement.' In an earlier literary venture I encountered Wellington's chaplain Samuel Briscall, warned by the great man to keep his sermons short: 'Briscall, say as much as you like in five and twenty minutes. I shall not stay longer.'

Padres were also much in evidence in British India, a subject that deserves a further book. I cannot deny a special regard for Father Bertrand (not, strictly speaking, an army padre at all, but a civilian clergyman) when he went about giving quiet consolation to the troops preparing to storm Delhi in 1857. He asked the commanding officer of the 75th Highlanders for permission to bless the men, saying: 'We may differ, some of us, in matters of religion, but the blessing of an old man and a clergyman can do nothing but good.' There was widespread approval.

However, it was when I was researching the British soldier on the Western Front in 1914–18 that I became especially concerned with the role and impact of the padre. It seemed to me that the debate on the merits of padres had, like so much else, been hijacked by the historiography of the 1920s and beyond. Officers and soldiers actually serving at the front during the war were, by the testimony of their letters and diaries, often far more aware of their own spirituality, and grateful for the solace provided by a good padre, than we tend to believe. Michael Snape and I certainly do not agree on every detail, but it is clear that we are both persuaded, as he puts it in an earlier book, *God and the British Soldier*, that 'the army's most senior and influential commanders in both World Wars shared the apparently reasonable and well-founded conviction that religion was a crucial and sustaining force for the morale of their citizen soldiers'. There was no escaping the fact that many soldiers judged religion not in terms of abstract theology, but by the men who brought it to them. Colonel Walter Nicholson, who spent most of the war on the Western Front, had a high regard for a particular Wesleyan padre ('I never met a finer Christian') but thought, more generally, that 'when the padres were good, they were very, very good, but when they were bad they were awful'.

It is remarkable that no proper history of the Royal Army Chaplains' Department, the branch of the service to which padres belong, had been undertaken before Michael Snape embarked upon this book. Of course, the subject is scarcely virgin territory. On the one hand Sir John Smyth's 1968 official history *In This Sign Conquer* provided a wonderful series of anecdotes of chaplains and chaplaincy, though it did not begin to chart the real history of the Department, interwoven, as it inevitably was, with rich and complex threads of political, ecclesiastical and military history. On the other hand, scholars have examined particular aspects of military chaplaincy, sometimes considering specific denominations or national groups, or considering the importance of military padres in a specific conflict. The question of the apparent role conflict between the chaplain as military officer and as minister of religion has also generated at least as much heat as light, and will no doubt continue to do so.

Yet the fact remains that a properly sourced history, beginning with the eighteenth century and taking the Department's story on to the twentieth, has been long overdue. Michael Snape's narrative has several great strengths. First, it is solidly based on primary sources. There are times when the author is evidently delighted to deploy a telling anecdote: when J. C. Edghill (a future Chaplain-General) installed a communion table in his church at Aldershot, the district commander, the evangelical General Sir James Hope Grant, sent round a Royal Engineers carpenter with orders to shorten its legs. Yet these individual stories never bend the book's structure out of shape, and that structure is forged from robust sources. Next, the Department's history is considered, as surely it must be, in the context of church history in Britain. Different denominations played their own social and political roles. We can scarcely think of the history of Ireland, that nursery of so many fine soldiers, without reflecting on Roman Catholicism's long ascent to emancipation. Presbyterianism had a particular importance for Scotland and Northern Ireland, while Methodism was to flourish with the Industrial Revolution, especially in areas like Wales and Cornwall. The Department mirrored the ebb and flow of army strength more generally: it had a Chaplain-General, 117 commissioned chaplains and 37 acting chaplains in August 1914, and by November 1918 contained almost two thousand Anglican padres, to say nothing of hundreds of chaplains of other Christian denominations, and sixteen Jewish chaplains too. And, like other arms and services, its status often reflected the whirls and eddies of ministerial bureaucracy.

Of course, there were tensions. Some clergymen, especially in the nineteenth century, felt that their officer status made it harder for them to relate to ordinary soldiers, and one Chaplain-General felt that it was a mistake to wear uniform. For many years Methodists were not prepared to accept commissions, though they would serve as acting chaplains. On the one hand, relations between chaplains of various denominations were not always comfortable; on the other, denominational hierarchies did not always work smoothly with the Department. There were repeated attempts to ensure that the Chaplain-General was a Church of England bishop, and a former Chaplain-General was barred from one diocese after carrying out a confirmation in barracks without the local bishop's permission. In war, many chaplains felt it difficult to be sure whether they were, as one put it, 'Mr. God or M. Cinema'. Were they primarily concerned with welfare support, or with saving men's souls?

Yet the story is, on the whole, a positive one. The Royal Army Chaplains' Department has evolved to reflect changes in religious practice and opinion. Although his appointment lies outside the parameters of this book, the Department now administers an imam on behalf of the Ministry of Defence. The crucible of war has often burnt off inter-denominational markings. In 1917 a Church of Scotland chaplain thought that: 'It might amaze our domestic bigots, of all faiths, to find Jesuit priest and Presbyterian minister working and sleeping in wondrous unity.' In 2004 the bodies of some Iraqi insurgents, killed in a fierce battle near Al Amarah, were taken back to the nearby British base and prepared for handover to their relatives. The process was monitored by the unit's padre, and there was widespread recognition amongst soldiers present that decency went beyond the detail of religious belief. At such a time, even the products of a non-deferential, interest-led society were clear that the padre could offer something that nobody else could.

I come to the subject with the shakiest of beliefs, and my opinion of this admirable book is not fuelled by personal religious conviction. Changes in liturgy have done away with so many of the comfortable words I learnt as a boy that I no longer know where I stand, and seldom a day passes when my belief does not lose its mental battle with agnosticism. Yet my dealings with chaplains across more than forty years have done much to sustain a spirituality that goes beyond creed or catechism. If I had to sum up the feelings of so many soldiers who reach that point when life's clock stops (sometimes just for a second or two, but sometimes for ever) as they confront mortal danger, it would be in the words of a padre who served in the Falklands in 1982. Many of his soldiers believed in a God who might not turn away a bullet, but who would not turn away a soul in need.

All my instincts as a historian persuade me that modern battle often resembles historical combat more closely than it does any other aspect of contemporary affairs, and that, in the words of a wise jurist, those engaged in it do not lose their responsibility to their fellow human beings and to God. As Michael Snape shows so well in the pages that follow, the Royal Army Chaplains' Department is the product of a complex process of evolution, and it would be unrealistic to expect that process to stop. Yet I have no doubt that there will be a Department to discuss in a century's time, for it stands like a rock, with the tides of popular religiosity, politics, and military bureaucracy surging about its base, testimony to the fact that the human spirit remains fundamental to soldiers and to soldiering.

Richard Holmes, November 2006

Acknowledgements

I am extremely grateful to the Ven. John Blackburn and to the Royal Army Chaplains' Department Association for inviting me to write this new history of the Royal Army Chaplains' Department. This project was facilitated by Prof. Iain Torrance, now of Princeton Theological Seminary, and was helped to completion by the unfailing support of the Rev. David Wilkes C.F. It was funded by a generous research grant from the Royal Army Chaplains' Department Association, to which all royalties will be paid. This project represents my third, and final, full-length study of the history of religion in the British army, my earlier books being *The Redcoat and Religion* (Routledge, 2005) and *God and the British Soldier* (Routledge, 2005). I am also very grateful to Prof. Stephen Taylor, Prof. Arthur Burns and Ms. Caroline Palmer for accepting this volume as part of Boydell's series of Studies in Modern British Religious History and I am indebted to Prof. Richard Holmes for kindly agreeing to write its foreword and to the Rev. Andrew Totten C.F. for his help in selecting its illustrations.

Many minds have helped to stimulate and inform this study. Among others, I am grateful to Prof. Gary Sheffield, Dr. John Bourne, Dr. Bob Bushaway, Dr. Bob Watt, Mr. Nigel Dorrington and Mr. Alun Evans of the University of Birmingham's War and Society seminar; to Prof. Hugh McLeod, Prof. John Briggs and Dr. Stephen Parker of the University of Birmingham's History of Religion seminar; to Prof. John Hick, Prof. Michael Goulder and Dr. Marius Felderhof of the University of Birmingham's Open End seminar and to Prof. Tim Larsen of Wheaton College; Prof. Callum Brown of the University of Dundee; Prof. Jim McMillan and Dr. Jeremy Crang of the University of Edinburgh; Prof. Keith Robbins and Prof. Densil Morgan of the University of Wales and to the Rev. Dr. Peter Howson for an early sight of his article on chaplains' casualties in the Second World War. I am also obliged to three of my research students, namely the Rev. Kevin Bell C.F., Mr. Neville Benyon and Mr. John Brennan, all of whom have been lively, informative and entertaining sources of inspiration.

Over several years of research and writing, I have incurred major debts to a number of archivists and librarians. The greatest of these is to Mr. David Blake, curator of the Royal Army Chaplains' Department Museum at Amport House, who has proved a constant source of references, timely discussion and sound practical advice. Quite simply, this study would have been impossible without him. Sr. Eileen Grant was also a generous and helpful host at the Department's Roman Catholic archives at Bulford Camp, as was Dom. Philip Jebb at Downside Abbey and Dr. Gareth Lloyd at the Methodist Archives and Research Centre at the University of Manchester. Special mention is also due to the inter-library loan staff at the University of Birmingham as they have been unfailingly helpful, and surprisingly successful, in dealing with a constant stream of obscure requests on my part.

Last, but by no means least, in the course of writing this book I have been massively reliant on the love, patience and understanding of my long-suffering wife, Rachel, and my fantastic daughters Katy and Helena. I can now look forward to spending much more time with all of them.

Copyright Acknowledgements

The author would like to thank Mr. C.L.J. Leaney, Rev. Arthur Royall, Mrs. Marjorie Jones, the relatives of C.I.S. Hood, Mr. Martin Rogers, Dr. M.E.N. Downing, Mrs. E. Franks, Mr. James Quinn, Mr. John and Mrs Rosemary Chambers and a Mrs. Ball for permission to cite from copyright material held in the Imperial War Museum's Department of Documents. He would also like to thank Mr. David Baron, the Trustees of the British Museum, the Trustees of the National Library of Scotland and the Trustees of Lambeth Palace Library for permission to quote or to reproduce material held in their collections. All Mass-Observation material is reproduced with permission of Curtis Brown Group Ltd, London, on behalf of the Trustees of the Mass-Observation Archive, Copyright © Trustees of the Mass-Observation Archive. All Imperial War Museum photographs are used with the permission of the Trustees of the Imperial War Museum, London. Every reasonable effort has been made to contact the owners of copyright material used in this book but this has proved impossible in certain cases. The author would be grateful for any information that might lead to further copyright acknowledgements in future editions of this book and extends his apologies in advance for any omissions in the present volume.

Abbreviations

A.A.G.	Assistant Adjutant-General
A.B.A.	Archdiocese of Birmingham Archives
A.C.G.	Assistant Chaplain-General
A.Ch.D.	Army Chaplains' Department
A.G.	Adjutant-General
A.L.R.P.C.	Angus Library, Regent's Park College
A.P.C.	Assistant Principal Chaplain
A.S.R.S.F.S.	Army Scripture Readers' and Soldiers' Friend Society
A.T.A.	Army Temperance Association
A.T.S.	Auxiliary Territorial Service
B.A.O.R.	British Army of the Rhine
B.A.S.R.S.	British Army Scripture Readers' Society
B.B.C.	British Broadcasting Corporation
B.E.F.	British Expeditionary Force
B.L.	British Library
C.B.	Companion of the Bath
C.C.S.	Casualty Clearing Station
C.C.W.W.F.	Committee of the Churches' Work for Women in the Forces
C.E.M.S.	Church of England's Men's Society
C.F.	Chaplain to the Forces
C.G.	Chaplain-General
C.M.S.	Church Missionary Society
C.M.S.A.	Church Missionary Society Archives
C.O.	Commanding Officer
C.O.P.E.C.	Conference on Politics, Economics and Citizenship
D.A.C.G.	Deputy Assistant Chaplain-General
D.C.G.	Deputy Chaplain-General
D.E.B.	*Dictionary of Evangelical Biography*
D.S.O.	Distinguished Service Order
E.I.C.	East India Company
E.N.S.A.	Entertainments National Service Association
G.H.Q.	General Headquarters
G.O.C.	General Officer Commanding
H.C.P.P.	House of Commons Parliamentary Papers
I.A.C.	Interdenominational Advisory Committee

I.C.F.	Industrial Christian Fellowship
I.E.E.	Indian Ecclesiastical Establishment
I.W.M.	Imperial War Museum
J.R.A.Ch.D.	*Journal of the Royal Army Chaplains' Department*
J.R.U.S.I.	*Journal of the Royal United Service Institution*
J.S.A.H.R.	*Journal of the Society for Army Historical Research*
K.R.R.C.	King's Royal Rifle Corps
L.P.L.	Lambeth Palace Library
L.R.B.	London Rifle Brigade
M.A.R.C.	Methodist Archives and Research Centre
M.C.	Military Cross
M.O.A.	Mass-Observation Archive
N.A.A.F.I.	Navy, Army and Air Force Institute
N.A.M.	National Army Museum
N.A.S.	National Archives of Scotland
N.A.T.O.	North Atlantic Treaty Organisation
N.C.L.	New College Library
N.C.O.	Non-commissioned Officer
N.L.S.	National Library of Scotland
N.M.B.S.	Naval and Military Bible Society
O.C.	Officer Commanding
O.D.N.B.	*Oxford Dictionary of National Biography*
P.O.W.	Prisoner of War
P.P.U.	Peace Pledge Union
P.R.O.	Public Record Office
P.T.	Physical Training
R.A.Ch.D.	Royal Army Chaplains' Department
R.A.F.	Royal Air Force
R.A.M.C.	Royal Army Medical Corps
R.A.P.	Regimental Aid Post
R.A.R.O.	Regular Army Reserve of Officers
R.C.C.	*Reports of the Church Congress*
R.G.A.C.S.	*Reports to the General Assembly of the Church of Scotland*
R.P.D.A.	Rawlinson Papers, Downside Abbey
R.S.C.S.	*Reports on the Schemes of the Church of Scotland*
S.C.F.	Senior Chaplain to the Forces
S.D.A.	Southwark Diocesan Archives
S.P.C.K.	Society for Promoting Christian Knowledge
S.P.G.	Society for the Propagation of the Gospel
T.F.	Territorial Force (Territorial Army after 1921)
Toc H	Talbot House
U.N.	United Nations
U.S.	United States
V.C.	Victoria Cross
W.A.A.C.	Women's Army Auxiliary Corps

W.C.M.	*Wesleyan Conference Minutes*
W.M.M.S.	Wesleyan Methodist Missionary Society
W.R.A.C.	Women's Royal Army Corps
Y.M.C.A.	Young Men's Christian Association

Introduction

On Sunday 22 April 1951 Padre Sam Davies and the three other chaplains of the British 29th Independent Infantry Brigade Group held services in its positions overlooking the Imjin River in central Korea. Although compulsory church attendance had been abolished for all but ceremonial occasions five years earlier, attendance was remarkably good. As Anthony Farrar-Hockley, then adjutant of the 1st Gloucestershire Regiment, observed: 'As ever, the expectation of battle swelled congregations.'[1] However, this was not the only source of support that British chaplains in Korea were providing. After joining the 1st Gloucesters earlier in the year, Sam Davies had already spoken to many time-expired regulars and recalled reservists who were anxious to know how long they would have to remain in the war-torn Korean peninsula. Significantly, this was a question that soldiers were reluctant to ask their regimental officers because 'those concerned had no wish to give the impression that they were looking for an excuse to leave their comrades in the midst of operations in a hard climate'. However, they had fewer inhibitions when confiding in their chaplains. According to Farrar-Hockley 'Their relationship with the chaplain was different; in such a matter he was better informed as to their state of mind.'[2]

Despite the anxieties of those who found themselves reluctantly embroiled in a distant war, for most of the 1st Gloucesters it would be years before they would return home and many would never do so. On the night of 22 April a huge Chinese offensive broke along the entire length of the British positions and attacks continued throughout the following day. By daybreak on 24 April, the 1st Gloucesters, holding the left of the British line, had been isolated and surrounded. Massively outnumbered, the battalion's survivors, now clinging to a single ridge, fought off repeated Chinese assaults until, on the morning of 25 April, their commanding officer, Lieutenant-Colonel J.P. Carne, ordered individual companies to break out and make for the relative safety of the nearest United Nations positions. However, only a handful reached their intended destinations; over the next few hours, the seriously wounded and hundreds of weary fugitives were rounded up by the victorious Chinese to begin nearly two and a half years in Communist captivity.[3] Besides Carne and Farrar-Hockley, Davies was among those taken prisoner. Throughout the battle he had worked at the regimental aid post, burying the dead, ministering to the wounded and carrying medical supplies. As the battalion dug-in to defend its final position, Davies had 'walked about talking to [the] men, trying to appear relaxed and hopeful, and feeling for encouraging words'. When it became clear that no relief would be arriving and that the battalion would attempt to break out, Davies chose to stay behind with the severely wounded. As he later recalled, he had concluded that 'Whatever happens it's my duty as chaplain really to stay with these few men who cannot move . . . my duty [was] to remain with them as chaplain to give what solace I could.'[4]

One of only four U.N. chaplains to be captured in Korea, Davies had the distinction of being the only one to survive captivity, three American army chaplains dying while prisoners-of-war.[5] However, captivity was not without its peculiar dangers for Davies as he soon became a key figure in an overarching ideological struggle between Marxist-Leninism, with all its internationalist trappings, on the one hand and British, Christian, democracy and its very different vision of international solidarity on the other. As neither North Korea nor the People's Republic of China recognised the Geneva Convention, in their P.O.W. camps they were free to implement 'The Lenient Policy' that had been applied to Nationalist captives during the Chinese Civil War and to pursue their self-appointed task of the political re-education of their prisoners. According to Farrar-Hockley:

> Each shared the view that military forces fighting against the Communist cause were, by definition, war criminals, political sinners. But they were sinners who should be given an opportunity to be brought to repentance by political education to join the struggle against imperialism and the capitalist camp.[6]

Although his Chinese captors initially had no conception of the chaplain's role in the British army and its 'reactionary' potential, after an interrogation in which Davies affirmed his faith in God – and in the U.N. – the battle lines were clearly drawn.[7] As Davies and his fellow prisoners were marched northwards during the first stages of their captivity, Davies held 'short, informal services and spoke of God'; after his arrival at Camp No. 2 on the Yalu river that autumn, he came to regard it as his 'parish behind barbed wire' and his congregation as 'the Church of the Captivity'.[8] With the permission of the camp authorities, Christmas Day 1951 was marked by a celebration of Holy Communion and by a carol service. As Davies recalled, 'Looking at the pictures of the dialectical materialists gazing down on the scene, St. John's words came to my mind, "This is the victory that overcometh the world, even our faith." ' The defiant note of these services was also marked by the first use of a Celtic stone cross that Carne had fashioned using 'two large nails and a primitive hammer'.[9]

Perhaps not surprisingly, the indulgence shown at Christmas 1951 soon wore thin. Two months later, Carne was subjected to a public trial for subversive activities and began nineteen months in solitary confinement.[10] Although a policy of 'Religious Freedom' had been developed on the basis of 'The Lenient Policy', it was beguiling in principle and increasingly capricious in practice. While candles, wine and bread were sometimes made available, requests for 'Bibles, hymn books, rosaries, Holy Communion vessels and vestments' were repeatedly refused. Davies was not allowed to visit British prisoners in Camp No. 1 ('in spite of requests from me and, as I learned later, from the men themselves') and, in February 1952, he was banned from attending the hospital at Camp No. 2; a request to visit prisoners held in solitary confinement was also denied that Easter.[11] From Christmas 1951, Davies' services were subjected to an increasing degree of censorship and he was required to submit a monthly report headed 'Religious Activities for the month of . . .'[12] As Davies summarised the situation: 'There was a degree of religious toleration – yes, but it was a toleration so hedged about with prohibitions, warnings, accusations, mental harassment, censorings, punishments, of giving here and taking away there, that to dignify it with the name of "Religious Freedom" would be farcical.'[13]

Although officialdom proved more co-operative over the matter of Easter services in 1952, an unsanctioned rendering of 'God Save the Queen' on Easter Sunday provoked a strong reaction from the camp authorities and Davies' attempts to explain the incident were curtly dismissed: 'You cannot out-manoeuvre us. We know that all priests are connected with politics.'[14] In June, weekday services were suspended and, in August, confirmation classes and even choir practice suffered the same fate.[15] When Davies ventured to criticise these policies in a sermon, as 'a cunning priest' he was consigned to solitary confinement on charges of 'illegal religious activities, and a hostile attitude'.[16] After nearly three weeks, Davies was released on the strength of a signed confession.[17] However, in his absence Sunday services continued and, on his first Sunday in the cells, hundreds of his fellow prisoners could be heard singing Frederick William Faber's hymn 'Faith of Our Fathers' in a calculated act of ideological defiance.[18] The battle of wills continued after Davies' release and the division of the camp in October 1952. Although material conditions improved in the months prior to the armistice of July 1953, there were still religious and political flashpoints; Davies' petition for an Ash Wednesday service was ignored and a further request for a service to mark the coronation of Elizabeth II in June 1953 was flatly rejected. Still, Davies held the service in secret and was later present at a clandestine coronation party that was discovered and broken up by the Chinese. On this occasion, Davies even tasked a Chinese officer with having insulted 'the British people' and berated him for being 'a stupid man'.[19] Unsurprisingly, as one of the camp's most prominent and persistent 'trouble-makers', Davies was among the last British prisoners to be repatriated that September.[20]

The significance of Davies and his status as a rallying point for resistance among the prisoners in Camp No. 2 cannot be gainsaid. However, religious activity also served as a focus for resistance in other camps. Those prisoners sent from Camp No. 2 to its new annexe in October 1952 continued to hold weekly services led by a 'lay-chaplain', Captain James Majury of the 1st Royal Ulster Rifles, who had been captured in January 1951. As Majury wrote of the home-made service book that was used in the camp: 'In my mind the book is a standing testimonial of the part religion played in upholding our morale and the trouble men took to put their faith before anything in face of the severest opposition.'[21] Although deliberately segregated in order to avoid the contaminating influence of their officers,[22] some other ranks in Camp No. 1 at Chongson also organised meetings for Bible-study and worship while Roman Catholics in Camp No. 5 at Pyoktong were led in their devotions by a lance-corporal of the 1st Royal Ulster Rifles, who even presided at a parade service on St. Patrick's Day 1953.[23] While

Correlli Barnett claimed that 'The solidarity of British prisoners, both officers and other ranks, in the face of ruthless and brutal Communist brainwashing . . . reflected credit on the discipline of the British soldier and on his unquenchable sense of humour',[24] the experience of British prisoners-of-war in Korea also says much about the underlying strength and significance of Christianity in post-war British society. Victorious in its recent struggle against Fascism in Europe and Japanese imperialism in Asia, 'Christian civilisation' was once again pitted against a cruel and godless foe, emerging victorious despite the clear, if unspoken, Communist agenda of eliminating religious faith as part of their prisoners' re-education.[25] Like the British army in the Second World War, the soldiers who were taken prisoner in Korea were a cross-section of British society, among them many recalled reservists and National Servicemen.[26] However, such was their stoicism in captivity that American observers, who were worried at the contrasting behaviour of many of their countrymen under the same conditions,[27] identified a stronger degree of religious faith as a prime reason for the lack of defections among British prisoners-of-war.[28] Still, the importance of Sam Davies (who was 'remembered by his fellow-prisoners with immense affection and respect')[29] was not simply due to the hidden strengths of British Christianity in the early Cold War period or to his personal dedication and charisma. As this book will show, in captivity as well as at the battle of the Imjin, Davies personified a model of practical service and moral and religious leadership that had been developed by the Royal Army Chaplains' Department over a period of generations.

The history of the Royal Army Chaplains' Department (or Army Chaplains' Department as it was known before 1919) is undeservedly obscure. No departmental history appeared prior to the First World War and, while histories of individual units proliferated in its aftermath, no equivalent history was published for the Chaplains' Department; even plans to publish purely denominational accounts of wartime chaplaincy came to nothing in the inter-war period.[30] While this pattern was largely repeated after the Second World War, a volume on Roman Catholic chaplaincy work appeared in 1947 under the title *The Priest Among the Soldiers*. However, this was a compilation of chaplains' memoirs rather than a history of Roman Catholic chaplaincy as such. Indeed, the only history of the entire Department to be published in the twentieth century was an official history by Sir John Smyth which appeared in 1968. Unfortunately, the value of Smyth's *In This Sign Conquer: the Story of Army Chaplains* is distinctly limited. Although able to draw on an impressive roster of helpers and informants (mostly senior officers and former or serving chaplains) Smyth based his book on virtually no archival research and it was, in effect, an account of the campaigns of the British army with the experiences of individual chaplains grafted on. Consequently, Smyth's chaplains were portrayed in a heroic vacuum, largely detached from the course of national politics and from key developments in the history of the churches, the army and military bureaucracy.

However, Smyth's accounts of clerical derring-do at least reflected a marked and enduring taste for biographies of the Department's more distinguished members; G.A. Studdert Kennedy (or 'Woodbine Willie'), 'Tubby' Clayton and

Theodore Bayley Hardy remain perennial favourites with amateur biographers.[31] Furthermore, while Chaplain-General in the late 1920s, A.C.E. Jarvis wrote a succession of long and detailed essays on his forerunners which he entitled 'My Predecessors in Office', an endeavour which helped to promote the beguiling cult of George Gleig, the longest serving Chaplain-General who headed the Department from 1844 to 1875. This preoccupation with the Department's most famous sons has been compounded by a tendency to view its history from narrow denominational perspectives. While very useful studies of Anglican, Roman Catholic, Church of Scotland and Free Church army chaplaincy have appeared in recent decades,[32] their inherent selectivity (and even partiality) has served to obscure connecting themes. Similarly, the strength of national identity in Scotland, Wales and Ireland has fuelled a tendency to examine Scottish, Welsh and Irish chaplains in isolation. In the 1960s, Alexander Dow wrote a lengthy history of Scottish military chaplains from the Middle Ages to the twentieth century, only the first volume of which found its way to publication.[33] More recently, Densil Morgan has studied the experience of Welsh chaplains in the First World War and the growing significance of 1914–18 as part of a unifying history for Irish Nationalists and Ulster Unionists has given rise to similar studies of Irish chaplains.[34] However, the problems of this approach are clear; national identity was by no means a clear-cut issue in the context of a unified British state. For example, despite his Irish origins, his 'rich Irish brogue' and his university education at Trinity College, Dublin, Studdert Kennedy was very much a product of the Church of England; indeed, much of his university education was acquired *in absentia* while studying at Leeds Grammar School.[35] Similarly, William Finn, the Roman Catholic chaplain of the 1st Royal Dublin Fusiliers and the first chaplain to be killed in action during the First World War, was born in Yorkshire, trained at Ushaw and ordained for the diocese of Middlesbrough.[36]

Besides the tendency to approach the history of British army chaplaincy from biographical, denominational or national perspectives, a much greater complicating factor has been the long-running pacifist agitation against military chaplaincy *per se*. During the twentieth century, and in response to the First World War, the Second World War, the Cold War and the Vietnam War, in the English-speaking world Christian pacifism spread far beyond its traditional sectarian constituencies and its precepts and sensitivities are now common among Christians in Great Britain and North America. Inevitably, the growth of Christian pacifism has been marked by strident attacks on the principle and institution of military chaplaincy, which has been strongly criticised for subordinating Christianity to the interests of the military and as an emblem of ecclesiastical subservience to the state. As we shall see, this critique was popularised in Great Britain by Dick Sheppard and by other Christian pacifists in the 1930s but it gained ground, and academic credibility, in the era of the Cold War, primarily through the work of Waldo Burchard, Gordon Zahn and Alan Wilkinson. Although it is hard to judge just how representative their opinions are of wider sentiment within the churches, these pacifist commentators have succeeded in creating an influential discourse on the insuperable problems of military chaplaincy in the American and the British contexts.

In 1954, in the immediate aftermath of the Korean War, Waldo Burchard published a seminal essay in the *American Sociological Review* entitled 'Role Conflicts of Military Chaplains'. This paper was partly inspired by the growing importance of the chaplain in the American armed forces, an importance that was reflected in the development of an inter-service 'Character Guidance Programme'. Boosted by the Communist subornation of American prisoners-of-war in Korea, this scheme made military chaplains responsible for 'a program of instruction in "godly patriotism" ', a programme which sought 'to equate the values of patriotism and religion by giving patriotism a religious basis'.[37] Burchard's indignant reaction to this initiative was to declare that the teachings of Christianity were 'manifestly incompatible with the aims of a nation at war', that it was 'impossible for the Christian in military service to put them into practice' and that the very situation of the military chaplain exposed 'the age-old problem of the relationship between church and state . . . whether the state or the church shall demand the first loyalty of its followers'.[38]

Working from the sociological premise that 'Each person has a "hierarchy of role obligations" ' and that these 'may be directly antithetical', Burchard argued that the conflict of social roles was 'extremely severe' among military chaplains because 'the ends specified by the two major institutions which define their social roles are in some respects mutually exclusive'.[39] In Burchard's view, this underlying conflict was apparent from the answers produced to a questionnaire circulated among seventy-one serving and former chaplains of the U.S. army, navy and air force 'in the San Francisco Bay area'. While not disclosing the precise wording of its fifty-seven questions, Burchard nevertheless maintained that the majority of his respondents justified their ministry with reference to the ancient Christian moral tradition of the just war. However, from his own implacably pacifist standpoint Burchard dismissed this position as 'moral relativism', claiming that the overwhelming response of his subjects to their patently untenable situation was either one of two 'escapes', namely 'Rationalization' or 'Compartmentalization'. Of these, 'Compartmentalization appeared to be the more successful of the two techniques, and more frequently used. Rationalization requires facing the dilemma and arguing away the conflicting elements. Compartmentalization involves refusing to recognize the conflict.'[40]

However, according to Burchard it was not only the fundamentals of Christian moral teaching that served to embarrass the military chaplain and trigger these evasive reactions. The chaplain was also an officer, a situation that posed another problem as his rank was 'a barrier to primary relations with enlisted men'. Despite the fact that his respondents were simply addressed as 'Chaplain', that they socialised freely with enlisted men and were generally of the opinion that 'if the individual chaplain were adequate he could overcome the barrier posed by rank', to Burchard all of this was yet more obfuscation: 'the usual response to questions suggesting a conflict between the demands of the chaplain's military office and those of his ecclesiastical office was to deny the existence of conflict by disclaiming the reality of his status as an officer'.[41] Besides being morally exceptionable and professionally irregular, Burchard also argued that the status of the American military chaplain was, in any event, unconstitutional because 'In spite of the traditional American ideology of the strict separation of church and state, military chaplaincy is a state supported religious institution – not actually an official religion, but a form of state established church.' Again, Burchard noted that the majority of his respondents chose to deny this incontestable truth: 'When asked for their reactions to the statement that the chaplaincy is a form of state established church, 68 per cent of the respondents disagreed, more or less violently.'[42]

With the exception of the constitutional separation of church and state in the United States, Burchard's work clearly offered scope 'for the student of role conflict'[43] in the British context. Inspired by Burchard's principles and example and no less convinced that military chaplaincy was an 'extreme manifestation' of role conflict,[44] Gordon Zahn, an American Roman Catholic priest and a veteran peace activist, published *Chaplains in the RAF: a study in role tension* in 1969. Working from the premise that 'religion is expected to be at odds with the world about it', Zahn's lengthier and more detailed study expanded upon the untenable position of R.A.F. chaplains in light of the obliteration bombing of Germany during the Second World War, the brutal nature of contemporary post-colonial conflicts and the terrifying prospect of nuclear war.[45] Twelve years later, Alan Wilkinson applied the same logic to the British army in an essay entitled 'The Paradox of the Military Chaplain'. While some of Wilkinson's arguments (especially that concerned with the chaplain's rank) had been adumbrated by individual members of the R.A.Ch.D. for many years, he based his case on the assertion that 'The very existence of military chaplains is a paradox' and that 'Their role is replete with ambiguities.'[46] He then went on to delineate some key examples in the form of eight propositions and questions. These were:

(1) The 'basic incongruity between Christianity and the military profession' and the consequent 'paradox of representing Jesus in a military institution'.
(2) The 'tensions created by [their] non-combatant role' and the 'feelings of marginality and helplessness' which this can induce among chaplains.
(3) The problem of 'tribal religion' and the dangers of betraying Christian 'catholicity while serving the national cause'.
(4) The 'tension of being both a priest and an officer' and the 'class bias of the Church and its ministers' which the chaplain's rank betrays.
(5) The 'tension between the priestly and the social' role of the chaplain, as exemplified by the salutary fact that men could crowd a chaplain's canteen while evading his spiritual ministrations.
(6) How far could the chaplain go to 'reinforce morale', especially given the moral challenge of the conscientious objector?
(7) How far could the chaplain 'exercise a prophetic role', especially if criticism of military policy was called for?
(8) 'The military and religious establishments' had widely employed 'Religious and chivalric imagery' in order to 'romanticise war', much to the disgust of ordinary soldiers and the inevitable detriment of the churches.[47]

While superficially impressive, the evidence employed to support his case was culled from a disparate range of sources including a selection of anti-war fiction, the reflections of certain Anglican bishops and military chaplains and the documents of the Second Vatican Council. In keeping with this eclecticism, the case of conscientious objection that Wilkinson invoked was that of Franz Jägerstätter, an Austrian Roman Catholic who was executed by the Nazis in 1943 despite the urgings of a military chaplain to relent.[48] Although generalised, highly coloured by pacifist perspectives and heavily influenced by the tensions of an escalating Cold War, these arguments gained a following even in the Royal Army Chaplains' Department. In 1996, Stephen Louden, its Principal Roman Catholic Chaplain, published a highly admonitory study entitled *Chaplains in Conflict: The Role of Army Chaplains since 1914*. Here, Louden concurred with Wilkinson that British army chaplains suffered from 'conflicting loyalties', that their ministry was largely geared towards meeting military needs and that chaplains 'must confront the qualities of ambivalence and paradox in their role' and answer the fundamental question 'Might there be some taint of evil in things good?'[49] Ten years later, Louden returned to the fray with an article that was unambiguously entitled 'Chaplains as whistle-blowers? You're having a laugh!', in which he concluded that:

> Confronted by the conflicting demands of authority and conscience, evidence demonstrates how unforthcoming Chaplains have been in bringing charges of own-side major military wrongdoing. The capability of any military organization depends to a large degree on effective socialization of its officers and soldiers. Loyalty and obedience have always been an essential element of that socialization which inhibits it would seem critical moral judgment in Chaplains . . . When whistle-blowing is called for, Generals can rest assured that a Chaplain will hardly be the one to expose anything seriously embarrassing to the military.[50]

Once again, however, the evidence was less compelling than the accompanying rhetoric; Louden's sources included sundry experiments on the phenomenon of group conformity, David Lean's Oscar-winning film *The Bridge On the River Kwai*, the conduct of *Wehrmacht* chaplains on the Eastern Front in the Second World War and the sins of omission ascribed to two American army chaplains in the aftermath of the My Lai massacre of March 1968.[51] Evidence of comparable misconduct by British army chaplains was notable by its absence. Indeed, rather than demonstrating the hopelessly compromised character of military chaplaincy *per se*, what these examples tend to illustrate is the key importance of differences in military culture and operational context in explaining the failures of military chaplains whether as groups or as individuals. For example, the uncritical support for the Nazi war effort that was evinced by many *Wehrmacht* chaplains in the Second World War was to a large extent dictated by their numerical weakness (only 1,000 chaplains served an army which numbered around 6,500,000 at its peak),[52] by the hostile ideological environment into which they were thrown and by the extreme brutality of Germany's genocidal war against the Soviet Union on the Eastern Front. Similarly, the chaplains implicated in the My Lai massacre (who were not present at the killing of 500 Vietnamese civilians by soldiers of the 20th Infantry Regiment but were later blamed by an official inquiry for failing to pursue their initial calls for an investigation) were clearly casualties of much deeper problems relating to America's war in Vietnam.[53] The atrocity and subsequent inquiry clearly and painfully exposed the military dilemmas and public unease that dogged American involvement; as Michael Maclear has stated, 'My Lai was a collective consequence of the individual emotional overload which almost every American ground combatant in Vietnam came to endure in a war without any recognizable front, enemy or cause, waged without national participation or unity.'[54] The case of British army chaplains in the Second World War provides an instructive and striking contrast to both these cases. Here, chaplains had the full support of the British state and of the British army in playing their appointed part in a war which had the overwhelming support of the British people. These chaplains were far more numerous and ubiquitous than their German counterparts (with nearly 3,000 serving an army which peaked at just over 3,000,000 in the summer of 1945)[55] and, against the Germans and Italians at least, they participated in a conventional conflict in which the rules of war were usually observed. Partly due to these factors, British army chaplains emerged from the Second World War with an enhanced reputation and their experience and situation has provided very little ammunition for critics of military chaplaincy as a broader phenomenon.

If the case against military chaplaincy too often rests on unqualified appeals against its worst manifestations, its failings can be exaggerated in other respects. For example, and as this study will show, the craven conformity which Louden associated with British army chaplaincy was often much less in evidence than the military authorities might have wished. Nevertheless, historians of military chaplaincy have been heavily constrained by the prevailing pacifist discourse on their subject. This is illustrated by a recent collection of essays on the history of military chaplaincy entitled *The Sword of the Lord: Military Chaplains from the First to the Twenty-First Century* (2004), from which Louden drew some of his inspiration for his article of 2006. Based on a conference held at Indiana's University of Notre Dame, the book chiefly consists of a number of well-researched essays on the history of military chaplaincy ranging from antiquity to the present day. Still, the whole exercise was framed by the pacifist critique of military chaplaincy; indeed, the final word went to Michael J. Baxter (a Roman Catholic priest and 'the national secretary of the Catholic Peace Fellowship') who concluded the volume with an attack on military chaplains in general: 'I regard their service', he declared, 'as service to a strange warrior god, not the God and Father of Jesus Christ, who calls His followers to embody His peace.'[56]

As William Temple, then Archbishop of York, wrote against the background of the inter-war peace movement and the outbreak of the Second World War, 'One of the unfortunate results of the pacifist controversy is that it compels those of us who hold that it might be right for a Christian to engage in warfare to appear as defenders of the institution of war.'[57] This is equally true today, as the historian who accepts the validity of the just war tradition and who does not subscribe to pacifist tenets on Christianity, war and military chaplaincy runs an appreciable risk of attack; indeed, the work of the present author has already been condemned by one pacifist commentator on these very grounds. In this case, his assailant was Kristofer Skrade, a Lutheran pastor based in Minneapolis, who is best known as the editor of various handbooks on contemporary Christian living, readers of his *Christian Handbook* being treated to a host of 'factoids', 'check-lists' and 'timeless biblical truths'.[58] When Skrade brought his acumen and subtlety to bear on *God and the British Soldier*, a revisionist historical study of the role of religion in the British army in the two World Wars, he was outraged to discover that its arguments did not tally with his pacifist predilections. Consequently, he denounced the book, and railed against its author, employing a combination of turgid satire, glib misrepresentation (notably of the pacifist nature of various world religions) and an assortment of historical fallacies and clichés that purported to be authoritative knowledge of the First World War. For example, according to Skrade's view of morality and history, between 1914 and 1918 an unholy alliance of chaplains and generals sent 'an entire generation of young men' to their deaths, the latter observing the tragic consequences of their blasphemous pact from the safety of 'distant hills' and the apparent comfort of their 'glossy, patent leather saddles'.[59] However, while the tired myths of a futile war, 'the lost generation' and 'lions led by donkeys' have been comprehensively debunked by revisionist historians of Britain and the First World War,[60] Skrade's ill-informed and splenetic tirades are still of significance to any study that seeks to shed new light on the history of British army chaplaincy.[61] As Hew Strachan has emphasised, the old mythology of the First World War has erected 'a barrier between our understanding of the war and that of those who fought in it . . . Hindsight bred arrogance, and – worse – misconception.'[62] Nevertheless, Skrade's protestations illustrate the continuing value of this lurid popular mythology of the First World War to pacifist critics of British army chaplaincy, who still seek to portray it as an awkward legacy of a shameful past and as a lesson against allowing the church to act as the spiritual lackey of the state.

Despite its many shortcomings, so simple and compelling is this negative discourse on military chaplaincy that it has even found its way into mainstream historiography, being appropriated by Joanna Bourke, a leading cultural historian, in her book *An Intimate History of Killing: Face-to-Face Killing in Twentieth-Century Warfare* (1999). Heavily influenced by the arguments of Burchard and Zahn, Bourke devoted a good deal of attention to the role of 'Priests and Padres' in this process. Drawing on a loose collection of British, American and Australian evidence, Bourke presented a series of vignettes to illustrate how military chaplains experienced 'role tension' and how they succumbed to military culture and to the primordial joy of killing.[63] However, quite apart from the disparate nature of her evidence, her arguments were problematic in other respects. The wider role of the chaplain was wholly eclipsed by her consuming interest in killing and her generic treatment of military chaplaincy made no effort to differentiate between its different national or service manifestations. In fact, and once more in the treatment of this subject, historical rigour was at a discount as many of her comments on the history of British army chaplaincy were plainly wrong. For example, Bourke claimed that chaplains 'joined the *British* Army' (my italics) in 'the thirteenth century'; that Welsh Nonconformist chaplains in the First World War were the products of a vigorous fighting tradition and that Roman Catholics and Nonconformists were only entitled to appoint their own chaplains 'after

1915'.[64] Once again, therefore, a simplified caricature of military chaplaincy was arraigned and duly condemned on the strength of a skewed and otherwise dubious body of historical evidence.

In the course of recent decades, it is clear that the historiography of military chaplaincy has been heavily encumbered by a pacifist agenda that has generated far more heat than light. However, besides breeding distortions of its own this agenda has helped to perpetuate others. In the British context, perhaps the greatest of these is the alleged uselessness of First World War Anglican army chaplains, a reputation that has proved extremely useful to pacifist critics of military chaplaincy because it portrays the accredited representatives of England's established church as inept as well as morally irresponsible.[65] Although fuelled by historic undercurrents of anticlericalism in British society and by the complaints of some frustrated chaplains, this reputation largely stems from the work of influential anti-establishment writers such as C.E. Montague and Robert Graves in the inter-war years. However, it is important to recognise that their criticisms were very largely contradictory; for example, while Graves presented the typical Anglican chaplain as malingering in the rear, Montague averred that 'He gladly frequented the least healthy parts of the line, and would frankly mourn the pedantry which denied him a service revolver.'[66] Similarly, while Graves alleged that Anglican chaplains remained aloof from the practical realities of war, the nub of Montague's criticism was that they were much too preoccupied by them and that they failed, in consequence, to engage with some of the religious questions to which the war gave rise. As Montague mused:

> What, indeed, could the average army chaplain have done, with his little budget of nice traits and limitations? How had we ever armed and equipped him? When you are given an infant earth to fashion out of a whirling ball of flaming metals and gases, then good humour, some taste for adventure, distinction at cricket, a jolly way with the men, and an imperfect digestion of thirty-nine partly masticated articles may not carry you far.[67]

What is also implicit in these portrayals of Anglican chaplains is the suggestion that their social background proved a major handicap in relating to their men. While this argument was developed by Alan Wilkinson in his book *The Church of England and the First World War* and has been duly echoed by Michael Moynihan and Richard Holmes,[68] there is in fact little evidence to support it. Although Graves played upon the differences between the rarefied chaplains of the Church of England (who 'were remarkably out of touch with their troops') and the earthiness of their Irish Roman Catholic counterparts, he ignored the fact that the Irish secular clergy comprised only a fraction of the army's Roman Catholic chaplains; in fact, almost half of the latter were drawn from the religious orders throughout the British Isles, orders that recruited heavily from their own grammar and boarding schools (and thus the Roman Catholic middle and upper classes) and among whom pastoral experience was severely limited.[69] Nevertheless, and in beguiling contrast with their Anglican equivalents, Roman Catholic chaplains have been consistently portrayed as a solidly working-class body, with

Richard Holmes even ascribing these origins to the Irish Jesuit William Doyle, who, as the son of a senior civil servant, was educated at a Roman Catholic public school in England.[70] There was, moreover, in pre-war British society a strong and discernible bias *in favour* of clerical recruitment from the middle and upper classes. While its *Report on the Supply and Training of Candidates for Holy Orders* of 1908 reflected the Church of England's existing sensitivity to charges of social elitism, it acknowledged that there was a 'long established prejudice in favour of one particular class' and that, in consequence, 'clergy drawn from the artisan and labouring classes are apt to be regarded both by their own people, and by other ranks, somewhat critically'.[71] Significantly, there was nothing in the least plebeian about the more celebrated Anglican chaplains of 1914–18. Theodore Bayley Hardy (whom even Montague described as a 'hero and saint'),[72] Studdert Kennedy and 'Tubby' Clayton were all university graduates and Clayton was a cousin of the Earl of Cavan.[73] All of these cases seem to demonstrate an essential continuity with the situation in civilian life where, as Sarah Williams has shown, it was force of personality that served to endear individual clergymen to their parishioners.[74] In view of these considerations, it can only be concluded that if the chaplains of the Church of England had any major and consistent handicap in relating to their flocks this lay in the fact that they ministered to 70 per cent of the British army and to much larger numbers of religiously uncommitted soldiers than did their Presbyterian, Roman Catholic and Nonconformist colleagues.[75]

While this historical study of the Royal Army Chaplains' Department seeks to challenge the fixed assumptions and conceptual thraldom of current perspectives on this subject, I must make clear that what it represents is not an exhaustive history of chaplaincy to the British army over a period of 250 years. For reasons of scale and coherence, this study is primarily concerned with full-time chaplains in the pay of the British army. This category includes regimental and ordnance chaplains and their commissioned successors of the Army Chaplains' Department. However, this approach is not to downplay the significance of other agents and agencies. Quite apart from the associated work of scripture readers and other lay missionaries to the British soldier, a vast and diverse array of clergymen ministered to the religious needs of the British army at various times and in sundry locations throughout the period of this study. This expansive category included officiating civilian clergymen in Great Britain and the colonies, the chaplains of the East India Company (and of the later Indian Ecclesiastical Establishment) and also a vast number of missionary clergy. In fact, many of the clergymen involved were not even British. In nineteenth-century India, the Roman Catholic priests who were paid to say Mass for their co-religionists in the army were very often Portuguese, Italian, French or even German missionaries. Hence, in their numerous petitions to Rome during the early nineteenth century Roman Catholic soldiers in India often stressed the need for English-speaking priests,[76] a need that was never adequately met. Similarly, in East Africa during the First World War the Roman Catholic clergy who were locally engaged as acting chaplains were a multi-national assortment of British, French and South African priests while in Uganda the French White Fathers 'volunteered to perform Chaplains' duties without payment'.[77] Even as late as the Second World War it was noted that Roman Catholic soldiers in at least one German P.O.W. camp were under the care of fellow prisoners in the form of French soldier-priests.[78] While aspects of this diverse and often *ad hoc* provision invite further study in their own right, for the present it is instructive to note that its importance can be seen in the origins of the term 'Padre', a term that became the universal appellation of the British army chaplain in the course of the nineteenth century. Although at first associated with Roman Catholic missionaries in India,[79] by the early 1800s it was also being used to denote those Anglican clergymen who were salaried servants of the East India Company. As Henry Shepherd, a former E.I.C. chaplain, explained in 1827 for the benefit of his English readership, 'PADRE, i.e. Father, is a term invariably applied to the Clergy by Europeans as well as natives.'[80]

Within these stated parameters, this book seeks to chart the origins and history of the Royal Army Chaplains' Department, the experience of serving chaplains and the development of the chaplain's role in the British army from the early eighteenth century to the Cold War. As a study, it incorporates elements of military, ecclesiastical, political, theological, social, imperial, cultural and gender history and it has been informed by a wide range of evidence drawn from military and ecclesiastical records, periodical literature, published and manuscript memoirs and oral history interviews. While it is hard to do justice to this subject in the span of a single volume, this book will have succeeded if it creates a new framework for understanding the history of British army chaplaincy and if it highlights some important areas for future research. These areas clearly include the history of British military chaplaincy in India, the history of British army chaplaincy in a comparative context and the long-term significance of the experience of military chaplaincy in two World Wars for the lives, thought and ministry of thousands of British clergymen over the course of the twentieth century.

1

The Origins and Early Years of the Army Chaplains' Department

Army Chaplaincy in the Eighteenth Century

Military chaplaincy was an ancient institution even at the beginning of our period; in fact, the Latin term *cappellani* is thought to derive from the term *cappa*, namely the cape of St. Martin of Tours, a potent relic that was carried into battle by the Frankish kings and which required the care of a dedicated band of clergy.[1] While military chaplains evolved from the eighth century into an important and conspicuous feature of medieval warfare throughout western Christendom,[2] their significance did not diminish with the Reformation or with the wars of religion of the sixteenth and seventeenth centuries. During the British civil wars of the 1640s and 1650s, chaplains played a prominent part in the armies of all the protagonists;[3] indeed, it was reputedly due to the influence of the over-mighty ministers of the Scottish Covenanting armies that David Leslie was persuaded to offer his army for destruction by Oliver Cromwell at the battle of Dunbar in September 1650.[4] Contemporary military organisation meant that commissioned chaplains were normally attached to regiments, chaplains being appointed by their colonels and commissioned by their army commanders.[5] While this model of regimental chaplaincy emulated practice in the Swedish army of Gustavus Adolphus, chaplains could also be found on the establishments of troops of horse and trains of artillery and an attempt was made to create a more cohesive 'Chaplains' Corps' in the Royalist armies in 1643–4. In addition, many clergymen were employed to serve as chaplains to individual garrisons.[6]

After the Restoration, regimental chaplains were embodied in the army of Charles II, where they were originally expected to 'every day reade the Common prayers of the Church of England to the soldiers . . . and preach to them as often as with convenience shall be thought fitt', and they were present in sufficient numbers in Flanders during the Nine Years War (1688–97) to warrant the appointment of a local Chaplain-General.[7] Thereafter, British military chaplaincy remained a largely regimental affair, with each regular, militia and fencible regiment having a chaplain on its establishment.[8] However, the militia was only a part-time force, fencible regiments were raised only during the American and French Revolutionary Wars and the size of the regular army waxed and waned over time. Hence, only chaplaincies in senior regiments of the regular army could really be seen as permanent appointments. Like other regimental commissions (and, indeed, presentations to parochial livings in the Church of England) these chaplains' commissions were a form of property that could be sold by colonels or hawked by chaplains themselves and there was a steady traffic in them until their abolition in 1796.[9]

While chaplains' commissions should only have been available to clergymen of the established churches of England and Scotland, the anarchic nature of the system ensured that clergy of the Scottish Episcopal church also served as regimental chaplains notwithstanding their status as Dissenters north of the border.[10] Furthermore, in 1794 George III unwittingly signed the commission of the Roman Catholic chaplain of the Glengarry Fencibles, despite the fact that Roman Catholics were debarred from holding military commissions in England and Scotland.[11] However, if this slip was singularly embarrassing, many contemporaries were convinced that, in general, very little care was taken in the appointment of chaplains. As one satirist wrote of the typical colonel, 'He's no mighty Friend to the Clergy . . . he usually keeps a Chaplain for the Battalion he commands, as he does a led Horse, more for Shew than Service.'[12] Similarly, another commentator saw the system of militia chaplains as particularly venal, some satirical *Advice to the Lord Lieutenants of Counties Commanding Regiments of Militia* warning that:

> You must take care to appoint a proper chaplain; that is, you must find out some parson who has a vote for your county, who would be glad to preach to a couple of regiments, which he will ludicrously call his parishes. He must swear, and drink and talk bawdy twice as much as an army chaplain; for I don't know how it is, but tho' I have seen some signs of religion and morality in the army, I never saw the smallest traces of either in the militia.[13]

In addition to regimental chaplains, a number of chaplains were also maintained at major fortresses and garrisons at home and overseas, either being appointed by their governors or by the Secretary at War.[14] As the garrisons of different stations could fluctuate in size, they were employed and paid in relation to local need, their pay sometimes being supplemented by allowances for fuel and candles. Hence, in 1741, when Britain was at war with Spain, there were thirteen fortress and garrison chaplains, the garrison chaplain at Portsmouth receiving 6s 8d per day while his counterpart at Edinburgh Castle, then a relative backwater, received only 2s 6d.[15] In years of crisis, however, the number of fortress and garrison chaplains could rise considerably and they numbered twenty-eight in 1776 and twenty-six in 1796.[16] Of these appointments, the most prestigious was that of chaplain to the Tower of London who, 'though never in the army', discharged to its garrison and inmates 'the duties of [a] parochial minister'.[17] Besides these regimental and garrison chaplains, the Board of Ordnance also maintained a small establishment of chaplains to serve the Royal Artillery.

Finally, when Crown regiments were deployed to the Indian subcontinent during the Seven Years War (1756–63), the chaplains of the East India Company were also drawn into the spiritual care of the British soldier.[18]

As there was no overarching supervision of regimental chaplains, these clergymen enjoyed considerable freedom of action. However, certain guidelines were available which were designed to ensure that they understood and performed the religious offices expected, though not necessarily specified, under the Articles of War. According to an order issued from Dublin Castle in July 1697, the chaplains of regiments on the Irish establishment were to be drawn exclusively from the ranks of the unbeneficed clergy; any chaplain who had a 'Benefice with Cure of Souls' had to choose between his chaplaincy or his parish. Chaplains were to furnish episcopal certificates of their godliness and learning and, if their regiments were widely dispersed, they were to take care to ensure that officers and men were not neglected. Chaplains were accountable to local bishops in matters of doctrine and morals and, unless they were already read by the parish minister, prayers were to be read every day, the catechism was to be expounded every week and Holy Communion was to be administered at least four times a year. Chaplains were also required to supervise the behaviour of the officers and men of their regiments, exhorting and reproving where necessary. By such means it was hoped that 'their Godly Admonitions, and Instructions may become Effectual, to the general Reformation of the Souldiers'.[19] Bennet Cuthbertson, the author of *A System for the Compleat Interior Management and Oeconomy of a Battalion of Infantry*, shared these aspirations in the 1760s. Cuthbertson saw one of the salient tasks of the regimental chaplain as being 'to improve the Morals of the Soldiers', recommending that his sermons be 'calculated' for their 'understanding' and that they point out 'such vices, as they have been most remarked in'.[20] He also attached great importance to the chaplain's work with the sick, urging that the chaplain 'endeavour to seize that serious season of reflection, for fixing in their minds a proper sense of religion, and morality, as the certain means of making them the better Soldiers, in case of their recovery'.[21] In addition to this, other evidence from the eighteenth century shows that chaplains were expected to conduct christenings, marriages and burials and to minister to soldiers under arrest.[22]

Despite attempts to prevent the beneficed clergy from serving as regimental chaplains, there were no real safeguards to prevent this from happening. In 1705, the Bishop of Worcester found that the parish of Binton was being served by neighbouring clergymen because its incumbent was 'chaplain to a Regiment of Horse in Flanders'.[23] Furthermore, Samuel Noyes served as regimental chaplain to the Earl of Orkney's Regiment from 1692 to 1709. At the same time, he accrued no fewer than three parochial livings and, in 1700–1, he was also a junior proctor at Cambridge. As his correspondence reveals, his military career was partly driven by a desire to ingratiate himself with influential patrons. In 1703–4, Noyes wrote fifteen letters to the Archbishop of York, letters that were military narratives intended to inform and entertain this powerful prelate. Furthermore, Noyes also regaled the Bishop of Ely with similar correspondence. As a strategy for preferment, a regimental chaplaincy seems to have paid dividends for Noyes as he ended his career as a wealthy pluralist and a prebendary of Winchester Cathedral.[24] Still, some pluralists could be attentive to their military responsibilities. While his regiment was encamped in Dorset during the Seven Years War, William Agar, then incumbent of two Lincolnshire parishes, gave a series of fourteen sermons to the officers and men of the 20th Regiment, these being published in 1758 under the title *Military Devotion: or, the Soldier's Duty to God, His Prince and His Country*.[25]

The prevailing system of regimental chaplaincy was not only compromised by the appointment of beneficed clergymen. A culture of absenteeism was also rife among regimental officers, with colonels usually setting a lead by leaving routine matters of command and administration to their subordinates.[26] If there was an institutional tolerance of absenteeism, regimental chaplaincy was also complicated by home deployments, postings which meant that regiments were likely to be served by garrison chaplains or, if they were billeted among the civilian population, by the parochial clergy. If it could be argued that these considerations compensated for the absence of regimental chaplains,[27] their habit-forming potential was all too clear. In the context of the Church of England and Church of Ireland, regimental chaplains risked being seen as interlopers within a rigid ecclesiastical system that regarded the rights of parochial incumbents as sacrosanct. Within this framework, the presence of another clergyman preaching and administering the sacraments, and depriving the parish incumbent of fees for baptisms, marriages and burials, was clearly problematic. Given these circumstances, it seems quite possible that ecclesiastical law served as an incentive for absenteeism. The generally pragmatic outlook of the eighteenth-century Anglican clergy also militated against regimental chaplains ministering to their regiments in England and Ireland. Recent studies have emphasised that the Anglican clergy tended to view their spiritual duties in the context of local need rather than professional obligation. Hence, where services were already provided by garrison chaplains or by the local clergy, there was simply no need for the presence of an extraneous clergyman.[28]

Given all of this, it is perhaps to the credit of many regimental chaplains that they went overseas at all. At least one contemporary remarked that a willingness to undertake active service compensated for his absence at other times. As Cuthbertson put it in 1768: 'Whilst a Regiment is in the Field, the attendance of the Chaplain is seldom dispensed with, though at other times (contrary to the custom of all other Christian armies) [it is] most shamefully neglected.'[29] One regimental chaplain drowned during the ill-fated expedition to Quebec of 1711[30] and the British component of Marlborough's army in the Low Countries benefited from the presence of a significant number of clergymen throughout the War of the Spanish Succession. Besides those chaplains ministering to individual regiments, Josiah Sandby served as chaplain to Marlborough's artillery train, as secretary to General Charles Churchill and as the official chronicler of the Blenheim campaign of 1704.[31] Furthermore, Dr Francis Hare, later bishop of St Asaph and of Chichester, was attached to Marlborough's headquarters, holding the local office of 'Chaplain General'. If details of Hare's role are sketchy (his surviving letters, like those of Samuel Noyes, are simply a commentary on

Marlborough's campaigns of 1704–11)[32] the British component of Marlborough's army at Blenheim in August 1704 was served by thirteen attendant chaplains, all of whom received a bounty of £20 for their contribution to this resounding Allied victory.[33] During the War of the Austrian Succession, regimental chaplains also appear to have been present in reasonable numbers among British troops on the continent; they protested the growth of Methodism among British regiments in Flanders and they were sufficiently numerous for the Duke of Cumberland to order that 'Prayers [are] to be read every Morning at the Head of each Brigade at nine: The Chaplains of each Brigade [are] to take it by Turns, beginning with the Eldest.'[34] During the War of the Austrian Succession, individual chaplains also found the opportunity to distinguish themselves on the battlefield, although stories of Adam Ferguson's heroics at the battle of Fontenoy (where, as chaplain of the Black Watch, he reputedly 'continued with the regiment during the whole of the action in the hottest of the fire, praying with the dying, attending to the wounded and directing them to be carried to a place of safety') may well be apocryphal.[35]

Regimental chaplains were also present among British troops in Germany during the Seven Years War. In north-west Germany in 1761, Corporal William Todd of the 12th Regiment noted how he and his fellow pioneers were detailed to construct a makeshift chapel in order to accommodate a service for more than a thousand men. A rudimentary church was thrown up in a matter of hours and Todd remembered that 'our Chaplin read prayers and preach'd an Excellent Sermon, & took his text from the 27 Psalm, Verse the 2nd and 3rd ["When the wicked, even mine enemies and my foes, came upon me to eat up my flesh, they stumbled and fell. Though an host should encamp against me, my heart shall not fear: though war should rise against me, in this will I be confident"]'.[36] Furthermore, as a result of the British build-up in North America from 1755, more regimental chaplains found themselves bound for the colonies. Whereas there were only three battalions and seven 'independent companies' of regular soldiers on the North American mainland in 1750, by 1757 the number of battalions had risen to twenty-one.[37] In 1755, Philip Hughes earned some distinction amid the chaotic defeat of General Braddock's army on the Monongahela River, rescuing the colours of the 44th Regiment despite being wounded in the battle.[38] Four years later, during the siege of Quebec, five regimental chaplains were present with the besieging army and Wolfe praised their dedication in a general order of August 1759.[39] Even as late as the American War of Independence, by which time regimental chaplains were often conspicuous by their absence,[40] there was still scope for some chaplains to distinguish themselves in this forbidding theatre of war. During the disastrous Saratoga campaign of 1777, a clergyman named Brudenell (who was described by one veteran as 'the chaplain to the artillery') performed some signal services for Burgoyne's beleaguered army. After the battle of Bemis Heights he presided at the burial of Brigadier-General Simon Fraser – despite the fact that the enemy 'with an inhumanity deserving the condemnation of every liberal mind, cannonaded the procession as it passed'. Later, he also acted as an escort to Lady Harriet Acland when she was allowed through rebel lines in order to attend her wounded husband, a scene that was greatly romanticised by artists of the day.[41]

Despite these salutary examples, the likelihood of clerical heroics on the battlefield diminished as the century progressed, largely because regimental chaplains were increasingly reluctant to join their regiments on active service. Several factors contributed to this growing disinclination. As regimental chaplaincies could be held for life, there were inevitably those who were either too old or too ill to accompany their regiments on campaign. Besides the age and incapacity of some, those who held regimental chaplaincies along with other livings could not be expected to prioritise their military obligations over their civilian duties. Significantly, this problem was not confined to the clergy of the Church of England. Alexander Dow has estimated that almost half of the clergymen who held chaplaincies in Scottish regular or fencible regiments during the latter half of the eighteenth century were parish ministers of the Church of Scotland, their dual commitments entailing high levels of absenteeism.[42] In addition to the many attractions of settled civilian life, the avoidance of regimental responsibilities may also be explained in terms of the low moral tone of army life and the fear of scandal that haunted all self-respecting clergymen. As one experienced officer admitted:

> No institution could have been formed so ingeniously contrived to defeat its own purpose as that of the establishment of regimental Chaplains. Imagine a young man of twenty-four or twenty-five, fresh from Oxford, who had just taken priest's orders, joining a regiment of noisy, rattling, young fellows, with whom he was obliged to live all day . . . constantly in the way of hearing all the jokes of every description, and witnessing scenes nowise fit for his contemplation, it could not be wondered at that he frequently joined in what was going forward. The devil was a mere bungler when he invented the temptations of St. Anthony – he ought to have made him a regimental chaplain.[43]

While few chaplains caused the same degree of scandal as Robert Newburgh of the 47th Regiment, who faced allegations of sodomy in 1774,[44] it was widely understood that chaplains were prone to succumb to the more unsavoury aspects of army life.[45] Duncan Wright, a Methodist soldier-preacher who served in several Irish garrisons during the Seven Years War, remembered that 'When we lay in one city the care of four or five regiments was left to an unhappy man, who was an object of common ridicule among the soldiers for his perpetual drunkenness.'[46] In the wake of the Seven Years War, their standing was such that the satirist Edward Ward could pen a very unflattering caricature of the regimental chaplain in *Mars Stript of his Armour: or the Army Displayed in all its True Colours*. According to Ward, it was only the dangers of campaigning that could curtail the chaplain's insatiable appetite for drinking and wenching:

> [W]hatever Inclination he has to be wicked, a Storm, or a Battle gives him such a Qualm of Conscience, that he shakes as much as any Quaker in *Great Britain*: But he's soon out of his Apprehensions, and in his old Pickle of Profaneness; for no sooner is the Storm over, or the Regiment marching into Winter-Quarters, but off goes the Glass, and up go Madam's fine Petticoats; 'tis handle your Arms, and to the Left about as you were.[47]

Significantly, the Articles of War of 1748 explicitly recognised the problem of the morally delinquent chaplain, their sixth article stipulating that: 'Whatever chaplain to a Regiment, Troop, or Garrison shall be guilty of drunkenness, or of other scandalous or vicious behaviour derogating from the sacred character with which he is invested, [he] shall, upon due proofs before a Court-martial, be discharged from his said office.'[48] Nevertheless, Ward held that military life was inevitably corrupting, forcing the chaplain to adjust to the milieu in which he found himself:

> He is far from being a Scandal to his Profession: He may drink, and wench to the end of the Chapter, yet he may plead with the missionary Jesuits in *China*, that he permits himself those Liberties with a Design to render his Person acceptable to the People . . . He seldom swears, but when he's full of *Brandy-Wine*, or good *Burgundy*; and then the Flesh yields to the Spirit: And he carries himself in such a Manner, as you'd imagine him, by his Dress and Behaviour, rather an *Irish* Grenadier or Dragoon, than the Soldier of a Crucified Master.[49]

Twenty years later, in his own satirical *Advice to the Officers of the British Army*, John Williamson agreed that any chaplain's scandalous behaviour could be largely ascribed to the corrupting influence of military life upon the clergyman's character. Indeed, he even addressed some facetious guidance to chaplains in this respect:

> You may indulge yourself in swearing, and talking bawdy as much as you please; this will show you are not a stiff high priest. Moreover, example being more effectual than precept, it will point out to the young officers the ugly and ungentlemanly appearance of the practice, and thereby deter them . . . Should you want to provide yourself with a deputy, be not over scrupulous respecting his character or morals. It would be a pity that he should be well disposed; for he would be sure soon to get spoiled among the officers.[50]

In addition to the invidious milieu of regimental life, finance was a further contributory factor to the problem of absentee chaplains. Whereas regimental colonels could profit from absenteeism by helping themselves to the pay of absentee chaplains,[51] other financial considerations could positively discourage chaplains from performing their duties in person. A burgeoning problem was the long-term decline in the relative value of a chaplain's pay, especially in the face of rising inflation in the latter half of the eighteenth century.[52] Throughout the 1700s, chaplains were paid 6s 8d per day, a level of remuneration that had remained unchanged since 1661.[53] During the reign of Queen Anne, this compared quite favourably with the pay of other regimental officers, a regimental chaplaincy being more remunerative than a majority in all but the most prestigious regiments.[54] However, this edge was lost under George I and George II. By 1740, the pay of regimental chaplains had slipped behind that of most captains and was less than half that received by infantry majors.[55] While inflation took its toll and their pay fell behind that of other officers, when present with their regiments chaplains could see much of it lost under the heading of subsistence, which was intended to provide for 'immediate maintenance'. In 1782, for example, deductions for subsistence stood at 5s per day (or £91 5s per annum) for chaplains of regiments on the British and Irish establishments. After other deductions were made, this could leave a regimental chaplain clearing as little as £22 6s 5d per annum.[56] Furthermore, while the chaplain was expected to make his home among the officers of his regiment, the costs that a regimental officer could incur as a result of his chosen profession were considerable, the expense of clothing, kit and the services of a horse and servant being daunting for much better paid officers than the regimental chaplain.[57] In view of these financial liabilities, the phenomenon of the absentee chaplain becomes ever more explicable. However, if the returns to be had from a regimental chaplaincy were undoubtedly in decline, it must be stressed that, even in the 1790s, pay amounting to £121 13s 4d per annum compared very favourably to the annual income of a great many Anglican clergymen. It also had the advantage of not having to be prised from the hands of reluctant tithe-payers or, in the case of ministers of the Church of Scotland, from the hands of their parish heritors.[58] In view of this, it is not surprising that a chaplain's commission was always regarded as a useful investment, one that could be maximised if a clergyman chose to invest in a senior regiment (which was less likely to be disbanded in years of peace) and if he stayed away from its officers and men.[59] Consequently, chaplains' commissions always fetched a good price and as late as 1796 they were being sold for as much as £800.[60]

Given the numerous factors involved, absenteeism was endemic among regimental chaplains even in the early years of the eighteenth century. On 26 May 1703, Noyes reported that eleven out of twenty-four regimental chaplains from Marlborough's army were absent in England or Ireland or their places were as yet unfilled by their colonels, who were skimming off their pay.[61] Such delinquency was officially frowned upon and it clearly offended the pious sensibilities of Queen Anne. Consequently, Lord Portmore was sent the following letter in November 1704:

> My Lord, Her Majesty being inform'd that the Chaplain of your Lordship's Regiment is remaining still in England without Leave, notwithstanding Her Orders to the contrary, does direct me to signify Her Pleasure that *Your Lordship do immediately appoint another in his room*.[62]

Similarly, two months later the Duke of Marlborough issued the following order demanding that chaplains return to their regiments:

> Whereas I have been informed that severall of the Chaplains of the Army have neglected to attend their Duty with their respective Regiments in the Low Country's; I do hereby Direct that no Chaplain of any Regiment do presume to be absent from his Duty after the 25 day of March next upon pain of having another Chaplain immediately Commission'd in his Room, and do further require the Chaplain Generall to give me immediat notice of any Chaplains that shall be Absent from their Regiments after the Five and Twentieth Day of March and to recommend at the same time fitting Persons to Supply their Places.[63]

Nevertheless, despite occasional crackdowns the problem of absentee chaplains appears to have become more acute as the years passed, a situation reflected in the 1748 Articles of War wherein it was stated that: 'No chaplain who is commissioned to a Regiment, Company, Troop, or Garrison, shall absent himself . . . (excepting in case of sickness or leave of absence) upon pain of being brought to a Court-martial, and punished as their judgment and the circumstances of his offence may require.'[64] Despite the spirit of this article, its loopholes were all too obvious and the problem of absenteeism remained unsolved. Some of the issues involved were reflected in Horace Walpole's correspondence with the Duke of Bedford, then Lord Lieutenant of Ireland, in January 1757. In a breezy letter to the duke, Walpole wrote:

> My friend Mr. Montagu's parson at Greatworth is chaplain to his brother's regiment in Ireland, and it will make Mr. Montagu, and consequently me, very happy, if your Grace will give Mr. James Miller (the clergyman's name) leave to be absent from the regiment now at Cork. Were I writing to the Archbishop of Canterbury, I could plead with great truth that while they have their present colonel, even the souls of the regiment will not suffer from the absence of their chaplain . . .[65]

In reply, Bedford made it clear that he thought very differently about the matter:

> I am truly very sorry, that it will be impossible for me to comply with your request . . . I have laid it down as an unvariable rule, that every chaplain in Ireland, shall constantly attend his duty either by himself, or a proper deputy, to be approved of by me, and recommended to me by the officer commanding the regiment, through whom every request of this nature, must come . . .[66]

While plainly an issue in Ireland, the problem of absentee chaplains was also apparent in Germany during the Seven Years War, with one chaplain being absent from his charge for a year before being compelled to resign.[67] However, the problem seems to have been particularly acute in North America. In this case, regimental chaplains faced a lengthy sojourn and the additional deterrents of an unpleasant trans-Atlantic voyage and the prospect of facing a savage Indian enemy in the depths of the American wilderness. In 1760, John Ogilvie, an Anglican clergyman who was then an S.P.G. missionary and rector of St Peter's, Albany, wrote to the committee of the Society informing them that he had taken a chaplaincy in the Royal American Regiment. However, he knew of three other regular regiments that had campaigned without one.[68] Nor were the fever-ridden West Indies any more congenial to chaplains of this time. After the capture of Guadeloupe in 1759, its governor wrote to Lord Barrington: 'Our new friends the French take us for atheists, as we have ne'er a Chaplain amongst us nor any signs of public Worship.'[69] Such was the seriousness of the problem that, by the end of the Seven Years War, it seems clear that requests for leave of absence were being determined only at the highest levels. In September 1762, General Jeffrey Amherst, the army's Commander-in-Chief in North America, informed 'Colonel Forster, or officer commanding His Majesty's Forces in Nova Scotia, Halifax' that:

> It is with great Reluctance that I can consent to a Chaplain's leaving this Country, as so very few attend their duty in it, altho' their presence certainly is Very Necessary: I have a Letter from Mr. Breynton representing the Necessity of his requesting Leave to go to England: You will therefore give him Leave of Absence till next Summer, if he thinks his affairs cannot be Settled without his presence, altho' I had much rather he would continue where he is.[70]

In the wake of the Seven Years War, a significant number of regiments were retained in the American colonies, some for as long as seventeen years thanks to a flawed system of rotation. By 1774, there were seventeen regiments in the colonies and, with the outbreak of the American War of Independence, by 1776 this number had risen to forty-six.[71] However, even in peacetime the unattractiveness of North America was all too evident. This was underlined by correspondence between the Secretary at War and the Commander-in-Chief in North America in 1766. Having been informed by Lord Barrington of complaints that had been made to the king 'relative to the Non Attendance of the Chaplains to Regiments serving abroad', and having being urged 'to enforce obedience to the King's repeated Orders given for their personal Attendance, or for providing sufficient Deputys',[72] General Thomas Gage reported that four of his fifteen regiments were unattended by either their chaplain or by a deputy.[73] However, the American War of Independence once again exposed the unwillingness of many chaplains to serve in North America. At one point, two of the four chaplains of the four battalions of the Royal American Regiment were in England and one regimental chaplain was noted to have been absent from his regiment for more than twenty years.[74] It was against this background that one military commentator, Thomas Simes, proposed in 1777 that the position of the regimental chaplain be combined with that of the regimental pay-master, an expedient that would augment the chaplain's 'inadequate' pay and 'for which consideration he should be obliged to reside constantly with his corps'.[75]

As the correspondence between Gage and Barrington shows, by the 1760s it had become commonplace for regimental chaplains to employ deputies to perform their duties, usually at the heavily discounted rate of 2s 6d a day.[76] However, this practice was not universally winked at and, as late as 1777, Simes wrote that 'The practice of allowing the duty to be done by deputy is scandalous, as [regimental chaplains] care not how their offices are filled by others; if they make an advantageous bargain, their main point is, not who will serve them best, but who will serve them cheapest.'[77] Nevertheless, the expedient proved acceptable to some senior officers; on a single day in August 1762, George Townshend wrote several letters on this very subject. That sent to the chaplain of the 51st Regiment at Liverpool was typical:

> Sir, I have received your letter of the 6th Instant. I have wrote to the commanding Officer of the 51st Regiment to report to me whether there is any person officiating in the Regiment as Deputy to you, if he certifies that there is there will be no occasion for you to repair to the Regiment 'til further notice is given you.[78]

Anglican regimental chaplains appear to have recruited these surrogates from the Church of England's unruly underclass of unbeneficed clergy, a group that was responsible for a good deal of clerical scandal and whose involvement did little to enhance the image of military chaplains in general. According to the Commissioners of Military Enquiry, a body created by parliament in 1805 in order to investigate the running of Britain's various military departments, by the end of the eighteenth century it had become the norm for regimental chaplains to appoint a deputy, it being the impression among them that their appointments were effectively sinecures. Indeed, the Commissioners even found that it had been common for buyers of regimental chaplaincies to be assured that 'personal Service would never be demanded of them, provided [that] they assented to the usual deduction from their pay to remunerate a Deputy'.[79]

Although the army was generally ill prepared for war with Republican France in 1793, its early campaigns exposed a chaplaincy system that had long been in a state of atrophy. In 1795, Miles Beevor, chaplain to the 1st Royal Scots, was noted to have been absent from his regiment since his commission was signed on 14 February 1786;[80] likewise, in 1796 it was noted that Peter Vataas, an octogenarian and the incumbent of livings in Oxfordshire and Essex, had been on paid leave of absence from the 14th Light Dragoons for a period of fifty-two years.[81] In August 1793, the Adjutant-General wrote to Lieutenant-General Cunninghame in Ireland explaining the factors that encouraged such abuses:

> [W]ith regard to Chaplains, their personal Attendance with their Regiments on their leaving Ireland, ought certainly, in strictness to be required, but their own Colonels generally speaking, assume an Authority of dispensing with it, if agreeable to them. All that Lord Amherst [the Commander-in-Chief] desired, on the late Embarkation of our Cavalry for the Continent was, that there should be at least one Chaplain, or his Deputy, to every Brigade; But several of the Colonels, without attending to this Indulgence from his Lordship, ordered their own Chaplains either to go themselves, with the Detachments of their Regiments, or to provide Deputies to do their duty for them.[82]

In 1809 it was found that 'there was only one Regimental Chaplain' present with the Duke of York's army in Flanders in 1793; four or five other clergymen eventually turned up, however, 'who acted as Deputies to their respective Employers'.[83] If this showing was decidedly poor, worse was to follow in 1795 when not a single regimental chaplain bestirred himself to accompany General Sir Ralph Abercromby's massive expedition to the West Indies. Although the expedition comprised a major proportion of the army's line regiments,[84] a journey to the West Indies 'was not to be seen so much as an exotic sojourn as a death sentence'.[85] As the Commissioners of Military Enquiry therefore discovered:

> [General Abercromby] directed an Order to be addressed to all the Chaplains of the Regiments under his command, requiring their personal attendance at his then Head-Quarters, in order to settle amongst themselves what number of them should accompany the Troops on that Expedition [but] no Chaplain appeared to the General's summons.[86]

The Army Chaplains' Department

The wretched inefficiency of the chaplaincy system in the British army during the early years of the French Revolutionary Wars left it dangerously exposed to the reforming energies of the Duke of York, who undertook the radical remodelling of British army chaplaincy as one of his many reforms as Commander-in-Chief. Although his reputation was later tarnished by his disastrous affair with Mary Anne Clarke, there is every indication that the duke (who was to become a strong supporter of the Naval and Military Bible Society and who was, until 1803, the lay Bishop of Osnabruck) felt a genuine concern for the religious welfare of the army, a concern that may have been sharpened given the place of religion as an ideological bulwark against the Jacobin tide then threatening to engulf Europe. In addition to the glaring inefficiency of the existing system and the possible dangers of neglecting religion, a further problem with regimental chaplaincy was its spiralling expense. The French Republic's declaration of war in 1793 prompted the expansion of the regular army, the embodiment of Britain's militia regiments and the raising of a new generation of fencible regiments, all of which meant more expenditure in maintaining an ineffectual chaplaincy system.

The seriousness with which the Duke of York took the matter of army chaplaincy is reflected in the terms of the instrument used to effect its reconstruction, namely the Royal Warrant of 23 September 1796. Given the 'nearly universal want of personal Attendance among the Chaplains of Regiments, and of care in providing proper deputies' and also 'the difficulty of finding clergymen to attend Corps serving abroad upon such a stipend as is usually stopped from the pay of the Chaplains for that purpose', the Warrant of 1796 ordered that all regimental chaplains join their regiments by Christmas Day or 'retire from [the] service on a reduced subsistence of four shillings per diem'. In order that the performance of returnees could be properly monitored, the Warrant required that commanding officers certify twice a year that their chaplains were engaged 'in the personal discharge of [their] duty'. Failure to do so would result in the deduction of the chaplain's pay from the funds paid to the regiment by the Paymaster-General.[87] The Warrant then went on to prohibit the appointment of regimental chaplains and deputy chaplains after Christmas Day 1796.[88] In view of the gradual abolition of regimental chaplaincies which the Warrant aimed to achieve (and the impact upon regimental colonels, who would thereby lose a valuable piece of patronage) the Warrant was sweetened by a War Office circular dated 30 September 1796 which announced the compensation to which colonels were entitled. Under the terms of the circular, each colonel was allowed to sell extra commissions in their regiment upon the death of their existing chaplain. By these means, the colonels of cavalry regiments were allowed to raise up to £700 and the colonels of infantry regiments up to £500 'in lieu' of their right to nominate a successor.[89]

Clearly, these terms were quite favourable to regimental colonels, who were often well-connected general officers and relatively powerful figures in the military establishment.[90] However, their chaplains were left smarting from the firm smack of reform, a sensation that was to become ever more familiar to the clergy of the Church of England and Church of Ireland in the course of subsequent years. In October 1796, 'A Chaplain of a Regiment' penned a heartfelt protest to the editor of *The Gentleman's Magazine*:

> Mr. URBAN, I am almost annihilated, spiritually and corporally . . . From a situation I deemed in sunshine, I am as suddenly covered with gloom and darkness as a candle under an extinguisher. Sir, I am a chaplain to a regiment. Four or five years ago I expended my inheritance and oeconomical accumulation, amounting to [£900] in purchasing a chaplaincy to an old regiment, then returning home from abroad, enjoying in anticipation an income of 6s. 8d. a day, the full pay of a chaplain. But, what was my dismay when I found, by the public papers, my regiment was immediately ordered to the West Indies, and 2s. 6d. a day withdrawn from my pay for a deputy, nominally so only; for, no duty was done! I quieted my mind, in daily hopes of peace, of my regiment returning home, and my enjoyment of full-pay. But, a few weeks since, an official communication told me I must join my regiment in person, must constantly personally attend it, or accept of an annuity for my own life of 4s. a day, or the alternative of forfeiture and extinction. Alas! Sir, what a privation of property, purchased under the sanction of fifty years usage, with the right of selling again! I hope some liberal military man in power will, at his hour of amusement, catch your general Publication; and, in compassion and benevolence, obtain for us our original full pay of 6s. 8d. a day for life . . . Such a benevolent act to us will be a shield and buckler of defence, in the day of battle and hour of danger, to the promoters of it.[91]

A more altruistic objection was entered in 1800 by an anonymous pamphleteer –'an old man, and an old soldier' – who protested that 'it is bad reasoning, from the abuse of a thing to argue against the use of it'.[92] Claiming 'that in abolishing the order of regimental chaplains, government trod rather too near the foot-steps of our enlightened Gallican neighbours' and that recent military setbacks on the continent could be attributed to divine displeasure at an ill-advised course of action,[93] he pointed out that less draconian measures should have sufficed to secure chaplains for the army:

> If the chaplain's duty was scandalously neglected, by the connivance of the Colonel in suffering it to be made a sinecure, in order to enhance the value of it; and any worthless clergyman was suffered to be sent as deputy, and in that capacity to officiate for half a dozen regiments; that evil might have been easily removed by a general order, that every chaplain should personally attend his regiment, or sell out, and resign to one who would. It would be a strange inference, to conclude, that, because a man neglects his duty in an office he may hold, therefore the office itself is of no consequence. At that rate, because an incumbent will not reside on his living, but leaves it to the care of a curate, who has perhaps, two or three more churches on his hands, we might argue against the use of parish priests: or 'because a Bishop may not have confirmed in his diocese for those nine years past,' we might plead the inutility of the episcopal order.[94]

Despite the cogency of this argument and their own indignation, the threat of compulsory service with their regiments ensured that the near universal response of regimental chaplains was to retire on their new pensions of £73 a year. It was, indeed, a poor reflection on the priorities of regimental chaplains of the day that only two returned to their regiments under the new dispensation. Even here, however, their duties were embraced with reluctance. Both were chaplains to the two regiments of Lifeguards,[95] whose specific functions had ensured that they had not seen active service since 1745. Moreover, even the demands of this gilded role proved too much for one of them, who retired within the space of a few years.[96]

Having effectively disposed of the encumbrance of regimental chaplaincies, the Royal Warrant of 1796 outlined the complex organisation of the new Chaplains' Department that would supersede them. In lieu of regimental chaplains, the Warrant stipulated that chaplains would be appointed to armies or to large garrisons overseas 'in the proportion of one to each Brigade, or to every three or four Regiments'. These were to be paid ten shillings a day and they were to be eligible for a pension of £73 per annum after twelve years' service. Additional chaplains were to be appointed to smaller overseas garrisons of one or two regiments with the pay of seven shillings a day, a pension of £73 per annum after twelve years and with the prospect of promotion to brigade chaplain 'as opportunity may offer, and as they shall be found deserving'. Whereas overseas chaplains were to serve as full-time functionaries on the staffs of their respective armies and garrisons, the Warrant envisaged a less exalted role for clergymen ministering to troops at home: 'For every barrack in the British dominions a neighbouring clergyman is to be employed as the curate to perform Divine Service every Sunday, and to be paid twenty-five pounds per annum.' For those regiments at home who were not stationed in barracks, a rather different system was prescribed whereby 'The Commanding Officer of every separate Regiment in quarters will attend with his Regiment at some Parish Church; or employ a neighbouring clergyman to perform Divine Service to the men.' Such clergymen were to be paid 'a just compensation' (not exceeding ten shillings a week) and were to claim their pay from the agents of the regiments in question, to whom they were required to submit full certification of their services.[97]

Having announced the advent and mechanisms of the new order, the Warrant concluded by stating that all regular chaplains were now subject to the orders of a Chaplain-General who was to receive his instructions from the Secretary at War, a junior government minister who oversaw military administration from the precincts of the War Office.[98] The new Chaplain-General was the Rev. John Gamble, a Fellow of Pembroke College, Cambridge, and a domestic chaplain to the Duke of York. Free of parochial responsibilities, Gamble had developed a strong and practical interest in military affairs. In 1788 he had purchased the chaplaincy of the 37th Regiment and exchanged this for that of the 11th Light Dragoons five years later. As the only regimental chaplain to accompany the Duke of York's expedition to Flanders, Gamble was appointed domestic chaplain to the duke in 1794 and exchanged his chaplaincy in the 11th Light Dragoons for a regimental chaplaincy in the Coldstream Guards in 1795.[99] In the same year, Gamble published a short treatise on telegraphy entitled *Observations on Tele-*

graphic Experiments. Or the different modes which have been, or may be adopted for the purpose of distant communication which he 'gratefully inscribed' to his royal patron.[100] Although he followed this with an essay on military signalling in 1797, Gamble's taste for system and his 'mechanical mind', as he described it, was also applied to the business of military chaplaincy, the Commissioners of Military Enquiry identifying him as the chief architect of the new Department.[101]

However distinguished Gamble may have been as a theoretician, the administrative problems facing the Chaplains' Department were formidable and not least among them was the question of finance. Given the administrative complexity of the new dispensation, and the fact that scores of regimental chaplains had retired in 1796,[102] a former War Office clerk was employed to assist Gamble (who seems to have based himself at the Horse Guards)[103] with the finances of the new Department. The task of Gamble's 'cashier' was to receive from regimental agents the pay that had hitherto been received by their regimental chaplains. As the Commissioners put it:

> These sums constituted a fund, out of which [the cashier] was to pay such compensations to Clergymen performing duties with the Regular and Fencible Corps at home, and other disbursements connected with the Service, as were directed by the Secretary at War through the Chaplain General.[104]

Whatever its other faults, the new Department appears to have been a model of shrewd financial management. By December 1797, the fund had generated a surplus of more than £7,000, a sum that had grown to nearly £13,000 two years later. Initially, this sat idle in the hands of private bankers but in 1800 it was decided to put these funds to public use and 'the Secretary at War directed the sum of [£15,000] to be purchased in the three-per-cent Consolidated Annuities'. By 1805, the sum invested in these annuities had risen to £55,000 and in 1806 the Treasury agreed that the rights to all dividends should be sold off, a sale that realised more than £33,000 for 'His Majesty's Exchequer'. This sale was prompted by the Secretary at War's proposal that the finances of the Department be simplified, with parliament voting an annual sum towards its maintenance. In 1806, this was estimated at £31,500, a figure that covered the pay of 130 officiating clergymen, 136 retired regimental chaplains, thirty garrison chaplains and eleven brigade chaplains.[105]

If the new Department was a triumph of economy, it is clear that it experienced considerable problems in other respects. Significantly, the Royal Warrant of September 1796 said nothing about the future of the chaplains employed by the Board of Ordnance, which was fiercely independent of the War Office. As the Board appointed chaplains for the Royal Artillery, its chaplains were largely tasked with ministering to the gunners who manned fortifications at home and overseas. It was emblematic of the independence of the Board of Ordnance and of the incremental nature of the reform of army chaplaincy at this time that Ordnance chaplains remained separate from the new Chaplains' Department until the abolition of the Board in the 1850s. Inevitably, the survival of this independent jurisdiction posed difficulties for the newly established Chaplains'

Department and was particularly galling for the Chaplain-General. As late as 1845, George Gleig bemoaned the existence of two Ordnance chaplains at Woolwich – 'independent, we cannot tell why, of all connexion with thc chaplain-general's office'.[106] One problem arose from the question of who should pay those local clergymen who ministered to mixed congregations of artillerymen (who were the responsibility of the Board) and other troops (who were the responsibility of the Department).[107] Furthermore, with the growth of Britain's coastal defences and the expansion of the Royal Artillery, the Board greatly expanded its chaplaincy provision in 1806–7, increasing the number of its full-time chaplains from zero to seven and its part-time chaplains from three to eight. As the Chaplain-General complained to the Commissioners of Military Enquiry, all of these appointments were made 'without any previous communication to me, who, as Chaplain General of His Majesty's Land Forces, cannot but consider that the Artillery is of that description'.[108] The Commissioners found that six of the Board's full-time chaplains received a salary of £120 per annum in addition to allowances for accommodation and, where appropriate, for forage. The plumb job, however, was that of chaplain to the Royal Artillery at Woolwich, a post that came with a salary of £182 10s per annum and a house of its own.[109] After assessing this situation and the Chaplain-General's complaints,[110] it was left to the Commissioners to recommend that:

> [It] would be convenient if the Ordnance Chaplains (although appointed by the Ordnance Board) were placed under the control of the Chaplain General, and made subject to His Majesty's Regulations, equally with every other Chaplain or Clergyman performing Ecclesiastical duties to His Majesty's Forces, by which all invidious distinction would be removed; the remuneration of all placed on an uniform principle; and double payments for the same service effectually prevented.[111]

While the independence of the Ordnance chaplains was a long-running irritant, a much greater problem lay in the system of brigade chaplains inaugurated in 1796, the policy of appointing chaplains to field armies proving an abject failure in practice. Much of the blame for this lay at the door of the Adjutant-General's Department, which was responsible for appointments of this kind, and with general officers in the field. The journal of D.P. Cosserat, who served as a brigade chaplain in Egypt in 1801, reveals a telling picture of administrative confusion. On arrival in Aboukir Bay in mid-July, Cosserat was politely received at the brigade headquarters of Major-General Sir Eyre Coote. However, Coote was puzzled as to what to do with Cosserat and with a second new chaplain named Matthews:

> General Coote [Cosserat noted] behaved with great civility and politeness, but said he could not open [my] letter [it] being addressed to the Commander in Chief, and advised me to write him an official letter at the same time, and begged I would call again at camp in the course of the week when most probably he would have received directions to put Mr M[atthews] and myself in orders.[112]

Five days later, Cosserat returned to Coote's headquarters, where the situation was still unresolved:

> Matthews and myself again went to camp to wait on General Coote, as we had no horses we were obliged to walk which tired us most amazingly, however the general behaved with his usual politeness, insisted on our dining with him and lent us horses to return to our boat. He could not give us any information relative to our being put in orders as he had not heard from the Commander in Chief, but advised us to come again to camp in the course of the week when if he did not hear he would take it on himself to employ us.[113]

A week later:

> According to General Coote's order Matthews and myself again went to camp, but found as Gen: Hutchinson [the Commander-in-Chief] was on his return from Cairo, [Coote] could not possibly put us in orders but advised us at the same time to find out the General and personally pay our respects to him and remind him of the letters of service we brought from England which had not been answered or at all noticed.[114]

When Cosserat and Matthews finally met the irascible Hutchinson at the beginning of August, the Commander-in-Chief was just downright rude:

> [The General] received us in a very cavalier manner, and told us we had been put in orders two days since, and were to go to camp immediately, as it was a pretty thing for chaplains to the army to remain on board ship, we asked him when we were to go, and he informed us in the course of two or three days.[115]

However, and despite Hutchinson's impatience, the question of their postings was far from being resolved:

> As it was needless for us to take our tent to camp before we knew to what Brigades we were to be attached . . . I went on horseback [and] was much surprised on calling first on Gen. Coote, and afterwards at Head Quarters to find we were not in orders and that it had been omitted by mistake. However as the form was absolutely necessary, our going to camp till it was gone through was of none avail. I was advised by Col. Kempt, secretary to the Commander-in-Chief, to write him an official letter on board the *Fondroyant* and the business would be settled immediately.[116]

A month after arriving in Egypt, Cosserat and Matthews were still without an official posting and it was not until the end of August that the former was able to preside at a parade service.[117] However, this proved to be a unique occasion during Cosserat's four month sojourn in Egypt, Cosserat noting in late September that: 'Such has been the bustle in camp, or rather such has been the disposition of our noble Commander in Chief that he has not once had duty performed since our arrival, indeed the day of the month only is regarded, and Sunday is the same as another day.'[118]

This combination of inefficiency and indifference helped to ensure that, in the aftermath of the short-lived Peace of Amiens, large bodies of troops left Britain's shores with little or no pastoral oversight.[119] No chaplain, for example, appears to have served with the troops sent to the River Plate in 1806–7.[120] In fact, in view of

Lieutenant-General Whitelocke's humiliating capitulation at Buenos Aires in July 1807, one brigade chaplain later remarked that 'in South America, the Spaniards were shocked at our army's being unprovided with chaplains, and attributed our calamities in great measure to this want'.[121] As late as the summer of 1808, the Commissioners of Military Enquiry found that Sir Arthur Wellesley had gone to Portugal with a force of nearly 9,000 men but without 'any Clerical Officer of any description'.[122] However, there was also the question of the quality as well as the quantity of brigade chaplains. Given the severe inflation of the war years, the pay awarded to brigade and garrison chaplains by the Warrant of 1796 rapidly lost its value. Consequently, by 1806 the Duke of York had concluded 'that, with few exceptions, the persons employed as Chaplains with the Army were, in point of conduct and character, extremely unfit for such a station'.[123] This was not an isolated opinion. In 1837, one veteran officer recalled the chaplains he encountered in Malta nearly forty years earlier:

> [T]he two persons who called themselves Chaplains at Malta, were discarded surgeons of the Navy. I saw one of these worthies one Sunday morning before going to church in such a state of nervous weakness from being drunk the night before, that he could not carry the spoon to his mouth – and at the funeral of Sir Ralph Abercromby these two respectable divines had nearly fallen to fisty-cuffs to decide who should have the honour of officiating, neither of them being sober at the time.[124]

Convinced that the pay of brigade chaplains in particular was insufficient to attract a better class of clergyman, in June 1806 the Duke of York wrote to the Secretary at War proposing that brigade chaplains should receive the same pay as infantry majors, namely 16s per day (or £292 per annum). Through such an increase, the duke maintained, these appointments would become 'objects of competition with Gentlemen of respectability in their profession'. Furthermore, by seeking to ensure that chaplains were appointed to brigades as soon as they were ordered overseas and remained attached to them thereafter, the duke maintained that 'by their example and precept, [they] may most effectually promote a due regard to Religion and Morality [which is] the best foundation of the discipline of an Army'.[125] Although the duke's proposal had found acceptance at the War Office and at the Treasury by April 1807, persistent difficulties in providing chaplains for the army's expeditionary forces showed that this enhancement was not sufficient to achieve the desired results. Accordingly, in June 1808, and at the duke's behest, the Adjutant-General, Sir Harry Calvert, approached the War Office with a more radical proposal. According to a new scheme devised by the duke, all full-time chaplains were to be made eligible for active service and confirmed in their status as staff officers. The system of officiating clergymen was to be abolished, not least because there was 'no adequate provision made for the discharge of other duties' besides their Sunday services. Hence, officiating clergymen were not 'calculated to establish that constant intercourse and communication between the Chaplain and the Soldier which is necessary to render the service of the former of real essential benefit'.[126] Members of the new and enlarged establishment of staff chaplains were to receive 16s a day (the pay of an infantry major) while serving at home, rising to 17s per day (the pay of an infantry lieutenant-colonel) while serving overseas. They were also to be eligible for half-pay upon leaving the service.[127]

Despite the duke's enthusiasm, the Secretary at War, Sir James Murray Pulteney, had doubts about the proposal. Although conceding the need for a system of half-pay and more generous allowances for brigade chaplains, Pulteney saw no grounds for giving them additional pay for serving abroad and nor was he convinced of the need to abolish the system of officiating clergymen. In his view, each garrison did not require its own staff chaplain because 'the perpetual change of Regiments precludes the idea of his having a personal influence and acquaintance with the men'. Furthermore, the army needed its connections with the parish clergy in order to gain access to civilian churches, an essential requirement given the inclemency of the British weather and the unsuitability of barrack accommodation for divine service. Instead, Pulteney proposed a compromise whereby staff chaplains would be appointed to garrisons at home 'where the Troops are too numerous to be attended by the Parochial Minister'. Even here, however, they would supplement rather than supersede the officiating clergy. By means of these new appointments, 'a certain number of Chaplains, adequate to the Duties of a Brigade, would at all times be in readiness, who might, as occasion required, be ordered to proceed on Foreign Service'. However, Pulteney doubted whether even these were strictly necessary as these posts could be filled by staff chaplains returning home with their brigades.[128]

The future organisation of army chaplaincy was still unresolved as Britain's military commitments in the Iberian Peninsula grew in the summer and autumn of 1808. By December of that year, Gamble could report to the Duke of York that there were ten brigade chaplains serving with the army in Spain and Portugal. Furthermore, the public enthusiasm for the patriot cause in Spain had resulted in a surfeit of applicants for brigade chaplaincies.[129] However, the army's ill-fated campaigns of 1808–9 only exacerbated some unresolved problems in the Department. One brigade chaplain, James Cooley, quickly succumbed to the rigours of campaigning and, although the pay of brigade chaplains had been confirmed at 16s a day in December 1808, it was unclear as to what his widow's entitlements were.[130] More seriously, the evacuation of Sir John Moore's army from Corunna and Vigo in January 1809 left the Chaplain-General unsure as to what to do with the six brigade chaplains made redundant by the evacuations. As Gamble put it in a letter to the Secretary at War, these clergymen had been posted to home garrisons on full pay and the cost-conscious Gamble felt compelled to air the question of their severance.[131] In the event, the problem was partly resolved by the despatch of an army of 30,000 men to the Scheldt estuary in July 1809, this new (and ultimately futile) campaign in northern Europe allowing Gamble to dispose of two of the Department's erstwhile brigade chaplains.[132]

John Owen as Chaplain-General

John Gamble retired as Chaplain-General in March 1810, just short of his fiftieth birthday. Clearly in poor health, he died the following year. With the demands of the war increasing, and with important changes pending in the Department, it was fortunate that his successor was a man of energy and ability. Unlike Gamble, who was essentially an administrator, John Owen brought to the office of Chaplain-General a marked pastoral zeal that was born of strong evangelical convictions. Owen's parents and family had strong Methodist connections and his father, a wealthy shipping agent, had been on intimate terms with John Wesley. Educated at Charterhouse and at Oxford, Owen held a fellowship at New College before serving in a succession of London curacies. However, the young Owen had much wider horizons than the metropolis and in 1784 he secured a chaplaincy in the East India Company. On his arrival in Calcutta, Owen served as chaplain to the garrison at Fort William, then the most important military station in British India. Although Owen was active in his support for the S.P.C.K. and for other charitable work in Calcutta, the local climate (of which he often complained) eventually proved too much and he resigned his chaplaincy in 1793. On his return to England, he held no ecclesiastical appointment until he became a brigade chaplain in 1799. After serving with the Guards brigade in Holland,[133] Owen was appointed to the archdeaconry of Richmond by the Bishop of Chester, an appointment that was a virtual sinecure.[134] In 1802, during the brief peace with France, he was also preferred to the united parishes of St Benet and St Peter in London. However, these civilian appointments do not appear to have satisfied his ambitions and, in 1808, he was among the first applicants for a brigade chaplaincy in the Peninsula, his commission from the Secretary at War being signed in July 1808.[135] Furthermore, and due to a direct application to the king, Owen appears to have been designated 'Senior Chaplain to the Forces destined to be employed in Spain and Portugal'.[136] Finally, in March 1810 he was appointed to succeed Gamble as Chaplain-General. Whereas Gamble was a protégé of the Duke of York (who, in 1810, was in a state of dishonourable retirement over a corruption scandal involving his mistress) Owen's appointment owed much to the esteem in which he was held by Spencer Perceval.

Perceval was appointed Prime Minister in October 1809, an appointment that gave the evangelical party in the Church of England unprecedented influence in government. Perceval's interest in the reform of military chaplaincy was probably a decisive factor in Owen's appointment, being a natural extension of the Prime Minister's enthusiasm for higher pastoral standards among the clergy of the Church of England. As chancellor of the exchequer, Perceval had already played a key role in securing the more flexible system of chaplaincy envisaged by the Duke of York. In January 1809, and as part of ongoing negotiations over the reform of the Department and its projected costs, Perceval wrote a lengthy memorandum outlining his views on the subject. Although he was in favour of retaining the system of officiating clergy 'where soldiers may be quartered in such numbers as would not require the Appointment of Chaplains', the chancellor was entirely at one with the Duke of York in preferring to have 'all the Military Chaplains on the same footing, even tho' it should lead to the abolition in some instances of the existing Garrison Chaplains'.[137] Furthermore, and providing that the efficiency of the new system could be ensured, Perceval was not prepared to let questions of economy stand in the way:

> I am so impressed with the propriety of adopting some new plan upon the principle proposed, that I will not suffer any consideration of what I should deem a most false economy to induce me to withhold my consent from the adoption of it . . . provided . . . the system which shall be introduced, shall ensure a real and efficient discharge of duty on the part of the chaplains.[138]

Noting that 'not one in ten' of overseas garrison chaplains were actually resident, the chancellor blamed the inadequacy of their pay, asserting that 'the present Salaries are so far below what they ought to be, that persons of due respectability and character could not upon these salaries be found to undertake the offices upon condition of residence'.[139]

In view of this, Perceval announced that he was prepared to defend any increased expenditure in parliament provided that certain conditions were met. Firstly, that all army chaplains 'should receive commissions which should hold them liable to serve when called upon, either at any Military Station in England, or abroad, or with any part of the Army on Foreign Service for the space of 8 years'.[140] Chaplains would then be eligible for half-pay at the rate of five shillings a day with bonuses if they remained available for future service. If circumstances required that they be placed on half-pay before the end of their eight years, they would not be allowed to hold a living or preferment that would prevent them from being recalled for the balance of this term. Secondly, garrison chaplains should be given 'the option of transferring their services to the Establishment formed under this measure'; if they did so, they would have to relinquish any other 'clerical occupation' and accept that 'for the purposes of discipline . . . they should, like all other staff officers, hold themselves available to be employed wherever their Services are required'.[141] Thirdly, brigade chaplains then serving in Spain would not be automatically taken onto the new establishment. Instead, their applications would have to be supported by the senior chaplain and by the Commander-in-Chief in the Peninsula. Fourthly and finally, Perceval required that the assistance of either the Archbishop of Canterbury or the Bishop of London (or, better still, 'both of them') be obtained in the appointment of new staff chaplains. He even looked forward to the day when either one of these prelates could take 'the whole of this subject under their immediate Control' as chaplain-general with 'a Deputy Chaplain General under him, and such assistance in Secretaries and Clerks as the extent of the Business might require'.[142]

The 'new modelling'[143] of the Department was achieved through the promulgation of a 'New Regulation' in December 1809 and it fell to Owen to develop the Department from this point onwards.[144] Under his direction, a system of recruitment was devised whereby the Chaplain-General interviewed applicants and endeavoured 'in every practicable way to ascertain [their] character and opinions'. He also inquired about their pastoral methods, 'ascertaining with care, if [they were] in the habit of finding out and visiting the sick'. Finally, he read sample sermons submitted by applicants, visited services at which they presided and tried to assess the state of their health. Only once these checks had been completed would he forward an applicant's papers to a triumvirate consisting of the Archbishop of Canterbury, the Archbishop of York and the Bishop of London, giving his own opinion as to the candidate's suitability.[145] Once episcopal approval had been obtained, the Chaplain-General would recommend the successful applicant for the king's commission.[146] By dint of the 'New Regulation' and its corollaries, the Department was able to eliminate pluralism among its more junior members. In a description of the system dating from 1818, Owen declared that:

> It has been determined for good reasons, by the late Mr. Perceval, by the Lord Archbishop of Canterbury, by the Lord Archbishop of York and by the Lord Bishop of London that no Person holding a Benefice with care of Souls, shall be eligible to the Office of Chaplain to the Forces, and no papers of such beneficed persons have, at any time, been forwarded to the Prelates by the Chaplain General.[147]

Significantly, fifteen chaplains resigned on the promulgation of the 'New Regulation', twelve of them garrison chaplains who had no stomach for the more adventurous life of a staff chaplain.[148] However, in 1811, and with the approval of Lord Palmerston, Pulteney's successor as Secretary at War, Owen introduced a new category of 'Home Chaplain'. These clergymen would minister to the larger garrisons in Great Britain on a full-time basis for £250 per annum – considerably less than the pay of a staff chaplain and with no entitlement to half-pay or other perquisites. These were to be recruited from among clergymen without cure of souls and their applications were to be approved by the Chaplain-General and the bishops' committee. They would be expected to undertake overseas service if called upon to do so but would not receive a commission until posted abroad by the Secretary at War. If a staff chaplain was to return to Great Britain for any reason, then the Secretary at War was free to dismiss a Home Chaplain in order to make room for him and to keep the number of chaplains at a sustainable level. As far as Owen was concerned, the precarious situation of the Home Chaplain was a major advantage of the whole system as they were, in effect, probationers:

> There will be opportunity of trying every Chaplain before he be received on the establishment. Those of the strongest mind and body will be taken in preference, and where there is reason to think any one fails in the requisite qualities, he may be dropped without pain to his feelings or those of his military superiors. It will be sufficient to allege that a Chaplain of the Establishment being in England for his health, the Home Chaplain must give place to him.[149]

In addition to creating this reserve of 'Home' chaplains and remodelling the means whereby staff chaplains were appointed, Owen also set about ensuring greater accountability on the part of the officiating clergy. In December 1810, he circulated a new scale of allowances to 135 civilian clergymen, together with new forms to be completed when claiming fees for their services. These services (and their rationale, wherever an additional Sunday service for soldiers was provided) were to be certified by commanding officers and claims for payment were to be made twice yearly.[150] Like any born bureaucrat, Owen was ruthless with defaulters. Earlier that year he had written a tart rejoinder to a clergyman in Barbados, who had submitted an uncertified claim for fees to which he felt entitled:

> Your readiness to serve the Military claims I am sure my fullest acknowledgments, which I beg you to receive. I am aware that there is no adequate remuneration for those who truly perform their duty with these poor fellows, but you will not miss your reward at the resurrection of the just.[151]

Likewise, in September 1814 a Scottish clergyman was the recipient of the following missive:

> The Chaplain General presents his Compliments to the Rev. Robert Auld and is under the necessity of returning the enclosed Certificate in order that the period during which the sick were visited only once a Week may be stated, and also the cause of the omission. Mr. Owen also begs to observe that the Average number of Men attending Divine Service should be stated, and not the Number of which the Depot consisted. Mr. Auld is requested in future to use the printed form of Certificate, of which some Copies are enclosed.[152]

If Owen derived a certain satisfaction from being unhelpful towards a representative of the Kirk, there can be no doubt about his feelings at having to remunerate the clergy of the Church of Rome. As clergymen of an established Church, ministers of the Church of Scotland were perfectly entitled to payment as officiating clergymen. However, Roman Catholic priests had been excluded under the law from official military chaplaincy for well over a century and their recognition as officiating clergymen in 1813 ranks as a major (if little known) development in the early history of the Chaplains' Department. The question of regular payments to Roman Catholic priests arose in consequence of the Interchange Act of 1811, whereby militia regiments from mainland Britain were freed for service in Ireland and vice versa. However, the Irish militia was largely composed of Roman Catholics and the Interchange Act had been rendered more palatable to them by the guarantee of freedom of worship whilst serving in mainland Britain.[153] Although there is evidence that certain discreet 'donations' had been made to Roman Catholic priests before this at the behest of the Secretary at War,[154] it was only after Bishop Collingridge visited Lord Palmerston in March 1813 that payments to Roman Catholic priests for their ministry to Irish militiamen were authorised as a matter of policy by the Secretary at War.[155]

Clearly, Owen did his utmost to resist this development. As a staunch Churchman and a strong evangelical, the thought of lining the pockets of Popish priests was anathema to him. However, he was careful to ground his opposition in practical considerations. For Owen the evangelical, the importance of preaching to soldiers could not be gainsaid and it was a source of great concern to him that many of the clergy who stood to benefit from their work with the Irish militia were in fact French émigré priests. In January 1812, Owen was approached by Major William Fitzgerald, the commanding officer of the Clare Militia, which had recently arrived in Ipswich, concerning the work of a 'Mr. Simon'. Owen's reply reflected his wider misgivings:

> I will lay the case of Mr. Simon before the Secretary at War . . . Will you permit me to ask if the Revd. Mr. Simon is a foreigner [and] if so how long he has been in England and whether he is perfect master of the English tongue. May I likewise beg of you to inform me what description of duty he has performed with the Regiment and where. I should judge it desirable that your Catholic clergyman be perfect master of the English tongue as you may reasonably propose much moral and religious benefit to the Soldiers from the sermons of a man of sense. I submit to you if a plain preacher discourse on the great points of duty to God and our neighbour be not calculated to improve the discipline and character of a Regiment.[156]

Later that year, Owen made the same point to the Secretary at War in relation to the claims of a priest named George Spain on the Isle of Wight:

> I sent the enclosed Papers to Major General Taylor and I requested to know if Mr. Spain could speak English intelligibly, and was of any real service to these soldiers by instructing them in good morals and the great doctrines of our common religion. I have reason to think very useless persons have in several instances taken possession of the Irish soldiers in their neighbourhood: to whom they could say nothing but in broken English, if they were otherwise well disposed. To pay such men would be a waste of public money. If any Priests of their persuasion were paid by the Public, it is to be wished they were Englishmen of good lives and a sober zeal to instruct the Soldiers in their duty to God and Man.[157]

However, such was Owen's distaste for this duty that he pressed his objections on other grounds as well, citing the supposed impiety of Irish soldiers and raising questions of equity in relation to officiating clergy of the Church of England. Further to the case of George Spain, he wrote to the Secretary at War in December 1812:

> The Irish soldiers I am informed often make their Religion a pretext for Idleness on the Sunday. Many who claim the right of going to Mass prefer the Alehouse. An emigrant French Priest, and such it is who commonly appear to call for remuneration, is not qualified to instruct the Soldiers. If the Doors of the Mass House be opened there is no account of the numbers who attend, nor is there any where by what I hear a separate Service performed for the Soldiers by a neighbouring Priest . . . Your Lordship is aware how precisely we are informed on the Honour of the Commandant and the Claimant of every thing that the Parochial Clergy perform for the Troops, and you are likewise aware of the very frugal manner in which these Services are paid. Without care Government may pay more in many instances to Foreigners for Services which perhaps were never performed and which we know they are not qualified to

> perform than to our own people who are bound to the completest Service and are paid only on Certificate of its actual performance.[158]

Even when Palmerston finally authorised the payment of Roman Catholic priests 'officiating to Irish Regiments in this country' at the same rate and under the same terms as the officiating Anglican clergy,[159] the Chaplain-General remained obstructive. In October 1813, he resumed the fight in relation to a priest named Bowland who had petitioned the War Office for payment on the strength of the visits he had made to Roman Catholic soldiers in various hospitals in England. In this case, much of his opposition hinged on his conviction that Roman Catholic priests could do no more for sick and wounded Catholics than the clergy of the Church of England:

> It is probable the zeal of Roman Catholic Clergymen thro'out the Kingdom has induced them for many years past to visit sick soldiers of their own Communion not that they would have been unvisited had the case been otherwise. From more than five and twenty years experience with Troops in Hospitals I have found the Catholic just as attentive to my exhortation and as ready to learn the Lords Prayer from my Lips, as any Protestant, the only exception I ever met with arose, as the sick men told me, from the positive prohibition of the Priest who had left the Room on my entering in. Lest I should have deceived myself on this point I have enquired of the most diligent and able Chaplains in the Service, what has been the result of their experiences and find it fully coincides with my own.[160]

To be fair to Owen, it is hard to overstate the importance that the remodelled Department attached to the chaplain's hospital ministry. Significantly, after the recent closure of general hospitals at Deal, Gosport and Plymouth, the importance of these facilities had been brought home to the British public by the evacuation of the battered and diseased remnants of Sir John Moore's army from Corunna in January 1809.[161] In his memorandum of that month, which he had written as the evacuation was taking place, Perceval had stressed the centrality of the chaplain's hospital work, citing it as a compelling reason for ensuring that garrison chaplains were resident in their quarters.[162] For his own part, Owen's prior experiences as a chaplain no doubt heightened his awareness of the desperate vulnerability of the British soldier. During the French Revolutionary and Napoleonic Wars, around eight British soldiers died from disease or accident for every soldier killed by enemy action.[163] If the army suffered devastating losses from disease in tropical stations,[164] even the health of the army at home was far from robust. According to Owen's calculations, one-twelfth of the army in Great Britain was hospitalised at any one time.[165] Although the Prayer Book's order for the visitation of the sick reflected the traditional importance of this office within Anglicanism, for evangelicals its importance was accentuated by the prospects it offered for the saving of souls. In many respects, hospitalisation represented the soldier's prime religious opportunity, for in hospital (with the evidence of mortality all around them) the stricken and convalescent often had the leisure to reflect on their own sinful state. The threefold process of conviction of sin, repentance and justification therefore lent itself to hospital work more than to any other aspect of military chaplaincy. Owen's sense of the urgency of his duty to the sick and the wounded is betrayed in a famous anecdote from the memoirs of John Stevenson, a Methodist guardsman, who served in the Dutch campaign of 1799. As we have noted, Owen was at this time chaplain to the Guards brigade and Stevenson remembered that:

> Here we were favoured with the zealous exertions of a pious clergyman, the Rev. Mr. Owen [who] on many occasions gave some excellent addresses. In the time of action he would be very forward in the field, so that one day one of the [men] called to him and said, 'where are you going Mr. Owen? you will be killed.' – 'I am going,' he answered, 'to see if I can be of any service to those that are departing this life.'[166]

From the earliest months of his term as Chaplain-General, Owen insisted that it was every chaplain's duty to visit the hospitals under his care at least twice a week. Indeed, in the autumn of 1810 he revised the payment forms for officiating clergymen in order to ensure that this was done. As he explained to Palmerston that September:

> The time of sickness is for the young and heedless the time for reflection. It is in the Hospitals that the soldier discerns the result of vice and intemperance [and] I have earnestly directed my efforts to obtain the attendance of Chaplains twice a Week, at least, at the Bed side of every Sick and wounded man. Where we have not Chaplains on our Establishment, it is provided by the Certificates of Duty now about to be circulated, that no Clergyman officiating to the Troops shall receive Pay without a declaration on his own Honour as well as that of the Commanding Officer that he has visited the sick twice a Week.[167]

Similarly, Owen wrote to Samuel Briscall (then the army's senior chaplain in Portugal) in March 1811, emphasising that his stress on the importance of hospital work was endorsed in the highest circles of government:

> I have promised Mr. Perceval that all the Hospitals shall be visited twice each week. He has directed that it shall be a law of the service and you will inform your Chaplains that I expect they will give you and me their word of honour that they have so visited them. The service they perform in them must be bona fide such as they can answer to me, to their consciences and to God. Mr. Perceval has with reason required me to see that we have no indolent men in our corps.[168]

Despite these cautions, Owen was fully aware that the presence of a chaplain could not be relied upon, especially in the case of troops serving overseas. Consequently, he also made strenuous efforts to ensure that suitable religious literature was made available in military hospitals. As Owen pointed out to the Secretary at War in September 1810, the need for such literature was heightened by the fact that military hospitals in Great Britain were routinely targeted by Nonconformists who fully recognised the saving potential of this work and over whose activities and publications the military authorities had little or no control.[169] In light of this,

Owen proposed that 'One Bible One Testament 1 Common Prayer [Book] and two or three Tracts' be provided for every ten men in military hospitals at home. He also recommended that any larger volumes be strongly bound, that all these publications should be supplied by the S.P.C.K. and that 'the custody of the Books in the Hospitals at Home should rest with the respective Barrack Masters. The King's Arms with a proper inscription should be pasted on the Inside board and they must be accounted for as His Majesty's Stores.'[170]

Whilst civilian sectaries were not as well placed to prey upon the military hospitals in Portugal, the Chaplain-General was conscious that the needs of these hospitals were in many respects greater than the needs of those at home, particularly as any books in English were in short supply. Initially, he even bought books for these hospitals at his own expense, entrusting them to individual chaplains as they went out to Lisbon.[171] However, chaplains could not travel with large quantities of religious literature, a fact that led Owen to propose that a devotional library be supplied to the general hospital at Lisbon. In November 1810, he reported to Samuel Briscall that the Secretary at War had proved amenable to this request and that a box of books was on its way to Portugal. Given the importance of this consignment, Owen gave detailed instructions as to how these books should be managed:

> I have applied to Government for Books to be distributed in the Hospitals at Home and I have desired we may have some for Lisbon. They have listened to me and I shall send a Box of Books to be delivered to the Purveyor of the General Hospital . . . The Box will be strong and have a key with it, and I have requested that orders may be given to the Purveyors of General Hospitals to remove the Box of Books whenever the Hospital moves . . . I know if the Books are not delivered out by a careful man and occasionally mustered they will not last a fortnight . . . In the Hospitals at home the Barrack Master is responsible for the Books but abroad this must be left with the Senior Chaplain. If you have a carefull Chaplain, as I would recommend at Lisbon, he will attend the General Hospital and look to mustering the Books. A few may be given to different Chaplains, who will be responsible for them. Consider my dear Sir that Testaments etc. are very important Instruments of the Business for which we serve and consider that the care of them lies on our conscience, for it is out of the question to have these Books often renewed.[172]

Some weeks later, and in a remarkable piece of micro-management, Owen wrote directly to the purveyor of the general hospital at Lisbon, describing the appearance of the box, the purpose and management of its contents and reminding him that they were to be treated with the same care as other hospital stores.[173]

Nevertheless, by the winter of 1810–11 all was not well with the staff chaplains in Portugal. Wintering in the shelter of the Lines of Torres Vedras, which protected the Portuguese capital from the depredations of the French, Wellington had leisure to turn his attention to the religious condition of his army. By this time, the growth of evangelical Nonconformity was causing a good deal of disquiet at home, particularly in view of the presumed link between religious and political radicalism. While the Tory administration at home grappled with the growing problem of itinerant preaching, in February 1811 Wellington wrote to the Adjutant-General, Sir Harry Calvert, voicing his concerns about the lack of chaplains in Portugal, the growth of Methodism to which this gave rise and its implications for 'military discipline and order'. In Wellington's view, an adequate supply of 'respectable and efficient clergymen'[174] was being impeded by the conditions of service under which chaplains were appointed:

> Notwithstanding all that has been done upon the subject, with a view to making these situations such as to induce respectable persons to accept of them, I fear that they are not yet sufficiently advantageous to insure the object. I believe the income, while they are employed abroad, to be sufficiently good, but that of retired Chaplains, after service, is not; and the period of service required of them is too long. You will observe that a man can scarcely be eligible to be an army Chaplain till he is 26 or 28, after an expensive education; and it can scarcely be said that the pay of a retired Chaplain, at 36 years of age, is what a respectable person would have acquired if he had followed any other line of the clerical profession besides the army. In my opinion, the period of service ought to be reduced from 10 [sic] to 6 years; but they ought to be years of service, without leave of absence, excepting on account of health; and the pay of the retired Chaplain ought to be augmented.[175]

However, and in addition to their lack of prospects, Wellington also argued that chaplains were lacking in zeal, a point he underlined with reference to the exemplary conduct of Samuel Briscall:

> I have one excellent young man in this army, Mr. Briscall, who is attached to headquarters, who has never been one moment absent from his duty; but I have not yet seen another who has not applied, and made a pitiable case, for leave of absence immediately after his arrival; and excepting Mr. Den[n]is at Lisbon, who was absent all last year, I believe Mr. Briscall is the only Chaplain doing duty.[176]

Owen's response to these blistering criticisms was to post four more staff chaplains to Lisbon (all that were then available at home) and to urge Briscall to take a tougher line with his subordinates:

> The Chaplains who have of late sailed received my directions to report themselves to you instantly on their arrival in Lisbon. You will please to take care that they receive directions . . . Be very peremptory in your Orders and give every Chaplain to understand that they must immediately obey. Inform yourself of everything and see that the proper orders be sent from the Adjutant General. Know from every man how often he does duty on the Sunday on his part of the line. Entreat my Lord Wellington to issue orders for the facilitating [of] Divine Service, a great deal is in his power. Direct, as I have done, every Chaplain to give a short discourse intelligible and suitable to the men.[177]

In a frank admission of the poor quality of some of his chaplains, Owen went on to recommend how Briscall should deal with Thomas Dennis, whom Owen knew from his own time as senior chaplain in Portugal:

> I am extremely mortified to find so many Sick for so long a period have been committed to Mr. Dennis. I never could trust him with an Hospital Duty. I have followed him repeatedly and I have found it was never done. I therefore did the whole of it myself and allotted him the Burial of the Dead only. When I found such an Office as visiting the Sick at Lisbon had been committed to him, I desired the Commander in Chief to recall him. Knowing that he was indolent I had before desired the Prelates not to nominate him to our Establishment . . . It is the universal law of the Service that the Sick be visited twice a week [and] I shall expect the same from the Chaplains with you. I expect that they will declare upon their honour that they have visited all the Sick who were not removed from their Division twice a week, and performed with them, according to their discretion, the requisite offices. The Chaplain at Lisbon must engage to do this.[178]

As Wellington's letter to the Adjutant-General of February 1811 emphasised, another vital function of the military chaplain at this time was to curb and control the religious enthusiasm of the army's Methodist soldiers. Clearly, Samuel Briscall enjoyed some success in this regard. Known (and even admired) among the army's Methodist soldiers,[179] Wellington said of Briscall:

> Mr. Briscall has his eye upon these transactions [i.e. the Methodist meetings at Cartaxo], and would give me notice were they growing into any thing which ought to be put a stop to; and the respectability of his character and conduct has given him an influence over these people which will prevent them from going wrong.[180]

From his own experience, Owen concurred that zealous and attentive chaplains were the solution to the army's Dissenting problem. In his lengthy advice to Briscall on the management of his chaplains, Owen wrote:

> Methodism is said to make progress among the Troops, I am sorry for it and my Lord Wellington rightly infers that the Zeal of the Chaplains is the surest obstacle to its progress. When Men in the ranks undertake to preach and pray extempore they become shocking coxcombs, and think all knowledge and Religion is centred in such as themselves. If they would be content on a Sunday evening in a little knot to let the best readers read a chapter or two and a few prayers they might be none the worse. But from the instant either preacher or hearer are for extempore prayers and harangues they assume a character that is highly injurious to themselves and others . . . Soldiers will have some Religion and Lord Wellington is right when he demands Zeal in his Chaplains. A little persuasion and management may keep some men from Enthusiasm and Methodistical self importance, who would otherwise be in danger of falling into these vices. If they see the Chaplain really cares for their religious improvement they will not refuse to hear.[181]

As part of this 'persuasion and management', Owen urged Briscall to ensure that chaplains preach short and pertinent sermons and suggested that Briscall acquaint his Methodist flock with the exemplary *Lectures* of Archbishop Thomas Secker.[182] However, the problem of religious enthusiasm was not only confined to the Peninsula. In March 1811, Owen wrote to Palmerston's secretary to ensure that the chaplain's house at Sheerness was rendered fit for the residence of J.F. Holloway, emphasising that:

> The trouble I have had to obtain a Man of Mr. Holloway's character for Sheerness is more than I can describe . . . All the Officers of the Dock Yard attend at the Garrison Chapel. The Place is full of Methodists and Dissenters and the Scandal to which we are exposed by having inferior Clergymen there is boundless. Will you, Sir, have the kindness to press this on the Secretary at War, and if it be possible let the House rest as heretofore with the Ordnance Department and if otherwise at least let it be made decent.[183]

Such was the concern surrounding the spread of Nonconformity in the army at this time that the Duke of York (who had been recently reinstated as Commander-in-Chief at the recommendation of Spencer Perceval)[184] stressed the importance of the chaplain's work in a circular of November 1811. Written by the Adjutant-General and addressed to commanding officers at home and abroad, it began:

> I have received the Commander-in-Chief's Commands to request your earnest Attention to a Branch of the Service placed under your direction, from which His Royal Highness expects, that the most essential Benefits will be derived, as well to the discipline of the Army at large, as to the Conduct of the Individuals of whom it is composed. I allude to the Establishment of Military Chaplains, and the Duties which attach to them.

Stressing that staff chaplains had been granted 'the Pay and Allowances of a Major' and that they had 'been selected, with the utmost Care and Circumspection by the first Prelates of this Country', the circular went on to insist that the regulations governing the chaplains' work be fully enforced:

> It is the Commander in Chief's Command, that the Chaplains shall visit the Sick and the Hospitals of their respective Divisions or Garrisons, at least twice in each week, and diligently perform the requisite duties therein [and] that Divine Service shall be performed each Sunday . . .

However, it also offered some very specific advice in view of the current threat posed by Dissent:

> His Royal Highness particularly enjoins, that more Men shall not be assembled for [divine service] than the Voice can reach (a Precaution very necessary to insure the Attention of the Soldier) but that the Chaplain shall perform the Service successively to the different Corps of his Division; and His Royal Highness desires, that the Service may close with a short practical Sermon, suited to the Habits, and Understandings of Soldiers. To this last part of the Service the Commander in Chief attaches much Importance, as being in conformity to the custom of the Established

> Church, and more than ever required at this time, which is peculiarly marked by the Exertions, and Interference, of Sectaries of various Descriptions.[185]

Despite the Duke of York's endorsement of the staff chaplains and their work, the Chaplain-General's plans for the reinvigoration of chaplaincy in the Peninsula unravelled in the course of 1811. Although the circular of that November was duly issued as a general order from Wellington's headquarters the following month,[186] in July Wellington had already written to Owen reporting that two of the four chaplains who had recently arrived in Portugal were now on their way home. One had speedily resigned whilst the second had secured a leave of absence before even joining the army in the field. Given this sorry performance, Wellington resumed his refrain as to the conditions of service for chaplains, insisting that 'The remuneration in the shape of half pay is not sufficient to induce respectable persons in a state of good health, who have any other prospect in the [clerical] profession, to accept the situation of Chaplains to the Army.'[187] Worse was to follow. A few weeks later, Briscall was also compelled to return to England 'on the grounds of ill health' and he was not ordered back to the Peninsula until the end of the following year.[188] As his position as senior chaplain at Wellington's headquarters was kept open for him, from the autumn of 1811 to the autumn of 1813 (when Briscall rejoined Wellington's headquarters in northern Spain) the immediate supervision of chaplains attached to Wellington's army in the Peninsula effectively ceased, no deputy being appointed in Briscall's stead.[189]

This lack of oversight in Spain and Portugal was compounded by a remarkable turn of events in England, namely the appointment of John Owen to the revived position of 'Chaplain General to the Fleet' by an order in council of March 1812.[190] Owen, of course, had never served as a naval chaplain and his appointment was greeted with a howl of protest from the thirty-nine serving chaplains of the senior service.[191] Nevertheless, and although the problems of army chaplaincy were far from being resolved, Owen enjoyed a decisive advantage, namely the support of influential evangelicals such as Admiral Lord Gambier and the confidence of the Prime Minister, Spencer Perceval, who had turned to Owen for advice on naval chaplaincy in December 1811.[192] While retaining the office of Chaplain-General to the army, Owen devoted considerable energy to meeting his commitments to the Royal Navy. Besides taking a role in the appointment of chaplains to larger vessels, a process that had traditionally concerned their captains and the archbishops of Canterbury or bishops of London,[193] Owen also helped to ensure the better provision of religious literature for sailors. Whereas this had hitherto been a matter for interested captains, the same order in council which appointed Owen as Chaplain-General to the Fleet also decreed that a New Testament and Prayer Book be provided for every mess on board ship. Consequently, the Navy Estimates of 1814 earmarked £1,500 for the purchase of religious literature and a new regulation was promulgated that reclassified this material as naval stores.[194] However, few were persuaded that Owen's dual role was a good idea. Captain C.V. Penrose, for example, aired his misgivings in the pages of the *Naval Chronicle*:

> We have lately a chaplain-general added to our naval establishment; and I apprehend that our first officer of that description is a zealous labourer in his avocation; but it seemed odd, that when the spiritual concerns of the navy were to have a nominal head, they should be thought so trifling as to be made over to a man whose hands seemed before sufficiently full of business and never, I believe in the navy.[195]

Suspicions that Owen had enough work to do as Chaplain-General of the army were definitely well founded. Besides the scores of officiating clergymen with whom the Chaplain-General always had to deal, the number of commissioned chaplains rose dramatically during Owen's early years in office. In November 1809, nineteen brigade chaplains were serving with the army; two were attached to each of the garrisons of Gibraltar, Malta, Sicily and Cape Town, two were with the troops on Walcheren, one was attached to each of the garrisons of Ceylon, Heligoland and Madeira and six were in Spain or Portugal.[196] However, four years later Owen was dealing with an establishment of thirty-eight staff chaplains. Although two postings were vacant, three staff chaplains were in England, sixteen were in Portugal or Spain, two were in Gibraltar, five were in Sicily, one was a prisoner of war and the rest were scattered in various garrisons across the British empire from Martinique to Ceylon and from Heligoland to the Cape of Good Hope.[197] Certainly, it seems that the Chaplains' Department derived little or no tangible benefit from this partial integration of military and naval chaplaincy and that the advantage derived from this arrangement was largely Owen's, whose salary consequently rose by 50 per cent from £800 to £1,200 per annum.[198]

Chaplains and the Peninsular War

Earlier accounts of British army chaplaincy in the Napoleonic Wars have assumed that the clergymen who served as chaplains were drawn from the ranks of the parochial clergy.[199] However, this assumption requires some qualification. As we have seen, in 1809 it became a matter of policy that clergymen with cure of souls were ineligible to apply as staff chaplains (or as Chaplains to the Forces, as they were also known). Hence, the Department was reliant on the services of a mixed body of clergymen consisting of jobbing curates, fellows of university colleges and well-connected individuals who had good prospects of preferment once their obligations to the Department ceased. For some, a gross salary of £292 per annum (plus the prospect of half-pay) was probably more than they could hope for in civilian life, a case in point being that of Thomas Ireland, who joined the Department as a non-graduate and who served for many years at the Cape and in Ceylon before returning to take his degree at St. John's College, Cambridge. Service as a military chaplain also served as an important outlet for patriotic and adventurous individuals among the fellows of Oxford and Cambridge. For these unmarried men (who seem to have comprised roughly a third of the establishment of staff chaplains in 1813) service as a C.F. also offered the opportunity to attract the eye of an influential patron .[200] This was definitely true of Samuel Briscall, the financially straitened son of a Stockport surgeon who embarked on his military career in 1808 as a fellow of Brasenose College, Oxford.[201] On the strength of his performance in the Peninsula, Briscall enjoyed the patronage of the Duke of Wellington for the rest of his life. In 1814, he became Wellington's domestic chaplain and attended the duke in Paris before and after Waterloo, mixing with the foremost members of the French aristocracy and with some of the leading figures in Europe.[202] Finally, in 1822, and while still attending Wellington in the dual role of domestic chaplain and assistant curate of Stratfieldsaye, Briscall was preferred to the remunerative rectory of South Kelsey in Lincolnshire through the good offices of his distinguished patron.[203]

Whether recruited from the fellows of the great universities or from starveling or well connected curates, the chaplains of this period had one thing in common, namely their complete lack of formal training for army work. This mirrored their lack of professional training for their ordained ministries and, as in the case of the parochial clergy, manuals of advice were made available by more experienced chaplains for the benefit of the novice. In the absence of any alternatives, the key work for the aspiring chaplain of the Napoleonic period may well have been William Henry Pratt's *Divine Service for Camp or Garrison, as performed at the Drum-Head; with the outlines of a few Discourses, or Field Sermons, adapted to the Understanding and circumstances of the private Soldier* (1808). Published just as the Peninsular War commenced, the author's credentials were only superficially impressive. Pratt was the rector of Jonesborough, County Armagh, and his background smacked more of a showy Irish Loyalism than of hard campaigning experience, Pratt being the chaplain of three Irish Volunteer regiments and the 'Officiating Chaplain to several Regiments of Cavalry, Infantry, the Line, Fencibles, and Militia, during the late and present Wars'. In view of this, it is doubtful to what extent Pratt's experience or advice (which had been honed in Ireland and which included 'A Sketch of the Form of Consecration of a Stand of Colours') could have been useful to chaplains who served overseas and for whom hospital work loomed large.[204]

Despite the fact that the number of commissioned chaplains doubled between 1809 and 1814, the recruitment of chaplains generally kept pace with official requirements. In part, this was achieved by enlarging their responsibilities, a policy reflected in the Peninsula by attaching chaplains to divisions rather than to brigades in the wake of the reorganisation of the Anglo-Portuguese army in June 1809.[205] However, it is likely that this situation also reflected the growing success of British arms, Wellington's triumphs at Salamanca and Vittoria in 1812 and 1813 no doubt boosting the appeal of military chaplaincy in clerical circles. Moreover, towards the end of the Peninsular War the lot of the chaplain seems to have improved, a development which was probably related to the significant improvement of military hospitals in this theatre of war under the direction of James McGrigor, Wellington's Surgeon-General from 1812.[206] Although an extreme example, George Watson's journal shows that he sailed for northern Spain three days before the surrender of Napoleon in April 1814. Consequently, his six-week sojourn to the seat of war largely consisted of a journey into France in the wake of Wellington's victorious army. During this period, he had extensive dealings with his fellow chaplains; on arrival at Pasajes, he was entertained by

Joseph Langley Mills, the 'Chaplain to the Depot', and met two other chaplains at Orthez a week later. On arrival at Toulouse, Watson 'visited three hospitals at this place for Mr. Frith the Chaplain at the Depot, and preached once before the Head Quarters in the Protestant Chapel'. From Toulouse, he travelled to Bordeaux where he spent a fortnight as chaplain to the 7th Division, where he struck up a friendship with a Protestant pastor and dutifully read prayers in its two military hospitals.[207]

However, Watson's journal belies the earlier realities of military chaplaincy in this theatre of war. Given the rigours of service in Portugal and Spain, the general shortage of chaplains on the ground and the frequent dispersal of their flocks when in the field, it was extremely difficult for chaplains to provide religious services for the army. Anecdotal evidence suggests that parade services were most regularly held at the beginning and towards the end of the Peninsular War and when Wellington's army was concentrated around the lines of Torres Vedras (outside the army's Lisbon base) in the winter of 1810–11. Significantly, the small British army that won Wellington's first notable victory in the Peninsula (that at Vimiero, on Sunday 21 August 1808) did so having held its parade services.[208] These also appear to have been fairly regular occurrences during the winter of 1810–11. Joseph Donaldson of the 94th Regiment wrote of this period, 'When settled in a place for any time, the brigade assembled on Sundays for divine service.' However, the benefits of a parade service for the men of the 94th Regiment were partly vitiated by the prospect of drill immediately afterwards:

> We were always in full marching order on these occasions: and not uncommonly had a field day after it. If a person were to judge from the hitching of knapsacks, and wry faces that were making, during this ceremony, he would have thought the soldiers would rather have dispensed with it; but I dare say, the anticipation of the drill that was to follow, prevented them from feeling much benefit from their devotions.[209]

Parade services were once again fairly routine in the winter of 1813–14. As one of Wellington's staff officers recalled:

> During the time when we were in winter quarters in St. Jean de Luz, we had Divine Service every Sunday in a field near the Sea. The D. of Wellington & all the Officers of Head Quarters attended. A Hollow square was formed by a Brigade of Infantry quartered in the Town, & under the Colors of one of the Regiments, was placed a big drum for a reading desk. A Serjeant acted as Clerk & Prayers were then offered up. The attention of Officers and Soldiers was exemplary, & doubly so when Psalms and Lessons were selected alluding to our situation, or to the uncertain tenure by which we held our lives. There was something affecting in the simplicity of this form of Worship, the most reverent we had it in our power to show to Him, who had been our constant Protector. The same service was performed every Sunday when we were not fighting, with every Brigade and Division of the Army.[210]

Although Wellington believed that his chaplains were lacking in commitment, this must be balanced against the fact that he was liable to be unfair in his treatment of subordinates, a trait that was best illustrated in the recriminations which surrounded his army's siege and retreat from Burgos in 1812.[211] Furthermore, and if Wellington's miscalculations lay at the heart of that failed campaign, it is hard to avoid the conclusion that he greatly underestimated the difficulty of the chaplain's role for, even in England, the vital duty of hospital visiting was no easy task. As Samuel Briscall wrote from Portsmouth in March 1809, his work at Haslar hospital among the troops who had been recently evacuated from Corunna was both demanding and depressing: 'all my Acquaintance lays among the sick and wounded, and of course is a little tinged with Melancholy'.[212] Although not as pestilential as the West or East Indies, the Iberian Peninsula took a heavy toll of the British army through disease alone; whereas nearly 9,000 British soldiers died in action or of wounds received in Spain and Portugal, nearly 25,000 died of disease.[213] Worse still, and as an officer of the 34th Regiment remembered, because they lacked any recourse to sacramental confession Protestant Britons were not easily consoled on their deathbeds:

> [When] once an alarming disease appears among them, they are overcome with surprise, they lose all elasticity of spirit, hope forsakes them, and they sink unresistingly to the grave. This does not proceed altogether from weakness of character; on the bed of sickness, the English soldier thinks more seriously of death, and his accountability hereafter, than perhaps any other, if we except the Protestant soldiers of the north of Germany. The inhabitants of the south of Europe, and the men who compose the mass of the continental armies, are, for the most part, members of the Roman or Greek church; and, certain it is, that on the bed of death all of these religious persuasions do appear to entertain a confidence of salvation, which, to the sober-minded and humble Protestant, however innocent and happy a feeling, seems mistaken, if not presumptuous.[214]

In such circumstances, hospital work could assume massive and forbidding proportions, a situation that was not helped by its surrounding squalor, especially before the advent of James McGrigor. As John Cooper of the 7th Royal Fusiliers recalled of the hospitals he experienced in the Peninsula:

> The Hospital at Olivenja was a long low room, with another at a right angle to it; crowded with fever patients; the ventilation bad; many deaths daily. The hospital at Villa Vicosa was in a convent; about 150 patients in the four corridors; next to no ventilation; small windows; great barrels or tubs for all purposes; the stench horrible; logs of fir burning at the four corners of the building, to drive away the infection; smoke blinding . . . The Hospital at Elvas; Into bomb proof barracks again. No ventilation, twenty sick men in the room, of whom eighteen died. In this place there was one door, and one chimney, but no windows . . . The hospital at Guarda, miserable like the above. The hospital at Celerico [where] there were about twelve of us in two small rooms [and where] there was not a single chamber utensil. A blanket was spread on the floor instead. Some made use of the window for every purpose. I saw neither basin, soap, nor towel. Such was the place and such our condition.[215]

In view of the conditions in which they were required to work, the high incidence of sickness among Peninsular chaplains is easily explained, bearing comparison with the fate of medical officers in major hospitals[216] and prompting the suspicion that they did their best work among men who did not live to tell of it. Furthermore, and notwithstanding Wellington's imputations, those chaplains who returned to England pleading sickness were not simply malingering. At least one brigade chaplain, James Cooley, 'died on service in Spain' in 1809 and James Allott, who served for years as a chaplain in Lisbon, died very shortly after his return to England in 1814.[217] Rightly concerned for the health of his chaplains and with hostilities in Europe seemingly over, in August 1814 Owen approached the Adjutant-General over the case of R.W. Tunney:

> The Rev. Mr Tunney Chaplain to the Forces lately returned from Spain has requested me to ask leave of absence for six weeks for the recovery of his health. This Gentleman has been indefatigable in the great Depots of Sick with which he has successively been placed, and I entreat you Sir to lay this request before his [Royal Highness] the Commander-in-Chief, subject however to any commands his R.H. may judge expedient in the interim.[218]

A fortnight later, Owen wrote a similar letter on behalf of another chaplain, John Cracroft:

> His Royal Highness the Commander in Chief was pleased to give leave of absence to the Revd. John Cracroft, Chaplain to the Forces, lately returned from the Peninsula from 25th July 1814 to the 1st Instant. Mr Cracroft was very ill of an intermittent fever, I have heard from him and he is yet so weak as to need what I take the liberty to request, a prolonged leave of absence for one month. He offers to send me medical Certificates, but as I have confidence in this Chaplain and I am acquainted with the truth of his plea, I have not asked for them on this second application.[219]

Inevitably, high wastage rates placed an even heavier burden on those chaplains who remained in the Peninsula. As one brigade chaplain wrote from Portugal in 1808:

> The spiritual care of the [Lisbon] garrison has devolved upon me; and ample occupation it affords to one person. There are five regiments here, besides the artillery, and to these I have to read prayers and preach respectively every Sunday. They are quartered in barracks, convents, and in the citadel, the ascent to which nearly incapacitates me for duty the remainder of the day.[220]

More onerous still was the hospital work which this posting demanded:

> My principal professional employment is that of visiting the sick in the numerous hospitals, which are every day filling with patients in fever, or dysentery . . . The sick of the artillery occupy the royal hospital of St. Joseph . . . The general hospital of the army is in the Estrella convent . . . There are, besides, seven or eight regimental hospitals in and near the

> town; the care of them all engrosses my time, and leaves me little leisure for any other occupation. For the dispatch of business, a regular hour is appointed for my attendance at the burial ground; and not a day has elapsed, within this fortnight, that I have not had to discharge my melancholy office from three to six times.[221]

In addition to the suffering and infection to which they were exposed in the course of their hospital work, Peninsular chaplains were also faced with other grim realities of contemporary military life. In 1811, and although a seasoned campaigner, Samuel Briscall felt moved to protest the manner in which the dead were disposed of in the hospitals at Elvas and Lisbon, their naked corpses being simply thrown into mass graves.[222] The rigours of military discipline also presented some problems. In 1812, one chaplain was faced with ministering to five deserters who had been captured while fighting alongside the French at Ciudad Rodrigo. As inveterate delinquents, they greeted their death sentence with a chorus of oaths and ignored his prayers at their execution.[223] The unease such duties could engender was expressed by Samuel Briscall, who wrote from Portugal in March 1810:

> My Time is far from a Life of Pleasure. The common Rounds of Duty, offices to the Sick and the melancholy Duties to those poor Fellows cut off by the Gallows or Coup de Fusil for their different Crimes, are continual Recurrences of so many Memento moris and do not pass but without a due influence upon my Mind.[224]

Nor, it must be stressed, were chaplains wholly at ease with the company of their fellow officers. Uncomfortably sandwiched between the expectations of the Church and the boisterous spirit of the officers' mess, they were placed in an invidious situation and some clearly fell prey to the latter. In January 1810, an officer of the 4th Dragoons wrote from Lisbon, 'We have some Chaplains with the army: were I to detail their mode of living, you'd be a little Surpriz'd: to be sure They preach, but don't ever make the appearance of following their doctrine.'[225] Although far from being a prude, in a letter to his sister, in which he also bemoaned the lack of music and the paucity of eligible widows in Portugal, Briscall betrayed a hint of disquiet when he observed that even 'well bred men . . . being acquainted with little or no Rule of Guidance but their Passions, are at once ignorant and depraved'.[226] Although Briscall did not elaborate, when George Watson arrived in southern France at the end of the Peninsular War he felt no compunction about reproving and exhorting where necessary. At Tarbes in May 1814, Watson scored a small victory for Christian propriety, noting that 'A ball was given, at which several English officers and the Commandant were present. I persuaded some not to go there as it would be an unjustifiable breach of the Sabbath.'[227]

Given the terrible conditions of their ministry and the perennially awkward situation of clergymen in the army, Oman was no doubt right to betray a certain sympathy with his subjects when he remarked of Wellington's chaplains: 'A good many of them were sent straight out from a country curacy to the front, had no special knowledge of soldiers and their ways, and were appalled at having to face the great facts of life and death in their crudest form day after day.'[228] However, Oman's sympathy is not widely reflected in the published recollections of Peninsular veterans. Although John Stevenson wrote approvingly of John Owen, Samuel Briscall and a third chaplain named Maurice James, whom he met at Antwerp in 1814,[229] other godly veterans were less happy with those whom they regarded as spiritually blind to the great truths of salvation. Quartermaster William Surtees of the 3/95th Rifles noted how one chaplain proved wholly incapable of helping him once he felt convicted of sin. As Surtees remembered:

> From the clergyman, though a kind and sympathizing man, I, alas! derived but little benefit. He did not direct me to the only source of a sin-sick being's hopes – the Lamb of God which taketh away the sins of the world. He tried to make my hopes centre more on good resolutions, and after-doings. How thankfully would I have accepted the true method of salvation pointed out in the gospel . . . The kind gentleman wrote me out prayers, and seemed much interested in my welfare. But reading and praying seemed more like an irksome task than an exercise which brought spiritual profit.[230]

Other memoirs betray a raw anticlericalism that would have resonated with large sections of their readership in the quarter century after Waterloo. In this troubled period anticlerical feeling reached new heights in British society as the clergy of the Church of England (who were increasingly affluent, largely Tory in sympathy and strongly represented among the magistracy) became a natural target for reformists and radicals of every stripe.[231] In memoirs of this kind, chaplains were liable to be portrayed as useless appendages to the army and as capable of inspiring only bemused contempt. The fact that staff chaplains were an exclusively Anglican body may have led Scottish veterans in particular to take the seat of the scorner. In the 1830s, Captain John Kincaid of the 1/95th Rifles drew the following portrait of a chaplain whom he had encountered in the Peninsula:

> He might have been a very good man, but he was not prepossessing, either in his appearance or manners. I remember, the first Sunday after his arrival, the troops were paraded for divine service, and had been some time waiting in square, when he at length rode into the centre of it, with his tall, lank, ungainly figure, mounted on a starved, untrimmed, unfurnished horse, and followed by a Portuguese boy, with his canonicals and prayer-books on the back of a mule, with a hay-bridle, and having, by way of clothing, about half a pair of straw breeches. This spiritual comforter was the least calculated of any one that I ever saw to excite devotion in the minds of men, who had seen nothing in the shape of a divine for a year or two.[232]

The same chaplain fell into the hands of the French shortly afterwards but, as Kincaid put it, 'conceiving good provisions to be thrown away upon him, they stripped him nearly naked and dismissed him [with] a kick in the breech, and sent him in to us in a woeful state'.[233] The same picaresque note was struck by George Bell of the 34th Regiment, who recalled that in 1813:

> A chaplain was now in reality sent out from England, and attached to [General] Hill's division. My regiment was here alone, and his reverence came to perform Divine Service; twenty minutes was the regulation time. A square was formed, the big drum placed in the centre to do the duty of a reading-desk; the parson entered, made for the drum at once, got one leg up, when the big drummer made a rush, caught him by the tail, and pulled him nearly over, saying, 'You'll be through it, sir; the only parchment in camp.' The poor padre thought, he said, it was to *elevate* him in reading the service. No one, of course, could keep his gravity during this scene.

The chaplain went on to compound this by preaching on the Lord's Prayer. As Bell recalled, 'I remember the text very well – in St. Luke iii. 14. There went a buzz through the ranks. The men knew very well that they were six months' pay in arrears, and their daily bread was killing and slaying their neighbours!'[234]

However, English veterans were also free with their criticism of the army's Peninsular chaplains. Sergeant William Lawrence of the 40th Regiment (a native of Dorset, whose memoirs were transcribed in the 1850s after decades of popular anticlericalism had made their mark on England's agricultural poor)[235] recalled how a parade service was ignominiously abandoned prior to the battle of Sorauren in July 1813:

> A square had been formed into which a parson entered to read prayers and preach, and a drum being placed for his books and a knapsack for him to kneel on, he had proceeded with the service for some little time, when all of a sudden up he jumped with his traps and made a bolt, before any one had hardly time to see the cause, amid the applause and laughter of the whole of the troops at his running, which was as fast as his legs could carry him, and looked then as if the poor man might be going on even till now. They used to say that the three scarcest things to be seen in the army were a dead parson, drum-major, or a woman; the explanation of this was to be found in the fact that they were none of them often to be seen on a battle-field; and I think in this case our parson must have told and frightened all the others in the kingdom, for never after that did we have any service in the field . . . But the cause of the sudden flight on the part of the parson proved not to be one entirely of enjoyment, for a large body of the enemy appearing, we likewise found ourselves running about pretty smartly and preparing for immediate action.[236]

While this account may have been coloured by later animosities, in his contemporary correspondence Private William Wheeler of the 51st Regiment also intimated that the army's chaplains were unimpressive. In June 1814, Wheeler wrote from the hospital at Fuenterrabia:

> In this house of misery how many fine brave young fellows have died without the assistance of a friend, mother, sister or wife to soothe their agony in their last moment. No minister of religion to cheer the dying sinner . . . The people of England little think how her soldiers are neglected respecting spiritual aid, or I believe it would not be so. If they could hear or see the agony of the dying, their prayers, their despair and the horrid oaths uttered by some in their exit from this world, I am sure

> this most of wants would be attended to. It is true there are chaplains with the army who sometimes perform divine service, but of what use are they, the service they perform has no effect, for their mode of living do not agree with the doctrine they preach. I have often heard the remark 'That a Chaplain is of no more use to the army than a town pump without a handle.' If these Reverend Gentlemen were stationed at the sick depots and made to attend to the hospitals, they would be much more usefully employed than following the army with their brace of dogs and gun, running down hares and shooting partridges etc. In winter quarters these men once on a Sunday (weather permitting), perform divine service, but when the campaign opens, it is seldome or ever an opportunity offers, every day then is the same, few trouble themselves about days or anything else.[237]

However, perhaps the most damning, and definitely the most self-serving, indictments of the army's Peninsular chaplains were the responsibility of George Gleig, an Anglican clergyman, protégé of the Duke of Wellington and future Chaplain-General who had served as a subaltern of the 85th Regiment in northern Spain in 1813. In the preface to his best-selling memoir *The Subaltern*, Gleig had much to say about the inadequacy of chaplains in the Peninsula and about the efforts of the Duke of Wellington to remedy the situation: '[The] absence, from the hospitals, of religious instruction and comfort was sorely felt. But the Duke of Wellington was not to blame for this; indeed, his public despatches prove, that he made many, though fruitless efforts, to remedy the latter evil.'[238] In addition to forsaking the army's sick and wounded, Gleig also maintained that chaplains routinely neglected their obligations to the dead:

> [As] to reading the burial service over the dead, that, during the wars of the French Revolution, was a thing unheard of. Into huge pits dug to receive them the slain in battle were cast, as manure is cast into a trench, and the victims of fever and privations were in a somewhat similar fashion disposed of. Even the officers, though interred apart, had no prayers read beside their graves, for this, among other reasons, that the chaplains of the army were very few in number, and of those few, not one, so far as I know, cared to make more than a convenience of the service.[239]

With all the malice reserved for an uncomfortably close rival for Wellington's favour, Gleig was particularly keen to denigrate the conduct and character of Samuel Briscall. Long after Briscall's death, Gleig damned him with faint praise in his *Personal Reminiscences of the first Duke of Wellington*:

> The Duke in his despatches speaks favourably of [Briscall], especially on the ground that he kept down Methodism in the army. I believe he did more than this, by performing divine service every Sunday, so long as the troops occupied winter-quarters, though I and many more never saw him but once, and then could not hear a word he said.[240]

Gleig also alleged that Briscall was averse to visiting the sick, that he grossly imposed on the duke's hospitality and that he was an unreliable and even fraudulent debtor. On the first count, Gleig claimed that in Spain 'a constitutional shrinking from encounters with pain and sickness kept [Briscall] from visiting the hospitals'; consequently, while curate at Stratfieldsaye, 'he had a nervous fear of infection, and could not bring himself, be the case what it might, to visit a dying parishioner'.[241] As for his financial situation, Gleig wrote that, 'though his ostensible expenses were moderate enough', Briscall was 'always in debt, and ready at any moment to give a note of hand in exchange for a loan to any one who might be good-natured enough to accommodate him'. However, he was 'less regular in repaying than in borrowing' and in 'an evil hour for himself' Briscall borrowed £500 from the duke which was 'payable in six months'. When it became clear that neither settlement nor explanation would be forthcoming, Wellington treated him 'ever after with marked coldness'. In fact, and as Gleig remembered with ill-concealed relish, 'The curate remained . . . in the rectory, and dined as usual, day after day, with the lord of the manor, but the lord of the manor took no more notice of him, either at table or afterwards, than as if he had not been present.'[242]

Summary

Although the prevailing system of regimental chaplaincy was never robust, habits of absenteeism and neglect clearly worsened among the regimental chaplains of the British army in the forty years after the outbreak of the Seven Years War, years in which unwelcome postings to North America became more common (at least until the end of the American War of Independence) and the relative value of chaplains' pay continued to fall. While this problem was symptomatic of wider pastoral attitudes among the clergy, it was tackled directly in 1796 with the creation of the Army Chaplains' Department. The formation of the Department represented a significant measure of ecclesiastical as well as military reform but its achievements were limited in the short term; chaplains employed by the Board of Ordnance were unaffected, retired regimental chaplains became a drain on the public purse, the administration of brigade chaplains was shambolic and the real value of chaplains' pay was eroded by the pressures of wartime inflation.

Despite the sustained interest of the Duke of York in improving religious provision for the British soldier, ongoing problems with the army's system of garrison and brigade chaplains necessitated further reform in 1809. Significantly, the godfather of the Department's 'New Regulation' was none other than Spencer Perceval, the country's first (and only) evangelical Prime Minister whose zeal for promoting religion in the armed forces was shared by his evangelical protégé, Archdeacon John Owen. As Chaplain-General to the army, Owen worked hard to enlarge and inspire the new establishment of staff chaplains, he demanded greater efforts on the part of the officiating clergy and he promoted the distribution of religious literature in the army at public expense. Nevertheless, these efforts proved insufficient to meet the heavy demands of the time, especially those of the protracted campaign in Spain and Portugal. Thrown into an invidious and often brutal military milieu, staff chaplains were required to prioritise their work in the army's pestilential hospitals, where they almost inevitably succumbed to sickness and returned home. Consequently, Methodism flourished, Wellington voiced his displeasure with the clergy and many Peninsular veterans, including a future and rather unscrupulous Chaplain-General, acquired an unwarranted disdain for their chaplains that was to be widely and unjustly aired in the politically unsettled and anticlerical climate of post-war Britain.

2

The Army Chaplains' Department from Waterloo to the Crimea

The Army Chaplains' Department after Waterloo

The years following Waterloo saw the army visited by the twin plagues of chronic retrenchment and massive demobilisation.[1] These developments were fully reflected in the reduction of the Chaplains' Department. By the end of 1813, the Department had an establishment of thirty-eight staff chaplains. However, when John Owen died in office in June 1824, he left his successor, Robert Hodgson, with only fourteen, these being scattered across the empire from Quebec to Ceylon.[2] In 1830, commissions ceased to be granted altogether (thus saving the Treasury the expense of half-pay) and so 'on fixed salaries, varying from £300 a year to £150, [chaplains] were sent forth to all parts of the world . . . to resign and starve as soon as health and strength should fail them'.[3] However, this was not before a sharp difference of opinion over expenditure had taken place between Hodgson and the Secretary at War, Sir Henry Hardinge. Consequently, in December 1829 Hodgson was dismissed and the office of Chaplain-General was downgraded to that of Principal Chaplain, its salary being cut to reflect its reduced status.[4] It was the unfortunate lot of Hodgson's successor, William Whitfield Dakins, to preside over the further decline of the Department. When Dakins retired in March 1844, he left a Department with only four staff chaplains still serving with the army.[5]

One of the factors that sparked the quarrel between Hodgson and Hardinge was that the coming of peace left the Department burdened by a disproportionate number of chaplains on half-pay. By 1830, there were sixteen chaplains on half-pay, more than the number on the active list.[6] As they had served for less than eight years, they were liable to be recalled in emergencies or to fill positions on the active list as they became vacant. However, this system proved to be highly unsatisfactory as chaplains who had settled into civilian life proved reluctant to return to the army after intervals of several years. For example, when a small British force was sent to Portugal in 1826, Hodgson had great difficulty in finding chaplains to accompany it. As Hodgson reported for the benefit of the Secretary at War in January 1827:

> [The] Rev. G. Stonestreet . . . made in the first instance a *Voluntary Offer* of Service and as I understood he was a man of great respectability I had no hesitation in accepting it. I received however a few days after a second Letter from that Gentleman, in which from motives of private convenience he declined the appointment. I then wrote to the Rev. R.G. Curtois who has lately returned from Gibraltar, where he had for several years discharged the duties of a Chaplain to the Forces in a very exemplary manner; but I am sorry to inform you, that he also has sent me a refusal, founded in similar reasons.[7]

By this time, Stonestreet was embarked on a civilian career that would eventually take him to a stall at Lincoln cathedral while Curtois had been appointed domestic chaplain to the Marquis of Queensbury and vicar of Oving in Sussex.[8] Although Curtois did not entirely forget the army, pangs of 'conscience' prompting him to write a catechetical *Soldier's Manual* for the S.P.C.K. in 1833,[9] it was against this background of retrenchment, organisational inefficiency and general European peace that the Chaplains' Department increasingly turned to non-commissioned garrison chaplains and officiating clergymen in order to meet the spiritual needs of the army in Britain and the empire.

This policy had much to recommend it, including the prime considerations of economy and efficiency. Garrison chaplains were employed wherever there were large concentrations of troops on terms which varied according to local conditions. Chaplains for overseas garrisons were sent out from home or recruited from the colonial clergy and larger charges (such as the London district) were eligible for the appointment of assistant garrison chaplains. At some stations, the availability of Royal Navy chaplains reduced the need for more garrison chaplains, Malta being a prime example.[10] Similarly, at Chatham in the early 1850s, the work of its two garrison chaplains was assisted by the presence of a dockyard chaplain and by a chaplain to the Marine Infirmary.[11] However, it was widely accepted that garrison chaplains were generally overworked and poorly placed to do much good. In an isolated plea for the revival of regimental chaplaincy, a letter to the *United Service Journal and Naval and Military Magazine* in 1843 observed that:

> The charge of a force exceeding 100,000 men, dispersed through both hemispheres, is entrusted to a few garrison Chaplains, who have usually around them four or five regiments, with a large proportion of women and children. These gentlemen are doubtless for the most part zealous and useful, but their task is so arduous, and apparently so hopeless, that they must frequently doubt where to commence. It cannot be expected that in the course of three or four years (the usual period of a regiment's service in a foreign garrison,) they should acquire that knowledge of the habits and dispositions of soldiers, without which their labour must be in a great measure unavailing, or take the interest in individual men necessary to stimulate and repay their exertions.[12]

Despite the claims of this letter, most of the chaplains who ministered to troops in Great Britain and Ireland were not garrison chaplains at all, but simply parish clergymen who had offered their services to the military. According to new regulations proposed by Hodgson and introduced by the War Office in 1826, these officiating clergymen were entitled to a guinea if forced to hold a separate Sunday service for soldiers and fifteen shillings for any second or subsequent service. Furthermore, and depending on the distance they had to travel and the numbers they had to serve, they could expect as much as ten shillings a week for ministering to sick and convalescent soldiers.[13] Although regulated by War Office certificates and very much a pragmatic response to the needs of the time, this system became the subject of much retrospective criticism. In 1931, A.C.E. Jarvis deplored the fact that 'Religion in the Army [had been] contracted out to a host of officiating clergymen at a price per head, determined by the positively hated certificate.'[14] Earlier, in 1887, when Lord Randolph Churchill had the audacity to propose that this odious system be revived, George Gleig wrote to *The Times* insisting that:

> Religion itself suffered among all ranks, because of the obvious contempt in which it was held by those in authority. A hurried service, often in the barrack square early in the morning, left the officiating clergyman free to take his proper duties at 11 o'clock, and that was all we saw of him throughout the week, except, perhaps, when a soldier died, and the vicar or curate read the funeral service over him. The good man never thought of visiting the sick in hospital. He took no interest whatever in the soldier or his family; he did not so much as ask whether a soldier's child were baptized, or in any other respect pretend to regard him, except as an outcast to be avoided. Could we blame him for this? Scarcely; he had his own people to attend to – a burthen as great as he could well bear, especially in large towns, in or near which troops were usually quartered, and he therefore did for birds of passage, whom the Government threw upon his hands, as much as appeared to him commensurate with the paltry guinea, which, subject to deductions as often as rain fell or threatened, the War Office grudgingly doled out to him.[15]

However, and as with so many of Gleig's self-serving commentaries on the subjects of religion and education in the army, these views are open to question. In fact, there is considerable evidence to show that, in this age of clerical and pastoral renewal in the Church of England, the system worked tolerably well and that many of the officiating clergy were earnest in their army work. In 1849, a former officiating clergyman wrote to *The Times*:

> During the period in which I was barrack chaplain I afforded accommodation to the troops in my church on Sundays. The sick in hospital were visited at least once during the week, generally twice, exclusive of Sundays, when invariably prayers were said and a sermon or lecture given between the church services . . . The school was visited and inspected once a week, and the children catechised with others of the parish, if sent to church for that purpose. It is scarcely necessary to add, that there were occasions of special sickness when it became the chaplain's duty to be in daily attendance . . . For all these duties the sum of 5s. a-week is paid, and any remonstrance addressed to the authorities at the Horse Guards upon the subject is unheeded. It is even required that a

> deduction be made for the one or two weeks when the barracks may be empty before a new regiment has marched in after the departure of that which had occupied the quarters for the preceding year.[16]

Similarly, in 1830 an officiating clergyman named E.P. Hannam produced *The Hospital Manual, or Soldier's Guide in the Hour of Sickness*. Published by the S.P.C.K., it was based on the experience Hannam acquired while visiting Regent's Park Barracks in London and it comprised 'a general Service for the Sick' (for use in hospitals) and 'a Manual of Prayers, for the benefit of soldiers individually'.[17] In fact, officiating clergymen were not without influence upon their military parishioners. Colour-Sergeant George Calladine, a veteran of the 19th Regiment, remembered that at Tynemouth in the 1830s the officiating clergyman was '[O]ne of the best preachers I ever heard, and also a most excellent Christian. During the many times we were there he gave us two farewell sermons, when there were few dry eyes in the barrack room, which was the only place of worship we had.'[18] Faced with signs of diligence and charges of neglect, in his voluminous history of the British army J.W. Fortescue could only conclude that:

> [The] extreme sub-division of the Army into tiny detachments practically compelled the employment of local clergy, who knew nothing of the men. These, being called upon to perform nothing beyond a certain routine of prayer-reading for a miserable fee, naturally, in the majority of cases, treated their charge, so far as possible, as a sinecure. [However] occasionally a chaplain was found [who] would throw his whole soul into the work of ministering to the sick soldiers and reclaiming the bad . . . The Anglican Church, let men decry it as they will, is never without its saints.[19]

Nor were garrison chaplains necessarily deficient in zeal or influence. A case in point was J.T. Twining, an evangelical clergyman who for many years ministered to the garrison of Halifax, Nova Scotia. In contrast to the officiating clergy in the growing towns of industrial Britain, soldiers at colonial stations could comprise the principal charge of a garrison chaplain. It was in this capacity that Twining ministered to the troops at Halifax, being instrumental in the conversion of two of the most celebrated 'soldier-saints' of the mid-Victorian period, Maximilian Hammond of the 60th Rifles and Hedley Vicars of the 97th Regiment. Although Twining's work does not appear to have been full-time in the first instance, his role eventually expanded to the point that he entertained hopes of a chaplain's commission.[20] However, these hopes were frustrated when he became embroiled in a controversy over his support for the Colonial Church and School Society. In the course of this controversy, George Gleig, now Chaplain-General, firmly sided with Twining's ordinary, Bishop John Inglis of Nova Scotia. As Gleig warned Twining in September 1847:

> I have not forgotten your wish to obtain a Commission, though hitherto the opportunity of pressing the point has not presented itself . . . But before any thing can be done in that way let me beg of you withdraw from the Colonial Church Society of which I have reason to believe that your Bishop does not approve, which is likely to work I fear, as much harm as

> good in the Colony . . . It is above all things necessary that Military Chaplains should set an example of the strictest attention to the wishes of their Ecclesiastical Superiors and I am quite sure from what I know of your character that you will act upon the point which I take the liberty to throw out . . .[21]

Given his differences with his bishop and the Chaplain-General, Twining's hopes for a commission proved elusive until the Chaplains' Department was remodelled and expanded in October 1856.

However objectionable the prevailing system of chaplaincy prior to the Crimean War may have appeared to commissioned chaplains of later years (who naturally resented what they regarded as the casualisation of the chaplain's role) it did at least have the advantage of remaining under the control of the Chaplain-General or Principal Chaplain. Besides receiving the certificates and reports of duty performed by the officiating clergy and garrison chaplains, the departmental head also had a say in their appointment.[22] In 1842, for example, William Dakins wrote to Thomas Poole, a garrison chaplain in the Bahamas:

> I have received your half yearly reports of Marriages, Baptisms and visits to the Military Hospital which are very interesting to me and have my perfect approbation indeed I rejoice on your having retained the Office to which I was the means of appointing you . . . It will always afford me satisfaction to hear from you at the usual periods and your communications shall receive due attention.[23]

In a similar vein, in April 1848 George Gleig wrote to the Archbishop of York requesting a reference for a curate in Dewsbury who had applied for recognition as an officiating clergyman.[24] However, this degree of control did not exist over other agents who were involved in the spiritual care of the soldier in the early decades of the nineteenth century. Given the impossibility of providing a chaplain for all soldiers in every circumstance, a significant aspect of the army's religious life during the eighteenth century was that officers often read prayers to their men in the absence of a clergyman. This, of course, paralleled the situation on board smaller vessels of the Royal Navy, whose commanders were traditionally obliged to read prayers for the ship's company. However, during the Napoleonic Wars the shortage of chaplains at key stations and with forces in the field obliged the War Office to go further in according officers a formal religious role. Remarkably, both John Gamble and John Owen were fully complicit in this development. In July 1809, for example, John Gamble wrote to Captain John Hitchcock of the 8th Veteran Battalion on Heligoland:

> I am favoured with your Letter of the 30th [June] enclosing a Certificate of your having performed Divine Service to the Troops at Heligoland from October 1807 until the arrival of Brigade Chaplain Bennet . . . In reply thereto, I have to acquaint you that on submitting the same to the Secretary at War, he has been pleased to authorize an allowance of Twenty Pounds being paid to you for the duty in question . . .[25]

This pragmatism went still further in 1811, when a War Office circular authorised any officer of captain's rank or above to perform the duties of a chaplain in the absence of a clergyman.[26] If Gamble and Owen were tempted to view this development as an acceptable response to the needs of the time, it was almost bound to cause problems in the longer term, particularly given the religious (and often narrowly evangelical) enthusiasm of many army officers.

In the aftermath of Waterloo, this potential for trouble was realised at the apex of the military hierarchy as a result of the Duke of York's support for the Naval and Military Bible Society. Established in 1780 at the height of the American War of Independence, the goal of this broadly based evangelical society was to ensure that Holy Scripture was available to every soldier and sailor who desired to read it.[27] By 1812, the Society claimed to have distributed 'nearly 50,000 Bibles, besides a great number of Testaments' to British soldiers and sailors since its foundation, following a distribution ratio of one Bible or Testament 'among ten individuals'.[28] By this time, its *modus operandi* was to invite senior army and naval officers to submit applications for Bibles on their men's behalf. As its appeal for funds proclaimed in 1812, 'Where then is the Briton who loves his king and country, who will not cordially lend his aid to put the Bible into the hands of their intrepid defenders, and who will not add his prayers that the divine blessing may attend the gift?'[29] In 1814, and in a flush of euphoria precipitated by the first (though not the final) defeat of Napoleon, the N.M.B.S. confidently predicted that 'the friends of religion and of their country, will, in a short time, enable [it] to furnish every soldier and sailor with a copy of the Holy Scriptures'. Significantly, William Wilberforce had been a founder member of the society and it was not lacking in powerful friends. By this time, the president of the society was the Archbishop of Canterbury and, at the society's annual general meeting of 1814, the Duke of York took the chair and the Adjutant-General was in attendance.[30] In 1818, and in furtherance of the society's goals, the duke lent his name to a circular letter issued by the N.M.B.S. which required regimental commanders to correspond with its committee 'with respect to the supply of Bibles and Testaments'.[31]

If this circular unduly confused the duke's position as Commander-in-Chief and patron of the society, the expanding role of the N.M.B.S. as a supplier of religious literature to the army clearly encroached upon the remit of the Chaplains' Department. Since the appointment of John Owen as Chaplain-General, the responsibility for acquiring religious literature for the army had been one of the Chaplain-General's responsibilities and a small budget of £1,000 per annum existed for this purpose.[32] What exacerbated this situation was that certain evangelical officers acting on behalf of the society were prepared to usurp the functions of the chaplain by distributing Bibles and Testaments themselves.[33] As a strong evangelical and an ardent champion of the cause of godly reading in the army, John Owen appears to have had little difficulty with this situation. However, Owen's successor, Robert Hodgson, took a very different view. If the methods of the N.M.B.S. and its supporters usurped the functions of the Chaplains' Department and its members, for a staunch High Churchman like Hodgson the society's non-denominational character also proved objectionable. When invited to become a vice-president of the society after being appointed Chaplain-General in 1824, Hodgson pointedly replied:

> [This] is an honour I must decline. I have a fixed personal objection to becoming . . . a member of any society for the distribution of the Bible without note or comment . . . I can get from the ancient and venerable Society for the Propagation [sic] of Christian Knowledge all the Bibles and Testaments I can possibly require, and at the same time the Book of Common Prayer, together with many admirable and most useful tracts calculated in an eminent degree to counteract and repress all heretical and erroneous opinion and to disseminate what I conceive to be the real doctrines and principles of our holy religion.[34]

After it overstepped the mark by issuing specific instructions to commanding officers concerning the purchase and distribution of Bibles, the society was finally reined in by the Duke of York in 1825, who charged it with conduct 'injurious to discipline' and for being 'highly objectionable in [its] tendency to set aside the Chaplain-General of the army'.[35] Henceforth, he directed the society to work exclusively through the Chaplain-General in supplying religious literature to the army. However, within a few weeks the duke met the aims of the society at a stroke. In a circular of March 1825 (which carried the endorsement of the two archbishops and the Bishop of London, all of whom were prominent in the N.M.B.S.)[36] the duke directed that every soldier who could read should be issued with a Bible and a Prayer Book and that a 'Depot' of religious books should be kept by each regiment, the costs of which were to be met from the army estimates. In terms of their supply, the Chaplain-General was to deal with requisitions from commanding officers and also with the purchase of religious literature from appropriate publishers.[37]

If Hodgson was victorious in fending off the threat posed to the role and authority of the chaplain by overzealous civilian agencies, he and his successor, William Dakins, were rather less successful in defending the Department's Anglican hegemony. Although not explicitly sanctioned by the Royal Warrant, an ineluctable consequence of the abolition of regimental chaplaincies in 1796 was that the commissioned chaplains of the Department became an exclusively Anglican body. Symbolised by the presence of an Anglican Chaplain-General at the helm and by the creation of an appointing committee consisting of the Church of England's leading prelates, this coup caused some resentment in the Church of Scotland. While ministers of the Kirk continued to supply the chaplaincies of Edinburgh Castle, Stirling Castle and Fort George and were not excluded, if resident in Scotland, from the post-1796 system of officiating clergy,[38] Presbyterians were naturally aggrieved by their new-found inequality, particularly as the Church of Scotland was an established church and the Scots were over-represented in the army at this time. These grievances were periodically aired at the Church of Scotland's General Assembly. For example, when a committee was created in 1812 to advance the Church of Scotland's interests in India, it was also empowered by the Assembly:

> To inquire into the arrangement recently made respecting the Religious Instruction of the Army [in its regimental schools and] to embrace any favourable opportunity which may occur, of stating in the most respectful terms, the Claims of this National Church, to have it provided, that some

> portion of the Army Chaplains should be Presbyterian Clergymen, whose character shall be duly certified by the Moderator of the General Assembly.[39]

However, the amelioration of Presbyterian grievances only gathered pace in the mid-1820s, its unlikely catalyst being Robert Hodgson, who took it upon himself to challenge the exclusive right of Britain's established churches to provide Protestant services and officiating clergy in their respective jurisdictions. Far from representing a gesture of goodwill to the established church of North Britain, Hodgson's campaign was that of a combative Churchman determined to assert the rights of fellow Anglicans north of the border. In many respects, this reflected the circumstances of Hodgson's appointment in 1824. As Dean of Carlisle with no prior experience of the Chaplains' Department, Hodgson had been recommended for the post of Chaplain-General by the Bishop of London and the two archbishops precisely because they believed that 'some distinguished dignitary of the Church' was required to champion the interests of the Church of England in the army.[40] Clearly, Hodgson saw the right of Anglican soldiers in Scotland to worship according to Anglican forms as fundamental to these interests and in 1825 the issue was brought to a head when the very legality of holding Anglican services in the chapel at Fort George was put to the Lord Advocate for his consideration.[41]

Hodgson's position was very much that the clergy of the Scottish Episcopal Church should be recognised as officiating clergymen. As Hodgson remarked in a letter intended for the Secretary at War in September 1826, such arrangements were not without precedent.[42] In fact, Hodgson even conceded that, if such a policy were to be adopted for the benefit of English regiments in Scotland, then the same could not be denied to Scottish regiments stationed in England or Ireland. However, and as Hodgson was at pains to point out, this concession was not intended to clear a path for the claims of other denominations:

> As to the idea of pecuniary payments out of the public revenue for the pure purpose of enabling Soldiers of *all* religious persuasions to have Divine Service performed to them, there cannot be a moment's hesitation in saying that it would be found totally impracticable if it were attempted and would be fraught with infinite mischief if it were possible to carry it into execution. It is necessary then to limit these payments to 'Members of the Church as by Law established', and I do not object in the least to his Lordship's principle that the rule, founded on this limitation 'ought in fairness to be applied to Scotland, as well as to England.' Unquestionably, 'The Presbyterian Church is as much and as completely the Church established by law in Scotland, as the Episcopalian is in England.' If a Scotch Regiment stationed in England applied on conscientious motives for the performance of their own mode of worship at the public cost, I should say, that the Application ought not in fairness to be refused.[43]

In the event, and after prolonged wrangling with the Secretary at War, the issue boiled down to one of finance and, somewhat surprisingly in this cash-strapped age, a decision was made in favour of Hodgson's position by the Lords of the Treasury in November 1827.[44]

In combination with the seismic political and constitutional changes of 1828–32, this victory helped to clear the way for the payment of Presbyterian ministers as officiating clergymen outside Scotland. Just after Hodgson's appointment in 1824, Palmerston had refused payment to a Belfast minister for officiating to the 72nd (Highland) Regiment on the grounds of protecting the rights of the established Church of Ireland.[45] However, in 1833 a Presbyterian minister at Mullingar obtained payment for his services to the 91st (Highland) Regiment, claiming 'the allowance, that in Scotland, Episcopalian Clergymen were paid' and threatening the War Office with an 'appeal to the Synod of Ulster'. A few months after Lord Howick became Secretary at War in April 1835, similar payments were granted to Presbyterian ministers in Limerick, Armagh and Galway.[46] In the latter case, there was even 'a contention between the Minister of the Established Church, and the Presbyterian Minister regarding the allowance',[47] the latter prevailing due to the fact that the 78th (Highland) Regiment to which he had ministered was a regiment 'composed almost entirely of Presbyterians'.[48] In October 1835, Howick explained these concessions to the Treasury in the following terms:

> [As] in 1828 the simple and proper arrangement of trusting to the National Church of each division of the Kingdom was given up, and it was admitted that English regiments in Scotland should be attended by Episcopalian clergymen, it is impossible to deny that Scotch regiments when out of Scotland should have similar indulgences, and should be attended by Presbyterian clergymen in connection with the Church of Scotland, *wherever they may be found.* That these claims which have hitherto been preferred in Ireland only, will probably be made in England also and, inconvenient as it may be, his Lordship, after the concessions already made, cannot resist them.[49]

Clearly, Howick was unenthusiastic at the prospect of adding to the costs of the Chaplains' Department but a semblance of economy was at least maintained by the fact that ministers of the Church of Scotland remained ineligible for a chaplain's commission or even, it would appear, for appointment as garrison chaplains outside Scotland.[50] This did not escape the attention or the complaints of the General Assembly, for in May 1839:

> The General Assembly called for the Overture on the appointment of licentiates of the Church of Scotland, or of the Synod of Ulster adhering to the standards of the Church of Scotland, as Chaplains of Presbyterian Regiments, and of Presbyterian schoolmasters for the education of the children in Presbyterian Regiments, – also of Presbyterian Chaplains in the large military garrisons throughout the British Empire. The General Assembly having heard several Members, approved of the Overture, and appointed a Committee to prepare a petition, to be laid before Parliament on the subject.[51]

However, the interest of the Assembly proved to be fleeting and it was not until 1844 that the Church of Scotland took up the matter of Presbyterian garrison chaplains with the new Principal Chaplain, George Gleig. In the event, Gleig's response was to play for time and he requested further clarification of the matter. Hence, at the General Assembly of that year, 'Principal Macfarlan communicated to the House a letter which he had received from the Chaplain-General [sic] of the Forces, in regard to the appointment of Presbyterian Chaplains to Colonial Stations. The General Assembly appointed a Committee to collect and transmit the information referred to in this letter.'[52] However, there is no evidence to show that the matter was pursued to its conclusion or that any clergyman of the Scottish Church was recognised as a garrison chaplain outside of Scotland before the Crimean War.

By the mid-1830s, circumstances were such that even Roman Catholics could not be denied their officiating clergy. As we have seen, there was a strong precedent for this concession given the provision that the War Office had made for Irish militia regiments in England during the latter years of the Napoleonic Wars. However, this provision had lapsed with the coming of peace and with the return and disembodiment of these largely Roman Catholic regiments. Although Roman Catholic soldiers were free to attend Mass, their priests were not eligible for remuneration from the state for saying it. Nevertheless, discretionary payments to Roman Catholic priests had resumed as early as 1831, when £15 was allowed to a priest at Gibraltar; furthermore, in 1833 Sir John Hobhouse (then Secretary at War) had authorised a small annual grant which was to be paid to priests who visited the sick in the military hospitals at Dublin, Cork and Chatham.[53] Although Dublin Castle agreed that the Irish grants were 'highly proper',[54] Catholic Emancipation in 1829 and the general elections of the early 1830s brought to Westminster a small but vociferous band of Irish M.P.s who were not only committed to the repeal of the Act of Union but were also determined to redress outstanding Catholic grievances. Given that Irish Roman Catholics comprised between 30 and 40 per cent of the rank and file of the army at this time, upon his appointment to the War Office in 1835 Howick (who had been a leading advocate of Emancipation in any event) was disinclined to quarrel with the Whigs' fractious Irish allies by denying Roman Catholics the same rights that he had just conceded to Presbyterians. Hence, in February 1836, and following requests for payment from priests in Portsmouth and Plymouth, the Treasury agreed to meet the additional expense. However, given the pitch of anti-Catholic feeling which had been generated in mainland Britain by the passage of Catholic Emancipation, this administrative decision was not advertised by the promulgation of a general regulation but was quietly conceded in principle, the Secretary at War being resolved 'to deal with individual applications as they might arise'.[55] Still, these concessions proved controversial, and not least for the Commander-in-Chief, Lord Rowland Hill. In April 1836, Hill wrote to Howick via the Adjutant-General expressing his fears for the future now that the agents of Rome were free to pursue their 'insidious meddling' in the army. In particular, Hill drew attention to the danger of clerical interference with regimental schools, with the running of military hospitals and with discipline in general. He also protested that priests would be responsible for the 'Incouragement of Marriages among [the] Catholic soldiery, contrary to the wishes of the C.O.' In the event, Howick brushed these objections aside, pointing out that the system of certificates that governed the payment of the officiating clergy should guarantee their good behaviour.[56]

Nevertheless, commissions for Roman Catholic priests and their appointment as garrison chaplains remained out of the question and this remained a source of complaint until the outbreak of the Crimean War. In 1842, the Catholic Institute presented a parliamentary petition that protested the injustice of the situation. The petition argued that, whereas one third of the army's rank and file were Roman Catholic, their spiritual needs claimed only one-fifteenth of the annual budget which was allocated for the religious needs of the army as a whole.[57] Although this petition proved fruitless, Frederick Lucas, M.P. for Meath and editor of *The Tablet*, used the annual debate over the army estimates and the prospect of war with Russia to press these longstanding grievances in the House of Commons in March 1854. In this speech, Lucas remarked that the sums allocated for the religious needs of Protestant soldiers were grossly disproportionate to those allocated for their Roman Catholic comrades. While Catholics 'formed one-third of the whole Army, they only received one-seventh of the grant for religious purposes', statistics which actually disguised the real discrepancy as the religious needs of Protestants were also being met under other budgetary headings such as the payment of officiating clergy at military prisons. In practical terms, this situation resulted in the flagrant exploitation of officiating priests by the War Office. Citing the case of a priest who received only £30 per annum (with no allowance for horse or forage) for ministering to Roman Catholic soldiers in scattered outposts at the Cape, Lucas complained that the government cared more for the religious needs of Protestant convicts than it did for its Catholic soldiers. He also hinted at the implications of this situation for recruitment in Ireland and stressed the need to redress these grievances while Roman Catholic support for the imminent war with Russia (dubbed by Lucas 'a barbarous Tartar empire') was still strong.[58]

George Gleig

When, 'in consequence of ill-health and infirmity',[59] William Dakins resigned the office of Principal Chaplain in March 1844, the staff chaplain hovered on the brink of extinction and the duties of the Principal Chaplain were chiefly confined to the pedestrian business of overseeing the army's officiating clergy and garrison chaplains. Of the army's four other staff chaplains, three were stationed overseas (at Malta, Trinidad and Mauritius) and none had been in service for less than twenty years.[60] In the absence of a more suitable candidate among the handful of remaining staff chaplains, the military and ecclesiastical authorities saw fit to appoint the frustrated and ambitious George Gleig to the office of Principal Chaplain. A man of staunch (if negotiable) Tory principles and a protégé of the Duke of Wellington, Gleig had been languishing as chaplain to the Royal Military Hospital at Chelsea for the past ten years. However, some time before Dakins retired, the duke had suggested Gleig as his successor and Gleig had registered his interest with the Archbishop of Canterbury, William Howley.[61] In the event, the

Secretary at War, Sir Henry Hardinge, suggested three candidates to the Bishop of London and the two archbishops, these being Rowland Grove Curtois, Samuel Briscall and George Gleig.[62] When the prelates selected Gleig in February 1844 they were not only responding to the strong preference evinced by Hardinge but also to the pressures of economy. In his letter to the prelates on the subject of this appointment, Hardinge indicated that the office of Principal Chaplain could be separated from that of chaplain to the garrison of London, a role which Dakins had discharged for many years. By these means, the Department would be able to add another staff chaplain to its establishment while retaining the services of J.H. Dakins, the Principal Chaplain's son, who had been appointed London's assistant garrison chaplain in 1838.[63] Moreover, the income of the Principal Chaplain could be kept at £600 per annum by combining the salary of that office with the £300 a year already received by Gleig as chaplain to the Royal Military Hospital.[64] Through such financial juggling, the Department's small cadre of staff chaplains was increased by one and its expenses were actually reduced.[65]

Despite the inauspicious circumstances of his appointment as Principal Chaplain, George Gleig is the towering figure in the lore and historiography of the Army Chaplains' Department. A later Chaplain-General, A.C.E. Jarvis, described him as 'the foremost educationist of his day' and claimed that Gleig's three decades in office were 'the golden years' of the Department.[66] In his dissertation on Gleig and army education, David Jones portrayed him as 'a tough, highly principled man, much concerned with the welfare of the British soldier' while, more recently, Kenneth Hendrickson presented Gleig as 'the father of institutional religion in the modern British army'.[67] Unfortunately, such positive appraisals largely stem from an uncritical acceptance of Gleig's own propaganda. Probably the greatest assets which Gleig brought to his role as Principal Chaplain (and later as Chaplain-General) were his talents as a popular writer and his awareness of the growing power of the press to influence military matters through the medium of public opinion. In particular, Gleig excelled in creating opportunities for himself by presenting damning descriptions of various aspects of army life, portrayals which endowed him (often undeservedly) with the air of an expert. As we shall see, this was most apparent in his approach to army education and in his vaunted role as Inspector-General of Military Schools.

In order to understand Gleig's career as Chaplain-General it is vital to understand his background as a soldier, a clergyman and a writer and the High Church views and intense personal ambition that inspired him. Born in Stirling in 1796, Gleig was the son and namesake of George Gleig, subsequently Bishop of Brechin and *primus* of the Scottish Episcopal Church.[68] Given the strongly Jacobite allegiance of Scottish Episcopalians throughout most of the eighteenth century, Gleig was born into a church which had only just secured toleration under the law. In the historically hostile and oppressive environment of Presbyterian Scotland, Gleig imbibed strong Tory and High Church principles and a certain sense of dependence on the more powerful and affluent established Church south of the border. In 1811, Gleig began his undergraduate studies at Balliol College, Oxford, where his principles were widely shared and where he cemented his friendship with J.G. Lockhart, the future editor of the influential

Quarterly Review.[69] Although Gleig found Balliol 'very agreeable', he aspired to a military life and became 'determined to serve the Crown were it only as a private'.[70] Despite the misgivings of his father, a free commission was secured for him in 1813 and he joined the 3rd Garrison Battalion in Ireland, from which he soon exchanged into the 85th Regiment on the grounds that 'my sole object in entering the Army was to win, if possible a good name in War, a chance for which service in a garrison battalion must have for ever have excluded me'.[71] Gleig subsequently served with distinction in Spain, southern France and the United States, leaving the army in 1816 on the strength of a pledge he had made to his father. Although parental pressure may have played a part in this decision, Gleig later confessed that his regiment's absence from Waterloo was the fatal blow to his military career: 'Not having had the good fortune to share in that triumph, to me the door of advancement to Military distinction was closed.'[72] Returning to Oxford as a half-pay officer and resident of Magdalen Hall, Gleig took his B.A. in 1818 and was ordained deacon the following year with a title to the curacy of Westwell in Kent. In 1819, Gleig also married and, more importantly for his future career, he visited Edinburgh and struck up a friendship with the publisher William Blackwood.[73]

His ordination as a priest in 1820 left Gleig as an assistant curate in an obscure Kentish parish, with only his half-pay (which he was eventually obliged to sell), a small allowance from his father and his first earnings as a writer to supplement his meagre stipend of £75 a year. In order to make ends meet, Gleig tried to open a boarding school in the parsonage. When this experiment failed, he was compelled to move to another curacy at Buddhover in 1822, the rector of which was 'an excellent specimen of the old fashioned English Divine' who 'resided on another benefice some twenty miles away and for his own amusement and that of his neighbours, kept a pack of harriers'.[74] Despite his situation, Gleig did enjoy one significant advantage, namely that his diocesan, Archbishop Manners Sutton, could not ignore the fact that the son of the *primus* of the Scottish Episcopal Church was present in his diocese and living in straitened circumstances. Although Gleig claimed to disapprove of Manners Sutton (whom he described as 'somewhat Cardinal Wolseyish' and as 'an admirable specimen of the Princely Prelate of the Georgian era')[75] the Archbishop had the good grace to present him to the perpetual curacy of Ash (worth £130 per annum) in 1822 and to the rectory of Ivy Church in 1823, this being worth another £350 per annum after the salary of a curate and other expenses had been subtracted.[76]

During his early years as a parish clergyman in Kent, Gleig was keen to prove his credentials as a solid but innovative High Churchman. In order to counter the potentially schismatic attractions of evangelical cottage meetings, at Westwell he commenced informal Wednesday evening services in the parish church.[77] However, and as he later recalled:

> I was not slow in discovering that these proceedings of mine gave little satisfaction to my clerical neighbours – the high and dry church party spoke of them contemptuously – the Evangelicals condemned them because in their view of the case no higher motive could be found for them than hostility to dissent.[78]

Furthermore, and 'finding it impossible to improve the dames school', Gleig 'opened a night school for growing lads' at which he taught twice a week.[79] In order to quieten the apprehensions of his more conservative critics, Gleig was a demonstratively keen participant in local field-sports and by these means found that he 'kept on excellent terms with all except rabid low Churchmen'.[80] In 1823, and ostensibly on behalf of 'the old established Society for the Propagation of the Gospel', he attacked the Church of England's evangelicals by publishing a critique of what he described as 'a combination of individual Clergy and laity of the Evangelical school which tho countenanced by only a few of the Bishops, took to itself the high sounding title of "The Church Missionary Society" '.[81] However, this sudden attack on the C.M.S. clearly backfired for, as Gleig later acknowledged, it 'brought me flattering letters from more than one prelate' but at the same time brought 'a hornet's nest about my ears and did no good whatever either to myself or the cause which it undertook to advocate'.[82]

Gleig's other publishing ventures proved rather more successful. Although he had published a translation of Aristotle's *Poetics* while at Oxford, Gleig soon found that his talents lay in more populist fare. As a young clergyman in Kent (and clearly not overtaxed by his work once installed at Ash) Gleig devoted 'all his spare time to literature'.[83] Besides writing several articles for *Blackwood's Magazine*, in 1820 he published a full-length narrative of the campaigns around Washington and New Orleans during the Anglo-American war of 1812–15. Though this was not a conspicuous success, his great breakthrough came in 1824 when he published his Peninsular memoirs anonymously in *Blackwood's Magazine* under the title of 'The Subaltern'. Although he later regretted having sold this series so cheaply to William Blackwood,[84] there can be no doubt that the success of 'The Subaltern' transformed his subsequent career. In 1825, the series was published in a single volume and, in 1826, the Duke of Wellington (who transpired to be a great admirer of *The Subaltern*) broke with personal convention in order to allow Gleig to dedicate the second edition to him, this edition firmly identifying Gleig as its author.[85] Now connected with one of the greatest men in Europe, Gleig was at pains to cultivate his acquaintance and, following further correspondence with Wellington, Gleig was finally invited to visit the duke, who was then Prime Minister, at Walmer Castle in August 1829.[86]

Once admitted to the charmed circle of the Duke of Wellington, Gleig threw himself into politics with a vengeance. Earlier in 1829, Gleig had identified himself with Robert Peel's position on Catholic Emancipation, a position that accepted the measure with great reluctance, viewing it as no better than a necessary evil.[87] However, by the time Gleig visited Wellington that summer, the battle had moved on. The Tory party was in disarray over the passage of Catholic Emancipation and the great struggle between Whig and Tory over constitutional questions was now beginning to focus on the question of parliamentary reform, a measure to which Wellington was bitterly opposed. While holding the line against agricultural disturbances in Kent (informally, at first, as a parish clergyman and then as a Justice of the Peace)[88] in the interests of his patron Gleig turned his mind 'towards the best means of working upon public opinion'.[89] Consequently, he pressed upon the duke the potential of the provincial press in checking the growing clamour for reform. In April 1831, and with a general election in prospect, Gleig wrote to Wellington (who was now in opposition) pointing out that the opponents of parliamentary reform were at a disadvantage in the country at large as they had 'no control over the periodical press'. As 'the London papers' were largely pro-Reform, it was vital for the Tories to capture 'the country newspapers'. As Gleig put it, 'the press is a very powerful engine, of which your opponents fully understand the value, and of which they wisely make use. My Lord, you must endeavour to do likewise, otherwise there can be no hope for you in the present or any other great struggle.'[90] With the apparent sanction of the duke,[91] this policy was acted upon, at least in Kent. According to Gleig, at this point Wellington admitted him into his 'entire confidence' and the two were in regular correspondence on the progress of the Reform Bill.[92] For his part (and now as editor and part-proprietor of the *Kentish Gazette*)[93] Gleig championed the anti-reform cause in the local press. However, all this effort proved to be in vain. In June 1832, and in the face of intolerable pressure, Wellington led a hundred Tory peers out of the House of Lords and the Reform Bill was finally passed.

Despite his enthusiasm and industry in their common cause, Gleig's unequal friendship with Wellington had not resulted in rapid preferment; in fact, Gleig's hopes in this direction were entirely frustrated. In March 1830, he received a letter from Downing Street informing him that the duke was inclined to offer him a Crown living in Devon but was not willing to involve himself in any 'question of leave of absence', insisting that it 'must be settled between you and the Bishop'.[94] Consequently, the proposal got no further, Gleig later claiming that he had refused it on the grounds that it would have added little to his income while being too far from London.[95] Later that month, Gleig received another disappointing letter from Downing Street which quashed his hopes for the chaplaincy of the Tower of London:

> My Dear Sir, I have received your letter this morning . . . I assure you that it will be quite useless to make an application to the Duke for the Chaplaincy of the Tower, as I know that the Duke has already destined it for another Person – That person, I may tell you privately, is the Gentleman who has performed all the Duties as Deputy, for many Years, but I believe the Duke has not yet announced to him his intentions.[96]

Inevitably, their comprehensive defeat over the Reform Act was a shattering blow not only for the Tories but also for Gleig's unquenchable ambition. However, help came from a surprising quarter and, once again, the fame of *The Subaltern* proved to be Gleig's salvation.[97]

In February 1834, Gleig received the following letter from Lord John Russell, the Paymaster-General and chairman of the commissioners of the Royal Military Hospital at Chelsea:

> Sir, In consequence of the death of the Senior Chaplain of Chelsea Hospital, and the present state of health of the second Chaplain, I expect that the Chaplaincy of that Establishment will speedily be vacant. Your former connexion with the Army, and your distinguished merit in your

present profession induce me to ask whether if the office were offered to you, you would be inclined to accept it.

Russell went on to point out the potential drawbacks of the situation in question:

> I should tell you that by a new Establishment of the Hospital there will in future be only one chaplain, instead of two as heretofore, and that consequently his services will be required for the constant duties of his station for nearly the whole of the year. Besides the ordinary performance of Divine Service the frequent deaths in the Hospital render this condition indispensable . . . The salary will, I expect, be £300 a year, with a comfortable apartment, and coals and candles, but no other allowances. Should you require any further explanation, before giving your answer, I shall be happy to afford it.[98]

Upon referring the matter to the Duke of Wellington, it transpired that Gleig's nomination had originated from the duke himself, who had passed it on to Russell through an intermediary. As Wellington explained, the matter involved more than a touch of dishonesty:

> I desired [Lord Fitzroy Somerset] to tell Lord John that you, as most other good clergymen of the Church of England, were a zealous Conservative politician, but that I did not believe you had ever been a party writer; that when I was in office I was anxious to promote you, on account of your ecclesiastical works, and that I had earnestly urged on you by all means to avoid party discussions; that I had never heard of you having engaged in them, and that I firmly believed you had not. *I think you had better keep this anecdote to yourself.*[99]

Despite Wellington's insouciant advice, Russell was not so easily fooled. Two days after Wellington penned this letter to Gleig, Russell wrote to the prospective chaplain of Chelsea Hospital indicating that he had heard more than an unhappy whisper concerning Gleig's recent political activities:

> I am sorry to say I have been again assailed with rumours that you were exceedingly active as editor or writer in a Kentish newspaper a year or two ago. This is so unpleasant for me that I must request an assurance under your hand similar to that which you gave me by word of mouth: viz. To the effect that you have not been a party writer in newspapers or periodical publications.[100]

In response, Gleig resorted to a combination of untruths, sententiousness and egregious flattery:

> I cannot for a moment, hesitate in assuring you, that I am not, nor ever was a party writer in any newspaper or other periodical publication. I believe, indeed, that very few men have written so much as myself – and so rarely discussed political questions at all.
> Having said this, I think it just both to your Lordship and myself to add, that during the heat of the Reform question I did contribute an occasional article to a Kentish newspaper. I did this, not as a partisan, but from a conscientious belief that the measure would disappoint its authors and

> prove fatal to the country. But as to being the Editor of that paper, or an active writer in it – the charge is wholly groundless. Many things were attributed to me during the excitement of that period of which I knew nothing, – and this is one of them.
> As I never wrote a line of what may be termed politics previous to the agitation of the Reform Question, so I entirely ceased to write after that measure was carried. I believed it to be my duty as a Clergyman to set an example to those around me of obedience to the laws, – and I have on that principle avoided as much as possible, even in conversation, the subject of party politics.
> I hope that this information will set your Lordship's mind at ease; and that it will enable you to treat lightly the complaints of those who seem desirous of taking from you the odour of having done a handsome thing in the most frank and high-minded manner.[101]

Apparently, Gleig repeated the same story in a subsequent meeting with the Paymaster-General and went on to publish his version of events in *John Bull* and the *Standard* in order to quell the murmurings that his appointment had provoked.[102]

And so Gleig went as chaplain to Chelsea Hospital, his appointment being the subject of a satirical piece in *Fraser's Magazine* of September 1834. This article purported to present 'a life-like sketch of the new chaplain of Chelsea' and remarked:

> The ex-lieutenant [Gleig] is a Tory [but] he is the only eminent man in the Church who has himself worn a sabre. The old heathens of the Hospital will perhaps listen to one who may be said to belong to their own – to a mere black and all black . . . they would undoubtedly turn the deafest of long ears.[103]

Clearly, the idea of being regarded as a fellow veteran ministering to the in-pensioners at Chelsea flattered Gleig's vanity and appealed to his old hankering for military life. As Gleig was at pains to point out in a brief autobiography composed in 1859:

> His removal from Ash did not take place without strong tokens of regard from the parishioners; who invited him to a public dinner and after the removal of the Cloth, presented him through the Chairman, with a handsome silver Epergne. He was equally popular in his new sphere of duties, where men and Officers alike greeted him, as a member of their own Profession.[104]

Although Gleig relinquished Ash, he retained the rectory of Ivy Church while at Chelsea, apparently unaffected by the gradual application of the Pluralities Act of 1838.[105] Gleig's ministry at Chelsea Hospital also afforded plenty of time to pursue 'his literary career'.[106] In 1835, he published *The Soldier's Help to the Knowledge of Divine Truth*, a volume of twenty-five sermons which he dedicated to serving and former soldiers and, more especially, to the pensioners of Chelsea Hospital before whom they were originally preached.[107] As Gleig put it, the purpose of the volume was 'to reduce to the level of the private soldier's capacity, a connected view of the whole scheme of man's redemption'.[108] Evidently, he was well qualified to do this, a Sunday visitor to Chelsea Hospital observing that 'Mr. Gleig has a very good voice; clear and emphatic in his sermon; distinct and well-measured in the prayers. His discourse, too, was well adapted to his congregation, whom he addressed as "soldiers".'[109] In 1839, and for the benefit of such visitors, Gleig published a guide to the Royal Military Hospital entitled *Chelsea Hospital and its Traditions*. This book has not endeared him to subsequent historians of the Hospital, one of whom deplored the fact that he described the pensioners 'in terms of living exhibits' and 'particularly recommended visiting on Wednesday or Friday, when the visitor might be fortunate enough to witness the touching and picturesque ceremony of burial'.[110] Nevertheless, it appears to have been well received by its intended readership, an article in the *United Service Journal and Naval and Military Magazine* describing it as an 'excellent work [of] admirable clearness'.[111] Moreover, Gleig retained his interest in political affairs while at Chelsea and, though conscious of his debt to Russell, he was inclined to resume the role of a concerned Tory churchman. In December 1836 and January 1837, he wrote unsolicited letters of advice to Sir Robert Peel, this time on the subject of ecclesiastical reform. Conscious of his temerity, he concluded the first of these missives with the plea:

> I would not have ventured to write at all [but] I see before me a prospect of disunion and acrimony within the church itself, to avert which I cannot think that any sacrifice of personal taking can be too great. And I throw myself for pardon on your [discretion] and express my most unbounded admiration of your character.[112]

Although Gleig had eagerly sought the position of Principal Chaplain when it fell vacant in 1844, in the event he was clearly disappointed with the terms of his appointment. As we have noted, the separation of the role of Principal Chaplain from that of chaplain to the garrison of London meant that the full financial dividends of this appointment were denied to him. Worse still, and because he was now admitted to the Department as a staff chaplain, he was no longer able to retain his remunerative living at Ivy Church, where he had been settling his accounts as late as 1840.[113] However, Gleig initially chose to view his appointment as a troublesome stepping-stone to something greater. Within weeks of accepting the post and being briefed upon it by the Secretary at War, Hardinge was appointed Governor-General of India in Lord Ellenborough's stead, an appointment which stirred Gleig's latent ambitions for advancement in the Indian church.[114]

By this time, Gleig had developed a strong interest in Indian affairs, having published in the early 1830s a three-volume *Life of Major General Sir Thomas Munro* and a four-volume *History of India*. Moreover, he had written several articles under the beguiling pseudonym of 'An Old Indian' and had published his *Memoirs of the Life of the Right Honourable Warren Hastings* in 1841, a biography that was later described by Macaulay as among the worst books ever written.[115] More poignantly, Gleig's awareness of the shortcomings of the ecclesiastical system in British India had been brought home to him by the death of one of his five sons from cholera at Nellore, near Madras, in 1837. As the officer who had attended the young ensign had informed Gleig:

> I talked and read to him, as he could bear it, and he asked me both at morning and evening to pray with him, joining me always in the Lord's Prayer. On the Saturday preceding his death, after dictating the accompanying Memorandum of his last wishes he expressed a wish to partake of the Sacrament on Sunday, but this was impossible, as there is no clergyman here.[116]

In combination, all this led Gleig to entertain hopes of becoming the next Bishop of Calcutta, an ambition that appears to have been quashed by Hardinge himself. Faced with the financial consequences of his appointment as Principal Chaplain and frustrated in his desire to be the Anglican metropolitan in India, Gleig took his revenge on Hardinge by publishing a spiteful article in *The Quarterly Review* in 1846 which was full of implied criticism of the Governor-General's handling of the First Sikh War. In response, Hardinge wrote several revealing letters concerning Gleig to his stepson, Sir Walter James. In August 1846, Hardinge stated:

> I placed Gleig in his present office of principal chaplain & I know him as the humorous & ingenious author of the *Subaltern*. He has also written the history of the Bible. He failed in his life of Warren Hastings & I can't say I admire his novels. He wished to be bishop of Calcutta & is somewhat a disappointed man & not at all times a very discreet man.[117]

However, Hardinge was not prepared to leave Gleig's challenge unanswered, and he wrote to Gleig about the article that September, telling his stepson that 'I never answer the abuse of the daily press, but mis-statements in the Quarterly are historical, & I have desired him to correct his errors.'[118] Even when Gleig penned a second article designed to moderate his earlier criticisms, Hardinge was suspicious of the draft he received and of Gleig's underlying motives:

> I have read the article. If it stands in the terms now sent, it is evident this clergyman very charitably means to raise ill-blood between me and Ld. [Ellenborough] . . . It shows his animus agt. me & his mortification that I did not back his application to be bishop of Calcutta.[119]

Whatever the means used to requite his grievances, it is all too clear that Gleig spent his first few months as Principal Chaplain crushed by frustration and resentment. Early in February 1845, he wrote a frank letter to the Prime Minister, Sir Robert Peel, from the Royal Military Hospital at Chelsea, a letter that fully conveyed his restless ambition and agitated state of mind at his stalled career:

> When you accepted office in 1835, and made choice of Sir Edward Knatchbull to be Paymaster General to the forces, he did me the favour to call upon me at this place, and said, – for I perfectly remember his words, 'of course you don't expect to remain long here.' . . . I confess that at that time my expectations ran in the channel which his observation [indicated]. But ten years – or nearly so – have run their course; and I am still here.[120]

Clearly, the passing of the years was weighing heavily upon him, for Gleig admitted that:

> when on the verge of fifty, I see myself passed by, day after day, by men younger than myself, and certainly not possessed of more moral weight in society, I trust that you will bear with me if I feel driven to ask for that, which would have come more pleasantly of its own accord, [namely] advancement to the honours and preferments of my profession.[121]

In order to add more moral weight to his predicament, Gleig invoked the declared intentions of the Duke of Wellington with respect to his languishing career:

> I therefore without so much as consulting his Grace on this subject, refer you to the Duke of Wellington, to confirm or reject the statement which I now make – that he has said to myself, and repeated the declaration to my kind friend Sir Henry Hardinge, – who has more than once cheered me by reminding me of the fact, that 'had the Duke of Wellington remained in office it was his intention to have promoted me in the Church.' Indeed I will go further – for the explicit words of Sir Henry are, 'the Duke has repeatedly said to me, that by your writings and general conduct, you were fitting yourself for the highest honours in the Church.'[122]

Finally, and now grasping the nettle, Gleig continued:

> I therefore venture directly to request, that for the sake of time gone by, – on account of my character as a man, a Clergyman and scholar, and a man of letters, as one who in seasons of extreme difficulty was induced to sacrifice his personal predilections to the prompting of others, and who, when the crisis was over, returned thankfully to his habits of peace-making and a total abstinence from the strife of parties both in Church and State – that you will consider me as a fit candidate for such preferment as the Crown may have to bestow, on those who have earned for themselves a good name and desire to fill a somewhat prominent place in the clerical profession.[123]

Having vented his personal feelings, Gleig turned to more official matters, deploring the debased condition of the office of Principal Chaplain.

> Through the personal kindness of Sir Henry Hardinge I am placed at the head of the Ecclesiastical Department of the Army; an office unknown in many respects, of small repute or influence, and remunerated at a rate not quite equal to the pay of a double-entry Clerk in the War Office.[124]

Invoking the support of the Secretary at War and of the Chancellor of the Exchequer, Gleig suggested a possible solution:

> I ask you, whether it be desirable to raise a depressed and neglected department of the army to something like respectability, [that] the individual at the head of it should be paid by a salary of three hundred pounds a year. Why! The Chaplains of London, Chatham and Portsmouth have all salaries larger than this which, as I have just stated, does not go beyond the pay of an ordinary Clerk in the [War] office . . . On public grounds I take the liberty of suggesting, that the best arrangements for the

> remuneration of the Chaplain General [sic], would be to attach to his office a stall either at St. Paul's or Westminster.[125]

However, the Prime Minister was unimpressed by Gleig's entreaties, whether made on his own behalf or on that of the office which he now held. On the following day, Peel honoured Gleig with a curt and noncommittal rebuff:

> I have appropriated the Church Preferment which has been at my disposal to the Reward and Encouragement of eminent Professional Learning and of long and faithful Services connected with the public Schools and Universities . . . I have found it very inadequate to meet the first Claim founded upon such qualifications for the favour of the Crown, and when I review the names of those who I have recommended for preferment, I must beg leave to say that I cannot admit the slightest ground for dissatisfaction or Complaint on your part . . . I beg leave in conformity with the Rule on which I have invariably acted – to decline giving any assurances in regard to the future Appropriation of the Church Patronage which may be vacant.[126]

Nevertheless, Gleig's inward resentment did not translate itself into outward lassitude. On his appointment as Principal Chaplain his duties were modest enough, Gleig having been informed that the primary duties of his office were to assist in the appointment of chaplains, to superintend 'the spiritual instruction of the troops, and the provision of religious books for their use', to guide staff chaplains in their work and to oversee the Department's records of births and marriages abroad.[127] However, conscious that he should at least be seen to succeed in his new post, Gleig chose to harness the power of the press and the dynamic of reform in the army in order to publicise and enlarge his existing remit. The energy which he brought to his new role is reflected in the fact that the level of outgoing correspondence from the Principal Chaplain's office increased dramatically during his first year in office.[128] Furthermore, and in pursuance of his own brief from the Secretary at War, in May 1844 he issued a new and comprehensive set of *Hints and Instructions to Military Chaplains*. These guidelines were addressed to staff and garrison chaplains and they dispensed advice on the deportment expected of them, the performance of divine service and the visitation of hospitals, schools and soldiers' families.[129] Under the first of these headings, Gleig stressed that a military chaplain 'is in many respects so peculiarly circumstanced, that a more than ordinary share of zeal . . . tempered by exceeding discretion, is required to direct him in the fulfilment of his duties, as well as in the general tone of his manners'. Because 'a thousand eyes' were always upon him, eyes which 'never fail to observe whatever may be objectionable in his deportment', Gleig stipulated that the chaplain should 'exercise great prudence and self-control'. In particular, he should be careful of his dress and conversation, especially in the officers' mess, and he 'ought never to play either cards or billiards'. Furthermore:

> [The chaplain] will do well not to attend public balls, or to hunt, or shoot, or to be seen on a race course, or to addict himself to any other pursuit which may be associated in men's minds with notions of laxity. In a

> private room and among familiar friends there can be no great harm in his doing as others do, but let him never commit himself by an unguarded proceeding in public.[130]

With respect to public worship, Gleig stressed the need for punctuality and for reading prayers 'reverently, devoutly, and with feeling'. With regard to preaching, he emphasised the goal of 'moral and religious improvement' and stated that the chaplain's sermons 'ought to be short, simple, and as intelligible as he can make them, and above all, as uniformly practical as is consistent with the spirit of the religion of which he is the appointed teacher'. While stressing that such preaching to soldiers did not exclude 'having the doctrines of the Atonement and of the Mediation of the Saviour judiciously brought before them', he ruled out preaching on 'all controversial points', insisting that 'They are out of place even in country churches: they are positively hurtful when dwelt upon in a garrison or a camp.'[131]

Lastly, and in terms of his specific pastoral responsibilities, Gleig averred that 'The heart of the military chaplain must be in his work. The hospitals, the schools, the libraries, where there are any, are placed especially under his care, and he will fail in his duty if he neglect them.' With respect to regimental schools, Gleig recommended that they be visited twice a week and that half an hour be devoted in each 'to the examination and instruction of the scholars' in matters of religion. Furthermore, he underlined the value of setting aside an hour every Sunday (throughout Lent at the very least) in order to teach 'the children both of officers and privates' the church catechism and 'the principal truths taught in the Bible'.[132] While care was also to be taken in supervising garrison and regimental libraries (and in liasing with the Principal Chaplain on the supply of religious books) the visitation of military hospitals retained its prime importance. Besides reading prayers in hospital on the Sabbath, Gleig maintained that:

> A conscientious chaplain . . . will visit his hospitals at least twice in each week – on Wednesdays for example, as well as on Sundays – and besides praying at the bedsides of dying men, he will speak kindly to all the patients, passing from room to room, and teaching them by his manner to feel that he is indeed interested both in their temporal and eternal welfare. Especially when men are lowered by sickness, he will strive to awaken in them a sense of true religion. He will see that the hospital is supplied with an adequate number of religious books and tracts, all of which will be furnished, when applied for, by the Chaplains' Department. And over and above all this he will, at some convenient hour on the Lord's Day, gather the convalescents together after prayers, and read and expound to them some chapter in the Bible. On these occasions he cannot speak too plainly, nor be too earnest in striving to press upon his hearers the truths, moral as well as doctrinal, of the Gospel.[133]

From these *Hints and Instructions* it is quite clear that Gleig viewed the principal business of the chaplain as lying in the moral reformation of the ordinary soldier. While this contrasted with the emphasis that John Owen had placed on leading the soldier to salvation, it was perfectly in tune with the reforming aspirations of paternalistic officers and enlightened politicians at this time. Although traditionalists such as the Duke of Wellington maintained a jaundiced view of the rank and file, put their faith in a draconian system of military discipline and poured scorn on those 'who declare we ought to govern our soldiers as nurses do children with lolly-pops and lectures',[134] to more enlightened opinion the work of moral reform represented a solution to besetting problems of indiscipline and inefficiency. As Peter Burroughs has put it, whereas traditionalists feared that any attempt to improve 'minds, morals, or conditions of service' would simply erode discipline and promote 'dissatisfaction and insubordination' among the other ranks:

> Paternalists and reformers, in contrast, evinced a more benevolent view of human nature and potentialities. They emphasized the environmental factors that influenced soldiers' conduct: the severe disciplinary code, the monotonous routine, the insanitary living conditions, the inducements to drunkenness and trouble-making. They believed that the State had a duty to promote the well-being of the ordinary soldier through material and moral improvements in army life.[135]

Whilst Gleig's complacent view of the army's pay, rations, uniforms and equipment showed that his sympathy for the common soldier had its limits,[136] there can be no doubt of his firm identification with the cause of pragmatic, relatively enlightened but essentially conservative reform. Significantly, this spirit was not only abroad in the army at this time but it was also characteristic of Peelite conservatism and of the policy of reformist High Churchmen such as the Bishop of London, Charles Blomfield, who had played a part in Gleig's appointment as Principal Chaplain.[137]

Hew Strachan has identified Gleig as one of the leading propagandists of army reform in the decade prior to the Crimean War, Gleig being particularly adept in the art of 'the creation, largely through the press, of an "intolerable" situation'.[138] In September 1845, Gleig published his most famous article on army reform in *The Quarterly Review*, addressing in this instance the pressing question of 'The Moral Discipline of the Army'. Here, Gleig painted a dismal picture of the moral and religious condition of officers and other ranks alike and stressed the wretched state of the current system of army chaplaincy. As Gleig argued, regimental officers were poor exemplars of moral virtue. Leading a careless and luxurious existence in the society of young, unmarried men, they had nobody to guide their general conduct. Furthermore, their lax example had a contaminating influence upon the rank and file, 'For the officers of the army deceive themselves quite, if they imagine that their proceedings, whether within the barrack-square or beyond it, pass unnoticed by the men, or that the latter are not acted upon, both for good and for evil, by the example which is set to them.'[139] As for the common soldier, the very act of enlistment wrenched him from the wholesome milieu of rural life and thrust him into a godless and profane environment:

> You take young men away from their village homes, where they were subjected to the wholesome restraints of domestic example, where the curate used to see and converse with them freely, not only during his pastoral visits at their fathers' cottages, but while taking his daily walk in

> the fields – you entice them to quit the place where Sunday after Sunday they were accustomed to array themselves in their best attire, and to worship God in his house of prayer, and to hear his holy word read and preached; – you induce them to relinquish all these chances at least of attaining to a right frame of mind – and you throw them into a state of society where there is no connexion that deserves the name between them and any minister of religion; where God's laws are habitually violated, however carefully the laws of men may be enforced.

The consequences of this situation were ruinous, not only to the morals of the individual but also to the discipline and efficiency of the army as a whole:

> [D]issolute talk, dissolute conduct – immorality, indecency, drunkenness, being considered as the mere outbreaks of youthful spirit . . . are certainly not discountenanced and condemned as they deserve; – and yet you lament that crime should be so common in the army, and wonder that the defaulters' list should be so extensive, and that the provost prisons should be so crowded, and barrack-cells never without their full complement of occupants. Moreover, you know that the root of most of the soldier's military offences is drunkenness, and yet if you do not entice him to spend his surplus pay on strong liquors, you furnish him [through the canteen] with a very convenient opportunity of doing so.[140]

In Gleig's view, the current system of army chaplaincy was wholly incapable of confronting these evils. Garrison chaplaincies overseas were poorly paid and, for those who left England with such appointments, the prospects of employment should they choose to return were poor to say the least.[141] As for full-time chaplains at home, whether commissioned or otherwise, 'All these gentlemen have their hands full, and all in some way or another stand in need of greater countenance and support.'[142] However, it was the ubiquitous system of officiating clergy at home that invited most criticism. These clergymen, so Gleig maintained, had work enough without the additional encumbrance of their military parishioners. Furthermore, sending soldiers to attend ordinary parish services made a mockery of public worship. When taken to parish churches, they typically marched there 'amid the jeers and jokes of idle and dissolute people'. Still worse was the fact that:

> Crowds of these follow them – and continue to loiter about the churchyard. Meanwhile the red coats come in, disturbing by the clatter which they make, the devout, and drawing off entirely the attention of the young and the thoughtless. They are then thrust into all manner of by-places, out of sight very often, and hearing too, of the clergyman; while beardless ensigns, and sometimes their elders, either steal away from the Church door or forget that they have passed beneath its portals for other purposes than to make merry. Not a soldier's wife, or child, except such as attend the regimental school, and not always these, accompany the battalion; there is no room for them, and nobody cares about it.[143]

Nor were separate services to be preferred. When they took place in the parish church, they aroused the same unseemly interest among the *hoi polloi* and the clergyman was thus compelled 'to cut his business short [and] our beautiful Liturgy is in consequence humiliated and defaced'.[144] While the liturgy was also mangled at services held on military premises, here accommodation posed a further problem as:

> [A] barrack square is cheerless in itself, and seems to ring continually with the drill-serjeant's sharp command, and the awkward recruit's low murmur. A barrack room is, for obvious reasons, not much better; but a riding-school is a positive abomination. The place of exercise for beasts during six days in the week, and of corporal punishment for men, whenever such may be inflicted, is surely no fit temple for prayer and praise.[145]

The very nature of the system of officiating clergy meant that meaningful contact between clergyman and soldier was lacking, a fact which rendered the ministry of those officiating clergymen who did bother to visit military hospitals wholly futile.[146] As Gleig put it:

> [T]he clergyman has no opportunity of becoming acquainted with the troops – or of reaching their hearts through the care which he may take in the moral and religious training of their children. The men have no adviser to whom they can go in case their minds be troubled, or their consciences check them. There is no kind friend at hand . . . there is a flock nominally Christian, but there is no shepherd.[147]

In order to remedy the situation, Gleig argued that two fairly modest changes were necessary. Firstly, military churches should be provided at all stations at home and overseas which had garrisons of more than 200 men. These would be simple chapels which could be easily and cheaply established by converting disused buildings or rooms at existing barracks. Secondly, at each of these stations a clergyman should be 'taken into the public pay, to whom the troops shall be accustomed to look as to their own pastor, and who shall be taught to regard the troops, their wives and families, as his especial charge'. These extra clergy could be obtained through negotiation with local incumbents, who would be asked to employ 'an additional curate' in return for a modest stipend payable from the War Office. Through such a system, so Gleig maintained, 'the curate will feel that the troops constitute his cure [and] he will pay to them the same unremitting attention that he would bestow upon a district of civilians'.[148] As Gleig saw it, once soldiers enjoyed the same clerical oversight as civilians, their moral reform could be effected:

> We venture to say that, were all this done, and canteens abolished, and athletic sports encouraged, and garrison libraries fostered in the liberal spirit which originated them, the unfavourable impression that prevails throughout the country as to the moral dangers attendant on the soldier's career would be got rid of, and a very superior class of young men would come forward to fill the ranks.[149]

While Gleig's article drew an extremely partial picture of the current situation, his reformist agenda made rapid progress. Key to its initial success was the active support of a sympathetic Secretary at War, Sir Sidney Herbert, to whom Gleig loftily announced in November 1845, 'Every question affecting the moral conduct of the soldier seems to me to belong legitimately to my province.'[150] Prior to publishing his thoughts on 'The Moral Discipline of the Army', Gleig had already stated his views on the officiating clergy to Herbert himself, his memorandum calling for the consolidation of their occasional payments into an annual salary.[151] Gleig's lobbying on this score quickly bore fruit when Herbert agreed to the creation of a new system of 'soldier curates' along the lines outlined by Gleig in *The Quarterly Review*. These curates were to receive a fixed stipend of £75 per annum for ministering to troops stationed in their parishes and their appointment was subject to Gleig's approval.[152] Following this early concession, in 1846 four new staff chaplains were appointed to the Department and Gleig embarked upon a prolonged visitation of the army's principal stations in Great Britain and Ireland, sending regular and unsolicited reports back to the War Office.[153] Although Fox Maule, the future Lord Panmure, succeeded Herbert in July 1846, Maule was no less enthusiastic for army reform and Gleig continued to enjoy the support of the Secretary at War despite the change from a Tory to a Whig administration.[154] In 1848, Gleig's crusade to improve the moral tone of the army was furthered by a prohibition on the sale of spirits in regimental canteens, a prohibition that he had demanded two years earlier.[155]

These successes were matched by the impressive progress of Gleig's own career. In 1846, Gleig scored a threefold victory when, upon being appointed Inspector-General of Military Schools, Herbert saw fit to restore the title of 'Chaplain General' and to raise the pay of this office from £300 to £500 per annum. As Herbert explained his decision to the Treasury:

> As the salary of the Principal Chaplain, placed as he is at the head of a vast number of clergy ministering both at home and abroad to the spiritual wants of the troops, is at present most inadequate for the position he ought to occupy, I propose that it should be augmented to £500 per annum, with the title of Chaplain-General . . . When it is considered that the office of Principal Chaplain is in the nature of an Archdeaconry, with a jurisdiction far more extensive than any that attaches to that office in England, and that the Inspector will be charged with the duty of inspecting all the regimental schools as well as the Chelsea and Hibernian Schools, I trust that the arrangement I propose . . . will not appear to my lords to be disproportionate . . .[156]

With his star clearly in the ascendant, in 1850 Gleig obtained the sort of preferment to which he had alluded in his correspondence with Peel five years earlier, becoming a prebendary of St Paul's Cathedral.[157]

Despite the progress made in other quarters in the decade following his appointment as Principal Chaplain, Gleig made his greatest impression in the field of army education. Although education was fundamental to the moral regeneration of the British soldier, Gleig had shown little interest in the field of popular education prior to 1845. Indeed, the issue did not feature very prominently in 'The Moral Discipline of the Army', where he had merely noted that the British army's system of education was inferior to that of the French and that its regimental schools were 'open to improvement'.[158] Even Gleig's admirers have been at a loss to explain the precise origins of this interest. David Jones, for example, conceded that Gleig was never an original educationalist and observed that he had published nothing on this subject prior to his appointment as Principal Chaplain. Furthermore, Jones raised the apposite question of why Gleig had done nothing to draw attention to the shortcomings of army education during his ten years as chaplain to the Royal Military Hospital, in which capacity he had lived next door to the Duke of York's School (or Royal Military Asylum as it was otherwise known) and had helped to select in-pensioners to act as teachers to the military orphans who were its inmates.[159] In sum, these facts would seem to indicate that this was a typical piece of opportunism on Gleig's part, the origins of his educational zeal lying in his realisation of the importance that his political masters attached to the cause of popular education, an importance which Peel's discouraging letter of February 1845 had only served to emphasise.

Although the army's system of regimental schools had been established by the Duke of York in 1812, they had tended to cater for soldiers' children rather than for soldiers themselves. Through the influence of William Dakins (who had abridged Andrew Bell's ideas into a pamphlet while acting as chaplain to the Guards in London) the new system had from the outset relied on the monitorial system which had been pioneered in Madras by Bell and which was also employed by the National Society.[160] In the short term, these monitorial schools seem to have enjoyed a measure of success, helping to reduce levels of illiteracy in the army in the years following Waterloo.[161] However, given improvements in elementary education in civilian life (and particularly those associated with James Kay-Shuttleworth, secretary of the Committee of the Privy Council on Education) the inadequate training of the army's schoolmaster-sergeants and the scant resources of its regimental schools were attracting considerable criticism by the 1840s. In 1842, an internal committee of inquiry chaired by the Deputy Adjutant-General confirmed the inadequacies of the army's existing educational provision and made several proposals. These included the recommendations that all barracks should be equipped with a dedicated schoolroom, that a training establishment for regimental schoolmasters be established at the Duke of York's School (this in emulation of Kay-Shuttleworth's Normal School at Battersea) and that chaplains should play a more active role in the inspection of the army's schools.[162]

Although it is unlikely that Gleig had a hand in these proposals, he quickly grasped the opportunity to become their noisiest advocate. In March 1846, *The Quarterly Review* carried yet another article by Gleig, this time calling attention to the 'Education and Lodging of the Soldier'. As Gleig announced:

> The schools connected with the army – from that at Chelsea, to the school of the last regiment which has returned in a disorganized state from the East – are miserably behind. All the schools of all well-regulated parishes in the kingdom have passed them by; and, what is worse, continue to render the interval between them every day wider.[163]

Consequently, Gleig called for the enrolment of all recruits in regimental schools, the formal training of the army's schoolmaster-sergeants and the establishment of a Normal School at 'the Chelsea Military Asylum'.[164] With the recommendations of 1842 also being pressed upon him from other quarters, the Duke of Wellington eventually capitulated to the pressure for reform in 1846.[165] At the same time, Gleig's vaunted enthusiasm for the cause of education in the army was recognised in his appointment to the new post of Inspector-General of Military Schools at £450 per annum, a post which he held concurrently with that of Chaplain-General and which allowed him to resign the chaplaincy of the Royal Military Hospital.[166] However, while this appointment reflected the seemingly boundless confidence of the Secretary at War, Gleig's promotion of educational reform in the army seem to have antagonised the ageing and archly conservative Duke of Wellington, who anticipated that the new breed of army schoolmasters could only serve to foment mischief among the rank and file.[167]

Gleig's dual role as Chaplain-General and Inspector-General of Military Schools involved a huge amount of work that was largely weighted towards the latter role. While Inspector-General, Gleig was responsible for the training and examination of army schoolmasters, the development of a new curriculum for its regimental schools and for the publication of a supporting series of textbooks which eventually covered subjects as diverse as hydraulics and sacred history.[168] Furthermore, Gleig's inspections of military stations continued apace and, in 1847, he was even sent on a fact-finding tour of the military schools of France, Belgium, Prussia and Holland.[169] In addition to all of this, Gleig's twin responsibilities involved him with the War Office, the Treasury and the Board of Ordnance in effecting substantial changes to barracks and stations across the empire. As we have noted, Gleig had insisted that the moral reform of the army required the creation of new chapels for its soldiers. However, his ability to act upon this was boosted by his appointment as Inspector-General, in which capacity he was charged with advising the Secretary at War as to where building work would be necessary in order to provide adequate schoolrooms.[170]

Given the continuing pressures of economy, the simultaneous need to provide chapels and schoolrooms for the army was met through the expedient of the 'chapel-school'. Conceived by Gleig in 1845, this was a dual-purpose building which, on the occasion of its introduction, saved the taxpayer the expense of providing separate chapels and schoolrooms at four new barracks then under construction in England and Scotland.[171] Introduced despite the initial reservations of Sir Sidney Herbert, chapel-schools certainly had the advantage of economy, that at Hounslow being completed in 1847 at a cost of little more than £600, much cheaper than the temporary brick and timber chapels which had come to Gleig's attention two years earlier.[172] In the course of time, standard plans were drawn up for chapel-schools and, as early as 1848, Gleig was tendering advice as to the best means of turning existing barrack space into a chapel-cum-schoolroom. According to his 'Memorandum of the fitting of a Room which shall serve the double purpose of a Chapel and School Room', a chapel-school consisted of two sections which served as nave and chancel. The latter comprised a raised platform which was curtained off during the week and fitted with two separate apartments which served as vestry and schoolroom store. A communion table was placed against the far wall, with a reading desk and pulpit on either side.

As for the larger section of the room, which doubled as a nave, this was fitted with three tiers of desks and benches along each of the three remaining walls. This section was furnished with a stove, additional benches for use on Sundays and a moveable master's desk. When configured for divine service, officers and their families were seated at the front while 'The Band and Singers [were] to occupy the Platforms on either side most removed from the Chancel.'[173] Despite their aesthetic shortcomings, chapel-schools were cheap, functional and, as venues for public worship, they were a marked improvement upon the army's riding schools, barrack rooms and barrack squares. Furthermore, and unlike the chapels in the historic fortresses of the realm, chapel-schools were unconsecrated and they were thus available for the services of all three of the army's recognised denominations. As Herbert explained in the House of Commons in 1854, the typical chapel-school was built 'out of the public funds, which were contributed by all denominations'. Consequently, 'he thought it perfectly just and fair that the clergyman of the Church of England and the Roman Catholic should perform divine service in it in turn, to such portions of the troops as were attached to their respective communions'.[174] Hence, the chapel-school was not only a dual-purpose building but it was also shared by all denominations, thus yielding further economies by forestalling demands for denominational places of worship. For all these reasons, chapel-schools proliferated from the late 1840s, eventually becoming a standard feature of military stations across the empire.[175]

The Crimean War

Despite Gleig's activism in the reorganisation of the Chaplains' Department and in the reform of army education, the coming of the Crimean War cruelly exposed the underlying shortcomings of the army's chaplaincy system. Owing to policies pursued since Waterloo, on the eve of war against Russia Gleig had at his disposal only seven staff chaplains.[176] There were no half-pay chaplains to call upon and the Chaplain-General had no authority to order any garrison chaplains or officiating clergymen to the seat of war. Furthermore, the army was still totally without commissioned Presbyterian or Roman Catholic chaplains. Nevertheless, some hasty expedients ensured that a complement of chaplains was scraped together for the 26,000 strong expeditionary force that began to assemble at Malta from February 1854. In order to meet immediate needs, two Anglican clergymen were commissioned on 24 March, four days before the outbreak of war, and through the good offices of the Secretary at War a Church of Scotland minister and two Roman Catholic priests were contracted to serve in the East as acting chaplains.[177]

After four decades of peace in Europe, it seemed at first that enough had been done. Early in March, Gleig even wrote to *The Times* assuring its readership that 'the Secretary-at-War has not overlooked the spiritual wants of the army now proceeding to the East'. Some chaplains had already embarked, more would soon follow and 'the spiritual wants of all denominations had been remembered'. Furthermore, and with reference to his own experiences in the Peninsula and in North America, Gleig declared that:

> Though no public stir has been made in this matter, neither Mr. Herbert or myself has been asleep. Indeed, I should have been most culpable, with my personal experience of such a want, had I failed to press for adequate means to supply it; and no pressure has been necessary . . .[178]

As we shall see, these words would return to haunt Gleig within the space of six months. However, the initial sufficiency of Gleig's endeavours was subsequently confirmed by Henry Press Wright, who was appointed Principal Chaplain to the Army of the East that September.[179] As Wright recalled in 1857, while the expeditionary force was being assembled at Malta between February and April 1854 'The sick were regularly visited, public worship was celebrated during the week, and on the Sunday, the sacrament of the Lord's Supper was frequently administered.' Furthermore, 'between 300 and 400 men were prepared for confirmation, and presented for that holy rite to the Bishop of Gibraltar'.[180] However, and in keeping with much of the army's thinking at this time, Napoleonic precedents set the pattern for the ensuing campaign and the old system of divisional chaplaincy was revived as the army moved eastwards to save the Ottoman empire from Muscovite aggression. By a general order of May 1854, by which time the army had moved to Gallipoli, five of the six Anglican chaplains in the expeditionary force were placed in charge of a division and Wright himself, as its senior staff chaplain, was attached to Lord Raglan's headquarters.[181]

Although clearly sufficient for the peacetime conditions that prevailed on Malta, the arrangements made at the War Office for the spiritual care of the army soon proved to be woefully inadequate under campaign conditions. Overstretched and completely unused to the demands of a ministry in the camps and hospitals of an army in the field, the difficulties of its chaplains were compounded by the ineptitude of Gleig himself. Despite the cooperative stance of the Secretary at War and his own public allusions to the shortage of chaplains during the Napoleonic Wars, the Chaplain-General made no provision for additional chaplains to be on hand to replace the Department's inevitable casualties in the East. This lack of foresight was dramatically exposed by the appearance of cholera among British troops at Varna in June 1854, an affliction that was to follow the army from Bulgaria to the Crimea that September.[182] Given their work among the sick, this lethal visitation (which had not troubled their predecessors in the Peninsula)[183] had a huge impact upon the chaplains of the expeditionary force. As Wright explained in a letter to Ernest Hawkins, the secretary of the S.P.G., sickness had all but wrecked the army's chaplaincy arrangements before it had even landed in the Crimea:

> At an early period of the War when our Army was encamped on the plains of Scutari the number of the Clergy was found painfully small but in Bulgaria the spiritual wants of the troops became so oppressive that a staff of eight Chaplains could not possibly contend with them – they laboured night and day during a season of raging cholera until their untiring zeal became the common talk of every regiment.[184]

Given their exposure to the disease, several chaplains quickly fell sick themselves. Consequently, and as Wright explained to Hawkins, with an ironic allusion to *The Times*,[185] 'when the Allies landed in the Crimea there were but four Chaplains to accompany the finest Army England ever sent from her shores'. However, George Mockler of the 3rd Division died soon after landing at Balaclava. Thereafter, the impact of disease, the battles of Balaclava and Inkerman and the terrible Black Sea storms of November conspired to produce a situation in which the ministry of 'a now sadly diminished' body of chaplains was rendered 'ineffectual'.[186]

The virtual collapse of the army's chaplaincy arrangements became apparent to soldiers in the Crimea during the autumn of 1854 and in the course of the following winter. As early as the battle of the Alma in September, there were not enough chaplains on hand to bury the army's dead.[187] Clearly, the priorities of its few remaining chaplains lay elsewhere for, as Wright later explained:

> [T]he first consideration with us all was the wounded. The chaplains could do little for the souls of three hundred lying in agony. We did our utmost to console them, and to allay their bodily sufferings. Wandering bottle in hand over the field, we stayed the burning thirst of the exhausted, and cheered them with a few kind and encouraging words, which are at such a moment so acceptable from the minister of God.[188]

Such efforts could not, however, disguise the fact that the army's chaplains were now far too few for the task in hand. In December 1854, Hedley Vicars wrote: 'There are very few chaplains left in the Crimea now; even if they all returned in health it would be impossible for them to reach half the spiritual wants of the army.'[189] That same month a pious corporal of the 9th Regiment wrote to the staff chaplain at Malta in words that bore eloquent testimony to the wretched situation which then prevailed:

> Dear Mr. Hare, we have, since the 28th of last month, buried fifty-seven men, all cholera cases, and I am very, very sorry to say, that a clergyman of any profession I have not seen since we left Malta, no not one; nor one hour of public prayer have I heard since sacrament Sunday in Malta.[190]

By this time, however, steps were being taken to address the situation, the principal agent of change being the committee of the S.P.G. With the prompting of sympathetic officers,[191] and actuated by the same spirit of patriotic and philanthropic zeal that had already prompted the N.M.B.S. to donate a New Testament for every soldier in the East,[192] in October 1854 the Society approached the Secretary at War offering to provide temporary assistant chaplains for the expeditionary force. Hardly a quixotic gesture, this offer had in fact been carefully prepared. From its inception, the proposal enjoyed the full support of the Bishop of London, Charles Blomfield, and the Society had established a special fund in order to support the scheme.[193] Furthermore, the High Church character of the S.P.G. made its offer of help more palatable to the Chaplain-General and it proved attractive to the Secretary at War because it obviated the need to appoint a large number of staff chaplains who would become financial liabilities once the war was over. In view of what it described as 'the extraordinary demands of an army in the field', the S.P.G. undertook to provide 'an additional body of clergymen, to be placed under the authority of the senior chaplain'. The Society would engage each chaplain for the term of a year and would pay him a salary of £100 providing that the War Office matched this sum and provided 'free passage, and the ordinary field allowances'.[194] This offer was promptly accepted by Herbert, who at the end of the month requested that six assistant chaplains be ready for embarkation within ten days.[195] By the end of November, *The Times* could report that twelve S.P.G. chaplains had been appointed and that 'Seven of the number have already sailed, and the remaining five will embark in a few days for the scene of their arduous labour.'[196]

It is significant that the mood and circumstances of the Anglican clergy ensured that there was no shortage of volunteers for these new posts. The first twelve assistant chaplains were chosen from more than a hundred candidates and complaints were raised because the beneficed clergy were ineligible to apply.[197] With the beneficed clergy now tied to their livings as a result of recent ecclesiastical reform, some were tempted to stress the benefits of a greater tolerance towards non-residence. One clergyman (who styled himself 'A BENEFICED CLERGYMAN WHO WOULD GLADLY GO') even wrote to *The Times* calling for legislation to enable bishops 'to give a year or two years' leave of absence to any beneficed clergyman for the purpose of carrying out any special mission'. This he claimed, would ensure that 'There will never then be found a lack of volunteers for any work worthy the risk of life or the loss of time.'[198] While agreeing that the call for assistant chaplains was primarily addressed to the unmarried and unbeneficed clergy, another correspondent hinted at an important reason for their willingness to come forward in such numbers. Service in the East, he argued, would bring them not only 'present gratification, but, on their return to this country, their previous services would, in all probability, act as a recommendation to many of the livings at the disposal of Government'.[199]

Whatever the motives of the volunteers, the new situation clearly threatened to undermine the position of the Chaplain-General. In October 1854, and in light of the S.P.G.'s growing involvement, Gleig composed a memorandum entitled 'Appointment of Assistant Chaplains' in which he asserted his authority in relation to that of the Society's Board of Examiners:

> Candidates for appointment to the office of Assistant Chaplain to the Army in the East may present themselves for approval in the first instance either to the Chaplain General or to the Board of Examiners.
> The Chaplain General will examine the several candidates who present themselves to him with a view to the satisfying of his own mind as to their qualifications, and having thus satisfied himself, he will, without expressing his judgment to the candidates themselves, send them with a private intimation of his opinion to the Secretary of the Board of Examiners.
> The Board, on its part, acting on the same principle, will, after examining the several candidates, communicate confidentially to the Chaplain General the names of those whom it has agreed to recommend for appointment.[200]

With his authority duly acknowledged, Gleig soon fell into line with the new arrangements. In early November, and at a special fundraising meeting held by the S.P.G. for the purpose of 'sending additional spiritual aid to our sick and wounded soldiers at the seat of war', Gleig even proposed a vote of thanks to the Society which was carried unanimously. Chaired by the Archbishop of Canterbury and attended by Bishop Blomfield of London and Bishop Tomlinson of Gibraltar (who had confirmed more than '5,500 members of both services' in the East that summer) this meeting represented an impressive display of support for the Society and an opportunity for the Chaplain-General to explain the circumstances that had led to the present crisis in the Crimea. Omitting his own poor planning, Gleig emphasised that the government had sent out during the first few weeks of the war 'a larger number of clergy than ever within the memory of man attended any army which had left the shores of England'. However, 'sickness did not spare a man in a black coat any more than it spared men in coats of scarlet or of blue'. Furthermore, to the perils of sickness had been added the burden of overwork:

> The toils and difficulties which the chaplains had undergone at the seat of war it was scarcely possible to describe . . . it appeared that for 16 days after the time of landing in the Crimea these clergymen never once had taken off their clothes . . . He did not want to make much of hardships which the chaplains had only endured in common with the rest of the army . . . but there was this difference between the soldier and the clergyman – when the march was ended, or the duties of the day in camp were brought to a close, the soldiers generally could lay themselves down and take their rest. When the march was over, however, the chaplain's duties were just beginning. The dying must be seen to; the sick were anxious for his presence; the wounded wished him to pray with them; the burial service must be read over the dead; and all night long he must go forth upon his ministrations.[201]

Despite the toll that the war continued to exact upon the army's chaplains in the East (of the first twelve S.P.G. chaplains to be appointed, three had died by the end of the following summer and two more had been invalided home)[202] it was largely due to the Society that the desperate shortage of Anglican chaplains was remedied. Early in 1855, a further twelve assistant chaplains were engaged through the S.P.G. under the same terms that the War Office had agreed the previous year.[203] In addition to these reinforcements, four regular commissions were granted in 1855 and more assistant chaplains were engaged by Gleig himself.[204] In fact, while some determined clergymen set out for the Crimea independently, the War Office was hard pressed to refuse certain applications. The Honourable Sydney Godolphin Osborne, rector of Durweston in Somerset, was able to use his exalted connections to secure his appointment as an assistant chaplain and later proved a trenchant critic of hospital arrangements at Scutari.[205] As a result of these rather disparate efforts, a total of seventy-two recognised Anglican chaplains served in the East during the course of the war, the great majority of them as assistant chaplains.[206]

In addition to demanding an increase in Anglican chaplains, the rigours of campaigning in the East also necessitated the engagement of more Presbyterian and Roman Catholic acting chaplains. These were appointed on the same terms as the Church of England's assistant chaplains and were engaged through direct negotiation with the War Office. The spiritual plight of their co-religionists in the East evidently struck a deep chord in the churches. Clearly dissatisfied with progress to date, in May 1855 the Presbytery of Edinburgh urged the General Assembly of the Church of Scotland 'to take into their serious consideration measures to provide for the Spiritual Edification of Presbyterians in our Fleets and Armies'.[207] No less concerned, the Free Church of Scotland secured the appointment of its own acting chaplains as a result of an approach from its General Assembly to the War Office. Hitherto ineligible to provide either officiating clergymen or garrison chaplains, the Free Church nevertheless claimed to be 'deeply impressed with the duty of ministering to the spiritual interests of her adherents among the soldiers engaged in the war'. Largely through the influence of Arthur Kinnaird, a staunch evangelical and its first civilian Under Secretary of State,[208] the War Office was 'prevailed upon to accede to the proposal', granting a salary of £100 per annum plus rations 'on condition that the Free Church gave a like [sum]'.[209] The first Free Church chaplain to leave for the East was Robert Boag Watson, who was despatched with much ceremony in November 1854.[210] Watson was one of nine Presbyterian chaplains to serve in the East, six of whom were attached to Highland regiments.[211] In addition to this multiplication of Presbyterian chaplains, episcopal pressure on Lord Aberdeen's government and the need to sustain recruitment in Ireland ensured that more Roman Catholic chaplains were appointed as the war progressed.[212] Although the army's first acting Catholic chaplains (namely John Wheble and Denis Sheehan) both died in the Crimea during the winter of 1854–5, reinforcements had been arriving in the East from the previous autumn. During the course of the war, more than twenty Roman Catholic chaplains ministered to soldiers in Turkey and the Crimea, usually in the capacity of hospital or divisional chaplains.[213]

It was indicative of the largely pragmatic and *ad hoc* manner in which chaplains were appointed that even the Wesleyan Methodists were eventually represented among the army's recognised chaplains. In January 1856, the Wesleyan press announced that the Wesleyan Foreign Mission Committee had sent Peter Batchelor, an Indian missionary then on home leave 'for the recovery of his health', to minister to Methodist troops in Turkey. Despite the state of Batchelor's health, it was thought that his earlier experiences of working with soldiers in India would give him 'the advantage of personal acquaintance' with some of his flock.[214] However, and because he was not officially recognised as a chaplain by the War Office, on arrival in Scutari Batchelor was politely informed that he could only 'be regarded as a camp follower, and had no claim on the Barrack Master for quarters'.[215] Nevertheless, Batchelor had better luck in the Crimea itself, where in February 1856 he was given a small hut and put on the strength of the 4th Division as 'an accredited Wesleyan Missionary' to the army.[216]

In consequence of these sustained if piecemeal efforts, a discernible improvement had occurred in the Crimea by the end of the winter of 1854–5. In February, a soldier of the 47th Regiment was able to report to William Hare at Malta that, in his division at Balaclava, there were now 'two ministers, who are zealous servants of the Lord'. Not only were they conducting three services every Sunday but they were also holding a weekly communion 'for the purpose of giving an opportunity to those who may be on duty one Sunday to attend the next'.[217] However, with the fall of Sebastopol that September, the War Office quickly distanced itself from the S.P.G. Understandably piqued by this development, Ernest Hawkins wrote to an officer at Scutari:

> Lord Panmure has just informed us that he does not intend to avail himself of the services of the S.P.G. any further, but that those who have already gone out on the recommendation of the S.P.G. will be retained on their present footing. The truth is that the War Office was bothered by the applications of all sorts of societies and has thus been driven at last to do what it ought to have done at first, namely, to send on its own responsibility and at its own cost, a sufficient number of Chaplains both for the Camp and the Hospital. Meanwhile, we may claim the credit of having compelled the Government to double at least the number it intended to commission . . .[218]

By the end of the war six months later, Wright estimated that there were no fewer than sixty chaplains serving with the army in the East.[219] The vast improvement in the situation since the winter of 1854–5 was reflected by the fact that the Highland Division alone had five chaplains on its strength – one Anglican, one Roman Catholic and three Presbyterians.[220] This establishment had been attained despite the high level of attrition suffered by chaplains themselves. As Wright noted, 'Of twenty chaplains who served with the army in the East during the winter of 1854–5, eight died and eight were sent away on sick certificate.'[221] By the time the Treaty of Paris brought hostilities to an end on 30 March 1856, the total number of deaths among chaplains had risen to twelve. Significantly, none had been killed as a result of enemy action. Rather, and as Sir Sidney Herbert explained to the House of Commons in April, they had succumbed to more insidious dangers, namely 'fatigue and exposure to fever and other epidemic diseases'.[222]

What undoubtedly contributed to the high rate of loss in the Crimean War was the sheer inexperience of the unseasoned chaplains who saw service in it. The first chaplains to be sent to the East in 1854 were not only too few in number but were hopelessly untried, their collective experience of campaigning amounting to one chaplain's service as a loyalist volunteer in the Canadian rebellions of the 1830s.[223] Significantly, when Robert Boag Watson of the Free Church of Scotland took leave of Edinburgh in November 1854, it was without any body of experience to draw upon. As Dr. Robert Candlish informed Watson in a farewell sermon: 'You will meet with many difficulties; you will have to adapt your ministry to a state of things so strange that we can give you no directions with regard to it. We can only bid you ask courage and wisdom from the Lord.'[224] While this was no doubt representative of the predicament of the army's assistant and acting chaplains, staff chaplains at least had the advantage of earlier acquaintance with officers and other ranks. This is clear from the case of Robert Crawford Halpin, who had been a staff chaplain since 1849. On his arrival in the Crimea,

Halpin was taken under the wing of an N.C.O. of the 63rd Regiment, a regiment he had known while stationed in Dublin.[225] Similarly, during the early stages of the campaign Henry Press Wright was supported by an officer of the Royal Engineers, whom Wright described as 'a fine soldier, an earnest Christian, and a true friend'.[226] However, prior acquaintance was also beneficial to soldiers themselves, a fact that was demonstrated when William Hare shipped warm clothing from Malta to the Crimea in the winter of 1854–5.[227]

As ever, the absence or availability of public religious services was seen as emblematic of the chaplains' effectiveness. While complicated by the ravages of sickness, in the Crimea the nature of military operations also affected this key aspect of the chaplain's ministry. In the siege lines outside Sebastopol, large concentrations of troops were highly vulnerable to Russian artillery fire, a fact that was brought home to Henry Clifford, a Roman Catholic officer of the Rifle Brigade, as early as October 1854:

> I have just returned from Church Parade. No Mass of course; poor Mr Sheehan has no means of carrying anything, but he said prayers. We formed the men into Squares – the Protestants were on the right and the Catholics upon the left about 100 yards apart. It was a curious thing, the moment we formed, though a ridge of hills hides us from the Russian forts, they opened a tremendous fire on us of shell and round shot, but we were almost out of range; but the noise of the 42 pound solid shot, made such a row each time they came along – all the men lay down, though I told them they were out of range, and poor Mr Sheehan had a most interrupted service . . .[228]

As most parade services had of necessity to be held outdoors, the local climate also conspired against the provision of public worship. As Henry Press Wright observed:

> Some have thought that the men suffered so much from exposure during the Sunday parades that they were not of much use to them. That many at times found such gatherings tedious, I know full well, but the soothing language of the liturgy, and the home thrusts of the minister of God, have an influence for good in spite of the weather.[229]

In the Crimean winter, extreme cold also contributed to lengthy interruptions in the provision of parade services. As Colonel Charles Ash Windham, then Quarter-Master General to the 4th Division, wrote on 1 April 1855: 'Church-parade was ordered at noon, but, owing to the cold, Sir John Campbell sent to the clergyman and told him not to come. I think he was right; but certainly it is a long time since we have seen a parson.'[230]

Despite the problems which surrounded the due performance of parade services, it was their work in regimental, divisional and base hospitals that dominated the ministry of chaplains during the Crimean War. Although an extension of the work of the chaplain (or officiating clergyman) in military hospitals in years of peace, the pestilential nature of campaigning in the Black Sea region accentuated this aspect of their ministry. Throughout the Crimean War, disease took a much heavier toll of British soldiers than enemy action; typhus, typhoid, malaria, dysentery and cholera were endemic and such were conditions at the end of 1854 that as many as 11,000 British troops were languishing in hospital.[231] British fatalities in the Crimea eventually numbered more than 21,000 and those who died from disease comprised 80 per cent of this total.[232] Given the sheer prevalence of disease and the frequent lack of chaplains to minister to the sick, this work was onerous, debilitating and dangerous. This situation was underlined by the testimony of E.G. Parker, an Anglican chaplain then on sick leave from the Crimea,[233] before the Select Committee on the Army before Sebastopol in March 1855. In the course of a prolonged examination, Parker answered more than 250 questions on the conditions he had witnessed during his two months in the Crimea.[234] Confirming that his 'whole time' had been occupied in the hospitals of the 1st Division, Parker described the condition of the sick as 'Most wretched; as miserable as you can possibly imagine it to be' and declared that:

> [T]he state of the hospitals was such, that I think, had I not been many years in South America, and been accustomed to attend yellow fever patients constantly, I should not have been able to bear the effluvia. Many times I was obliged to leave the hospital tents. I knew the case of a brother clergyman, Mr. Egan, who fainted in one of the marquees from the dreadful effluvia.[235]

The misery of the sick in Crimean field hospitals during the winter of 1854–5 was also described by Edward Eade, an S.P.G. chaplain attached to the Light Division: 'Since I have been up here, I have visited most of the hospital tents of my division. No one can conceive the scene of misery they present. Fevered, agued, frostbitten wretches, most of them suffering as well from dysentery or diarrhoea, all huddled together.'[236] The strain this work entailed was conveyed in a letter written by Lawrence John Parsons, another S.P.G. assistant chaplain, in May 1855. With cholera once again raging among the men of the 4th Division, Parsons wrote:

> I am just taking shelter in my tent after a long morning of hospital work and funerals . . . as I went round this morning I found a man just brought in, writhing in a most piteous manner, and what I have not seen much before very blue. Cholera kept seizing him by fits as I was reading to him, and then he called out to those who waited upon him to rub him violently till the life returned to his limbs. I do not suppose I will see him again [and] I fear occupying the same bed of anguish.[237]

Their civilian backgrounds and the squalid conditions they encountered in military hospitals during the Crimean War prompted some chaplains to lend their voices to the public outcry over the state of the army's hospitals and medical services. In a letter from Sebastopol dated 16 January 1855, Edward Eade declared that 'a very great proportion of sickness and suffering might have been prevented, had proper means been taken in time'.[238] While Sydney Osborne had much to say about the situation at Scutari when interviewed by the Select Committee on the Army before Sebastopol,[239] when giving evidence before the same body E.G. Parker decried conditions in the army's overcrowded hospital tents. As Parker put it, 'I never could get my foot between any two men to perform my ministrations [and] I was never able to kneel beside any individual.'[240] He also declared that he had made representations to the Adjutant-General in the Crimea 'as to the state of the hospitals and the sick'.[241] While many complained, some chaplains were able to effect changes on the spot. Alexander Fraser of the Free Church of Scotland was able to improve conditions in the regimental hospital of the 93rd Highlanders due to his influence over the regiment's commanding officer. As Fraser wrote in his journal:

> [10 July 1855] Major [Ewart] desired me, if I observed anything deficient as to the comforts of the men in Hospital, to inform him, and that he would immediately get them supplied. I had formerly directed his attention to the fact that many of the patients of the 93rd had nothing but their great coats, or a thin blanket between them and the ground, when the patients in the Hospitals of the 42nd and 79th had bedsteads, or at least mattresses to lay on. He immediately set about getting this rectified and got the men made comfortable. I now brought him to see the state of two wounded men who had been brought in yesterday and though they lay on bedsteads, they had nothing between their bodies and the rough ticking and ropes and their over blanket was dirty and bloody. He immediately got them made more comfortable.[242]

In addition to arousing their ire, the general state of the hospitals in which chaplains worked was probably the chief cause of the high rate of sickness and mortality among them. Clearly, this situation applied to all denominations. In August 1855, for example, a ship sailed from Balaclava with two of the nine Presbyterian chaplains who served in the East during the war, both having fallen sick.[243] However, ill health seems to have been the lot of the army's Roman Catholic chaplains in particular. Of the twelve chaplains who died in the Crimea, none were Presbyterian, six were Anglicans and six were Roman Catholics. In relative terms, however, at least one in every four Roman Catholic chaplains died of sickness whereas the proportion for their Anglican colleagues was one in twelve.[244] These statistics may suggest a correlation between casualty levels and the nature of denominational ministrations to the sick. Whereas Protestant chaplains preached and held services in hospitals (reading to and praying with individual patients when appropriate) Catholic chaplains had a sacerdotal duty to hear the confessions of those able to make them and to physically anoint the dying, duties which required close and recurrent contact with patients suffering from contagious and potentially lethal diseases.[245] Certainly, Henry Clifford was convinced that the death of Michael Canty after only two months in the Crimea was due to the overwhelming burden of his hospital work, his fever being 'brought on by the hardships he has gone through here visiting the sick'.[246]

Despite the dangers of their hospital ministry, chaplains in the Crimea were at least spared a battlefield role. To an extent (and especially during the early stages of the war) this was because of their scarcity. As John Wheble noted, the two Roman Catholic chaplains with Lord Raglan's army at the battle of the Alma were compelled to remain in the rear with the surgeons while their French counterparts were sufficiently numerous to be present with their troops on the battlefield as well as in their field hospitals.[247] However, it seems clear that this was also a function of military policy, British commanders regarding chaplains as being of most use to the wounded and dying. George Lawless, an Anglican chaplain to the 2nd Division, remained in the rear ministering to the wounded during the battle of Inkerman in November 1854.[248] Similarly, and although he had ventured into forward trenches during quieter periods in the siege of Sebastopol,[249] on the eve of the bloody assault on the Great Redan in June 1855 Alexander Fraser was reminded that his place was with the surgeons and not in the front line:

> In the evening Sir Colin Campbell rode past my tent at the front of which the Revd Mr Campbell and I happened to be standing. He called me to him, and told me the Division was to start from the camp at 3 o'clock in the morning to support the Regiments that were to assault Sebastopol – that there was a general order that no amateurs were to be allowed to advance beyond a certain prescribed line – but that he did not consider me as included in that class – that probably there would be some of the brigade seriously wounded and that it might be a comfort to them to see a clergyman and therefore that I and Mr Campbell might accompany the Doctors. I thanked him for his information and permission, and said I would consider it my duty to be there. I feel not the slightest alarm at the prospect, but rather a feeling of satisfaction that I am called to the discharge of duty, where I may be useful in perilous circumstances.[250]

A complicating factor in the chaplains' ministry was the general attitude of the military authorities towards them and their place within the military hierarchy. Whatever their perceived value, assistant and acting chaplains (who comprised the great majority of chaplains in the Crimea) were in the ambiguous situation of being civilians temporarily attached to the army. Because they were also, for the most part, attached to support units, major hospitals or larger formations they operated outside the regimental family and were thus often left to fend for themselves. Although he was commissioned as a staff chaplain in March 1855,[251] E.G. Parker testified that he had great difficulty in securing proper supplies and accommodation as an assistant chaplain in the Crimea. If he received a bell tent, an officer's rations and a horse, he got no hay for the latter and its barley was provided by a sympathetic commissariat officer as 'a sort of kindness'.[252] Furthermore, and despite his complaints to the Quartermaster-General, he was not issued with a marquee (to which he felt entitled as a field officer) and so could not accommodate his congregation at communion services.[253]

Clearly, many of these clergymen could be dismayed by military culture and by army bureaucracy. Not only did they encounter numerous problems with their pay and allowances but they were often treated with scant respect.[254] In October 1855, an assistant chaplain attached to a hospital in the East felt compelled to write to *The Times* complaining of his lot. Prior to embarkation, he claimed, prospective chaplains were informed 'that they will be treated in every respect as field-officers'. Experience, however, had proved otherwise. At the seat of war the chaplain was treated as 'a sort of necessary nuisance' and even as a simple 'camp-follower'. Despite the dignity of their calling, chaplains were not accorded the courtesy of a salute and, although a chaplain was considered 'a useful personage so long as men are sick and dying', they met 'with indifference' when they themselves fell ill. Because chaplains had no prescribed insignia or uniform, the clerical estate was further demeaned by their dress: 'Each chaplain here pleases his own taste, by wearing some airy but unbecoming style', attire which made them look like 'hedge schoolmasters'. Consequently, the letter pleaded that 'military chaplains be treated in all respects as commissioned officers' and that they be given a proper uniform; only then, it argued, would soldiers 'treat their chaplains with the respect they deserve'.[255] Significantly, this letter provoked some animated debate in *The Times*. While applauded by one correspondent, who felt that such measures would recognise the sacrifice made by men who had resigned their livings in order to serve as chaplains,[256] it was greeted with alarm by others. In two letters from Scutari and Kulali, no fewer than ten hospital chaplains disclaimed 'all participation in the sentiments and statements of that letter', stating that 'there is nothing in our position that ought to deter clergymen from giving their services as chaplains to the forces in the East'.[257] In a further letter from Gibraltar, William John Coope, who had just served with the Royal Artillery,[258] deplored any suggestion that such trappings were necessary for military chaplains, exclaiming: 'God forbid that it should be needful for them to coerce the attention and respect of those who are committed to their care by external tokens of secular rank or temporal authority.'[259]

Another significant feature of the joint letters from Kulali and Scutari was that one Presbyterian, two Roman Catholic and seven Anglican clergymen put their signatures to them. This reflected an important development within army chaplaincy at this time, namely that confessional and denominational differences were often put aside in the gruelling context of active service. In the Crimea, chaplains were under the notional authority of the Principal Chaplain, Henry Press Wright, who was succeeded in this office by a newly commissioned Anglican chaplain, Henry Egan, in January 1856.[260] As Principal Chaplain, Wright was responsible for his Anglican colleagues and he also advised the Adjutant-General on the posting of Presbyterian and Roman Catholic chaplains. However, Wright generally allowed the Presbyterians to manage their own affairs, repeatedly assuring them 'that he did not wish to interfere with the Presbyterian Chaplains, but left them to arrange their own matters'.[261] Although there were disagreements when Wright was perceived to have unduly interfered with Presbyterian business and quarrels between Anglican and Presbyterian chaplains over who had a prior claim on specific regiments,[262] relations between them were usually cordial. Indeed, the prevailing harmony among chaplains was a source of some relief to Wright himself, who wrote to the secretary of the S.P.G. in October 1855:

> [This] I attribute partly to the wise selection made by the Society of Clergy known for piety and not party and partly to the fact that men with hundreds of sick and thousands of strong, daily requiring their attention, have no time for disputing. The platform of the Camp stirs up more of sympathy and love than of vanity and hatred.[263]

Notwithstanding the strength of anti-Catholicism in contemporary British society and the 'Papal Aggression' which had been widely construed in the restoration of the Catholic hierarchy in England and Wales in 1850, even Roman Catholics were embraced by this general mood of forbearance. While High Church dominance of the selection process for Anglican chaplains probably served to weed out Protestant extremists, a common Orthodox enemy and the Catholicism of Britain's French and Sardinian allies probably helped to moderate anti-Catholic sentiment. Although parliamentarians and the British public had long been subjected to complaints about the treatment of Roman Catholics in the army, Denis Sheehan sounded a different note in a letter to *The Tablet* at the end of November 1854. Referring to allegations 'that Catholic chaplains to the British army in the East have been obstructed in the discharge of their duties, especially in the administration of the sacraments', Sheehan declared that he had met with 'no such obstruction' and nor had any been encountered by his colleague, the late John Wheble. In fact, neither he nor any of his 'new colleagues' had suffered 'any hindrance to the exercise of their ministry' – 'It is', he concluded, 'of importance that no misunderstanding should exist on this matter, as an apprehension that impediments were put in our way would naturally carry anxiety and unhappiness into many homes in Ireland.'[264] Although there was trouble at Scutari in 1855 (where Michael Cuffe disputed the authority of the Principal Chaplain and where there was controversy over perceived proselytising by the Irish Sisters of Mercy and by a Jesuit chaplain, William Ronan)[265] personal relations between Protestant and Roman Catholic chaplains were usually amicable. Henry Clifford noted that Michael Canty of the Light Division was so widely respected that, when he died outside Sebastopol in February 1855, an Anglican chaplain and a Protestant officer followed his body to the grave.[266] Similarly, William Howard Russell of *The Times* alleged that Thomas Unsworth had incurred the suspicion of Cardinal Wiseman precisely because of his good relations with his Anglican colleagues.[267]

If an increasingly diverse body of chaplains learned to live with each other amidst the common hardships of the Crimean War, in what light were they viewed by the army in the forty years that separated the battle of Waterloo and the fall of Sebastopol? The answer to this question is complicated by two factors. Firstly, the great majority of British soldiers were not ministered to by commissioned chaplains of the Chaplains' Department. Instead, they were the responsibility of full and part-time garrison chaplains, of the chaplains of the East India Company, of hundreds of officiating clergymen and (in the Crimea at least) of dozens of assisting and acting chaplains. Secondly, and as in the Peninsular War, it seems likely that the chaplain's best work was done while on campaign among the sick, wounded and dying, a constituency that left little in the way of testimonials to their efforts. However, it is possible to arrive at some tentative conclusions. Clearly, the army's officiating clergymen and garrison chaplains were not as ineffectual as George Gleig insisted they were. As the testimony of George Calladine and the fame of J.T. Twining serve to illustrate, soldiers were not necessarily neglected under their care and they could respond positively to committed civilian pastors. Likewise, while there were few staff chaplains to complain of in the pre-Crimean period, it is clear that those who went to the East in 1854 were able to rely on the goodwill of officers and other ranks alike. Furthermore, the correspondence of William Hare (which was eventually published in 1857 as

Religion in the Ranks; or, letters from Soldiers in the British Army) indicates that he was a diligent evangelical chaplain who, despite the frequent upheavals of military life, showed a strong and sustained concern for the spiritual and material well being of ordinary soldiers.[268] Finally, there is ample evidence of the support and affection that acting Roman Catholic chaplains were able to command in the Crimea, a phenomenon that no doubt reflected deep reserves of sectarian identity and nationalist feeling among the army's Irish Catholic soldiers. Henry Clifford observed that the ministry of Michael Canty was enthusiastically received by the Roman Catholics of the Light Division in the winter of 1854–5. Later, Denis Sheehan was honoured by the men of the 88th Regiment (the Connaught Rangers) who erected a memorial to him in his former church at Clapham in recognition of his work in the Crimea.[269]

Summary

The Chaplains' Department was an inevitable casualty of massive post-war retrenchment. In the thirty years after Waterloo, the title of Chaplain-General was suppressed, its cadre of commissioned chaplains dwindled to the point of extinction and a heavy emphasis came to be placed on the services of non-commissioned garrison chaplains and officiating clergymen. The modest contribution of Anglican commissioned chaplains to the moral and religious state of the army in these years was also necessarily limited by the large proportion of Roman Catholic and Presbyterian soldiers in its ranks and by the existence of a separate system of military chaplaincy maintained by the E.I.C. in India, a destination to which increasing numbers of British soldiers were being sent in this period. Against this background of departmental decline, civilian agencies such as the Naval and Military Bible Society intruded upon the Department's shrinking remit and the Church of England's near-monopoly on officiating clergymen was eventually broken by pressure from Scottish Presbyterians and Irish Roman Catholics in a process that was part of a more general decline of the Anglican ascendancy in British national life.

However, in its reduced state the Department found a saviour of sorts in 1844 in the person of the clergyman and former soldier, George Gleig. A shameless self-publicist and endowed with all the ambition of a determined outsider, the Chaplains' Department was definitely not Gleig's first choice as a vehicle for advancement in the Church. Nevertheless, exploiting his fame and talents as a writer, his native mendacity and his own taste for conservative reform, as Principal Chaplain and later as Chaplain-General, Gleig was able to ride and direct the reformist tide which was then flowing in the army. Capitalising on his military background and upon the enlightened and fashionable cause of the moral and intellectual improvement of the soldier, Gleig established himself as a champion of army education and as the originator of the ubiquitous 'chapel school', a process that won him new and powerful patrons while it lost him the friendship and patronage of the Duke of Wellington. By these means, Gleig advanced his own career and the cause of the Department, which experienced a growth in its public profile and in the number of its commissioned chaplains prior to the Crimean War.

Nevertheless, while Gleig prepared the Department for the long-term and essentially peacetime project that was the reform of the British soldier, he could not prepare it for the Crimean War. Not only were there too few commissioned chaplains to sustain a protracted ministry to the army in the East, but there were no commissioned Presbyterian or Roman Catholic chaplains to call upon. In the event, the Department's work was only saved from the wreckage of a blighted campaign by War Office expedients which chiefly included the temporary employment of dozens of assistant and acting chaplains, chaplains who included Roman Catholic, Presbyterian and even Nonconformist clergymen. While most of the blame for this fiasco did not lie with Gleig, it is clear that he at least gravely misjudged the needs of the war in the first instance, a remarkable error for a seasoned campaigner (and strident critic of the army's chaplains in the Peninsular War) to make as Chaplain-General. Much to Gleig's chagrin, Anglican chaplaincy in the Crimea in the winter of 1854–5 was effectively rescued by a civilian body in the form of the S.P.G. and the Crimean War was largely over before the Department's early reliance on the society abated. Nevertheless, and as we shall now see, the moral and political capital accrued by the deaths of a dozen Crimean chaplains would stand the Chaplains' Department (and the Chaplain-General) in good stead with the coming of peace in 1856.

3

The Army Chaplains' Department from the Crimea to South Africa

Reform and Reconstruction

The political impact of the Crimean War was far-reaching. Stirred by the reports of William Howard Russell of *The Times*, a wave of public outrage at the mismanagement of the war toppled Lord Aberdeen's coalition government in January 1855. At the instigation of the radical M.P. J.A. Roebuck, a Select Committee on the Army before Sebastopol was formed to inquire into the condition of the army in the Crimea and to investigate those governmental departments responsible for its maladministration. On the formation of Lord Palmerston's government, the office of Secretary at War was absorbed into that of the Secretary of State for War and was finally abolished in 1863.[1] Although the last Secretary at War, Sir Sidney Herbert, was a notable casualty of the Crimean debacle, Gleig was fortunate that another old ally, namely Lord Panmure, was appointed Secretary of State for War in 1855. Undoubtedly, Gleig's handling of the war had left much to be desired and, on the strength of the ill preparedness of the Chaplains' Department, there would have been good grounds for dismissing him. However, even if Gleig had not been one of Panmure's protégés, he at least had an established reputation as an army reformer. Furthermore, given the limited pool of commissioned chaplains available to fill the post of Chaplain-General, there was probably no alternative to Gleig.

As Olive Anderson observed, the Crimean War saw the religious condition of the soldier become 'a matter of topical concern' for the British public.[2] This interest was reflected in the chaplains who were dispatched to the army in the East, who eventually totalled well over a hundred, and also in the dozens of civilian scripture readers who made their way to Turkey and the Crimea under the aegis of private patrons or of civilian organisations such as the Army Scripture Readers' and Soldiers' Friend Society.[3] However, the British soldier at home also benefited from this unprecedented level of public interest. The wartime expansion of the army to around 200,000 men was accompanied by the growth of existing military camps in England and by the establishment of large new camps at Aldershot and the Curragh. Despite the evil reputation that Aldershot and the Curragh quickly acquired, the soldier's moral and spiritual needs were not forgotten by the War Office. The building of iron churches at both camps was authorised in March and April 1855 and similar churches were also erected that year at Shorncliffe and Colchester. While they were apparently 'of the rudest and cheapest character', they at least had a purely religious function and the plans for these churches included accommodation for their incumbent chaplains.[4]

An important and fateful reflection of the public's concern for the religious welfare of army was the gratitude and sympathy which was shown to those chaplains who had served in the East. While the dead were memorialised in the garrison church at Portsmouth,[5] questions were raised in the House of Commons as to suitable rewards for the living. Less than a fortnight after the coming of peace, the Radical M.P. Sir George De Lacy Evans (who had commanded the 2nd Division in the Crimea and who was passionately committed to army reform)[6] declared in the House of Commons that 'The chaplains with the army in the East had had a more arduous duty to perform than the chaplains in any other war of the same duration.' Consequently, 'it was his duty to bring the subject of their meritorious, but ill-requited, services before the House'. Emphasising the paltry remuneration of the officiating clergy and stressing the fact that some garrison chaplains 'might serve several years – ten, he believed, at least – without receiving a commission' Evans demanded to know 'what recognition, if any, might be hoped for in respect to the services of the chaplains of the army during the war'.[7] In reply, the Prime Minister delivered his own eulogy on the recent work of the army's chaplains in Turkey and the Crimea:

> The chaplains, whether of the Church of England, whether of the Presbyterian persuasion, or of the Roman Catholic, have vied with each other in the zealous performance of their duty, and the success which has attended their efforts has been attested by the invariable good conduct of the troops. Those Gentlemen spared no pains to carry on their good work, and shrank from no exposure to the dangers of the hospital or of the field, while, at the same time, they displayed to the world the highest example of Christian charity, being the best practical comment on the religion they professed.

Whilst expressing his personal satisfaction with the existing system of officiating clergy, Palmerston assured De Lacy Evans that the Crimean chaplains would be looked after. A few had already received commissions and his government would be 'glad to take any opportunity that may arise of evincing our high sense of them'.[8] At this point, Sir Sidney Herbert rose 'to state his entire concurrence in all that had been said with respect to the admirable conduct of the chaplains' and 'to throw out a suggestion to Her Majesty's Government'. Pointing out that many of them would return home with 'no resources to fall back on' he expressed the hope that the Lord Chancellor, with around 800 benefices in his gift, would ensure that some of his patronage was 'dispensed among those clergymen who had served in the East'. Furthermore, and in view of the larger concentrations of troops at home which the war had generated, he hoped that 'Government would find room for the appointment of a larger number of commissioned chaplains'.[9]

These exchanges helped to ensure a decisive shift in War Office policy towards the Chaplains' Department, a shift symbolised by the expansion and restructuring of the Department in October 1856. Thirty-six new commissions were awarded and the Department was subdivided into chaplains and assistant chaplains in line with East India Company practice.[10] While all of the chaplains concerned were Anglican, they were a mixture of chaplains commissioned before and during the Crimean War, of pre-war garrison chaplains and of assistant chaplains who had proved their worth (and discovered their military vocations) in the course of the recent war. The senior class of twenty chaplains was largely composed of the existing commissioned chaplains, eleven of whom were commissioned before April 1855. Of the remainder, at least six had served as assistant chaplains with the army in the East. In contrast, the junior class of thirty assistant chaplains seems to have been dominated by former garrison and assistant chaplains, with J.T. Twining, the distinguished garrison chaplain of Halifax, at last receiving his commission.[11] Clearly, this remodelling of the Department amounted to more than mere expansion. Although some chaplains on the new establishment had been employed by the War Office prior to the Crimean War, their new commissions gave them better pay and allowances and entitled them to an army pension.

Further developments occurred in November 1858, when a Royal Warrant (which took effect on 1 January 1859) introduced new rates of pay, allowances and half-pay for all chaplains on the new establishment. It also replaced the short-lived classes of chaplain and assistant chaplain with four new classes of Chaplains to the Forces, each of which was endowed with a relative rank. Thus, the Chaplain-General was to hold the relative rank of major-general, chaplains of the First Class that of colonel, chaplains of the Second that of lieutenant-colonel, chaplains of the Third Class that of major and chaplains of the Fourth Class that of captain. Basic pay started at 10s per diem for a Fourth Class chaplain with less than seven years' service, rising to 22s 6d for First Class chaplains with thirty years' service or more. Furthermore, all commissioned chaplains were entitled to an allowance for lodging and an allowance for a servant, chaplains of the First and Second Class being eligible to claim a forage allowance providing a horse was 'actually and necessarily kept'. On retirement, the scale of half-pay commenced at 5s per diem for between five and fourteen years' service, rising to 17s 6d for thirty years' service or more. Except for those discharged on the grounds of ill health, a chaplain could retire after twenty-five years' service and his widow's pension was paid in relation to his relative rank.[12] Given that even the most junior Fourth Class chaplain serving at home stood to receive, in pay and allowances, a minimum of £241 16s 3d per annum (or well over twice the average curatal stipend in the Church of England)[13] this was handsome remuneration indeed. Furthermore, the basic pay and emoluments of First Class chaplains in 1859 (namely £528 17s 9d per annum) gave them an income comparable to that of the most affluent parochial livings in the Church of England.[14]

The relative value of departmental pay and allowances at this time must also take into account the distinctive lifestyle of chaplains to the forces. Unlike the beneficed clergy, chaplains were not responsible for the repair, maintenance or even building of parsonages and nor were they required by dint of custom to provide for necessitous parishioners or to subsidise parish charities out of their own funds.[15] Furthermore, and unlike most officers, their non-regimental status and the dignity of their calling spared them the sometimes riotous company and considerable expenses of the regimental mess.[16] In addition to this, chaplains could expect promotion on the basis of seniority, a system that offered entry to the Third Class after fourteen years, to the Second Class after twenty-one and to the First Class after thirty. In fact, it was not until November 1859 that a slightly amended Warrant was issued which allowed for promotions on the basis of distinguished service.[17] Thus, from the end of the 1850s, the remodelled Chaplains' Department offered decent pay, security in retirement and (saving death or ill health) a clear career path which was not susceptible to those vagaries of patronage that influenced advancement in the civilian church.

Ironically, the immediate catalyst for the Royal Warrant of 1858 may well have been the domestic problems that Gleig was then experiencing. When he was suddenly deprived of what he described as his 'official residence' in Chelsea Hospital in 1858, the new Secretary of State for War, Major-General Jonathan Peel, felt compelled to authorise a new lodging allowance for Gleig commensurate with that of a major-general. However, this was queried by a percipient clerk on the grounds that the Chaplain-General held no relative rank.[18] This experience may have served to focus Gleig's mind on the ambiguous situation of the chaplain within the military hierarchy. As we have noted, the Crimean War had provoked a vigorous if inconclusive debate in *The Times* as to whether or not the normal trappings of the Queen's commission would help or hinder the chaplain in his work. Although his role in driving post-war policy is unclear, it seems evident from his connivance that Gleig believed that chaplains would benefit from being treated as officers. This would benefit their conditions of service, it would clarify their position in the military hierarchy at home and on campaign and it would confer a greater authority on the chaplain in his role as moral reformer. Hence, while the terms of the Warrant of November 1858 resolved Gleig's immediate problems and enhanced the position of his subordinates, it also helped to blur the distinction between chaplains and the bulk of the officer corps. This process was furthered by a general order of May 1860, by which the Commander-in-Chief, the Duke of Cambridge, introduced a black uniform for chaplains and ordered that it should be worn 'in the field, in Home Camps, and in Garrison towns when visiting the Hospital or otherwise engaged in military duty'.[19] Two months later, a further general order stipulated that soldiers were now required 'to salute all Military Chaplains, paying them the compliment due to their relative rank'.[20]

Chaplains and Moral Reform

Alongside these changes, the members of the Chaplains' Department developed their role as agents of moral reform within the army. From February 1857, Gleig had an unfettered opportunity to advance this work after resigning his post as Inspector-General of Military Schools.[21] This move was precipitated by disagreements with Panmure over his powers as the new Director of Military Schools, powers that Gleig was characteristically keen to see enlarged. However, with the expansion of the Department Panmure was prepared to accept Gleig's resignation on the practical grounds that the Chaplain-General now had 'plenty to do in the purely clerical line'.[22] Gleig's resignation also had the unforeseen consequence of prompting the removal of 'Regimental and Garrison Day Schools' from the oversight of chaplains.[23] Consequently, in March 1857 Gleig issued a revised version of his *Hints and Instructions to Military Chaplains*. Although the chaplain was now no longer empowered to inspect the army's libraries and day schools,[24] Gleig stressed that he could still exert his influence in other ways. As the chaplain's involvement in these schools had been curtailed, it was imperative that more effort be put into Sunday schools and other means of religious instruction outside of school hours.[25] In terms of soldiers themselves, Gleig invoked the opportunities presented by the cause of rational recreation in the army: 'The Chaplain may make himself extremely useful, if, with the concurrence of the officer commanding, he takes general charge of the library, and gets up lectures on scientific and other subjects, for the instruction and rational amusement of the men.'[26] Furthermore, he drew attention to the unrealised potential of local help:

> As it is clearly impossible for any one man to make his personal influence continually felt for good in a community of some hundreds of persons, the Military Chaplain is recommended to look out from among the officers, non-commissioned officers and privates of his charge, as many earnest and humble minded men as may be willing to labour with him; and to employ them in the capacity of Scripture Readers in the hospitals, in the barrack rooms, and wherever a door of usefulness shall seem to be opened, to bring God's Word within the reach of their comrades, and encourage them to study and be directed by it.[27]

Finally, Gleig stressed the need for clear, intelligible and pertinent preaching at parade services, when virtually all of the chaplain's flock would be present: 'Address your audience so that they may feel that you are speaking to them about matters which concern themselves, not delivering an essay which may or may not touch their wants or interest their feelings.'[28]

For their part, the military authorities continued to recognise the chaplain's expertise and authority in a range of issues connected with the moral and professional improvement of its soldiers. As Chaplain-General, Gleig appeared before a committee of inquiry into the army's barracks in May 1855. In the course of his questioning, Gleig stressed the need to ensure that married and unmarried quarters were 'distinct and separate'; this would be 'an important step towards raising the moral tone of the Army' and would encourage younger soldiers 'to abstain from improvident marriages' by giving them an incentive to marry with the knowledge and permission of their commanding officers. He also argued for more libraries, chapel-schools and sporting facilities:

> [The] more home-like, the more comfortable you can make the barracks, the less disposed the soldier will be to break out of them and get into trouble . . . Having provided schools, chapels, good quarters, libraries and

gymnasia, I am confident that it will be the fault of the officers if crime does not virtually disappear from among the troops.[29]

Given his recognised interest in these matters, Gleig was also a natural candidate to sit on an eight-man commission of inquiry into the army's libraries and reading-rooms that reported to the Secretary of State for War six years later. Chaired by Major-General Eyre, this commission ventured well beyond its official remit, eventually producing a report and recommendations on the army's entire recreational provision in August 1861. While Gleig urged the opening of 'Military Chapels and Chapel Schools at suitable hours for purposes of private devotion',[30] the commission also canvassed chaplains' opinions on the desirability and regulation of soldiers' institutes, a new phenomenon that had emerged during and after the Crimean War as an expression of public concern and sympathy for the common soldier. Hence, Henry Press Wright gave a glowing account of the salutary influence of a soldiers' institute that had been opened through the generosity of the people of Canterbury, claiming that 'The institute has tended to make the garrison of Canterbury an exemplary one.' With typical pragmatism, Wright predicted that educational meetings 'would destroy the institute in a few months' and even confessed to being in favour of linking it to the garrison canteen, adding that 'I have laid my plan before the Chaplain-General, who will gladly explain it to the Committee.'[31] However, a rather different note was sounded by George Dacre at the Curragh, who voiced his exasperation with the seemingly endless task of keeping the British soldier on the straight and narrow:

> There is no problem more difficult to solve than how to amuse the British soldiers. Give them football or quoits, and they will play for a week. Give them cricket, and unless the officers play with them, very few will avail themselves of it. Give them athletic games, and unless you add prizes it is in vain. Give them plots of ground for gardening, and unless they can make large profits by selling the produce, they will not raise as many vegetables as will supply their own mess . . . the only game I have seen persevered in is skittles *near a canteen*; away from the canteen it was a failure: – all [of] which shows that the moral condition of these men is merely an animal existence; and if we shut our eyes to this we shall only be disappointed in our expectations.[32]

Gleig, however, remained optimistic as to the improving potential of the burgeoning leisure facilities of the mid-Victorian army. Furthermore, as Chaplain-General and a constant visitor to home garrisons, his opinion seemed to carry weight. As one survey of the army's home stations put it in 1867:

> There are 208 recreation rooms, and refreshment bars have been established in 107 corps . . . [The Chaplain-General], who has visited the rooms at all hours, considers them, when established regimentally and upon a suitable scale, to be thoroughly successful, stating that it is delightful to observe the enjoyment of the men, and the good order that is maintained. Other inspectors confirm the statements.[33]

However, keeping the soldier entertained was but one aspect of the chaplain's work on behalf of personal morality and professional efficiency. With the steady decline of flogging in the Victorian army (it was largely abolished in 1881), imprisonment became the principal form of punishment for military defaulters.[34] In the context of this more enlightened system chaplains were expected to play a key role in the reform and rehabilitation of offenders through their visiting of inmates in their cells and their general ministry to military prisons. Indeed, a lack of departmental input into the report on military prisons for 1870 provoked outrage in the pages of *Colburn's United Service Magazine*. While condemning other aspects of the report, one critic deplored the fact that chaplains had so little to contribute to it, with only the chaplain of Millbank having anything of substance to say:

> Soldier-prisoners they should remember are men open to conversion as well as conviction, not malefactors doomed to eternal punishment; and if they are but treated kindly and humanely by chaplains, we are certain the latter will reap a rich reward, in gaining the grateful remembrances of those they had shown compassion to when in trouble. A prison chaplain's motto should be 'Kind words cost little but are worth much'. We hope that the next Report will contain extracts confirmatory of our hopes.[35]

Despite this episode, it seems clear that military chaplains of the mid-Victorian era worked diligently to promote the soldier's moral and religious welfare in the army's barracks, prisons and hospitals. A case in point was that of William Sykes, an acting chaplain who went to the Crimea under the aegis of the S.P.G. before being commissioned in 1855. Sykes' career spanned more than three decades and he served at six different stations before retiring in 1888. However, the greater part of his career was spent at Plymouth, where he was stationed from 1860 to 1866 and from 1868 to 1879. During his years at Plymouth, Sykes' correspondence shows that he was heavily involved in causes affecting the moral and religious welfare of his flock. One of his first letters to the War Office complained of the lodgings that married soldiers were obliged to take in the town due to the shortage of married quarters in the Royal Citadel:

> [The] lodging houses in the vicinity, with very few exceptions, are brothels, the language is filthy, the sanitary arrangements very objectionable, and the rent very high. The general effect on the children is very bad. I hope the [Secretary of State for War] may be able to do something to remedy this state of things.[36]

Sykes was also attentive in his duties at the military prison, visiting prisoners in their cells and holding four services each week, three of them on weekdays.[37] While his correspondence shows that he would have preferred to see a proper chapel and chaplain's quarters built at Devonport, he did his best with the chapel-school that had been established in 1858. However, in his battle to preserve its dignity as a place of worship, he was obliged to protest its use for dances and other entertainments and was even forced to complain about the removal of its seats for use at a review.[38]

The chaplain's role as the foremost moral guardian of the soldier did not diminish as the years passed. When questions were raised in 1887 about the cost of maintaining the Chaplains' Department in its existing form, J.C. Edghill, then Chaplain-General, quipped in a letter to Gleig:

> Lord Wolsey [sic] is trying to do away with the Chaplains on the ground of expense. Saving a paltry few hundreds of pounds is of more weight than saving men's souls and bodies . . . I hold efficiency is cheaper and I am quite prepared to prove that in my twenty three years of Chaplain's work I saved my pay over and over again in rescuing men from drunkenness and impurity . . . It was always my boast that I was a *saving* machine for the State.[39]

The role of the chaplain in promoting the cause of morality and efficiency in the army was forcefully invoked by Edghill when questioned by a Select Committee on army expenditure the following year. As Edghill put it:

> I hold that there are two things more than anything else which make the army expensive; these are intemperance and impurity. The best manner in which you can face that, and deal with it, is by the chaplain, who must live amongst the men, and become one with them, and exercise influence upon them: in that way he saves infinitely more to the country than the difference between the payment to the officiating clergy and the chaplain on the Establishment.[40]

The strength of this argument was underlined by Edghill's own role in promoting temperance work at that time. Given that drunkenness had long been the army's besetting sin, chaplains had been involved in organised temperance work among soldiers since the creation of the Church of England Temperance Society in 1862. However, their efforts ran parallel to the work of similar organisations of an evangelical and pan-denominational character, most notably the National Temperance League, the International Order of the Good Templars and the Soldiers' Total Abstinence Association. It was also rather complicated by the army's indulgence of alcohol and its provision of 'wet' canteens. No doubt prompted by such problems, in 1887 Edghill wrote to the Commander-in-Chief, the Duke of Cambridge, urging the creation of a single, consolidated organisation that could advance the cause of temperance and abstinence throughout (and under the aegis of) the army. This plan was realised in 1893, when Lord Roberts, who had already forged a single Army Temperance Association for the Indian army, returned to Britain and gave his support to the creation of the Army Temperance Association (Home Organisation), a body that subsumed the work of the National Temperance League and the Church of England Temperance Society and which enjoyed the backing of the War Office. Both Roberts and Edghill gave addresses at the inaugural meeting of the new organisation in June 1893, its aims being 'The promotion of sobriety in the British Army at home and abroad through the formation of branches, whose object is to establish a strong regimental opinion in favour of strict sobriety, uprightness of character, and decency of language in the fear of God'.[41] In the pursuit of its goals, the A.T.A. drew on tried and tested means; rooms were provided in barracks for the use of its members, proven abstainers earned medals and other distinctions and the Association sponsored a wide range of sporting activities.[42]

While the A.T.A. stoked the passion for competitive sport that was characteristic of British military and civilian society at this time,[43] army chaplains were also keen promoters of sport in their own right, a role that was encouraged by the growing influence of the cult of 'Christian manliness', their largely male clientele and by the emphasis that the army placed on physical fitness in the wake of the Crimean War. Speaking at the Church Congress held at Stoke-on-Trent in 1875, Henry Press Wright emphasised the importance of 'manly games' for the soldier and declared that in the ministry of an army chaplain 'every recreating occupation, every pleasing pursuit which tends to develop the body, and occupy the mind, should . . . be carefully encouraged. It is impossible to over-estimate the influence of those amusements within and without the barracks, which encourage the soldier's self-respect, and so keep him from low and degrading society.'[44] Although the chaplain's interest in sport was clearly well established by the turn of the twentieth century, the sobering lessons of the Boer War and the renewed drive for higher standards of physical fitness in the post-war army called for even greater efforts on the chaplain's part. In 1907, the army's new Committee on Spiritual and Moral Welfare was advised that chaplains should only be selected from among 'men of physical activity and skill in many games' and that 'To gain an influence for good with soldiers [chaplains] must first gain . . . respect and affection by comradeship with them in sports, games, hardship etc.'[45] Consequently, while the Edwardian Chaplains' Department under Bishop John Taylor Smith recruited virile young sportsmen such as Harry Blackburne, who played 'rugger' for Aldershot Command, and James Rowland Walkey, a well-known rugby international,[46] others urged the importance of sport upon the rank and file. In 1912, Walter Bristow, a retired chaplain, reminded new recruits that:

> Much of the healthy condition and moral life of [soldiers] is due to their physical exercise on the playground, and the happy rivalry to be found therein. So . . . join the fun and enterprise of athletics and healthy games of all sorts, whether in the playing-field or in the recreation-room. It is the deadly hours of lounging and loafing about which are so dangerous and so full of terrors. The simple killing of time, which brings in its train so many disasters, undermining the physical, mental, and moral condition, is the fatal factor in our midst.[47]

There were, however, many other ways of improving the tone of army life. One of the army's abiding problems throughout the nineteenth century was that of 'improvident marriages'.[48] Typically, these were unions undertaken by younger soldiers without the permission of their commanding officers and without the assistance which the army afforded to a privileged minority of families, usually those of N.C.O.s or other tried and tested soldiers. Whereas these army families were provided with quarters, fuel and rations, marriages 'off the strength' were unsupported and often resulted in moral catastrophe. As one chaplain, E.J. Hardy, wrote in the *United Service Magazine*:

> [When] nothing comes in except five shillings a week, the result is misery and too often immorality on the part of the wife. The husband wearies of the contest, and, perhaps not having money to pay his wife's fare when

the regiment moves, takes the opportunity of deserting from his matrimonial obligations.[49]

Unfortunately, this infidelity was often reciprocated. While stationed at Plymouth in the 1890s, Hardy raised a subscription to pay for some unsupported wives whose husbands had recently moved to Belfast to join their husbands in the north of Ireland. However, this well-intentioned initiative foundered when many of these women simply found replacement spouses among the soldiers of an incoming regiment.[50] In the light of such problems, chaplains were keen to ensure that soldiers' wives were found honest and gainful employment whenever possible. When giving evidence before a committee on barrack accommodation in 1855, Gleig declared that having the army's laundry done by soldiers' wives in its own barracks helped to 'furnish occupation for the women and keep them moral'.[51] For the same reasons, by the 1880s chaplains were even procuring and managing clothing contracts for the army.[52] During his ministry at Devonport, William Sykes purchased calico for 2,000 shirts that were to be made by the wives of soldiers at the station.[53] Although all chaplains could do this much, the expansion of the army's married quarters during the latter half of the nineteenth century put married chaplains at an advantage in ministering to soldiers' families, for they could always delegate the visitation of married quarters to their wives. At Aldershot in 1904, for example, Harry Blackburne's wife visited married quarters and taught at the garrison's Sunday school. Similarly, at Bordon camp in 1913–14, J.L. Findlay's new bride was put to work doing 'many things among the married quarters' in addition to organising mothers' meetings and sewing parties.[54]

The importance of the soldier's home background was also recognised in one of the most promising initiatives to emerge from the Edwardian army. Pioneered in Scotland by the United Free Church, the so-called 'Mackay Scheme' aimed to encourage recruitment from the more respectable working classes by ensuring that their sons would be closely supervised during their years with the colours. This was to be achieved by encouraging communication between civilian pastors and army chaplains. Extended to England in 1911, the scheme was supported by the Secretary of State for War, Richard Burdon Haldane, and it was running in all of the army's home commands by the summer of 1914.[55] Among others, the Presbyterians and the Wesleyans were greatly impressed by its success. In 1909, J.T. Bird, a Church of Scotland chaplain at Aldershot, reported that, 'The new system of sending information to the chaplain regarding recruits joining the station from Scotland is, I consider, a good one. The chaplain is brought more into touch with the recruit when informed [of] him by the minister in Scotland, to whom his past history is known.'[56] Similarly, the Wesleyan Royal Navy and Army Board heard in 1912 that 'The number of Wesleyans who have been enrolled as entering the Army in the Northern Command shows a great increase upon the numbers previously enlisting [and] the Chaplains find that the scheme helps them in their pastoral work among the soldiers in the various Depôts.'[57]

Although widely welcomed, the Mackay Scheme would have remained a relatively minor Presbyterian initiative had it not gained the support of an entirely new body that had been created by the War Office some years earlier. Christened the Advisory Committee on the Spiritual and Moral Welfare of the Army, this twenty-strong committee was formed in 1906, its work comprising one aspect of Haldane's far-reaching army reforms. Inter-denominational in character, the committee possessed a broad remit, being tasked with advising the newly formed Army Council on 'all matters affecting the spiritual and moral welfare of the Army' and considering 'the best means of ensuring the greater efficiency and organisation of the work of the Chaplains of the different denominations'. The committee was chaired by the Chaplain-General (who was by then Bishop John Taylor Smith) and it counted Lord Roberts (the last Commander-in-Chief of the British army), Robert Brindle (the Roman Catholic Bishop of Nottingham and a retired army chaplain) and several M.P.s among its members.[58] Although it began its work by reviewing the situation in the army's home commands, the committee gave early signs that it intended to be proactive. In August 1907, a circular was issued from the War Office by Sir Reginald Brade, the Permanent Under Secretary of State, which emphasised the importance of its work:

> I am commanded by the Army Council to acquaint you that at a meeting of the Advisory Committee on the Spiritual and Moral Welfare of the Army it was agreed that it is desirable that whenever possible the Chaplains and Commanding Officers in the various garrisons should meet from time to time to consider the possibility of combined action and organisation for dealing with the questions of drink, gambling and sexual morality . . . I am to inform you that the Army Council leave it to General Officers Commanding-in-Chief to give practical effect to the above resolution.[59]

How far the committee may have gone to reform the work of army chaplaincy is unclear as it was suspended after the outbreak of the First World War in August 1914. However, its brief work had a twofold significance. Firstly, and as J.H. Thompson has argued, it showed that 'inter-church co-operation was achievable in matters to do with the army'.[60] Secondly, the formation and work of the committee demonstrated that the work of moral reform in the regular army continued to lie at the heart of the chaplain's duties.

In 1888, J.C. Edghill insisted that there was 'no doubt' that chaplains had already done a great deal to improve the character of the army.[61] However, given the broad and varied nature of moral reform in the Victorian army it is difficult to assess the impact of their contribution to this process, which by the 1880s had at least produced a decline in drunkenness as a military crime.[62] In addition to the work of chaplains, improvements to the soldier's accommodation, education and leisure opportunities were ongoing from the 1840s and the mid-Victorian period also saw the development of army temperance organisations and the rise of the soldiers' home. Moreover, although soldiering continued to appeal primarily to the unskilled working classes, the general calibre of the army's recruits may have improved as, owing to the Education Acts of 1870 and 1880 and the Army Enlistment Act of 1870, the army was better placed to engage the services of more educated recruits for a more limited period of time. In view of these factors, the relative contribution of the Chaplains' Department to the moral improvement of the army was probably quite modest. Furthermore, and because chaplains to the forces operated from within the military hierarchy, their contribution could shade into broader army initiatives, as their consultative role regarding barrack accommodation and the recreational needs of the soldier serves to illustrate. This close identification with the military authorities also posed problems in other respects. To the mid and late-Victorian public, the worst and most public symptoms of the soldier's moral incontinence were the Contagious Diseases Acts of 1864, 1866 and 1869. This legislation was designed to curb the spread of venereal disease in ports, camps and garrison towns by the rigorous policing and inspection of suspected prostitutes. Though urged as necessary from a military perspective, these Acts were very widely regarded in civilian society as morally outrageous and they inspired a broadly based campaign which eventually secured their suspension in 1883 and their repeal in 1886.[63] Despite the agitation of purity campaigners and the chaplain's role as the custodian of public and private morality in the army, it is significant that both George Gleig and Bishop Piers Calveley Claughton (Gleig's successor as Chaplain-General) eschewed public confrontation with the military authorities over this delicate and deeply embarrassing issue. Indeed, such caution was justified. The limits of what the military authorities were prepared to tolerate from their chaplains in the cause of moral improvement were illustrated in 1891, when an Anglican chaplain offended the G.O.C. at Aldershot by preaching a sermon in which he attacked 'the canteen arrangements of the Army' and declared that 'the Canteen was a place to make a man a drunkard'. This trenchant criticism was construed as insubordination and the senior Anglican chaplain at the station was subsequently directed to forbid his chaplains from making 'any remarks which reflect on the orders of His Royal Highness the Commander in Chief'.[64]

Anglican Chaplaincy under George Gleig

In his management of the enlarged, post-Crimean Chaplains' Department, Gleig showed his usual zeal as an administrator, employing methods which compared to those associated with the reform of the diocesan machinery of the Church of England.[65] Like many reforming bishops of the age, Gleig sought to make his authority more proximate to his subordinates. For most of his years as Chaplain-General, he took full advantage of Britain's expanding railway network and proved a regular visitor to the army's home stations. As Gleig made clear in 1868, 'Once a-year the Chaplain-General visits each military station in England, and as often as circumstances will allow, in Ireland also; when, besides examining the young people under religious instruction, he looks closely into the general work.'[66] In November 1872, when old age was rendering these tours of inspection less practicable, he sought to maintain this level of supervision by reserving fixed hours at the War Office for interviews with 'such of the Chaplains as desire to confer with me in person'.[67] From his base at the War Office, Gleig issued a steady stream of advice and memoranda on matters ranging from the proper dress to be worn by chaplains at royal levees to the means whereby religious instruction might be improved in army schools.[68] While it is tempting to see his *Hints and Instructions* as the departmental equivalent of episcopal visitation charges,[69] in 1867 (and in a development which very clearly paralleled the growth of diocesan synods in the wider Church) Gleig convened the first departmental conference at the Guards' Chapel in London.[70] Ever mindful of the power of the press, Gleig continued to exercise his talents as a publicist for the Department. In March 1868, he published an essay on 'The Church in the Army and Navy' in *Blackwood's Edinburgh Magazine* and, upon his retirement in 1875, he sent copies of his farewell address as Chaplain-General to no fewer than eleven newspapers and periodicals including *The Times*, the *Daily Telegraph* and the *Morning Post*.[71]

By virtue of these efforts, Gleig retired in good standing with his political masters. Upon his retirement, the Conservative Secretary of State for War, Gathorne Hardy, made a successful application to the Treasury that Gleig be allowed to retire on his full pay of £1,000 per annum.[72] In his farewell address, Gleig presented a roseate picture of the Department's progress over the past thirty years. Contrasting the situation in the mid-1870s with the pre-Crimean world of officiating clergymen, pastoral neglect and Anglican exclusiveness, Gleig reminded his fellow Anglican chaplains that:

> You are now associated in a great work with Presbyterian and Roman Catholic chaplains to the forces. You have your churches, your chapels, and your chapel schools – the latter open alike to all three persuasions – in which to conduct public worship, and the brotherly feeling which prevails among you, and has prevailed ever since the department was reconstituted, proves that good and earnest men may conscientiously differ on many points without breaking the very bond of peace and of all virtue, the noblest of all Christian gifts – charity . . . with rare exceptions, the common work has been carried on with marvellous harmony, and the results are seen in the growing interest which is taken by all ranks in its progress.[73]

Despite his ample pension and the confident tone of his address, Gleig's appraisal of the Department's progress very much belied the problems of authority that had plagued the Department (and undermined the position of the Chaplain-General) since the Crimean War. Significantly, these problems did not arise from the post-war equality of Anglicans, Roman Catholics and Presbyterians. Rather, they arose from tensions with the parish clergy and the bishops, from relations with unrecognised denominations and from the response of influential officers towards the Ritualist tendencies which were showing themselves among Gleig's subordinates.

Almost inevitably, the multiplication of commissioned chaplains and the expansion of the army's infrastructure of chapels and chapel-schools provoked trouble with the bishops and parochial clergy of the Church of England and Church of Ireland. As early as the 1830s, with the building of the new Guards' Chapel at Wellington Barracks, problems had surfaced concerning the rights of ordinaries over new military churches. In this case, the Bishop of London, Charles Blomfield, had insisted that a second gallery be installed in order to accommodate the poorer members of the local civilian population, who were 'almost wholly destitute' of 'the means of public worship and religious instruction'.[74] This intervention dismayed and embarrassed the Principal Chaplain, William Dakins, it delayed the completion of the chapel until additional funds could be found and it infuriated the Adjutant-General, Sir John Macdonald, who wrote:

> I . . . can conceive no arrangement more uncalled for, or indeed more open to objection, than the building of a Chapel upon the Barracks site in the Bird Cage Walk for a promiscuous congregation. I can discover no one circumstance in favour of such a scheme, whilst I can see manifold objections to it . . . A part of Dr. Dakins' design is to instruct and catechise the children of the soldiery of the Household Troops in the proposed Military Chapel, but he cannot undertake to admit the children of the inhabitants of Westminster to that instruction, there being now between two and three hundred soldiers' children for admission to it.[75]

After the business of the gallery was resolved, the Principal Chaplain went on to demonstrate his formidable ignorance of government procedure and ecclesiastical law by inviting Blomfield to consecrate the new building, a service which required that the site of the Chapel be surrendered to the diocese of London. Such a surrender of Crown property was, of course, impossible and the new chapel was formally opened without episcopal consecration.[76] This stalemate over the consecration of military churches offended Gleig's High Church sensibilities and cast a shadow over the army's new generation of chapels and chapel-schools. In March 1846, Gleig even approached Blomfield with the aim of having the necessary powers of consecration vested in himself.[77] In the event, it appears that a compromise of sorts was reached in 1856 when, in exchange for episcopal consecration, the War Office agreed to supply written guarantees to the bishops concerned that the site of a new burial ground at Aldershot and of a new church at the Royal Small-Arms Factory at Enfield would be reserved for sacred uses.[78]

In addition to these difficulties with local ordinaries, the multiplication of military churches and commissioned chaplains following the Crimean War heightened tensions with the parochial clergy, many of whom resented the invasion of their parishes and the consequent loss of income which this entailed. Although the War Office had received legal advice in 1858 that upheld the right of its chaplains to minister to soldiers 'without the license of the Bishop or the assent of the incumbent',[79] on closer scrutiny the chaplain's legal position *vis-à-vis* the bishops and the parochial clergy was precarious to say the least. This became evident in 1863, when the legality of burials conducted by a commissioned chaplain was disputed by the rector of Woolwich. On this occasion, and contrary to earlier advice, the War Office was informed that the legal right of chaplains to conduct burials or solemnise marriages was extremely doubtful.[80] As a result, a Bill was drafted regarding 'The performance of rites in the United Church of England and Ireland by military chaplains'. This sought to clarify the anomalous position of the commissioned chaplain by giving the Chaplain-General the title and powers of a bishop and by constituting the army's camps and barracks as a separate diocese. However, when the draft was sent for perusal to Bishop Tait of London in 1865, he rejected it out of hand. In an age where bishops were busily strengthening their control over their dioceses, the prospect of a roving bishop 'intruding into their Dioceses and interfering with their proper work'[81] was anathema. However, Gleig was very much in favour of the plan proposed to Tait. As we have noted, he had long aspired to episcopal office and he could draw encouragement from the fact that many reformers within the Church of England were clamouring for 'more bishops and more dioceses'.[82] Furthermore, Gleig could not fail to be aware that the Roman Catholic chaplains of the British army were under the control of the Bishop of Southwark and he certainly knew that there were several continental precedents for an army bishop. The armies of Italy, France and Austria were all served by army bishops and even in Protestant Prussia (which, through its victory in the Austro-Prussian War of 1866, was setting new standards of military efficiency) the army had its own superintendent, in keeping with what Gleig described as Prussia's 'semi-episcopalian constitution of superintendency'.[83]

While the shape of army chaplaincy was under consideration in England, matters came to a head in Ireland in 1867. With the disestablishment of the Church of Ireland in the offing, its clergy were naturally sensitive to the encroachments of army chaplains. The ministry of army chaplains was technically illegal and, to add insult to injury, it deprived parochial incumbents of the income that could be earned by officiating clergymen. Against this background, Thomas Mills (the incumbent of St. Jude's, Kilmainham) brought an action against Herbert Tudor Craig (the chaplain at Richmond Barracks) for ministering in his parish without authorisation. As Gleig explained:

> [Craig], like his predecessor, and in obedience to orders issued on the spot . . . officiated regularly in the barrack chapel. Besides officiating in the chapel he placed himself towards the officers and soldiers and their families in the relation of a parish priest, administering the sacraments, visiting the sick, catechising the children, and preparing the young of both sexes for confirmation.[84]

However, and as Gleig fully accepted:

> [Craig] had no authority whatever so to act, either from the incumbent of the parish or from the bishop of the diocese. It was believed, both at the Horse Guards and in the War Office, that such authority was not necessary to a chaplain holding Her Majesty's commission; and the opinion thus entertained rested itself upon two grounds: 1st, that as of old fortresses were supplied with chaplains, the same being exempt from ecclesiastical jurisdiction, so barracks in general, and this particular barrack among the rest, had taken in law the place of fortresses; and, next, that in the independent status of the chapels of the royal dockyards, and of the chaplains officiating therein, a precedent existed establishing, apart from episcopal authority, the validity in things sacred of the Queen's commission.[85]

Whatever assumptions were held in London, the lack of sympathy shown to

Mills by the military authorities in Dublin rebounded on Craig.[86] The case, which was heard in the highest ecclesiastical court of the Province of Dublin, resulted in a bruising verdict that threatened to destroy the whole system of military chaplaincy. The judge, Dr George Batterbsy, ruled that:

> The Queen can doubtless commission as many chaplains as may please Her Majesty, but she has no authority to order them to break the law of the land . . . Mr. Craig by ministering within the barracks . . . has broken the common law, the civil law and the canon law. He has not a leg to stand upon . . . no clergyman of the Church of England and Ireland has any right to read prayers, preach, administer the Lord's Supper, visit the sick, speak one word of religion ministerially to his own brother, if he were dying, in another clergyman's parish without his permission; and not only so, but he must have also the licence of the archbishop or bishop of the diocese.[87]

Although Battersby pronounced that 'This is a criminal case, and Mr. Craig has done a criminal act', he acknowledged that Craig had been acting in good faith and so withheld punishment on these grounds. Nevertheless, he admonished Craig to desist from his ministry and awarded costs against him.[88] The War Office followed the case very closely and with more than a little apprehension.[89] Furthermore, following Battersby's ruling Gleig took the opportunity to state his case for 'the erection of a military episcopate' in *Blackwood's Edinburgh Magazine*. This new office would embrace the Royal Navy as well as the British army and he urged this scheme on Bishop Tait.[90] Consequently, an Army Chaplains Bill was prepared which sought to endow the Chaplain-General with the powers of a bishop, including those of licensing.[91] However, it was heavily criticised by the bench of bishops and it was radically reshaped by a committee of the House of Lords. Ultimately, a very different solution to that envisaged by Gleig emerged in the form of the Army Chaplains Act of 1868.[92]

Under this legislation, the Crown was empowered to turn military stations into extra-parochial districts – subject to a clear delineation of their boundaries and the consent of the bishops concerned. Furthermore, the Secretary of State for War was empowered to appoint clergymen to these extra-parochial districts 'to perform the Functions of an Army Chaplain'. The chapels of these districts could be consecrated or unconsecrated but, in the latter case, their use for sacred purposes had to be certified to the diocesan authorities. Stopping well short of constituting the army as a separate diocese under its own bishop, the Act gave the Crown the power to 'declare all or any of [these] Extra-parochial Districts . . . to be under the exclusive Jurisdiction of [an] Archbishop or Bishop' at some unspecified point in the future.[93] According to Tait, the intention of the bishops was simply:

> [To] vest this authority in one of the two Archbishops, or in the Bishop of London, but it was left to the Secretary of War to put in motion the machinery of the Act . . . But it was understood in the discussions at the time that it would be impossible for either of the two Archbishops or for the Bishop of London *personally* to undertake the duties contemplated by the Act, and the Archbishop of Canterbury expressed his conviction that,

> if he was called upon to become responsible in the matter, he must be allowed to delegate all the duties implied in the Act to some other [bishop].[94]

However, problems of a political and practical kind ensured that the Act was never implemented. According to the War Office, Tait 'announced his readiness to accept the jurisdiction' but took the opportunity to present a list of other demands. These were:

> (1) That the name of every candidate for a Chaplaincy should be submitted for his approval before appointment.
> (2) That every Chaplain to the Forces should in addition to his commission from the Crown receive a license from the Archbishop, the revocation or suspension of which would prevent his officiating anywhere to troops.
> (3) That all questions of unsound doctrine, vesture, and ornaments, and the mode of performing their public duties should be referred to the Archbishop for his summary decision and
> (4) That the Act should be extended to the Navy.

These demands were simply impossible; the Admiralty refused to co-operate and Tait's proposals threatened 'removing all control, except as regards pay and station, from the Secretary of State' for War. Furthermore, the Act met with 'considerable opposition' from parochial clergy and diocesan bishops alike and 'the technical difficulties of defining the areas' in question sealed its fate. An attempt to apply the Act to Chatham and Woolwich met with hopeless complications and its application to Aldershot would have involved no fewer than nine separate parishes.[95] While there was a certain feeling abroad among the bishops that the Church of England 'had too many unattached Bishops already',[96] Gleig disagreed and deplored the Act as a lost opportunity. After the appointment of Edward Cardwell as Secretary of State for War in December 1868, he complained to the Permanent Under Secretary, Sir Edward Lugard, that the Army Chaplains Act had done nothing to regularise the position of the military chaplain within the polity of an episcopal Church, especially as military chaplains continued to minister without licence under the oversight of a Chaplain-General who was not himself a bishop:

> [It] is of the essence of the Church of England that all her Presbyters and Deacons shall be superintended by some Bishop and receive authority to perform their functions either by induction or license. Induction can never take place in the Army, and therefore a license must be had somehow or else the whole Church system is destroyed . . . the whole of our proceedings are and have been, since 1796, illegal . . . This miserable Act only makes us worse than we were before it was passed. It will be a constant thorn in our sides. If I were in Mr. Cardwell's place I should get it repealed, and bring forward another of far simpler construction. Whether the Church of England remains in unison with the State or not, she will always be an Episcopal Church.[97]

If Gleig denied any personal ambition in the matter (he in fact continued to lobby for a military bishop even in retirement)[98] his failure to see the office of the Chaplain-General dignified with episcopal status was without doubt a personal setback. However, this was not the only defeat that he had to endure in the 1860s. In 1856, the Wesleyan minister and missionary Dr. William Harris Rule arrived at Aldershot with a view to establishing a Wesleyan mission at the camp. Even to his admirers, Rule was 'an unwearying fighter; pertinacious, domineering and difficult to work with'[99] but to his Anglican antagonists at Aldershot he was simply a constant irritant. Rule had emerged as the champion of Methodist interests in the army while ministering at Gibraltar from 1832 to 1842.[100] The Rock had a long tradition of army Methodism and had seen recurrent friction between Methodist soldiers and its garrison chaplains.[101] However, in July 1839, and as a result of pressure from India, the Commander-in-Chief, Lord Rowland Hill, had given the soldier 'full liberty to attend the worship of Almighty God according to the forms prescribed by his own religion, when military duty does not interfere'.[102] Nevertheless, this order had distinct limitations. According to Rule, 'It acknowledged the right of the soldier to enjoy liberty of worship, but it did not instruct the Commanding Officer to enable him to exercise the right. It gave the officer no order, and where no order is given there is no authority conferred.'[103] Furthermore, this concession was not the same as granting Wesleyan Methodists (or any other Nonconformists for that matter) formal recognition and nor was it always acted upon.[104] Within months of the order being issued, the commanding officer of a regiment at Gibraltar had banned his men from attending Methodist worship and had even reduced a Methodist corporal to the ranks for the unlikely offence of hypocrisy.[105] While Rule prosecuted a successful campaign against the governor in order to ensure that the spirit of Hill's order was observed on the Rock,[106] the fact remained that, even where Nonconformists were allowed to attend their own chapels on the Sabbath, their ministers were not recognised as officiating clergymen. By the time Rule returned to England in 1842, an uneasy compromise had emerged:

> In rare instances, by the good-nature of commanding officers, Wesleyans were sent to their own places of worship. At Woolwich it was managed by permitting Wesleyan men to fall out with the Presbyterians, and then march to the Wesleyan chapel. All were returned as Presbyterians, and capitation grant was paid for them under that head, but not to the Wesleyan minister. Indeed the Conference did not desire that its ministers should be paid by Government, all that was asked being that Wesleyan soldiers should be permitted liberty of worship.[107]

Despite Rule's zeal for the cause of the Wesleyan soldier, his enthusiasm was not widely shared by fellow Wesleyans until the Crimean War, when Peter Batchelor, an Indian missionary, was belatedly despatched to join the army in the East. In Rule's sardonic words, during the course of the war 'indifference to the moral condition of the soldier' had been 'happily succeeded by a lively concern for his spiritual welfare'. Consequently:

> I caught that opportunity for proposing that our Foreign Missionary Committee should send a minister to the seat of war. [Batchelor] was

> indeed named, and Secretary Lord Panmure gave him a free passage out, with authority to act in Camp. But the choice of suitable ministers was as imperfect in that time as the supplies of the Commissariat; and the change from the exhaustion of an Indian mission to the horrid grandeur of a campaign was too violent for our improvised Chaplain to sustain. Happily for him the war ended soon after his landing, and he returned forthwith without fairly coming into use.[108]

Despite a lengthy interval in his military work, Rule was irresistibly drawn to the new camp at Aldershot, visiting it on his own initiative in 1856 and arranging meetings with its commanding officer, Lieutenant-General W.T. Knollys. Although Knollys refused Rule's request that a Wesleyan minister be admitted to the camp in order to hold services for its Wesleyan soldiers, the War Office was more encouraging. Whereas Knollys had declined Rule's request on the grounds that it would set an awkward precedent for other unrecognised denominations, Arthur Kinnaird (who had already proved sympathetic to the Free Church of Scotland and its claims upon its soldiers) led Rule to understand 'that if a church was built within a reasonable distance of the camp the men would be permitted to attend it'.[109] Fortunately, the Crimean War had stirred sufficient interest in Wesleyan circles for Rule to obtain permission at the Conference of 1856 to begin raising funds for Wesleyan work at Aldershot. Consequently, a committee of ministers was convened to manage this income and Rule 'went from circuit to circuit advocating the cause of those sons of Methodists who were serving their country in the army'. By dint of these efforts, land was acquired near the boundary of the camp and, in clear emulation of the Church of England, a temporary iron church and a chaplain's house was erected thereon.[110] Significantly, and possibly due to his own volatile mien, Rule was not the connexion's first choice to serve at Aldershot, this honour falling to Peter Batchelor of Crimean fame. However, 'feeling unequal to the task, [Batchelor] relinquished the post, and Dr. Rule was himself put in charge of the work which was due to his own initiation and untiring energy'.[111]

Because Wesleyan Methodism had a doubtful status in the army, the opening of the new church at Aldershot in July 1857, at a cost of £4,800, smacked of a very costly gamble. In fact, 'No one knew, except Dr. Rule, who kept his own counsel, that the question of the troops being marched to the church on Sunday was as yet unsettled.'[112] From the outset, therefore, it was clear that Rule would have to be active to the point of aggression in his assertion of Wesleyan rights. At the same time, Rule had to justify the connexion's lavish and risky investment in this new field of work. As the proceedings of the Wesleyan Conference of 1859 showed, even in the wake of the Indian Mutiny a sizeable number of Wesleyans regarded this new departure with distaste and they were particularly uncomfortable with Rule's use of the term 'Wesleyan soldier'.[113] As Rule remembered:

> Some of the most excellent members of the Conference revolted from the sound, as with sacred horror. They were accustomed to confine the venerable name to consistent members of the Wesleyan Societies, devout attendants in the Class-meetings, and thereby accredited as worthy to partake of Holy Communion at the Lord's Table, the Communicants

> being distinct from the mere members of Congregation. Words were not wanting wherewith to condemn the application of this name to the red-coated drunkards, whose very presence in our towns was pestilential . . .[114]

Despite their reservations, this dissentient element eventually yielded 'to the force of reason, of Christian Charity, and of fatherly affection' and the controversial designation was grudgingly conceded.[115]

Meanwhile, in the months and years which followed the opening of the mission at Aldershot, Rule insinuated himself into the life of the camp, assuming the role of a *de facto* Wesleyan chaplain. However, Rule's presumption aroused the strident opposition of the camp's Anglican chaplains. Three factors seem to have contributed to the ferocity of the Anglican response. Firstly, Gleig's role in the selection and appointment of chaplains had created a High Church bias within the Department and many of Gleig's chaplains were inclined to take a dim view of pushy Dissenters. Secondly, the army had accorded the chaplain a major role in the moral reform of the soldier and Wesleyan incursions threatened to undermine this key aspect of the chaplain's work. Thirdly and finally, given the new military rank and status that was awarded to chaplains in 1858, Rule's unauthorised labours at Aldershot represented a flagrant subversion of military authority by a maverick civilian. Hence, Rule's pretensions did not go unchallenged and he encountered many 'angry clerical opponents'.[116] On one occasion, the camp's senior chaplain reported C.H. Kelly, Rule's principal assistant at Aldershot, to the War Office as 'an unauthorised person visiting the camp'.[117] Later, a new senior chaplain greeted Rule with the words: 'You have too great a footing in this camp, where you ought not to have any, and I shall do my utmost to *live* you down, *work* you down, and *pray* you down.'[118] Gleig himself (who, according to Kelly, was one of 'the old school of parsons – high, dry and bitterly opposed to Nonconformists')[119] instigated a ban on Rule visiting Aldershot's military hospitals.[120] When Conference appointed Kelly to Chatham in 1861, further controversy ensued, with the commanding officer at Chatham choosing to stand by military regulations. Consequently, he made an attempt to ban Kelly from visiting Chatham's military hospitals and, in March 1862, he also banned Wesleyans from attending Wesleyan chapels during parade services.[121] At Aldershot, meanwhile, the conflict had come to focus on who should bury Wesleyan soldiers.[122] Although the Wesleyans won this bout, the practice of giving details of Wesleyan services in garrison orders ceased abruptly, a development which threatened 'the very existence of Methodism in the army'.[123]

Rule's response was a characteristic mixture of guile, tenacity and audacity. In August 1858, and with his Protestant sensibilities outraged at the prospect of Roman Catholic priests being commissioned as chaplains, Rule wrote to the new Secretary of State for War, Major-General Jonathan Peel, demanding capitation grants for Wesleyan ministers and a commissioned Wesleyan chaplain for the camp at Aldershot.[124] Though this met with a firm refusal, Rule's strategy of exploiting differences and uncertainty among the military authorities proved more fruitful. When banned from visiting the hospitals at Aldershot, he wrote directly to the Commander-in-Chief, the Duke of Cambridge, invoking a precedent set by the Duke of Wellington, who as Commander-in-Chief had allowed the inmates of military hospitals to request the assistance of a Dissenting minister if desired. Partly out of deference to his illustrious predecessor, Cambridge cancelled the prohibition despite having been a party to it.[125] By 1860, Rule's hand had been strengthened by the formation of a Wesleyan Methodist Army Committee, which in that year lobbied the Secretary of State for War, Sir Sidney Herbert, for the formal recognition of Wesleyan Methodism by the army. However, although this pressure led the Duke of Cambridge to convene a court of inquiry into the treatment of Wesleyans at Aldershot in March 1860, its proceedings went badly for Rule and his charges of systematic harassment were speedily dismissed.[126] Shortly afterwards, Lieutenant-General Sir John Pennefather replaced the more sympathetic Knollys at Aldershot and the position of the authorities hardened to the point where Wesleyan interests were simply ignored. As Owen Spencer Watkins put it, 'At Aldershot Dr. Rule was now informed by [Pennefather] that he was not permitted to recognize officially the word "Wesleyan" in any public documents, returns, or reports. This amounted to total prohibition . . . The opponents of Methodism were victorious.'[127] However, Rule was able to snatch victory from the jaws of defeat through a chance meeting with the Earl of Shaftesbury while lobbying at the House of Commons. Besides being the nation's leading evangelical layman, Shaftesbury was an unofficial adviser on ecclesiastical affairs to Lord Palmerston's administration and he exerted this influence to good effect on Rule's behalf.[128] In June 1862, Sir Edward Lugard wrote to the chairman of the Wesleyans' Army Committee, notifying him that Wesleyans would be marched to their own services at Chatham. Furthermore, Lugard stated that the Secretary of State for War, Sir George Lewis, and the Commander-in-Chief, the Duke of Cambridge, had agreed to extend the range of the army's recognised denominations. Henceforward:

> Wesleyan Soldiers ought not to be classified under any of the three denominations into which the Army is at present divided [but] a fourth class [will] be formed under the title of 'Other Protestants,' to include all men who are neither Episcopalians, Roman Catholics, nor Presbyterians – this class to be borne on the monthly Regimental Returns rendered to the Horse Guards, and the name of the Denomination placed over the beds of such Patients in Hospital as may belong to that class. In this suggestion His Royal Highness has signified his concurrence, and Orders have been issued for carrying both arrangements into effect accordingly.[129]

Thwarted in his schemes for an army bishopric and unable to check Wesleyan encroachments, Gleig's later years as Chaplain-General were also dogged by fierce controversy over Ritualism in the Chaplains' Department. The Ritualist question was, of course, a major problem for the Church of England as a whole and it is no coincidence that it reached its climax in the army in the late 1860s and early 1870s, years in which it also came to a head in civilian life.[130] Although overlooked in recent studies of Ritualism and its attendant controversies,[131] the difficulties posed by Ritualism in the Chaplains' Department were probably more acute than they were for the civilian Church. In the context of the army, the issue of Ritualism was complicated by the lack of episcopal authority over Anglican chaplains, by its implications for military discipline, by the shared and non-denominational nature of the army's own places of worship and by the opposition of some very senior Low Church officers.

The rise of Ritualism in the army was in part a function of the Department's High Church bias following the Crimean War, leanings that did not escape the attention of some hostile officers. As early as 1857, Lieutenant-General Knollys had felt obliged to take 'stringent action' at Aldershot against what he regarded as 'the encroachments of certain High Church chaplains'.[132] Although details of these 'encroachments' are unclear, the principal scourge of Ritualism in the mid-Victorian army was Lieutenant-General Sir James Hope Grant. A successful and respected soldier, Grant was raised a Presbyterian but seems to have attached himself to the Church of England during his military career, even becoming an Anglican communicant. Famous for encouraging 'temperance, thrift, and, above all, the diffusion of the precepts of the Bible among the soldiers throughout the army',[133] Grant was known to hold daily prayer meetings which he expected his servants and his staff officers to attend.[134] However, Grant was no sectarian bigot. Evelyn Wood (who was married to a Roman Catholic and who was serving as a staff officer at Aldershot when Grant arrived) found that his fears on this account were quickly dispelled. As Wood recalled, Grant had:

> [T]he reputation of being very Low Church, and I seriously contemplated resigning my appointment, but was deterred by the wiser counsels of my wife, who urged me to wait and see whether her religion would in any way interfere with the smoothness of my relations with the General. She was right, for both he and his wife became two of our most intimate friends, as kind as any we ever had, and we enjoyed their friendship till they died.[135]

In light of this, there seems little reason to doubt the verdict of Grant's biographer, Sir Henry Knollys, who claimed that Grant was not motivated by blind prejudice in his dealings with the Chaplains' Department but was simply 'disgusted with those who ate the bread of one faith and preached the doctrines of another'.[136]

After lengthy and distinguished service in India and China, Grant had returned to Britain in 1865. Appointed Quartermaster-General, he assumed command at Aldershot five years later. However, in both capacities Grant opposed Ritualism at every turn. In 1867, he challenged an Anglican sisterhood over its work in military hospitals and even rebuked Gleig after discovering that chaplains at Shorncliffe and Devonport 'were carrying on the church services in the most ultra-High-Church fashion'.[137] These chaplains, so Grant believed, had taken their cue from 'a code of instructions issued by Mr. Gleig, in which it was notified that voluntary services would be carried on "in an attractive manner" '.[138] Here, Grant was referring to a set of guidelines on public worship which Gleig had circulated in 1865. However, far from urging popery on his subordinates, Gleig had actually required full compliance with Prayer Book rubric and had forbidden the wearing of any liturgical garment other than the surplice in military services.[139] Nevertheless, and no doubt misjudging the authority and influence of the Chaplain-General, Grant placed the blame for Ritualist innovation squarely on Gleig's shoulders. Indeed, Grant's suspicions eventually became the subject of 'an angry discussion' with Gleig in front of the Duke of Cambridge. As Grant recalled, '[Gleig] ended by saying, in a bland manner, "he trusted I should become more liberal in my views," to which I answered that "I was very sorry to find him in the situation of Chaplain-General" '. Much to Grant's satisfaction, it seemed that the Commander-in-Chief 'did not approve of the views of Mr. Gleig, who consequently stopped the chaplains from using Roman Catholic forms, and as a punishment sent one of them away to Dublin'.[140] Nevertheless, only a few days after this victory over the Chaplain-General, Grant was incensed by a roster of guest preachers at the military chapel at Chatham. This had been approved by Gleig and included a certain priest who belonged 'to the most Ritualistic Church in all London'. The clergyman in question was also the author of a Romanising tract which he had distributed among soldiers. Consequently, Grant complained once again to the Commander-in-Chief, even sending him a copy of the tract in question with the offending passages obligingly marked in pencil.[141] Although not named by Grant in his memoirs, the offending priest was the prominent Ritualist A.H. Stanton, who had preached at Chatham barracks in 1866 and who, besides circulating his *Pathway of Faith*, had urged sacramental confession upon his congregation.[142]

Significantly, Gleig was not only a High Churchman by conviction but also a product of the Scottish Episcopal Church, a church that was to prove highly receptive to Ritualist innovation during the course of the nineteenth century.[143] However, and publicly at least, his quarrels with Grant turned on questions of authority rather than liturgical forms. As we have seen, Gleig had doggedly defended his authority and that of his chaplains in the face of Wesleyan incursions at Aldershot and it seems clear that he regarded Grant as yet another unwelcome trespasser upon his jurisdiction. After Grant's renewed complaints to the Duke of Cambridge, Gleig banned Stanton from military premises in a strongly worded letter[144] but he also wrote a second intemperate missive to Grant in which he deplored his unwonted interference:

> No man can be more opposed than I to what is called Ritualism . . . But I object to the mode of action which, if adopted in any other department of the service than my own, would immediately be put a stop to. What would you say of me if I, discovering, or supposing that I discovered, irregularities in the professional conduct of officers on the Quartermaster-General's staff, were to carry my tale direct to [the Duke of Cambridge], or to the Secretary of State for War, without communicating with yourself . . . ? It is my duty to see that false doctrines and sheer nonsense are not taught as religious truths to soldiers. I don't think that any such duty devolves upon the Quartermaster-General of the army, or upon any other belligerent officer, and I would therefore request for the future, when it seems to you that mischief of this sort is brewing, you will be so good as to draw my attention to the particular case.[145]

In his reply, Grant condemned Gleig for issuing guidelines that had fostered Ritualist error and insisted on his personal right to intervene against 'the practises now carried on by several of the chaplains' – practices that he described as 'a source of increasing danger to both the Church and the army'.[146] In turn, so Grant recalled, Gleig replied 'in a bitter spirit, and without dealing with a single one of my representations'. However, Grant believed that his intervention 'was attended with a good effect', namely that of 'causing the Chaplain-General to warn his clergy against the practices in question, and to promulgate another code of regulations which materially mended the evils'.[147]

The second code of regulations to which Grant referred was issued by Gleig at the Department's first general conference in June 1867. Despite its significance, this meeting at the Guards' Chapel was not a happy occasion and the tenor and content of Gleig's lengthy address were indicative of his beleaguered situation, a predicament which was hardly helped by wider developments within the Church of England. By June 1867, anti-Ritualist agitation had grown to the extent that a Clerical Vestments Act had only just been averted and a Royal Commission on Ritual was about to begin its deliberations. In view of the wider situation, Gleig was obliged to be blunt. Beginning with the stark warning that 'we have lost of late, or seem to be in danger of losing, our hold upon the authorities under whom we act, and, as a necessary consequence, upon the Army',[148] Gleig threatened those chaplains who repeatedly flouted departmental instructions with the loss of their commissions.[149] Because 'a clergyman who accepts a commission as a Chaplain to the Forces becomes, by that act, an officer as well as a minister of religion',[150] Gleig insisted that delinquents were at fault on two grounds:

> In his capacity of a minister of religion [a chaplain] is bound to teach as the Church teaches, and to use in his public ministrations only the Church's liturgy. As an officer, he is subject to the very same rules of military discipline which extend to other officers.[151]

Hence, Gleig utterly rejected the notion that it was possible for a commissioned chaplain 'to plead conscience as authorising disobedience to the orders of his superior'.[152] He then cautioned against chaplains confusing their teaching with that of other churches and warned against tampering with the interiors of army churches and chapel-schools.[153] Gleig also insisted that the letter and spirit of Prayer Book rubric be followed at all times; chaplains should wear only their surplices, black stoles and academic hoods. The wearing of vestments, the elevation of the elements during the communion service and 'all uncalled-for posture-making' was forbidden. Any breach of these regulations was to be treated as 'an offence against discipline'.[154] The Chaplain-General concluded by stressing the paramount authority of superior officers, urging chaplains to 'be sure that you make the commanding officer your first referee, and take counsel with him. Do nothing, indeed, without his concurrence'.[155]

Unsurprisingly, this crude blend of menace and erastianism sparked outrage in the Department. However, because of Gleig's tough new line on discipline, it was left to an anonymous 'OFFICER IN THE ARMY' to enter the necessary protests. In a pamphlet entitled *The Church in the Army; a Letter to the Right Honourable*

Sir J.S. Pakington, Bart., G.C.B., M.P., Secretary of State for War, the author denounced Gleig's strictures as a departure from 'the wisdom and justice' of the army's tradition of religious toleration.[156] It condemned Gleig's perception of the Church as wholly subsidiary to 'the "Discipline of the Army" ' and deplored his implication that commissioned chaplains were:

> [No] longer administrators of the Word of God and the Sacraments according to the law of the church of the land, but mere machines to carry out the views and fancies of commanding officers, who may be sincere Churchmen, but who may also be Roman Catholics, Protestant Dissenters, Indifferentists, or positively hostile to religion in any shape or form.[157]

Indeed, the freedom of a chaplain from the control of his commanding officer was claimed to be as important as that of the surgeon, not least because 'officers and soldiers instinctively dislike the idea of their religion being made a matter of military regulation, and in any degree placed in the power of secular military authority'.[158] It was also pointed out that the regulations were issued without real ecclesiastical authority and that they supplied 'the want of the proper official sanction by a superabundance of threats and expressions which would be appropriate enough when used against a parcel of convicts, but which become insulting when spoken to men of education and integrity and ministers of religion.'[159] In sum, Gleig's regulations were themselves irregular, they were injurious to the interests of the Church and they amounted to 'a slur on the administration of the War Office, and an insult to the clergy and laity of the Church of England within and without the Army'.[160]

In the event, these controversial regulations failed to provide a solution to the army's Ritualist problem as it once again raised its head in 1873, this time sparked by the unsanctioned adornment of military chapels at Aldershot. According to Queen's Regulations, it was the duty of commanding officers at home and abroad to ensure that divine service was duly performed and to report 'any irregularities that may occur in this respect' to the Commander-in-Chief or Secretary of State for War. The same also applied to any matter touching the interior arrangements of military chapels and chapel-schools, which were not to be adjusted without permission from the War Office.[161] However, J.C. Edghill, then a Third Class C.F. at Aldershot, showed little regard for these requirements. On one occasion, the installation of a communion table in one of the camp's iron churches provoked a dramatic confrontation between Edghill and Sir James Hope Grant. Hearing of the new addition, Grant inspected the table and sent for a Royal Engineers carpenter in order to have 'the length of the legs summarily reduced'. Outraged, on the following Sunday Edghill announced his resignation from the pulpit and it required the intervention of the Duke of Cambridge to defuse the situation.[162] Similarly, in 1873 a shared chapel-hut also became the subject of Edghill's innovations, his Eastertide decorations prompting a complaint by a Presbyterian chaplain and a boycott of the building for the purposes of Presbyterian worship. Roused by this protest, Grant reported the matter to the Adjutant-General, emphasising that Edghill's actions were not only 'painful' to 'many

Episcopalians' but grossly offensive to members of the Church of Scotland and especially to the 93rd Highlanders who were 'almost to a man strict Presbyterians'. In view of the imminent arrival at Aldershot of another Scottish regiment, the Scots Greys, Grant claimed 'that much annoyance may occur if such proceedings are not put a stop to'.[163]

Although relations between Anglicans and Presbyterians were placed under considerable strain by the adornments crisis, the issue was exacerbated when some Anglican officers joined the fray by voicing their own concerns over 'certain proceedings which had taken place during the Church of England services' at Aldershot.[164] These included the use of Ritualist ceremonial and a graphic sermon on Bathsheba which had been preached by T.W. Belcher of Saint Faith's, Stoke Newington,[165] a Ritualist clergyman who had been invited to officiate at the camp by H.N. Wheeler, its senior Anglican chaplain and an old Crimean hand.[166] Consequently, Grant peremptorily ordered Wheeler to remove Belcher and complained to the Adjutant-General about the offensive sermon. However, and as with his earlier protests over Edghill's Easter decorations, Grant received no response from the Adjutant-General's office. Instead, Gleig arrived at Aldershot to investigate but, as the Chaplain-General sided with Belcher, his visit only triggered another row with Grant. Eventually, Grant was summoned to the War Office where he was received by the Duke of Cambridge who, much to Grant's disgust, sided with Gleig and told him that he had 'promised [the Chaplain-General] not to have any disagreements with the chaplains on church matters'.[167] Grant replied that the present trouble had been triggered by Presbyterian complaints and that he would have his orders obeyed at Aldershot or else he would resign his command.[168] The issue dragged on for several months, Grant taking his stand on Queen's Regulations and on his authority as commanding officer of the camp while reinforcing his position with the threat of resignation.[169] Faced with Grant's intransigence and public standing, and no doubt swayed by the passage of the anti-Ritualist Public Worship Regulation Act, which received the royal assent in August 1874, Cambridge caved in and switched his support to Grant. However, this was only after several months of prevarication and his capitulation occurred despite the opposition of the Secretary of State for War, Gathorne Hardy, who was a staunch High Churchman, to this new and controversial legislation.[170]

Typically, Grant relished this further victory over Gleig, noting his sense of triumph over 'the crafty Chaplain-General' and his belief that in this matter he had 'been supported in a most marvellous manner' and guided by 'that great Hand from above who rules all things'.[171] The duke's support for his position was communicated by Grant 'to Mr. Wheeler, Mr. Edghill, and chaplains of the Presbyterian and Roman Catholic persuasions' at Aldershot. As Grant remembered, 'I told them in plain terms that I was their commanding officer, and that they were as much under my command as any officers in the garrison, and that I trusted I should be obeyed'.[172] However, this victory proved to be the last of a distinguished army career, for Grant died suddenly in 1875, the same year in which Gleig retired as Chaplain-General. Fortunately for the Chaplains' Department, no senior officer stepped forward to assume Grant's mantle after his death. In fact, even one of Grant's admirers conceded that:

> In his quarrel with the High Church chaplains at Aldershot [Grant] was doubtless in the main in the right. It was they who exhibited intolerance. It is obvious that where Presbyterians, Roman Catholics and members of the Church of England worship in succession in the same building, there must be some give and take in the matter of adornment. On the other hand, it is certain that it was by no means only the aggressive chaplains who received the impression that Sir Hope Grant exerted his military authority to favour certain specific religious opinions, and it is difficult to think that a considerable part of the trouble was not connected with Sir Hope's incapacity for putting what he wanted to say, and what was in the main sound and right, in a way to commend itself to other people.[173]

Besides being plagued by jealous bishops, presumptuous Wesleyans and interfering officers, the position of Anglican chaplains in the mid-Victorian army was also complicated by the numerous evangelical organisations involved in army work. Here, however, Gleig was able to hold his own. In 1856, a wave of resignations from the civilian and non-denominational Army Scripture Readers' and Soldiers' Friend Society (which had been formed in 1838 and which had recently sent scripture readers and a vast quantity of religious literature to the Crimea)[174] led a deputation of former members to approach Gleig with a scheme for a new society. In contrast to the A.S.R.S.F.S., this would be dominated by the Church of England and commissioned chaplains and army officers would play a leading role.[175] Dubbed the British Army Scripture Readers' Society, its formation compelled the A.S.R.S.F.S. to reconsider its position and to explore the possibility of union, especially after the new organisation was favoured with a War Office charter in 1856.[176] Despite Gleig's assertion that the subsequent negotiations were 'conducted on both sides in a most Christian spirit',[177] they were in fact quite acrimonious and suspicions of Gleig and his High Church chaplains were widely aired. One former officer and B.A.S.R.S. committee member feared a clerical coup, suspecting that the consolidated society would be too broad and 'priest-ridden' and condemning J.E. Sabine, a commissioned chaplain and one of Gleig's principal henchmen, as the Crimea's 'greatest opposer' of 'evangelical truth'. For his part, William Carus Wilson, who had inaugurated a mission to soldiers in Portsmouth during the Crimean War, also had his doubts about the Chaplain-General, describing Gleig as a 'snakish man' and adding that 'A more complete Jesuit never existed'.[178]

According to William Harris Rule, these suspicions proved to be all too prescient. Initially, Rule seems to have been persuaded of the evangelical 'catholicity' of the consolidated society and was an early and influential supporter of its work at Aldershot. In fact (and despite their differences over the status of Wesleyan Methodism in the army) it would appear that he and Gleig collaborated in scrutinising the society's tracts and in examining prospective scripture-readers.[179] However, Gleig's duplicity soon became apparent. As Rule remembered:

> [Under] cover of this 'catholicity,' [Gleig] was quietly so corresponding with the chaplains on various stations that complaints came to me from several readers that they found it impossible to be excused from going to

> the Parade Services of the Church of England. In private conversations I called his attention to this departure from our constitution and breach of rules; but he defended every case in detail, suddenly took occasion at a Public Meeting to declare that he found it 'difficult to work with Nonconformists,' and when the sense of our Committee was pronounced against those proceedings of his, he stood upon his authority, which no officer present could presume to dispute in form; and as I could not remain there without resisting, I quietly withdrew, stating my reason in regretful correspondence, and avoiding the maintenance of conflict where nothing should disturb the work of peace.[180]

The United British Army Scripture Readers' and Soldiers' Friend Society was formally inaugurated in May 1859 and, despite Rule's sobering experiences, the society appears to have prospered in subsequent years. According to its report for 1864, its patrons included the archbishops of Canterbury and York, the Chaplain-General and the Earl of Shaftesbury. Among its seventeen vice-presidents, there were ten army officers, six clergymen and only one lay civilian. At the same time, the Chaplain-General chaired its 'Sub-Committee for Examining Tracts' and two serving chaplains were among the Society's six 'Examiners of Scripture Readers'.[181] As the same report made clear, the society's agents were 'superintended in most cases by the Garrison Chaplains'[182] and this strict subordination of scripture readers to chaplains was to remain a constant feature of the society's *modus operandi*. During the 1860s, scripture readers were detached from their work with individual regiments and, like chaplains, posted to individual stations. The need for such close supervision was revealed in a set of instructions which Gleig issued in September 1871, instructions that very much stressed the need to preserve the army's fragile religious harmony. Describing the army's scripture readers as 'as a rule, simple-minded men; earnest [and] God-fearing', Gleig advised his chaplains that they be employed in such a way that they were prevented from holding forth on controversial subjects. Also, and rather than allow differences of opinion to occur between chaplains and scripture readers, Gleig warned that:

> [The] Reader should be charged to avoid controversy; not indeed to turn away from difficulties when they are raised by others, but, instead of venturing upon decisive dogmas himself, he should refer the questioner to the Chaplain, or minister of the persuasion to which he is known to belong, for that answer which an educated man is better qualified to render correctly.[183]

Besides the policy of the society, the background of its scripture readers also served to ensure their subordination. As a society publication put it in 1879, 'The true office of the Army Scripture Reader is to supplement, but in no wise to supplant the functions of the Military Chaplain . . . A large majority of the Readers have seen service in the ranks, and are consequently inured to regimental discipline.'[184] Indeed, Rule later argued that it was this habit of obedience to military authority which had allowed Gleig and his chaplains to stage their takeover of the United British Army Scripture Readers' and Soldiers' Friend Society and:

> [To] appropriate to the exclusive service of the Church of England the whole body of Army Scripture Readers, most of whom, if not all, were at that time Wesleyans, as they had been when non-commissioned officers. One by one, these good men, being superintended by Anglican Chaplains, were persuaded, or, if persuasion was insufficient, were compelled, to absent themselves from their own worship, contrary to the original constitution, rules, and practice of the Soldiers' Friend Society.[185]

However, Gleig could not count on such leverage with respect to those civilian ladies who, along with their soldiers' homes, formed the vanguard of evangelical missionary work in the army from the 1860s onwards. Although these homes had the support of influential officers and civilians (and could even enjoy the moral and financial backing of the War Office) to Gleig and his subordinates they and their largely female personnel were simply more interlopers to be guarded against. After the strong resistance put up by the camp's Anglican chaplains to W.H. Rule's early ministry at Aldershot, the likes of Louisa Daniell and Sarah Robinson also met with a frosty reception. Sarah Robinson remembered that the Chaplains' Department was decidedly hostile towards Louisa Daniell's pioneering institute when it opened at Aldershot in 1862 and that Gleig forbade one chaplain, John Francis Browne, from attending its opening services. According to Robinson, after the opening of the institute Browne began to preach extemporaneously and became increasingly bold 'in preaching Christ crucified'. Consequently, and as some 'godly officers' predicted, he was soon posted elsewhere.[186] Some years later, in 1874, Robinson met with similar opposition from the senior chaplain at Plymouth who objected to the Bible classes held in her newly opened institute.[187] Given the High Church and even Ritualist leanings of the Chaplains' Department, these evangelical homes reciprocated this coolness, it being noted at the Church Congress of 1900 that 'though worked on a so-called "unsectarian" basis, these homes were conducted on very strict lines indeed, and the army chaplains were neither invited nor encouraged to attend them'.[188]

Anglican Chaplaincy under Bishop Claughton

Despite the positive tone of Gleig's farewell address and posterity's perception of his 'brilliant reign' as Chaplain-General,[189] it is clear that by the time Gleig left office in April 1875 the Anglican branch of the Chaplains' Department was in serious disarray, with the need for episcopal supervision of some kind being accentuated by the army's recent Ritualist controversy. Although Gleig had been frustrated in his bid to endow the office of Chaplain-General with episcopal rank, on his retirement the Secretary of State for War hastened to recommend an existing bishop, Dr. Piers Calveley Claughton, for the post of Chaplain-General. However, and with the aim of avoiding trouble with the bench of bishops, Gathorne Hardy hesitated to invoke the Army Chaplains Act which would have endowed Claughton with full episcopal powers over his chaplains. Consequently, and as one critic of Claughton's appointment observed, 'Bishop Claughton has not the shadow of Episcopal power in the Army [as] all his acts will be by permission.'[190] Although Claughton was not equipped with the kind of power which Gleig himself had sought, in his farewell address the outgoing Chaplain-General nevertheless welcomed the fact that Claughton was at least in episcopal orders. As Gleig put it:

> To part from you is very painful, yet the pain is mitigated by the thought that in my successor, a Bishop of the Church of Christ, and your Bishop, you will find one, for obvious reasons, more capable than I of advising and sustaining you in your difficulties, should such at any time, or under any circumstances, beset you.[191]

While the idea of having a bishop at the helm of the Chaplains' Department may have appealed to Gathorne Hardy's High Church sensibilities, there was more than a hint of expedience in his decision to nominate Claughton as Gleig's successor; as an assistant bishop of the diocese of London, Claughton was handily resident in the capital. More than sixty years of age when he became Chaplain-General, Claughton had enjoyed a distinguished university career and had spent fourteen years as a parish clergyman before becoming Bishop of St. Helena in 1859. Translated to Colombo in 1862, on his return to England nine years later he was appointed Archdeacon of London and a prebendary of St. Paul's. Otherwise distinguished as an originator of the modern Harvest Festival, Claughton's experience of the army was meagre in comparison with that of some senior members of the Chaplains' Department. While Claughton claimed to have maintained constant contact 'with bodies of troops in the Colonies' and had supervised 'clergymen who were in spiritual charge of troops' as a colonial bishop,[192] this paled in comparison to the record of the other obvious candidate, namely Henry Press Wright. Already Archdeacon of British Columbia, where he had served in the 1860s, Wright had served as a garrison chaplain in Cephalonia and Corfu, as Principal Chaplain in the Crimea and now had almost thirty years' service to his credit as well as being chaplain to the Duke of Cambridge.[193] With these credentials Wright naturally saw himself as Gleig's rightful successor and was outraged at 'an Ex Colonial Bishop with already £1400 a year coming in and taking £800 more' as Chaplain-General.[194] In fairness to Wright, it does indeed seem that Claughton had very little to offer the Chaplains' Department apart from his episcopal title, his High Church proclivities and his own emollient temper. This situation was not helped by his lack of proper episcopal authority over his chaplains or by his continuing responsibilities as Archdeacon of London, an office that bound him to eight months' residence per year in the diocese of London under the Pluralities Act of 1838.[195]

From the outset, Wright was sceptical as to Claughton's capacity for his new post, pointing out that the bishop 'had already as Archdeacon and Canon of St. Paul's plenty of work for the most active mind and body'.[196] Nevertheless, Claughton put a happier gloss on his questionable qualifications and competing commitments. In June 1875, he convened his first chaplains' conference at the War Office and gave an address in which he explained the advantages of his position:

> [Although] he was very far from undervaluing the advantage of a professional knowledge of the Army, he could not disguise from himself that such knowledge sometimes had its drawbacks also. It tended to narrow men's views unless carefully guarded against, while on the other hand a wider and non-professional experience might conduce to a more comprehensive and unprejudiced judgment.[197]

Likewise, Claughton stressed the advantages of his position as Archdeacon of London, stating that:

> [He] believed it was for the good of the Chaplains' Department that he should retain his appointment of Archdeacon, as he trusted this position in the Diocese of London would not be without advantage to the Service, and would lead in some degree to breaking down the wall of exclusiveness that had before in a great measure separated the Army Chaplains from the Parochial Clergy – a separation which he regarded as injurious to the Chaplains. It would also give him facilities for inducing suitable young clergymen to enter the Department, whilst it might also enable him to find openings for those Chaplains who, after a certain period of Army service, desired to devote themselves to parochial work.[198]

Whatever their perceived benefits, Claughton's civilian background and lack of familiarity with the army fostered a perceptible slackening of discipline within the Department. As early as the chaplains' conference of June 1875, Claughton signalled that his touch would be a light one. In stark contrast to Gleig's autocratic approach, Claughton emphasised that collegiality would be the keynote of his management of the Department:

> [His] previous experience convinced him that speaking openly and unreservedly with his clergy was the best course, and as it had succeeded with other bodies of clergymen who had been under his charge, he confidently hoped [that] it would procure the same effect with the Chaplains of the Army.[199]

With reference to the volatile question of Ritualism, Claughton declared that he would allow 'legitimate latitude in non-essentials' but emphasised the necessity for consultation over any liturgical practice that seemed of 'doubtful legality'. He followed this statement of policy with the mildest of threats:

> He expected to be previously consulted in all such matters, and though he should be very loth to use it, and hoped he should never be compelled to do so, he was aware that the War Office Regulations gave him power of enforcing his orders not possessed by other Bishops.[200]

Rather than dwelling on possible divisions, Claughton promised to strengthen the position of his chaplains 'by every means in his power' and sought to rally the Department around two pressing issues. Firstly, there was the need for 'better places for the celebration of Divine Worship'. Though this did not necessarily mean an end to unconsecrated places of worship, it did encompass the provision of 'better furniture and accompaniments'. Secondly, Claughton identified the need 'for Chaplains' rooms or offices where they could see the members of their flock, and get over the difficulty of either having to meet the men in their barrack room or see them in their own quarters'.[201]

Despite his good intentions, Claughton's gentle approach fostered a long-term reaction against many of the policies that had developed under his predecessor. Furthermore, this rebellion acquired a public platform through the Church of England's annual Church Congresses. Although these had begun in 1861 and were devoted to practical matters,[202] it was significant that Gleig had not taken chaplaincy business to them. However, only six months after becoming Chaplain-General, Claughton led a deputation of chaplains to the Church Congress at Stoke-on-Trent in order to discuss 'Church Work in the Army'. Here, and regardless of Claughton's presence, Henry Press Wright gave his forthright views on 'the office and qualifications and work of the Chaplain-General' and also pronounced on 'what kind of men the chaplains of the army should be, how they should be chosen, and how supported'.[203] He also criticised the role of the Secretary of State for War in the appointment of chaplains and called for an end to the chapel-school system, claiming that he had even heard Gleig admit that 'the school-chapel system [had] proved a failure'.[204] The subject of chapel-schools raised its head once again at the Church Congress of 1885, when Canon Beach, the senior Anglican chaplain at Aldershot, condemned the 'bare, uncongenial, unsanctified school barrack schoolroom' as a place for divine worship and denounced the army's 'so-called churches' as 'big wooden structures, devoid of all ecclesiastical ornament [and] possessing no single recommendation save that of being constructed to hold 1,000 men'. These churches, he reminded his audience, were frequently shared by Anglicans, Presbyterians and Roman Catholics and were reduced to the absurd lengths of being supplied with wheeled altars that could be pushed in and out as required.[205] Significantly, these complaints appear to have been heeded at the War Office. By the late 1880s, the army estimates were allowing £1,000 per annum for 'improving or adding' to church accommodation at stations in Great Britain, a long-term process that involved the gradual conversion of chapel-schools into dedicated chapels.[206]

Under the long shadow cast by General Charles Gordon's pseudo-martyrdom at Khartoum in 1885, other aspects of Anglican religious provision were also in contention at Church Congress later that year. In one strident address, Lieutenant-Colonel J.B. Walker of the Royal Artillery challenged the wisdom of commissioning chaplains and the existing system of relative rank, describing an officer's rank as 'one of the greatest obstacles' to the chaplain's ministry and alleging that he had seen convalescents spring to attention in military hospitals when a chaplain arrived on their ward. He concluded his address by inquiring:

> Did Jesus Christ have any official rank? Did the apostles have any official rank? Were men bound to spring up to attention and salute them [?] How can a man unfold what is nearest to his heart to one who he feels is his official superior and whom he cannot approach without giving a military salute?[207]

Given that the Church Congress essentially served as 'a barometer of opinion' within the Church of England,[208] this issue was quickly taken up by the national press. In October 1885, *The Times* echoed Walker's criticisms by expressing its own reservations over commissioned chaplains, a view that was refuted from retirement by Gleig himself:

> There may be – in my time there unfortunately were – some chaplains who thought more of their rights as officers than of their high duties and privileges as chaplains. These were, or if any of them still cumber the 'Army List' they continue to be, worse than useless. But look at the other side . . . You may take the word for it of one who knows the Army well, both as a combatant officer in the old war, and as Chaplain-General for 30 years and more, that your misgivings on the point referred to in your leading article are illusory. Silly and worthless chaplains may make light of their proper duties, just as silly and worthless rectors and vicars neglect their parishioners, or shoot over their heads. But the commission which the chaplain holds, while it renders him amenable to discipline . . . gives both to officers and soldiers, claims upon his services such as they could not otherwise advance . . .[209]

In addition to hearing criticisms of commissioned chaplains and of the army's places of worship, the Church Congress of 1885 also heard Canon Beach call for the resurrection of the regimental chaplain.[210] Although their numbers had greatly increased during Gleig's years as Chaplain-General, Anglican chaplains remained attached to stations and were rotated every five years.[211] However, in 1885 Beach claimed that the current system led to an uneven standard of pastoral care and that it did not provide the army with enough Anglican chaplains:

> It is impossible for one clergyman to do all that is in his heart to do for a Brigade consisting of three regiments, especially when these regiments are constantly changing from station to station . . . The number of chaplains should be increased if the spiritual and moral condition of our soldiers is to be really improved, and the Church should strongly represent this to those who have the power to increase them.[212]

Far from being a new demand, this call had been made as early as 1843, when an editorial in the *United Service Journal and Naval and Military Magazine* had pointed out that garrison chaplains could hardly minister effectively to their charges when they were often responsible for 'four or five regiments [along] with a large proportion of women and children'.[213] Indeed, this case had been reiterated by Henry Press Wright in 1858. Against the backdrop of the Indian Mutiny, Wright had urged the appointment of a regimental chaplain for every regiment ordered overseas. In India alone, he argued, 'Viewed simply as a moral policeman, a sensible, earnest-minded clergyman, walking daily among a thousand men, each of whom, on Indian soil, is worth at least £100 to the State, would be a source of gain instead of expense to the Treasury.' With reference to the failings of the system prior to 1796, Wright argued that 'under the old regime [when] every corps in the service had its chaplain, that chaplain was generally appointed without any consideration whatever as to his qualifications'.[214] However, the same would not now be true because the current pay and conditions of chaplains served to ensure that the army would always find 'a faithful clergyman to be a pattern to all ranks of the service'.[215]

Despite these undercurrents of discontent, Claughton discharged the functions of the Chaplain-General in a conciliatory manner that occasionally veered towards the inept. In February 1878, he issued an address and supplementary set of instructions to his chaplains which sought to stimulate the liturgical life of the army while avoiding any suspicion of Ritualist zeal. Hence, he emphasised the need for including the communion office at parade services at least once a month and recommended the institution of voluntary services on Sunday evenings and on every day of the week if possible. However, this was to be achieved while avoiding controversy and remaining within the rubrics of the Prayer Book. Thus, for example, chanting was permissible at parade services but chaplains had to be careful not to give offence – 'It is one of the things which are lawful, and may be claimed as such when plainly also expedient, which it cannot be when it is not consonant with the feelings of the congregation'.[216] Conscious of his episcopal office, Claughton also embarked upon two extensive tours of military stations in the British Isles in order to hold confirmations in garrison churches and chapels, a gesture that may not have been welcomed by diocesan bishops.[217] In May 1879, his benign naivety was once again displayed by his announcement that the relationship between senior chaplains and their subordinates at military stations was 'not precisely that of a junior officer to his senior' because senior chaplains were charged with monitoring their subordinates and reporting 'any neglect or objectionable proceedings to the Chaplain-General, through the General Officer Commanding'. Furthermore, he weakened the chain of command still further by granting chaplains the right of 'direct communication with the Chaplain-General on any purely ecclesiastical matter which may require his opinion or advice'.[218]

Anglican Chaplaincy under J.C. Edghill

Claughton died in office in August 1884. In view of his handling of the Department, it is hard to dispute Jarvis' verdict that he had 'no outstanding aptitude for the task' and that 'he made no contribution of worth either of leadership or administrative advance in the Department'.[219] Certainly, following his death the Anglican hierarchy was not anxious to repeat the experiment of making a Chaplain-General out of a bishop. In November 1884, and with the office still vacant, Sir Ralph Thompson, the Permanent Under Secretary, wrote to Gleig informing him that:

> Lord Hartington [the Secretary of State for War] has had a sort of joint representation from several of the Bishops urging him to appoint one of the Army Chaplains as Chaplain General. He has not made up his mind to do so, but he would like to know something about the fitness of the Senior Chaplains for the post and he has asked me to ask you if you will kindly give him confidentially your opinion on the merits of the Chaplains who are in the First Class – [J.C.] Edghill has been strongly recommended from various quarters . . .[220]

Although it is not clear whether Gleig endorsed Edghill's candidature, among Edghill's supporters was Prince Edward of Teck, a minor royal and a nephew of the Duke of Cambridge. Edghill was eventually appointed Chaplain-General in January 1885 and, in a letter of thanks to the prince, he wrote:

> I never expected the offer and I know I owe it entirely to the kind interest so many have taken in me, and their appreciation of the little I have attempted to do for the Army . . . The only claim I have for the post is an intense desire to do soldiers good, and a general belief that the religion of Jesus Christ is just what is wanted to make them brave and loyal . . .[221]

Now fifty years old, Edghill was much younger than his predecessor and was in fact ranked among the most junior First Class chaplains. While his High Church predilections were fairly typical of the post-Crimean Department, Edghill was very much a professional army chaplain and had served in Gibraltar and at Halifax, Nova Scotia, as well as at several home stations.[222] Commissioned in 1861, he had risen to the rank of chaplain First Class by September 1881 and he was to remain in post as Chaplain-General until 1901.[223] Appointed on a salary of £800 per annum, Edghill's income was much less than that of Gleig or Claughton and he at first found it 'impossible to live in London and fulfil my duties upon [£800] a year', a fact that demanded his appointment as Chaplain to the Tower of London on a further £150 a year.[224] Such generosity was warranted by the fact that Edghill's abilities were not only recognised inside the army. In 1887, the Synod of Nova Scotia, a colony where the S.P.G. had traditionally been strong,[225] unanimously elected him as successor to Bishop Hibbert Binney. Although the synod offered to raise the bishop's income by $2,000 per annum, in an open letter written that July Edghill revealed the pastoral and providential reasons that obliged him to decline:

> No one who knows anything of the circumstances of my selection as Chaplain-General can doubt for one moment that God called me to it; that He had a special work for me to do in this post. The Archbishop says: 'No post within my knowledge and recollection cost authorities, civil and ecclesiastical, so much trouble as yours did in the filling of it. That God has you there with your special gifts and special experience no man can doubt.' For two years and a half I have met with nothing but helpful kindness and consideration from all those in authority in carrying out what I believe to be necessary for the well-being of the Church in the army. But as yet the work is but beginning . . . The work is peculiar, unique. 'There are many Bishops,' says the Archbishop, 'but *one* Chaplain-General.' The Secretary of State writes to me: 'I feel strongly that your loss to us *just now* would be almost irreparable.' Thus strengthened by the judgment of those whose position enables them to judge so well, I can but believe that God has called me distinctly to my present work, and that *I have not completed it*, and if I gave it up thus prematurely I should be thwarting God's purpose . . .[226]

As Edghill stated in 1888, his responsibilities as Chaplain-General included the supervision of Anglican religious instruction in army schools, the selection and inspection of Anglican chaplains and in 'advising the Secretary of State as to the religious and moral welfare of our soldiers'.[227] However, although capable and experienced, Edghill's early years as Chaplain-General were fraught with difficulty.[228] Indeed, it was ironic that within weeks of declining the see of Nova Scotia, the very post of Chaplain-General was under threat. Given the size of the Army Estimates, which had reached between £16 million and £18 million per annum by the mid-1880s,[229] public expenditure on the Chaplains' Department had become a salient aspect of a sensitive political issue. In August 1887, and only eight months after the scale of the Army Estimates had led to his resignation as Chancellor of the Exchequer, Lord Randolph Churchill drew attention in the House of Commons to what he considered to be the unjustifiable expense of the Chaplains' Department, whose costs had risen by nearly £13,000 since 1874.[230] By this time, a Select Committee had been established under Churchill's chairmanship to investigate the whole issue of army expenditure, a committee that was to show great interest in the complicated finances of the Chaplains' Department.[231] With nearly £60,000 about to be voted under the heading of 'religious services for the army':

> [Churchill] expressed his opinion very strongly that among the votes which the [Select Committee] had examined there was no vote which showed itself more susceptible of revision and reduction than the present one. In a great many cases it would be desirable to substitute the services of an officiating clergyman paid by a capitation rate in lieu of an Army chaplain on the establishment, who would become entitled to a pension; and he suggested for consideration whether the office of Chaplain-General could not be done away with.[232]

To this, the Secretary of State for War, Edward Stanhope, smoothly replied that while 'he wished to effect every practicable reduction' to the Army Estimates he felt that judgment on this issue ought to be suspended until the Select Committee had considered all the evidence.[233]

Alarmed by this rather lukewarm defence, Gleig wrote to Stanhope imploring him 'to stand between the Chaplain[s'] Department of the Army and the evil with which it is threatened'. Indeed, he was even able to suggest means whereby economies might be achieved:

> The Church patronage of the Crown is great and we live in an age when any proposal to utilise it for the public good would be most popular. Instead of paying the Chaplain General, as is done now, why not advise the Crown to connect the office with a Canonry in St. Paul's or Westminster or Rochester – or even in Canterbury [?] This would serve the double purpose of drawing the line of connexion closer than it is now between the Church in the Army, and the Church in civil life and of showing that Crown patronage is a public benefit, not a means of providing for Court favourites.[234]

While he was prepared to acknowledge the financial burden placed on the taxpayer by retired chaplains, Gleig had an appropriate remedy to hand:

> The non-effective list of Chaplains is a heavy expense. You might I think greatly lighten this by extending the period of compulsory retirement to

> 65 – and connecting the pension with the acquisition of preferment in private life. You are aware of course that Naval Chaplains are retired on Dockyard Chaplaincies, and on benefices in the gift of the Commissioners of Greenwich Hospital. Is there any reason why the benefices in the gift of both the Crown and the Lord Chancellor should not in like manner be utilised [?][235]

It was indicative of Gleig's continued standing with the War Office that Stanhope favoured him with a swift reply, reassuring him that 'With regard to the Chaplains as a body, the work that they are doing is well appreciated, and I do not fear that even the House of Commons will be disposed to dispense with them.'[236] In the event, and after its close questioning of the Permanent Under Secretary, the Chaplain-General and the Accountant General in April 1888, the Select Committee found no evidence of extravagance and simply concluded that 'a more extended employment of officiating clergymen would in all probability result in a sensible economy'.[237] Consequently, and with Churchill's star in decline among his fellow Conservatives, his budgetary challenge to the Department quickly disappeared.

However, in 1890 the size of the army estimates and the findings of the Select Committee once again put the Department under the spotlight, the issue at stake being the necessity of maintaining commissioned chaplains in Ireland. In this case, financial considerations were complicated by three other factors. Firstly, there were the liturgical differences between the Church of England and the Church of Ireland after the latter's revision of its Prayer Book and canons in a more Protestant direction in the late 1870s;[238] secondly, there was the hostile posture of the Irish Catholic church towards commissioned Roman Catholic chaplains and, thirdly, there were the overarching politics of Irish Home Rule. In March 1890, a Nationalist M.P. challenged the Secretary of State for War over the cost and propriety of maintaining Anglican chaplains in Ireland:

> Mr. MacNeill suggested that some steps should be taken to permit the parochial clergy in Ireland to perform the duties now discharged by Army Chaplains. The total cost of the Army chaplains now on duty in Ireland was £9,500 a year, whereas the services they rendered might be given by the parochial clergy for about £2,000 per annum . . . a very substantial saving could be effected by allowing the clergy of the disestablished Church to minister to the troops in Ireland as the Catholic clergy did. Representing as he did the most Roman Catholic constituency in this great Empire, he was satisfied that in trying to do justice to their Protestant fellow-countrymen he should receive their sympathy and support.[239]

Nonplussed, Stanhope agreed to look into the matter. With the hounds now unleashed, Viscount Wolseley (the Adjutant-General, an Irish Low Churchman and patron of several evangelical causes in the army)[240] took the opportunity to take a swipe at the Chaplains' Department, sending Stanhope the following memorandum:

> The enclosed has been sent to me anonymously – 'To send Army Chaplains to Ireland is like sending inferior coals to Newcastle. In Ireland the

> Clergy of the [Church of Ireland] are even still numerous and have always had an excellent reputation. It seems to me that we spend a great deal more than is necessary on our Chaplains, and Ireland is just the place where economy on this score could most easily and with best advantage to the army, be effected'.[241]

However, too much was being made of the virtues of officiating clergy in general and of the Irish clergy in particular. Although Dr. George Wheeler, the incumbent of nearby Ballysax, attracted large crowds of soldiers from the Curragh to his Sunday evening services between 1865 and 1877 on the strength of his 'simple and telling discourses',[242] Edwin Mole of the 14th Hussars was bemused by the quirky style of the Dean of Tuam, who 'constituted himself our chaplain' during the Fenian disturbances of the 1860s:

> [He] visited us twice a week. He invariably began his ministrations by ordering a pint of beer all round, and after we had drunk it would say: 'Now, men, your pots are empty, let us pray.' And when devotions were over he ordered us another pint of beer all round before going away.[243]

The basic unfitness of the Irish clergy to minister to the army was one of the reasons cited by Edghill in a memorandum that flatly rejected any idea of surrendering Ireland's larger garrisons to the clergy of its disestablished Church. As Edghill observed, the scale of the task involved would entail the appointment of additional curates, a fact which raised the crucial question of whether the selection of men for this delicate and important ministry could be entrusted to individual incumbents. Furthermore, Edghill stressed the established view that officiating clergymen were not in a position to discharge the manifold duties of an army chaplain:

> Officiating Clergy have been tried and found wanting. The G.O.C. at the Curragh felt the neglect and mode of work of the Rector of Newbridge very much, and recommended again and again that the Chaplain at the Curragh should take it over. There is now a request from the G.O.C. at Belfast asking for a Chaplain (commissioned) to be sent there for the same purpose . . . Soldiers also greatly prefer their own Chaplains. I continually hear from them grave complaints as to the little that is done by officiating Clergy. The only service is from 10 to 11 a.m. on Sunday mornings. The clergy cannot do more, their own work requires their time and care . . . If the Secretary of State thinks that one hour on Sunday is enough for useful work; if the somewhat perfunctory parade service is to be regarded as all, I should go much further in the way of economy and dismiss all *Chaplains and Officiating Clergy* at once.[244]

Edghill also deplored the sheer selfishness of the proposal. The Chaplains' Department already included twelve commissioned clergymen of the Church of Ireland – 'a much larger proportion of Irishmen than can be fairly sustained' – and some of these were serving as senior chaplains in England. The basic question was one of fairness and the Irish Church was doing very well out of the current system. As Edghill pointed out:

> It cannot be equitable to take our Chaplains from Irish Garrisons and then to bring Irish Chaplains to English ones. This would be one-sided Home rule. I may mention that from some English Garrisons I have had complaints of the accent and pronunciation of my Irish Brethren, but I have been able to allay the little irritation . . . My rule is to treat Englishmen and Irishmen alike and to approve the best men I can get from either Church. Surely the Irish Clergy so long as they are fairly represented in the Department are gainers by the present arrangement.[245]

Most significantly, however, Edghill stressed the need to insulate the army from the political and religious strife that prevailed in Ireland. Under the existing system, Anglican worship in the army was conducted solely in accordance with English forms. This policy helped to ensure uniformity and it was informed by the fact that the great majority of Anglicans in the army were English:

> But hand over the large body of our Troops with their Chapels to the Parochial Clergy of Ireland and what will the result be. At present happily among our soldiers there is but little *party spirit*: this abounds in Ireland. But with the abolition of Chaplains Irish uses would come in and parties would be formed. When the men come again to England they would find much that they had been taught to abhor tolerated and loved.[246]

As a concrete illustration of these dangers, Edghill compared his own tact and discretion with the bigoted mendacity of the clergyman who would claim responsibility for the Curragh:

> I preached last year at the Curragh [to] a crowded congregation of soldiers at a voluntary service. I preached a plain practical Sermon which no Christian could rightly object to. There was not a hint of any disputable doctrine or practice in it. I was the more careful as there were a large number of Scotsmen in the Church. Yet the Rector of Newbridge writes to the papers misrepresenting all I said, and deliberately tried to stir up bad blood, through lies. Yet this is one man to whom we should hand over a large body of men.[247]

Clearly persuaded by the force of these arguments, Stanhope and his subordinates took the side of the Chaplain-General. In a memorandum to the Permanent Under Secretary, Stanhope wrote:

> I would have snubbed the proposal at once, but that (1) it appeared to come from the Archbishop of Dublin, though why he should have adopted this means of making it is hard to understand (2) the vote had to be passed. I am quite prepared, when it comes on for serious discussion, to reject the proposal.[248]

Although this threat receded, the Department remained exposed to questions of cost. Two years later, for example, Edghill was obliged to agree to the raising of the Chaplain-General's retirement age.[249] Individual chaplains also remained vulnerable to the interference of senior officers. While belligerent Low Churchmen of the stamp of Sir James Hope Grant were in a dwindling minority by the end of the nineteenth century, there were still senior officers who seemed determined to dictate to their chaplains. In 1888, and during the deliberations of the Select Committee on the army estimates, Sir Henry Havelock-Allan breezily informed Edghill that 'having had 40 years' experience of the Army, I have never found that there was any difficulty in getting rid of a non-effective chaplain, by giving him such practical hints as to how he was held in favour or disfavour as would incline him to seek some other occupation'.[250] One letter from an army chaplain to the *Church Times* in April 1901 complained of precisely this attitude:

> As is well known, a commanding officer is supreme in his own sphere in most matters, and is not unusually an autocrat, sometimes even worse. I have seen in my experience some terrible instances of tyranny exercised by these gentlemen. It has been a long and severe lesson to teach these men that they cannot tyrannise over the chaplain, though they often 'try the game on,' and make the Church's work very difficult to accomplish.

Such officers, it was claimed, had a tendency to carry such attitudes into retirement, when 'they settle in some unhappy parish, and at once endeavour to introduce the barrack-square system into their dealings with their parish priests'.[251] This letter had been prompted by recent disturbances in the church of St. Mary-le-Bow at the election of A.F. Winnington Ingram as the new Bishop of London. Led by John Kensit, the leading Protestant agitator of the day, 'the Kensit brawl in Bow Church' had been sparked by Winnington Ingram's well-known Ritualist sympathies and it involved three former or serving colonels enter loud objections against the new bishop, particularly on the matter of auricular confession.[252] While Winnington Ingram claimed that 'it certainly was fun to see those Protestant Colonels from Ireland turn up to protest against my being confirmed as Bishop of London',[253] for High Church chaplains of the day this incident (which the King had deplored as a 'disgraceful scene')[254] was clearly symptomatic of an intractable problem that still threatened their work.

Another ongoing difficulty for the army's Anglican chaplains was that their role seemed to render them peripheral to the ministry and concerns of the civilian church. Significantly, on accepting the position of Chaplain-General, Edghill wrote that 'by accepting this appointment for seven years I am really giving up all chances of other preferment, and taking this as my life work'.[255] Given these perceptions of the marginal place of the Chaplain-General in the national life of the Church, at the Church Congress of 1885 Canon Beach (who held his canonry in St. John's Cathedral, Hong Kong, where he had previously served as a colonial chaplain) suggested that the Chaplain-General should be made an *ex-officio* member of Convocation and that Convocation should maintain a standing committee on the Church's work in the army and navy. Furthermore, and whilst acknowledging the interest of the current Bishop of Winchester, Edward Harold Browne, Beach went on:

> I cannot forbear saying, with all respect, that if the bishops generally would summon chaplains to hear their Charges at their Visitations, as his lordship kindly does, it would be a help to us, making us feel that we were truly one with our brother clergy in civil life, bound by the same solemn vows and obligations, and engaged in the same holy work.

Beach also claimed that chaplains would regard invitations from rural deans to join their chapter meetings as invaluable 'opportunities of meeting and conferring with the clergy of the neighbouring parishes'.[256] However, the marginal status of Anglican chaplains was most keenly felt on their return to civilian life. When Henry Press Wright retired from the Chaplains' Department it was to return as archdeacon to British Columbia. Clearly, this was not what Wright had hoped for after thirty years' distinguished service and after his disappointment at not becoming Chaplain-General. Although Gleig lobbied the Lord Chancellor for a Crown living on Wright's behalf,[257] Wright felt compelled to write to *The Times* in December 1876:

> I would fain make a last appeal on behalf of my brother Chaplains. Inasmuch as Chaplains to the Forces are cut off from all Church preferment in the gift of Bishops, I may fairly ask, would it not be an act of justice and, I may add, of wisdom were one or two livings of £300 or £400 a year placed by the Crown at the disposal of the Chaplain-General, to be conferred, as circumstances may suggest, on Chaplains who have done good service to the State?
>
> During the past 30 years the Crown has never bestowed a living on an Army Chaplain. If when I am at work in a far off colony I can only learn that Mr. Disraeli or his successor has graciously considered the military career of distinguished Chaplains, it will be cheering intelligence indeed, and I am sure you, Mr. Editor, will be glad to have in any way served a department of the Army which gave 12 of its little band to rest in honour with their comrades in the Crimea.[258]

Despite these hopes, things had not improved by the turn of the twentieth century. In December 1902, a former chaplain, D.D. Bennett, wrote to *The Times* concerning the prospects for those chaplains who had served in the Boer War. While echoing the call for 'a certain number of livings in public patronage' to be placed 'at the disposal of the War Office', he deplored the meagre pensions of former chaplains in comparison with those of other army officers, if not of other clergymen. While J.C. Edghill had maintained that 'the greatest incentive to thorough good men to become Army chaplains is the pension',[259] Bennett pointed out that whereas a medical officer could retire on £1 a day at the end of twenty years' service, a chaplain could expect only 12s 6d. Furthermore, the retired chaplain had no hope of preferment because 'when a clergyman joins the Army he severs his connexion with his diocese and becomes a sort of "nobody's child," ecclesiastically speaking, and is practically obliged to begin life de novo when he retires, and that under great disadvantages'. Worse still was the lot of those chaplains who, like Bennett himself, were invalided from the service. Not only was their pension proportionately less (they received 5s per day for their first five years' service but only 2s 6d for every further five) but they also had to scrabble for work in order to live. Since leaving the army in 1892, Bennett had served a two-year spell as a continental chaplain in Stockholm and had been an assistant curate in two English parishes. However, the fact remained that 'after 30 years' work in the Church' he was without a benefice. Pressing his point, Bennett compared the complete indifference of the Church of England to the favour and solicitude that the Church of Rome evinced to its former chaplains:

> Father Virtue [sic] was appointed Bishop of Portsmouth; Father Bellord (wounded at Tel-el-Kebir), Bishop of Gibraltar; and that gallant soldier-priest, Father Brindle, first assistant Bishop to Cardinal Vaughan, and then Bishop of Nottingham. Of course all her retired chaplains are not made Bishops, but I am confident that an independent sphere of work would be found for any priest if, after good service, he had, like me, to retire through injured health. He would not, like a Church of England chaplain, be left to shift for himself, be knocked about from pillar to post, and have to advertise for work . . . The reproach ought to be rolled away from the Church of England that she is less mindful of her old chaplains than the Church of Rome.[260]

Anglican chaplains also grappled with what they perceived to be a lack of influence over the rank and file of the army. Proportionately fewer than their Presbyterian and Roman Catholic counterparts, Anglican chaplains were posted to larger stations at home and overseas where each was often responsible for an entire brigade of three regiments.[261] Besides the daunting scale of their responsibilities, regimental redeployments meant that their work could be undone with depressing regularity. As one member of the Select Committee on army estimates put it in 1888, 'It has been stated that chaplains, however zealous they may be, get weary of their work, owing to the constant changes of regiments; they lose their congregations, and find it wearisome to get fresh men and fresh congregations time after time.' Edghill concurred, stating that 'there is great pressure upon the various Army chaplains', adding that 'it is a very difficult thing for any Army chaplain not to fall into the hands of giant despair'.[262] Similarly, one officer who had served in the ranks in the 1870s before being commissioned, wrote in 1881 that:

> The whole question about chaplains, and how they can get at the men, is very difficult, and I know they are not satisfied at present, for I have talked the matter over with many of them . . . as long as regiments (which are like small parishes of 500 or 600 souls) are moved about, and come under fresh chaplains every year or two, it will be impossible for much good influence to be brought to bear. The chaplains and men are perpetual strangers.[263]

For reasons such as this, one historian of the late Victorian army has claimed that 'the influence of most chaplains hovered near zero'[264] and there is indeed evidence to suggest that relations between Anglican chaplains and Anglican soldiers could be rather distant. In his recollections of army life in the 1890s, Horace Wyndham remarked that chaplains could feel 'a certain diffidence about visiting barrack-rooms – thinking, perhaps, that, in doing so, they would be unduly intruding'.[265] Of chaplains as a breed, Wyndham was inclined to be dismissive, claiming that:

> [These] members of the Church Militant are generally in a vastly superior position to their over-worked, harassed, and often poverty-stricken

> brethren who work in the uncongenial surroundings of great towns and cities. Parochial work, with all its kindred worries and anxieties, is, to the Army Chaplain, quite unknown . . . In point of work, too, he seems to have a fairly easy time of it. Beyond the two services on Sundays, and the usual Church Festivals, his time is to a great extent very much his own. In places where there are three or four chaplains to share the extraneous work, such duties as visiting the sick, &c., do not press very heavily. In fact, in many stations the chaplain's proficiency at tennis is uncharitably ascribed to his having such ample opportunities for practice![266]

Nevertheless, away from the settled patterns of garrison life the shared hardships and dangers of campaigning could serve to enhance the standing of that minority of Anglican chaplains who saw active service. John Gordon, a former soldier of the 1st Black Watch, was very much impressed by the chaplains he encountered in the Sudan in 1885. In contrast to Wyndham, Gordon remarked that chaplains of all denominations were 'Indispensable . . . leading sacrificial, benedictive lives, devoted to the service and comfort of sick and wounded, and performing last rites for [the] dying and dead'. He also observed that they were generally 'good sports' who could 'play as well as pray'.[267]

Besides the problems associated with the number and posting of Anglican chaplains, the suspicion that their commission and relative rank were major handicaps to their ministry was widely and deeply held in Anglican circles. Although the Church Congress of 1885 heard stories of how convalescents were compelled to come to attention and salute chaplains visiting their wards, the vicar of St. Stephen's, Lewisham, had told an earlier Congress of an ex-soldier who had resolved 'never [to] enter a church again' or 'to have anything more to do with the clergy' after his experience of chaplains and parade services in the army.[268] In view of these concerns, the policy of Claughton and Edghill during the last quarter of the nineteenth century was to reduce the distance between the chaplain and the common soldier as much as possible. In 1875, Claughton had stressed the necessity of chaplains' rooms where they could meet soldiers on a relatively private and informal basis. However, as this would place pressure on accommodation in barracks, a better alternative was the privately funded Church of England soldiers' institute. The first of these institutes was opened in rented rooms in Aldershot in 1880. However, after determined fundraising by Canon Beach, a purpose-built institute on Aldershot's main street was opened on St. Michael's Day 1883. Foremost among its benefactors was the former Secretary of State for War, Gathorne Hardy, now Lord Cranbrook, who as 'a simple donation from a private person' gave £1,000 towards its building costs.[269]

Given the success of the Aldershot experiment, soldiers' institutes soon sprang up elsewhere, their multiplication being driven by the surge of public interest in Christian work in the army that was triggered by the death of General Gordon at Khartoum. The spread of these institutes was co-ordinated by local committees, which were often formed on a diocesan basis, and also by the Church of England's Soldiers' Institutes Association. At its annual meeting in 1900, this national body heard that nine institutes were in existence across the empire and that two others were being planned.[270] Six months later, Church Congress heard

Colonel R.H. Jelf – a spokesman for the Association – report that these institutes were making a vital contribution to 'the spiritual and moral welfare' of the soldier.[271] Like the soldiers' homes they resembled, these facilities partly aimed to provide the soldier with wholesome means of recreation. In a fundraising letter to the *Church Times*, A.W.B. Watson (who had lately served as the senior Anglican chaplain in the Sudan) described the contribution that a soldiers' institute would make to the tedious lives of the Cairo garrison:

> [For] the rank and file, Cairo is probably one of the dullest of stations; and, let it be well remembered, the most fruitful parent of vice is dullness. There are hardly any outside his barracks, who speak his native tongue, to offer social intercourse to the soldier, while Greek vendors of the vilest kind of liquors abound, with harpies not far off lying in wait for their prey. It is no exaggeration to say that no British town would tolerate the state of things existing in Cairo, by which the soldier is tempted so much and so often . . . A place which can attract and amuse men, without forcing them to go to the town for relaxation, is a need, and the Church of England's Soldiers' Institutes Association is collecting a sum towards that purpose.[272]

However, and as Jelf made clear in his address to the Church Congress, the 'primary idea' of these institutes was that they should be places where the Anglican soldier could 'find and talk to his chaplain'. Similarly, they afforded an opportunity for chaplains 'to make the personal acquaintance of their men, and on occasion to offer them words of spiritual comfort and advice'. By these means, and alluding to the current war in South Africa, Jelf claimed that 'the good resolutions formed on the battle-field, in camp, or bivouac may be fostered and strengthened, and the bad influences that will meet the returning soldier on every side, be avoided and overcome'.[273]

Part of the impetus for these soldiers' institutes was provided by the Guild of the Holy Standard, a military counterpart of the Ritualist guilds which emerged in the Church of England during the mid-Victorian period.[274] As with so many religious initiatives in the army at this time, the Guild of the Holy Standard originated in Aldershot, being founded in 1873 by J.C. Edghill with the purpose of supporting Anglican communicants and of giving 'Christian soldiers working for Jesus Christ the requisite "help and a sense of comradeship" '.[275] Embracing chaplains, officers and other ranks alike, the Guild's early adherents included the future Lord Kitchener (who was also a member of the English Church Union) and those responsible for establishing the first Church of England Soldiers' Institute at Aldershot.[276] Enthusiastically supported by Bishop Claughton, an annual 'festival service' at St. Paul's Cathedral soon became a fixture of the Guild's calendar. At one of these gatherings, Canon Beach delivered an address that detailed the duties of the guildsmen. These included almsgiving, the visitation of 'the sick and needy', assisting at services, acting as Sunday school teachers, befriending new recruits, circulating 'the Holy Scriptures, Prayer Books, and tracts etc., approved by the Chaplains' and encouraging soldiers and their families to present themselves for baptism and Holy Communion.[277] At its annual general meeting in 1898, Edghill praised the rules of the Guild as 'simple, manly, and English' and promised that 'everything was possible for the chaplain who had round him a number of guildsmen, honest and true-hearted, faithful witnesses for Christ'. Nevertheless, by this time it was already apparent that the Guild was in difficulties. While even Edghill accepted that it was an object of suspicion to some chaplains, W.F. Thompson (a chaplain of the Indian Ecclesiastical Establishment who was then on leave from India) noted a worrying decline in membership. Additionally, it was noted that guildsmen were being outshone as communicants by members of the evangelical and non-denominational Soldiers' Christian Association, an offshoot of the Y.M.C.A.[278]

Besides fostering links with the ordinary soldier through soldiers' institutes and the Guild of the Holy Standard, there was also a discernible shift towards a more populist style of ministry. By 1896, for example, Ewen Macpherson, a junior chaplain at the Curragh, was providing magic lantern shows and leading temperance outings to local beauty spots in commandeered ambulance vehicles.[279] This approach was very much to Edghill's taste, the Chaplain-General having declared eight years earlier that 'I hate what is called an officer's chaplain [and] I do everything to discourage such tendencies in every possible way.'[280] Significantly, this pastoral style may well have proved most congenial to Ritualist chaplains who claimed to be more conscious of their sacerdotal status than of their relative rank. Paul Bull, for example, a priest of the Community of the Resurrection, was a tireless and familiar visitor to his flock in their barrack rooms while serving as a probationary chaplain at Aldershot on the eve of the Boer War:

> I used to preach in every barrack-room in my charge, sit down and have tea with the men – 'muck in' with them, as they call it – and then say, 'Now, lads, I want to talk to you about our Saviour.' They would call the men from the other rooms, and when forty or fifty were assembled I showed them pictures of our Lord's sufferings.[281]

Furthermore, Bull very much endeavoured to assist individual soldiers, being particularly attentive to the plight of new recruits:

> Spending most of my time among the men in their barrack-rooms, I soon was able to form a fairly correct opinion as to when [the tyranny of drill sergeants over recruits] was becoming unbearable; and often by a word to the adjutant could get a man transferred to another company, where, under better influence, he could make a fresh start and pick up heart again to do his soldiering well.[282]

However, by the end of the Boer War it would appear that such an approach was generally adopted by junior chaplains; while on manoeuvres in South Africa in 1903, William Drury, a newly commissioned Low Churchman, was diligent in visiting soldiers in their tents, he presided over a tented 'recreation room' and was notably critical of a colleague whom he deplored as an 'officer's chaplain'.[283] Apparently, the scale and duration of the Boer War had done much to promote that affinity between chaplains and soldiers that Edghill had long encouraged and which had characterised the experience of active service in earlier years. In his address to the Church Congress of 1900, Colonel Jelf had drawn attention to the 'energetic, zealous, self-denying young clergymen' who comprised 'the present set of Army chaplains' in South Africa:

> Tramping with the men in their long and weary marches, often helping to carry their rifles or ammunition, bivouacking with them in the open, sharing their homely rations (or, not infrequently, want of rations!), fearlessly exposing themselves when the battle begins, attending and praying with the wounded and dying when it rages most – these are the things that have drawn men's affections to the chaplains, and that have won their hearts to God.[284]

By dint of their example and through the familiar and invigorating style of their services, Jelf insisted that soldiers were at last learning to 'value their chaplain as their friend, and his ministrations as their blessings'.[285]

Emblematic of these developments were the essays of E.J. Hardy, a senior Anglican chaplain who portrayed the ordinary soldier with remarkable sympathy and candour. Although some were published in the 1890s in the *United Service Magazine*,[286] a collected edition of Hardy's essays appeared in the aftermath of the Boer War under the title *Pen Portraits of the British Soldier*. In this volume, Hardy was keen to stress the rapport that now existed between chaplains and the other ranks:

> When a Chaplain goes into a barrack-room, and sits on a form or on a man's cot, and talks to a group of soldiers who are cleaning their things for parade or guard-mounting next day, he learns from them their sentiments and ways of looking at things as their own officers could not. A man is settling the small amount of property that his black box and kit bag contains. He shows you a book or some other keepsake from a mother or teacher, and the fact that this is treasured up gives an insight into his character. One day not long ago I sat down to have a yarn with the men of one room round the fire. Before long a man got up, went to his kit box, and producing a cigarette, asked me with the grace of a perfect gentleman to accept it, as he had nothing else to offer.[287]

However, such testimony was not sufficient to allay persistent doubts as to the chaplain's commission and relative rank. When the Convocation of Canterbury discussed the means of providing supplementary chaplains for South Africa in February 1900, the Bishop of Coventry enthused about the case of a clergyman in the diocese of Worcester who had gone out to the Boer War as:

> [A] trooper Chaplain in the Yeomanry, having obtained the Bishop's sanction. He goes through the drill with all the other privates; but he means to act as a chaplain as well as a trooper. We have heard some of the difficulties of officer-chaplains. One wonders if it would be possible that we could have chaplains enlisted as privates . . . I was told this young clergyman has gone out, and that he was very popular, and they say that he is the right man in the right place.[288]

In reply, the Archdeacon of Exeter expressed reservations about combining the role of clergyman and combatant but instead waxed lyrical about another 'special chaplain' whom his diocese had dispatched to work among 'Devonshire troops in

South Africa'. Although he would be under the orders of the Chaplain-General, he would not be an official member of the Chaplains' Department, the archdeacon observing that 'it is desirable that we should have men with not quite so much of the official stamp about them as the ordinary chaplain'.[289]

In view of this strong and apparently consensual opinion against the chaplain's rank and its concomitants in the higher reaches of the Church of England, Edghill was encouraged to decry its overt distinctions. Hence, in December 1899, the Chaplain-General announced:

> I dislike intensely the chaplain who wants to be an officer. I dislike the chaplains wearing uniform. I have never worn it myself. I want our chaplains to feel that they are simply clergymen, and then they will have infinitely more power over the men. If you go to a man dressed as a colonel then he treats you officially; but go as a simple chaplain, with no military rank, go as a minister of God, and you will be able to get to the heart of the man.[290]

While Edghill made no mention of this fact, the style of chaplaincy he was advocating was already established in the Royal Navy. Although naval chaplains had been commissioned since 1843, they held no relative rank and wore no official uniform, the object being that naval chaplains (though armed with a commission) would be better placed to fulfil their intended role of being 'the friend and adviser of all on board'.[291] Significantly, and because of the prevailing unease over the rank and uniform of army chaplains, the Department's peacetime uniform was quietly abolished in 1902.[292]

Presbyterian Chaplaincy

In the wake of the Crimean War, the War Office was quick to commission Presbyterian chaplains, the Secretary of State's decision to commission five Presbyterian chaplains being formally announced in June 1858.[293] In contrast with its Anglican counterpart, Presbyterian chaplaincy in the post-Crimean army evolved quite smoothly over the next fifty years. The Presbyterian ministers of the Chaplains' Department were not unduly disturbed by Wesleyan assertiveness, troubled by formal legal challenges to their ministry or dogged by lengthy controversy over the rise of Ritualism. Nevertheless, Presbyterian chaplaincy was still complicated by the competing claims of Britain's several Presbyterian churches and by the practicalities of ministering to a religious, and largely ethnic, minority.

Although gravely weakened by the Disruption of 1843,[294] as Britain's only established Presbyterian Church the claim of the Church of Scotland to the lion's share of these commissions was never in doubt. The first Church of Scotland Chaplains to the Forces were commissioned on 1 July 1858,[295] that of Francis Cannon being antedated to April 1855 in recognition of his services in the Crimea.[296] However, by 1858 other Presbyterian churches were also heavily involved in army chaplaincy; the Free Church of Scotland had furnished acting chaplains for the Crimea and Presbyterian ministers in England and Ireland were serving as officiating clergymen, a Presbyterian minister being employed on a full-time basis at the Curragh on a salary of £175 per annum by 1856.[297] Perhaps because of its connections with the Curragh, the General Assembly of the Irish Presbyterian church was especially anxious to make itself heard in chaplaincy matters. In May 1855, it rebuked the War Office over the scale of allowances that had been introduced for officiating clergymen the previous year, claiming that the preferential rates afforded to Anglicans were unjust, especially because 'the course of preparatory Education' for Presbyterian ministers was both longer and more expensive 'than that which is required in the Church of England'.[298] Irish Presbyterians also called for Presbyterian ministers to be commissioned as Chaplains to the Forces.[299] However, having secured the Secretary of State's agreement to commission two Irish ministers, the Irish General Assembly lost the initiative by badly mishandling its nominations in July 1858.

With a majority in the Assembly wishing to assert the independence and authority of the church, it proceeded to make two nominations rather than send a list of candidates to the War Office from which the Secretary of State could make his selection.[300] Given this attitude, and the unseemly divisions which these nominations had caused within the Assembly, Peel turned to the Church of Scotland for his remaining appointments, the Irish Moderator being curtly informed that '[The Secretary of State] cannot consistently with his public duty select any gentleman for these posts who he has not reason to believe are generally acceptable to the Presbyterian [church] in Ireland, without reference to party or political opinion.'[301] Although the Secretary of State seemed to relent in November 1858, when he at last granted a commission to one of the Assembly's nominees, the *Belfast Mercury* quickly perceived the point he was making and complained that:

> [T]he Assembly has made a sad bungle of this chaplaincy business from first to last. In nominating two members only, it was thought Government could not act otherwise than ratify the appointments. The Government asked for the privilege of a choice – for the right of making a selection; but this was denied, and now we have the Government turning the tables on the Assembly, and out of two selecting one.[302]

For its part, the *Irish Presbyterian* professed to be appalled by the Assembly's actions and drew the attention of its readers to the grubbier issues of faction and patronage that had surrounded these appointments:

> When the Government announced their intention of appointing and supporting a number of Presbyterian chaplains, it is humiliating to find a rush made for the appointments – a regular scramble – even before the negotiations had terminated. The struggle for the appointments very soon assumed a political aspect, so that two political parties in the General Assembly were speedily arrayed against each other, and the struggle resolved itself into the question of their relative strength. There is a great outcry on the part of some, as if the independence of the church were at stake. This is all a sham. It would be far nearer the truth to represent the whole affair, so far as the Assembly has been convulsed by it, as a contest for 10s 6d a-day between two political sections of the General Assembly.[303]

Despite this shambolic intervention from Ireland, Presbyterian chaplaincy was largely a Scottish affair. However, the proportion of Scots and of Presbyterians in the British army was in chronic decline throughout most of the nineteenth century. Whereas nearly 14 per cent of the army's rank and file were Scottish in 1840, by 1899 this proportion had fallen to only 8 per cent. Consequently, whereas Presbyterians comprised nearly 11 per cent of the army's other ranks in the early 1860s, by the late 1890s they comprised only 7 per cent.[304] Hence, the number of Presbyterian Chaplains to the Forces was never very large. Only five commissions were granted to Presbyterian ministers in 1858 and this number of commissioned Presbyterian chaplains was the same twenty years later.[305] In the 1880s, however, the demands of occupation duties in Egypt and the comparatively favourable ratio of Presbyterian chaplains to soldiers allowed by the War Office saw this number climb to eight.[306] On the eve of the Boer War eight Presbyterian chaplains remained on the Army List, a number that nevertheless represented only 10 per cent of the Chaplains' Department.[307]

Despite their modest representation in the Chaplains' Department, the General Assembly of the Church of Scotland was not content to consign its chaplains to the management of an Anglican Chaplain-General, least of all one brought up in the Scottish Episcopal church. In 1860, the General Assembly appointed a standing committee to oversee the work of its chaplains in the army and the Royal Navy.[308] Four years later, the Moderator was made an *ex officio* co-convenor and the committee was endowed with the authority to liase with the War Office over chaplaincy matters. In a further curtailment of Gleig's shrinking powers, in 1864 the War Office excluded the Chaplain-General from any direction of Presbyterian chaplains and made them directly accountable to the Permanent Under Secretary.[309] However, this close relationship between military officialdom and the Church of Scotland did not preclude other Presbyterian churches from pressing their claims upon the War Office. In 1877, the newly formed Presbyterian Church of England appointed a Soldiers and Sailors Committee of its own, a committee which soon established that no English minister was serving as a Chaplain to the Forces. Although the War Office rejected a claim for parity from this quarter in 1882 on the grounds that the small number of commissioned Presbyterian chaplains it required could easily be supplied from Scotland or Ireland (where the vast majority of the army's Presbyterian soldiers hailed from in any case) ministers of the Presbyterian Church of England continued to serve as officiating clergymen at several stations in England.[310]

However, a much less marginal case was that of the Presbyterian Church in Ireland. An insight into the pressures that could be brought to bear on the War Office from this quarter (particularly given the electoral and religious cross-currents of the Home Rule question) is provided by the correspondence which eventually resulted in the appointment of J.M. Simms in 1887. In February 1885, the General Assembly wrote to the Marquis of Hartington recommending three Irish ministers for a commission – despite the fact that there was then no vacancy on the Department's Presbyterian establishment.[311] However, a letter in support of one of these candidates stated the compelling pastoral and political reasons for an additional Irish Presbyterian chaplain:

> My Lord, The Presbyterians of the North of Ireland have requested me to draw your attention to the small proportion of their ministers who hold chaplaincies in the army . . . You are well aware that the most reliable regiments, and the regiments most frequently chosen for the most difficult and arduous duties are members of the [Presbyterian] Church. They therefore more frequently need spiritual advisers: surely then it is the duty of the government to see that they are well supplied. The General Assembly have recommended to your special notice the Rev Robert Taylor Bailey [of Strangford] as a gentleman well fitted for this work, and have I understand sent you his name which has been unanimously chosen by them. I am positive that your granting their request would be accepted with gratitude, indeed this small favour would be an acknowledgment of your desire to encourage the most loyal Liberals in Ireland.[312]

A further letter written by an M.P., Dr. John Kinnear, also alluded to the electoral implications of the issue, urging that '[Bailey's] appointment will gratify much the Presbyterian Church of Ireland, who, through her official Committee, has warmly commended him.'[313] Undeterred by the unenthusiastic response of the Permanent Under Secretary, whose concerns were primarily financial,[314] the General Assembly wrote another letter to the War Office in June 1885 suggesting the name of J.M. Simms for equal consideration.[315] In the event, and with an eye to the army estimates, Hartington stood his ground and it was left to one of his Conservative successors, Edward Stanhope, to appoint Simms in February 1887 upon the retirement of James Spiers, a long-serving chaplain of the Irish Presbyterian church.[316]

In contrast to the English and Irish Presbyterian churches, the principal problem of the Church of Scotland was not the intransigence of the War Office but a degree of uncertainty about the place of military chaplaincy within the overall scheme of the Church's ministry. In 1878, the General Assembly turned its hitherto independent Committee on Army and Navy Chaplains into a sub-committee of its Committee on Colonial Missions and this administrative and financial subordination was only brought to an end in 1900. By this time, the war in South Africa (and the heroic death of one of the sub-committee's more active members, Major-General Andrew Wauchope, while leading the charge of the Highland Brigade at Magersfontein) had served to underline the importance and distinctiveness of its task.[317]

At a local level, the work of the Committee (or Sub-Committee) on Army and Navy Chaplains largely consisted in making sure that the religious needs of Presbyterian soldiers were being met. This task was complicated by the limited supply of Presbyterian Chaplains to the Forces, by the thin sprinkling of Presbyterians at many home and overseas stations and by the shifting deployment of the army's 'Scottish' regiments. While the General Assembly reserved the right to nominate chaplains for commissions, the primary duty of the Committee's convenor was to oversee the Church's provision for the forces as a whole, inspecting the army's home stations and liasing with the War Office as necessary.[318] In view of their scattered constituency, commissioned chaplains of the Church of Scotland were usually posted to stations in England, their deployment being subject to frequent review.[319] Furthermore, the Committee on Army and Navy Chaplains employed a small number of additional chaplains to supplement those 'in the pay of the Government'.[320] Extensive use was also made of officiating Presbyterian clergymen and even of ministers of other denominations. For example, prior to the arrival of a commissioned Church of Scotland chaplain at Preston in 1865, Presbyterian soldiers were marched 'to an Independent chapel' near Fulwood Barracks.[321] While an expedient that was sometimes seen in Great Britain, the need for this kind of pragmatism was even greater overseas. In 1884 a general order was issued which formalised existing practice by stating that 'Where a minister of one of the three recognised Protestant denominations is not available, officers and soldiers of that denomination may attend the services of either of the other denominations that they may elect.'[322]

Given the Anglican hegemony in the Chaplains' Department (and the High Church to Ritualist leanings of many Anglican chaplains) Presbyterians and Wesleyans were often pushed into an alliance with one another. For example, Rule's protégé, the acting Wesleyan chaplain C.H. Kelly, struck up a close and lasting friendship with the Crimean veteran Francis Cannon, whom Kelly described as 'a very broad churchman' despite his allegiance to an established, Presbyterian church.[323] Nevertheless, this alliance of convenience between two churches so very different in their theology and traditions was not always productive of happy results. As Permanent Under Secretary, Sir Ralph Thompson noted that 'the Presbyterian church bodies' were basically uncomfortable with having to surrender Presbyterian troops to the care of other denominations and, at Cairo in the 1880s, one Presbyterian soldier was even imprisoned for refusing to attend local Wesleyan services.[324]

Wesleyan Chaplaincy

Wesleyan work in the army mushroomed after W.H. Rule began his pioneering venture at Aldershot, the Wesleyan Conference of 1859 denoting 'the ministration of the Gospel to the Wesleyan portion of the Army' as 'a long-neglected duty'.[325] Roused by the mutual exhortations of their respective conferences, from the late 1850s Wesleyans across the empire threw themselves into this burgeoning work.[326] In 1860, the Army Committee, which had been established the previous year, unanimously recommended to Conference 'the appointment of Chaplains on principal military stations, so far as funds may be available for that purpose'.[327] By 1878, no fewer than twenty-four 'acting chaplains' (i.e. 'ministers without a commission, but devoting the whole of their time to the troops')[328] were working at twenty-two home and colonial stations, their flocks consisting of sailors as well as soldiers at major naval bases such as Portsmouth, Chatham and Malta.[329] However, this represented only part of the connexion's commitment to the army as 122 Wesleyan clergymen were engaged in full or part-time work with soldiers by 1888.[330]

The co-ordination of this work was initially the responsibility of the Wesleyans' Army Committee. Originally composed of W.H. Rule, the president and secretary of the Wesleyan Conference and those members of its Home Missionary Committee who happened to be resident in London,[331] this body was completely reorganised in 1878 in order to include more 'Ministers and Laymen interested in Methodist work in the Army and Royal Navy'.[332] Re-designated the Army and Navy Sub-Committee, it was accountable to the Wesleyan Home and Foreign missionary committees – although its work was largely financed from Home Mission funds.[333] Besides liasing with the War Office and advising Conference on military matters, one of the principal duties of this body was to appoint ministers for army and navy work. In keeping with the precedent of Rule's mission to Aldershot (which had been established under the aegis of the London District) and no doubt conscious of the friction that could arise between the chaplains and clergy of other denominations, the Wesleyans at first tried to ensure that their chaplains operated within the established hierarchy of circuits and districts.[334] However, given the conflicting pressures involved, this attempt to ensure harmony by integrating chaplains into normal church structures proved unsustainable. Hence, in 1888 Conference decided that:

> Ministers who are appointed to Army and Navy Work are not to be considered as Ministers of the Circuit in which they may be stationed, so as to be claimed for Circuit work, unless special arrangements be made with the Army and Navy Sub-Committee. After their proper work has been efficiently done, they may give such help to the Circuit as they can, but only by arrangement in writing between the Superintendent of the Circuit and the Army and Navy Sub-Committee. Their personal conduct is to be under the cognisance of the Superintendent of the Circuit and the District Synod, subject to the before-mentioned conditions.[335]

In 1901, and in further recognition of the separate status of their work, the Army and Navy Sub-Committee resolved:

> [T]hat a meeting of our Ministers set apart for Army and Navy work and of such others officiating for the benefit of our Methodist Soldiers and Sailors . . . be held not less than once in six months for conference and inquiry as to the conditions of the work in the various stations, as well as for mutual counsel and encouragement.[336]

The onerous ministry of the diligent Wesleyan chaplain at a home station was captured in the memoirs of C.H. Kelly, who was appointed to Chatham in 1861 with the additional brief of initiating work 'for Wesleyans in the Royal Navy' at Sheerness.[337] Fifty years later, Kelly reflected on his six years at Chatham:

> When I look at my pile of written sermons I sometimes wonder how, with the daily work in hospitals, visitation of barracks, prison, and my classes, both religious and secular, almost every night, they were ever so carefully written . . . My sermon-book shows that I preached for military parade services 556 times, at voluntary services at Manor Street Chapel 96, and, in addition, voluntarily in the chapels of the Rochester Circuit 167. These are all entered with dates and texts, but do not include all; still, without counting those sermonettes preached in hospital, they total up to 819.[338]

Notwithstanding his heavy preaching commitments, Kelly's principal success at Chatham lay in his creation of a Wesleyan soldiers' home in 1861. Its facilities were necessarily basic (it was begun in the basement of Manor Street Chapel) but the institution proved to be a great success, its foremost attraction being the evening classes provided by Kelly and his assistants for soldiers aspiring to promotion.[339]

From 1870, the professional needs of the army and the example of other agencies led the Wesleyans to pursue a policy of supporting Wesleyan soldiers' homes wherever they could be established.[340] In contrast to the limited amenities afforded by Kelly's makeshift home at Chatham, a new generation of purpose-built soldiers' homes provided refreshments, accommodation, libraries, prayer rooms and other facilities. Consequently, by the end of the nineteenth century they had become the focus of Wesleyan work in the army, providing an ideal setting for the missionary work of the Wesleyan chaplain despite their ostensibly open and non-denominational character. Although they were established through local initiatives and were managed by local committees, the Wesleyan authorities were keen to ensure that ultimate control lay elsewhere. In 1887, Conference charged Wesleyan chaplains with rendering an account of local homes in their quarterly reports to district synods.[341] It also decreed that:

> In addition to the Connexional sanction already required by our Rules before any property can be acquired for Methodist purposes, Ministers or other persons connected with our Societies contemplating the erection or acquisition of a Soldiers' or Sailors' Home shall communicate with the Army and Navy Sub-Committee; and no binding arrangements shall be entered into until the written consent of the Home Mission Committee and of the Foreign Missionary Committee respectively shall have been received.[342]

In 1900, Conference tightened its control by creating a standard set of rules and a single board of trustees for all Wesleyan homes. These rules confirmed their policy of openness to soldiers and sailors of all denominations while upholding their teetotal traditions and stipulating that the worship and teaching which occurred on these premises should be in accordance with Wesleyan doctrine.[343]

By 1899, no fewer than thirty-two Wesleyan homes were in operation throughout Britain and the empire, representing an investment by the Army and Navy Sub-Committee of more than £42,000.[344] However, besides the generosity of the Wesleyan church, government support for these homes had also been a vital factor in their expansion. Recognising the value of their work, the War Office, the Admiralty and the India Office made government land available during the latter decades of the nineteenth century, a fact that did not escape the jealous attention of the Chaplain-General, J.C. Edghill.[345] In addition to grants of land, the costs of Wesleyan army work were partly defrayed by the grants and capitation fees paid by the War Office from 1881. By this time, the financial strain under which the Wesleyan church had been placed in pursuing its army work had been evident for some years and, notwithstanding an ingrained reluctance to countenance 'State aid', by the 1870s there was 'a growing feeling in the Connexion that it was not right that the trustees of chapels to which troops were marched for divine service should make provision for them without receiving any remuneration for the seats thus occupied'.[346] Hence, in the late 1870s the Army and Navy Sub-Committee was involved in tortuous and ultimately fruitless negotiations with the War Office for the payment of 'seat rents'. However, with the advent of Gladstone's Liberal government in April 1880 the War Office conceded much more than the Sub-Committee's original demands by granting capitation payments to Wesleyan ministers in January 1881, thus according them full recognition as officiating clergymen.[347] Furthermore, the War Office began to pay grants towards the maintenance of Wesleyan chaplains at nine of the army's largest stations in mainland Britain. By 1898, these grants amounted to more than £1,500 per annum – the equivalent of one-third of the Home Mission Fund's expenditure on army work.[348]

While Wesleyans were willing to accept a measure of state recognition and support, commissions for their chaplains were ruled out until the outbreak of the First World War. Besides the delicate questions surrounding the barriers raised by rank, the possible temptations of the officers' mess and the acceptance of further assistance from the state, it was widely feared that the commissioning of Wesleyan 'Army Ministers' would weaken the authority of the church and would impact in particular on the freedom of Conference to dispose of its ministers.[349] Ruled out by the Army and Navy Sub-Committee in 1891, an offer by the War Office to grant permanent commissions to five Wesleyan chaplains in 1900 was discussed at length but eventually rejected in 1903, after the Sub-Committee had resolved that:

> Conference should be advised that it will best promote the true efficiency of its work in the Army . . . by not receiving Commissions for its Ministers, but by continuing to place them at the disposal of the Secretary of State as Acting Chaplains, whilst at the same time retaining them in that complete and intimate relation to itself which has hitherto obtained.[350]

However, this decision caused deep frustration in certain quarters. While it may have prompted at least one acting chaplain to resign and transfer his allegiance to the Church of England,[351] in 1906 Owen Spencer Watkins (who was already a veteran of the Sudan and South Africa) insisted that the issues involved were not insuperable.[352] His resentment was not assuaged by some tantalising precedents; Wesleyan chaplains had been treated as commissioned officers in previous colonial campaigns and, more recently, extraordinary commissions had been granted to facilitate Wesleyan participation in key public events. In 1900, R.W. Allen, the Secretary of the Army and Navy Sub-Committee and the Wesleyan chaplain to the London garrison, was given a temporary commission so that he might join a deputation of army chaplains at the celebrations for the inauguration of the Commonwealth of Australia. Furthermore, in Allen's absence his deputy, James Fletcher, was given a uniform and a twenty-four hour commission so that he could participate in the state funeral of Queen Victoria. In fact, when Allen formally retired as a Wesleyan chaplain in November 1901 he was granted the honorary rank of Chaplain First Class and 'as a special case, a pension of

£91–5–0 per annum'.[353] This unconsummated relationship with the army was underscored in 1903 when the names of Wesleyan acting chaplains – along with those of other denominations – were made eligible to appear in the Army Lists.[354]

Although commissions remained objectionable to the Wesleyan authorities, there can be no doubt of their attraction to Watkins and his colleagues. While an enduring system of regular ministerial rotation in the Wesleyan church helped to prepare acting chaplains for the upheavals of army life,[355] it was naturally galling to serve alongside commissioned chaplains at home and overseas and to be denied the salary, status and perquisites accorded to them. In 1879, the minimum salary for a Wesleyan minister was £150 a year if married and £80 if unmarried, much less than the salary afforded to even the most junior Fourth Class chaplains.[356] Likewise, and instead of the generous pension paid to a chaplain First Class upon retirement, as late as the early 1900s a Wesleyan minister with forty years' service could look forward to a pension of only £54 per annum.[357] The disparity between the lot of the acting chaplain and that of his commissioned counterpart was even more glaring on campaign. As Watkins complained in 1906:

> The experience gained during the war in South Africa has shown that the position of the Wesleyan chaplain might and should be improved. Up to the present all Wesleyan chaplains going on active service have been given rank and pay merely on the authority of a 'War Office Letter'. The result has been that the chaplain's position is hard to define, and he may find himself treated either as a military officer or as a civilian, according to the convenience of the general under whom he is serving, or as the chief of staff may see fit to interpret his credentials.[358]

To add insult to injury:

> At the close of the campaign also, when officers are rewarded for their services, and chaplains amongst them, receiving special promotion, and such honours as the 'Distinguished Service Order', no reward of any sort is given to Wesleyan chaplains. During the South African War three at least of the Wesleyan chaplains should have been so rewarded, chaplains of other Churches whose service was no more distinguished receiving rewards; the only reason that could be given for passing over the Wesleyans being that they were not eligible, as they were civilians.[359]

Despite their ambiguous status, from the early 1870s the Wesleyans sent many acting chaplains overseas with the help of a letter of introduction from the War Office. In 1874, Edward Cardwell allowed John Laverack to sail to the Gold Coast to minister to troops preparing for Wolseley's campaign against the Ashantis. Laverack's letter of introduction entitled him to rations and lodgings at Cape Coast Castle but he held no military rank and received no pay for his subsequent part in the Ashanti War.[360] However, for the Egyptian campaign of 1882, the War Office was in a more magnanimous mood, two Wesleyan chaplains enjoying the pay, allowances, uniform and notional status of Fourth Class chaplains.[361] Thus, by the outbreak of the Boer War, which has been hailed as 'the apogee of Wesleyan chaplaincy work',[362] the Army and Navy Sub-Committee was well practised in the selection and deployment of its acting chaplains for active service – Wesleyan chaplains having seen service in West Africa, Zululand, the Transvaal, Egypt, the Sudan and Burma.[363] Accordingly, shortly after the outbreak of war with the Boer republics, it sent E.P. Lowry to Cape Town to serve as the senior Wesleyan chaplain in South Africa. Once again, the War Office obliged by granting notional rank, Lowry's being that of a Third Class chaplain while his subordinates enjoyed the status of Fourth Class chaplains.[364]

Roman Catholic Chaplaincy

Even after the Crimean War, the agitation of Catholic Irish M.P.s, an apprehension of the seditious potential of dissident Irish priests and the bigotry of many British Protestants conspired to ensure that the commissioning of Roman Catholic army chaplains remained a sensitive and contentious issue. Consequently, when the War Office grasped the nettle in June 1858 the business was undertaken with the least possible fanfare. In a letter from the War Office, the Bishop of Southwark, Thomas Grant, was requested to recommend a number of priests 'for the office of Assistant Chaplain, for [the] consideration and approval of the Secretary of State'.[365] Three days later, the impending appointment of Roman Catholic 'assistant-chaplains' with the pay and allowances of their Anglican counterparts was announced by the Deputy Adjutant-General in a circular to all commanding officers.[366] Grant's nominations were eventually made in January and February 1859 and nineteen Roman Catholic chaplains were duly commissioned the following April.[367] Of these, four were currently serving as acting chaplains in India (and being paid by the Government of India) and eight were veterans of the Crimean War.[368] Despite the caution that surrounded these appointments, the management of Roman Catholic chaplaincy proved to be remarkably uncontroversial for the War Office in subsequent years, especially in comparison with its Anglican equivalent. In a letter to *The Times* in October 1885, Gleig ascribed this situation to the episcopal oversight which was exercised over the army's Roman Catholic chaplains by the Bishop of Southwark:

> The Roman Catholic Army chaplains are under the pastoral supervision of a special prelate . . . On his recommendation all appointments are made. From him each chaplain receives his faculties. Under his eye and by his instructions all spiritual functions are discharged, and a mandate from him severs at once the military priest from his flock, whether the Government be willing to lose his services or not . . . By this same prelate, also, the soldiers and their children are confirmed, the soldiers' burying places are consecrated, and the soldiers' altars hallowed. The Roman Catholic soldiers have, in short, their spiritual head, whose word is with them law. And do not let me forget to add that in consequence of all this the Roman Catholic chaplains are confessedly most zealous in the discharge of their duties, and to the authorities at the War Office and the Horse Guards the least troublesome of all Army chaplains.[369]

However, the situation was not as straightforward as Gleig imagined. Firstly, he greatly exaggerated the authority of the Bishop of Southwark, who was by no means an army bishop in the continental mould. In the wake of the Crimean War, the Vatican's Congregation for Extraordinary Ecclesiastical Affairs had made it very clear that it did not wish to see a Roman Catholic bishop for the British army; nevertheless, Rome did grant extraordinary faculties to commissioned chaplains on a trial basis in April 1859.[370] Secondly, and for a combination of nationalist, jurisdictional and financial reasons, the Roman Catholic hierarchy in Ireland refused to accept the presence of Chaplains to the Forces in their dioceses. In fact, due to such *amour propre*, the first commissioned chaplains to be sent to Ireland had to be withdrawn and, in 1863, Bishop Grant of Southwark had to concede that in Ireland the army's Catholic soldiers would be served by officiating clergymen.[371] Hence, by 1865 pastoral care of the Curragh had passed to the dioceses of Kildare and Leighlin, with the parish priests of Newbridge and Naas being paid, respectively, allowances of £70 and £10 per annum for their ministry to Roman Catholic soldiers in the camp.[372]

If the Irish bishops were determined to guard their dioceses against intruders appointed in England, Irish M.P.s continued to show an active interest in the spiritual welfare of the Roman Catholic soldier. Although a growing hostility towards the army among Irish nationalists helped to reduce the proportion of Roman Catholics from 28.7 per cent of the army's rank and file in 1868 to 17.7 per cent thirty years later,[373] the spiritual interests of the Catholic soldier were still being championed from the Irish benches in the House of Commons. For example, soon after the outbreak of the Zulu War in 1879, the Secretary of State for War, Colonel Frederick Stanley, was taken to task over the provision of Roman Catholic chaplains for the troops in South Africa. As *The Times* reported:

> Mr. [George] Errington [M.P. for Longford] asked the Secretary of State for War whether he had already arranged that Catholic chaplains should accompany the reinforcements for the Cape; if not, whether he would take the necessary steps in order that the Catholic officers and soldiers should not be left without the assistance of ministers of their religion.[374]

Stanley meekly replied that one commissioned chaplain had been chosen to join the troops in Zululand and that Lord Chelmsford had 'already engaged the services of a local priest'.[375] However, attention later focused on the provision of Roman Catholic chaplains on troopships bound for India, the largest of which were provided by the Royal Navy and so constituted a jurisdictional no-man's land.[376] Significantly, interested Protestants appear to have been inspired and even chastened by this kind of pressure upon the authorities. Roused by Errington's questions on the subject of Catholic chaplains for Zululand in 1879, other M.P.s soon raised questions on behalf of Presbyterian and Wesleyan chaplains.[377] At the Church Congress of 1885, J.C. Edghill invoked the salutary example of the Catholic approach to chaplaincy matters in general, declaring that 'The Roman Catholic soldiers are cared for by the Roman Catholic Church in a manner that ought to shame us.' He then proceeded to compare the fruits of Catholic activism with those of Anglican inertia, stressing in particular the role played by Roman Catholic M.P.s:

> Not long ago it was customary for only the Church of England chaplains to sail in our troop ships, but the Roman Catholic body said, 'Our soldiers are unprovided for in these ships, and it is the duty of the State to see that these men have chaplains sent with them.' I should like to know when the Church of England would have said that to the State . . . Year by year the number of Roman Catholic clergy thus required is increasing, for their Church takes good care to make its wants known . . . I hope there are some members of Parliament present; it must have struck everybody who read the papers to see how frequently questions have been asked in the House of Commons about Roman Catholic soldiers and chaplains. Some time ago a return was called for of the number of chaplains serving in Egypt, and it was found that the Roman Catholic chaplains were only one less in number than those of the Church of England, although the proportion of Roman Catholic soldiers is only one to three compared with those belonging to the Church of England. They had taken good care that their interests were looked after, whilst we had been asleep.[378]

However, the successful development of Roman Catholic chaplaincy in the army also owed much to the background and diplomacy of Bishop Thomas Grant of Southwark. Such were Grant's achievements in dealing with government that Bishop Ullathorne of Birmingham wrote on Grant's death in 1870: 'All our really successful negotiations with Government for military chaplains, for mitigation of aggressive laws, for the navy, for workhouses, etc., etc., have been, directly or indirectly, accomplished through him.'[379] Significantly, Grant had been born among the army of occupation in France in 1816, his father being a veteran of Waterloo and a sergeant in the 71st Highlanders.[380] Very much a son of the regiment, he had attended the regimental school of the 71st and may even have served as one of its drummer boys.[381] However, despite his Irish ancestry and his early upbringing in a Scottish regiment, Grant's clerical formation was emphatically English. Placed at the age of ten in the care of a Catholic priest in Chester, he later trained for the priesthood at Ushaw and at the English College in Rome before being ordained in 1841. After serving as the secretary to Cardinal Acton, Grant became the rector of the English College in 1844. As the agent of the English Vicars Apostolic in Rome, Grant played an important role in negotiating the restoration of the Catholic hierarchy in England, his performance earning him the admiration of the English bishops and strengthening his reputation as 'the foremost canon lawyer in the English Church'.[382] Appointed to Southwark in 1851, Grant was young, capable and endowed with an exceptional knowledge of the army. Furthermore, he was distinctly out of sympathy with Irish nationalism, once saying of the Irish and their politicians 'They abuse the Government till they get something, and then they frustrate it if they can.'[383]

The original diocese of Southwark comprised the whole of the south-east of England and much of the south coast, embracing many of the country's most important military and naval stations. Hence, in the running of his new diocese Grant was dealing with the War Office from a very early stage.[384] During the Crimean War and the Indian Mutiny, the War Office turned to Grant for help in providing acting Roman Catholic chaplains and he was ideally placed to negotiate the appointment, control and direction of Roman Catholic Chaplains to the Forces. In January 1859, Jonathan Peel, the Secretary of State for War, finally agreed that 'while the selection of [Roman Catholic] Chaplains will be left to their own spiritual superiors, the right of rejecting any gentlemen so recommended, is reserved to the Secretary of State for War, who can alone recommend them for appointment by the Crown, and advise the recall of their commissions'. Despite this blunt assertion of his authority, Peel agreed to revoke the commission of any Roman Catholic chaplain whose faculties had been withdrawn and to place Catholic chaplains under the military direction of the Permanent Under Secretary. These concessions served to safeguard episcopal control over Catholic chaplains while freeing them from the authority of an Anglican Chaplain-General. Nevertheless, Grant was warned that the lot of Roman Catholic chaplains would be similar to that of their Protestant peers in other respects and he was advised that 'They will . . . equally with Chaplains of the Churches of England and Scotland be required to fill up all returns and obey all such secular instructions as are issued to them.'[385]

Given that much has been written about the role of the Irish priest in the Irish ghettoes of Victorian Britain,[386] it is significant that the Roman Catholic soldiers of the British army, who remained largely Irish by birth, were increasingly served by English-born priests from English dioceses. While this may have been reassuring for the military authorities, it was also a function of the means whereby Roman Catholic chaplains were appointed. Under the new dispensation, applicants were obliged to secure the permission of their ordinaries before approaching the Bishop of Southwark with a view to being recommended for a chaplain's commission.[387] This situation militated against Irish applicants for, while the Irish hierarchy had rejected the system of commissioned chaplains from the outset, there was a growing hostility towards the army among the Irish clergy throughout this period. In December 1895, a prospective chaplain and son of a former soldier wrote from Toronto to Bishop John Butt:

> I can supply all the testimonials required, but would rather that no communication should be sent to my Archbishop until my appointment would be certain, for the very natural reason that as unfortunately nearly all Irishmen look upon it as a disgrace to be connected with the Service in any way my life in the diocese as a candidate for army chaplain would not be very happy. More than once my brethren in the clergy here have cast it up to me as something of a disgrace! that my father served his Queen and country.[388]

In view of this situation, the majority of priests who were commissioned were recruited from England. Of the twelve Roman Catholic commissioned chaplains on the Army List in 1899, only one had been born in Ireland; ten had been trained in English seminaries at home or abroad and at least eleven had been ordained for English dioceses.[389] It was also indicative of the strong links which had developed between the army and the southern dioceses of England that none of the army's chaplains in 1899 were regular priests and all but two came from the dioceses of Westminster, Southwark and Portsmouth, the latter having been carved out of Southwark in 1882.[390]

When the Roman Catholic hierarchy was restored in England and Wales in 1850, the average stipend of diocesan priests was in the region of £35–£40 per annum, with their curates receiving even less.[391] Obviously, a commission in the post-Crimean Chaplains' Department was vastly remunerative in comparison. Furthermore, and in stark contrast to the situation that obtained in the Church of England, former army chaplains were often promoted after retirement as their careers had provided them with a significant public role and equipped them with vital experience in dealing with the British establishment. This was dramatically illustrated during the Zulu War, when James Bellord had the unenviable task of receiving the body of the Prince Imperial after his death in an ambush in June 1879, a stunningly embarrassing blow to the British army and to the British government alike. As Prince Louis Napoleon was a devout Roman Catholic, Bellord was called upon to help salvage some dignity from the proceedings. A contemporary photograph of the funeral parade shows him in his biretta and stole reading prayers over the prince's coffin while another witness described an 'R.C. priest in his full stoles etc.' walking in front of Lord Chelmsford in the funeral procession.[392] By virtue of their experience and connections, by 1900 several former Roman Catholic Chaplains to the Forces had been chosen by the Vatican to become bishops of dioceses with strong military connections. These included John Butt (who became auxiliary Bishop of Southwark in 1884 and Bishop of Southwark in 1885); John Vertue (who was the first Bishop of Portsmouth); Robert Brindle (who became auxiliary Bishop of Westminster in 1899) and James Bellord (who in 1899 was appointed Bishop of Milevis and Vicar Apostolic of Gibraltar).[393] In any event, throughout their army careers Roman Catholic chaplains were more integrated into civilian church life than were their Anglican counterparts. In fact, several used their substantial means to finance new missions while posted to stations in southern England. James Bellord, for example, inaugurated a new mission while attached to the fortifications at Fareham.[394]

Despite the national differences between English Roman Catholic chaplains and their largely Irish flocks, there is no evidence to suggest that these worked to their disadvantage. By the later decades of the nineteenth century there was little difference in Roman Catholic devotional life on either side of the Irish Sea and by this time Roman Catholics throughout the British Isles shared an exalted, Ultramontane view of the priesthood that served to place Roman Catholic chaplains on a rather different plane from their Anglican, Presbyterian or Wesleyan equivalents.[395] Given the complete ascendancy of the Roman Catholic clergy in their church and the relatively small number of Roman Catholic officers in the army, a distinct advantage enjoyed by the Catholic chaplain (especially over his Anglican counterpart) was that his authority was much less likely to be challenged by opinionated officers. A further factor that strengthened their spiritual authority was that the army's Roman Catholic chaplains clearly viewed their rank as subordinate to their sacerdotal office. When the idea of a chaplain's uniform was still being mooted in 1859, Bishop Grant had complained to John Vertue:

> I have just heard that a chaplain's uniform is being talked of . . . When the chaplains had a uniform in France they had to attend parade, and it will do

> more than anything to subject them to military authorities. How could you, a Monsignor, wear a military uniform? Try to find out if this news be true. I shall hate the sight of soldiers for ever if priests are to be thus reduced.[396]

Roman Catholic chaplains clearly benefited from a general recognition that their rank was transcended by their priestly status, a situation that enabled them to relate to both officers and other ranks with comparative ease. Even Byron Farwell, a historian who is largely dismissive of the chaplain's role in the late Victorian army, acknowledged that 'For the most part . . . it was the Roman Catholics who won the respect of the troops, whatever their denomination.'[397]

To a significant extent, the good reputation of Roman Catholic chaplains in the late Victorian army rested on the fame of Robert Brindle ('Father Brindle' to all ranks) who was widely celebrated on account of his extensive service in the Sudan. During the Gordon Relief expedition of 1884–5, Brindle marched with the men instead of riding with the officers and took his turn at the oars as the men of the 1st Royal Irish Regiment rowed up the Nile.[398] If this was a populist approach, Brindle's efforts were nevertheless highly regarded by senior officers. For his part in the expedition, Brindle was promoted to chaplain First Class and awarded the D.S.O.[399] As Sir Evelyn Wood testified:

> Father Brindle was doubtless the most popular man in the Expedition. His own flock naturally loved him, and he was respected by everyone, from Bugler to Lord Wolseley, who more than once tried to get him knighted. He had a pony which he never rode, it being used to carry foot-sore men in turn.[400]

Furthermore, in 1900 Winston Churchill made an unfavourable comparison between Anglican chaplains in South Africa and 'the venerable figure and noble character of Father Brindle', who had served as senior chaplain in the Sudan two years earlier.[401] After its reconquest in 1898, Kitchener resumed attempts to secure a knighthood for the army's favourite Roman Catholic priest but the honour was finally 'ruled out as inappropriate for a chaplain'.[402] Nevertheless, by this time even the Wesleyans had joined the chorus of Brindle's admirers, Owen Spencer Watkins writing of his fellow chaplains in the Sudan:

> [C]hief among them [was] that man beloved of all ranks, Father Brindle, of the Roman Catholic Church. No other man in the Chaplains' Department has seen so much service as he – no Nile campaign, it is said, is complete without Father Brindle; and though over sixty years of age, he marches as gaily and carries himself as straight as any boy. During the Expedition I was indebted to him in many ways, for the old campaigner, if he has the will, can do much to help one who is inexperienced.[403]

The Chaplains on Campaign

A notable feature of the Anglican component of the Chaplains' Department in the years between the Crimean and the Boer wars was the fact that its members saw very little active service. In April 1888, J.C. Edghill said of the Anglican chaplain, '[H]e has to regard his soldiers as his parishioners, and to do for them what a good local clergyman would do for his parish.'[404] When, in the following month, he was asked by the War Office to nominate an army chaplain for the post of honorary chaplain to the Queen, Edghill was surprised as well as gratified, remarking that 'The real work for which we employ Chaplains is done in our garrisons at home, but no honour [and] no promotion could be given to those men who did it best.'[405] As Edghill went on, extraordinary awards and promotion were never given 'except for active service, whereas the hard grind of a Chaplain's life is in the daily unseen routine of Barrack or Camp life'.[406] Of sixty-five Anglican chaplains on the Army List in 1899, only six had seen active service as Chaplains to the Forces and, notwithstanding nearly forty years of service in the Department, Edghill was not among them.[407] Indeed, part of the Treasury's case for raising the retirement age of the Chaplain-General in 1892 rested on the view that 'the duties of a Chaplain General are akin in their nature to Civil duties [and] that there is no reason why a Chaplain General should be less fit for his duties up to 65 than the head of an important Civil Department'.[408]

The reasons for this remarkable lack of active service experience are not hard to locate. Chaplains were commissioned with a view to the needs of the army's larger stations at home and overseas. Because of the heavy concentration of Presbyterian and Roman Catholic soldiers in Scottish and Irish regiments and the greater availability of Anglican clergymen to act as officiating clergymen in Britain and the colonies, the system was weighted in favour of the former denominations. As the Permanent Under Secretary explained in 1888, at larger stations an Anglican chaplain was needed for every thousand Anglican soldiers whereas the threshold for Presbyterians and Roman Catholics was 500, the rather complacent rationale being that 'there is always a Church of England clergyman in every parish; but there is not always a Presbyterian or Roman Catholic minister'.[409] In practical terms, this meant that Presbyterian and Roman Catholic chaplains often enjoyed what were effectively regimental postings, following (outside India at least) the army's Scottish and Irish regiments wherever military requirements took them. In comparison, Anglican chaplains were burdened with larger and more impersonal charges in both peacetime and on active service.

Furthermore, throughout this period many of the army's major campaigns continued to be waged from India, where Anglican soldiers were very much the responsibility of the Indian Ecclesiastical Establishment. In fact, the first ever chaplain to win a Victoria Cross was J.W. Adams of the I.E.E., who earned his V.C. for rescuing soldiers under fire at Killa Kazi in December 1879 during the Second Afghan War.[410] In contrast, the Chaplains' Department became extensively involved in other colonial campaigns only when expeditionary forces, or substantial bodies of reinforcements, sailed from Great Britain. For example, only one commissioned chaplain (the Anglican George Ritchie) was in Natal on the unexpected outbreak of the Zulu War in January 1879 and, when the Department did respond, it was very much a case of too little, too late.[411] In June 1879 the Archbishop of Canterbury received a letter complaining of the spiritual plight of Anglican troops in Natal. This letter, which had been written from Stanger three months earlier and sent to a female missionary on leave in Ireland, complained that 'There are now 6 English Regiments up here besides Bluejackets, Engineers and Artillery and neither with the Regiments or at any of the Hospitals is there a *clergyman.*' Its author, a local woman, also described how:

> Here at Stanger there is always *at least* one company . . . then about 4 miles from here is the Hospital [where] there are now over *100* ill . . . [In] the last fortnight or 3 weeks 3 officers and several men have died there and there is *no clergyman* or any one who would speak of God to them. They simply take their medicine and die and are *sewn into their blanket* and put into the ground [and] who ever the officer is here generally reads the service . . . is this as it should be – does England only count her soldiers as so many *things* to fight! And I *know* how the men *themselves* want some good man and ask for a clergyman. The other day a young fellow I know, and about the very least you would have thought of doing such a thing, when near death *asked for a clergyman, some one to pray with and for him and there was no one*.[412]

When Archbishop Tait took the matter up with Claughton, the Chaplain-General reported that the Church of England now had three regular and two acting chaplains in South Africa and that he had 'taken part in sending out several Army Scripture Readers (besides the Chaplains) to the Army in Zululand'. Two further Anglican chaplains were also dispatched at the end of June, although much too late to render any service to the 32,000 British and colonial troops who served in the campaign.[413]

Even when a major expedition was actually planned and mounted from Great Britain, the needs of home and overseas stations and the age and fitness of available men still meant that chaplains could be in short supply. In 1882, only six Anglican chaplains accompanied the four cavalry regiments, nineteen infantry battalions, eight artillery batteries and miscellaneous support troops who were assembled from the army's home and Mediterranean stations for the invasion of Egypt. In comparison, the Presbyterians and Roman Catholics supplied one and four chaplains respectively, a balance that struck even a later Chaplain-General as decidedly 'peculiar'.[414] The following year, the lack of commissioned Anglican chaplains, and even of local missionaries who could be recruited as acting chaplains, meant that the great majority of the British garrison in Egypt experienced a terrible cholera epidemic without the benefit of adequate pastoral care. On 17 August 1883, a *Times* correspondent relayed a familiar message from Alexandria: 'The staff of the Church of England Army chaplains serving in Egypt with the force of occupation is insufficient. One clergyman has to act as chaplain at Suez and Ismailia, and one, assisted by a local civilian chaplain, takes charge of the force at Cairo.'[415] Worse still, C.H. Butcher, the 'civilian chaplain' at Cairo, wrote a letter of complaint to Tait's successor, Archbishop Benson, in September

1883 about the quality of the army chaplains sent to Egypt, men whose 'conduct and character' had 'occasioned repeated and serious scandal'. Of the four Anglican chaplains attached to the army of occupation, one had been 'harassed by domestic troubles' and had taken to the bottle; eventually, he had been 'sent home invalided after causing a disgraceful scene at a public hotel'. The second proved to be a hypochondriac who rarely left his room and was 'liable to sudden illnesses described by his physician as like hysterics in a woman'. The other two had malingered to such an extent that they had been 'officially censured . . . for callous neglect of duty during the cholera'. Although 'the regulation Church parades' had been duly performed, Holy Communion had not been administered in military hospitals and confirmation candidates had not been catechised.[416] Significantly, Claughton made no attempt to defend his subordinates. Instead, he meekly acknowledged the veracity of these reports, writing to Benson: 'I [can] not tell you the pain that has been caused to me by the state of things among the Chaplains at Cairo. Although some of the facts are strongly stated there is only too much truth in the account'.[417]

As early as 1868, a shortage of available Anglican Chaplains to the Forces had prompted the Secretary of State for War to adopt the expedient of employing acting chaplains using funds earmarked for the payment of the army's officiating clergy. As a War Office memorandum later explained, '[The] Secretary of State in lieu of employing officiating clergymen at the capitation rates of pay, sanctioned the appointment of two Acting Chaplains . . . with pay at 10s a day, the lowest rate for Commissioned Chaplains, but without the allowances to which the latter are entitled.'[418] This was done on the understanding that these acting chaplains would be granted commissions as soon as vacancies occurred and that their previous service would count towards future pay and promotion.[419] However, far from proving a temporary measure, these chaplains became a permanent, if slightly irregular, addition to the Chaplains' Department. By 1877, when the War Office sought to formalise these arrangements with the Treasury, there were four Anglican clergymen serving in this capacity. As the War Office explained, 'the pay of 10/- a day or £182 10s a year is less than in many cases would be paid for the partial services of a local clergyman under the capitation arrangement, and it enables the Secretary of State to secure the whole services of the Acting Chaplain'.[420] In 1878, by which time one Presbyterian minister and two Roman Catholic priests were also being employed by the War Office as acting chaplains, the Chaplain-General even suggested that the War Office incorporate its acting chaplains into a larger establishment of commissioned chaplains but this proposal was rejected on the grounds of the additional costs it would involve.[421] In time, however, what began as an expedient evolved into a formal probationary system. As J.C. Edghill explained in 1888, an Anglican acting chaplain was not commissioned 'until he has been a year on probation, and has been well recommended by a senior chaplain', Anglican acting chaplains also being subject to the inspection and approval of the Chaplain-General.[422]

However, because of the chronic shortage of Anglican commissioned chaplains in particular, for many of the colonial wars of the later nineteenth century the army was heavily reliant on acting chaplains temporarily recruited from among the missionary and colonial clergy. The deficiencies of the post-Crimean Chaplains' Department were exposed as early as 1865 when, during the protracted course of the Third Maori War, it was claimed in the House of Commons that there was only one Anglican Chaplain to the Forces among the 10,000 troops then serving in New Zealand, a situation which had led the Bishop of New Zealand, G.A. Selwyn, to volunteer 'the services of himself and several of his clergy'. Although exaggerated, this claim betrayed an uncomfortable truth. At the end of December 1864 there were only two Anglican, one Presbyterian and two Roman Catholic commissioned chaplains in this theatre of war, the greater part of the army's spiritual needs being met by sixteen other clergymen of the same denominations.[423] Whatever else, it is indicative of the militaristic temper of late Victorian Christianity that many missionaries and colonial clergymen were only too happy to volunteer their services to the army. Several Wesleyan missionaries (including Owen Watkins, the father of Owen Spencer Watkins) served as acting chaplains during the Zulu War.[424] Furthermore, on its outbreak in January 1879, George Smith, one of the most celebrated members of the late Victorian Chaplains' Department, was an S.P.G. missionary and the incumbent of Estcourt in Natal.[425] Described as 'something of a fire-eater and a rabid High Churchman', Smith had served as an acting chaplain in the amaHlubi rebellion of 1873–4 and his leading of parade services was thought to be exemplary.[426] After distinguishing himself by distributing ammunition at the defence of Rorke's Drift, his 'unquenchable enthusiasm for military life' was rewarded by the grant of a regular commission in 1880 and the nickname of 'Ammunition Smith'.[427]

The employment of acting chaplains of all kinds reached new heights in the Boer War of 1899–1902. In February 1900 the War Office announced that:

> Forty-three commissioned chaplains to the Forces and acting chaplains (including a limited number of unpaid acting chaplains representing the different denominations) have been, or are about to be, sent to South Africa. Of these, 25 are Church of England, six are Presbyterians, eight are Roman Catholics, and four are Wesleyans.
> In addition, the military authorities in South Africa are employing local clergy of the various religious denominations wherever necessary . . . There is no present intention of sending out additional chaplains, and the services of clergymen volunteering for South Africa cannot, therefore, be accepted.[428]

While it was also reported that Lord Roberts was 'very well satisfied with the number of chaplains' already sent out to South Africa by the War Office,[429] this early confidence proved misplaced and more chaplains were soon on their way to the seat of war. In July 1900, the House of Commons was informed that:

> The War Office has sent to South Africa or given direct authority for employing 49 Church of England chaplains, nine Church of Scotland and other Presbyterians, 22 Roman Catholics [and] five Wesleyans . . . Besides these the Commander-in-Chief in South Africa has had a free hand to employ colonial clergy, and large numbers of all the denominations mentioned are known to have been employed, but no returns of their numbers or denominations have been sent to the War Office.[430]

In this manner, the army provided employment not only for missionaries and colonial clergymen in Natal and Cape Colony but also served as a haven for British clergymen who had fled the Transvaal and the Orange Free State as refugees on the outbreak of war.[431]

Despite these expedients, there were inevitably cases when chaplains were conspicuous by their absence and when denominational niceties had to be ignored. As it was quite impossible to secure a chaplain for every one of the army's recognised denominations on every troopship that sailed from a British or imperial port, problems often began with the outward voyage. Hence, when sailing from Southampton to Cape Town on board the *Nubia* in 1899, E.P. Lowry took charge of all the Presbyterians as well as his fellow Wesleyans. However, this still left the Anglican and Roman Catholic majority unprovided for. While alternative arrangements were made for the Anglicans, the latter went without an organised service for the whole of the voyage.[432] Although Wesleyans and Presbyterians had a history of collaboration, extreme situations could demand a broader pragmatism. When ministering to large numbers of sick and wounded men after the battle of Paardeberg in February 1900, Robert McClelland, a Church of Scotland acting chaplain, was briskly informed by an Anglican colleague that 'You will do for my people, and I will do for yours equally well in this sort of work.'[433] Inevitably, there were also situations when no chaplain of any description was available and officers had to step in. After Gordon's would-be rescuers had won a hard-fought battle around the wells at Abu Klea in 1885, one veteran of the relief expedition recalled that 'The day after the battle was a Sunday and a service was held which was conducted by General Stewart himself.'[434] Similarly, on board the *Nubia* in 1899:

> In the absence of an Anglican chaplain, Surgeon-Colonel McGill, the principal medical officer, read prayers with the men of the Royal Army Medical Corps. The captains of the various regimental companies did the same for the Church of England men; while in the main saloon the ship's captain conducted worship with as many of the naval and military officers as found it convenient to attend.[435]

In terms of their work on campaign, the chaplain's ministry remained largely unchanged. Despite denominational variations, whether in garrison or in camp chaplains were responsible for providing parade and voluntary services, for ministering to the sick and for burying the dead. However, in discharging the former duty they were liable to attract some adverse criticism. In particular, controversy erupted when Winston Churchill, then a war correspondent for the *Morning Post*, impugned the usefulness of army chaplains after hearing one of them preach in February 1900. Only days after General Buller's bloody defeat at Spion Kop (and with the prospect of more hard fighting to come) Churchill was shocked by how otiose this sermon was:

> I attended a church parade this morning. What a chance this was for a man of great soul who feared God! On every side were drawn up deep masses of soldiery, rank behind rank – perhaps, in all, five thousand . . . It was one of those occasions when a fine preacher might have given comfort and

> strength where both were sorely needed, and have printed on many minds a permanent impression. The bridegroom Opportunity had come. But the Church had her lamp untrimmed. A chaplain with a raucous voice discoursed on the details of 'The siege and surrender of Jericho.' The soldiers froze into apathy, and after a while the formal perfunctory service reached its welcome conclusion . . . As I marched home an officer said to me: 'Why is it, when the Church spends so much on missionary work among heathens, she does not take the trouble to send good men to preach in time of war . . . ?'[436]

Significantly, Churchill's theme was taken up by another correspondent who complained of a poor Christmas sermon given by an army chaplain during the siege of Ladysmith. These reports prompted a spate of anxious letters to the press and a flurry of complaints to the Chaplain-General.[437]

Nevertheless, an officer of the Imperial Yeomanry sprang to the defence of the chaplains in South Africa, writing to the *Church Times*:

> An Army chaplain (Rev. J. Blackbourne, BA) looks after our spiritual welfare, and nothing can possibly be brighter or more cheerful than the services he conducts, and no sermons can be more to the point and yet full of interest to the many who attend the services . . . Mr. Blackbourne attends to his daily duties of visiting the sick and wounded in the hospital (some 500 now) besides holding other classes in religious instruction. I venture to think that the majority of Army chaplains of the Church of England in South Africa are more of the stamp of Mr. Blackbourne than those described by Mr. Winston Churchill.[438]

Similarly, the war correspondent of the *Daily Chronicle* dismissed Churchill's tales by stressing the minor place of the sermon in the chaplain's work:

> I am not at all prejudiced in favour of the Church, but during the siege [of Ladysmith] I could not help coming across the work of at least two of the chaplains then present, and I have no doubt the work of others was as good. I never heard any of them preach. In war time it is too late to preach, but for kindness to the sick, for politeness in the midst of privations, for cheerful encouragement to all in distress, for fearlessness in the face of shells and bullets, and (what to me is a far more trying ordeal) for fearlessness in the face of all the deadly plagues which infested town and hospital alike, and breathed from the mouths of the dying as the last rites were administered, there were many of us to whom these chaplains might have served as examples . . . If [these correspondents] knew the chaplains and the privates and the poor, they would also know that the ten minutes' sermon once a week counts simply as nothing at all in comparison with the innumerable labours of a good parson, whether in camp or parish.[439]

The force of this point can be appreciated by the fact that, despite some considerable advances in military medicine since the Crimean War, two thirds of the British army's 22,000 fatal casualties during the Boer War were due to disease – principally typhoid, or enteric fever – and thousands of other soldiers had to be invalided home.[440] This meant that the greatest burden for most chaplains was, as ever, their hospital work. As James Robertson, the senior Presbyterian chaplain in

South Africa, confirmed to the Church of Scotland's Committee on Army and Navy Chaplains as the war drew to a close: 'Hospital work to those of us near large district hospitals has been very heavy.'[441] As in the Peninsula and the Crimea, disease did not discriminate between chaplain and layman. W.S. Jaffray, a commissioned chaplain of the Church of Scotland, was invalided home in July 1901 'after a severe attack of enteric fever' and Cathel Kerr, an acting chaplain of the United Free Church who had been sent to South Africa to minister to Gaelic-speaking Highlanders, died of typhoid at Kimberely in 1900.[442]

The ministry of the chaplain was no less onerous in the field. Jaffray had the unusual experience of conducting a service under fire during Lord Roberts' march across the Boer republics in the spring of 1900. He also wrote of this dramatic phase of the conflict:

> It is sometimes forgotten that the chaplain has often harder times than the men to whom he ministers. Not only has he the long and weary march to perform with the others, but should the day be a day of battle, when action is over, and those safe and well go into camp to rest and sleep, the chaplain's work only begins. The dying call for constant and careful ministration, the wounded require consolation and strengthening, and for the dead arrangements must be made for laying them to rest.[443]

During the protracted guerrilla war that followed the fall of Pretoria in June 1900, the army's lengthy lines of communication and its growing lines of blockhouses served to prolong the itinerant ministry of many chaplains. Prior to leaving South Africa, Paul Bull spent several weeks visiting troops in the Komati Poort Valley of the north-eastern Transvaal:

> I devoted ten days to each station, gathering the men each night for a service, walking or riding along the [railway] line to the detached companies who were guarding bridges, etc., and giving them a Bible-reading and prayers. In camp at Godwan River we often mustered from 100 to 200, and at all of the outlying stations I received a ready welcome . . . In this loathsome valley . . . where fever and dullness were sweeping whole regiments away, my visit used to break the monotony of their uneventful lives.[444]

Similarly, William Drury, another acting chaplain, was tasked with serving a line of blockhouses in the Transvaal in 1902. As Drury explained in a letter from the town of Warmbaths:

> I have orders that my duty is from Nylstroom north of here to Waterval in the south, about 60 miles of blockhouses [with] garrisons at the extremes. My plan will be to work Sunday to Wednesday or Thursday south one week, and north the next, taking a day off at Warmbaths at the end of each week. I can take the horse by train on Saturday night, and then ride home calling along the line at the blockhouses . . . I have a parish 60 miles long, magnificent country, with real men building the Empire with stone and steel.[445]

Drury's bravado masked the dangers of such work, particularly in view of the ubiquitous threat of the Boer 'bitter-enders'. On one occasion, an Anglican chaplain and his soldier-servant were apprehended by Boer guerrillas and even threatened with execution before making their escape.[446]

Although the Geneva Convention of 1864 had confirmed the status of chaplains as non-combatants and had counted them as ambulance personnel,[447] their diverse provenance, their lack of formal training and the brutal realities of so many of the army's colonial campaigns meant that the terms of the Geneva Convention were often ignored by chaplains themselves. One Wesleyan acting chaplain even carried a revolver and served as a dispatch rider during the Egyptian campaign of 1882. Twenty years later, Owen Spencer Watkins defended these actions by arguing that they were 'perhaps permissible in a war in which the Geneva Convention played no part'.[448] Being something of a kindred spirit, Watkins felt similar temptations at the battle of Omdurman in September 1898. Although a spectacularly one-sided victory for Kitchener's Anglo-Egyptian army, he made his way to the firing line on the pretext of proving his 'skill in bandaging'. Although no such help was required, Watkins lingered to savour the experience of battle:

> I was enabled to speak words of cheer to many, and exchange a hurried grip of the hand and a 'God bless you' with not a few, whilst more than one looked over his shoulder and shouted the Christian soldier's watchword 'Four-Nine-Four' (meaning Hymn 494, in *Sacred Songs and Solos*, 'God be with you till we meet again').[449]

However, the 'civilised' nature of the enemy helped to ensure that the part played by chaplains in the pitched battles of the Boer War was far more in keeping with the terms and spirit of the Geneva Convention. At the battle of Belmont in November 1899, E.P. Lowry scoured the field for wounded in the company of some stretcher-bearers. As he recalled, they spent much of the day moving from rock to rock in order 'to find shelter from the bullets that made music all around us'. Eventually:

> I found myself, as soon as the heaviest fighting on the left was over, among the wounded Guardsmen, giving them water from my bottle, or a bit of biscuit; helping the Bearer Company with my own knife to cut away the straps of the wounded, and assisting as best I could in first aid work, or whispering words of Christian consolation.[450]

Nevertheless, the prudence and practical value of scampering around the battlefield in the face of an enemy armed with modern artillery and magazine-loading rifles was soon called into question, the consensus being that chaplains were of much greater use further to the rear. As a letter to the *Church Times* pointed out in August 1901:

> [At] the time of Belmont and Modder River some newspaper correspondents made mistakes as to the place a chaplain should occupy in battle, and it was then pointed out to them that a chaplain's place in action is with the hospital staff in the rear, not in the firing line; and though some of us did not always keep to this arrangement, common-sense and experience seem to point out that one can do very little with men suddenly stricken down by bullet or shell, because the shock is in most cases severe and the

> pain of some wounds very great indeed. After such wounds are dressed, and the effects of the shock have passed, there is much more chance of one's ministrations receiving attention and being helpful . . . In the firing line the chaplain's movements will attract the enemy's fire, for which the men will not be grateful; and on the field, where ambulance men and doctors are at work, he is likely, in his official capacity, to be decidedly in the way.[451]

Naturally, the role of the chaplain on the battlefield was not without risk and enemy action took a small but steady toll of the army's commissioned and acting chaplains during the colonial campaigns of the later nineteenth century. In 1869, C.M. Clode noted that 'One Chaplain (at least) has a ball lodged in him, which he received in front while attending the wounded' during the Second China War of 1856–60.[452] The regimental attachments of the army's Roman Catholic chaplains and their tendency to be at hand in order to administer the sacraments to the wounded and dying entailed a predictable trickle of casualties. Significantly, the only chaplain to become a combat casualty during the Egyptian campaign of 1882 was James Bellord who was wounded at the battle of Tel-el-Kebir; likewise, it would seem that the only chaplain to be wounded in action during the Boer War was Joseph Rockliffe, who was hit by shrapnel during the march on Pretoria.[453]

Whatever they did on the battlefield, chaplains were expected to steel their soldiers for action. Although soldiers could be encouraged by a cheery presence in the firing line, this was obviously in tension with the chaplain's prescribed role under the Geneva Convention. Consequently, the best and least controversial method of preparing their men for battle was the pre-battle sermon. Although Churchill was manifestly disappointed by the sermon he heard before the advance on Ladysmith in February 1900, John Gordon of the 1st Black Watch was more impressed by a service held before the battle of Kirbekan in February 1885: 'church parade, the first for weeks; we hardly remembered how to behave. We formed a square, and our Chaplain in the centre made an address, offered prayer, and led us in singing.'[454] Similarly, just before Omdurman in 1898, an Anglican chaplain gave a stirring sermon that likened the present campaign to a crusade and which portrayed the union flag as a sacred banner comprising the crosses of St. George, St. Andrew and St. Patrick.[455]

However, by this time certain Liberal and Radical elements at home were calling into question the army's conduct on campaign. Liberal and humanitarian concern over the army's behaviour in the Sudan and in South Africa reached its apogee in Sir Henry Campbell-Bannerman's ringing denunciation of the 'methods of barbarism' that were being employed against the Boers by 1901, methods which included the razing of Boer farmsteads and the creation of concentration camps for Boer civilians.[456] Given the chaplain's vaunted role as the moral guardian of the soldier and the perceived success of Christian work in the army since the Crimean War, public criticism of this kind was potentially very damaging for the Chaplains' Department. Hence, while many British officers in South Africa came to admire their Boer adversaries,[457] a strident and defensive tone tended to characterise chaplains' accounts of the war. Indeed, chaplains themselves became targets for anti-war writers and their views featured prominently in a post-war publication entitled *The Churches and the South African War. Lest We Forget.* This indictment of churchmen's pronouncements during the Boer War noted the following outburst of a commissioned chaplain who had written to the *Daily Telegraph* on the eve of the conflict:

> If Great Britain is not ready to draw the sword, and give the signal to her marksmen to sight their rifles for justice, liberty, and freedom . . . then the [Boer] half-breeds will get first blood, and their hangmen will find halters for every tree . . . We must strike for life and honour such a blow as will make all Boerdom reel. [President Kruger] will swim through seas of blood, Psalm-singing with every stomach stroke, and not the least off colour all the while. Whilst we are politically procrastinating, he is prayerfully preparing, and whilst some of our Radicals are calling on the hucksters of the party to curse our cause and bless our enemies, he is in pious prostration before the Lord of Hosts. Meanwhile his myrmidons can all do murder at a pinch, and to ravish they are not ashamed.

Significantly, it was noted that even the Church of England's *Guardian* newspaper had misgivings about this chaplain's 'ultra militant and scarcely clerical sentiments in regard to Mr. Kruger'.[458]

However, chaplains were steadfast in their defence of the British soldier in South Africa. In his 1904 account of the war, Paul Bull said of the capture of Bloemfontein in March 1900: 'Not a shop was looted, not a home was violated. There was no plundering, no crime, no outbreak of violence. I believe the annals of warfare can show no greater example of patient self-restraint.'[459] As for the burning of Boer farmsteads, Bull had made his feelings known to the *Daily Chronicle* while the war was still in progress:

> I think it will help us to get rid of this atmosphere of sickly sentiment if we remember that a farm in South Africa is much more than a peaceful home. It is in many cases a fortress, a food dêpot, an arsenal where thousands of rounds of ammunition lie buried, a look-out post which commands fifty miles of country, and too often a death-trap for our soldiers.[460]

Indeed, of the war in general Bull was only prepared to concede that:

> It is probable that small detached bodies of troops, who were isolated and free from the control of public opinion, were guilty of crime [but] If an army of 250,000 archdeacons were to march through Africa, I have no doubt that some would momentarily forget themselves and 'commandeer' an occasional gaiter button or a casual apron string.[461]

In 1905, Bull's account of the occupation of Bloemfontein was echoed by an anonymous clergyman in *The Times*. Roused by the allegation 'that when Bloemfontein fell into the hands of the British our troops tried to make it absolutely uninhabitable for the Boers', 'AN ACTING CHAPLAIN WHO WAS THERE' wrote:

> A more absurd statement it would be impossible to imagine. Absolutely no damage was done to the town, no looting was permitted, and, as Sir A. Conan Doyle [author of *The Great Boer War* and *The War in South*

> *Africa: its Cause and Conduct*] says, 'nothing could exceed the gentleness and good humour of the troops. Indeed, there seemed more need for an order which should protect them against the extortion of their conquered enemies.'[462]

An identical position was adopted by chaplains of the Church of Scotland, not least in their published reports to its Committee on Army and Navy Chaplains. In 1902, for example, T.A. Cameron reported that he had visited the concentration camp at Pietersburg, which was then home to 6,000 people. With reference to the prevailing conditions, Cameron declared:

> On this point I can confidently say that if all the camps were as well managed as ours the Boers had not only nothing to complain of, but might frankly admit that they had never been so comfortable in their lives. There were *no* complaints, and all the outcry about 'methods of barbarism' and the like hurled against our gallant and humane soldiers, as well as against our hard-wrought and kindly officials in these camps, is the outcome of an overheated imagination.[463]

That same year, Robert McClelland published his recollections of the war under the unambiguous title *Heroes and Gentlemen: an army chaplain's experiences in South Africa*, the purpose of which was to 'speak the truth about our British soldiers' despite 'misrepresentation at home and calumny abroad'.[464] Far from falling victim to a licentious soldiery, McClelland insisted that abandoned women and children had been treated with the greatest solicitude by British soldiers during the advance on Pretoria in June 1900:

> [Never] a finger was lifted nor a word said to increase that fear or deepen that grief by our brave and true men; their passage through the country was a splendid object lesson on the honour of Tommy Atkins, and an utter refutation of the base calumnies and vile slanders (some of them too filthy even to name) that had been scattered broadcast by the enemy.[465]

Given the divided state of Nonconformist opinion on the nature and direction of British imperial policy around the turn of the twentieth century, the army's Wesleyan chaplains were equally active in their efforts to vindicate the conduct of the British soldier. In his 1899 account of the reconquest of the Sudan, Owen Spencer Watkins devoted a whole chapter to refuting charges of British cruelty after the victory at Omdurman. According to E.N. Bennett, an amateur journalist who had covered the reconquest of the Sudan for the Liberal *Westminster Gazette*,[466] Kitchener's British and Sudanese troops had either killed or culpably neglected thousands of Mahdist wounded after the battle. Furthermore, they had looted Omdurman itself, dismembered the Mahdi's corpse and shelled civilians as they tried to escape.[467] In reply, Watkins debunked these charges, his spirited defence being moved by his conviction that 'Throughout the whole campaign – and probably I saw more of the inner working of things than did Mr. Bennet – both officers and men acquitted themselves, under conditions of hardship and danger, in a way that any Briton might be proud of.'[468] In 1901, and with the war in South Africa still raging, Watkins resumed his defence of the army in another book entitled *Chaplains at the Front: incidents in the life of a chaplain during the Boer War*. By this time, Watkins was addressing a deeply divided body of opinion among the British Free Churches,[469] with the Wesleyan Methodists being the most firmly pro-war.[470] In *Chaplains at the Front*, Watkins evinced great impatience with those who sympathised with the Boer enemy. When describing Boer treatment of 'Christian natives' at a mission station in Natal, he remonstrated: 'Oh that the ignorant "at home" would make note of this! These were the men of whom the deluded still speak as "the simple, godly, Bible-reading Boers".'[471]

While Roman Catholic opinion was also deeply divided over the Boer War, with many Irish Nationalists being either anti-war or positively pro-Boer,[472] Roman Catholic chaplains dutifully praised the behaviour of the army in general and lauded the piety of its Roman Catholic soldiers in particular. Charles Swarbreck, an English-born priest of the diocese of Liverpool who served as an acting chaplain in South Africa in 1901, wrote of the capture of a Boer wagon train near Middelburg in the Transvaal:

> The women and children were a pitiable sight; they had been in the open a long time, and their clothes were badly worn. They were delighted when they heard they would be sent back to their homes in Middelberg [sic], where they would be no longer afraid to stay after the kind treatment they had experienced from the troops.[473]

More reassuring still was the veneration of the cross by some Irish troops at Philjohn's Drift on Good Friday 1901:

> The Cork Militia were on guard here, and nearly all were Catholic. As many as could assembled round our [railway] carriage, and we said a few encouraging words and supplied them with medals, rosaries, and such things as we had. Fr. Scannell gave them a crucifix for the regiment, and a delightful little episode followed. All the men knelt down and kissed the cross . . . some thirty rough soldiers, bronzed with heat, and their khaki uniforms all stained and torn with long service, filled with faith, kneeling on the railway track late at night, and kissing the cross with intense devotion . . . I hope I may never forget the rough faces of those grand Catholic soldiers . . . The men went back to camp proud of their treasure, and glad to have seen the priest.[474]

Summary

In the wake of the Crimean War, the Chaplains' Department was expanded in terms of its size and broadened in terms of its denominational profile. However, the post-war reconstruction of the Department also saw it integrated more closely into the officer corps as commissioned chaplains were given relative rank and accorded the trappings that went with it. In part, this was intended to augment their authority in the moral reform of the soldier, a long-term and rather elusive process that remained a key part of the chaplain's role throughout this period. While Anglican chaplains in particular were diligent in their promotion of temperance, rational recreation and organised sports among the rank and file, the overall success of their efforts is difficult to determine. Not only did they face indirect competition from soldiers' homes and other civilian agencies but the chaplain's work was rather embarrassed by the Contagious Diseases Acts and by the existence of the army's 'wet' canteens. In addition, their efforts comprised only one strand of a sustained public policy towards the army which sought to achieve the physical, moral and intellectual improvement of the soldier through a wide variety of means. Furthermore, in the strongly hierarchical milieu of the Victorian regular army the chaplain's relative rank came to be seen as a stumbling block, rather than as an aid, to the chaplain's work, a perception that led to the growth of a more informal style of ministry among Anglican chaplains in the last quarter of the nineteenth century.

However, Anglican chaplains had other problems as well. If Gleig's controversial and rather vainglorious bid for an army bishopric came to nothing, the anomalous position of Anglican chaplaincy *vis-à-vis* the normal structures of the church was never satisfactorily addressed. The parish clergy (and especially the Low Church clergy of the Church of Ireland) were liable to resent army chaplains as interlopers and the Army Chaplains Act of 1868 did nothing to resolve the chaplain's relations with the diocesan bishops or with the parish clergy. Sensitive questions of church order also lay at the heart of the army's Ritualist controversy of the 1860s and '70s. The legacy of the Crimean War and the preferences of George Gleig led to strong High Church leanings within the Department. However, Ritualist innovation was liable to be fiercely resisted by senior Low Church officers, a situation that underlined the continuing influence of laymen on the army's religious affairs, an influence that may even have been strengthened by the erastian undertones of the post-Crimean militarisation of the Department. If Gleig had to contend with the interference and complaints of militantly Protestant officers, he was also faced with the claims of Wesleyan and other evangelical missionaries to the army. While successful in bringing the army's official scripture readers under departmental control, he met his match in W.H. Rule and Wesleyan claims to recognition were finally conceded by the War Office in 1862 after a period of bitter confrontation at Aldershot and Chatham. Furthermore, Anglican chaplains were unable to check the encroachments of female evangelists and their ostensibly non-denominational soldiers' homes, though they did eventually pay them the flattery of imitation in the form of the Church of England's soldiers' institutes which emerged as vehicles for the chaplains' work from 1880.

In comparison with the trials and tribulations of Anglican chaplaincy, the difficulties that beset its Presbyterian, Roman Catholic and Wesleyan equivalents were relatively minor. While several Presbyterian churches competed for a limited number of Presbyterian commissions and Roman Catholic chaplains were swiftly debarred from serving in Ireland, both denominations had the distinct advantage of being closely identified with the army's Scottish and Irish regiments – regiments to which their chaplains were usually attached. Consequently, the Roman Catholics in particular could rely on powerful political support from Irish Nationalist M.P.s despite the attitude of the Irish hierarchy to the Chaplains'

Department and the declining Irish presence in the late Victorian army. While a reluctance to allow their ministers to become subject to the army meant that the Wesleyans eschewed permanent commissions, from the early 1880s they accepted state aid in the form of government grants by which they were able to subsidise and expand their existing network of acting chaplains and soldiers' homes.

Nevertheless, irrespective of denomination the Department was fundamentally geared towards peacetime garrison work and it was hard pressed to cope with the demands of far-flung colonial campaigns. Hence, the army's recognised denominations were compelled to fall back on expedients of various kinds. While this sometimes meant that Presbyterians and Wesleyans shared their chaplains on active service, it more commonly involved the recruitment of additional acting chaplains. While some were probationary members of the Department or, if Wesleyans or Presbyterians, ministers who were employed by their churches for full-time army work, in the vast majority of cases these were civilian clergymen who were temporarily recruited as chaplains from Britain or the colonies. However, regardless of their professional background the nature of their role on active service and the rigours of campaigning were liable to generate a strong and often overweening identification with the army. Consequently, during the Boer War there was a discernible tendency for chaplains to become heavily identified with their soldiers and with the controversial conduct of the war, a fact that incurred criticism from anti-war writers in a manner that prefigured much larger developments during and after the First World War.

4

The Army Chaplains' Department and the First World War

The Pre-war Years

J.C. Edghill retired from the Army Chaplains' Department in 1901.[1] The first choice of Lord Roberts, the hero of the war in South Africa and the new Commander-in-Chief of the British army, was Arthur Winnington Ingram.[2] Bishop of Stepney and a canon of St. Paul's Cathedral since 1897, Winnington Ingram was a rising star in the Church of England. A veteran missionary to the East End and a celebrated public speaker, he had shown great interest in military matters and warmly endorsed the quasi-military work and ethos of the newly formed Church Lads' Brigade, which had its origins in the diocese of London.[3] Furthermore, Winnington Ingram (like Gleig, Claughton and Edghill) was a staunch High Churchman and was also known to be sympathetic to Ritualism (or Anglo-Catholicism), which was strongly represented in the Chaplains' Department. However, the talents of Winnington Ingram were not only apparent to Roberts and nor were they suitable only for the office of Chaplain-General. Hence, the prospect of Winnington Ingram succeeding Edghill was nullified when the promising Bishop of Stepney was appointed Bishop of London on the death of Bishop Mandell Creighton in January 1901.[4]

In the event, the vacancy was filled from a relatively unexpected quarter. The new Chaplain-General, who was appointed in November 1901, was Bishop John Taylor Smith, a fervent evangelical and a veteran C.M.S. missionary to West Africa. Trained at St. John's, Highbury ('a distinctively evangelical' theological college) Taylor Smith was ordained in 1885 and spent five years as an assistant curate in Upper Norwood before being appointed 'Canon of St. George's Cathedral, Sierra Leone, diocesan missionary, and chaplain to the Bishop of that diocese'.[5] Although he had no prior experience of the army, he served as an acting chaplain to British forces in the Ashanti campaign of 1895–6, a campaign that was to profoundly alter the course of his career. Here, he had the good fortune to minister to a hapless member of the royal family, namely Prince Henry of Battenberg, Queen Victoria's adventurous and somewhat wayward son-in-law, who succumbed to a fatal attack of fever. Subsequently, and with the purpose of communicating Prince Henry's last messages to Queen Victoria and Princess Beatrice, Taylor Smith sailed for England where he was informed that both were in the south of France. Summoned to Nice, he delivered his messages in a private interview in which he knelt to lead the bereaved women in prayer. After further impressing his talents on the queen by means of a comforting sermon preached before the royal household the following day, he was quickly appointed an honorary chaplain to the queen.[6] Having earned the favour of the royal family, Taylor Smith was chosen by Archbishop Frederick Temple as the obvious successor to Bishop Ingham of Sierra Leone. Although this meant that he had to resign his honorary chaplaincy, his consecration in St. Paul's Cathedral in May 1897 was attended by Princess Beatrice 'who had travelled all night from Balmoral in order to show her appreciation of her friend'.[7]

However, the Ashanti campaign had provided Taylor Smith with other potential patrons. During the campaign, he had struck up a friendship with Edward Ward, a future Permanent Under Secretary at the War Office. According to the bishop's biographer:

> [There] is no doubt that the natural healthiness of the temporary chaplain in his talks with the men, his advice to the officers, and his strong commonsense way of presenting religion, appealed to the future [PUS], who 'made a note of' the abilities and manliness of this vigorous missionary.[8]

Significantly, it was Ward who instigated Taylor Smith's appointment as Chaplain-General in 1901. After securing the support of Lord Roberts for his nomination (Roberts had met Taylor Smith and heard him preach, the bishop demonstrating his 'powerful and penetrating voice' and an apparent ability to communicate with 'men and boys') Ward was able to recommend Taylor Smith to the Secretary of State for War, William St. John Brodrick. With Brodrick's agreement and the enthusiastic support of Edward VII and Archbishop Temple, who was anxious to see a bishop at the helm of the Chaplains' Department, only the bishop's consent was required. However, this was not so easily obtained. Initially, Taylor Smith, who was in England for the funeral of his father, was inclined to refuse the offer on account of his missionary commitments in West Africa. However, after a persuasive interview with the Assistant Adjutant-General at the War Office and consultations with the Archbishop and the C.M.S., he agreed to take spiritual charge of what the A.A.G. had artfully described as 'the largest missionary society in the world – namely, the soldiers of the British Army'.[9]

Although Taylor Smith had the support of the king, the War Office, the Archbishop of Canterbury and the Commander-in-Chief, he was much less acceptable to the Chaplains' Department. On a personal level, the bishop's style was rather disconcerting; not only was he in the habit of soliciting a 'beautiful thought' from everyone he met but, as a legacy of his West African days, he also kept a pet monkey named 'Bobbo'. Such was Taylor Smith's affection for his pet that 'Bobbo' became part of departmental folklore: 'All intending Chaplains had to undergo "Ordeal by Bobbo"; they were invited to lunch at the Chaplain-General's flat, with Bobbo sitting at the table for his meal. If they passed this test they were accepted.'[10] Besides these personal eccentricities, there was also the obvious professional problem that Taylor Smith had little knowledge of the army or of his new Department, considerations that led him to adopt a somewhat hesitant style of leadership. As E.H. Thorold wrote:

> He had little experience of the Army, though he soon felt at home in it. He went to work quietly, visiting all the stations at home and staying with the Chaplains in unceasing rotation, and making many foreign tours. His methods of promoting efficiency were unobjectionable, as he did not interfere with anyone who seemed to him to be doing good work, but contented himself with setting an example of evangelistic zeal. He made few enquiries about the conduct of the routine duties of his Chaplains, believing that they were too well trained to need his supervision, and feeling himself ill-equipped to inspect them owing to his ignorance of their traditions . . . Gradually he obtained the confidence and generally the friendship of the senior members of the Department in these early years, and as vacancies occurred he began to appoint younger men who were more ready to adopt his ideas. He found no particular difficulty in his work of administration at the War Office, where he always had the benefit of good advice and usually followed precedents. His judgment was invariably sound: and though he showed little initiative, he did not neglect anything which plainly demanded his attention.[11]

The evidence seems to confirm that Taylor Smith was generally conscientious in dealing with the Church of England, the War Office and his military superiors. In June 1902, the new Chaplain-General attended a meeting of the Church Navy and Army Board, a committee which had been established by the Convocation of Canterbury in the aftermath of the Boer War in order 'to promote the moral and religious welfare of sailors and soldiers and their families'. At the meeting, Taylor Smith joined with the Chaplain of the Fleet in welcoming 'trained lay help, in due relation to Church order, as a supplemental agency in promoting the moral and religious welfare' of the two services.[12] Furthermore, he acquiesced in the creation of a 'Chaplains Branch' at the War Office in 1908, a small body of civil servants who would work under the direction of the Secretary of State for War. The primary task of this new sub-division was the 'Administration of the Chaplains' Department for all denominations other than the Church of England'. However, under the direction of the Chaplain-General it also undertook 'Clerical work . . . connected with the administration of the Chaplains' Department for the Church of England' and 'Secretarial duties in connection with the Committee on the Moral and Spiritual Welfare of the Army, and with the Presbyterian Chaplains Advisory Committee'.[13]

Much more important than his co-operation in this bureaucratic fine-tuning was Taylor Smith's role in the preparation of the Chaplains' Department for a future European war. Under the guidance of Major-General Sir Henry Wilson, then Director of Military Operations, from 1910 the British army was actively planning to send an expeditionary force to the continent in the event of war with

Germany.[14] As shown by a comprehensive mobilisation schedule from August 1914, Taylor Smith had a clear conception of the Department's contribution to the British Expeditionary Force. Fifty-five chaplains were earmarked to accompany the B.E.F. to France. Each had a place and date of mobilisation and the majority were attached to its seven fighting divisions, with each division being allocated one Presbyterian, one Roman Catholic and three Anglican chaplains. All of these were to be attached to brigade field ambulances, of which there were three per division. In addition, there was at least one chaplain for each of the B.E.F.'s twelve general hospitals and two chaplains for the supporting 'Army Troops'. In total, thirty-one Anglican, nine Presbyterian, ten Roman Catholic and four Wesleyan chaplains would sail for France under the direction of the senior First Class chaplain in the Department, the Presbyterian Dr. J.M. Simms.[15]

If Taylor Smith's civilian background raised immediate questions about his suitability for the post of Chaplain-General then his churchmanship was no less controversial. Born and brought up a Methodist, his ordination and career in the Church of England did nothing to dampen the bishop's youthful evangelical zeal. According to Thorold, Taylor Smith regarded 'the work of spiritual evangelisation' as 'the prime purpose for which he had been born', work in which he indulged 'in season or out of season, in the office, in the drawing room, in the train, or in the street'.[16] After Gleig, Claughton and Edghill, the appointment of such a keen and assertive evangelical was bound to prove disruptive to the Department and to its High Church – even Ritualist – traditions. Despite an otherwise tentative approach to his chaplains, from the outset the bishop was keen to curb those Ritualist tendencies that had flourished in the Department for decades.[17] The potential for conflict became clear in 1903 over a memorial service for the South African War. Planned by the Guild of the Holy Standard, the service was to take the form of a choral celebration of the Eucharist and was to be held in St. Paul's Cathedral. However, despite being approved by the dean and chapter of the cathedral the intended form of service was 'denounced in Parliament and by Mr. Kensit'[18] and, also offended by its form of prayers for the dead, Taylor Smith quarrelled with the clergy of St. Paul's and withdrew his support from the Guild.[19]

As an alternative to the Guild of the Holy Standard, the new Chaplain-General sought to promote an army branch of the Church of England's Men's Society, a broadly based organisation that had been launched by Archbishop Temple in 1899. Because it 'stood for the Church, and not for sectionalism', it was hoped that the C.E.M.S. would eventually embrace all shades of opinion and incorporate 'every section of the Church's work among soldiers'.[20] In 1905, the C.E.M.S. duly commenced its work in the army, hoping in time to absorb the Guild of the Holy Standard and its members. This goal, however, was strongly resisted by the Guild itself and, in 1907, it merged with its sister organisation, the Guild of St. Helena, to form a new and larger Army Guild.[21] Needless to say, Taylor Smith was strongly opposed to the united and defiant Army Guild. Hence, in May 1907 he forbade chaplains from working with former members of the Guild of St. Helena and even urged that those women who were dissatisfied with the Army Guild form themselves into a separate society.[22] Consequently, the Army Guild appealed to Archbishop Davidson so that it 'might obtain at least toleration and be let alone'. Davidson, however, remained passive, conscious that the C.E.M.S. had a more 'comprehensive character' and that it had the advantage of enlisting 'civilians as well as soldiers and thus holds good for a man's life whether he is in the Army or not'.[23] Greatly encouraged, Taylor Smith stepped up what the Guild described as his campaign of 'persecution'. According to a list of grievances which it compiled in 1908:

> In the present year, the Brothers of the Guild have not been allowed to meet the Sisters for business and social purposes in a Chaplain's room. Again, for the last 27 years it was a valued privilege of Guild Members, men and women, to join in a corporate act of Communion on their anniversary day at the Guards' Chapel in Wellington Barracks, where 2 of the handsome Altar-candlesticks were presented at Easter 1907 by the London Branch of the Guild as a mark of their appreciation of this privilege. This year the service was forbidden at the instance of the Chaplain General.[24]

Hence, and despite an otherwise timid approach to the Department, within a few years Taylor Smith had become identified in Anglo-Catholic circles as an obnoxious evangelical autocrat, a reputation that would return to haunt him after the outbreak of the First World War.

If Anglican chaplaincy experienced some internal problems in the first years of the new century, then its Roman Catholic counterpart, which had hitherto been so trouble free, was positively racked with dissension. In 1903, the War Office accepted without demur Rome's designation of Francis Bourne, who had been Bishop of Southwark since 1897, as 'Superior of all Catholic Commissioned Chaplains attached to the service of the British Army, and Delegate of the Holy See in all questions regarding the spiritual welfare of the Catholic soldiers'.[25] However, unlike his immediate predecessors at Southwark, Bourne was not content with being a remote figure of authority. As Bourne described the situation prior to his new appointment:

> The situation was clearly anomalous and unsatisfactory. The Bishop of Southwark had no real jurisdiction over the Chaplains, who were practically subject only to military control. He granted them their first faculties but they were not dependent on him for their renewal. He had no official knowledge of their removal from one station to another. He could not call on them for a report of their work. In case of difficulties with other Ordinaries he was not entitled to intervene. Such difficulties, arising mainly from the use of diocesan buildings by commissioned Chaplains not belonging to the Diocese, were frequent and increasing. Moreover it was well-nigh impossible to withdraw from military service Priests who from the military or ecclesiastical point of view, even without serious fault on their part, had nevertheless outgrown their period of useful service. Lastly it became more and more difficult to obtain the consent of Bishops to the withdrawal from their Dioceses for an unlimited period of the very Priests who on account of their exceptional qualities were most needed as Military Chaplains . . .

Such was Bourne's determination to overthrow the old dispensation that, with permission from Rome and with the connivance of the War Office, he retained his control over the army's Roman Catholic chaplains following his translation to Westminster in September 1903.[26] In view of the fact that the Archbishop of Westminster already had responsibility for Catholic chaplains in the Royal Navy, Bourne thus secured complete ecclesiastical control over every chaplain in both of the nation's armed services. This coup was confirmed in 1906 when Propaganda announced that 'the Archbishop of Westminster had been permanently constituted Ecclesiastical Superior of all the Military and Naval [commissioned] Chaplains' and also as 'Delegate of the Holy See for the British Army and Navy'.[27] Armed with these formidable powers, Bourne persevered in his efforts to eliminate the worrying independence of Roman Catholic army chaplains. In 1909, and possibly taking advantage of the prevailing current of reform in the army as a whole, Bourne formulated a new scheme of short-service commissions for Catholic army chaplains, a plan which was duly approved by the Army Council. According to this new scheme, the Archbishop of Westminster was to place 'suitable Priests at the disposal of the War Office'. Each of these was to serve a probationary year and:

> At the end of the first year the Chaplains, if approved, will be re-engaged for a further 2 years for home service or of 3 or 5 years for foreign service, according to the nature of the foreign station . . . At the expiration of this period a Chaplain may be re-engaged for a further period of 3 or 5 years, with the possibility of the service being renewed at the expiration of each period.

Clearly, in Bourne's judgement it was crucial to divest these chaplains of the impertinent delusions that an officer's status seemed to give them. Accordingly, their pay was to be fixed at £200 per annum, they were to draw no allowances ('except field and travelling allowances'), they were to receive no pension ('except in special circumstances, e.g. physical disability from wounds or disease arising from military service') and, though commissioned officers, they were to have 'no military rank, but will simply be "Roman Catholic Chaplains to the Forces" '.[28]

While existing chaplains were unaffected by these new arrangements, their long-term implications were all too apparent and opposition to these measures was widespread.[29] In fact, Bourne's policies remained deeply controversial in Roman Catholic circles up until the outbreak of war. In May 1913, some leading Catholic peers and army officers petitioned Pope Pius X concerning 'the disadvantages of the methods by which the spiritual needs of Catholics serving in the British Army are now provided for'. The petition claimed that it was essential that one individual should have the exclusive task of watching 'over all the questions that arise with Catholics in the army' and insisted on the value of 'the former method of appointing Catholic chaplains', a system that served to ensure 'long service and experience' among them. It concluded by calling for 'The appointment of a [Catholic] Chaplain-General' and for the formation of a Catholic advisory board 'similar to those boards formed by Presbyterians and other denominations'. Naturally, Bourne very much opposed these proposals and vented his anger by scrawling on his copy of the petition comments such as 'Untrue', 'Inaccurate' and 'Unfair'.[30]

In stark contrast to the partisan wrangling which beset Anglican and Roman Catholic chaplaincy in the decade following the Boer War, Presbyterian chaplaincy was characterised by a growing sense of harmony. In part, this was dictated by the wider agendas of the Church of Scotland and the United Free Church, whose policy of convergence was to culminate in formal union in 1929.[31] However, it was also driven by administrative convenience. Since the first Presbyterian chaplains were commissioned in 1858, the War Office had been obliged to deal with the competing demands of several Presbyterian churches over the limited number of commissions available in the Chaplains' Department. Hence, the creation of a Presbyterian Chaplains Advisory Committee by Richard Burdon Haldane, the new Secretary of State for War, in 1906 was an important step forward from an administrative as well as an ecclesiastical point of view. The brief of the new committee was 'to consider the appointment and distribution of Presbyterian Chaplains and Officiating Clergymen and to make representations thereon to the War Office'. The four principal Presbyterian churches (namely the Church of Scotland, the United Free Church of Scotland, the Presbyterian Church of England and the Presbyterian Church of Ireland) each sent a representative, the War Office provided a secretary and the committee was chaired by Lord Balfour of Burleigh, a political heavyweight and the recent Conservative secretary for Scotland.[32]

For their part, Wesleyan chaplains continued to bask in the warm appreciation of the War Office. In September 1910, E.P. Lowry was gazetted as an honorary chaplain First Class and Owen Spencer Watkins as an honorary chaplain Third Class, 'the said classes being', as Haldane explained in a memorandum to King George V, 'those which substantive Chaplains to the Forces reach by a similar length of service'.[33] Given that Wesleyan Methodists had made the running in furthering the rights and standing of Nonconformists in the army since the 1850s, the members of the Wesleyan Army and Navy Sub-Committee seem to have been genuinely gratified when in 1903, and acting in concert, the Baptists and the Congregationalists followed the Wesleyan example and at last accepted formal recognition from the army.[34] Although Baptists and Congregationalists comprised only a tiny element of the army's rank and file (less than 1 per cent in 1904, a reflection of the negative light in which professional soldiering had been generally viewed by Victorian Nonconformists)[35] this development created new denominational categories for the purposes of attestation. Consequently, it allowed Baptist and Congregational ministers to be recognised and remunerated as officiating clergymen, of whom there were sixty-six, thirty-four Baptists and thirty-two Congregationalists, by 1914.[36]

One of the most far reaching of Haldane's reforms was the reorganisation of the army's auxiliary forces and the creation of the Territorial Force, which came into being in April 1908. Largely composed of the old Volunteer Force, which had been raised in 1859 in response to fears of French invasion, the T.F. was recruited and administered in peacetime by County Territorial Force Associations and its primary role was that of home defence. Although the volatile state of Irish politics meant that the Territorial system was not extended to Ireland, the T.F. in mainland Britain comprised nearly a quarter of a million men by 1913. These were organised into fourteen regional infantry divisions and fourteen regional cavalry brigades, their military potential being enhanced by the fact that soldiers of the T.F. were free to volunteer for Imperial Service overseas in the event of war.[37] The creation of the T.F. was accompanied by the inauguration of its own Chaplains' Department. Although the Chaplain-General dutifully convened conferences of Territorial chaplains, Territorial chaplaincy was steered from 1909 by a new Territorial Force Chaplains' Advisory Committee which was appointed by the War Office.[38] However, the response of the churches to the T.F. was very mixed, broadly reflecting the extent of their earlier association with the Volunteer Force. In May 1909, the General Assembly of the Church of Scotland was informed that chaplains' appointments would be 'made by County Associations' on the recommendation of 'the governing bodies of the various Presbyterian churches'. However, after consultations between the Church of Scotland and the United Free Church, it was agreed that 'as far as their services could be utilised, chaplains who held appointments in the Volunteer Force . . . should receive appointments as chaplains to the Territorial Force'. On this basis, it was hoped 'that comparatively few Volunteer chaplains who are under the age of sixty-five, and who have expressed their willingness to serve, will be left without appointments'.[39] Earlier links with the Volunteer Force were also revealed in the debate over whether uniforms should be worn by Territorial chaplains in peacetime. As we have seen, regular chaplains had discarded their peacetime uniforms in 1902. However, Territorial chaplains proved to be much more attached to their military attire. The first meeting of the T.F.'s Advisory Committee in December 1909 was deeply divided on this issue, with 'a strong minority' (namely 'the representatives of the Church of Scotland, the Baptists and the English Presbyterians') being in favour of a uniform, a position that was shared by the Anglican chaplains of the West Yorkshire Division.[40] Although the majority of the committee favoured conformity with the regulars, the issue was only resolved in September 1911 when new dress regulations permitted both regular and Territorial chaplains to wear a distinctive forage cap and chaplains' badges 'on the collar of the clerical frock coat or short jacket' if desired.[41]

If the question of uniform seems to have preoccupied the T.F. Advisory Committee, individual denominations had different policies towards Territorial chaplaincy. Although the Roman Catholics were represented on the Advisory Committee by Monsignor Manuel Bidwell, one of Bourne's most trusted protégés, the Territorials were given a low priority by the Archbishop of Westminster. Consequently, no Roman Catholic chaplain was appointed to the Territorial Force prior to August 1914, notwithstanding the existence of historically Catholic Volunteer (now Territorial) units such as the London and Liverpool Irish.[42] In contrast, and despite their tiny representation in the T.F. as a whole, the Nonconformist churches were quick to claim more than their share of Territorial chaplaincies. As a result of a special concession by the War Office, three English Presbyterian and four Wesleyan chaplains were appointed (two of the latter to Territorial battalions of the Duke of Cornwall's Light Infantry) and a Baptist (or

Congregationalist) chaplain was also put on the national establishment, a Baptist chaplain being attached to the 3rd Welsh Field Ambulance on the outbreak of war.[43] However, the concern of the Free Churches for the religious condition of the Territorial Force went much deeper than the provision of chaplains. Obliged to make the most of its annual, fifteen-day summer camps, the Territorial Force was no respecter of the Sabbath. Besides the movement of large numbers of part-time soldiers to and from camp on Sundays, its training regime required the use of firing ranges on the Lord's Day. All of this did much to offend sabbatarian feeling and a deputation of Free Churchmen even waited upon the Secretary of State for War in 1912, protesting (with little success) at this public and systematic violation of the Sabbath.[44]

War, Expansion and Reorganisation

In August 1914, and besides the Chaplain-General, the Army Chaplains' Department comprised 117 commissioned chaplains plus thirty-seven acting chaplains, their principal charges being the 247,000 soldiers of the regular army and their dependants, a third of whom were routinely stationed in India and were thus the responsibility of the Indian Ecclesiastical Establishment.[45] However, this modest total was wholly insufficient to meet the needs created by the huge expansion of the British army in 1914–15, months that saw the recall of more than 200,000 reservists, the mobilisation of the Territorial Force and the raising of Lord Kitchener's vast 'New Army' of thirty divisions. Moreover, from early 1916 the ranks of these regular, Territorial and volunteer soldiers would be replenished and reinforced by hundreds of thousands of conscripts. Consequently, between August 1914 and November 1918 a further 5,053 commissions were granted to chaplains of all denominations.[46] Like the British army as whole, in the long term the vastly expanded Chaplains' Department rose to the unprecedented demands of the war but this proved to be a painful process fraught with difficulty and controversy.

Given that around 70 per cent of the 5.7 million soldiers who served in the British army during the First World War gave their religion as 'C. of E.',[47] the demand for Anglican chaplains was particularly acute. On 4 August 1914, Bishop Taylor Smith had at his disposal ninety-seven full time Anglican chaplains, of whom seven were on probation as acting chaplains.[48] Two years later, there were 1,270 Anglican chaplains serving under regular, temporary and Territorial commissions. By the end of the war in November 1918, this number had climbed to 1,985.[49] Although Anglican chaplaincy expanded at a rate that actually outstripped that of the army as a whole, the demands of the army's training camps, overseas bases, lines of communication and fighting units were unrelenting. Worse still, the pool of available clerical manpower was distinctly limited. In addition to the natural reluctance of bishops to release too many men to the armed forces, the Anglican clergy were ageing as a body, the Church of England having seen a declining number of ordinations in the decades prior to the war.[50] Furthermore, there were other forms of military service available to the clergy. While some Anglican clergymen were recalled to the colours as reservists, a much larger number volunteered to serve in the combatant arms of the army and, less controversially, as non-combatants in the Royal Army Medical Corps.[51] Over and above all this, beneficed clergymen were deterred from coming forward by the pastoral demands of their parishes, by the difficulty in finding suitable locums and, if married, by the meagre pay and perquisites that the army afforded to its temporary Fourth Class chaplains, their pay being equivalent to that of subalterns.[52] As one chaplain complained in 1917: 'Our pay is none too generous, and, like other officers, there is no separation allowance for our wives and children, and no honest man is willing to draw the stipend from his parish for duties he is not performing.'[53] Because the service of temporary chaplains was limited to twelve months for most of the war, for reasons such as these many seasoned chaplains did not renew their service when their contracts expired.[54] Speaking at the Convocation of Canterbury in February 1918, Archbishop Davidson stated that 2,472 Anglican chaplains had held commissions since the start of the war and that 668 had relinquished their commissions, a total representing more than four times the number of Anglican chaplains who had been killed or wounded.[55]

Given these chronic difficulties, various solutions were mooted or applied in the course of the war. While a reduction in the term of service for temporary chaplains was under consideration in 1915,[56] the opposite course of action was eventually adopted in June 1917, the period of service for chaplains posted to Mesopotamia and other distant theatres of war being raised to two years. This term was eventually applied to all chaplains 'whenever possible' from March 1918.[57] However, Taylor Smith grew increasingly impatient with the manpower situation. In October 1917 he wrote to Archbishop Davidson reporting that the leakage of Anglican chaplains from the B.E.F. amounted to 'nine per week',[58] a predicament which, in turn, led Bishop Gwynne to urge the conscription of clergymen as chaplains, a move that was widely supported by his subordinates in France.[59] In response to this pressure Davidson engaged the help of his fellow bishops in a subtler scheme that required them to draw up lists of interested or eligible clergymen in their dioceses. These lists were then forwarded to the Chaplain-General for further action, action that appears to have taken the form of a direct approach to the individuals concerned. By February 1918, a list of 900 clergy had been compiled, a third of whom were deemed 'first-rate men available at once'.[60] Aided by the introduction of family allowances for temporary chaplains and by new pensionary arrangements for their widows,[61] by these means the Church of England seems to have weathered its manpower crisis, with more than 500 chaplains being commissioned between February 1918 and February 1919, when it was announced that 3,030 Anglican chaplains had served in the Army Chaplains' Department since August 1914.[62] Nevertheless, the success of Davidson's 'Lambeth scheme'[63] came much too late for some Anglican chaplains, Julian Bickersteth complaining in June 1917:

> It is very sad to see how short we are of chaplains. Vacancies take ages to fill up and, as far as I can make out, many divisions are short. Why this should be, goodness only knows. It makes me despair of the Church of

> England. Rome makes no mistakes. We have no fewer than five Roman priests in our division for barely 400 R.C.'s, and at the present moment only six C of E chaplains. Frantic appeals for more make no difference.[64]

Ironically, despite the chronic shortage of wartime chaplains, the Chaplain-General had been inundated with volunteers in the first weeks of the war. In October 1914, he told Davidson that he had 'over 1,200 volunteers for duty and there has been little difficulty in selecting good and suitable men of all shades of Church thought'.[65] In 1916, the Chaplain-General was reported to have received more than 4,000 applications for temporary commissions and it was estimated that he conducted roughly the same number of interviews throughout the course of the war.[66] Even without the presence of 'Bobbo', these interviews with Taylor Smith were the stuff of legend. As Everard Digby wrote in November 1917:

> The questions he will ask the applicant will refer solely to his suitability for Army work. What work has he done amongst men? Can he address large bodies of men, and can he tackle them individually? Does he realise the greatness of his opportunity, and is he prepared to make the most of it? If he wishes to serve overseas, he will be asked to sign an agreement binding him to remain abroad for twelve months. If he is going to France, he will be questioned as to whether he can ride, and as to his knowledge of French, etc. If accepted, he will have to be medically examined as to physical fitness by an Army doctor. In every case the Chaplain-General will always kneel and pray with his visitor ere the interview closes.[67]

Although Taylor Smith insisted on his fairness to 'all shades of Church thought',[68] this view was open to question. Significantly, nearly 60 per cent of a wartime total of 7,169 applications ended in failure, a pattern that was most pronounced in the early stages of the war.[69] Although Digby insisted that 'No reference is likely to be made as to the applicant's "views" ',[70] the key question that applicants faced concerned their intended ministry to the dying, with the demonstrative bishop being known to lie on the floor of his office in order to mimic the recumbent posture of a stricken soldier.[71] As a satisfactory meeting with the Chaplain-General was vital to the success of his interviewees, Anglo-Catholics felt that they were at a disadvantage, it being widely believed that he was unlikely to welcome any reference to sacramental confession or absolution. As Digby conceded, 'This interview is often dreaded by men who are of what is sometimes called the advanced School in the Church. The Chaplain-General is a well-known Evangelical, and many stories are told of these interviews, which make him out to be a bitter partisan of a very brutal type.'[72] While Digby maintained that this was far from being the truth, it appears that Taylor Smith was hard pressed to conceal a certain animosity even towards those Anglo-Catholic candidates of whom he otherwise approved. As Ernest Raymond wrote of his interview with Taylor Smith in the summer of 1915:

> I look back across fifty years to that interview with the Chaplain General in his War Office room . . . He is standing before me, a heavy man of fifty-five in full episcopal array: black frock-coat, pectoral cross, black sashed apron, and buttoned black gaiters . . . Bishop Taylor Smith, whose

> manner is brisk and brusque, as though he would say, 'There's a war on, and no time to waste', shoots at me a fusillade of questions. He has been Bishop of Sierra Leone, and I am wondering if this quick, sharp manner has been acquired among the Negroes of that 'White Man's Grave', or from his brother generals all around him in this War Office where he has been Chaplain General for fourteen years. Most of his questions I answer well enough, but the last one foolishly. Thus:
> Bishop (a low churchman): 'What would you do if a soldier came to you and said he was tired of his sins and wanted to be a Christian?'
> E.R. (determined to be loyal to his high Anglo-Catholicity, even if it cost all): 'I should tell him to come and make his confession.'
> Bishop: 'Wouldn't understand what you're talking about. Go down to the [medical officer] and see if you're fit for service abroad.'[73]

Regardless of his treatment of Anglo-Catholics, it does appear that, as in the pre-war years, a more masculine and virile type of Low Church chaplain was overtly favoured by the Chaplain-General. Mervyn Evers, who had met Taylor Smith at the Keswick convention of July 1913, believed that he sprang to the top of a 1,200-name waiting list when he wrote to the Chaplain-General early in the war 'reminding him of Keswick days and asking him if he had a job for me'.[74] Taylor Smith's preferences were also evident in his sympathy for the Y.M.C.A., then an emphatically evangelical organisation. The Chaplain-General had endorsed its work at T.F. camps in the pre-war years and went on to hail its initial wartime work as a 'magnificent effort' in the autumn of 1914.[75] Conversely, he seems to have been prey to traditional Protestant suspicions of Anglo-Catholic effeminacy, even homosexuality, and was not above noting the 'mincing manner' of certain Anglo-Catholic candidates for commissions.[76] The bishop's understanding of what was required of a chaplain and the fact that a 'weak-kneed, wobbly kind of religion was anathema to him'[77] no doubt led Taylor Smith to suspect that Anglo-Catholicism was essentially incompatible with military chaplaincy, especially given the pre-war model of the army chaplain as a sportsman and a man's man. In view of these prejudices, one of Taylor Smith's earliest and most questionable decisions was to appoint an elderly Territorial chaplain as S.C.F. of the 7th Division, a regular division that was sent to Belgium in October 1914. As a younger man, Edmund John Kennedy had evangelised with the London City Mission, soldiered with the London Scottish Volunteers and played rugby for the Harlequins. Furthermore, from 1884 to 1894 he had served as the general secretary of the Y.M.C.A. However, at fifty-nine years of age Kennedy was well past his peak and was not equal to the demands of the Western Front. Consequently, he served for only twelve months, half of which were spent recovering from a riding accident, before returning to England, where he died in October 1915. Although the Chaplain-General consoled Kennedy's widow with her husband's 'quick promotion',[78] the dubious effects of such patronage were evident on a much wider scale. After attending a chaplains' conference during Archbishop Davidson's tour of the Western Front in May 1916, Julian Bickersteth wrote that this gathering (and the discussion of the National Mission which ensued) had done much to betray the preferences of the Chaplain-General:

> [It] soon became apparent, all the more so when speeches were made at the conference . . . that the majority present were much after the Chaplain General's own heart . . . I had not realised before how successful the CG had been in appointing men of his own way of thinking. There were quite a few padres there with moustaches, and as they wore khaki collars they looked very much like combatant officers . . . Several chaplains spoke, in a rather fervid way, of the importance of assuring men that Christ was their Saviour and their Friend, ignoring the fact that what the Archbishop wanted were practical methods.[79]

Nevertheless, the pretext for change in the Department was not the Chaplain-General's alleged bias but the insupportable workload that the war had placed upon him. As E.H. Thorold remembered:

> His routine work in the office was very heavy, and visitors on every kind of business were numberless . . . His baggage and an express train were frequently in the background of his thoughts, for he was perpetually travelling all over the Kingdom to conduct confirmations, to preach and to visit hospitals: from which he seemed to return refreshed to peruse files, decide problems and answer conundrums in scores of personal letters. Meanwhile, the Churches, and particularly the Church of England had much to say.[80]

This was undoubtedly true. Inspired by his pioneering visit to the Western Front that Easter, a visit that had met with scant encouragement from the Chaplain-General,[81] in July 1915 Winnington Ingram gave 'a long, critical speech'[82] in the Upper House of the Convocation of Canterbury that deplored the state of Anglican chaplaincy in the B.E.F. and which stressed the need for an Anglican bishop who could administer confirmation and 'be a Father in God to the chaplains' in France and Belgium.[83] Significantly, Davidson responded sympathetically, agreeing that it would be a first step towards ensuring necessary changes.[84] Consequently:

> [The] Bishops unanimously called upon the Archbishop of Canterbury, acting in 'conjunction if it may be, with the Archbishop of York,' to arrange a private conference between the War Office authorities and certain representative Bishops to discuss the whole question of religious ministrations to the troops both at home and abroad.[85]

This conference took place at Lambeth Palace less than a fortnight later and considered 'the Chaplains' Question' in its entirety. The participants duly agreed to create an Anglican advisory committee and to appoint a deputy for the Chaplain-General on the Western Front.[86] With the support of Lord Kitchener (the Secretary of State for War and a staunch High Churchman)[87] both measures were quickly effected. When the War Office announced that Davidson and Kitchener had agreed to appoint Bishop Llewellyn Henry Gwynne 'to represent the Chaplain-General at the Front and to be his deputy there',[88] the Anglo-Catholic *Church Times* was elated, crowing that it was 'to be hoped that the other suggestions made by the Bishop of London in his Convocation speech . . . may meet with equal acceptance'.[89]

It may, however, have been of some consolation to the Chaplain-General that his new deputy shared a very similar background. Besides their colonial experience and C.M.S. attachments, Gwynne and Taylor Smith had been contemporaries at St. John's, Highbury, and Gwynne even regarded his fellow bishop as an 'intimate friend'.[90] As late as 1918, the two could converse freely 'about the things of God', a faculty that led Gwynne to describe the Chaplain-General as 'a really spiritually minded man'.[91] Ordained only a year after Taylor Smith, Gwynne had acquired 'much parochial experience' as a clergyman in the industrial East Midlands (where he had even played as a centre-forward for Derby County) before going out to the Sudan as a C.M.S. missionary in 1899, commencing this work in the aftermath of the Anglo-Egyptian reconquest.[92] As part of his work in the Sudan, Gwynne also served as an officiating clergyman to its British garrison and there he made the acquaintance of Kitchener himself, who encouraged Gwynne's ministry to the military as a more prudent alternative to evangelising local Muslims.[93] In 1908, Gwynne was consecrated suffragan Bishop of Khartoum, which was then part of the diocese of Jerusalem, and was on leave in London when war broke out.[94] Although over fifty in August 1914, an age that Taylor Smith came to regard as the upper limit for temporary chaplains,[95] Gwynne promptly offered his services to the War Office as a temporary chaplain. Despite Taylor Smith's reluctance to accept him, Gwynne's connections and perseverance eventually prevailed and, at the end of August 1914, he arrived in France as a temporary chaplain Fourth Class.[96] Thereafter, the Bishop of Khartoum served at Rouen, St. Nazaire and Boulogne before being posted as a brigade chaplain to the 2nd Division in December 1914.[97]

If his episcopal orders, exalted connections and military experience rendered Gwynne acceptable to the Anglican hierarchy and to the War Office, as D.C.G. he also transpired to be genuinely popular with the Anglican chaplains of the B.E.F. Indeed, George Bell subsequently claimed that 'Hardly any man in the Army was more welcome than [Gwynne], wherever he went, and no priest or bishop in the whole Chaplains' Department was more appreciated in his pastoral ministry.'[98] Unlike the Chaplain-General, Gwynne's approach to his subordinates was characterised by its sensitivity and tact, a manner that endeared him even to Anglo-Catholics.[99] Typical of this style was an episode from May 1917, when Gwynne felt obliged to take Neville Talbot to task for his controversial *Thoughts on Religion at the Front*. As Gwynne noted in his diary:

> I took Neville Talbot out for a walk in the woods and we sat under [a] tree while I talked to him like a father about the mistakes I thought he had made. I told him my experiences of God's special providences to me in the Sudan [and] all the misunderstandings between us vanished.[100]

Furthermore, and although two controversial Anglo-Catholic chaplains were sent home after his appointment,[101] Gwynne refrained from interfering with matters of worship or the 'reverent experiments' of his chaplains, latitude that allowed Anglo-Catholics to celebrate Holy Communion during parade services and others (including Gwynne himself) to participate in joint services with other Protestant chaplains.[102] F.R. Barry, who served as a brigade chaplain, a divisional S.C.F. and eventually as a D.A.C.G. on the Western Front, believed that Gwynne was ideally suited to his task:

> [M]any of us, I think, would have gone under or have suffered shipwreck of their faith had it not been for the pastoral care and guidance of the great and saintly Bishop Gwynne, Father in God to a whole generation of young men . . . he exercised an outflowing love and goodness which drew out the best in anyone who had contact with him . . . A burly man, and a Welsh footballer, he was every inch masculine, a man's man. Yet he was patient and gentle as a mother . . . [his appointment] at once raised the status of the Department and got it properly recognised by the Top Brass. (He had known some of the Army commanders when they were subalterns serving in the Sudan.) He made himself felt all over the Western Front; what he did for his chaplains can never be told in words . . . He was a commanding figure in that period; and his place is on the roll of the Church's heroes.[103]

However, Gwynne's timely appointment as D.C.G. was only one of several measures that served to divest the Chaplain-General of much of his power. Within a few weeks, the new Anglican advisory committee was about its business. Though small, consisting of only four members plus a War Office secretary, the committee made up in influence what it lacked in numbers. Chaired by the fourth Marquess of Salisbury, its secretary was Sir Reginald Brade (the Permanent Under Secretary at the War Office) and it comprised the bishops of Winchester and Ripon and Field Marshal Lord Grenfell. As Kitchener conceived it, the task of this committee was 'to advise the Chaplain General on various questions which may arise regarding the Church of England Chaplains'.[104] However, by means of two successive reports on the state and requirements of the Anglican branch of the Army Chaplains' Department, by early 1916 the committee had secured a complete reorganisation and a major augmentation of Anglican chaplaincy work. In January 1916, an Assistant Chaplain-General was appointed to each of the army's home commands and an additional A.C.G. (namely E.H. Pearce, a Territorial chaplain and a Canon of Westminster) was also appointed to help Taylor Smith with interviewing applicants and with the day-to-day running of the Department.[105] An A.C.G. was also appointed to each army headquarters and major base on the Western Front.[106] The chain of command in the B.E.F. was also tightened. Whereas the senior chaplains of its constituent armies had exercised no control over senior divisional chaplains (their work being confined to the supervision of chaplaincy work in rear areas) divisional chaplains were now brought under the control of their respective A.C.G. The appointment of another tier of senior corps chaplains was also urged by the Anglican advisory committee, although this did not take effect until December 1916 when each of these functionaries assumed the title of Deputy Assistant Chaplain-General.[107]

Soon after these adjustments were made to the higher organisation of Anglican chaplaincy, the War Office also agreed to increase the number of Anglican chaplains from seven (an establishment fixed in March 1915) to nine in each English (and largely Anglican) division. It also accepted the committee's proposed quota of chaplains for hospitals, bases and lines of communication, concessions that instantly created 129 vacancies for Anglican chaplains in the B.E.F. alone.[108] Significantly, much of this success was achieved through backstairs lobbying. As the son of a former Prime Minister and a major figure in the Conservative party,[109] Lord Salisbury was able to secure a private meeting with Herbert Asquith in November 1915, a meeting in which he briefed the Prime Minister on the committee's aims and objectives. By this time, Salisbury had already accompanied Lord Grenfell on a visit to the B.E.F. where they had discussed chaplaincy matters with its Commander-in-Chief (Sir John French), with his chief of staff (Sir William Robertson) and with the D.C.G., Bishop Gwynne. All of these had expressed a firm conviction that the number of Anglican chaplains should be increased. In fact, the D.C.G. had even argued for twelve Anglican chaplains per division, effectively endorsing the Bishop of London's call for an Anglican chaplain to be appointed to every infantry battalion.[110]

Besides being a reaction to Taylor Smith's handling of the Chaplains' Department, the radical reorganisation of Anglican chaplaincy from the summer of 1915 was also a response to the *ad hoc* system that had arisen in France and Belgium since the despatch of the B.E.F. in August 1914. As we have seen, Taylor Smith had drawn up a mobilisation schedule for the Chaplains' Department. However, this was not incorporated into the official mobilisation tables of the B.E.F., an omission that was widely attributed to 'a Printer's error'. In fact, what actually happened was that the mobilisation tables, which had been compiled some years earlier when the future size of the Department had been in doubt, had never been updated, their reference to a single senior chaplain being intended as an *aide memoire* rather than as a fixed establishment.[111] Hence, and with the exception of the Principal Chaplain, who was attached to G.H.Q., there was no official provision for any of the chaplains who originally sailed for France. Consequently, and in the spirit of Taylor Smith's schedule, chaplains attached themselves to their general hospitals and field ambulances as unexpected, if not unwelcome, guests. As Harry Blackburne remarked of the early weeks of war on the Western Front:

> [Those] of us who went out with the original B.E.F. are not likely to forget how difficult it was to fit ourselves into a machine which had been wonderfully woven together, and in which no clear decision had been made about the Chaplains' Department . . . It was disconcerting, to say the least of it, to be greeted wherever one went with, 'Hullo, Padre, what on earth are you doing out here?' The Medical authorities, into whose arms we were thrown, did what they could for us, and provided us with homes in the Field Ambulances and in the Hospitals; but for the first few weeks of the War it was always a matter of some difficulty to get one's modest kit carried on wagons which were already fully loaded with authorised equipment, as laid down in those carefully constructed mobilisation regulations; and in which, except for the Principal Chaplain, the Chaplains did not appear.[112]

The only mitigating factor was that the chaplains concerned were pre-war regulars and were thus reasonably well placed to get on and make do; as one of their number put it, 'The situation was very fluid, and initiative was the only saving quality.'[113] However, personal resourcefulness could not offset a bigger problem, namely the lack of suitable reinforcements and replacements. Quite simply, the hallowed system of promotion by seniority had created a top-heavy Department in which a large proportion of chaplains were simply too old to take the field. As a War Office committee reported in 1928, 'The result of this system was that the establishment in 1914 consisted too largely of elderly men in high classes, whose qualifications did not always justify their rank and pay.'[114]

If the mobilisation of chaplains for the regular divisions of the B.E.F. verged on the shambolic, the mobilisation of Anglican chaplains for the Territorial Force, which began to see action in France in the autumn of 1914, descended into farce. The T.F. had a much larger establishment of chaplains than the regular army and it was planned that 163 Territorial chaplains would be mobilised in the event of war.[115] As a memorandum to Archbishop Davidson explained, the lavish establishment of Territorial chaplains was emblematic of the good will of the War Office, which had always recognised the value of church work among these part-time soldiers.[116] Hence, a certain local standing and an ability to stimulate recruitment had been prime considerations in the appointment of Anglican chaplains to the T.F. As one of their number recalled, many Anglican Territorial chaplains were 'middle-aged clergymen who were selected by the lord lieutenant of the county and the bishop of the diocese . . . as being, according to War Office Regulations, of such a position that [they] "could influence recruiting for the Territorial Force" '.[117]

However, with the outbreak of war two factors served to limit the usefulness of such chaplains. Firstly, although the Territorial Force had been largely intended for home defence, its role was rapidly transformed as more than 90 per cent of its officers and men volunteered for service overseas.[118] Secondly, the criteria upon which its chaplains had been appointed meant that many T.F. chaplains were senior Anglican clergymen who were simply unable to extricate themselves from their civilian duties, the bishop of London being a prime example of this phenomenon. At the beginning of August 1914, Winnington Ingram was at Beachy Head attending the annual training camp of the London Rifle Brigade, whose chaplain he had been for thirteen years. Although he then accompanied the L.R.B. to Bisley, where he proved useful in helping to persuade thousands of London Territorials to volunteer for overseas service, the bishop was hardly in a position to accompany the L.R.B. to the Western Front and he was eventually obliged to return to London, leaving the regiment in the care of a deputy.[119] Although only six chaplains were mobilised for each of the fourteen Territorial infantry divisions, for reasons such as this it proved impossible to meet even these requirements and Anglican clergymen in particular did not respond to their summons. According to the memorandum prepared for Davidson, this reflected the naivety with which many had accepted Territorial chaplaincies in the first place:

> It has not been easy to secure Chaplains who were both able and willing to respond to the call which mobilisation makes and to go off with their men. This difficulty has been partly due to the unexpectedness of a call for distant external service, the Chaplains having regarded their work as mainly local. Probably in originally accepting the Chaplaincy position to

> a Territorial force they had neglected to consider what mobilisation would involve.[120]

Indeed, in a letter to Davidson of October 1914, the Chaplain-General warned that 'all these Territorial Force Chaplains when mobilised are under the Army Act and I can only hope that military discipline will not pursue them'.[121] What also added to Anglican embarrassment was the efficiency of the Presbyterian churches north of the border. When the Territorial Force was mobilised, thirty-two ministers of the Church of Scotland and the United Free Church turned out to serve its units at home and the four general hospitals in Scotland. However, as the bulk of Scotland's two Territorial divisions remained in Great Britain for several months,[122] a deal was soon struck with the War Office whereby Presbyterian chaplains of the T.F. were required to serve for only three months and, by May 1915, fifty-five ministers of the Church of Scotland had already seen service on this basis.[123]

Apart from the partisan rivalries and organisational problems that beset Anglican chaplaincy in the first year of the war, a further goad to the Chaplain-General's many critics was the fact that the Principal Chaplain of the B.E.F. was an Irish Presbyterian who owed his position simply to his seniority in the pre-war Chaplains' Department. Born in 1854, Dr. John Morrow Simms was on the verge of retirement in August 1914 and was the oldest serving member of the Chaplains' Department, having seen active service in the Sudan, South Africa and East Africa in the course of nearly thirty years as a commissioned chaplain.[124] Nevertheless, on the Western Front in the autumn of 1914, this 'genial, forceful Irishman'[125] turned out to be an able administrator who did much to create order out of chaos in partnership with the B.E.F.'s Adjutant-General, Sir Nevil Macready. In November 1914, Macready held a meeting which aimed to reorganise the Chaplains' Department in France and Belgium while respecting denominational differences and maintaining the authority of the Principal Chaplain. Attended by Simms, Ewen Macpherson and William Keatinge (the senior Anglican and Roman Catholic chaplains of the B.E.F.) its results were threefold. Simms established an office at Rouen, which was later transferred to St. Omer, and was provided with an assistant; Macpherson and Keatinge were each given cars and assistants of their own and tasked with advising Simms in matters relating to their respective denominations. Finally, the establishment of chaplains in each division was raised from five to thirteen, the denominational preponderance depending on the denominational composition of each division.[126] In conjunction with Macready, Simms then began a process of redeployment, many regular chaplains being withdrawn from their brigades in order to assume greater responsibilities in larger formations, an important move given the inexperience of chaplains arriving (or due to arrive) with Territorial and New Army divisions. Furthermore, Simms introduced a scheme whereby experienced chaplains were temporarily attached to new divisions in order to help their chaplains adjust to their new situation.[127] More chaplains were also posted to the B.E.F.'s bases, rear areas and lines of communication.[128] Lastly, and all too aware of the difficulties inherent in administering a multi-denominational entity, in May 1915 Simms officially appointed senior chaplains for his Anglican, Presbyterian, Roman Catholic and Wesleyan chaplains, his rationale being to ensure that administrative and denominational matters were kept separate and that proper ecclesiastical control was maintained over chaplains of each denomination.[129]

On his return from France in March 1915, the army's senior Jewish chaplain announced that he was 'deeply impressed by the whole-hearted unanimity with which the different religious bodies are working. Church of England, Presbyterian, Methodist – all are as one'.[130] According to J.E. Edmonds, the system that Simms devised worked 'smoothly and satisfactorily, but certain influential persons at home were not entirely satisfied with the absence of any local episcopal atmosphere for the Church of England chaplains'.[131] This was certainly true. As the Archbishop of York, Cosmo Lang, argued in June 1915:

> Is it not involved in the principles of an Episcopal Church that the supervision of a work of such overwhelming opportunity and importance should be in the hands of one who has received episcopal consecration? He ought to be more than an administrative officer; but a Father in God both to the Chaplains and also to the Officers and men. It is needless I think to press this point.[132]

These arguments contributed to the appointment of Gwynne as D.C.G. in July 1915. However, the creation of this new position (which was endowed with 'the local and temporary rank of Major General')[133] and the promotion of Gwynne over the head of Simms (who was ranked only as a brigadier-general) was fiercely resented by the Principal Chaplain and his allies. In fact, Simms responded by threatening his resignation and the Church of Scotland led demands that he should be granted the same rank as Gwynne, a request that Kitchener brusquely rebuffed with the words, 'I'll make him a General when you make him a Bishop.'[134] Although parliamentary lobbying eventually ensured that Simms was promoted, 'the invidious and inconsiderate treatment' meted out to the Church of Scotland 'in common with other non-Anglican Churches'[135] fed a common sense of grievance.

However, the most obvious consequence of Gwynne's appointment was that it shattered the fragile unity of the Chaplains' Department and created 'a dual organisation' of chaplains in the army's most important theatre of war. After July 1915, chaplains in France and Belgium served in either the Anglican D.C.G.'s branch or the polyglot branch of the Department run by the Principal Chaplain. Despite the resentment it caused, a clear advantage of Anglican separation and reorganisation in 1915 was the greater degree of cohesion that it generated within Anglican chaplaincy. Endowed with a formidable combination of military and ecclesiastical authority, from April 1916 Gwynne was able to gather his most senior chaplains together for regular conferences, meetings that played a major role in defining the policy and practice of Anglican chaplaincy on the Western Front. At these conferences, of which a dozen were held between April 1916 and January 1918, numerous matters were debated and thrashed out, ranging from the allocation of 'battle posts' to chaplains (a standard scheme being agreed in June 1916) to the disposal of profits generated by Church Army huts.[136] In contrast, there was comparatively little in the way of general policy and immediate guidance in the Principal Chaplain's branch, prompting one chaplain to complain to Cardinal Bourne in November 1917:

> There is, in fact, no *practical* organisation. Each man has to fend for himself . . . To give an instance: my own Division, the 48th, was engaged in the battle of the Somme 4 times. On no single occasion was there anyone to tell us the best place to go or to organise our efforts for the men. When your eminence realises that a Brigade may be sent into the line one day, attack the next, and be withdrawn, the day after, you will see the absolute necessity of someone able to give information about an unknown locale, and advice to the distracted and overworked Chaplains. With us, there was no such person.[137]

The tone of this letter also reflected widespread dissatisfaction with the wartime development of Roman Catholic chaplaincy. On the outbreak of war, Catholics had comprised the second largest group of commissioned chaplains in the Chaplains' Department.[138] However, there were no Roman Catholic chaplains in the Territorial Force and Taylor Smith had allotted only ten Catholic chaplains to the B.E.F., with seven being attached to divisions and the remainder to general hospitals – a clear breach with the traditional practice of allocating a Catholic chaplain to every Irish battalion.[139] In the chaos of mobilisation and the confusion attendant on the B.E.F.'s retreat from Mons, this establishment proved wholly inadequate. At the end of August, for example, the absence of a chaplain of their own meant that a German priest ministered to the dead and wounded of the 2nd Royal Munster Fusiliers after their stand at Etreux.[140] As more Roman Catholic chaplains joined the B.E.F. that autumn,[141] Macready invited William Keatinge to propose a proper establishment for them.[142] Keatinge recommended that one be allotted to each Irish battalion, four to each infantry division and that others should be sent to the army's bases and lines of communication. However, this desideratum (even if only partially met in the spring of 1915) placed heavy demands on the Roman Catholic church in mainland Britain, particularly given the competing demands of the New Army and the lack of any Catholic chaplains in the pre-war Territorial Force. Indeed, it was a demand that proved extremely difficult to meet, especially as each applicant for a temporary commission needed the agreement of his bishop or superior prior to offering his services to Bourne and the War Office.[143]

Bourne's response was to call upon the religious orders and the Irish hierarchy to help supply the priests required, despite the fact that they had been very minor contributors to the Chaplains' Department in recent decades. Although Cardinal Logue nominated eight chaplains for the 10th and 16th Divisions after they were formed in southern Ireland in 1914,[144] throughout the war the Irish hierarchy proved unable or unwilling to send priests in sufficient numbers.[145] If Ireland's clerical resources were thinly stretched (Irish missionaries were, for example, called upon to replace many of their French and German counterparts in the African mission fields)[146] there was also a discernible reluctance to volunteer on the part of the diocesan clergy.[147] Besides a shortage of enthusiasm for the Allied cause, there was a lingering conviction that Roman Catholic army chaplains were underpaid and overworked in comparison with their Protestant counterparts.[148] A further disincentive may have been that Bourne expected Catholic priests to serve for the duration of the war, notwithstanding the War Office system of fixed-term contracts. Whatever its causes, the lack of Irish chaplains was both obvious and alarming. By March 1916, Dublin, Ireland's largest see, had supplied only twelve army chaplains and it seems that as few as seventy-three Irish diocesan clergy served in the Chaplains' Department during the course of the war.[149] In fact, according to Bourne's biographer, by Easter 1915 the archdiocese of Westminster had sent more diocesan clergy to the army than all of the Irish dioceses put together.[150]

Given the muted response of the diocesan clergy of Catholic Ireland, the principal burden of providing chaplains fell upon the religious orders and on the diocesan clergy of England and Wales (the Scottish dioceses appear to have released only twenty-one priests).[151] It was indicative of the heavy reliance on the former that, in May 1915 and as 'Delegate of the Holy See for the British Army & Navy', Bourne addressed a circular letter to the superiors of the male religious orders throughout Great Britain, announcing that:

> There is now a very urgent need for another large increase in the number of Priests to do duty as Chaplains in the Army or Navy. Would you very kindly let me know if you have any Fathers available whom you can specially recommend as in every way suitable for these duties. I should be grateful if you would be good enough to state in each case if the Father prefers one of the Services to the other, so that I may be able, if possible, to satisfy this preference. Any Priest accepted for duty of this kind must be at the disposition of H.M.'s Government until the end of the War.[152]

Such pleas did not fall on deaf ears, the orders providing around 40 per cent of the army's Roman Catholic chaplains.[153] Making a virtue out of a necessity, one Catholic commentator even wrote that 'Monks came forth from the cloister, scholars laid aside their books, schools reduced their staffs [and] preachers of eminence gave themselves to the care of the soldier.'[154] Through these expedients, there was a sustained and significant increase in the army's Catholic chaplains; there were 400 by August 1916 and 643 by November 1918.[155] Indeed, such was the number of Roman Catholic chaplains in France in 1915 that Archbishop Davidson was even moved to complain that there was an 'inordinate number' of them – 'some of whom have hardly anyone to minister to'.[156] Furthermore, and partly because of poor levels of recruitment in Ireland, the proportion of Roman Catholic soldiers actually declined as the war progressed, generating a chaplain to soldier ratio that Julian Bickersteth rightly identified as a distinct advantage to his Roman Catholic counterparts.[157]

While their numbers grew, the organisation and leadership of the army's Roman Catholic chaplains underwent considerable change, especially on the Western Front. Named the B.E.F's Senior Catholic chaplain in May 1915, William Keatinge was appointed Principal Chaplain to British troops in Salonika in the autumn of 1916, his place being taken by his assistant, Bernard Rawlinson, a Benedictine who had served as an acting chaplain in the Boer War. However, as part of a wider reorganisation of the Principal Chaplain's branch in the winter of 1916–17, the title of Senior Catholic chaplain was abolished and Rawlinson became an Assistant Principal Chaplain.[158] While Catholic chaplains seem to have been prepared to serve in the Principal Chaplain's branch under a Senior Chaplain of their own faith (especially as Keatinge was a First Class chaplain in his own right) doubts were expressed at what seemed to be the unequal partnership of Simms and Rawlinson. As one old regular, E.M. Morgan, wrote to Bourne in January 1917:

> Fr. Rawlinson has, I understand, been promoted to the post of Assistant Principal Chaplain, Headquarters. Probably, Dr. Simms will make use of him to deal with Catholic Chaplains, and so, on the surface, things will seem very much as they used to be. But we have no guarantee how long Fr. Rawlinson's appointment will last. Dr. Simms need not have appointed him. He can move him from Headquarters any day and select any of the Non Church of England chaplains to fill the post. If Dr. Simms employs him to deal with Catholic matters he does so at his own pleasure . . . The only safeguard is to appoint a Catholic Deputy Principal Chaplain to deal with Catholic chaplains and Catholic affairs. Dr. Simms would then be the means of communication between the Catholic chaplains and the Adjutant General.[159]

The new designation of 'non-C. of E.' for all chaplains embraced by the Principal Chaplain's branch also grated with Morgan, who complained:

> Personally, I have always thought that we should have followed the example of the Church of England. They found the present system intolerable and broke away from it. I think it a pity that we did not do the same. Catholics can never settle down in a happy family made up of Presbyterians, Wesleyans (Primitive or otherwise), Baptists, United Board, Jews, Congregationalists and all the variegated sects who, with ourselves, now rejoice in the proud title of Non Church of England. If the War Office can recognise two religious organizations in the Army there ought to be no difficulty in their recognizing three.[160]

Although Bourne expressed his full confidence in 'the satisfactory results of the re-organization of the Chaplains' Department' in the autumn of 1917,[161] simmering away in the background were longstanding tensions over his exalted position as 'Delegate of the Holy See for the British Army & Navy'. Bourne's 'excessive powers' in the appointment of army chaplains were resented by the Irish and the Scottish bishops alike and moves were soon afoot in Rome to divest him of them.[162] According to an alternative scheme devised in August 1915 (and seriously considered by the War Office and by the Foreign Office) an advisory committee on Roman Catholic chaplaincy would be established which would include representatives of the Scottish and Irish hierarchies. Furthermore, and following Anglican and other European precedents, a Catholic Chaplain-General (or equivalent thereof) would be appointed to the British army. Although this scheme was sabotaged by Bourne,[163] lobbying at the Vatican was incessant, particularly on the part of the Irish bishops.[164] Indeed, Bourne's stubborn refusal to surrender any of his powers in chaplaincy matters even alienated Pope Benedict XV.[165] Consequently, his resistance was unavailing and he was only able to postpone the inevitable.[166] In November 1917, the Pope appointed William Keatinge *Episcopus Castrensis* for the British army. Returning home from Salonika, Keatinge was consecrated bishop in Rome in February 1918 and he assumed responsibility for all Roman Catholic chaplains the following month. Some weeks later, the War Office bestowed upon him the title of Principal Roman Catholic Chaplain – thus requiring the grant of equivalent titles to the army's senior Presbyterian, Wesleyan and United Board chaplains.[167]

In contrast to the Anglicans and Roman Catholics, the Presbyterians expanded their chaplaincy work without experiencing serious political difficulties. In August 1914, the regular army had eighteen commissioned or acting Presbyterian chaplains, including nine ministers of the Church of Scotland, four of the United Free Church, three of the Presbyterian Church of Ireland and two of the Presbyterian Church of England.[168] While the mobilisation of Territorial chaplains for home service went smoothly north of the border, there was also a glut of applications for the limited number of temporary commissions that were also available. Hence, in May 1915, its Committee on Army and Navy Chaplains reported to the General Assembly of the Church of Scotland that more than two hundred parish ministers ('besides a number of probationers') had offered their services as temporary chaplains. Faced with a surfeit of applicants, the committee's convener, Dr. J.A. McClymont, had found their selection to be a 'difficult and delicate task' in which he had 'endeavoured to keep in view the claims of different parts of the country and of the various Territorial regiments, as well as the personal qualifications required'.[169] By this time, thirty-six Church of Scotland chaplains were serving abroad; of these, six were regulars, fifteen were pre-war Territorial chaplains, four were chaplains drawn from the Indian Ecclesiastical Establishment and the remainder (a small minority) were temporary chaplains.[170] By 1916, however, potential chaplains had become much scarcer as the expiration of annual contracts, pressure on ministers to return home, the loss of ministers to other branches of the army and the growing establishment of chaplains stretched the clerical resources of the Presbyterian churches to the limit.[171] Nevertheless, and led by the Church of Scotland, which was always ready to assert its equality with the Church of England, the Presbyterian churches continued to demand an establishment of chaplains in line with that granted to the Church of England. By August 1916, the number of Presbyterian chaplains had risen to 175 and, despite an ongoing lack of available clergy, the reorganisation of the Principal Chaplain's branch in January 1917 created vacancies for an additional thirty.[172]

By 1917, it was clear that Presbyterian resources were close to breaking point, despite the fact that smaller Presbyterian churches, such as the Free Church of Scotland and the Free Presbyterian Church, had also joined the Presbyterian Chaplains Advisory Committee and were sending ministers to the Chaplains' Department.[173] In 1917, worrying shortfalls were reported to the Church of Scotland's General Assembly.[174] The 52nd (Lowland) Division was two chaplains short of its revised establishment of nine Presbyterian chaplains and shortages were also apparent in largely English divisions.[175] Consequently, from as early as 1915, and on the condition that those transferred served for the duration of the war, the War Office sanctioned the transfer to the Chaplains' Department of Presbyterian ministers who were then serving in the Royal Army Medical Corps.[176] As the shortage of chaplains worsened, pressure mounted for the release of more ministers from this and other branches of the army, it being noted in 1916 that eighty-five Church of Scotland ministers were serving in other capacities whereas only eighty-three were serving as chaplains.[177] Although these transfers ceased in April 1918,[178] the Chaplains' Department gained at least sixteen ministers of the Church of Scotland by these means. While a modest number in overall terms, they could make a significant difference in certain theatres of war. In 1918, for example, it was reported from Salonika that a local transfer of ministers had brought the Presbyterian chaplains up to strength after a long period in which they had been 'much below establishment' owing to significant casualties and poor communications.[179]

The transition of Wesleyan chaplaincy to a wartime footing in many respects mirrored the Presbyterian experience. In 1914, and in addition to the small number of Wesleyan chaplains in the Territorial Force, fifteen of the regular army's thirty-six acting chaplains and three of its four honorary chaplains were Wesleyans.[180] Four Wesleyan chaplains accompanied the B.E.F. to France and, as their presence grew on the Western Front, Owen Spencer Watkins was appointed their Senior Chaplain in May 1915.[181] By August 1916, the Wesleyan component of the Army Chaplains' Department had experienced the exponential growth that was so typical of the period. At this point, 160 Wesleyan chaplains were serving with the army, a figure that was to reach 256 by the end of the war.[182] However, this expansion was not achieved without placing great demands on available manpower, particularly as ministers and senior theological students were lost to the army in other ways. A few, like John Boullier, were army reservists recalled to the colours on the outbreak of war. Others, like T.L.B. Westerdale, Robert Rider and eighteen of Rider's fellow students at Handsworth College, volunteered to serve in the ranks, often (although not always) in the R.A.M.C.[183] By 1916, and in order to ease the strain on the connexion's circuit ministers, many were being reclaimed and transferred to the Chaplains' Department, where they acted as a useful leavening of experienced men who had seen service in the ranks.[184] In addition to its vastly increased size, Wesleyan chaplaincy also became more closely integrated into the Army Chaplains' Department. As the policy of the War Office was to issue temporary commissions rather than letters of introduction, Wesleyan chaplains were commissioned from August 1914 and the Wesleyan Conference accepted this *fait accompli* the following year.[185] Furthermore, with the reorganisation of the Principal Chaplain's branch at the end of 1916, Wesleyan chaplains acquired new and greater responsibilities. In November 1916, Owen Spencer Watkins became Assistant Principal Chaplain to Third Army and, by the end of the war, he was serving as Principal Chaplain to British forces in Italy.[186]

Despite being formally recognised by the army in 1903, neither the Baptists nor the Congregationalists had any commissioned or acting chaplains when war broke out, the same being true of the Primitive and United Methodist churches. However, the strength of Nonconformist influence on Britain's Liberal government ensured that this situation was swiftly rectified and temporary commissions were granted to ministers of these denominations from the end of August 1914.[187] However, the War Office was not thrilled by the prospect of having to deal separately with a plethora of smaller denominations and sought to create a generic category of Free Church chaplain, a bid that foundered on a rock of Wesleyan opposition.[188] Furthermore, Kitchener himself was distinctly unsympathetic to the claims of the Free Churches. As Lloyd George maintained:

> Kitchener's rigid point of view and its reactionary arrogance showed itself in other directions . . . He vehemently opposed the recognition of Nonconformist denominations not already included in the Army List, and his refusal to appoint chaplains of what he evidently thought were superfluous and eccentric sects provoked the most angry scenes I have ever witnessed at a Cabinet. The Army only recognised three or four denominations. The others, not being on the Army List, had no existence for him. He did not realise that with an army that was being multiplied tenfold and drawing recruits from classes, or types, untapped by the ordinary recruiting sergeant, the variety of religious beliefs held must necessarily be greater. To his mind the religious services provided for the regulars of the old army ought to be good enough for these amateur soldiers.[189]

However, Kitchener eventually capitulated, more or less gracefully, to pressure from his cabinet colleagues:

> When he gave way, however, he did it thoroughly. I well remember how, when he had been overruled by the Cabinet on the question of chaplains he took a piece of paper, started writing, and turning to me said: 'Come now, tell me the names of these sects for which you want padres. Is this list right? Primitive Baptists, Calvinistic Wesleyans, Congregational Methodists . . . ?' It was not intended to cast ridicule; he simply had never heard the correct names of these great religious bodies. I gave him the right titles. He wrote them all down carefully. As soon as he returned to the War Office he took steps to invite representatives of all these denominations to attend a Chaplains Committee there. It functioned right through the War without any friction.[190]

The solution to which Lloyd George referred was the creation of a United Navy and Army Board, whose purpose and functions closely resembled that of the Presbyterian Chaplains Advisory Committee. Composed of representatives of the Baptist, Congregationalist, United and Primitive Methodist churches, the United Board first met in November 1914.[191] Under the chairmanship of J.H. Shakespeare, the dynamic secretary of the Baptist Union and a confidante of Lloyd George,[192] as far as the War Office was concerned the main purpose of the board was to recommend ministers for temporary commissions in the Chaplains' Department. Initially, this was done by rotation but in November 1915 a fixed ratio was agreed upon; for the remainder of the war one third of the board's nominees would be Baptists, another third would be Congregationalists whilst the remaining nominations would be equally divided between the Primitive and the United Methodists.[193] Balancing appointments between denominations was no easy task, particularly in the face of determined lobbying. In March 1915, for example, the board considered the following memorandum from a Baptist minister in Lancashire:

> As Secretary of the Burnley, Nelson, Colne, and Padiham Baptist Ministers Fraternal, I hereby send you the Copy of Resolution passed on Feb. 8th, 1915—
> 'That we point out to the Rev. J.H. Shakespeare, M.A., that as so many men have left the Churches and Schools of the North East of Lancashire to serve with the Forces, we suggest that if possible, a minister from this North East District be appointed Chaplain to H.M. Forces'.[194]

Other churches also lobbied for admittance to the board. By April 1917, the Moravians and the Wesleyan Reform Union were seeking chaplains of their own. However, although the board was sympathetic to the case of the Moravians, their intended chaplain was killed later that year while serving as a lance corporal in the Royal Scots.[195]

Despite these problems, the board's overall success was reflected in the fact that by October 1916 there were 134 United Board chaplains serving with the army, a number that had risen to 251 by the time of the Armistice.[196] Furthermore, in 1918 the Primitive Methodist Conference heard that forty-one of its ministers were then serving as chaplains, a fair reflection of the scrupulousness with which the board observed its denominational quotas, the Primitive Methodists being entitled to one-sixth of its nominations.[197] Nevertheless, the board's component churches were hard pressed to meet the demands of this dramatic growth. The Primitive Methodists inaugurated an Army Committee of their own in September 1914, its purpose being to interview applicants for temporary commissions. However, after two years had elapsed it was clearly scraping the barrel and was increasingly looking to the army to supply its current needs through the transfer of serving personnel.[198] Although pressure on the Army Committee mounted during the course of the war (and especially when the transfer of ministers was prohibited in 1918)[199] it was clearly determined to supply the right calibre of chaplains to the United Board. As late as March 1917, the committee received an appeal from an unsuccessful minister asking it 'to re-consider his position with regard to his application for a chaplaincy'. Not to be swayed, it simply reiterated its position 'That we do not consider he is likely to stand the strain involved by the work of a Chaplain at the Front. We assure him of our confidence in his character and worth and regret we cannot alter our former decision.'[200] So closely did the committee adhere to this line that in the spring of 1917 it even formed a special 'Chaplains' Selection Committee' which sat under the chairmanship of a serving chaplain for the purpose of selecting the best possible candidates.[201]

If the United Board proved to be a fairly successful coalition, several smaller Nonconformist denominations failed to secure any commissioned chaplains of their own. Besides the Wesleyan Reform Union and the Moravians, these included the Independent Methodists and the Swedenborgians, whose requests for chaplains were rejected as late as 1918.[202] However, even the Salvation Army, which had a high profile presence in almost every theatre of war,[203] had difficulties in this respect. Although Salvation Army officers were recognised as chaplains by the Australian, New Zealand, South African and Canadian governments, full recognition was not extended to their British equivalents until April 1918, when four Salvationist chaplains were commissioned as temporary chaplains for the Western Front.[204] However, even then a request for a further Salvationist chaplain for Salonika was refused as there were 'only 158 men of that faith in the Force'.[205] The position of the War Office was questioned in the House of Commons in November 1916, where it was explained that 'the difficulty in meeting the needs of the Salvationists lies in the fact that they are spread in small numbers over the whole of the Armies'.[206] However, this ungenerous spirit was keenly resented and, as early as the autumn of 1915, a letter to *The Times* claimed that the Salvation Army (which it described as 'an active spiritual and social force with world-wide influence, highly organized, and vibrating with energy') was ideally placed to furnish the kind of chaplains required by the army:

> Its officers, if they have not matriculated at any of the great universities, have graduated in 'the University of Humanity,' the term used in later years by the late 'General' Booth to describe our training colleges. The Salvation Army is well disciplined, and the courage and zeal of its officers have not been questioned . . . The Salvationist chaplain was the first and for some days the only chaplain in the trenches on the Gallipoli Peninsula after the landing of the Australian troops.[207]

In contrast to the Salvation Army, the Welsh Calvinistic Methodists were early beneficiaries of the wartime diversification of the Chaplains' Department. This was largely due to their concentration in the principality and to Lloyd George's determination to rally Nonconformist Wales behind the war effort. In particular, the raising of the 38th (Welsh) Division offered Welsh-speaking volunteers a context in which they 'would be able to use their own language and where their religious needs would be met to the full'.[208] Although they initially contemplated joining the United Board, by November 1914 the Welsh Calvinistic Methodists had seen their opportunity and had decided to 'seek recognition direct from the War Office'.[209] Consequently, their first chaplain was commissioned in 1914 and by the end of the war ten of their ministers were serving as chaplains.[210]

The vast expansion of the army in the first months of the war also had a profound impact on the development of Jewish chaplaincy. From the late 1880s, Jewish soldiers had been free to attest themselves under their own religion. Although there were only nineteen declared Jews in the army in 1889, the 1890s saw a growing number of soldiers identify themselves as Jewish and, in 1903, it was estimated that around 1,200 Jews had served in the army during the Boer War.[211] In keeping with the emulative tendencies and integrationist strategies of the Anglo-Jewish elite,[212] in 1892 the Visitation Committee of the United Synagogue applied to the War Office for the appointment of an accredited Jewish chaplain. Accordingly, Rabbi F.L. Cohen, then minister of the Borough Synagogue, was appointed to the new post. In view of the small numbers involved and the scattered distribution of his flock, the duties of the army's 'Jewish Chaplain' were part-time and akin to those of an officiating clergyman, mainly involving the organisation of occasional services for Jewish soldiers, the promotion of Jewish life and the careful monitoring of Jewish numbers in the army.[213]

However, the enlistment of thousands of naturalised Jews following the outbreak of war rendered these arrangements wholly inadequate. In response to the new situation, a central register of Jewish soldiers was compiled, the country was divided into districts overseen by officiating rabbis and in June 1916 a Jewish War Services Committee was created that worked in conjunction with the office of the Jewish Chaplain and which helped to nominate both Jewish chaplains and officiating clergymen.[214] In common with some of his Christian counterparts in the pre-war army, this wartime expansion swept Dr. Michael Adler (the army's Jewish Chaplain in 1914 and a member of Anglo-Jewry's most powerful rabbinical family) into a new and exalted position. Commissioned as a Territorial chaplain in June 1909,[215] Adler was not mobilised with the original B.E.F. However, in January 1915 he embarked for France, becoming the first Jewish chaplain to serve with the British army overseas.[216] Adler was to serve on the Western Front until July 1918, when ill health compelled him to return to England. Nevertheless, a second Jewish chaplain received a temporary commission in January 1915 and, by November 1918, the army had sixteen commissioned Jewish chaplains, twelve of whom were serving overseas.[217]

In addition to the difficulties caused by the rapid expansion of their chaplaincy work, in 1915–16 most churches also shared a sense of grievance over the preferential treatment accorded to the Church of England by the War Office. However, as long as Kitchener remained Secretary of State for War, few of their representatives were willing to suffer his wrath by pressing their demands. However, this situation changed dramatically with the intervention of the German navy and the death of Kitchener on board the cruiser H.M.S. *Hampshire* after it struck a mine in June 1916. With the unexpected demise of Kitchener, Lloyd George became Secretary of State for War and the churches were free to push at a door that was already swinging open. Instigated by the Church of Scotland, which was still smarting at the failure of the War Office to treat it as an established Church,[218] a coalition of the discontented was rapidly formed and a deputation of Protestant churchmen was received by Lloyd George at the House of Commons at the end of July.[219] At a meeting held at Baptist Church House the previous day, the deputation had orchestrated its joint demands. Because of Wesleyan opposition, the demand for a non-Anglican Chaplain-General was discarded, much to the chagrin of the Church of Scotland.[220] However, the list of demands presented to Lloyd George included a call for more non-Anglican chaplains (especially for bases, general hospitals and hospital ships) and for the appointment of senior non-Anglican chaplains at divisional level.[221] The response of the Secretary of State for War was wholly sympathetic. Indeed, Lloyd George took the opportunity to announce to the deputation his intention of forming a new Interdenominational Advisory Committee on Chaplaincy Services that would serve to 'secure impartial treatment for the various Churches working in the Army'.[222] Despite some wrangling as to its composition,[223] the Interdenominational Advisory Committee met for the first time at the War Office in mid-August and it was to meet monthly thereafter.[224]

Until April 1918, the I.A.C. was chaired by the Earl of Derby, who served for most of the intervening period as Secretary of State for War. The committee's task was to advise the Army Council on chaplaincy affairs and it consisted of a representative of the Roman Catholic church, the Church of Scotland, the United Free Church, the Presbyterian Church of England, the Presbyterian Church in Ireland, the Wesleyan Methodist church, the United Board and the Welsh Calvinistic Methodists. Although the Chaplain-General sat on the committee as its sole Anglican member, the work of the I.A.C. was mainly geared towards addressing and managing the needs of the other churches, a point that was underlined when an application for membership from the Jewish War Services Committee was rejected in December 1916.[225] The first major task to be undertaken by the I.A.C. was the enlargement and restructuring of non-Anglican chaplaincy, especially in the B.E.F. This was the subject of its first meeting in August 1916 and the necessary changes were implemented on the Western Front four months later by Lieutenant-General George Henry Fowke, the new Adjutant-General of the B.E.F.[226] In parallel with the structures of Anglican chaplaincy, Assistant Principal Chaplains were appointed to each army and major base with the rank and pay of chaplains First Class; Deputy Assistant Principal Chaplains were appointed to each army corps with the rank and pay of chaplains Second Class and Senior Chaplains ('non-C.of E.') were allocated to each division with the rank and pay of chaplains Third Class. Furthermore, the establishment of chaplains per infantry division was fixed at seventeen in every theatre of war, the denominational balance varying in accordance with the national identity of each. In 'English' divisions, the establishment was fixed at nine Anglican, four Roman Catholic and four Presbyterian or Nonconformist chaplains. In 'Scottish' divisions, nine Presbyterian chaplains were complemented by four Anglicans and four Roman Catholics and, in southern Irish divisions, nine Catholic chaplains worked alongside four Anglicans and four Presbyterians or Nonconformists.[227] In addition, December 1916 saw the creation in France of 'a small reserve pool of Chaplains for both C. of E. and Non C of E. Denominations to meet emergency needs, and to allot for work in hospitals, bases, &c.'[228] In the fullness of time, the benefits of the enlarged divisional establishment were enhanced by the reorganisation of the infantry divisions of the B.E.F. in February-March 1918, a process that resulted in the disbandment or amalgamation of 153 infantry battalions as the number of battalions per division was cut from twelve to nine.[229]

Although the reorganisation of December 1916 was the committee's major wartime achievement, the work of the I.A.C. touched upon many aspects of religious provision for the army, its members being free to advise the War Office on 'other matters affecting the religious interests of the soldiers both at home and abroad'.[230] By the end of the war, the I.A.C. had made a significant impact on the Chaplains' Department and upon the moral and religious life of the army more generally. In terms of the Chaplains' Department, it had achieved further refinements in its organisation and nomenclature. As a result of previous discussions, it was announced at its meeting of May 1918 that Presbyterian, Wesleyan and

United Board Principal Chaplains were to be appointed to the Chaplains' Branch of the War Office and that Assistant Principal Chaplains would be appointed to every Home Command.[231] Furthermore, the same meeting agreed that the 'obnoxious title "Non-C. of E." ' should be abolished with reference to chaplains 'who do not belong to the Church of England'.[232] In addition to guiding War Office policy in relation to the Army Chaplains' Department, by the end of the war the I.A.C. had also organised a programme of purity lectures for soldiers in Home Commands, it had made representations to the military authorities on 'the decent observance of the Lord's Day in Camps at Home' and its Protestant members had begun to compile a new hymn book for the army which was intended 'to supersede the various denominational hymn-books which are at present supplied by the War Office'.[233]

Development and Diversification in the Chaplain's Role

Despite the huge efforts devoted by the churches and the army to the expansion and reorganisation of military chaplaincy in the early years of the war, one of the most striking aspects of chaplaincy work at this time was its ill-defined nature. This problem was exacerbated by the total lack of specialised training given to temporary chaplains for most of the war, a problem that was only partly remedied in its latter stages. As E.C. Crosse ruefully remembered of his experiences in 1915:

> [The chaplain] received no sort of preliminary training to equip him for his new life. He went straight from his parish to his unit, and was left almost entirely to gain his experience for himself. Even one month spent at some preliminary school of army training would have paid a handsome dividend, and saved him many needless efforts.[234]

This lack of preparation was no less true of the army's 'non-C. of E.' chaplains. As one Presbyterian chaplain wrote of his posting to France in September 1915, 'At that early period of the war . . . a temporary chaplain was given no special training of any kind for service with the Forces; he merely received his commission and was told to get into uniform.'[235] The Roman Catholic experience was no different. One Catholic chaplain with the B.E.F. remembered that 'We were a disorganised body, each playing his own lone hand. There was no definite public policy, no one to train us, no one to lead. Each had to learn his work by experience of his own failures.'[236]

The predicament in which chaplains could find themselves during the early months of the war was illustrated by H.A.R. May in his *Memories of the Artists Rifles* (1929). According to May, the 1/28th London Regiment (Artists Rifles) acquired an unofficial chaplain quite by chance in October 1914, the chaplain in question stumbling across the battalion in his quest for a unit to which he could offer his services. As May recalled of their first encounter:

> He informed me that he was a clergyman – that his name was Gibb – that he was a 'fourth class Army Chaplain' – that he had come out to France

> hoping to find a job as Chaplain to some British troops – that someone on the Staff at Headquarters at St. Omer had informed him that 'a new lot' had recently arrived from England without a Chaplain [and] had suggested that we (being the new arrivals) might be glad of his services.[237]

As the battalion's commanding officer, May agreed 'to his staying with us, unofficially, as Chaplain till something better turned up for him to do'.[238] However, even then it was not at all clear what his role would be, an issue that led to further frustration for Gibb. As May remembered:

> Later in the evening, after our evening meal, when I was engaged in the solution of the many novel problems that are constantly arising in a novel situation, our energetic unofficial chaplain tackled me again on the subject of his work, and pressed for some definite job, but at the moment I could think of nothing except that he should talk matters over with the Quartermaster, the Surgeon and the Company Commanders, and see how he could best assist us, and that I would be willing to consider any suggestions that occurred to him.[239]

While chaplains had difficulty in finding their feet in France, as new divisions were raised in Britain in 1914–15 it appears to have been the accepted practice to allow chaplains to adjust themselves to their work by simply sharing the training of the units to which they were attached. Posted to Aldershot Command in September 1914, a raw Anglican chaplain of a New Army division remembered that his period of induction meant throwing himself into every sphere of brigade activity:

> Route-marching, Hospital visiting, concerts, boxing, meetings and classes – each and all of these (even boxing) gave scope for what, I can only repeat, is the essence of a chaplain's work under such conditions – personal touch with officers and men, and the endeavour to use each 'contact' as a spiritual opportunity . . . On Salisbury Plain we had the great advantage of large and well-equipped Y.M.C.A. Huts with good canteens. This made social and religious activities possible on a larger scale. I made it an invariable practice to close Concerts and Meetings of any kind with very short 'family prayers' . . . This may have been open to criticism, but I have never found it resented either by the audience or by the artistes . . . Occasionally manoeuvres took place, and a chaplain might either take the day off or accompany the men as a free-lance – no duties were assigned to him and he was responsible to no man.[240]

However, as the war developed it was widely accepted that such a regime was not sufficient to prepare chaplains for the demands of active service. As the Archbishop of York put it in December 1917:

> In the early days it was a great advantage that the Chaplains should go through the home training with their units and then go out with them to the front; but I gather that now the circumstances have entirely changed, the units are so divided and drafts so continually sent out from home that there is not the same point in Chaplains remaining for some time in home camps before they are sent abroad.[241]

During the latter half of the war, the obvious deficiencies in the initial training of chaplains were partly addressed through a number of local initiatives. A course of instruction for chaplains seems to have been running at Woolwich by early 1917 where, among others, Mervyn Haigh learnt 'to find his way about the army, visiting in the military hospitals, discovering how to take church parades, and so on'.[242] Later that year, a basic training school for Anglican chaplains was also opened at Ripon. This was the result of a personal initiative by Archdeacon Armstrong Hall and it offered everything from canteen management to anti-gas drill. However, although its effects were apparent in France from January 1918 (when Gywnne posted a number of new chaplains who had been to 'the Ripon School of Instruction')[243] its two-month courses trained only twelve chaplains at a time and it was thus quite incapable of offsetting the chronic unpreparedness of Anglican chaplains for their wartime ministry.[244]

Rather more ambitious than the Ripon School of Instruction was the initiative launched by H.A.R. May while commandant of the officers' school of instruction at Tidworth. While May had been conscious of the lack of training for chaplains since his chance encounter with Gibb in October 1914, his subsequent experience in France had accentuated his concerns:

> On one occasion, when walking with a 'General' at St. Omer, we passed a Chaplain, newly arrived (apparently) from England [and] (apparently) inexperienced in military matters. He gave a most original flourish of his arm as he passed. 'Who the deuce is that?' asked the General, wrathfully, 'And what is he doing? – blowing me a kiss or what?' 'He's a Chaplain, sir, and he's saluting you,' I replied. 'Well, why the devil doesn't someone show him how to do it?' responded the General. This remark puzzled me a little at the time, and I thought about it afterwards. Why didn't someone show him how to do it? Whose business was it to teach him?[245]

After his posting to Tidworth, May resolved that its officers' school should inaugurate 'a scheme for training newly-appointed Army Chaplains without military experience',[246] an initiative that met with the approval of his commanding officer and with the encouragement of the War Office.[247] An avowedly non-denominational venture, May and his team of instructors eschewed questions of theology and churchmanship and sought 'only to try and teach a newly-appointed and inexperienced Army Chaplain how in war-time he could best help at all times and in all circumstances the men of the unit to which he was attached, and also to teach him enough about his military duties to enable him to carry them out with credit'.[248] With this in view, May's syllabus included an overview of the chaplains' work, basic drill, military law and procedures, map-reading, cycling (or riding) and elementary first aid.[249] The first 'experimental' course of five days' duration took place in April 1918, with fifteen 'non-C. of E.' chaplains and an equal number of Anglicans in attendance. Generally deemed to be a success, extended courses of two weeks' duration commenced in May with the support of the I.A.C. and the War Office, these courses being capable of training sixty new chaplains a month.[250] Nevertheless, and despite the potential of this programme, which one graduate judged to be of 'immense benefit',[251] the end of the war in November rather confirmed May's venture as another case of too little, too late.

The general absence of preliminary training for new chaplains was exacerbated by an initial dearth of detailed and authoritative guidance on chaplaincy work, a situation that can hardly have been helped by the steady leakage of experienced chaplains back into civilian life. This problem may have been at its worst among chaplains of the United Board, whose component churches had no tradition of army chaplaincy to draw upon. As late as 1916, some *Memoranda of Information* issued by the United Board baldly stated that:

> A Chaplain's duties are very vaguely defined. As in the civilian ministry, most of his work is left to his own initiative.
> He must arrange Divine Services and classes of instruction; visit the Hospital and see any of his men who may be ill. In general terms, it is his duty to have regard to the material and religious welfare of his men.[252]

However, things were not much better even for chaplains of the Church of England. Although *Hints and Instructions* had been issued by the Chaplain-General's office in the nineteenth century, these had been geared to the settled existence of garrison life in the regular army of the Victorian period. However, for temporary chaplains of the Church of England in the massively expanded citizen army of 1914–18, there was very little scope for overseeing regimental schools, visiting soldiers' families and attending to the inmates of garrison hospitals and military prisons. Hence, and as E.C. Crosse remarked, 'the specific duties' which a temporary chaplain was expected to perform were remarkably 'few in number'.[253] Apart from his obligations to conduct parade and voluntary services and to preside at burials, the chaplain was to a large extent left to determine his own role. The results were predictable, with ignorance and confusion characterising the early experiences of many. Writing as late as November 1917, Everard Digby complained that 'The working of the Army Chaplains' Department is wrapped in mystery . . . the Chaplain, newly appointed, gropes his weary way along in a fog as to what he may and may not do, his rights, if any, and the redress of his many wrongs.'[254] Indeed, it was with the aim of ameliorating this situation that Digby wrote a pamphlet entitled *Tips for Padres: A Handbook for Chaplains*. However, its impact was limited by the fact that the war was entering its final months by the time it was published and, because Digby's experience was confined to two years' work in home camps, he had little advice to tender regarding the trials and tribulations of active service.[255]

Despite Digby's impression that little had been written for the benefit of chaplains,[256] a growing volume of information was made available to them, not least through the steady stream of books that were written and published by chaplains during the course of the war. Typical of these were Tom Pym and Geoffrey Gordon's *Papers from Picardy* (1917) and F.B. MacNutt's *The Church in the Furnace*, an edited collection of chaplains' essays published the same year. Although both were forward-thinking volumes aimed at a broad church readership, specialised pamphlets and manuals for chaplains also began to make their appearance on the Western Front from the winter of 1915–16.[257] In effect, these represented the Department's contribution to a flood of manuals and pamphlets that were published in and for the army during the course of the war, a flood that reached its peak in 1917 'as the lessons of the Somme were digested and disseminated'.[258] In January 1917, and in his capacity as the senior Catholic chaplain on the Western Front, Bernard Rawlinson published a substantial pamphlet entitled *Roman Catholic Chaplains. Information and Hints. British Armies in France*. As Rawlinson explained in its preface, 'This is not meant to be an exhaustive treatise on the duties of Chaplains, but merely to give a few general ideas and practical hints which may be useful to a Catholic Chaplain.'[259] The booklet described the various spheres of a chaplain's work, ranging from the division through to the base, and it proffered advice on how the chaplain's work should be arranged in each. It also provided 'A Few General Hints' on topics such as military courtesies, impromptu confessions and relations with other chaplains, concluding with a discussion of burial procedures and a warning against Catholic churches being used for Protestant worship.[260]

Reissued in a second edition in 1918,[261] Rawlinson's pamphlet was indicative of the greater sense of organisation and system that now prevailed in the Department as a whole. This development was also illustrated in March 1917, when the War Office published some *Notes on Service in the Army Chaplains Department*. These were devised for prospective applicants for temporary commissions and they briefly explained the duties of the army chaplain and furnished details of pay, outfit and allowances.[262] In June 1917, a more specialised pamphlet was published entitled *Practical Advice for the Guidance of Church of England Chaplains Attached to a Division in the Field.* Probably written by Harry Blackburne, the dynamic A.C.G. of First Army, the pamphlet clarified some key administrative and organisational issues, it described the varied nature of the chaplain's work with a front-line division and it discussed the proper deportment and attitude of the divisional chaplain.[263] This diffusion of knowledge and experience was also facilitated by *The Chaplains' Bulletin*, which began publication in October 1917.[264] Edited from the chaplains' school of instruction at St. Omer, the paper was aimed at the B.E.F.'s Anglican chaplains and its purpose was essentially practical. As B.K. Cunningham explained in his first editorial:

> The objects of this Paper are primarily practical. It is hoped that it may serve to some extent to keep us chaplains in touch with one another and afford an opportunity for the interchange and pooling of experience; that it may give to the chaplains suggestions in regard to reading and thinking; and that it may serve as a medium for calling the attention of all the chaplains in the field to any information which it concerns them as a body to know.[265]

There was clearly much that was useful in *The Chaplains' Bulletin*; it gave notices from the school of instruction, it covered church affairs at home and provided details of organisations willing to make grants of books, pictures and church hangings.[266] Nevertheless, there was a distinct impression among some of its readers of stable doors rattling shut. As one correspondent wrote in January 1918:

> Sir, – May I make two suggestions which would be helpful to us if they could be acted upon?
> 1. The chaplains joining the B.E.F. for the first time should receive a short course of instruction before they join their units. The Y.M.C.A. workers have such a plan, why should not we? When I first arrived in France I was sent straight to a hospital without any previous instruction. Fortunately I had worked in civilian hospitals for four years previously, but I feel that my army work might have been less inadequate had I had some preliminary schooling.
> 2. That a handbook for chaplains, containing official and non-official matter, be published. From time to time excellent pamphlets relating to special kinds of work reach us, but it would be of more practical use if these publications could be gathered together under one cover, together with non-official matter which it would be of real use for the chaplains to know. To some extent the BULLETIN meets this need, but a handbook would be even more helpful . . .[267]

A notable consequence of this lack of specialised training and direction was that it placed chaplains in an awkward position in relation to their commanding officers. As Everard Digby was keenly aware, the ill-defined nature of the chaplain's role meant that chaplains were often distracted in their work, especially by pushy superiors:

> [The] absence of regulations regarding the Chaplain is apt to tempt a certain type of Commanding Officer to assume an authority he does not possess over a Chaplain attached to his unit. Such usurped authority should be resisted at once, not for your own sake alone, but for the sake of your successor and the entire Department . . . It should be pointed out to such Commanding Officers that you are merely an attached officer, subject to your own Department, and controlled by it in regard to your work.[268]

While Digby urged his readers to work 'in complete accord' with their commanding officers, asking his advice and permission whenever necessary,[269] he still insisted that a degree of independence be maintained:

> If you are really good at any sport, play for the Battalion team, but don't take on committee work, and never be the secretary. Certainly sing at the concerts, if you can sing well, but don't be responsible for the entertainments. It is not your job; you are not 'the only man with nothing to do in the Battalion,' although the Commanding Officer may think so, and you have not the time for these things, unless your work is to be neglected . . .[270]

Despite this sound advice, it was clearly all too easy for chaplains to be drawn into the day-to-day running of the units to which they were attached. One of the most common tasks to be shuffled onto the shoulders of the chaplain was the censoring of soldiers' letters, an onerous and thankless chore which junior officers were generally glad to relinquish. As S.F. Leighton Green, then serving as an Anglican chaplain to 22nd Casualty Clearing Station, wrote to his Norwich parishioners in May 1916:

> [This] is no essential part of a Chaplain's duty, but it is a duty he is usually asked to undertake by the Commanding Officer, and I was appointed Field Censor No. 1,504 soon after my arrival . . . It is sometimes a heavy task. The daily letter bag from here totals from 100 to 250 letters.[271]

Though sometimes undertaken voluntarily by the chaplain and even rated as 'part of the Padre's education',[272] the burden of censoring an endless stream of mail proved irksome to many. In November 1915, C.I.S. Hood, an Anglican chaplain at Gallipoli, wrote in his journal that this was 'a job which seldom repays doing more than once or twice', bemoaning the fact that 'Of the censoring of letters there is no end.'[273] However, such duties did not end with the scrutiny of soldiers' mail and they varied according to context. For example, while attached to a base hospital at Rouen in the spring of 1915, the Anglican chaplain Charles Doudney was persuaded to work as a radiologist on the strength of his amateur interest in electronics.[274] Besides the ubiquity of such pressures, the different needs of the Church of England's large and diverse membership meant that the position of the Anglican chaplain in particular was complicated by an unresolved tension inherited from the clergy's pastoral work at home. As Geoffrey Gordon put it in 1916:

> At bottom, the alternatives before [the chaplain] are not different from those which face a parish priest at home, who is in danger either of becoming so much occupied with organisations, institutes, clubs, etc., that the spiritual in him is altogether swamped, or of wasting many hours of his time over the wholly unimportant devotional eccentricities of pietistic ladies.[275]

According to Gordon, the dilemma of the brigade chaplain lay in choosing between two extremes. As Gordon put it:

> Either he will elect to stand strongly, definitely, and exclusively for spiritual things, in which case he will have to be content to come in contact with only a very few men; or, in order to get to know the battalion as a whole, he will have to throw himself into a number of minor activities, and run the risk of getting but rarely on to a higher spiritual level.[276]

In simple terms: 'Mr. God or M. Cinema – for which does the chaplain stand? Does the soldier think of his Padre in the main as the representative of God, or chiefly as the provider of canteens, cinemas, and creature comforts?'[277]

This preoccupation with the soldier's recreational needs was not, however, simply an extension of the pastoral and missionary strategies pursued by the churches at home. In fact, it had a compelling military rationale. By the winter of 1914–15, and with the war having reached a state of deadlock on the Western Front, it was vital to maintain the morale of troops in the front line and to provide wholesome comforts and recreations for troops in base areas, in hospitals and on lines of communication. Although this work was to be embraced and popularised by the Y.M.C.A., the Church Army and other civilian religious agencies during the course of the war,[278] given the early shortage of such facilities and the initial organisational problems faced by civilian bodies, chaplains had a pioneering role to play in the provision of clubs, canteens and similar amenities for the troops.[279]

In a report to the Church of Scotland's Committee on Army and Navy Chaplains in the spring of 1915, W.S. Jaffray wrote:

> The comfort of men at the Front has not been lost sight of. I was requested by Divisional Headquarters to establish clubs in every brigade area to break the monotony of life during the quiet winter months. These clubs contain reading, writing, and game rooms, and a refreshment bar where the men can obtain hot coffee . . . Lectures and concerts have been given, and everything possible has been done to brighten the soldier's life.[280]

Bishop Gwynne was also an early pioneer of these institutions on the Western Front. By April 1915, and in the space of only four months with the 5th Infantry Brigade, he had established three recreation rooms and taken charge of 'a motor coffee-cocoa car' whose task was to distribute hot drinks to men returning from the trenches.[281] From the first winter of the war, many chaplains also threw themselves into running sporting competitions and similar entertainments. In the winter of 1914–15, D.P. Winnifrith, the Anglican chaplain of the 14th Infantry Brigade, devoted much of his time to organising a football tournament.[282] According to a colleague, 'Friends in England supplied him with footballs, a suitable field was selected, hop-poles improvised into goal posts, teams chosen [and] a 14th Brigade Association Football League was formed.'[283] In combination with the provision of lectures and concerts,[284] these efforts on the part of chaplains were clearly intended to promote the morale as well as the moral well being of the men. As Gwynne wrote of a soccer tournament which he organised in March 1915, 'I thought it splendid that [the men] should forget all about the war for a time and that the Germans would give up in despair to see how calmly and cheerfully Thomas Atkins takes the greatest war in the world.'[285]

By the autumn of 1915, it is clear that many senior officers attached great importance to this deceptively mundane work. When Major-General C.W. Jacob took command of 21st Division after its mauling at the battle of Loos, he evinced a keen interest in efforts of this kind. As one Roman Catholic chaplain noted in his diary:

> Another activity has been the starting of a club. This is the outcome of a suggestion of General Jacob, Divisional G.O.C., who has recently replaced General Forestier-Walker. He signalised his arrival amongst us by making himself known to everybody and inspecting every department of the division, and seeing everything at work . . . The General even takes an interest in chaplains – a cheery benevolence being the best that we had got before, with apparent indifference on the part of Forestier-Walker. But General Jacob called all the chaplains together one evening and told us he wanted to help us in our work . . . And he suggested that I ought to start a club for Catholic soldiers. This I have now done.[286]

The desirability of this work was also apparent to lords Salisbury and Grenfell when they visited the B.E.F. on behalf of the Anglican advisory committee in September 1915. As the committee stressed in its second report on the state of Anglican chaplaincy:

> It must be remembered that in addition to the purely spiritual work which is their first and most important duty, Chaplains are of the greatest use on the social side and in helping forward the recreation of the men when not actually in the trenches. As is well known the effect of this on the morale of the troops is of great value.[287]

Although this work found its most celebrated expression in 'Everyman's Club' at Talbot House in Poperinghe, which was opened by Philip ('Tubby') Clayton in December 1915,[288] the recreational and welfare work of chaplains was striking in its scope and ubiquity. In May 1916, S.F. Leighton Green observed that his 'secondary' duties at the 22nd Casualty Clearing Station were essentially those of a field censor, a caterer and concert manager. Clearly, he did not begrudge these responsibilities, writing that:

> The canteen is practically the R.A.M.C. Club, and I try to get in for a few minutes each night in order to smoke a pipe with the handful of men off duty. The canteen is a capital thing, and does a world of good. Our R.A.M.C. men work hard, and in spare moments they like to get there. It keeps them together, and makes for the spirit of comradeship.[289]

Similarly, Robert Wearmouth, a Primitive Methodist chaplain attached to another C.C.S., spent much of his time engaged in this kind of work:

> At that time [1916–17] we had as our O.C. an outstanding soldier, a V.C. Colonel, full of sympathy and understanding for the wounded lads. Calling me into his office one day he said, 'Look here, Padre, I want you to do all you can for the lads. You cannot do too much.' I was running the men's canteen at the time and we had a good balance in the fund. I suggested selling cakes at less than cost price . . . He agreed to that and it was done for a long time. I also suggested the purchase of a small Pathé Projector, worked by hand and generating its own electricity. He agreed to this and one was bought from Paris . . . There was no doubt about the success, the running expense being covered by the profits of the canteen. Again and again the marquee or the tent was full of sick and wounded lads seeking a bit of joy out of the cinema show.[290]

By the summer of 1917, Wearmouth had even formed 'a small and efficient orchestra' in order 'to provide entertaining music at every show' and was under instructions to take his film projector into the surgical wards.[291]

While being of enormous value to the army, this recreational work was also of considerable benefit to chaplains themselves as it gave them a prominent and tangible role, helping many to find their feet and prove their worth in an unfamiliar milieu.[292] F.R. Barry wrote of the canteen which he established as a raw chaplain at Ismailia in the winter of 1915–16:

> I spent all the evenings there with the men and was thus brought into much closer contact. This little effort changed the whole tone of the camp. And it gave me a much needed confidence. I had lived hitherto a very sheltered existence and had hardly encountered human life in the raw, and I had been scared stiff at the prospect of living with 'brutal and licentious soldiery'. But I had now been taken into their hearts.

> Companies would wave to me as they passed. Lorry drivers would stop and give me a lift. Everyone I met smiled and seemed pleased to see me. I discovered that there was dormant in me something of what it takes to be any kind of leader.[293]

However, not all were convinced of the value of this work. This was particularly true of certain Roman and Anglo-Catholic chaplains who were prone to regard it as a distraction from their sacramental ministries and demeaning to their sacerdotal status. Although Everard Digby expressed reservations in his *Tips for Padres*, as early as the autumn of 1915 another Anglo-Catholic chaplain had eschewed this role, the senior chaplain of the 5th Division informing Bishop Gwynne that J.A. Pickworth would not 'help to provide men with rest-rooms and recreation saying he is a priest not a publican'.[294] Shortly after the war, E.C. Crosse was also inclined to question the worth of these endeavours, arguing that they had evolved out of the chaplain's initial confinement to the army's rear areas and that the chaplain's recreational value had soon been eclipsed by the work of other agencies:

> Chief among [the chaplain's] works of supererogation at the beginning of the war were perhaps the organisation of concerts, and the supervision of battalion canteens – 'holy grocery', as Neville Talbot called it. Many a chaplain in the early days of the war practised as an unlicensed tobacconist to the great satisfaction of his flock . . . The demand however for their services in these unofficial capacities diminished rather than increased as time went on . . . Commodities of such vital importance to an army as music, tobacco, and beer could not for long be entrusted to the fitful administration of The Church, and gradually the padre's improvisations in these spheres gave place to the Y.M.C.A., the Church Army, and later to Divisional canteens and concert parties.[295]

Whatever the pros and cons of this type of work, the nature of the chaplain's ministry varied according to his religious affiliation and to less constant factors such as his posting and the immediate military situation. For Roman Catholic chaplains, and despite competing claims on their time, the administration of the sacraments remained of paramount concern. In 1916, Geoffrey Gordon wrote of his Roman Catholic counterparts:

> [T]hey are frankly sectarian and have dealt with their own particular flock alone. In peace-time warfare, as we who have been in Picardy describe rest billets or ordinary trenches, they refuse steadily to have anything to do with canteens and the like; and even during a battle you see the results of their deliberate choice, for they always try to deal with their flock almost exclusively on spiritual levels.[296]

True to his own evangelical convictions, as an Anglican brigade chaplain Mervyn Evers strove to support like-minded men in their own faith and to promote the spread of the gospel. Consequently, he formed a Christian union in both of the battalions under his care, each having its distinctive membership card 'which each member was to sign and keep giving his allegiance to Jesus Christ [and] promising to carry out His commands and wherever possible to win others for His cause and kingdom'.[297] The Wesleyan chaplain John Boullier also acted on the evangelical imperative of winning 'decisions for the Lord', leading him to hold nightly services in a 'Gospel Hall' at Béthune at the height of the battle of the Somme.[298] For Jewish chaplains, who had the greatest difficulty in ministering to their scattered co-religionists, their overtly religious work (which largely consisted of leading services, officiating at burials and even organising Jewish 'officers and men so that they might hold services for themselves') took precedence over everything else. In addition to three base chaplains, by 1918 there was still only one Jewish chaplain for each of the five British armies on the Western Front, a fact that rendered the ministry of Michael Adler so peripatetic that he became known as the 'Wandering Jew'.[299]

However, the ministry of chaplains was also modulated by force of circumstance. Many who served overseas experienced a succession of different postings. On the Western Front, it was common for an Anglican chaplain who had just arrived in France to be sent to a base or to a base hospital before being posted nearer the front line, usually to a C.C.S., which was effectively a field hospital, or to an infantry brigade.[300] Furthermore, while the role of a brigade chaplain differed from that of a chaplain at base or at a C.C.S., it too was liable to change according to whether his brigade was in the line, in reserve or at rest. Despite the progression of postings towards the front line, there was no clear hierarchy of ease. For those chaplains charged with ministering to soldiers at base, the unruliness of men out of immediate danger posed problems of another sort. As Noel Mellish remembered, his first posting to an infantry depot at Rouen in 1915 was very uncomfortable. The commandant was plainly 'incompetent' and many of his flock were former convalescents who were 'completely fed up and very often almost on the point of mutiny'.[301] In this context, one of the chaplain's principal duties was to ensure that drafts of replacements for the front actually reached the railway station. As Mellish recalled:

> The streets [of Rouen] were lined with estaminets and more often than not men would fall out from the drafts to have a last drink and never arrive at the station at all, miss the draft and be for punishment when found. I found it was desirable to go down with the drafts and help men out of the estaminets and shepherd them to the train and at least save them from the women and men who fattened on the British soldier and robbed him of his money, health and honour.[302]

However, such were the mores of the base that, on one of these excursions, Mellish unwittingly entrusted his bicycle to the care of 'a passing corporal' and 'never saw that bicycle again'.[303]

Chaplains posted to base hospitals or to casualty clearing stations could also see the burden of their work fluctuate dramatically. C.E. Doudney wrote of his base hospital at Rouen:

> When I first arrived [early in 1915] the hospital was very empty and there was not much for me to do. No bad cases, and I could see all the men in a couple of afternoons. There are 23 wards altogether and in several there were but two or three patients. But, later, we have become crowded out.

> In one day and night there arrived no fewer than 458 wounded and all the staff have been pressed to desperation.[304]

Given the uneven rhythms of hospital work, chaplains at casualty clearing stations were even encouraged to assume responsibilities for surrounding units. As S.F. Leighton Green wrote in 1916:

> A Casualty Clearing Station Chaplain has a fixed anchorage, but, fortunately, he is not confined to home waters. He is told to roam at large in search of troops who have no Chaplain, and to give a helping hand to Chaplains of Divisions who may be understaffed or overworked. Consequently I have always had a squadron of the Royal Flying Corps to look after.[305]

Nevertheless, periods of intense fighting brought tremendous strains in their wake. J.M.S. Walker, a chaplain at the hitherto quiet 21st Casualty Clearing Station at Corbie, saw his workload spiral out of control with the commencement of the battle of the Somme in July 1916:

> In those three months I buried up to 900 who had died at the C.C.S. We have had 1,300 [cases] in twenty-four hours, one night 700 came in after 11 p.m. Sometimes one was in the moribund tent practically all day and night dealing with those who were given over to die or whose wounds were too numerous to deal with when so many others were waiting attention.[306]

The growing size and firepower of the Royal Artillery on the Western Front also meant that an increasing number of men were detailed to serve as specialised artillery chaplains. The pressing need for such chaplains was officially recognised by the War Office in 1917, when it was decided 'to post one additional Church of England, and one additional non-Church of England chaplain to France for each group of ten heavy and siege batteries of artillery'.[307] However, given that these long-range guns could be deployed in individual batteries and sections over a very wide area this was itinerant work that Bishop Gwynne described as particularly 'undefined and lonely'.[308] Having already distinguished himself as a brigade chaplain, Noel Mellish was chaplain to the heavy artillery of XIII Corps from November 1916 to June 1917. Although he found this task to be congenial enough he nevertheless recognised that: 'A padre to Gunners had not perhaps the same opportunity of identifying himself with a unit as he had with an Infantry Brigade, because of the great number of batteries and the area over which they were distributed.'[309] Similarly, W.T. Croxford, a Wesleyan chaplain, recalled that:

> I had over sixty Battery positions to visit, arrange services if possible and meet officers and men at their work; and, of course, these positions were constantly changing . . . services at the Batteries or sections were difficult to arrange. Indeed, sometimes, when arranged they could not be held. Sometimes in the middle of a service the men would be called to the guns. Often one was reduced to short conversations and one never knew the result.[310]

Given the problematic and even prosaic nature of other postings, the infantry brigade was undoubtedly the most glamorous and rewarding sphere of the chaplain's work. In this context, from 1915 onwards it was increasingly common for the brigade chaplain to be allotted to one of the infantry battalions under his care, sometimes even moving between them.[311] Naturally, this situation led to the forging of strong bonds between certain chaplains and individual battalions. For instance, on the disbandment of the 1/12th London Regiment in 1918 Julian Bickersteth felt moved to write:

> There is only one job for a chaplain in France and that is with the battalion. They are the fighting men, the men who bear the brunt of war, who get wounded and recover, return to the trenches, and get wounded again until the time comes and they die. It is good to live with dying men – dying men who are in the full vigour of health and strength, whose comradeship is something past understanding, but sacred and wonderful.[312]

However, not all brigades or battalions were the same. William Doyle, an Irish Jesuit, was jubilant at being posted to the largely Roman Catholic 16th (Irish) Division rather than to an English or Scottish formation:

> I often congratulate myself [he wrote] on my good fortune in being appointed to [an] Irish Brigade, more especially as the last vacancy fell to me. The vast majority of the chaplains at the Front seldom see anything more dangerous than the shell of an egg of doubtful age. They are doing splendid work along the lines of communication, in the hospitals or at the base. Even those who are attached to non-Catholic Divisions have little time to get to the trenches, their men are so scattered; but we with the Irish Regiments live in the thick of it. We share the hardships and dangers with our men, and if we have less polish on our boots and belts than other spruce padres, let us hope we have something more to our bank account in a better world.[313]

In contrast, Oswin Creighton was deeply upset at his transfer from a New Army brigade to a regular brigade of the 29th Division in January 1915. For Creighton, his stint with the Kitchener volunteers was congenial because 'Among the officers there were men preparing for Ordination, men I had been at school and college with, and the military life was no stranger for me than for them. I had formed many close friends, and was much interested in my work.'[314] However, his new brigade consisted of hard-bitten regulars newly returned from India; two of its four battalions were Irish and its field ambulance was 'mainly composed of Scotch Presbyterians'.[315] On leaving England for Egypt that March, Creighton complained that 'The men are really just like so many children. They have been writing reams of mawkish sentimental letters to the Nuneaton girls, which the officers have had to censor. I don't know of a single man who thought of buying a book or magazine for the journey.'[316]

For Anglican chaplains in particular, the role of the brigade chaplain evolved slowly and hesitantly between 1914 and 1916. Unlike Roman Catholic and Presbyterian chaplains, who had for decades often served as *de facto* regimental chaplains to the battalions of the army's 'Scottish' and 'Irish' infantry regiments, Anglican chaplains had usually been attached to larger garrisons and, when on campaign, to major field forces. Because of this, the army had no comparable tradition of Anglican regimental chaplaincy and this had little chance of developing in the circumstances of 1914–15. During these months, chaplains were under orders to remain with their respective field ambulances (that is, to the rear of the front-line trenches) orders that were in keeping with the Geneva Convention of 1864 and which were administratively and logistically convenient for the army. At Rouen in the late summer of 1914, Bishop Gwynne was perturbed to hear from a regular chaplain and a veteran of the Boer War that 'the present war would be run on much the same lines' and that 'none of us would be allowed within forty miles of the front line'.[317] Upheld by many senior chaplains and commanding officers, this unpopular policy was defended by the War Office and widely criticised by leading churchmen. In view of the sacramental needs of Roman Catholic soldiers, the Irish Roman Catholic hierarchy roundly condemned the policy, a position that was endorsed by sections of the Roman Catholic press in Great Britain.[318] However, resentment was no less acute in the Church of England. In December 1914, Archbishop Davidson scorned 'the unwillingness of the War Office authorities to send non-combatants to the fighting line with all the addition to the cost and trouble of transport and supply'.[319] By March 1915, the archbishop was convinced that Kitchener himself was responsible for official obduracy in this regard: 'I know that Kitchener, and probably others, have at times, during our long-drawn endeavour to get more Chaplains, said things [such as] "A Chaplain is not only a Chaplain; it means a servant and kit, and perhaps horse, and extra luggage for ecclesiastical use, and so on." ' Although Davidson had made it clear to the Secretary of State for War that Anglican chaplains were prepared to forego these perquisites, Kitchener had remained bullish, telling the archbishop that he was only prepared to defer in this matter to the opinion of Sir John French, the Commander-in-Chief of the B.E.F.[320] Although a committee was appointed in France to consider this question of deployment,[321] nothing was done before French was replaced by Sir Douglas Haig in December 1915. Hence, as late as the autumn of 1915, chaplains were still technically forbidden from being in the front line. Indeed, when E.C. Crosse joined his division in France that September he was 'absolutely forbidden' by his senior chaplain from venturing into the front line as there was at that time 'no conception of [brigade chaplains] having any sort of function in the line itself'.[322]

While this ban may have helped to stimulate the chaplain's recreational work in rear areas, it was also widely disregarded. Given the state of Roman Catholic opinion and the historic links between Roman Catholic chaplains and Irish battalions, Roman Catholic chaplains often defied higher authority by venturing into the firing line regardless of official policy, a course of action that was widely acclaimed. As early as December 1914, Francis Gleeson accompanied the 2nd Royal Munster Fusiliers in a counter-attack at Givenchy, an exploit that he repeated at Aubers Ridge five months later.[323] However, Anglican chaplains were no less ready to go forward. On 8 October 1915, George Ogden, who was then attached to the 36th Field Ambulance, even visited troops who were not his responsibility, confiding in his diary: 'Afternoon Germans shelled the line for 6 hours. Simply Hell. Went out to [the 9th Essex Regiment of 35th Brigade]. Very hot. Stayed about a couple of hours talking to the men.'[324] Likewise, Edmund Kennedy noted how, at the First Battle of Ypres in the autumn of 1914, Neville Talbot (a temporary chaplain, veteran of the Boer War and son of the Bishop of Winchester) had ventured into the front line in order to recover the body of his younger brother who had been serving in the Rifle Brigade.[325] In fact, another of Kennedy's chaplains had been wounded in the same battle:

> The Rev. and Honourable B.M. Peel was badly hit in the head and left leg, in charging with the [1st Royal Welch Fusiliers]; true, he had no right to be there from a military point of view, but I believe the O.C. had given him permission, and certainly his heroic action inspired the men, and has left a splendid memory in the minds of those who were with him.[326]

It is, in fact, rather revealing of the blind eye that was commonly turned to army policy that Kennedy should write in 1915:

> The padré will sometimes have difficult and perchance dangerous work allotted to him, such as carrying messages under fire, or tending wounded men in exposed places. He must also be prepared to lend a hand in carrying the wounded; and, in short, render himself as useful as possible . . . The question is often asked, 'Should a chaplain be under fire?' It is impossible to avoid it if he is serving troops under fire, and he must take his chance with every one else.[327]

Besides widespread defiance, other factors served to render official policy untenable in the course of 1915. As the front line achieved a greater degree of permanence on the Western Front, brigade field ambulances effectively became advanced dressing stations whose objective was to evacuate their wounded 'with the greatest possible speed'.[328] If this role meant that they were not an ideal setting for the chaplain's ministry, they were also unable to absorb the growing number of chaplains who were joining the infantry divisions of the B.E.F. in the course of 1915, especially after the divisional establishment of chaplains was increased to thirteen in the spring of that year.[329] While this augmentation served to raise the number of Anglican chaplains to two per brigade in most divisions,[330] it also meant that brigade chaplains were increasingly obliged to mess with one or other of their battalions rather than with their field ambulances.[331] Furthermore, prevailing conditions on the Western Front meant that rear areas could be as dangerous as the front line itself. C.E. Doudney, the first chaplain to die from enemy action in this theatre of war, was mortally wounded by long-range shellfire in October 1915 while driving through Ypres in an ambulance vehicle.[332] Similarly, though chaplains at Gallipoli were originally ordered to stay with their field ambulances[333] the narrow confines and resulting dangers of the British beach-heads meant that a more pragmatic approach was called for. As Oswin Creighton recalled:

> [O]perations on the peninsula did not at all follow the book, and later on the principal chaplain laid it down quite clearly that, while under normal

> circumstances the above rule is the best to follow, each chaplain must use his own discretion and be where he feels he can be of greatest use.[334]

What finally overturned the prohibition on chaplains serving in the front line was the appointment of Sir Douglas Haig as Commander-in-Chief of the B.E.F. in December 1915. From this point onwards, a heavy and explicit emphasis was placed on the role of the chaplain as a morale-builder for the army's citizen soldiers. Within weeks of assuming command of the B.E.F., Haig invited Bishop Gwynne to dine at G.H.Q. and assured him that 'A good chaplain is as valuable as a good general', marking his approval of Gwynne's efforts to date by having his Christmas sermon published and distributed among the troops. Furthermore, Haig declared that 'no one could do more than a chaplain to sustain morale and explain what our Empire is fighting for' and he encouraged Gwynne to dismiss chaplains who were lacking in 'spiritual force'.[335] As Haig noted of this conversation with Gwynne, 'I spoke to him regarding the importance of sending a message to all the clergy to preach of the great object of the war viz. the freedom of mankind from German tyranny.' The chaplains, so Haig thought, 'were too narrow in their views. They must be enthusiasts to do good.'[336] Significantly, Haig made these views known to a wider circle during a conference of army commanders at Cassel on 15 January 1916. According to Haig's diary, here it was agreed that:

> Every effort must be made to raise the 'moral' of the troops. Amusements, games, etc. etc. must be organised. I also called attention to the large number of clergymen who are now being sent to join the army. Army commanders must look to the efficiency of these men as well as to any other part of their commands. We must have large minded, sympathetic men as Parsons, who realise the *Great Cause* for which we are fighting, and can imbue their hearers with enthusiasm.
> Any clergyman who is not fit for this work must be sent home.[337]

Without doubt, Haig's appointment and the subsequent conference at Cassel marked a watershed in the army's policy towards its chaplains. Hitherto, chaplains had been required to discharge their prescribed functions of leading services and burying the dead. In addition, since the winter of 1914–15 they had been widely expected to provide entertainment and to ensure the well being of troops when out of the trenches.[338] The role of the chaplain as envisaged at Cassel was essentially open-ended, with no limit being placed on their potential usefulness.

The appointment of senior chaplains to each army headquarters in January 1916 ensured that, among Anglican chaplains at least, this new conception of chaplaincy work could be developed and implemented. As a newly appointed A.C.G., Harry Blackburne's first interview with Sir Charles Monro, Haig's successor as commander of First Army, was greatly encouraging:

> My first interview with him was most entertaining . . . he talked about my future work and said he would do all he could to help me, as indeed he did. He himself took me round in his car, to introduce me to the generals of corps and divisions as well as many others who would be able to help me in this new appointment.[339]

The effects of the new dispensation became increasingly evident during the prolonged preparations for the battle of the Somme. When Archbishop Davidson visited Haig's G.H.Q. at Montreuil in May 1916, the primate 'could not elicit anything except laudation' from Haig on the subject of chaplains, the Commander-in-Chief being 'strong on the great value of the changed administrative order which now encourages the chaplains to go forward into the trenches, if they will do so, instead of being, as formerly, kept behind at the casualty clearing stations, or even further back'. Besides speaking warmly of Gwynne's work, Haig was notably 'enthusiastic about the fine type of young Padre now at work in all parts of the line'.[340]

As Haig no doubt intended, the chaplain's duty as a morale-builder was most vividly reflected in his sermons. Given that King's Regulations still required that all soldiers attend a parade service once a week whenever practicable,[341] the chaplain's sermon on such occasions was a clear and direct means of instilling troops with the required spirit of determination and even aggression. Evidently, the chaplains of the B.E.F. did not disappoint. In a private letter to King George V dated 28 June 1916, only three days before the attacking divisions went over the top on the Somme, Haig wrote:

> Everywhere I found the troops in great spirits and full of confidence of their ability to smash the enemy when the moment for action arrives. Several officers have said to me that they never have known troops in such enthusiastic spirits . . . We must, I think, in fairness give a good deal of credit [for] this to the parsons. I have insisted on them preaching about the cause for which we are all fighting and encouraging the men to play their part. Some parsons too that were no use have been sent home. But, taken as a whole, they have done well and have been a very great help to us commanders.[342]

Significantly, in a further letter written in early August upon the second anniversary of the outbreak of war, Haig wrote to Gwynne:

> My Dear Bishop,
> Very many thanks for your most friendly letter. I appreciate most truly your kindly appreciation of my efforts to help you in your great work. That the troops are in such splendid heart and moral, and fight 'without counting the cost' is largely attributable to our chaplains who have so successfully made our men realise what we are fighting for and the justice of our cause.
> Please accept my dear Bishop my heartfelt thanks for your share in this great work and believe me
> Yours very truly
> (Sgd.) D. Haig.[343]

The pressure on chaplains to vindicate Britain's role in the war proved unrelenting. In September 1916, a meeting of all the chaplains of First Army was held at Lillers. Convened at the behest of General Sir Richard Haking, then one of First Army's corps commanders,[344] the Wesleyan chaplain John Boullier described the proceedings:

> The general desired, first of all, to thank all the chaplains for their work during the past months. They were not to be discouraged, though they might not have seen fruits for their labours. Their work had been appreciated, and, speaking for the whole of the army, had done much good. They had the sympathy of the army officials. To them were given golden opportunities of raising the morale and moral tone of the men, and, in consequence, make them more fitted for the tasks they are called to accomplish.[345]

Although Boullier recalled that, on this occasion, 'We all returned to our different spheres of work assured that we had the sympathy and full support of our devoted new commander [sic] in the furtherance of the cause of our Master and Lord',[346] other encounters with the top brass could be more disconcerting. Edward Archibald Forbes was dismayed by the attitude of 'a certain gallant General' who delivered an address at a chaplains' conference later in the war. In urging them to preach constantly on the 'High ideals of Honour, Duty, and Discipline', the speaker recalled 'being at a Church Parade' one Pentecost Sunday where 'The Padre gave us an elaborate account of what happened in some upper room in Jerusalem nearly 2000 years ago. As if that had anything in the wide world to do with us in the 20th century!'[347] No less striking was the attitude of the commanding officer of a South African battalion attached to the 9th (Scottish) Division. As one soldier remembered of Easter Sunday 1917, the eve of the battle of Arras:

> Today the Padre preached to us on the text *Love your enemies, do well to them that do spitefully use you.* Afterwards the Colonel gave us a little heart-to-heart talk on the desirability of remembering that we had bayonets on our rifles and using them accordingly. No encouragement to take prisoners unless they can be of value for information. Dead men tell no tales and eat no rations, etc. ad nauseam. The Church cannot be allowed too much rope lest we lose the war![348]

Despite these discordant notes, it is likely that most chaplains had no reason to doubt the justice of their cause or to disappoint the army's expectations of them in this regard. Whatever schemes or pressures may have induced them to join the army, chaplains remained volunteers by definition and, for those who found their duties uncongenial, there was usually the prospect of an escape to civilian life at the expiry of their annual contracts. Most notably, G.A. Studdert Kennedy achieved both celebrity and official approval by preaching what was required of him. Although his populist style could prove controversial, there can be no doubting Studdert Kennedy's consistency in this regard. In a typical address with the arresting title of 'What the ---- is the Church doing Here?', Studdert Kennedy directly confronted the question of the church's role in the front line as personified by the chaplain. As far as he was concerned, the church (and, by extension, the chaplain) was 'trying to fill the army and to keep it filled with the Spirit of the Cross, the spirit of strong love of Right which will triumph at all costs in the battle against wrong'. Moreover, it was committed 'to help the fighting men against two temptations, the temptation to dull despair which endures because it has to endure, and not because it wills to conquer, and the temptation to become brutalized, and to live as do the brutes'.[349]

While lacking the popular touch of 'Woodbine Willie', Bishop Gwynne was equally assiduous in steeling men for the fight. One sermon preached to men of the 50th (Northumbrian) Division after their experiences at Passchendaele commenced:

> i. A great pleasure to be here to-day
> ii. I know how well the Division has fought
> iii. I saw two men of your Division a few days ago who had lost their way. I had a talk with them on the road as I was putting them right. They were very proud of their Division [but] They were fed up and they wanted to go home, but they did not want the Germans to win
> iv. I think that is the feeling in every army to-day except perhaps in the American army who, thank God, have all their strength in reserve
> v. I know sometimes there is a great temptation to think it a misfortune to have lived in times like these. Why wasn't I born 100 years ago to have escaped this or 20 years hence when all this war is over?[350]

Gwynne then went on to invoke the early 'champions of Christianity' who were 'Thrown to the beasts – Tortured' and exhorted his listeners to 'Endure hardness', 'lay aside every evil' and 'Quit you like men' in the light of their salutary example. He ended by urging them to 'stick it' because their fallen comrades had done so and, if they did not, 'all we have suffered is lost [and] our children will have to fight for what we could not finish'.[351] Throughout his career as D.C.G., Gwynne reinforced his sermons with a series of rousing pamphlets that included his *Letter to the Church of England Troops on the Second Anniversary of the Commencement of the War* (1916) and *Religion and Morale: the Story of the National Mission on the Western Front* (1917). In the autumn of 1917, when morale seemed to sag throughout the B.E.F., Gwynne composed a further pamphlet and developed plans for an ambitious scheme of army education that would be run by the Chaplains' Department and which would impress upon soldiers the prospects of a better post-war society that was only achievable through victory.[352]

Apart from giving direction to their sermons and confirming the value of their work in rear areas, the new role that was conceived for chaplains in the winter of 1915–16 also gave them access to the front line itself. Although this was a gradual development, by June 1916 the principle was sufficiently well established for a formal scheme to be agreed in First Army which specified the 'Battle Posts' of divisional chaplains in formal offensive operations. This scheme, which carried the endorsement of Sir Henry Horne and of First Army's Director of Medical Services, ran as follows:

> I) S.C.F. (C. of E.) where he is in touch with all the Chaplains. The Headquarters of the Division should be informed where the S.C.F. is to be found when required.
> II) *Three Chaplains* for the three Field Ambulances. They should be the Chaplains who in normal times have the Field Ambulances under their care. When any of the three ambulances are not working, the Chaplain unemployed should be posted to Advanced Dressing Stations or Regimental Aid Posts.

> III) *The [Royal Artillery] Chaplain* should decide on some central place where messages can be sent, he being free to move from battery to battery wherever his services might be needed.
> IV) *The remaining Chaplains* at Advanced Dressing Stations or Regimental Aid Posts, which are sometimes brigaded.
> V) When opportunity offers, after a fight, the Chaplains might accompany the Battalion Medical Officer and Stretcher Bearers to bring in the wounded.
> These Battle Posts will vary according to varying conditions.[353]

However, in Fourth Army, which was to bear the brunt of the initial attack on the Somme, less latitude was in evidence. Eight days before his divisions attacked on the Somme, Lieutenant-General Henry Rawlinson issued the following order through his A.C.G.:

> It is the Army Commander's Instruction that Chaplains should be posted, during an Engagement, where they can best serve the wounded, and it is his order that Chaplains should, under no circumstances, advance with their Regiments or Brigade, or, except in the case of Chaplains allotted to [the Royal Artillery], take up positions other than with a Medical Unit. This order is to be strictly obeyed, and S.C.F's. C/E are responsible for making it known to all C/E Chaplains in their Division.
> The Army Commander does not consider that Regimental Aid Posts and Advanced Dressing Stations are suitable positions for Chaplains, as the accommodation is restricted, and opportunities for aid to the wounded necessarily limited; where however such arrangements have been made with the consent of Corps Commanders or G.O.C s. of Divisions, and by desire of the Medical Authorities, they can be allowed to stand.[354]

Significantly, this attempt to restrict the chaplain's freedom of action provoked a furore, with one Roman Catholic chaplain viewing confinement even to forward medical posts as 'a merely vexacious [sic] and irritating ruling which serves no useful purpose'.[355] Indeed, one report in *The Times* in late July 1916 even spoke of ' "Insubordinate" Padres':

> [T]he Chaplains, I believe, have been the most insubordinate – the only insubordinate – men in the Army, for when they are commanded to stay with Field Ambulances and Dressing Stations they keep turning up in the front-line trenches and going with the men where they have no right to be. There are many battalions in which the Padre is known to be one of the bravest officers of the lot; too many, also, which have no Padre now.[356]

However, the offending order had already been rescinded and G.H. Fowke, the B.E.F.'s Adjutant-General, had issued a circular that standardised policy throughout the B.E.F.:

> Some doubt appears to exist as to the positions Chaplains should occupy during active operations. It is considered that, provided their presence in no way hampers the operation in progress or in contemplation, no restrictions should be placed on their movements; and that Chaplains should be encouraged to go where the Senior Chaplains, Church of England,

> Nonconformist and Roman Catholic, of divisions, decide that their services can be most advantageously employed, and where they can be of most use to the troops.[357]

This ruling, which was to be reiterated in April 1917,[358] confirmed the chaplain's freedom of action for the remainder of the war, a situation that led to a dramatic rise in casualties among chaplains and a growing tally of honours and awards. Indeed, by the later years of the war there can be no doubting the keenness of many brigade chaplains to be in the thick of any attack. As one of their number recalled:

> We underlings in the folly of our youth and the pride of our worldliness wanted to be in things; we thought it rather a disgrace to be sent down the line for a battle; perhaps we feared that it might seem to attach to us some stigma in the eyes of others; perhaps there was the ambition of a decoration.[359]

Such ambitions were not held in vain. Three Victoria Crosses were awarded to members of the Army Chaplains' Department during the First World War, the departmental total exceeding that of many of the army's infantry regiments.[360] The first of these V.C.s went to Edward Noel Mellish, formerly an assistant curate at St. Paul's, Deptford, for rescuing dozens of wounded men under fire at St. Eloi in March 1916.[361] Two other awards were subsequently made to Anglican chaplains for similar exploits; to William Addison for his part in the recovery and tending of wounded at Sannaiyat in Mesopotamia in April 1916 and to Theodore Bayley Hardy for his role in the rescuing of wounded men near Bucquoy in April 1918.[362] However, these were only the most celebrated examples of clerical courage and many others could be cited; Anglican chaplains alone earned 37 D.S.O.s and 205 M.C.s and bars.[363] One very worthy case was that of H.E. Hubbard, in civilian life the assistant curate of the Yorkshire parish of Skelton-in-Cleveland. In less than two years on the Western Front, Hubbard was twice mentioned in despatches and was awarded the M.C. and the D.S.O. As was usually the case, Hubbard's recommendation for the M.C. was based on his care of the wounded:

> April 12–14, 1918 [Hubbard] displayed great bravery and untiring devotion to Duty. When [his] R.A.P. was obliged to move back owing to heavy shelling he remained for rest of day at [an] advance aid post under very heavy shell fire, so that he could direct any cases that came in to the new aid post. His bravery and care of wounded are worthy of the greatest praise.[364]

Similarly, when recommending P.M. Northcote for the M.C. in 1917, the commanding officer of the 118th Infantry Brigade wrote of this Roman Catholic chaplain:

> For a period covering the last 18 months he has been most indefatigable in carrying out his duties and has rendered admirable service to the men of my Brigade. He has always accompanied the 1/6th Cheshire Regt. in the trenches, comforting the men when in pain and personally attending

> to their wounds, encouraging them when under shell fire by his personal disregard of danger, and ever solicitous for the welfare of the men irrespective of their religion. During the operations of Sept. 3rd 1916 at the SOMME he rendered most valuable service to the wounded, carrying out his duties under heavy shell fire and being ultimately wounded himself and losing the sight of one eye. Not deterred by this immediately on recovery he returned to my Brigade in January last at YPRES and has at all times been of the greatest assistance.[365]

On the award of Mervyn Evers' first Military Cross in December 1916, Bishop Gwynne assured him that 'Your ministry will now be doubly appreciated by your flock for they will recognise in you soldierly qualities which appeal to them.'[366] However, while they served to enhance the Department's reputation and the stature of their recipients, these decorations were not cheaply obtained. The first chaplain to be killed in action during the First World War was Fr. William Finn, who died in the surf at Sedd-el-Bahr in April 1915 while ministering to the men of the 1st Royal Dublin Fusiliers during their landings on the Gallipoli peninsula.[367] This kind of ministry prefigured the model of front-line chaplaincy which evolved throughout the British army from the winter of 1915–16 and casualties among chaplains rose dramatically during the Somme offensive of the subsequent year. At Passchendaele in 1917, casualties among the Anglican chaplains of 25th Division were so heavy that they were exactly proportionate to losses among its infantry, namely 'five out of nine'.[368] The realities of heavy losses among chaplains during periods of intense fighting were conveyed in a letter from Bernard Rawlinson to Cardinal Bourne of June 1918, a letter that detailed casualties among Roman Catholic chaplains over the previous week:

> Your Eminence will be sorry to hear of the following casualties to priests on this front:
>
> 1. Revd. C. WHITEFORD, Shrewsbury Diocese, wounded on 29th May and died on 30th. According to information, he was badly wounded and passed through the Corps Main Dressing Station . . . He was then taken to a Canadian Stationary Hospital where he died. A few minutes after his death, the Germans bombed the hospital badly, and it was completely destroyed by bombs and fire. Unfortunately his body could not be saved . . .
> 2. Revd. T.L BAINES, Liverpool Diocese, wounded on 30th May and died on 31st. He was attached to Divisional Artillery, and was with a number of officers in a house when the Germans started bombing the place. Fr. Baines went outside to see if he could see the airoplane [sic], and a bomb fell close to him almost immediately badly shattering both legs and taking off his right hand. He was removed to a C.C.S. [and] lived till 1 p.m. of the following day, and was conscious most of the time . . .
> 3. Revd. J. Nolan, Clogher Diocese, is reported missing since the night of the 27th May, and is presumed a prisoner of war.[369]

Although definitive casualty figures are hard to establish (partly because of the vagaries of record keeping and partly because war-related deaths could occur years after hostilities had ceased) a recent estimate has put the number of chaplains who were killed as a result of enemy action in the First World War at 102. Of these, at least ninety-five chaplains were either killed in action or died of wounds after the commencement of the battle of the Somme.[370] Among these was Basil Plumptre M.C., formerly an assistant curate at St. Mary Magdalene, Bermondsey, who died in 1917 while serving as a brigade chaplain with 142nd Brigade. Emotionally and militarily attached to the 1/22nd London Regiment, a Territorial battalion with strong Bermondsey connections, a local newspaper reported his death in the following terms:

> The young Chaplain knew Bermondsey from end to end, and knowing it loved it and the people it contained. He had several offers of preferment, but his heart was in these South London streets and here he preferred to remain . . . Mr. Plumptre was as devoted to his work in the Army as he was to his duties in London. Just before his death an officer found him with his men within fifty yards of the German lines and remonstrated with him for taking such risks. 'I just wanted to keep the men cheery,' was the reply he received. A shell landing in the dug-out shortly afterwards put an end to a devoted career.[371]

If some chaplains were reckless in courting the perils of the front line, its stark realities were a terrible trial for others. F.R. Barry wrote of his service on the Western Front from 1916 to 1918:

> Having landed in France [the 5th Dorsets] were sent straight up to the front and almost immediately to the Somme. I was with them in some terrible engagements, notably in the assault on Mouquet Farm, in which about half my brigade was annihilated. I had never seen a dead man before, much less bloody bits and pieces of men, and as near as nothing I turned and ran. They thought I was brave, but in fact I was too innocent fully to appreciate the dangers! The real test of courage comes later, when a man's nerves are beginning to wear down. What needs courage and resolution then is not walking about in no-man's land but managing to hold on at all. Towards the end of the war I would sweat with fear even in comparatively safe places; but I don't think anybody was aware of it.[372]

Inevitably, some chaplains cracked altogether. During the battle of the Somme a Roman Catholic chaplain became so traumatised by his work at an advanced dressing station that he became 'hysterical and cursed and swore at people (including a general and two colonels who came and spoke to him), hardly knowing what he was saying'.[373] For another chaplain, who had served as an ordinary infantryman until joining the Chaplains' Department in 1916, the breaking point came in October 1918. As he remembered:

> We were believed to have an easy task, but camouflaged machine guns made [the attack] a tragic fiasco. There was an aid post on a sunken road which was safe until you turned the bend that led into the village we were to capture. Then it was under direct observation and almost point-blank range from machine guns in and round the village church tower. I had taken a casualty back as dawn was breaking. My nerve had gone. Instead

> of returning to my work, I cowered in the side of the road trembling like a leaf. When walking wounded came I walked as though I was going forwards and then when they had passed I hid again. This went on for half an hour.[374]

The symptoms of breakdown were spiritual as well as psychological. In June 1918, Rawlinson wrote to Cardinal Bourne concerning P.G. Prevost, a priest of Brompton Oratory, who had been an object of complaint in February 1916. In that instance, a sergeant of the 16th Manchester Regiment had written to his parish priest claiming that his battalion had not seen Prevost for six weeks, an allegation that was speedily brought to the attention of Bishop Casartelli of Salford. When confronted with this accusation by Rawlinson, Prevost simply pleaded that:

> I am not so well equipped as a priest accustomed to parish work . . . devoting most of my time to private study chiefly Canon Law, useless to say I would only be too pleased if any body else would take my place here, these Northern Catholics are most exacting and although our London boys are by no means as devout I would give anything to be amongst them once more . . . I have done as much as I could under the circumstances more even, another priest might have done more, but I could not and I am far from well, however I hope to be able to stick it until our division is relieved . . .[375]

Although Prevost persevered for another two years, by the summer of 1918 he was a broken man, with his career as a chaplain and his vocation as a priest in tatters. As Rawlinson wrote to Bourne:

> I am afraid the poor man has lost his faith entirely. I have wired him to come and see me, but fear that nothing can be done for him but send him home immediately as unsuitable from the ecclesiastical point of view. I very much hope he will go to see you on his arrival in England, and will certainly urge him to do so.[376]

However, in most cases those chaplains who could not cope with the stresses of the front line were quietly posted elsewhere. One Anglican chaplain observed that 'If a padre comes down the line to a hospital, he is probably not at his best and is unfit to do spiritual work of great and immediate urgency.'[377] Barclay Baron, a senior Y.M.C.A. worker at Le Havre, confirmed that ill-adjusted chaplains were all too common in the army's French bases:

> I have to confess that, on the whole, we did not see the best of the Chaplains' Department at the base. Some who came out were not judged fit enough to go up to the trenches, others had been up and were sent down again because their physique or their moral courage had broken down under the strain. One of them, an old friend of mine, was a very delicate man but a fine scholar. He had made a plucky attempt in vain and now sat in his tent in one of the camps among two thousand potential parishioners lamenting that the College library at Oxford would not send him out the books he needed for his theological studies.[378]

Despite the stresses of front-line work, it should be remembered that, given the prevailing rhythms of trench warfare, brigade chaplains spent very little of their time in a battle situation; as one of their number put it, life in the trenches could be 'very boring', even 'a great loaf'.[379] However, although a common shortage of dugout accommodation meant that brigade chaplains were usually compelled to sleep in reserve trenches or in the transport lines rather than in the front line itself,[380] with the advent of unrestricted access to the trenches, comprehensive visiting routines were quickly developed and perfected. As E.C. Crosse remembered, 'whereas in 1915 a padre in the trenches was regarded as quite out of place, no sort of general restrictions prevailed after 1916, and most chaplains [came] to regard visits to the trenches as the best part of their work'.[381] Crosse certainly recognised the military benefits of such visits. First, the chaplain could provide company for tired sentries and, second, he could talk to the men in their dugouts, allowing him to give their conversations 'a less pessimistic turn'.[382] However, given the pastoral maxim that 'A house-going parson makes a church-going people',[383] he was also fully aware of the missionary as well as the military potential of this work:

> [If] the military value of these visits came to be generally admitted, the religious value was certainly no less. Never indeed have the clergy of the Church of England had such a chance to get to know the manhood of the nation as was offered to them in the days of trench warfare in France. Visiting is generally recognised as the most important part of a parson's life at home, but at home it is usually only possible to call at 'the home', and at a time when only 'mother' is usually in . . . The padre who spent most of his time in the line could rest assured that he would find little difficulty in preaching to his men when he came out, and for the first time on a big scale the gap which so often exists between the clergy and the people was temporarily bridged.[384]

The burial of the dead was, of course, a common accompaniment to these visits, being one of the few specific duties expected of a chaplain throughout the war and, in the period 1914–15, the only legitimate pretext by which most chaplains could gain access to the front line.[385] Burials in or near the front line were as unpleasant as they were dangerous, a task made worse by the fact that chaplains were not only responsible for burial services but were also involved in the collection and identification of human remains. Julian Bickersteth, then the Anglican senior chaplain of 56th (London) Division, penned a vivid description of his work during the fluid fighting of September 1918:

> The battle being for the moment comparatively quiet, I turned my attention to burying, and went out all day till the evening with our Divisional Burial Officer and a large party, collecting and burying the dead. We were clearing up from the back area forwards, and as a party were engaged in burying horses as well, [so] our progress was naturally slow. However, there was no difficulty in identifying our dead, as we could follow up soon after the battle. It is piteous work this collecting of dead and committing their poor bodies to the earth. After three or four days in the forward area too, it tries the nerves and causes a curious kind of irritability which was quite infectious – all the party being cross and out of temper, and it was quite easy to find oneself heatedly arguing some trivial

> point for no apparent reason. I buried about seventy of our lads today [including] two of the Queen's Westminster officers, one of whom I had known well, only married three months ago, whose bodies the battalion had managed to get away from the battlefield. I took no services today – how could I?[386]

More harrowing still was the task of 'clearing the battlefield', sometimes through the burial of corpses that had been decomposing for weeks, months or even years. In January 1918, E.F. Campbell, a regular army chaplain and Irish rugby international, was awarded the D.S.O. for just this kind of work. In his recommendation for the award, Lieutenant-General Sir Edward Fanshawe praised Campbell's grim achievements during the summer of 1917 and, in particular, Campbell's:

> [D]evotion and perseverance in [the] burial of numerous dead in [the] Serre-Beaumont Hamel area. A most arduous duty, the majority of bodies being in [an] advanced state of putrefaction. Between 5000 and 6000 bodies were buried during about 15 weeks. Only Mr. Campbell's determination enabled him to perform the work; his assistants and working parties had frequently to be changed.[387]

Even after the work of interment had been completed, the chaplain's responsibilities to military officialdom, the dead and to their next of kin were not yet over. As Everard Digby stressed, they also had the duty of liasing with the Graves Registration Commission which had been created in March 1915:

> Every Saturday each chaplain, officer, or other person who has officiated at a burial is required by General Order to send by post all particulars to the head of the Commission. It is required by the same authority that every grave be marked so as to be easily identified pending the erection of a cross bearing all particulars. The course recommended is to write all details on a sheet of paper, then, having placed it in a bottle carefully stoppered, to bury the bottle neck downwards in the filled-in soil, so that only the bottom can be seen. In a few days, if the man's regiment does not take responsibility for marking the grave, there comes a cross from the G.R.C. bearing the necessary particulars.[388]

Although this task was onerous in itself, before the work of the Graves Registration Commission gathered momentum, the establishment and maintenance of graves and cemeteries largely devolved upon chaplains. In fact, and as E.C. Crosse remembered, until the Commission 'undertook the location and supervision of cemeteries, there was no one other than the padre to undertake this work, and he could profitably devote almost any amount of his time to the lay-out and care of proper cemeteries'.[389]

Besides conducting burials and tending graves, chaplains usually wrote to the relatives of killed and wounded soldiers under their care. Hence, during the Third Battle of Ypres, the Anglican chaplains of the 56th (London) Division wrote between three and four thousand letters to next of kin.[390] The burden of this and other correspondence could be extremely heavy, especially as it was held that a chaplain could 'rapidly endear himself' to his flock by writing 'to a man's people on any matter, however trivial'.[391] Victor Tanner, an Anglican brigade chaplain, remembered that:

> Quite a large amount of correspondence devolved upon a Padre in connection with his job. There were not many occasions when the post did not bring with it a letter from some anxious or bereaved relative asking for information about their husband, brother or son.
> From a country parson 'Dear Padre, may I commend to your pastoral care our dear boy . . .
> From a widow 'Dear Sir, I am worried to death wondering about my dear boy, he is my only son . . .
> And quite frequently something of this kind: –
> 'Dear Sir, I have just heard the terrible news that my boy has been killed in action. He was such a good lad, always cheerful and I do miss his cheery letters. Can you tell me what were his last words before he died (or) Can you send me the watch (or ring) that he was wearing (or) I should be grateful if you could send me a photograph of his grave.'[392]

The redefinition of the chaplain's role in 1916 prompted action to redress the prevailing lack of initial training provided for chaplains. In this as in many other matters, a key role was played by Harry Blackburne, the dynamic A.C.G. of First Army, who began to develop 'Courses of Instruction for chaplains' in 1916, his original idea being 'to fetch one or two chaplains from each Division to a central place, where comfortable billets can be found, and then to have two days for lectures, discussion and devotion'.[393] Because Blackburne's initiative met a recognised need, these refresher courses were widely welcomed.[394] Indeed, in view of the specialist schools of instruction that were flourishing in the B.E.F., they were soon dubbed 'Chaplains' Bombing Schools'.[395] Whatever their designation, their value in providing what Bishop Gwynne described as 'a spiritual gingering up'[396] was recognised in 1917 when the D.C.G. prevailed upon the War Office to authorise a central school of instruction for chaplains at St. Omer, 'which was, at the time, the seat of his office and situated fairly conveniently between the armies in the field and the large bases on the coast'.[397] Opened in February 1917, the principal of the school was Canon B.K. Cunningham, the genius behind Farnham Hostel, a theological college that had trained an elite band of ordinands (known as 'the Farnham Brotherhood') between 1899 and its closure through lack of students in 1915.[398] Because of Cunningham's expertise in the training of young clergymen, the Farnham regime naturally influenced the courses on offer at St. Omer. These normally consisted of collective worship and devotional exercises in addition to lectures and seminars on more practical subjects and stimulating walks in the company of Cunningham.[399] Julian Bickersteth, who passed through the school in June 1917, was impressed by his experience, writing just after his arrival:

> We had a wonderfully interesting discussion last night before the Retreat began; starting on Preaching, it developed into what was the general duty of a chaplain at the Front, what the ideal he should put before himself, how far divide his time to lifting the general 'morale' of the whole number of men under his care; what we were to make of the religion

> prompted solely, as far as we could see, by fear – each point led on really from the last.[400]

However, the impact of the school on the Anglican chaplains of the B.E.F. should not be exaggerated. While it could never fully compensate for a lack of preliminary training, it also failed to reach a large proportion of Anglican chaplains on the Western Front. In 1919, Cunningham claimed in *The Chaplains' Bulletin* that 873 chaplains had passed through the school during its existence, an impressive total given that there were nearly 900 Anglican chaplains with the British army in France and Belgium in November 1918.[401] However, these figures are belied by Cunningham's own diary which shows that only 600 chaplains attended the school between February 1917 and March 1919 (many of them twice)[402] and that a proportion of those who did attend were Commonwealth chaplains or chaplains of other denominations (the school's first 'Mixed Week' took place in December 1917).[403] Furthermore, between February 1917 and November 1918 the chaplains' school was closed for no less than eight months, first because of its relocation to Blendecques and later because of the critical situation at the front between April and November 1918.[404]

Besides taking the initiative in chaplain training, Blackburne also took the lead in promoting better relations between the estranged branches of the Department on the Western Front. With the co-operation of senior Presbyterian and Nonconformist chaplains, Blackburne organised a joint service that was held in the Grand Place at Béthune in August 1916 to mark the second anniversary of the outbreak of war, a service that was attended by 'two hundred and fifty officers and over four thousand men'.[405] This was followed in October by a two-day, interdenominational chaplains' conference at Aire, which Bishop Gwynne described as 'the first of its kind held in France'.[406] Although a voluntary gathering which was shunned by the Roman Catholics, the conference was organised by an interdenominational committee and attended by seventy chaplains, including the D.C.G.[407] The list of speakers included Blackburne, who spoke on 'A Chaplain's Duties', and A. H. Gray, a Scottish Presbyterian chaplain and Blackburne's chief collaborator, who held forth on 'The Religion of a Soldier'; B.A. Barber of the United Board and Owen Spencer Watkins were on hand to lead the conference in prayer.[408] One of the unexpected highlights of the event was 'an impromptu discussion on "Our Differences" ' in which 'opinions were expressed with the utmost candour [but] no one even began to lose his temper'.[409] Encouraged by the apparent success of the conference, and with the backing of Bishop Gwynne, Blackburne had its proceedings published 'in the hope that in other places similar conferences might be held'.[410]

All of this, however, represented more than a spontaneous effusion of ecumenical feeling. In fact, to a large extent these developments were driven by an anxiety on the part of senior chaplains to demonstrate that unity of purpose which general officers wanted to see among the chaplains of the B.E.F. The concord of the two-day conference at Aire clearly owed much to a sense of military discipline and to the expectations of senior officers. As Blackburne put it, amidst the divergences in churchmanship among those who attended, 'the most unifying factor [was] the physical training exercises which took place every morning before breakfast'.[411] Similarly, John Boullier remembered that the presence of First Army's new commander, Lieutenant-General Sir Henry Sinclair Horne, did much to inject a sense of common purpose, not least because of his appreciative and encouraging address.[412] Such was Horne's interest in the conference that he not only agreed to the publication of its proceedings but also wrote a foreword for the resulting pamphlet, which was published the following year, in which he stated:

> Religious feeling is strong in the Army in France to-day. We fight for a Cause, which the Prime Minister, Mr. Lloyd George, has described as 'a conflict of Christian civilization against organized savagery.' A great call, therefore, has been made upon our Chaplains. It is in order to decide how best to meet this call that we find our Chaplains in Council.[413]

These interdenominational conferences flourished as the war progressed. In September 1917, another two-day conference of First Army chaplains took place at Aire with 122 chaplains in attendance;[414] in August 1918, an interdenominational committee of First Army chaplains was busily preparing a third, this time in collaboration with the senior chaplain of the American 78th Division.[415] These conferences also spread to other armies and even involved Roman Catholic participants. In August 1918, Francis Drinkwater, whose 46th (North Midland) Division was then part of Fourth Army, attended two conferences for the chaplains of I Corps. At one of them, 'a paper on Militarism, Pacifism and Christianism' was read by another Roman Catholic chaplain and Drinkwater noted that this elicited 'curiously Tolstoyan views from one or two Nonconformists, who seem to believe strongly in the unlimited perfectibility of mankind en masse'.[416]

Despite inevitable differences, it seems clear that these ecumenical initiatives paid dividends in practical terms. By March 1917, Blackburne was able to issue the following circular to the senior Anglican chaplains of First Army:

> In the event of active operations, you should keep the S.C.F. (non C. of E.) informed of the whereabouts of C. of E. Chaplains.
> The A.P.C., First Army, is giving a similar order to S.C.F.s (non C. of E.) so that as far as possible all Chaplains may know where the Chaplains of other denominations are to be found.
> During heavy fighting it is obvious that such mutual courtesy between Chaplains will be invaluable in helping all to minister to men of their own flock.[417]

Furthermore, by October 1917 all denominations and both branches of the Chaplains' Department were rallying behind Bishop Gwynne's projected education scheme. Exploratory meetings held that autumn involved Harry Blackburne, Neville Talbot, 'Tubby' Clayton, J.M. Simms, A.H. Gray and G.S. Duncan (who was, in effect, Haig's personal chaplain at G.H.Q.). At the same time, the scheme was discussed with Haig himself and with Cardinal Bourne in the course of his second visit to the Western Front in October 1917.[418] When the co-ordinating committee held its first meeting four months later, Gwynne noted that: 'Although there was not much business the Chaplains' Department displayed a unanimity never seen before for all the denominations were represented. We lunched together and had a good opportunity of getting to know each other.'[419]

If a spirit of common endeavour and mutual co-operation was revived on the Western Front from the summer of 1916, personal relations between chaplains of different denominations were, in any event, usually polite and even cordial. Moreover, it must be stressed that the Western Front was exceptional insofar as the Department maintained a unified structure in every other theatre of war – including the Dardanelles, Mesopotamia, Salonika and Italy. However, certain issues could strain this concord. Given the sacrifices that the British army was making on the Western Front, an inevitable source of rancour was the refusal of local Catholic bishops to sanction the use of abandoned Catholic churches for Protestant worship. As Mervyn Evers recollected:

> When we were first in Plug Street [sic] in 1915 I can clearly remember my disgust under the following circumstances: The Nieppe Parish Church had been badly shelled and the R.C. Congregation had moved to a hutment Church and had allowed their bombed Church to be used by the troops as a drill hall and when I asked that I might use it for my Church of England Services, my request was turned down whether by the local cure or the Brigade R.C. padre I can't remember, but ever since then I have disliked the R.C.s.[420]

Roman Catholic policy held firm despite some hard lobbying from Bishop Gwynne and the Bishop of Birmingham, Henry Russell Wakefield, who vainly pleaded the Catholic credentials of the Church of England at a meeting with the Bishop of Arras in 1915.[421] This intransigence required the building of special church huts in base areas and demanded considerable powers of improvisation on the part of Protestant chaplains on the Western Front. As a brigade chaplain in the 56th (London) Division, S.F. Leighton Green held services in a French Protestant church, in a barn, in a cinema, and in a number of temporary churches near the front line, including 'St. George on the Western Front' at Laventie.[422]

Questions of how far the ordinary constraints of church life could be relaxed in the extraordinary context of war affected Protestant worship in other ways. Although frowned upon by High Churchmen, many evangelical Anglicans held united services with Presbyterian and Nonconformist chaplains[423] and the friction this caused was obvious even to non-Anglicans. In September 1915, Francis Drinkwater, who, as a Roman Catholic priest, was presumably a neutral observer, wrote of his fellow chaplains in the 84th Infantry Brigade: '[30 September 1915] Clayton (Nonconformist) came in to see Hogg. They have joint services, which Scott (the other C of E) doesn't like.'[424] Similarly, at the Church of Scotland's General Assembly in 1916, a Presbyterian chaplain 'home from the front' regaled his audience with tales of Anglican intolerance, especially concerning the vexed issue of inter-communion, whose practice at a missionary conference at Kikuyu in 1913 had provoked a fierce reaction in Anglo-Catholic circles and had sparked a theological furore in the Church of England: 'The sinister shadow of Kikuyu [he declared] has in some ways succeeded in extending itself even over the battlefields of France, especially in respect of the Communion Service.'[425]

Despite these problems, a strong and eminently practical inducement to harmony was that chaplains were often billeted together and so were obliged to make the best of available company. As early as September 1915, one Baptist chaplain testified to the readership of *The Scottish Baptist Magazine*: 'We – the chaplains – have a very comfortable mess near divisional headquarters – 4 Church of England, 2 Roman Catholic, 1 Presbyterian, 1 Wesleyan, and 1 Baptist, all reside together . . . We live together and work together and help each other in the heartiest manner.'[426] Similarly, early in 1916, Philip Fisher, a Primitive Methodist, found himself billeted with one Anglican and two Roman Catholic priests. Despite their differences, Fisher found their company highly congenial:

> In my ignorance I always imagined an Irish priest to be a very narrow, impossible sort of person, until I lived with these two . . . The Anglican was of a far 'Higher' order than I had previously had anything to do with, but in spite of all probabilities we found a great deal in common, and soon became firm friends . . . We were not the several irreconcilable humbugs wallowing in error that a sectarian tradition would have had us believe. And we were really all out on the same job . . . In fine, we helped one another respecting the common object which had brought us there together. If either came across a member of another's flock, he put shepherd and sheep in touch with one another. We helped each other in various ways, such as finding suitable places for services, and we made our round of the trenches in company.[427]

In those theatres of war where the Department retained a unitary structure under a single Principal Chaplain, relations between the denominations were closer still. When Owen Spencer Watkins was appointed Principal Chaplain in Italy in August 1918, his appointment elicited a protest from the Vatican. However, during a later audience with Benedict XV, the Pope told Watkins: 'You have been like a father to my priests. I think it is a beautiful thing that Christians should work thus together. The whole Army must thus be edified thereby.'[428] Despite its critics, a surprising degree of fruitful co-operation was also achieved within the Principal Chaplain's branch on the Western Front. By October 1916, the exigencies of active service had ensured that two Roman Catholic chaplains were serving with the 36th (Ulster) Division, a division that had been originally raised from the militantly Protestant Ulster Volunteer Force. One of these was attached to the 14th Royal Irish Rifles, a battalion recruited from among the Young Citizens' Volunteers and which even had its own Orange Lodge.[429] Less dramatically, from 1916 the affairs of the Principal Chaplain's branch flourished at Boulogne under the direction of J. Esslemont Adams, a chaplain of the United Free Church. On his departure in May 1918, a memorandum was signed by ten senior chaplains of various denominations which praised 'the unfailing fairness of [his] administration, the soundness of [his] judgment, and especially the inspiration of [his] friendship'.[430] Furthermore, in the Ypres salient in 1917 the Roman Catholic and the Presbyterian chaplain of the 146th Infantry Brigade made their daily rounds together. In the course of a typical day, they buried a number of dead and visited a captured pillbox, where the former administered Holy Communion to some machine-gunners and the latter 'spoke a few words to the others'.[431] In the light of such collaboration, a Church of Scotland chaplain wrote in 1917:

> What a lesson for the divided Churches at home is often given us here . . . It might amaze our domestic bigots, of all faiths, to find Jesuit priest and Presbyterian minister working and sleeping in wondrous unity. I shared a tent for some time with a Jesuit Father, and we were both content to have the flag of Scotland flying at the door of it. We were often quietly teased as 'the Incorporated Society of St. Peter and St. Andrew.'[432]

In the Principal Chaplain's branch, this ecumenical tone was undoubtedly set by the example of Simms, Keatinge and Rawlinson. As Francis Devas, a Roman Catholic chaplain and a Jesuit to boot, wrote to Rawlinson in March 1919:

> I found it, and I'm sure the other chaplains did too, such a comfort, in the strange new world we had got into, to know that our own G.H.Q. was a very human thing, not merely an office with official instructions . . . I used to take a pride in telling other officers how smoothly our Department worked . . . The more I think of it too, the more I am pleased with that arrangement that used to be called 'non C. of E.' and I should think many of us will find our relations with Nonconformists and Presbyterians much more cordial than before the war . . . I had meant to write to Dr. Simms – but I am a bad letter writer, and it would be merely adding to his correspondence – so would you when you see him, remember me to him, and tell him what a pleasure I found it to be loyal to such a kindly chief.[433]

Practical Problems and Critical Voices

In view of the wide variety of contexts in which they worked, the high-level support of senior officers and the reasonably harmonious nature of relations between the different denominations, some of the most intractable problems to confront chaplains were distinctly practical in nature. Foremost among these was the issue of transport, which remained a persistent problem throughout the war and despite the enhanced importance of the chaplain's role from the winter of 1915–16. For senior chaplains in particular, the success of their work hinged on their ability to visit and supervise subordinates who might be scattered over hundreds of square miles. Early in 1916, the Wesleyan Royal Navy and Army Board came into conflict with military officialdom over a motorcar for Owen Spencer Watkins. By this time, a group of Wesleyan laymen had bought a car for 'the efficient performance of his duties' but their generosity had been nullified by the refusal of the B.E.F.'s Quartermaster-General to sanction the use of a private car by the senior Wesleyan chaplain. As a result, the Board passed a resolution which claimed that it was impossible for Watkins 'to regularly visit the 52 [Wesleyan] Chaplains' in France and Belgium and that an army car had been 'granted without question to the Anglican, Presbyterian, and Roman Catholic Churches'. It concluded by warning that 'If such a refusal is persisted in, it cannot fail to create great disappointment, and a most disagreeable impression throughout the Wesleyan Methodist Church.' To add to the pressure on the military authorities, a copy of the resolution was sent to 'all the Methodist Members of Parliament'.[434] Nevertheless, the prohibition held and within a few weeks the Board was meekly negotiating with Haig for the use of an army car.[435] However, even the Church of England had problems in this respect. When Archbishop Davidson visited the Western Front in May 1916, he was unable to secure a car for each A.C.G., despite his plea that for them to be without motor transport was like 'choosing with much pride four first-rate horses and then insisting that they should remain in the stable'.[436]

For ordinary chaplains, the question of transport was still more problematic. Apart from lines of communication and artillery chaplains, whose ministry tended to be itinerant, even brigade chaplains required transport when ministering to their units when out of the line. Consequently, Charles Doudney of the 18th Infantry Brigade (who estimated that his division normally occupied an area of 'about two miles by ten miles in depth') was fortunate to receive a motorcycle as a present from his Bath parishioners in the summer of 1915.[437] Of course, most chaplains were not so lucky. According to E.C. Crosse, the terms of the annual contract signed by temporary chaplains entitled each to his own horse. However, few chaplains could ride on joining the army and 'by no means all' took the trouble to learn.[438] Still, chaplains had the option of using a horse or a bicycle[439] until 1917 when, as horses became scarcer, the chaplains of the B.E.F. were equipped solely with bicycles.[440] While this loss may have been offset by the diminishing size of divisional areas (one chaplain estimated that a division was typically 'spread over an area of 15 or 20 square miles' in 1914–15 but occupied only four or five square miles by 1917)[441] the loss of their horses was resented by many chaplains. As Mervyn Evers complained to his S.C.F. in April 1917:

> I understand that orders have been issued for the withdrawal of our horses. Might I ask you [to] protest against this. When we are out at rest and the billets are widely scattered a horse is invaluable. It is also of the greatest possible service in getting from the trenches to the Transport for services and classes. We use our horses on the average more [than] any of the other officers with the exception of the [transport officer].[442]

Others saw the development as another indication of the ungenerous treatment accorded to chaplains by army bureaucracy. As E.C. Crosse alleged, this was 'just another illustration of the old idea that [the padre] had no "military" value, which lingered on at G.H.Q. long after it had been outlived at the actual front'.[443]

If transport was a common problem, then so too were the numerous factors that complicated the organisation of services. Even after the war on the Western Front had settled into the dismal business of static trench warfare, church parades and other services could be seriously curtailed by the periodic movement of troops and by the obvious hazards of concentrating large numbers of men in or near the front line. In front-line trenches, church services were usually forbidden and even William Doyle was prohibited from saying Mass in the forward trenches of the culturally Catholic 16th (Irish) Division early in 1917.[444] In the Ypres Salient later that year, Maurice Murray was forced to hold a succession of parade services for the Anglicans of the 13th Royal Sussex Regiment, a standing order allowing only fifty men to gather at any one place at any given time.[445] Besides the constraints imposed by the range and power of enemy artillery on the Western Front, the vagaries of war meant that chaplains could not always rely on officers prioritising church parades or on soldiers being notified of voluntary religious services. In this respect, the frustrations experienced by Francis Drinkwater in the summer of 1915 were no doubt fairly typical. As a temporary chaplain attached to the 84th Infantry Brigade, it proved a difficult task for Drinkwater to assert himself in a brigade that was largely Protestant and mainly composed of regular soldiers. On 23 June 1915, Drinkwater noted in his diary, 'Went to say Mass at the huts of the Fusiliers and E[ast] Surreys, but no one turned up as the [commanding officers] had evidently forgotten our arrangements of the day before yesterday.' The following day brought more frustration, 'Mass for the Buffs in a barn', he wrote, 'The E[ast] Surreys didn't turn up – again!' By mid-July, however, there were more encouraging signs: 'Got round Y[ork] & L[ancaster]s C.O. for a confession-parade and Mass on a weekday; but he doesn't much care for padres.' However, this glimmer of hope soon faded, Drinkwater writing on 10 August: 'Last Sunday apparently the [York and Lancaster] Adjutant forgot the R.C. service and the 2nd [King's Own] C.O. made it voluntary on account of the weather. Hence smallness of the congregation.'[446]

Given that the overwhelming majority of chaplains were essentially civilians, it was inevitable that the issue of rank and its trappings should once more raise its head. This was especially true among Anglicans. As Hugh McLeod has said of the Anglican clergy, by the turn of the twentieth century 'a new style of clergyman was emerging, especially in urban working-class parishes, who was trying to get away from the image of clergymen as "gentlemen" and who cultivated a democratic style'.[447] Although this tendency found its ultimate wartime expression in the person and ministry of Studdert Kennedy, it also fed debate about the chaplain's place in the military hierarchy, a controversy that was further fuelled by the salutary example of the French army's conscript 'soldier priests' and of those Anglican clergymen who had chosen to enlist as ordinary soldiers. While this debate was aired in the national press,[448] Neville Talbot wrote in his *Thoughts on Religion at the Front*, which was published in 1917:

> There is something wrong about the status of chaplains. They belong to what the author of *A Student in Arms* calls 'the super-world' of officers, which as such is separate from the men . . . We are in an unchristian position, in the sense that we are in a position which Christ would not have occupied. He, I am sure, would have been a regimental stretcher-bearer, truly among and of the men.[449]

Everard Digby agreed that being treated as an officer posed a serious pastoral problem:

> It is a very moot question as to the value of the military title, and the writer and many of his brother Chaplains are strongly averse to it. To invest a Chaplain with badges of rank, etc., seems to put a gulf between him and the rank and file, which makes a real difficulty in one's work . . .

> Men like their Chaplain to be in khaki as they are, but they dislike immensely the difficulties created by his being an officer. To have to come to attention and say, 'May I speak to you, sir?' makes a very bad beginning for spiritual conversation, and the Chaplain is handicapped by this extra difficulty in an always difficult job.[450]

However, despite these opinions it seems likely that these problems were overstated and that they fostered a climate in which it was easy for ill-adjusted chaplains to blame their problems on their military rank. Whatever else, this vaunted issue belied the fact that the temporary chaplains of the First World War were not the remote figures that the regular chaplains of the Victorian era had often been. To a large extent, this was dictated by the very different composition of the British army in 1914–18 and by the very different dynamic of officer-man relations that prevailed in these years. As Gary Sheffield has remarked of the Territorial Force, which eventually furnished more than a third of the British army's infantry divisions, 'A whole series of factors, not least the social composition of the ranks and the officer corps, and the practical difficulties involved in enforcing strict discipline on a part-time amateur army, produced a style of officer-man relations and discipline very different from the Regular varieties.'[451] If the discipline of the pre-war Territorials was widely regarded as lax by the standards of the regular army,[452] this was also true of the New Army, which also contributed more than a third of the army's infantry divisions and where it was not unknown for soldiers to address their officers by their Christian names.[453] In the First World War, the British army represented a fusion of the regulars, the Territorials and the New Army. Hence, officer-man relations tended to be distinguished by a conscious paternalism on the part of officers, a due (but not uncritical) deference on the part of the other ranks and by cordial relations between the two.[454] Hence, if officer-man relations were usually very good,[455] chaplains had little practical reason to fret at their officer status. Over and above all this, the chaplain was very much in 'a caste of his own'.[456] Although chaplains wore badges of rank and were entitled to the courtesies and perquisites accorded to officers,[457] the army's temporary Fourth Class chaplains were not paid a captain's salary and nor did their relative rank permit them to be addressed by this rank.[458] Furthermore, and in marked contrast to ordinary regimental officers, they were usually in the enviable position of being allowed to return home on the expiration of their short-term contracts. For all these reasons, temporary chaplains were not regarded or treated by the army as ordinary officers, a point that Everard Digby was keen to impress upon new chaplains:

> You are expected to salute all officers of the rank of major and upwards. If in doubt, salute everybody is an excellent rule. You are not expected to know how to salute correctly, being only 'an old fool of a padre,' and not a soldier; but it should be obviously a salute, and not a half-hearted lift of the hand . . . As you are a priest, and feel like a 'pal' to the men, you can take the edge off by accompanying your salute with your best 'parochial smile,' or, better still, a cheery 'Good-day,' and you can be sure of a hearty response as a rule . . . The only parades, other than Church Parade, which you are expected to attend are those of the General Officer

> Commanding. On such parades a Chaplain's proper place is on the extreme left flank of the Battalion, in a line with the front rank of the men and three places away. As a matter of fact, the Adjutant, who thinks your figure will spoil his parade, is almost sure to put you in the extreme rear of the Battalion, with the Quartermaster and the regimental goat.[459]

For his part, Harry Blackburne, a pre-war regular chaplain, was convinced that those who bemoaned the military status of the chaplain were missing a more fundamental point. In a forceful memorandum written while A.C.G. of First Army, Blackburne took exception to Neville Talbot's pronouncements concerning the 'unchristian position' of commissioned chaplains, pointing out that such misgivings over the chaplain's status were part of 'a far larger problem', namely 'the social position of the clergy in relation to the varying conditions of [the] men to whom they minister'. Dismissing criticisms of the chaplain's rank as 'merely sentimental', Blackburne argued that the vaunted 'soldier priests' of the French army would happily change places with British army chaplains because the free exercise of their ministry was entirely subject to the whims of their commanding officers and 'because they know by experience that they cannot do their work as Priests properly if it has to be done as an addition to the heavy work of a soldier in wartime'. Furthermore, in countering the view that the clergy could be better employed by the army in another capacity, Blackburne invoked the telling example of the clergymen who had enlisted in the ranks of the British army on the outbreak of war and who had since found their way into the Chaplains' Department:

> The strongest evidence of all against this theory comes from nearer home. Hardly a month passes in which chaplains' commissions are not given to Clergy who have served honourably in the ranks of our own Army, often as combatants: while, in the writer's experience at any rate, the reverse is rarely heard of. And these men will always give the same reason for the change – they wish [to] become Chaplains in order that they may do the work for which they were ordained.

In Blackburne's opinion, if there was a barrier between chaplains and the other ranks it lay in the fact that the clergy were perceived as remote and aloof figures in civilian life – 'It is exactly the same "barrier" as kept a third-class smoking carriage nearly empty on a crowded train, because there was a Parson visible, sitting near the window.' However, he maintained that this popular aversion to 'anything that savours of official righteousness' was receding in the context of the present war, with the shared dangers and discomforts of the trenches serving to engender a greater 'spirit of comradeship and friendliness' towards the clergy than had ever been felt at home.[460]

Besides friction with military officialdom and disagreement over their commissioned status, chaplains were also troubled by questions of sexual morality. While concern over libidinous soldiers and illegitimate births was aired at the Convocation of Canterbury as early as July 1915,[461] moral questions were exacerbated on the Western Front by the existence of regulated brothels in France and by the army's surreptitious expedient of running similar institutions of its own, a practice which had met with some success in nineteenth-century India but which had always proved obnoxious to moralists at home and in the army.[462] Although senior officers such as Kitchener and Haig had always preferred the urging of restraint and moral purity, as a result of growing pressure from the churches regulated brothels were closed to British troops in 1918 and the army was compelled to embrace 'continence and self-control' as the best solution to temptation of this kind.[463] Besides being a source of grief and concern on moral and religious grounds, sexual promiscuity was a sad reflection on the self-discipline and military efficiency of the British soldier, especially as venereal disease took thousands of men away from their duties (hospital admissions for venereal disease in France and Flanders peaked at more than 60,000 in the critical year of 1918).[464] Thus, in the complementary interests of Christian morality and military efficiency, chaplains sought to combat the problem by promoting alternative recreations for soldiers and, more directly, by demanding purity and self-restraint.[465]

Sometimes this urging could be conciliatory in tone. In the light of a visit to Le Havre in August 1916, Bishop Gwynne wrote in his diary:

> One of the saddest things one has to do here is to visit and preach to the VD Hospital. There are now more than 4,000 men and officers in for treatment . . . I went for something positive instead of dwelling on the lower level of animal passions and tried to lift them up to a higher plane by talking on the friendship with God.[466]

However, other chaplains preferred a more combative approach. While stationed in England in the winter of 1914–15, Oswin Creighton prowled the streets of Nuneaton having heard rumours 'of soldiers leaving their billets at late hours to meet girls in back streets'.[467] Similarly, while seated with friends in a disreputable café in Armentières, where British soldiers were queuing to patronise the women in residence, Sergeant George Ashurst was spotted by his battalion's chaplain. As Ashurst remembered:

> The padre came over to us. We sat there, me and Tom and a couple more at a little table. You can imagine how he dressed us down. 'Have none of you any mothers? Have none of you any sisters?' and all that sort of thing. He said, 'I shall report this to the colonel.' He reduced our time in the town.[468]

Despite his celebrity as a populist preacher, Studdert Kennedy was no less zealous in his denunciation of impurity and the dangers it entailed. While eschewing any desire 'to lead a new movement with a new name: Kennedy's Anti-drink Crusade or Padre's Pioneers of Purity',[469] in a particularly trenchant sermon he harangued his listeners with the debilitating effects of venereal disease:

> The prevalence of venereal disease, both gonorrhoea and syphilis, among the troops is a continual source of anxiety and distress to those who lead our Army. It constitutes a continual daily, weekly, drain of men from the fighting strength which is worth a great deal to the enemy.[470]

Accordingly, he urged his listeners to rid the army's bases of 'all that weakens our national force, all that fetters our freedom and prevents our putting forward all our strength'.[471] While denouncing the regulation of brothels as sinful both in principle and in practice, he condemned prostitution as 'slow murder' and compared the evils of commercial sex with the worst atrocities of the Germans: 'It is better to rip a woman open and leave her disembowelled in the mud than to drive her into deadly sickness, to satisfy a self-created craving that we are too weak to fight.'[472] Rounding on the plea that such sexual activity was natural and unavoidable, Kennedy broadened his theme into a general denunciation of the seedier aspects of army life:

> Come off it . . . You make it necessary. You rouse your passion and then you submit. Why buy post-cards of naked women and keep them, and show them round? Why use continually the word for intercourse that makes your passion hot? Why talk about the traffic as an everlasting joke? Why make a dead set at a man who wants to keep his body clean? Why talk smut, think smut, and feed your soul on smut?[473]

Although the chaplains' stand against vice could be confrontational, their championing of Christian purity was at least to be expected of the clergy. Much more problematic in terms of their relations with the soldiers of the B.E.F. in particular was the chaplains' persistent (and, from 1916 onwards, their *ex officio*) advocacy of the war. Given the mounting human costs of the struggle in France and Belgium, it seems likely that this advocacy struck a discordant note with an increasing number of officers and men, a fact that was perceived by informed observers of the British army on the Western Front.[474] As Philip Gibbs, the official war correspondent of the *Daily Telegraph* and the *Daily Chronicle*, wrote just after the war:

> God and Christianity raised perplexities in the minds of lads desiring life and not death. They could not reconcile the Christian precepts of the chaplain with the bayoneting of Germans and the shambles of the battle-fields. All this blood and mangled flesh in the fields of France and Flanders seemed to them – to many of them, I know – a certain proof that God did not exist, or if He did exist was not, as they were told, a God of love but a monster glad of the agonies of men.

According to Gibbs, this was 'the thought which our Army chaplains had to meet from men who would not be put off by conventional words. It was not good enough to tell them that the Germans were guilty of this crime, and that unless the Germans were beaten the world would lose its liberty and its life.'[475] If the arguments propounded by the chaplains of the B.E.F. proved inadequate to many then their example likewise failed to resolve this underlying dilemma. As Gibbs put it:

> The devotion of military chaplains to the wounded, their valour, their decorations for gallantry under fire, their human comradeship, and spiritual sincerity, would not bridge the gulf in the minds of many soldiers, between a gospel of love and this argument by bayonet and bomb, gas-shell and high-velocity, blunderbuss, club and trench shovel.[476]

Chaplains also struck C.E. Montague (who, in civilian life, was a chief leader writer for the *Manchester Guardian*)[477] as unable to resolve the religious and moral difficulties of the average soldier. In Montague's opinion, even the conspicuously devoted and strongly egalitarian chaplain was not entirely satisfactory. This kind of chaplain, who 'had his counterpart in all the churches', undoubtedly had 'notable merits', being affable, brave, warlike, entertaining and 'a running fountain, more often than not, of good cigarettes'.[478] However, despite the theological problems and nascent religiosity engendered by the war, no 'man of apostolic genius' was to be found 'fishing in the troubled waters' of the British army on the Western Front. Instead, so Montague claimed, rather than engagement with their deeper concerns soldiers were presented with the bluff and jovial figure of the padre:

> [As] if chance had planned a kind of satiric practical epigram, came the brigade chaplain. As soon as his genial bulk hove into sight, and his cheery robustious chaff began blowing about, the shy and uncouth muse of our savage theology unfolded her wings and flew away. Once more the talk was all footer and rations and scragging the Kaiser, and how 'the Hun' would walk a bit lame after the last knock he had got.[479]

As this character sketch serves to illustrate, the perceived failure of the chaplains to address a major area of soldiers' concern was compounded by a high degree of assimilation to military culture. The misgivings that this evoked have to be understood in the light of the clerical self-consciousness and assertiveness that had marked 'the clerical renaissance' in Britain's largest churches during the nineteenth century.[480] Ironically, while the clergy had for decades sought to cultivate their distinctiveness in civilian life, in the military context these concerns seemed much less in evidence. Despite their limited terms of service and the subtly different way in which they were regarded and treated as officers by the army, chaplains frequently demonstrated a strong identification with their units and with their temporary status as officers and soldiers. Barclay Baron, a Y.M.C.A. worker at Le Havre from 1915 to 1917, remembered that:

> There was a sprinkling of chaplains, whom I respected least of all, who spent a deal of time at the bar in the officers' mess and traded in bawdy stories which the other ranks, at any rate, sincerely resented from such a source, who were very fussy about salutes to their officers' uniform and liked to write below their signatures 'Chaplain Captain', a rank [not] to be found in the Army List.[481]

Stephen Graham of the 2nd Scots Guards wrote of one such chaplain who was 'an extraordinary believer in discipline, quite a Prussian in his way [who] liked men to stand to attention when speaking to him, and say "Sir" and the rest'.[482] Another indicator of this phenomenon was the adoption of unauthorised dress and insignia. As Everard Digby observed in 1917, even in training camps at home chaplains frequently discarded their clerical collars in favour of the shirt and tie worn by their fellow officers and sported regimental insignia instead of the badge of the Chaplains' Department.[483] If chaplains stood on their dignity and assumed affectations of dress, their adoption of titles that were not properly theirs clearly irked senior chaplains. In 1916, a memorandum was issued from First Army headquarters stressing that it was wrong to address chaplains by rank, a point which had already been made by the Adjutant-General of the B.E.F. This affectation had apparently taken root in emulation of practice in the Canadian Expeditionary Force but Harry Blackburne was determined to emphasise 'that padres are padres, and not officers'.[484]

One of the most telling ways in which chaplains demonstrated their identification with the army as an institution was in their acceptance of a harsh system of military justice that led to nearly 300 British soldiers being 'shot at dawn'.[485] However, this should not be confused with a lack of sympathy for those who were tried for military offences and still less with indifference towards those who were executed for crimes such as cowardice and desertion. Significantly, the army encouraged its chaplains to take the part of defaulters as an aspect of their established role as the soldier's friend; as Gwynne noted in his diary on 1 May 1917, 'General Jacob of the 2nd Corps addressed our Chaplains at the [Chaplains'] School to night. He gave a very good address full of hints [and] asking the Chaplains to identify themselves with the men and not to be afraid of the officers.'[486] Consequently, chaplains were often expected or invited to act as 'prisoner's friend' at courts martial. Towards the end of the war, many were trained for this role at schools of instruction and Mervyn Haigh enjoyed considerable success in this capacity while serving in East Africa, securing the acquittal of five defaulters in succession.[487] Similarly, one chaplain wrote to the widow of Harry Farr, a regular soldier who was shot for cowardice in October 1916, assuring her that 'A finer soldier never lived.'[488] Nevertheless, the collective silence that was observed by army chaplains on the issue of executions for military offences clearly amounted to tacit support for the army's ultimate means of maintaining discipline.[489] This support was reflected in the case of Noel Mellish, who was summoned to attend an execution only days after he had earned his own Victoria Cross at St. Eloi. As Mellish remembered:

> At the end of March [1916] a man who had deserted was caught, tried by Court Martial and sentenced to be shot. It was a bright spring morning when the battalion was drawn up for his sentence to be promulgated. I had to prepare him for his tragic end which he seemed not to realise himself. Whether his mind was deficient I do not know, but he seemed benumbed, showing no signs of fear or any emotion. Early in the morning I went with him and the escort and there at one side of a field the firing party stood. The man's eyes were blindfolded and as I turned away and went apart the volley rang out and the poor lad passed to his account.[490]

While Mellish hardly revelled in these proceedings, it is significant that his chief complaint was that the wrong man had been shot that morning, the condemned man having been the dupe of a serial deserter who twice escaped the death penalty in the course of the war.[491]

Given that nearly 90 per cent of death sentences awarded by courts martial were commuted or suspended,[492] the involvement of chaplains in the preparation of condemned prisoners was far greater than the number of those actually executed implies. Indeed, this difficult ministry even produced its own specialists. Some chaplains attended more than one condemned prisoner and Bishop Gwynne noted in July 1916 that L.G. Dickenson, the S.C.F. of the 25th Division, was: 'Reported on by [the A.C.G. of Fourth Army] as a good man at preparing prisoners under death sentence.'[493] Whatever their skill and sensitivity may have been, the business in which they were involved was highly controversial. Edward Roe, a regular soldier serving with the 6th East Lancashire Regiment, recalled the execution of a soldier of his battalion at Gallipoli in December 1915:

> This youth barely 19 years of age was shot by twelve of his comrades for taking 'French Leave' from his Regiment on two occasions and attaching himself to the Anzacs. Not by any stretch of imagination could my comrades or I catalogue it as desertion, as 'twas impossible to desert from the Peninsula even had he so desired . . . I was one of the firing party; he was marched from a dugout about 80 yards away, to a kind of disused quarry where the final scene was enacted. A clergyman preceded the doomed youth and his escort, reading prayers for the dying (the mockery of it all).[494]

If these executions could arouse strong feelings even among hard-bitten regulars, a Roman Catholic chaplain noted that opposition to the death penalty was most keenly felt among the volunteers of the New Army.[495] Frank Crozier, who witnessed the execution of a young soldier of the 9th Royal Irish Rifles in February 1916, contrasted the resentment felt by the volunteers of this New Army battalion with the willingness of their chaplain to play his part in the proceedings. In fact, Crozier even doubted the need for a chaplain's presence at all on the grounds that:

> In the eyes of God, of course, he had committed no specific sin demanding repentance; therefore the Chaplain's task was easy . . . why the culprit had to make his peace with God when the only trouble he had at the time was with the Commander-in-Chief of the British Armies in France, I do not know.[496]

Apart from the emotive question of military executions, it was widely considered that many chaplains resented their status as non-combatants. As the high incidence of clerical enlistment for combatant service serves to illustrate, clergymen of military age were often loath to shun a combatant role. As late as April 1918, an officer of the 2nd Royal Welch Fusiliers met one Anglican chaplain who had not lost his original compulsion to smite the enemy:

> One of the Brigade chaplains, who shares our cellar, defied his bishop, enlisted in the artillery, and was a bombardier when he was reclaimed and transferred. To save his gold denture and best kit from roughing it down here, he left them in the Divisional Dump up north which the Germans have captured, all but ten lorry loads. Now he wants to kill Germans.[497]

According to C.E. Montague, this type of chaplain was common enough in the army – 'the man who, urged by national comradeship, would have been a soldier but that his bishop barred it; to be an army chaplain was the next best thing'.[498]

If chaplains widely mourned 'the pedantry which denied [them] a service revolver',[499] some nevertheless slid into a combatant role. At Messines ridge in June 1917, Mervyn Evers seized an abandoned machine gun, purportedly with the intention of 'handing it over' to the first machine gunner he met. Be that as it may, a story soon arose that during its capture he was seen 'charging up the hill with a machine gun'. On another occasion, during the German offensives of the following spring, Evers seized a rifle and threatened to fire upon a soldier who was falling back without orders.[500] However, such chaplains were not confined to the Church of England. In a training exercise in the spring of 1916, a Roman Catholic chaplain maimed himself and killed his commanding officer while throwing a hand grenade (or 'fooling around with bombs', as Keatinge sourly noted).[501] Two years later, the Jesuit brigade chaplain Henry Day assumed command of some leaderless troops who had found themselves surrounded by Germans. When asked 'Shall we hoist a handkerchief on a bayonet?' Day rejected the idea 'because I knew that would mean surrender and imprisonment, and the end of the war in France for me, just when I was beginning to enjoy it'. In the event, he led a costly breakout to the British lines.[502] However, one of the most egregious violations of a chaplain's non-combatant status came at an unlikely time and from an unlikely quarter. F.P. Crozier, who commanded the 119th (Welsh Bantam) Brigade of the 40th Division from 1916–1918, remembered that:

> On one occasion I came upon a Welsh Nonconformist chaplain indulging in rapid fire from a shell-hole at fleeting enemy targets. It was almost at the end of the war, when we were practically in open warfare in circumstances which called for no emergency . . . this Welsh chaplain was doing 'for fun' what most of us were heartily sick of doing in grim necessity. I simply took the rifle away from him, unloaded it, handed it to a sergeant and asked the chaplain to lunch with me. In privacy we had it out. And I came to the conclusion that the man should never have been a clergyman at all. I was driven to tell him so . . . There is a sequel. He renounced his vocation and joined up as a private. He did quite well, and I was told that he had the finest flow of language in the regiment, which, being Welsh, was saying a good deal.[503]

For some chaplains, this ineluctable assimilation to military culture shaded into an unseemly brutalisation of attitude and demeanour. Despite his own unhappy war and his inter-war career as an active pacifist, as a serving chaplain Charles Raven was thoroughly committed to Allied victory, even writing to one correspondent in the dismal autumn of 1917: 'I fancy it is the politicians and the pacifists who have wrecked Italy more than the generals. If [Lloyd George] wants to save England I'm inclined to think that a drastic slaughter of the Pro-German peace-mongers would do more than the establishment of a war council.'[504] Indeed, one of C.E. Montague's more striking claims was that:

> I never met a regimental officer or 'other rank' who wanted a day more of the war for himself, his friends, or his country after the Armistice. But I have heard more than one chaplain repining because the killing was not to go on until a few German towns had been smashed and our last thing in gas had had a fair innings.[505]

For his part, Henry Day condemned what he saw as a premature peace in November 1918 – only to be later snubbed by Haig as 'the padre who denounced the Armistice'.[506]

In addition to their visceral belligerence, some chaplains adopted a persona that seemed distinctly at odds with their sacred calling. According to Stephen Graham:

> They ate Germans for breakfast, tea, and supper, and were often more bloodthirsty than the men. One or two of them drank whisky with gusto, and spoke the gaudy language of the army. 'Graham', said one, 'if there's one thing more than another that is important in this war, it is that the whisky supply should not get low.'[507]

Graham also remembered that one chaplain, the padre with alarmingly 'Prussian' tendencies, 'told me [that] he had a physical loathing for the Hun, and was ready to see the whole race, man, woman and child, exterminated'.[508] Similarly, Philip Gibbs was struck by how many chaplains seemed to revel in the macabre humour of the trenches. On one occasion 'a military chaplain (Eton, Christ Church, and Christian service) described how an English sergeant stood round the traverse of a German trench, in a night-raid, and as the Germans came his way, thinking to escape, he cleft one skull after another with a steel-studded bludgeon'. Gibbs also remembered how some chaplains 'treasured' an anecdote concerning soldiers shovelling the remains of a comrade into a sandbag.[509] In adopting the vernacular of the army, some chaplains even fell foul of their superiors. In August 1918, Bernard Rawlinson was compelled to send Fr. Francis Richmond home in disgrace for causing grave scandal in the 38th (Welsh) Division. Several officers had complained of his foul language and the division's senior medical officer had on this account banned him from its field ambulances. As another chaplain explained to Rawlinson:

> No doubt the excess complained of is due to a mistaken notion of army life, which is not so ruddily Kiplingesque as a newcomer might imagine. When Fr. R. learns this fact that the soldier, with all his faults, follows the priest, some closely, most with attention and respect, and all of them with at least judgment, he will no doubt be able to make a new start in another sphere, and be most useful with this unfortunate experience behind him.[510]

This invidious tendency for chaplains to conform their outlook and behaviour to their new milieu was not helped by inadequate training, by their isolated position and high profile in their units or by negative perceptions of the clergy that were brought into the army from civilian life. As Hugh McLeod has shown, while the churches were not threatened by a popular anticlerical movement in the pre-war era 'Anticlerical attitudes remained significant in the private sphere' and these sentiments 'could have a significant influence both on the collective mentalities of certain groups and on the outlook of many individuals'.[511] Anticlerical feeling of this kind was inspired by a melange of personal grievances and prejudices which could give rise to resentment of the clergy's social position, of 'priestcraft' and all priestly pretensions, of clergymen's supposed hostility to science and progress, of their status as custodians of a restrictive moral order, of their apparently feminine proclivities and, finally, of their irritating naivety. While such sentiments informed dozens of anticlerical cartoons in *Punch* in the decades prior to the First World War, anti-clerical feeling was most conspicuous not among the polite, middle-class readership of *Punch* but among Protestant, working-class males – or precisely the constituency that made up the great bulk of the British army in the First World War.[512]

As Edward Madigan has remarked, in view of the unflattering image of the civilian clergy that was widely held by Britain's citizen soldiers, many chaplains felt compelled 'to work hard to bridge the sheer cultural distance between themselves and the men they encountered'.[513] While this fuelled debate over rank among chaplains themselves, many were liable to err by making too much of an effort to embrace military culture and the brutal business of war. As C.E. Montague observed, in his dealings with soldiers:

> [The brigade chaplain] seemed to be only too much afraid of having it thought that he was anything more than one of themselves. He had, with a vengeance, 'no clerical nonsense about him.' The vigour with which he threw off the parson and put on the man and brother did not always strike the original men and brothers as it was intended. Your virilist chaplain was apt to overdo, to their mind, his jolly implied disclaimers of any compromising connection with kingdoms not of this world.[514]

However, an unduly aloof or sanctimonious manner could equally invite censure and scorn, confirming Hugh McLeod's point that all too often 'the parson found that he was "damned if he did, and damned if he didn't" '.[515] William Drury, a brigade chaplain of the 56th (London) Division, remembered the instructive example of a Baptist colleague, Samuel Hamill Wilkinson, who was 'generally known as "Wilkiebard" on account of his extreme unlikeness to a popular comedian of that name. He was also inappropriately called "Sunny Jim" .'[516] Similarly, in 1922 a former chaplain complained that he saw 'no reason why the Army should not insist that some test should be given to chaplains that they can talk to men, that they are manly, and that they have some knowledge as to what should be said to men'. As an example of bad practice, he cited his experiences in Palestine in 1917:

> I remember on the Sunday before the second battle of Gaza . . . we had our last brigade parade service. All the officers and chaplains knew that the engagement would be a very severe one, but we had a chaplain in our brigade who preached a sermon to his men on that Sunday morning, two days before action, on the subject of swearing! He told the men that every time they swore they prolonged the war. The 19th of April, the Thursday of that week, was our fatal day, when our brigade was almost annihilated, and this chaplain held a service three days afterwards, and preached to the remainder of the men on the value of foreign missions . . .[517]

Wartime Trends in Theology, Politics and Churchmanship

Because the wartime composition of the Army Chaplains' Department increasingly reflected the religious diversity of the nation, the Department tended to reflect the variety of theological opinion that had been present in the mainstream Protestant churches in the pre-war period, a variety of opinion that ranged from conservative evangelicalism to, in the Church of England at least, liberal Anglo-Catholicism. Although liberal theology was rendered suspect because of its German origins and associations,[518] as in civilian life there was no clear correlation between a clergyman's theology and his support for the war.[519] Chaplains were volunteers by definition and their fixed-term contracts served as a further means of self-selection; consequently, whether they saw the war as a judgment on the modern world or, in a more liberal vein, as a painful harbinger of the Kingdom of God, virtually all could agree on Germany's depravity and culpability and on the need to fight the war to a victorious conclusion.

However, the war did have a discernible theological impact upon chaplains, an impact that arose from their close and sometimes problematic identification with their men. As F.R. Barry put it, 'We had to re-examine our fundamentals and to hammer out a working theology which could stand the test of battle-conditions and give men a faith that could overcome the world.'[520] Naturally enough, one facet of this inspirational 'working theology' was the emphatic rejection of traditional theologies of salvation. In the midst of unprecedented bloodletting on the Western Front and elsewhere, it would seem that liberal Protestant chaplains in particular were inclined to see death in battle as redemptive in itself, views that were communicated in letters of condolence to next of kin and which fed and affirmed the growth of similar perspectives in the churches at home.[521] As Oswin Creighton wrote in 1915, 'I don't think that the war makes people more religious at once. But it makes them a great deal more serious and unselfish . . . The men who are killed I feel absolutely sure must have many sins forgiven.'[522] Similarly, Studdert Kennedy likened the example of the British soldier to that of Christ himself in suffering to bring forth a better world.[523] Hence, in *The Hardest Part*, which he described as 'a fairly faithful and accurate account of the inner ruminations of an incurably religious man under battle conditions',[524] Studdert Kennedy argued that the war had served to broaden the parameters of salvation:

> There are many men who die fine deaths who have no faith, or at least no conscious faith, in God or Christ as Son of God. How about them? Well, God is greater than the Churches. He is the source, and the only source, of all fine life of the spirit. If a man dies for duty's sake a death which is for his spirit not defeat but victory, he dies in Christ. That is how it looks to me. Christ is the Lord of all good life. He is the only source of the splendid life of the spirit which turns defeat in death to victory. This gift of the 'life eternal' is indeed poured out upon men through the Church and the appointed means of grace, but we cannot confine God to His covenants. The river of eternal life breaks through a thousand channels and finds the soul of man.[525]

In addition to fostering a more inclusive theology of salvation, the war saw the radicalisation of the social and political outlook of many chaplains and fuelled the incipient drift towards Christian socialism among the Anglican clergy in particular.[526] Though strongly supported by senior officers, part of the fame of Talbot House lay in its highly egalitarian ethos, an ethos that was reflected in the famous notice above 'Tubby' Clayton's door which read 'ALL RANK ABANDON YE WHO ENTER HERE'.[527] According to F.R. Barry, the war greatly strengthened the appeal of the social gospel, leading many Anglican chaplains to ask 'Was not Christianity something about human life as God wills it to be, and the Lordship of Christ, not in the Church only, but in the whole social and economic order?'[528] Such thoughts were clearly in the mind of Julian Bickersteth, who wrote from France at the end of August 1918:

> The employer of Labour, however sympathetic, can never really appreciate the sweat of the men, let us say, in the iron foundry, until he lives their life. A visit to the foundry is as much use to initiate him into the feelings and attitude of the worker as a Staff Officer's hurried and periodical walk round the trenches is. I assure you Socialism or socialistic ideas grow apace in such an atmosphere as that which I have lived in recently.[529]

Among Anglicans, this current was also fed by the consequences of the National Mission of Repentance and Hope. Christian socialism infused the 1918 report of the Fifth Committee of Inquiry into church and nation which the National Mission had given rise to. This committee was charged with considering the question of 'Christianity and Industrial Problems' and its findings inspired the formation of the Industrial Christian Fellowship, an organisation to which many radical chaplains such as Tom Pym, F.B. Macnutt and F.R. Barry gave their support and to which Studdert Kennedy, although wary of socialism per se, devoted his post-war career. As Edward Madigan has remarked, in his work for the I.C.F. Studdert Kennedy's persona was very much 'that of the worker's friend just as his wartime persona had been that of the soldier's friend'.[530] However, this leftward drift in socio-political attitudes was by no means confined to Anglicans and it even extended to Roman Catholics. Indeed, a strong sense of political outrage actually prompted the resignation of Francis Drinkwater from the Army Chaplains' Department just after the Armistice. In December 1918, Drinkwater wrote to the War Office and to Bishop Keatinge explaining why he could no longer remain in the army:

> An essential part of a chaplain's work is to encourage the troops, by speaking in public addresses and private conversation, on the justice of the cause for which they are called on to kill other men and risk their own lives. I have always been able to do this wholeheartedly during the last 3½ years; but I cannot do it honestly in the case of soldiers who may be sent to the present British expeditions in Russia. The same would be true of most of the uses to which the Army may conceivably be put in the near future, such as further operations against the new Germany, or military coercion of Ireland, or repression of industrial troubles at home. I do not see how I could even observe silence on such matters.[531]

In addition to influencing their theology and politics, among Anglican chaplains the war also heightened concerns over church order, strengthening the developing case for loosening the Church of England's ties with the state. A Fourth Committee of Inquiry spawned by the National Mission was tasked with considering the 'Administrative Reform of the Church' and it eventually called for 'freedom of legislation' through the Church of England's 'own representative assemblies'.[532] Significantly, when a Padres' Fellowship was established in October 1918, a body with the avowed aim of helping Anglican chaplains apply the lessons of the war to the post-war world, one of its key demands was self-government for the Church of England.[533] In all of this, the Padres' Fellowship was at one with the wider Life and Liberty movement which had been founded by H.R.L. (or 'Dick') Sheppard some time earlier and which enjoyed broad and even outspoken support among Anglican chaplains.[534] Although Sheppard had served for only eight weeks as a civilian chaplain in France in 1914, it was indicative of the support for Life and Liberty within the Department that Harry Blackburne was among the speakers at the movement's inaugural meeting at Queen's Hall in July 1917.[535]

Also illustrative of this enthusiasm for ecclesiastical reform was the support which chaplains evinced for the recruitment of clergy from working-class backgrounds, an issue that had been raised early in the war and which was a notable concern of the Fifth Committee of Inquiry and its subsequent report. During his ministry at Talbot House 'Tubby' Clayton had sedulously recruited prospective ordinands from among its many visitors and, as F.R. Barry recollected, in the wake of the Armistice:

> The time had now come to trace them and follow them up . . . As part of the plans for demobilisation, the Army authorities had prepared a scheme for setting up a number of schools in all manner of trades and professions in which men could be re-trained for civilian life. The DCG had obtained a promise that men 'volunteering for the Church' – a wonderful phrase – should have a school of their own, which would be in charge of the Chaplains' Department.[536]

In the event, separate theological schools were opened in France for officers and other ranks.[537] The latter was established at Le Touquet and placed under Barry's direction, with Gwynne scraping together the necessary staff 'from chaplains who had been dons or schoolmasters'. As Barry described the school at Le Touquet:

> This was a pre-pre-theological college . . . We gave lectures on whatever we could remember [or] whatever any of us happened to know, all improvised and without any books. Of course, it was hopelessly amateurish. All we could do and all we were trying to do was to help the men's minds to reawaken and to find healing and recuperation in an atmosphere of friendship and happiness, within a framework of regular worship.[538]

Whatever its academic limitations, the school attracted visits from leading churchmen and it was at Le Touquet that Archbishop Davidson confirmed his pledge that 'no man accepted for ordination by competent authority after due testing' would be 'debarred by lack of means from training'.[539] In March 1919, a formal 'test school' was duly opened in a former prison at Knutsford with the aim of separating 'the grain from the chaff on evidence of educatability'.[540] Between 1919 and 1922, more than 600 students passed through the Ordination Test School of whom two-thirds proceeded to ordination, thus providing the Church of England with an infusion of badly needed manpower and saving its parochial system from incipient collapse.[541]

However, the clamour for reform that emanated from the Chaplains' Department could provoke an adverse reaction from senior Anglican churchmen, particularly as it was often presented by 'over-wrought' heroes and couched in a 'radical brashness'.[542] As F.R. Barry, now a bishop, admitted decades later:

> [We] were getting tired and 'frustrated' and developed our own version of 'We and They' – the chaplains at the front and the home Church. We tended to blame everything on 'the system' and particularly on 'the bishops', always the whipping boys of dissatisfaction . . . Harry Blackburne [who was] then ACG at [Lieutenant-General] Horne's headquarters, was grossly rude to Archbishop Davidson when he bravely came out to visit the armies [in May 1916]. 'The bishops are sitting like a lot of old hens on eggs which they do not know how to hatch.'[543]

After his own visit to the Western Front in 1917, during which he visited the new chaplains' school and attended several chaplains' conferences, Cosmo Lang, the Archbishop of York, confided to a friend who was then serving as a chaplain in France:

> It is good to see the discontent which [prevails] with the conventional ways of the church – a sign of new life: & naturally the Chaplains view the church and its problems from the point of view of the Army. But they have much need of a sense of proportion: are very ignorant of the position & problems of the church at home; & as I think you once said are in some danger of adjusting the Church to the Army rather than of lifting the Army to the Church. Here & there were signs of a rather carping sort of criticism: & of an attitude towards the Bishops which is unjust & not very seemly among men who ought to be learning the discipline of respect to superior officers.[544]

Indeed, in the light of his experiences Lang even felt obliged to write an open letter to the Chaplain-General, a letter which addressed the 'question of the service of the clergy during the war'[545] and which refuted the uncharitable and even self-righteous complaints he had heard from chaplains concerning the wartime role of the civilian clergy:

> If it should be found at any time that there is a considerable number of clergy of military age and physically fit who are not serving or waiting to serve as chaplains and whose essential parish work might by some means be handed over to others for the period of the war, we are ready again to take counsel with the military authorities as to whether there is any special way in which they could be so employed as to give them additional and more direct opportunity of sharing the life and dangers of the army.[546]

Lang also protested that chaplains did not understand the lot of the clergy on the home front:

> I cannot but feel that some of the chaplains who have been for some time serving abroad do not adequately realise the difficulties which the clergy at home have to meet under the conditions and in view of the problems which the war has created . . . 2,400 of the most vigorous of their brethren have been called away to serve as chaplains. Scarcely any men are now being ordained to fill up the vacancies in the ranks of the clergy inevitably caused by illness, old age, or death. Many of the best lay workers are serving in the Army; others, both men and women, are engaged at home in special war work or under circumstances of exceptional pressure.[547]

Another prominent bishop, Herbert Hensley Henson, was inclined to be harsher in his views. Highly suspicious of the pretensions, goals and Catholic churchmanship of the Life and Liberty movement, in his New Year message of 1919 to the clergy and laity of the diocese of Hereford, Henson observed 'that there was nothing in their experiences' that qualified army chaplains 'for the task of dictating the policy of the Church'. He then went on to remark:

> I have read a great many books by chaplains or groups of chaplains and though some of them have considerable merit I cannot say that I have found much which seems to me to assist us in the difficult problem of ecclesiastical reconstruction. Mostly these books have impressed me by the frank ignorance of the ordinary religious condition of English parishes which they disclose in the authors, and which is, of course, explicable enough when one remembers that clergymen were selected for chaplains not on the ground of knowledge and experience, but because they were young, generous, enthusiastic, adaptable and physically strong.[548]

However, the war does appear to have driven the theology and practice of many Anglican (and even Nonconformist) chaplains in a Catholic direction. While this may have been objectionable to churchmen such as Henson, who was 'in temper and habit a Protestant',[549] its cause is easily explained. First, Roman Catholic doctrine and practice seemed to offer the benefits of religious certainty in troubled times. In June 1917, Oswin Creighton wrote:

> I often wonder if it would not be better if all the men were RCs. For men who don't think, and have no initiative, what can you have but a dogmatic, authoritative, externally imposed religion? And even the men who do think are often quite prepared to submit to authority and accept unquestioningly the dogmas for the sake of the unity and strength that are gained. I am always absorbed in insoluble problems, the RCs have none. Everything of immediate importance is settled. I believe that is what makes most RC padres so unfailingly cheerful, often boisterous.[550]

However, similar observations were also made about Anglo-Catholics. On the basis of his experiences with the R.A.M.C. at Gallipoli, H.A. Thomas, a Broad Churchman and in civilian life curate of Alsager, wrote:

> I here set it on record, without prejudice, that the few to whom Religion was anything more than a name were definitely High Churchmen and the centre of their Faith was the Sacrament of Mass, as they preferred to call it. They took a definite stand on definite teaching. The ordinary ex-Sunday School scholar and ex-choirman – the great mass of Broad or Low Church production – were as 'reeds shaken in the wind' or 'houses built on sand,' without strength or stability. This I mention merely as a fact which came so strikingly to my notice that the suppression of it would be to misrepresent deliberately actual experience . . .[551]

A second factor that favoured Catholic fortunes was the vital question of numbers. Although this strained their resources, the Roman Catholics enjoyed a comparatively high ratio of priests to soldiers; in November 1918, Roman Catholic priests comprised nearly 20 per cent of British army chaplains. However, Roman Catholics probably comprised only 7 per cent of those who served in the British army between 1914 and 1918.[552] In addition, the Anglo-Catholic wing of the Church of England was well placed to supply chaplains to the army, especially after the power of the Chaplain-General was effectively broken in the summer of 1915. While celibate Anglo-Catholics were undeterred by family ties and responsibilities, Anglo-Catholic male religious communities provided additional reserves of manpower.[553] Furthermore, dioceses such as London and Winchester, both of which were Anglo-Catholic strongholds with historic links to the army, appear to have released much larger numbers of clergy to the Chaplains' Department than more 'Protestant' dioceses such as Liverpool and Manchester.[554]

Thirdly and finally, although the churches generally regarded the war as a missionary opportunity, Roman and Anglo-Catholic confidence was boosted by the catholicising influences of the war on the Western Front. With Britons being exposed to a Catholic landscape and culture on a scale unprecedented since the Reformation,[555] British soldiers proved highly responsive to the figure of the crucified Christ in wayside shrines and also to Catholic devotional aids such as rosaries and miraculous medals, if only for their talismanic value. Furthermore, for many soldiers mass mortality and recurrent exposure to extreme danger appeared to vindicate the value of prayers for the dead and frequent communion.[556]

Among Anglo-Catholic chaplains, all of this helped to fuel existing dissatisfaction with the Book of Common Prayer. As chairman of a preparatory committee for the National Mission, in 1916 J.P. Maud, the Bishop of Kensington, canvassed 1,300 army chaplains and 300 naval chaplains on 'the chief difficulties and deficiencies in the religion and religious life' of servicemen and invited their suggestions as to how these might be overcome.[557] Among Maud's respondents, a consensus emerged that Prayer Book services were a major problem and that matins and evensong were especially 'difficult and dull'.[558] Consequently, the need for 'a simpler Prayer Book' was emphasised and it was argued 'that Holy Communion should be explicitly treated as the principal Service of the Sunday'.[559] Although the report was in effect suppressed (partly because it was suspected of Anglo-Catholic bias and partly because the

Archbishop of Canterbury thought it might antagonise some senior officers)[560] chaplains' demands for Prayer Book revision could not be stifled. Two essays in *The Church in the Furnace* (which was also dubbed 'The fat in the fire') addressed the worship and services of the Church of England, with Eric Milner-White claiming that the war had also revealed the Prayer Book's communion and burial services to be woefully deficient.[561] Chaplains also made their mark on the National Mission's Second Committee of Inquiry into 'The Worship of the Church', its report accepting the central role of Holy Communion in public worship, the need for Prayer Book revision and greater scope for prayers for the dead. In additional statements, Neville Talbot, F.B. MacNutt and H.K. Southwell pleaded for 'bold and wise experiment', for a revised and simplified Prayer Book and for communion services to be held at times that would be convenient for all.[562] However, not all Anglican chaplains were impressed by this Catholic groundswell. Oswin Creighton, for example, regarded Anglo-Catholic 'spikery' as intellectually inadequate and, in Belgium in 1917, Maurice Murray scoffed at Roman Catholic hopes 'that Thomas Atkins may see and yet be saved as the result of his sojourn in this land of tinselled altars'.[563]

The currency of Catholic belief and practice also evinced different reactions from Nonconformist chaplains, many of whom developed a stronger sacramental consciousness as a result of the war.[564] For Thomas Tiplady, who served as a Wesleyan chaplain with the 56th (London) Division on the Somme,[565] the allure of Catholicism was apparent in the wayside calvaries of France, in well-frequented French churches and even in the precarious situation of the Golden Virgin of Albert, a war-damaged statue of the virgin and child which hung from the dome of the town's basilica and which was visible from much of the Somme battlefield.[566] Robert Rider, another Wesleyan chaplain, fully conceded the advantages enjoyed by Roman Catholicism on the Western Front, reflecting that:

> [T]he Roman Church had enjoyed many advantages . . . The war had been fought in countries where 'Roman Catholic' was the state religion [sic]. The general populace was of that faith; most villages had, at both entries, the sacred figure of the Crucifix, as well as a common public shrine inviting men's religious courtesies; and the village church with its resident priest and in many cases its general ecclesiastical equipment was at the service of Roman Catholic troops.[567]

Philip Fisher, a Primitive Methodist, even described how Nonconformist worship regularly took place in a Roman Catholic shrine (formerly an old barn) on the Somme in 1916:

> Months ago French soldiers erected a rough altar there, setting above it a broken image of the Virgin, saved from the ruined church, and gathered there from time to time for prayer. Catholics of our own men reverently inherited it, dressed it with such white textures as they could get, and now adorn it week by week with fresh flowers. There they receive the ministrations of their own priest. There, a little later in the day, the Anglican padre gathers his men. And there, later still, the lads of our own Free Churches gather for their simple service. The worshippers come quietly

> in little groups of two and three, set their rifles against the wall, doff their steel helmets, and bow their heads in prayer.[568]

However, a third Wesleyan chaplain, T.L.B. Westerdale, was much less impressed and remained strongly convinced of the virtues of a virile evangelical Protestantism: 'We *must* preach a strong, manly, vigorous, humour-loving, winsome Jesus' he declared in 1917:

> Believe me, Tommy likes a good sing and a good manly sermon all about the Saviour in a strong spiritual atmosphere in which alone the soul lives and flourishes, an atmosphere which leaves a burning fire and a clinging sweetness in the soul, with just a Communion Service now and then. If he gets that from the padre he will come to the services. Priestly pretensions simply alienate men in the army.[569]

Significantly, Westerdale even blamed Anglo-Catholic chaplains for alienating the majority of soldiers, claiming that the low proportion of Anglican communicants was attributable to the excessive influence of Anglo-Catholicism in the army. In his view, the Church of England had 'a preponderance of High Churchmen among her chaplains . . . quite sixty to seventy per cent, and many of these are very High Churchmen, much too high to appeal to the tastes of the Tommies who are marched to their Parade Services':

> Many of these High Churchmen light their candles, put images of Christ and the Madonna on their improvised altars, and use the Missal, St. Swithin's Prayer Book, and other Roman Catholic manuals in their services. Tommy is suspicious of these practices. He is as true as a die himself. He may never have heard of the Jesuits. But he feels that all is not quite as it should be, so he fights shy.[570]

The Aftermath of Victory

While the numerous lessons of the war were still being identified and digested, the end of hostilities in November 1918 brought in its wake a new raft of problems. In January 1919, the Chaplain-General presided at 'a New Year's Thanksgiving and Intercession service' organised by the World Evangelical Alliance where, in view of worrying developments elsewhere in Europe, he declared that 'there was never a time when prayer was more needed, when there was such manifestation of the unruly affections of sinful man in Russia and Ireland and various parts of the earth'.[571] Significantly, the Army Chaplains' Department was not immune from these 'unruly affections'. For those who saw their jobs as done, the desire to be released was acute. Although nearly 60 per cent of the 3,475 chaplains serving in November 1918 had been demobilised by the following August,[572] progress was slow for those who wished to engage in the more urgent task of shaping the peace. In March 1919 a flurry of correspondence took place in *The Times* after it was claimed that 'only 20 or 30 out of more than 2,000 Church of England chaplains' had been demobilised while more than two million men had returned to their homes. Consequently, there were 'hundreds of involuntary chaplains still in the garrisons and camps at home, either utterly idle perforce or else wasting their time in trivial jobs'.[573] Furthermore, the troubled state of Ireland unsettled some Roman Catholic chaplains. While the threat of coercion helped to prompt Drinkwater's resignation in December 1918, another Roman Catholic chaplain was arrested in Ireland that November for being absent without leave from France. In this case, the Army Council resolved not to press charges but chose to 'recommend that he should not remain as a chaplain in the Army'.[574]

Nevertheless, for many chaplains victory brought in its wake a flurry of rewards in church and state. Following a call for the Lord Chancellor to make livings available for returning chaplains, in February 1919 *The Times* reported that former army chaplains were 'being appointed to important posts at home, where the experience they have gained abroad may be specially valuable'.[575] In 1920, Archdeacon H.K. Southwell, formerly A.C.G. of Fourth Army, became Bishop of Lewes, being the first Anglican army chaplain to become a bishop since the foundation of the Army Chaplains' Department. Another beneficiary was Studdert Kennedy who, after becoming a chaplain to the King in 1919, was appointed to a non-parochial cure in the City of London in 1922, an appointment that supported his work with the I.C.F.[576] Outside the Church of England, J.M. Simms was made a Companion of the Order of the Bath in 1918, 'being the first Chaplain to receive this honour', and was elected Moderator of the Presbyterian Church of Ireland the following year.[577]

While Bishop Gwynne was made a Companion of the Order of St. Michael and St. George and a Commander of the Order of the British Empire, in contrast to Simms advancement in the home church was not forthcoming. Although Gwynne was widely expected to remain in Great Britain, where 'it was assumed by all who knew him that he would be the next Chaplain-General', he eventually returned to his old mission fields along the Nile and to the newly created diocese of Egypt and the Sudan.[578] If his many admirers ascribed this to Gwynne's natural humility and missionary zeal, there were clearly political factors at work; in fact, Gwynne had made a powerful enemy in Lloyd George, who was returned to power as Prime Minister in the general election of December 1918. While the two had always been diametrically opposed over the disestablishment of the Church of England in Wales (a cause that had prevailed in 1912), in the months in which Lloyd George had served as Secretary of State for War prior to becoming Prime Minister in December 1916, Gwynne had clashed with him on two occasions. Firstly, there was Lloyd George's designation of the 38th (Welsh) Division as a Nonconformist division. Although this gesture was intended to boost support for the war in the principality, Gwynne was outraged; in the wake of disestablishment it was a further injustice for Welsh Anglicans as it threatened a reduction in the division's establishment of Anglican chaplains when it was actually more than 60 per cent Anglican in composition. When Gwynne threatened to resign, the matter was resolved by allowing no fewer than twenty-four chaplains to serve the 15,000 men of the division, namely nine Anglicans, four Roman Catholics and eleven Nonconformists, whom Gwynne dismissed as 'wet nurses and not chaplains'.[579] Secondly, Gwynne had strongly opposed the formation of the I.A.C., which he saw as more tokenism on the part of Lloyd George. When told of its creation,

Gwynne had made it known that 'I was getting rather tired of the interference of politics in the army and said Lord Derby's committee was not a consultation committee at all, but only a certain number brought together to hear statements from Lloyd George through Lord Derby.'[580] Besides his own differences with Lloyd George, Gwynne was also the elder brother of Howell Gwynne, the controversial and ultra-right wing editor of the *Morning Post*, whom the bishop held in awe and had even entertained in France while D.C.G.[581] Howell Gwynne was strongly critical of civilian direction of the war (in fact, he favoured a military dictatorship as the best means of ensuring British victory) and in February 1918 he stood trial under the Defence of the Realm Act for disregarding government instructions not to publish details of the Allies' Supreme War Council meeting at Versailles in the *Morning Post*, a misdemeanour that his elder brother defended to Archbishop Davidson, condemning government vindictiveness and denouncing Howell's prosecution as 'tyranny of the worst sort'.[582] In other words, the brothers Gwynne had crossed the 'Welsh Wizard' too often and, by the end of 1918, the door of preferment in the home church was firmly barred against the Bishop of Khartoum for the foreseeable future.

If Gwynne was snubbed by a hostile premier, in March 1919 it was announced that the Chaplains' Department was to receive a new title: 'In recognition of the splendid service rendered by the Military Chaplains during the War, the King has been pleased to direct that in future the Department shall be known as the "Royal Army Chaplains' Department" .'[583] Furthermore, the honorary rank of C.F. was bestowed on thousands of temporary chaplains who had served to the satisfaction of the military authorities, a distinction that allowed them to wear uniform 'when attending ceremonials or entertainments of a military character' and a chaplain's scarf when 'called upon to conduct religious services for troops'.[584] All of these honours were emblematic of the favour that the Department had enjoyed among the army's senior commanders on the Western Front and of their conviction that their chaplains had made a significant contribution to Allied victory. As Simms recognised, his accession to the Order of the Bath reflected his standing with Haig and served as 'an expression of our great chief's approval of the work of our Chaplains in the Field';[585] indeed, soon after the Armistice Haig had written to Simms expressing his deep appreciation of the work of the Principal Chaplain's branch on the Western Front.[586] While Gwynne returned to the Sudan (much to the regret of F.R. Barry, who believed that 'had he accepted an English diocese he would have brought a tired and dispirited Church a galvanic and creative touch as leader of the demobilised armies')[587] General Herbert Plumer of Second Army nonetheless credited him with having done more than anyone else to ensure eventual victory.[588] Similarly, and speaking at the Royal United Service Institution in 1922, General Henry Horne, formerly commander of First Army, testified to the contribution that chaplains had made to sustaining the morale of the B.E.F.:

> [I]n most cases the Chaplain filled his place in the life of his unit with great advantage both to officers and men and with credit to himself. It may be fairly claimed that the padre gained the esteem, respect and affection of all ranks, and as a general rule he became one of the best known men in his unit. He certainly earned it by his example of gallantry and

> devotion in attending to the wounded on the battlefield and in the dressing station; by his forethought and consideration for their comfort, bodily and mental, in the trenches and in the hospitals and behind the line; by his organisation of coffee stalls, reading rooms, and other institutions; and by an example of patience and cheerfulness under trying conditions, an example which did much to encourage all ranks and which undoubtedly tended to the maintenance of morale.[589]

This sympathetic view of chaplains was no doubt widely shared by many veterans of the war. As early as 1919, E.C. Crosse made the telling observation that the term 'Padre' had passed into civilian usage and that 'in general, wherever it is used, it carries with it a sympathetic connotation which is one of the assets of the war'.[590] From the perspective of 1939, another former Anglican chaplain also reflected on what he saw as a dividend of the First World War:

> The ex-chaplain is a member of the comradeship of men. He is in quite a different position from that which he occupied before he became a chaplain. In his own lesser position he stands with [St.] Paul rather than with [St.] Peter. [St.] Peter might be the Prince of the Apostles, [St.] Paul was in the comradeship of men and became the chief evangelist of the Church. He shared the experience of courtiers, soldiers, sailors, manufacturers, scholars, slaves and jail-birds. They welcomed his society. He could speak their language, and when he wanted he could give his message in it . . . Something of [St.] Paul's familiarity belongs to the ex-chaplain. The Church has benefited greatly by it, both in the work of conversion and in the subtler influence that it checks the drift from religion by the personal touch of many non-religious people . . .[591]

Seemingly assured of the affections of the wartime generation, many former chaplains went on to play a major role in ex-servicemen's associations in the inter-war period. In religious terms, perhaps the most important of these was the Toc H movement, which was inspired by the spirit of Christian service and sacrifice that had been fostered at Talbot House in Poperinghe. The leading figure of the movement was, of course, 'Tubby' Clayton and it flourished in the inter-war period, benefiting from the patronage of the Prince of Wales and from the award of a Royal Charter in 1922; eight years later, Toc H was one of the largest men's societies in the British Empire.[592] Former chaplains also played a prominent part in the commemoration of the war, being responsible for a plethora of unit histories and memorials.[593] Their role was no less marked on a national level. Though his wartime credentials were open to question, in 1925 Dick Sheppard campaigned against the unseemly tone of the annual charity ball that was held at the Albert Hall on Armistice night. As a result of this campaign, the ball was discontinued and Sheppard was given the use of the Hall for his more sober festival of remembrance.[594] More famously, David Railton, formerly a brigade chaplain with the 34th and 47th Divisions on the Western Front,[595] was the moving force behind the Tomb of the Unknown Warrior, a national memorial that commemorated 'the average of the men who died' and which was consecrated amidst much pomp and ceremony in Westminster Abbey on Armistice Day 1920.[596] Inevitably, former chaplains also presided at countless services of commemoration in the inter-war period, often harnessing their preaching to demands for the social, economic and moral reconstruction of British society in order to honour the nation's debt to its war dead.[597]

Summary

The First World War had a profound impact on the Chaplains' Department. In addition to its numerical expansion, the Department was considerably broadened in religious terms. In August 1914 roughly 120 commissioned chaplains represented three denominations; four years later, nearly 3,500 chaplains represented eleven, four of which were subsumed into the United Board. As in earlier decades, diversification was driven by civilian politicians who remained conscious of (and even beholden to) the political power and influence of the British churches, a consideration that was also reflected in the multiplication of advisory committees and in the creation of additional senior posts in the Department itself. However, although the War Office and its political masters proved amenable to denominational claims and interests, there were significant tensions within and between the churches. While the recruitment and management of their chaplains encouraged faction, jealousy and discord within the Church of England and the Church of Rome, there was also considerable friction between the established churches of England and Scotland. Indeed, the latter found willing allies among the Nonconformist churches in its struggle against what was perceived to be Anglican privilege and presumption.

Although the Interdenominational Advisory Committee provided a veneer of unity among the churches from the summer of 1916, there was no disguising the fact that the Chaplains' Department was dismally unprepared for the demands of the new conflict. The despatch of regular chaplains to France with the B.E.F. was chaotic and there were too few chaplains in the field and too few in reserve. Meanwhile, the mobilisation of the Territorial Force also went awry; there were no Roman Catholic chaplains in the T.F. and its Anglican chaplains, many of whom were senior civilian churchmen, were badly wrong-footed by the unexpected willingness of Territorial units to volunteer for service overseas. Despite an early surplus of clerical volunteers for temporary chaplains' commissions, the length of the war and the growth of Britain's military commitments meant that the churches were hard-pressed to meet the demand for chaplains in the longer term. This situation was not helped by the loss of frustrated candidates to other types of military service in the early months of the conflict, by a system of fixed-term contracts that ensured the return of hundreds of experienced chaplains to civilian life before the end of the war, or by inter-denominational jealousies which served to inflate official requirements at times of existing shortage.

If a combination of denominational initiatives and War Office expedients helped to ameliorate the manpower crisis, it was ironic that the chaplain's role remained ill defined until 1916. Although chaplains were required by military regulations to take parade services and to conduct burials, temporary chaplains were, with very few late-war exceptions, wholly untrained and their practice was varied by different pastoral imperatives, by the diverse nature of their postings and by a widely resented and often flouted prohibition on chaplains working in, or even near, the front line. However, if their initial ban from the front line had the effect of stimulating their recreational work behind the lines it was only with the advent of Douglas Haig as Commander-in-Chief of the B.E.F. that a broad and coherent vision of the chaplain's role began to materialise on the Western Front. From early 1916 there was a strong consensus among the commanders of the B.E.F. that chaplains should do all they could to promote the uncertain morale of the citizen soldiers under their care. Hence, chaplains were ordered to preach on the justice of the national cause, their recreational work was strongly encouraged and brigade chaplains were given unfettered access to troops in the front line – even during offensive operations. This new concept of chaplaincy work was promoted and disseminated by senior chaplains and its progress was marked by a heightened emphasis on conferences, courses and training manuals for chaplains, by a flood of decorations and by a growing number of fatalities among brigade chaplains in particular.

However, if chaplains became more useful to the army then this development brought its own dilemmas. To existing problems posed by military bureaucracy, the morality of the serving soldier and discord over the chaplain's rank was added the question of how far the chaplain could sustain or decently pursue the new role allotted to him. The evidence suggests that, while some buckled under the weight of expectation, another element pursued their role further than civilian (or even military) proprieties would allow, especially given the background of 'the clerical renaissance' of the nineteenth century and the anticlerical sentiments that were common in pre-war civilian life. Nevertheless, victory seemed to vindicate the overall performance of the army's chaplains and, invidious though it could be, their close identification with the men who won it assured former chaplains of at least a hearing in the post-war churches, a conspicuous place in veterans' associations, a role in the turbulent realm of industrial relations and a significant part in shaping and interpreting the commemoration of the war.

5

The Royal Army Chaplains' Department and the Second World War

Reorganisation, Recrimination and Revival in the Inter-war Years

With the rapid demobilisation which followed the Armistice of November 1918, the R.A.Ch.D. reverted to its pre-war role and outlook. Given the host of organisational changes precipitated by the war, rationalisation was the order of the day. In the afterglow of victory, the Army Council approved the commissioning of regular chaplains of all denominations, thus ending the anomalous status of Wesleyan and other 'acting chaplains'. Following the experiences of 1914–18, the denominations concerned showed little inclination to cling to pre-war precedent. After a joint meeting between their Committee of Privileges and their re-designated Royal Navy, Army and Royal Air Force Board, the Wesleyans accepted the principle of commissioned Wesleyan chaplains in January 1919. Consequently, five names, including that of Owen Spencer Watkins, who had lobbied hard in favour of change, were put forward for regular commissions in February 1920. As a gesture of goodwill, the War Office backdated these commissions to when the chaplains in question commenced their full-time work with the army.[1] However, the Wesleyans were still wary of potential conflicts between military and ecclesiastical discipline. This issue was finally resolved by requiring Wesleyan chaplains to formally acknowledge the continuing authority of their church and by a policy document drawn up by J.H. Bateson which outlined the separate disciplinary procedures that were to be followed by the military and the Wesleyan authorities.[2]

For its part, the United Board inquired about regular commissions in December 1918.[3] Although Primitive Methodist chaplains of whatever kind were a very recent phenomenon, even they accepted the offer of regular commissions in July 1920. However, like the Wesleyans the Primitive Methodists had concerns about the dual control of their 'permanent Chaplains'. In the event, commissions were accepted providing that each Primitive Methodist chaplain agreed to the following conditions:

1. That he shall render a Quarterly Report, or at such other times as may be required by the Army Committee . . .
2. That wherever he may be stationed as a Chaplain he will, as far as his military duties permit, associate himself with the Primitive Methodist Church, and render it such service as he can.
3. That he will resign the appointment at any time the Committee or Conference may desire him to do so, such desire to be expressed in writing.
4. That he shall have the same right of resigning the appointment with the opportunity of returning to Circuit work and receiving the appointment of Conference.[4]

Strong competition for these commissions was further evidence of the shift in Primitive Methodist attitudes, with thirteen candidates vying for seven nominations. However, the requirements of the post-war regular army proved much more modest and only five chaplains were eventually commissioned to represent all four denominations of the United Board.[5]

Plans for the post-war configuration of the Department were being discussed at the War Office from as early as January 1918 and they were debated by the I.A.C. from September 1919 to March 1920.[6] As Sir Reginald Brade was forced to retire through ill health at the end of 1919, it was left to Sir Herbert Creedy, his successor as Permanent Under Secretary, to negotiate and finalise the reorganisation of the R.A.Ch.D. Although Bishop Keatinge insisted that Roman Catholic chaplaincy would remain independent of a fully unified Department, there was little opposition to the principle of reintegration from other members of the I.A.C. In fact, Taylor Smith even volunteered a blueprint for the new Department which was supported by J.H. Bateson for the Wesleyans and by J.H. Shakespeare for the United Board.[7] According to the Chaplain-General's scheme, the Chaplain-General would be the administrative head of all denominations and would be supported at the War Office by an Anglican Staff Chaplain and by a Deputy Chaplain-General of another denomination. Each of the eight home commands would have an Assistant Chaplain-General, three of whom would be of denominations not represented at a higher level. Finally, the Church of England's advisory committee would be merged with the I.A.C.[8] Significantly, only J.A. M'Clymont of the Church of Scotland, who was still galled by the preferential treatment accorded to the Church of England during the war, raised strong objections to these proposals, arguing that the A.C.G. of Scottish command should always be a Presbyterian and that the administration of the Department could be left to the Adjutant-General.[9]

Given the lack of unanimity on the I.A.C., Creedy produced a final scheme that was agreed in March 1920 for a trial period of four years.[10] In a report produced for the Army Council, Creedy gave full details of the new dispensation. The Permanent Under Secretary would remain answerable to the Secretary of State for War for the running of the army's chaplaincy services, being guided in matters of policy by the I.A.C. The military administration of the Department would be left to an Anglican Chaplain-General, to a D.C.G. belonging to a different denomination and, 'while necessary', to a Staff Chaplain. In each of the eight home commands, an A.C.G. would be responsible for chaplaincy matters and would be accountable to its commanding officer. In order to ensure a fair distribution of these higher offices, they were to be rotated and their tenure limited to four years. To help communication between the churches and the War Office, each of the main churches ('or group of Churches' in the case of the United Board and the Presbyterians) would appoint an 'accredited representative' who would nominate candidates for commissions and officiating clergymen for the home commands. Although the Roman Catholics would maintain their representation on the I.A.C., their chaplains would be 'administered independently' of the new structures. While Creedy accepted that these arrangements were not ideal (particularly given the 'exclusion of the Roman Catholics', whom he hoped would 'eventually consent to fall into line') he argued that they at least made for unity and economy and that their viability had been proven in all theatres of war where chaplains had been 'under one Principal Chaplain, irrespective of denomination'.[11] Notwithstanding its limitations, after it came into effect in October 1920[12] the new scheme at least harmonised with a groundswell of post-war ecumenism among the mainstream Protestant churches, a mood that was reflected in the proceedings of the 1920 Lambeth Conference of Anglican bishops and in the positive response of the Free Churches to its 'Appeal to all Christian People'.[13] In time, the army and the War Office also deemed the scheme a success; it was renewed indefinitely in 1924 upon the expiration of its four-year trial period, the Secretary of State for War announcing that 'from the Military standpoint the Unification Scheme was a great success, and that all the Command General Officers considered the Scheme effective from the standpoint of Army Administration'.[14]

Along with the structures of the Department, the pay and conditions of regular chaplains were also dramatically altered in 1920. A probationary period of three years was established, which was to be served as a temporary chaplain, and promotions were made more open to merit. Stringent age limits were imposed on each class of chaplains, with First Class chaplains being expected to retire at the age of 60.[15] Furthermore, for the first time since 1873 a new pay warrant came into force. Prior to the warrant of March 1920, chaplains' pay compared unfavourably to that of combatant officers and to the pay of officers in 'other departmental branches' of the army such as the Royal Army Medical Corps.[16] The impact of the new pay warrant (which saw the pay of permanent Fourth Class chaplains rise to £1 3s per diem plus allowances) was dramatic, particularly as the war years had seen the cost of living soar by more than 100 per cent.[17] As the Church of Scotland's Committee on Chaplains noted in May 1920, 'the pay of permanent commissioned chaplains has been raised to more than double what it was before the war, in order to meet the higher cost of living and induce young ministers who have a taste and capacity for the work to offer their services'.[18]

After these radical alterations to the structure of the Department and to the prospects and pay of regular chaplains, it remained only to determine the size of the post-war Department and the number of chaplains each denomination should have. In 1922, Sir Bertram Cubitt, the Assistant Under Secretary of State at the War Office, convened a committee to consider these questions. Recognising that tens of thousands of British troops would be served by the Indian Ecclesiastical

Establishment or by officiating clergy of the colonial churches, using a ratio of one chaplain to 1,000 co-religionists a departmental establishment of 150 chaplains was decided upon, a quarter being temporary commissions. Excluding the Chaplain-General, current attestation figures gave the Church of England 105 chaplains, the Presbyterians twelve, the Roman Catholics twenty, the Wesleyans seven and the United Board five. Five years later, this distribution was reviewed by another committee under Cubitt's successor, A.E. Widdows, and due adjustments made. Excluding the Chaplain-General, a reduced establishment of 141 chaplains was recommended. While the United Board gained another chaplain, the number of Roman Catholic chaplains was reduced to sixteen in consequence of the disbandment of several Irish regiments on the creation of the Irish Free State in 1922.[19]

The radical overhaul of the Department in the early 1920s was partly undertaken with a view to preparing it for a lengthy period of peace. This prognosis was enshrined in the 'Ten Year Rule', a maxim devised by Winston Churchill while Secretary of State for War and embraced by British governments from 1919 to 1932:

> It should be assumed that the British Empire will not be engaged in any great war during the next ten years, and that no Expeditionary Force is required for this purpose . . . The principal function of the Military and Air Forces is to provide garrisons for India, Egypt, the new mandated territory [e.g. Iraq and Palestine] and all territories (other than self-governing) under British control, as well as to provide the necessary support to the civil power at home . . .[20]

In this context, the role of the regular army chaplain largely reverted to its pre-war form. Although sometimes attached to specific battalions for the purposes of 'messing and accommodation', most chaplains were posted to stations rather than to units and, as one chaplain described them, their duties in the inter-war period chiefly consisted of:

> [T]he usual services on Sunday, commencing with early celebrations of Holy Communion, and the Church parade services for various units; generally a Sunday School in the afternoon, and the voluntary service at night. Duties during the week consist of hospital visitation; visitation of detention barracks (where there happens to be one); religious instruction to recruits, and to the children in the day schools; visitation of married quarters, and of the troops in barrack rooms.

It was also thought advisable for the chaplain to visit 'the institutes either of the NAAFI or the philanthropic institutes' in order to 'get to know his men this way', to get involved in 'the organisation of the social activities of units' and to accompany them on route marches and field manoeuvres.[21] As it was clearly business as usual in camps and garrisons across the empire, the Department quickly abandoned the training initiatives that had been developed during the war years. Despite the launch of a departmental *Journal* in 1922 and the holding of a departmental conference in June 1925 (at which papers were given on themes such as 'The Work of a Chaplain in a Single Station', 'Work Amongst Boys' and

'Voluntary Services, How to Make them Effective')[22] there was no attempt to enhance the training of new chaplains. Instead, and as in pre-war days, temporary chaplains were posted to larger stations in order to learn their trade under more experienced colleagues.[23]

Fittingly enough, there was little change at the top, with Taylor Smith remaining in office until his retirement in April 1925. While his critics had raised questions in the House of Commons in 1918 concerning his continuance as Chaplain-General and citing his alleged 'lack of energy, initiative, and care' for his chaplains,[24] on his retirement Taylor Smith's admirers were quick to judge his career as Chaplain-General in terms of the agenda he had inherited from his predecessors rather than in the light of the demands made by the First World War:

> The departure of Bishop Taylor Smith from the Padreship-in-Chief marks a distinct epoch in the spiritual and moral uplift of the Army . . . [He] took hold of the Army spiritually on its return from the Boer Campaign. He drew the troops closer to the Churches, regimental and religious institutes successfully competed with the canteen, chaplains entered into and led Army sports, and the soldier's outlook was enlarged. Drunkenness decreased, education advanced, moral qualities superseded old vices, until at last, one day in 1908, General Sir Horace Smith-Dorrien abolished the military piquets in Aldershot Town because the soldier had outgrown the centuries old custom of vigilance outside the alehouse. From that day the soldier, long since really emancipated from such overlook, took his honourable place with citizens as a responsible being.[25]

Despite the problems they had posed in certain respects, his Low Church sympathies in fact made Taylor Smith an ideal figure to lead the unified Department in the post-war years, his magnanimous approach to reunification being warmly received by J.H. Shakespeare in particular.[26] Furthermore, A.C.E. Jarvis, formerly A.C.G. of Northern Command and Taylor Smith's successor as Chaplain-General, was of a very similar stamp. Like Taylor Smith, Alfred Charles Eustace Jarvis came from a Methodist background. He had trained for the Wesleyan ministry at Handsworth College and had served as a Wesleyan acting chaplain in South Africa before being ordained into the Church of England in 1908. Commissioned in 1909, he had won the M.C. in the First World War and had served in the Dardanelles, Salonika and Egypt before becoming Principal Chaplain in Mesopotamia, where he did much to improve the shambolic situation he inherited.[27] In his opening address to the chaplains' conference of June 1925, Jarvis waxed lyrical about his predecessor, praising Taylor Smith's zeal for souls and announcing to the assembly that 'we are the possessors of a great spiritual heritage, it is for us to conserve it and if possible carry it to fuller fruition'.[28]

Rather ironically, even the issues that dogged the Department in the 1920s would have been familiar to another age. One of these was the hoary old question of how the army's chaplains, barracks and garrison churches stood in relation to the episcopal hierarchy and diocesan structures of the Church of England. In 1925, and following discussions with Sir Herbert Creedy, Jarvis sought to revive the Chaplain-General's claim to episcopal status in a memorandum on 'the

Ecclesiastical status of the Chaplain General of the Forces and the Chaplains serving under him'. Written as 'Chaplain General (Designate)', Jarvis argued that the terms of the Army Chaplains Act of 1868 could be fulfilled by conferring episcopal orders on the Chaplain-General, a solution that would 'so regularise the position of [the] Chaplain General that it will carry with it the regularisation of all the Chaplains serving under him'. If the Chaplain-General could be consecrated a suffragan bishop to the archbishops of Canterbury and York, individual chaplains 'could be licensed in a special form of license by the Archbishop through the Chaplain General and if canonical obedience is deemed essential it could be taken to the latter'. This, Jarvis argued, would preserve one of the most valuable aspects of Taylor Smith's tenure of the Chaplain-General's office, namely 'the privilege (valued throughout the Army) after 23 years experience of the Chaplain General performing all Confirmations within the Army'.[29] This line of argument aroused some sympathy at the War Office. Although Taylor Smith had been able to conduct confirmations by writing to all diocesan bishops 'asking for permission to move freely within their dioceses' the situation was clearly unsatisfactory. As a War Office memorandum observed:

> We can only be on safe ground if (1) the Army Council have power to declare any [War Office] property (or, to allow for increases of the Army in any future war, any area occupied by H.M. Troops) to be extra-parochial and extra-diocesan and (2) if the Chaplain General is a Bishop with all these extra-parochial and extra-diocesan precincts as his diocese. The Church of England Chaplain to the Forces would then be in the proper relationship to a duly constituted superior, and that superior would be a recognised officer of the hierarchy of the Church.[30]

However, the Archbishop of Canterbury was not impressed by these arguments and made it clear that from his point of view 'it was undesirable to seek the status of a Bishop or Archdeacon for the Chaplain-General'. Instead, Davidson sought a solution that would reinforce existing episcopal authority. Hence, in a special service held at Lambeth Palace in May 1925, Jarvis was presented with a new 'Commission to the Chaplain General to His Majesty's Land forces'. This was issued under the seals of the archbishops of Canterbury and York and it entrusted Jarvis with 'the spiritual supervision and direction of the Chaplains to His Majesty's Land Forces and the general superintendence of the work of the Church of England among the officers and men of His Majesty's Army'. Furthermore, in July a royal warrant was issued which stated that:

> [A]ll Chaplains belonging to the Church of England shall, after appointment for service with His Majesty's Army, receive a special Ecclesiastical licence or permission from the Archbishop of Canterbury and his successors, such licence or permission to be one capable of recognition by all Bishops and other authority of the Church of England throughout the world during the period that such Chaplains shall be on the Active list of the Army . . .

Although this system served to bring army chaplaincy into line with canonical norms, it clearly fell short of what Jarvis and the War Office had been contemplating. Undeterred, the Chaplain-General made another attempt to revive his case in 1927 after Taylor Smith, who was still confirming British troops at home and abroad, was banned from the diocese of Southwark after confirming candidates at the Guards Depot without prior permission.[31]

Another problem that would have been familiar to Jarvis' Victorian predecessors was the issue of Anglican public worship in the army. During the 1920s, the campaign for liturgical revision gathered momentum in the Church of England. In July 1927, the Church Assembly, which had been created by the so-called Enabling Act of 1919, followed the lead of the convocations of Canterbury and York and voted overwhelmingly in favour of a Revised Prayer Book for use alongside the 1662 Book of Common Prayer. However, when Church Assembly referred this measure to parliament for legal enactment under the terms of the Enabling Act it was passed by the House of Lords but rejected by the House of Commons in December 1927, mainly foundering on Protestant objections to the Romanising tendencies of the Revised (or Alternative) Prayer Book. Consequently, a toned-down version was quickly prepared, approved by both convocations and by the Church Assembly and once again rejected by the House of Commons in June 1928.[32] While some Anglo-Catholics were concerned that revision had not gone far enough, Evangelicals were to the fore in opposing the whole process and Jarvis lent his support to their campaign. In August 1927, the military case against revision was made in a letter to parliament's Ecclesiastical Committee by Lieutenant-General Sir Henry Beauvoir De Lisle, a former corps commander on the Western Front. De Lisle claimed that the Revised Prayer Book would be a gross and unfair imposition on the armed forces:

> [The] members of H.M. Services, the Navy, Army and Air Force have had no representations in Convocation or in the Church Assembly.
> In consequence, should the Deposited Prayer Book become law there is no provision made to allow the Services to decide whether the old or the new Prayer Book should be used.
> There are no parochial Church Councils in any of the three Services, nor has there been any need of any such Council hitherto. Should attendance at Divine Service continue to be compulsory as it is now, in accordance with the King's Regulations, part of the congregation must then be treated with injustice and contrary to the spirit and the wording of the Enabling Act . . .[33]

In his opposition to the Revised Prayer Book, Jarvis was helped by the fact that Taylor Smith had issued a new set of *Instructions for the Guidance of Chaplains of the Church of England in their Ministrations to His Majesty's Army* as recently as 1924. With these in mind, in October 1927 Archbishop Davidson assured Jarvis that 'the present modes and manner of conducting public worship in the Army must continue unaltered' for at least a year. Although the War Office was keen to appear neutral in the controversy, which soon assumed the aspect of a major crisis in church-state relations, the Chaplain-General was much less equivocal. In September 1927, Jarvis wrote a War Office memorandum emphasising the 'practical difficulties' associated with the Prayer Book measure, pointing out that the *Instructions* of 1924 sought to 'preserve and enforce a uniform use in all congregations', something that was 'not only desirable but essential' for the army. He also argued that the Revised Prayer Book would generate disputes between chaplains and their congregations and there was no proper authority to which these could be 'referred for settlement'. Even the logistics of the measure were forbidding as 120,000 new prayer books would be immediately required for the army.[34]

However, the problems generated by Prayer Book revision were as nothing compared to the threat that was posed to the Department by the wide-ranging reaction in British society to the trauma of the First World War. At the height of the war, the public standing of chaplains had been such that a chaplain had been cast as the hero of the propaganda film *It is For England!* (1916), in which the Rev. Christian St George was reincarnated as his namesake in order to return home to unmask a German spy and to warn self-interested politicians, businessmen and trades unionists against the dangers of national disunity.[35] However, this exalted image soon faded after the Armistice and, no doubt helped by the absence of any official history of the Department's part in the war, criticism of wartime chaplains began to accumulate in memoir literature in the 1920s.

In 1922, C.E. Montague, who had served as a sergeant in the 24th Royal Fusiliers and subsequently as an intelligence officer at Haig's G.H.Q., did much to undermine the standing of Anglican chaplains in *Disenchantment*, a reflection on the war on the Western Front that was as critical of the B.E.F.'s chaplains as it was of its high command.[36] Seven years later Robert Graves published *Goodbye To All That*, where he conjured the caricature of the cowardly, malingering and implicitly Anglican chaplain that has remained a stock feature of First World War folklore ever since. Claiming to speak on behalf of his fellow soldiers, Graves declared that 'For the regimental chaplains as a body we had no respect. If the regimental chaplains had shown one tenth the courage, endurance, and other human qualities that the regimental doctors showed, we agreed, the British Expeditionary Force might well have started a religious revival. But they had not.'[37] Although excluding Roman Catholic chaplains from this generalisation, Graves went on to state:

> The fact is that they were under orders not to get mixed up with the fighting, to stay behind with the transport and not to risk their lives. No soldier could have any respect for a chaplain who obeyed these orders, and yet there was not in our experience one chaplain in fifty who was not glad to obey them. Occasionally on a quiet day in a quiet sector the chaplain would make a daring afternoon visit to the support line and distribute a few cigarettes, and that was all . . . Sometimes the colonel would summon him to come up with the rations and bury the day's dead, and he would arrive, speak his lines, and hastily retire.[38]

In addition to impugning the courage of army chaplains, Graves also lampooned their stand on moral purity, claiming that chaplains were a conspicuous element among the patients of the venereal hospitals of the B.E.F. and that 'The troops took a lewd delight in exaggerating the proportion of army chaplains to combatant officers treated there.'[39]

However, other depictions and appraisals of army chaplains were more guarded or ambivalent. Although the war had inflamed Siegfried Sassoon's resentment of organised Christianity (the war being an outrage 'in which the principles of Christianity were either obliterated or falsified for the convenience of all who were engaged in it')[40] his view of chaplains was much less caustic than the criticism he reserved for the Anglican hierarchy.[41] In *Memoirs of a Fox-hunting Man*, the first instalment of his 'lightly fictionalised autobiography' which was published in 1928, Sassoon described a burial under fire in which a brigade chaplain did what he could to provide some dignity to the interment of a fellow officer.[42] Similarly, in *Memoirs of an Infantry Officer*, published two years later, Sassoon described how one 'emotional padre' had been unable to supply much help at an Advance Dressing Station other than 'stand about and feel sympathetic'.[43] Perhaps unsurprisingly, he had encountered the worst of the Chaplains' Department well to the rear, the chaplain of an infantry depot at Rouen being an 'alcoholic R.C. padre who managed the mess', supplying bad food at exorbitant prices.[44] While Sassoon presented a rather mixed picture of army chaplains, this was also true of John Brophy and Eric Partridge, who had both served in the ranks on the Western Front.[45] In 1930, they published *Songs and Slang of the British Soldier: 1914–1918*, in which occurred the following entry:

> PADRE. – Chaplain. From the Portuguese and Spanish Padre – Father, priest. Perhaps a survival from the Peninsular War, more probably originated in Gibraltar [sic]. A chaplain had few definite duties: he could make himself useful or he could slack. In general, it may be said that all Roman Catholic *padres* were respected, because they came into the line and because they lacked the haw-haw voice. Church of England and Nonconformist *padres* could be roughly divided into three classes: (1) The-man-of-the-world who swore and overdrank; despised and disliked; (2) The earnest but ineffectual; despised but tolerated; (3) The spiritual but determined, who made himself useful as a first-aid man and distributor of cigarettes; this sort was respected as a person, but not as a parson. Men would even say, 'A pity old So-and-so's a padre; he's not a bad sort' . . .[46]

Despite these different perspectives, Graves' views on the unreliability (if not the immorality) of army chaplains had gained widespread acceptance by the early 1930s.While Graves could invoke a well-known dispensation which had governed their deployment for part of the war, by the late 1920s the tone and content of his allegations may have resonated with a heightened mood of anticlericalism caused by the confusion and timidity of the churches during the coal dispute and General Strike of 1926.[47] Furthermore, Graves was able to amplify his criticisms through the recollections of a literary protégé, Frank Richards, a former miner and regular soldier of his old battalion, the 2nd Royal Welch Fusiliers. Richards published *Old Soldiers Never Die* in 1933, a highly successful memoir that betrayed much Gravesian influence in terms of its style and content.[48] Harbouring a longstanding contempt for organised religion, Richards corroborated the presence of a lascivious element among the army's chaplains, claiming that one 'parson' was denounced as 'a dirty old pig' because of his designs on a young French girl on whom he had been billeted.[49] He also echoed

Graves' assertion that 'Parsons always stayed with the transport when we were in the line', adding that one chaplain only ventured into the front line in order to drink company officers out of their whisky.[50] For good measure, Richards castigated the clergy of Britain and Germany for their conflicting appeals to the Almighty and for their refusal to carry arms: 'The Clergy on both sides were a funny crowd: they prayed for victory and thundered from the pulpits for the enemy to be smitten hip and thigh, but did not believe in doing any of the smiting themselves.'[51] Still, and notwithstanding his claims of clerical misconduct and malingering, even Richards offered several examples of chaplains being in the front line. On one occasion, 'A young frail Wesleyan minister' obligingly shouldered his rifle while Richards tended to a wounded comrade[52] and two chaplains were cited as accompanying his battalion during its capture of Villers Outreaux in October 1918. On this occasion, an Anglican padre was present 'to see what he could do for the wounded'[53] while the battalion's Wesleyan chaplain was felled by machine-gun fire while in the van of the attack. As Richards described his death:

> I found the frail Wesleyan Minister I have mentioned with ['A'] company. I liked him very much, although he had chastised me several times for my language. I told him the attack would start in about five minutes and he told me that he was going over with the first wave of attacking troops, so that he could attend the wounded as soon as they were hit. I told him that he was different from all the chaplains of my experience and that I admired his pluck but not his sense. It would be far better if he waited a few minutes until after the first wave had gone over; then he would be able to go forward and attend the wounded. But if he went over with the first wave it was quite possible he would get knocked out himself and would not be able to attend anyone. He would not take my advice and went over with the first wave, dropping dead before he had run ten paces.[54]

Rather more consistent than Richards' reminiscences was Guy Chapman's book *A Passionate Prodigality*, another officer's memoir which also appeared in 1933. While the relative merits of chaplains of different denominations had become a favourite (and often specious) topic of debate during the war years, Chapman took up Graves' refrain of extolling Roman Catholic chaplains at the expense of their Anglican counterparts. Recalling the visits of James Leeson to the trenches of the 13th Royal Fusiliers, Chapman wrote:

> These Catholic priests impressed one. Leeson never dropped a word of religion in my hearing; but one felt a serenity and certitude streaming from him such as was not possessed by our bluff Anglicans. Already there was a growing dislike of these latter. They had nothing to offer but the consolation the next man could give you, and a less fortifying one. The Church of Rome sent a man into action mentally and spiritually cleaned. The Church of England could only offer you a cigarette. The Church of Rome, experienced in propaganda, sent its priests into the line. The Church of England forbade theirs forward of Brigade Headquarters, and though many, realising the fatal blunder of such an order, came just the same, the publication of that injunction had its effect.[55]

1. 'The Church Militant' by John Collett, 1779. Echoing William Hogarth's famous depiction of 'The Sleeping Congregation' (1736), Collett's painting was an apt commentary on the state of regimental chaplaincy in the last quarter of the eighteenth century.

2. Archdeacon John Owen, Chaplain-General, 1810–24. A strong evangelical, Owen's family were close to John Wesley and Owen owed much to the patronage of Spencer Perceval.

3. Robert Hodgson, Chaplain-General, 1824–29. A staunch High Churchman, it was Hodgson's misfortune to preside over the Department during years of prolonged retrenchment. He was unceremoniously sacked after quarrelling over expenditure with the Secretary at War, Sir Henry Hardinge.

4. G.R. Gleig, Chaplain-General, 1844–75. A self-serving opportunist and publicist, Gleig made the best of his appointment as Principal Chaplain in 1844, although it was far from being the limit of his ambition. However, Gleig secured the restoration of the Chaplain-General's title before the Crimean War and presided over the expansion and reorganisation of the Department in its aftermath.

5. Bishop P.C. Claughton, Chaplain-General, 1875–84. A well intentioned but ineffectual figurehead, Claughton's appointment as Chaplain-General was largely dictated by the fact that he was a surplus bishop and resident in London.

6. J.C. Edghill, Chaplain-General, 1885–1901. An experienced and influential chaplain, Edghill was a High Churchman who fostered a new and informal pastoral style among his subordinates.

7. Bishop John Taylor Smith, Chaplain-General, 1901–25. Taylor Smith was the second colonial bishop to be appointed Chaplain-General in the space of thirty years and the first evangelical to hold this office since John Owen. Hard working and probably more partisan in his actions than he actually realised, Taylor Smith incurred strident criticism for his handling of the Department in the early months of the First World War.

8. Henry Press Wright with fellow chaplains in the Crimea. Wright is seated at the left of the picture. Despite his experience as Principal Chaplain in the Crimea, Wright's hopes for succeeding Gleig as Chaplain-General were sorely disappointed in 1875. Library of Congress, Prints and Photographs Division, LC-USZ62–68796.

9. Chaplains in camp in South Africa, c.1900. This group reflects the Department's relative diversity by the turn of the twentieth century. Standing from left to right are Fr. O'Donnell (Roman Catholic), A.V.C. Hordern (Church of England), J.G.W. Tuckey (Church of England) and S.H. Hardy (Wesleyan). Seated from left to right are T. Murray (Presbyterian), O.S. Watkins (Wesleyan) and A. Pennington (Church of England). Only Hordern, Tuckey and Murray were serving with the A.Ch.D. on the outbreak of the Boer War.

10. Bishop Arthur Winnington Ingram preaching to London Territorials, c.1910. Lord Roberts hoped that Winnington Ingram would succeed Edghill as Chaplain-General in 1901. After being appointed Bishop of London, Winnington Ingram became chaplain to the London Rifle Brigade, a Volunteer formation that was incorporated into the Territorial Force in 1908.

11. J.M. Simms, Principal Chaplain, British Expeditionary Force, 1914–18. An Irish Presbyterian and the most senior of the Department's First Class chaplains in 1914, Simms proved himself a competent and respected manager of a disparate body of non-Anglican chaplains on the Western Front from 1915 to 1918.

12. Bishop L.H. Gwynne, Deputy Chaplain-General, British Expeditionary Force, 1915–18. Gwynne had developed strong links with the British army while serving in the Sudan and he arrived in France as a temporary chaplain in August 1914. Appointed Deputy Chaplain-General the following year, Gwynne was highly esteemed by Anglican chaplains on the Western Front. However, his appointment shattered the unity of the Department in this principal theatre of war and his differences with Lloyd George ensured his return to the mission fields with the coming of peace.

13. A British chaplain helps to escort a wounded German prisoner to the rear, 1916. While the spruce appearance of the chaplain contrasts with that of the Tommy to his right, from early 1916 brigade chaplains were encouraged to go into the front line and began to suffer heavy casualties in consequence.
Photograph courtesy of the Imperial War Museum, London. IWM Q4505.

14. A chaplain assists with the evacuation of the wounded, La Boiselle–Amiens road, July 1916. While this photograph was taken behind the front line in the early stages of the battle of the Somme, from early 1916 chaplains earned hundreds of decorations for similar services to the wounded while under fire.
Photograph courtesy of the Imperial War Museum, London. IWM Q721.

15. The 'United Parade Service' held at Bethune, Sunday 6 August 1916. Conducted at the height of the battle of the Somme and marking the second anniversary of the outbreak of the war, this joint service marked a growing rapprochement between the divided branches of the A.Ch.D. on the Western Front. This reconciliation was strongly encouraged by the high command and the service in question included a stirring address from General Sir Charles Monro, G.O.C. of First Army. Photograph courtesy of the Imperial War Museum, London. IWM Q54987.

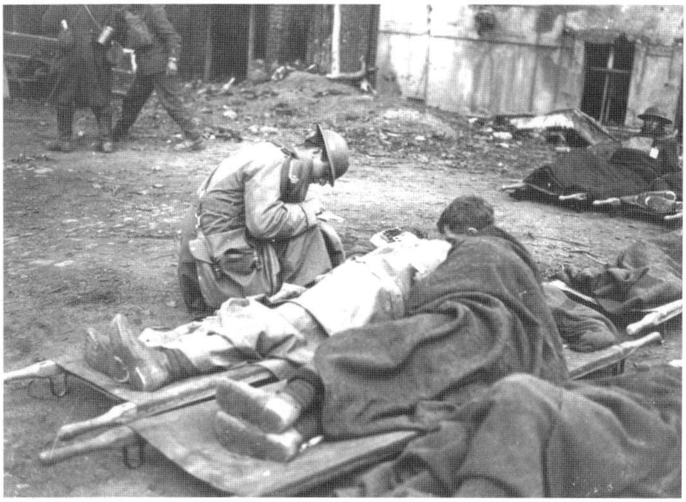

16. A chaplain writes a postcard for a wounded man, Noyelles, October 1918. By the last year of the war, the chaplain's duties were clearly defined and, despite overall shortages, chaplains had never been so numerous among front-line troops on the Western Front. Victory that November appeared to vindicate the new model of chaplaincy that had developed since 1916. Photograph courtesy of the Imperial War Museum, London. IWM Q9518.

17. Theodore Bayley Hardy, a brigade chaplain of the 37th Division, receives his Victoria Cross from King George V, Frohen-le-Grande, August 1918. Hardy was one of three members of the Department to win the V.C. in the First World War and he was mortally wounded near Cambrai in October 1918. Photograph courtesy of the Imperial War Museum, London. IWM Q11128.

18. Parade service on the Struma front, Macedonia, November 1916. Although this was one of the war's many 'sideshows', the Department maintained its unified structure in every theatre of war other than the Western Front. Although this parade service is Anglican, at this point in the war the Principal Chaplain in Salonika was a Roman Catholic, William Keatinge. Photograph courtesy of the Imperial War Museum, London. IWM Q32579.

19. Joint service of thanksgiving in Baghdad, 1918. A.C.E. Jarvis, the Principal Chaplain in Mesopotamia and a future Chaplain-General, is the figure in the mortarboard. Photograph courtesy of the Imperial War Museum, London. IWM Q24484.

20. Burial service at Arkhangelsk, north Russia, c.1919. In a remote outpost of British influence, a chaplain gives a dignified burial to a deceased soldier. Although the context is Allied intervention in the Russian Civil War, this aspect of the chaplain's work was crucial to soldiers' morale in the two World Wars. Photograph courtesy of the Imperial War Museum, London. IWM Q16266.

21. Owen Spencer Watkins and A.C.E. Jarvis at the War Office, April 1925. The two had much in common. Both had served as a Principal Chaplain in the First World War and both came from Wesleyan backgrounds, each serving as a Wesleyan acting chaplain in the Boer War. However, while Jarvis secured his career in the Department through a timely defection to the Church of England in 1908, Watkins persevered in his anomalous situation and finally reaped the rewards of full Nonconformist integration into the Department in the wake of the First World War.

22. E.H. Thorold, Chaplain-General, 1931–39. A highly experienced and capable administrator, the state of Thorold's health prevented his continuation as Chaplain-General in 1939.

23. Chaplains of the unified Department in Aldershot Command, May 1932. Thorold is seated at the centre of the front row while Percy Middleton Brumwell is seated third from right. On the extreme left is the much-decorated John Thom, who earned the Military Cross and two bars as a temporary chaplain in the First World War. Standing fifth from left in the second row is J.W. Steele, then only a probationary chaplain. A dynamic and controversial figure, during the Second World War Steele rose from the rank of Fourth Class chaplain to serve as A.C.G. of First Army in 1942–3 and as A.C.G. of Second Army in 1943–5.

24. C.D. Symons, Chaplain-General, 1939–44. A man more sinned against than sinning, Symons was undermined by the Anglican hierarchy, and in particular by Archbishop Temple, and he was widely despised by his unruly subordinates in the wartime Department. However, his resignation in 1944 was compelled as much by his personal as by his professional problems.

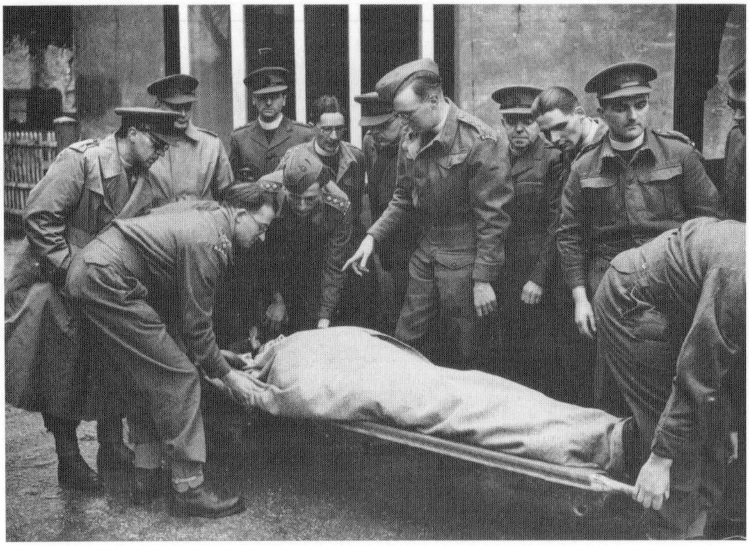

25. New chaplains undergoing medical training, probably at Tidworth, c.1942. The extent and quality of chaplains' training was greatly enhanced over the course of the Second World War, finding its ultimate expression in the chaplains' battle school opened at Church Stowe in September 1943.

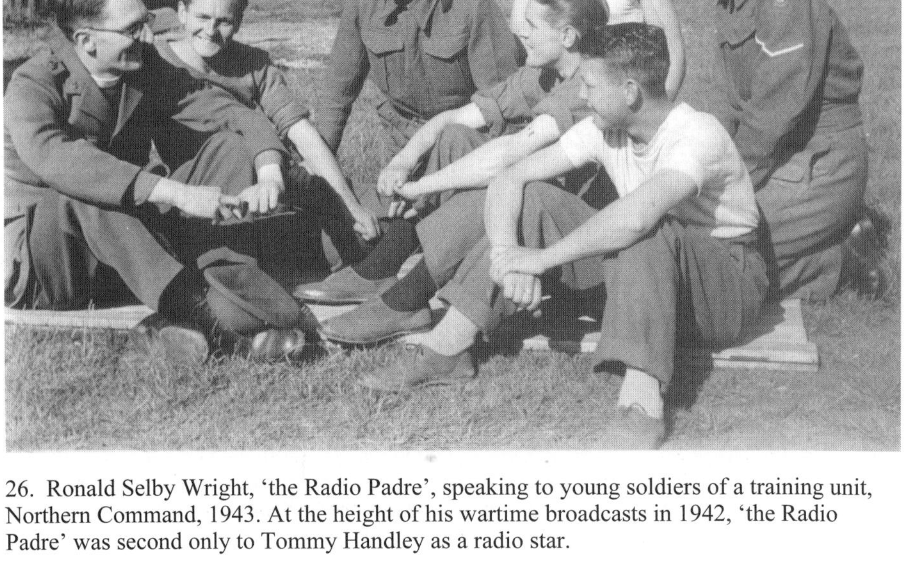

26. Ronald Selby Wright, 'the Radio Padre', speaking to young soldiers of a training unit, Northern Command, 1943. At the height of his wartime broadcasts in 1942, 'the Radio Padre' was second only to Tommy Handley as a radio star.

27. F.L. Hughes as A.C.G. of Eighth Army, 1942–44. Although he benefited from Montgomery's patronage, to his subordinates Hughes was a charismatic and sympathetic figure. He was also the first Territorial chaplain to become Chaplain-General, a telling reflection of the internal politics of the R.A.Ch.D. in the war years. Photograph courtesy of the Imperial War Museum, London. IWM E21919.

28. Field service conducted from the turret of an armoured car, North Africa, c.1942. A propaganda photograph, its imagery confirmed the strong public conviction that the Second World War was being fought by Great Britain on behalf of Christian civilisation. Photograph courtesy of the Imperial War Museum, London. IWM E12254.

29. The motorised church of St Paul, c.1944. Two of these specially constructed vehicles accompanied the British army to North-West Europe in 1944. Their novelty value obscured the fact that Protestant chaplains were once again prohibited from holding their services in Roman Catholic churches. Photograph courtesy of the Imperial War Museum, London. IWM B12000.

30. Anglican field service in Normandy, July 1944. H.J.L. Taylor, the chaplain shown here, was chaplain of the 3rd Royal Tank Regiment, 11th Armoured Division and was awarded the Military Cross for rescuing wounded soldiers under fire. He was fatally wounded in Holland that September while seeking to rescue a wounded British soldier and some injured Dutch children.

31. Field Mass in Burma for soldiers of the 36th Division, January 1945. Note the informal dress of the congregation.

32. Sam Cook, chaplain of the 9th Cameronians, 15th (Scottish) Division, receives his Military Cross from Field Marshal B.L. Montgomery, September 1944. Despite attempts to ensure a preponderance of Church of Scotland chaplains for Scottish divisions, this was not always possible. Cook himself was an Anglican. Photograph courtesy of the Imperial War Museum, London. IWM B10000.

33. Victor Pike (left), D.C.G. Middle East, and F.L. Hughes (second from left), Chaplain-General, 1946. Previously A.C.G. of Eighth Army, Pike was also a former Irish rugby international and he succeeded Hughes as Chaplain-General in 1951.

34. The R.A.Ch.D. Training Centre and Depot, Bagshot Park, 1947. This facility was a new peacetime departure for the Department and its creation was a telling reflection of its prestige in the wake of the Second World War.

Amidst the greater and lesser criticism that was aimed at the Chaplains' Department in published memoirs and memorials of the war, the most stinging attack came in the form of a novel. In 1930 Charles Benstead, a former officer of the Royal Garrison Artillery and a veteran of the Western Front, published *Retreat: A Story of 1918*, its subject being the physical, moral and spiritual collapse of an Anglican artillery chaplain during the climactic year of the war. Significantly, Benstead was serving as a naval officer when he wrote *Retreat*,[56] which was dedicated 'In Respect and Affection' to a naval chaplain, a dedication that pointedly implied a more positive experience of chaplains in the senior service. In contrast, Benstead's portrayal of his novel's central character, Elliot Warne, was utterly damning. News of Warne's arrival at brigade headquarters on the morning of the great German offensive of March 1918 is greeted with horror, ' "Oh Hell! Here's another bloody parson." '[57] Although an experienced and successful parish priest at home, in the course of subsequent weeks Warne proves utterly incapable of adjusting to 'the bewildering life' of an artillery chaplain.[58] In time, the extent of his failure is underlined by a telephone conversation between a battery commander and the brigade adjutant in which the former exclaims: ' "Look here . . . this is the second time you let that tame priest of yours loose on us. It's beyond a joke . . . He lowers our morale. Honestly, that face of his is enough to make a sow litter. For God's sake, Cheyne, tie him up." '[59] The novel concludes with the hapless Warne dying from influenza in June 1918, his demise being preceded by his loss of faith and his sanity.[60] While *Retreat* drew criticism from *The Times Literary Supplement* for being too far-fetched and was dismissed by Brophy and Partridge as 'a melodramatic account of an ultra parsonical padre', it greatly antagonised the *Church Times* and many former chaplains.[61] Noel Mellish, who had served in the same role as the fictional Warne, identified the book as part of an ongoing pacifist conspiracy against the R.A.Ch.D. and 'Tubby' Clayton, who had won his M.C. while ministering to artillery units in the Ypres Salient, felt obliged to write a lengthy rebuttal in the *Evening Standard*.[62]

However, other wartime chaplains also joined this war of words on their record between 1914 and 1918. In 1927, Edward Thompson, a former Wesleyan chaplain who had won the M.C. in Mesopotamia,[63] published *These Men Thy Friends*, a vivid, semi-autobiographical novel set against the backdrop of the Mesopotamian campaign. Although its central character was a former medical missionary turned army medical officer, the novel portrayed chaplains in a critical but generally sympathetic light, the novel's self-effacing Nonconformist chaplain (or 'Fancy Religions merchant' as he was known by one critic) proving his mettle while attached to an old regular battalion dubbed the 'First Loamshires'.[64] While keen to represent the work of Nonconformist chaplains in particular, *These Men Thy Friends* was viewed favourably by Brophy and Partridge, who described it as 'a much better book and a more reliable guide to the ways of *padres*' than Benstead's *Retreat*.[65] In 1932, Harry Blackburne also entered the lists with his memoir *This Also Happened on the Western Front*, a title that deliberately echoed that of Erich Maria Remarque's sensational anti-war novel *All Quiet on the Western Front*. However, while Remarque's novel, which had appeared in English in 1929 and which was released as a Hollywood blockbuster the following year,[66] purported 'to tell of a generation of men who, even though they may have escaped its shells, were destroyed by war', Blackburne's rather prosaic recollections simply recounted his own experiences as a senior chaplain and were intended to respond to some of the 'undeserved' criticism which the Chaplains' Department had incurred since 1918.[67]

Still, it did not help the Department's situation in the early 1930s that some prominent former chaplains were in the forefront of the contemporary peace movement. Charles Raven, who had served in the Army Chaplains' Department in 1917–18, was appointed Regius Professor of Divinity at Cambridge in 1932; that same year, he also became chairman of the Fellowship of Reconciliation, a Christian pacifist organisation inaugurated at Cambridge in December 1914 and which was now an international movement.[68] Although Raven was fond of invoking his wartime experiences as a chaplain, a habit that led his biographer to claim that he had 'served with distinction in the trenches of Flanders',[69] Raven had not proved a success as a brigade chaplain with the 2nd Division on the Western Front. Despite making a favourable impression on Harry Blackburne,[70] in his private correspondence Raven had confessed to his loathing of the role, which he saw as 'a separate incarnation' and as 'a sojourn in Gehanna'. It was not only the emotional strain of corresponding with next of kin and 'the sheer recurrence of death in its most ghastly forms' that troubled him but also a profound sense of social and intellectual isolation. Having conceived an early and violent dislike for the medical officer of one of his battalions, Raven wrote despairingly in May 1917:

> Here I am with my academic past, my more or less trained taste and instincts, my intellectual snobbishness, and my fastidious slowness to make friends . . . shot down into a mixed medley of all types and classes except my own and compelled to see the best in them all – or else chuck up the job.[71]

That September, and on the basis of his recent attendance at the chaplains' school, B.K. Cunningham deemed Raven to be 'too highly strung' for a front-line role, a verdict that may have led to his transfer to a base hospital in January 1918. Significantly, and despite the prevailing shortage of chaplains, to his unbounded relief Raven was not pressed to renew his initial contract on its expiry three months later.[72]

Notwithstanding his unhappy career as a chaplain, Raven brought energy, talent and some useful military and academic credentials to the pacifist cause and he spent much of the 1930s trying to popularise a liberal theology of Christian pacifism. In 1935, his recent Halley Stewart lectures were published as *Is War Obsolete? A Study of the Conflicting Claims of Religion and Citizenship*. Here, disclosing his preoccupation with science and religion and his commitment 'to a theology of evolutionary process',[73] Raven pronounced that:

> [I]n the course of evolution the struggle for existence has become increasingly an effort to achieve moral and spiritual values . . . in history we can see the gradual development of man's appreciation of such values [and] this development takes place step by step as accepted standards are

> challenged and primitive instincts sublimated [and] in this matter of war we have now reached a point at which it has become an intolerable anachronism.[74]

Three years later, and as the threat of war gathered, Raven returned to his anti-war theme in *War and the Christian*. Noting the unfinished business of the C.O.P.E.C. deliberations on war in 1924, the phenomenal growth of the Peace Pledge Union (which was then 'enlisting more recruits each month than the Army, Navy and Air Force combined') and describing the problem of war as 'the dominant moral and religious issue of the day',[75] Raven called for the churches' full and immediate engagement with the question, even warning of pacifist schisms in the event of another European conflagration:

> [The churches] agree that war is evil. That will count for little so long as they cannot agree upon any steps to be taken to remedy that evil, or decide to what degree the Christian can associate himself with it . . . It is probable that if Europe became again involved in war a pacifist secession from all the Churches would take place on a large scale and that the seceders would constitute a sect of their own. If, as has often been asserted, its attitude towards war is the acid test of the survival or fall of the Church as an institution commanding popular respect, it is even more evident that disagreement about it may well destroy the present [ecumenical] prospect of co-operation and still further mutilate the divided body of Christ.[76]

Despite Raven's intellect and the trenchancy of his pronouncements, the 'outstanding popular leader'[77] of the inter-war peace movement was the charismatic Dick Sheppard, who announced his conversion to pacifism in *The Impatience of a Parson*, a personal manifesto for church reform that was published in 1927.[78] Capitalising on his national fame as 'the first radio priest' and already well known as a peace activist,[79] Sheppard launched a war-renouncing initiative through the press in October 1934, asking all who shared his abhorrence of war to send him a postcard bearing the simple pledge, 'I renounce War and never again, directly or indirectly, will I support or sanction another.'[80] This initiative developed into the Sheppard Peace Movement in 1935 and into the Peace Pledge Union the following year.

A sensitive and well-connected clergyman at the outbreak of the First World War, Sheppard's traumatic wartime experiences went on to inform his later, highly emotive brand of pacifism.[81] Quixotically abandoning his new parish of St. Martin-in-the-Fields in August 1914, Sheppard embarked for France as a civilian chaplain attached to the Australian Volunteer Hospital. However, after only a few weeks he returned home in a state of 'complete breakdown', having been shattered by his experiences in hospital and on the battlefield, where he had somehow contrived to involve himself in a *French* infantry charge.[82] While his later claims to have served as a temporary commissioned chaplain for the remainder of the war were in fact false, Sheppard did receive a campaign medal for his work in France in 1914 and he made efforts to cultivate distinguished and reformist chaplains such as Studdert Kennedy, 'Tubby' Clayton and Tom Pym during and after the war.[83] Indeed, Sheppard seems to have so closely resembled his contemporaries who had seen service in the Chaplains' Department that Adrian Hastings mischievously described him as very much 'the gentleman populist, enclosing within the populism a very recognizable type of rather woolly and gushing C. of E. padre'.[84]

The credibility of the P.P.U., and of inter-war pacifism in general, was boosted by the sympathy and support of former chaplains who had a more distinguished wartime record than either Raven or Sheppard. The radicalising effects of the First World War, their close and traumatic proximity to death and suffering during the war years and the development of an anti-war reaction in British society during the 1920s propelled a vocal element of former chaplains into the inter-war peace movement. Many saw the maintenance of peace as one of the nation's most critical obligations to the fallen.[85] Furthermore, in view of the numerous disappointments of the post-war era, and the irony of Lloyd George's famous pledge to build 'a country fit for heroes to live in',[86] some even began to look askance at their own wartime records.[87] As Studdert Kennedy famously declared in a speech at Westminster Hall on Armistice Day 1921, a year in which the unemployed comprised 11 per cent of the British workforce,[88] 'I was mad – crazy. We got decorated for doing things that we did when we were mad.' He also caused consternation by pronouncing that the war had been 'futile'.[89] With the growing threat of war from the early 1930s, such convictions called for action as well as words and a leading exponent of pacifist activism was A.H. Gray, a Presbyterian chaplain who had been one of Harry Blackburne's closest collaborators on the Western Front. In 1931 Gray joined the Fellowship of Reconciliation and, in response to the Japanese invasion of Manchuria, with Dick Sheppard he played a leading role in mustering a so-called 'Peace Army' whose avowed (if abortive) aim was to insert itself between the warring Chinese and Japanese.[90] While such grandiose gestures were hardly the norm, F.R. Barry, who was then a canon of Westminster and rector of St. John's, Smith Square, believed that most veterans of the Department shared Gray's pacifism by the 1930s and he counted himself among them.[91]

While British secularists scoffed at this widespread retreat from wartime attitudes and pronouncements,[92] it was no help to the Department that the pacifist sympathies of many former chaplains reflected and encouraged strong and widely held feelings in the churches. Although falling short of a blanket condemnation of war, in 1924 the interdenominational Conference on Politics, Economics and Citizenship (C.O.P.E.C.) concluded that 'all war is contrary to the spirit and teaching of Jesus Christ', a view that was echoed from an Anglican standpoint by the Lambeth Conference of 1930.[93] According to Charles Raven, the growing strength of pacifist sentiment became evident in 1928 with the tenth anniversary of the Armistice,[94] a year which saw the death of Douglas Haig and the fuelling of the national debate over the conduct of the war on the Western Front.[95] With the example of Mahatma Gandhi encouraging a warm conviction 'that mobilizing popular opinion was more important than marching with tanks and guns',[96] from the late 1920s there was a flowering of Christian pacifism inside the churches. While this boosted the well-established and interdenominational Fellowship of Reconciliation, which saw its membership rise to nearly

10,000 by 1939,[97] denominational peace societies also flourished. Methodist, Congregationalist and Anglican peace societies were established in the early 1930s and a Council of Christian Pacifist Groups was created in 1933, a body that embraced organisations as diverse as the Church of Scotland Peace Society and the Unitarian Peace Fellowship.[98] In 1935, and as incoming President of the National Free Church Council, F.W. Norwood declared: 'I see no alternative for the Churches but the complete and final repudiation of war.'[99] Encouraged by these developments, and no doubt conscious of the failed Peace Army initiative, in *Is War Obsolete?* Charles Raven cheerfully proclaimed that a Peace Army was already in existence 'and its name is the Church of Jesus Christ'.[100] Such optimism seemed quite justified at the time, for when the P.P.U. came into being in 1936 it was obvious that this new and broadly based organisation owed 'its origins and its most important leaders to Christian pacifism'.[101]

However, the growth and assertion of pacifist sentiment in the churches did not go unchallenged, conservative misgivings being strengthened by pragmatic concerns over the deteriorating international situation. In March 1936, a conference of church leaders convened at Lambeth and declared its support for the government's policy of rearmament, a gesture that elicited a challenge from the Council of Christian Pacifist Groups.[102] These differences were also played out at a denominational level. After a charged debate in the General Assembly of the Church of Scotland in 1933, its Church and Nation Committee condemned war in general but upheld the principle of the just war. As a result, a pacifist resolution was voted down in 1934. Nevertheless, pacifism remained a significant tendency in the Church of Scotland, being identified with the Iona Community and its founder, George McLeod, 'the Dick Sheppard of Glasgow',[103] a minister and former infantry officer who embraced an uncompromising pacifism in the mid-1930s.[104] The Church of England also reflected these divisions. As early as 1935, Archbishop Temple and Charles Raven were exchanging accusations of heresy and apostasy in the pages of *The Times*.[105] In 1937, Church Assembly heard Dick Sheppard (who, according to Archbishop Lang, was by now 'swept off his feet by this Pacifist excitement') denounce war as 'mass murder, a betrayal of God and a blasphemy against the future of man'; it was unconvinced, and when Temple spoke against pacifism Sheppard considered resigning from the priesthood.[106] However, such zeal was not unusual among his sympathisers. Although he lived to regret these sentiments, F.R. Barry recalled that:

> When Hitler occupied the Rhineland [in 1936], I well remember saying to J.C. (Viscount) Davidson, then a member of Baldwin's government, 'If you allow our people to be involved once again in the Franco-German quarrel, you cannot justify it to God or man' . . . I used to vow that if war did break out I would use the Abbey pulpit to disseminate 'disloyal' and anti-war sentiments; and I must admit with shame that after Munich I shared in the popular hysteria.[107]

While it sowed discord in the British churches, this pacifist agitation inevitably had repercussions for the R.A.Ch.D. In March 1931 the House of Commons saw heated words and a remarkable division among Labour Free Churchmen when

C.J. Simmons, a Primitive Methodist and the Labour M.P. for Erdington, proposed an amendment for the radical reform of the Chaplains' Department during the annual debate on the Army Estimates. As Simmons put it to a committee of the House, everything turned on abolishing chaplains' salaries:

> By moving this Amendment I am not attacking religion or suggesting that religion be denied to the men who are serving in His Majesty's forces . . . I am moving to delete only the remuneration of the chaplains, so that if they still desire to carry on their ministrations to the troops without pay, there will be nothing to prevent them doing it, and they will be following the example of their Master . . . If the Government pay, they control what the chaplains preach, and in doing that, we are likely to have a repetition of what happened [between 1914 and 1918] when the Church crucified Christ on the Cross of Armaments . . .[108]

This proposal was seconded by Reginald Sorensen, a Unitarian minister and the Labour M.P. for Leyton West, who claimed 'that it is not a wise spending of public money to spend £63,000 on employing this section of the officer class to preach a diluted and perverted type of religion', one that to him seemed 'absolutely degrading and blasphemous'.[109] Their arguments were supported by James Hudson, a Quaker and the Labour M.P. for Huddersfield, who inquired, 'Is it not the case that the chaplain is paid in order to teach Christianity to the men, and if it can be proved that he cannot, by the nature of his office, teach Christianity to the men, may it not be argued that he should not be paid?'[110] However, Herbert Dunnico, a Baptist minister, the Labour M.P. for Consett and the deputy chairman of the Ways and Means committee, flatly refused to be drawn into debate 'as to what is and what is not Christianity'.[111] Furthermore, Tom Shaw, the Secretary of State for War and Labour M.P. for Preston, repudiated the suggestion that the War Office instructed chaplains 'as to the doctrine that they should preach' and, while he had nothing in particular to say in their favour, he defended their influence as generally positive.[112]

If the proposed amendment was consequently rejected by the House of Commons, that same year another blow was aimed at the R.A.Ch.D. from another quarter when F.W. Norwood, the chairman of the Congregational Union of England and Wales, sought to suspend the nomination of Congregational chaplains to the armed forces.[113] In 1935, and as his peace movement gathered momentum, more pressure was placed on the Department when Dick Sheppard turned his attention to armed forces chaplaincy in *We Say 'No'; The Plain Man's Guide to Pacifism*. Here, Sheppard presented an updated vision of army chaplaincy that was very similar to that which had been championed by Simmons and his confederates in 1931:

> A clergyman who had signed the Peace Pledge could not, in my view, serve as a chaplain, either in war or peace; but he could accept a Church appointment as a missioner to the Army, Navy or Air Force. He would then be a civilian, not an officer, and his loyalty would be to God and the Church.[114]

If the churches could be persuaded to declare 'definitely for peace and against war' then 'It would be known that the missioners had accepted this work not to give sanction or support to the war system, but in order to minister to souls who would otherwise be without spiritual comfort and guidance.'[115] While debate raged in the Protestant churches over the legitimacy of war and the implications of this question for military chaplaincy, the Roman Catholic hierarchy made it known that it did not hold this work in high regard either. In 1930, Bishop Amigo of Southwark refused to meet Bishop Keatinge to discuss the appointment of one of his priests as a naval chaplain.[116] Amigo's high-handed conduct was encouraged by the disdain that had emerged among the English hierarchy for the Bishop to the Forces and his paltry jurisdiction. After James Dey succeeded Keatinge as Bishop to the Forces and Principal Roman Catholic Chaplain in April 1935, 'he was almost ostracized by his fellow-bishops, and was not allowed to attend the Bishops' Conference except when service chaplaincies were discussed'.[117]

Although pacifism was strong in the British churches and in British society in general, a combination of the weight of conservative opinion, Sheppard's premature death in October 1937 and the direction of German and Italian foreign policy in the mid to late-1930s ensured the survival of the Department. Indeed, by the end of the 1920s, and despite the currency of the 'Ten Year Rule', plans for its mobilisation had formed one of the few substantive issues for discussion at the now infrequent meetings of the I.A.C. As early as 1926 Jarvis had raised the creation of a 'Regular Army Reserve of Officers' for the Chaplains' Department. As he informed Sir Herbert Creedy, no fewer than 127 chaplains would be required 'to proceed abroad with the Expeditionary Force' in the event of another European war. This number far exceeded the 63 regular chaplains who could be released from home stations and it took no account of the inevitable need for reinforcements. Ironically, the Territorial Army already had its own reserve of chaplains and, as Jarvis put it:

> The formation of such a Reserve, in my opinion, is the only satisfactory solution to this urgent question . . . I think I am right in saying that ours is the only Department or Arm of the Service without a Regular Army Reserve of Officers, and the position should be regularized at an early date.[118]

The War Office fully concurred and, at the I.A.C.'s meeting of November 1927, Creedy announced that:

> [S]teps were being taken to form a Regular Army Reserve of Chaplains for which the temporary Chaplains who served during the War would be eligible as well as the retired Regular Army Chaplains. He would arrange for copies of the relevant Royal Warrant to be sent to the members of the Committee in due course, with a letter explaining the scheme and asking for their co-operation in making the Reserve a success.[119]

Despite the disillusionment of Studdert Kennedy and other wartime chaplains, it was symptomatic of a certain hankering after the army among some of their former comrades that the new reserve of chaplains had attracted a hundred recruits by the following year.[120] However, by 1930 there was a definite problem of recruitment among Presbyterians, Free Churchmen (although, significantly, not Wesleyans) and Roman Catholics. At the I.A.C. meeting of that year, Creedy announced that the reserve had grown to 152; however, three quarters of these reservists were Anglicans and 'there was still room for improvement as regards Presbyterian, Roman Catholic and United Board Chaplains', who in total made up only 10 per cent of the new reserve.[121]

Besides his anxiety to secure an adequate reserve of chaplains in case of war, Jarvis was also concerned about the organisation of the Department in this eventuality. As he saw it, efficiency would depend on unity and this would require the renunciation of Catholic separatism and the complete integration of the Department in any future expeditionary force and, preferably, in all other respects as well.[122] Jarvis' position was bolstered by a War Office memorandum which revealed that, during an I.A.C. meeting in 1920, Keatinge had 'not challenged' the suggestion that Catholic chaplains should be part of a 'unified administration of Chaplaincy Services' in a future expeditionary force. It also surveyed 'the organization of the Chaplains in the various theatres in the Great War' and concluded that 'Except in France and Flanders, there was a unified system of administration, which appears to have worked quite smoothly, and the dual system obtaining in France and Flanders was apparently not an administrative necessity, but rather an embarrassment.'[123] While Sir Herbert Creedy was wary of expecting too much, he eventually wrote to Keating in December 1929 recalling the success of the 'unified system, embracing chaplains of all denominations' and reminding him that he had been 'Principal Chaplain at Salonika in charge of some 140 Chaplains'. Having thus prepared the ground, Creedy then broached the question:

> [W]hat we are anxious to know is whether in the field, and for the duration of the operations only, we may include the Roman Catholic Chaplains in one administrative system with the rest of the Royal Army Chaplains' Department. If this were agreed, you would of course have your share of the administrative appointments in the same way as Chaplains of other denominations.[124]

Pressured by the Permanent Under Secretary, embarrassed by the precedent that he had helped to set and probably even encouraged by the remote prospect of the events in question, Keatinge duly agreed 'in the event of war, and for the duration of the war only . . . to include the Roman Catholic Chaplains in one administrative system' on the grounds that 'a dual system would not work satisfactorily in the field'. His one condition was that a Senior Roman Catholic Chaplain should be attached to the G.H.Q. of any future expeditionary force in order to 'advise the Deputy Chaplain-General on all Roman Catholic matters'. Ideally, this chaplain could also double as the D.C.G.'s 'Assistant' and would thus come second in the chaplains' chain of command.[125] Clearly pleased, Creedy wrote a breezy letter to Keatinge in March 1930 in which he assured the bishop that:

> Our mobilisation arrangements contemplate and make provision for two appointments at G.H.Q., a Principal Chaplain or a Deputy Chaplain-General and an Assistant, and the latter appointment will be earmarked for a Chaplain of the Roman Catholic Church. This will give you the

assurance for which you ask, and I think it will be found that the consequential details will all fall naturally into the picture.[126]

With his retirement on the horizon, a further success for Jarvis came in February 1930 when a Chaplain Commandant was authorised for the Department. As Jarvis saw it, this new functionary would have a broad remit, his duties being:

1. To keep in touch with the Universities and Theological Colleges.
2. To nominate suitable candidates for commissions in the Department.
3. To act in an advisory capacity to the Chaplain General on all matters on which he is consulted, such as titles, changes in dress, memorials and departmental customs.
4. To maintain a close connection between the Regular, Territorial and Reserve Chaplains.
5. To keep in touch with the Chaplaincy Departments of the Dominions and Colonies.[127]

Although 'no sinecure', the position of Chaplain Commandant 'would be a worthy distinction and award for exceptional and meritorious service'. With this in mind, Jarvis proposed that the first Chaplain Commandant should be J.D.S. Parry Evans, the Department's most senior First Class chaplain who was due to retire as A.C.G. of Aldershot Command where he had been 'entirely responsible for the training of new entrants'. With the retirement age of the Chaplain Commandant set at seventy, Parry Evans could thus look forward to further years of useful service, helping to ensure continuity and being a source of guidance and support for the next Chaplain-General.[128] Indeed, the practical value of this office was demonstrated in 1932 when a second Chaplain Commandant was appointed to the Department in the form of W.S. Jaffray, a Church of Scotland chaplain who had served from 1891 to 1925.[129]

When Jarvis retired to become vicar of Sheffield in 1931, he was succeeded as Chaplain-General by E.H. Thorold. An Oxford graduate and the son of an Anglican clergyman, Thorold was very much a mandarin of the Department. Commissioned in 1906, between 1914 and 1918 he served as an assistant to J.M. Simms and then to Bishop Gwynne on the Western Front. Returning to England, he had acted as a staff officer to Taylor Smith (whom he rather admired) and, in the 1920s, he had served as A.C.G. of the Rhine Army and of Western and Southern Commands. When appointed Chaplain-General, Thorold was presiding over departmental affairs at Aldershot. In view of this vast experience, it was duly announced in the departmental *Journal* that 'In Dr. Thorold we have a combination of the sagacity of the statesman, the delicate touch of the scholar, the understanding of a friend, and the penetrating knowledge of the needs and possibilities of the Department.'[130] However, Thorold's years as Chaplain-General were quiet in comparison to his predecessor's and he was not in good health as the nation prepared for war. Although his term as Chaplain-General was extended by a year in 1938,[131] by June 1939 Thorold was in hospital and Joseph Lynn, the Presbyterian D.C.G., had taken temporary charge of the Department, with C.D. Symons, the A.C.G. of Aldershot Command, acting as his adviser in 'Ecclesiastical matters connected with the Church of England'.[132]

War, Mobilisation and Expansion

As a result of its internal reorganisation in the inter-war period and the army's lengthy preparations for war (conscription had commenced five months earlier), the R.A.Ch.D. was much better prepared in September 1939 than it had been in August 1914. In addition to 174 permanent and temporary chaplains serving with the regular army, there were 240 chaplains in the regular army reserve of officers and just over 400 in the Territorial Army and its reserve.[133] Furthermore, the experiment of the volunteer New Army (with all the problems that it had entailed in terms of the recruitment and organisation of chaplains) was not to be repeated; the Territorial Army provided the organisational framework for the army's wartime expansion and conscription acting as its main driving force.[134] The preparedness of the Department was also reflected in the temporary redundancy of the I.A.C. Although its business had declined in the inter-war period, the Committee did not meet at all between 1939 and 1943, when it met primarily to discuss the vexed question of chaplains' pay.[135] However, its real revival did not begin until the autumn of 1944, when demobilisation became its main preoccupation. After such a lengthy wartime hiatus, its reactivation seems to have come as something of a surprise to Archbishop William Temple, who wrote to Bishop Fisher of London:

> I never knew there was such a Committee. It seems to have doddered on since the last war, until the outbreak of this one, when it fell into a complete coma; then suddenly it revived itself . . . in order to discuss the pay of Chaplains as compared with the pay of doctors in the R.A.M.C.! 'Oh Lord, how long?' as the Saints beneath the altar justly wailed![136]

Besides its readiness for war, there were other important contrasts between the Department in 1914–18 and the Department in 1939–45. Most obviously, there were significant differences in the conditions under which chaplains served. Although nearly 80 per cent of all wartime chaplains received 'emergency' commissions after the outbreak of war,[137] the wartime release of able-bodied chaplains was exceptional as all were expected to serve for the duration of the conflict rather than for a fixed term of one or two years.[138] The contrast between the two World Wars was also marked in terms of the size of the Department. Far fewer clergymen served as commissioned chaplains between 1939 and 1945 than had served between 1914 and 1918, a natural corollary of the eschewal of fixed term contracts, the smaller size of the British army in the Second World War and the workings of the quota system. Echoing Sir John Smyth, Alan Robinson estimated that 3,692 chaplains of all denominations served between 1939 and 1945.[139] While post-war demobilisation statistics suggest that this figure may be too high, even this total is significantly less than the 5,170 chaplains who served in the First World War.

Another major difference was in the temper of serving chaplains, a temper that reflected the less deferential mood of the British army in the Second World War. If there was widespread concern that the army as a whole was cursed by too many incompetent and reactionary 'blimps' in senior positions,[140] the Chaplains' Department was not immune from these suspicions and, whereas Taylor Smith had been able to ride out a storm of criticism, they eventually claimed the career of the Chaplain-General, Charles Douglas Symons. Given the mood of the time, it was rather ironic that Symons should fall victim in this manner as he certainly did not have the same departmental pedigree as his immediate predecessors, both of whom had been commissioned chaplains in the regular army prior to the First World War. Indeed, Symons had only joined the Chaplains' Department in February 1916 after serving for a time in the R.A.M.C. Having won an M.C. on the Western Front in 1918, he was granted a regular commission but his post-war career was undistinguished and it was not until August 1937 that he became an A.C.G. and chaplain First Class. Hence, and in marked contrast to his immediate predecessor, Symons had served for only two years in a senior administrative position when he arrived from Aldershot Command to replace E.H. Thorold as Chaplain-General in October 1939.[141]

Significantly, even before Symons formally assumed the duties of Chaplain-General, his position was under threat. Mindful of the precedent of Bishop Gwynne's appointment in 1915 and of the mood and sensitivities of the clergy who were taking 'emergency commissions', in the course of a meeting with Symons in September 1939 Archbishop Lang stressed the need for episcopal control over the chaplains of the new B.E.F. As Lang noted:

> I put before him the view expressed by many of the Bishops that there ought to be a Bishop in spiritual charge of the Chaplains in France. He pointed out – (a) that Mr. Naylor, the appointed Deputy Chaplain General in France, was well qualified to look after the spiritual side of the Chaplains' work as well as its administrative efficiency; (b) that conspicuous as were Bishop Gwynne's merits in the last war there were difficulties on the administrative side; (c) that it would be very difficult for the Deputy Chaplain General if side by side with him there were some Bishop to whom Chaplains might have recourse apart from him.[142]

In his determination to defend the unity and integrity of the Department, Symons would only concede 'the need when conditions became more settled of sending out Bishops from this country to undertake Confirmations etc.'[143] Such a stand was unlikely to endear him to the Anglican hierarchy. In September 1941, Archbishop Temple of York wrote to Lang:

> I do know that many Chaplains are still feeling very much isolated and needful of opportunity to talk over their problems with people to whom it seems to them natural to go and whose counsel they would value, and most of them do not feel either of these things with regard to their S.C.F. or A.C.G. However we [bishops] have evidently got to develop the use of our opportunities as they are now to the utmost . . . If we can put a very large bomb under the Chaplain General's department at the end of the war

> it would be useful – but you have yourself intimated that such treatment of the entire Church of England might be salutary![144]

By this time, Temple and Symons had already clashed over the propriety of inter-denominational communion services at the chaplains' reception centre and depot at Chester. Keen to uphold denominational distinctiveness within the unified Department, Symons had sought to suppress the practice. As he reported to Lang in September 1940: 'The Principal, the Reverend H.S. Astbury, was ordered to the War Office for an interview, and informed officially that unless the practice ceased forthwith the School would be closed.' However, ecumenical feeling was strong among the trainee chaplains at Chester, and some even 'signed a paper expressing approval of the practice'.[145] Worse still, Temple took up the cudgels on Astbury's behalf and in March 1941 Symons was forced into a humiliating capitulation, being forced to write to the A.C.G. of Western Command in March 1941:

> Kindly inform the Commandant of the Royal Army Chaplains' Department Reception Centre and Depot that in accordance with paragraph 42 of the findings of the Lambeth Conference of January, 1933, it is permissible to hold a service of Inter Communion once in each course . . . In the opinion of the Lord Archbishop of York, the Royal Army Chaplains' Department Reception Centre and Depot at Chester, which is situated in the Province of York, comes within the meaning of the paragraph referred to above. This does not apply to any gathering of the Royal Army Chaplains' Department situated without the precincts of the said Reception Centre and Depot.[146]

By 1942, and in the face of high-level lobbying by Bishop Bell of Chichester and by the Bishops' War Committee chaired by the Bishop of London,[147] Symons had been forced to concede a greater role for the Anglican bishops in chaplaincy matters. That January, a memorandum addressed to all A.C.G.s in home commands stated that:

> There has been some slight misunderstanding through the misreading of official orders regarding administration. The Chaplain-General asks all Assistant Chaplain-Generals to make it clear that all Church of England chaplains are at perfect liberty to consult the Bishop of the Diocese in which they may be serving at the time, or their own Diocesan, on spiritual matters; as their Father-in-God.
>
> No other policy has ever been advocated. It was always the custom in peace time for regular chaplains to do this.
>
> The Chaplain-General hopes this custom will always continue.[148]

Still, even this did not satisfy the bishops. On the threshold of retirement, Lang had a further meeting with Symons in March 1942, of which the archbishop wrote:

> I said that I hoped that his Department would welcome the appointment of a certain number of specially qualified men [i.e. suffragan bishops] who could be made accessible to the Chaplains in the different Commands here in England and who might wish to hear them or to speak

> to them on their spiritual life without any share in administration or rank. He assured me first that personally he would welcome the help of such men, but secondly that it would not be well to make the use of them too public as it would inevitably move the R.C. and Nonconformist members of the Chaplains' Committee at the War Office to press for similar opportunities which would not be desirable . . . Unfortunately he renewed his plea that though personally he was very fond of Bishop Neville Talbot his arrival would not be largely welcomed at least by the Senior Officers because of his apparently inveterate tactlessness. I hope that now some steps may be taken in this direction and that the new Archbishops may in co-operation with the Chaplain General select some men and second them, so to say, for spells of this special work.[149]

The bishops were evidently encouraged in their campaign against Symons by the dissatisfaction which many chaplains felt with the running of the Department. An early bone of contention was Symons' decision to simply republish the same Army Prayer Book that had been used in the First World War. As one former chaplain complained:

> The reason why no attempt was made to produce a new and suitable book of prayers and worship (what a unique opportunity the Chaplain-General had!) is because the type was still set up for the printing of the old book and it was cheaper to print another few million copies. Anyone who cares to compute carefully the cost of printing a new Army Prayer Book will find that it could not exceed the price of a couple of tanks. The head of the Chaplains' Department had to allow the spiritual work of chaplains throughout the army and throughout the war to be ludicrously handicapped by a piece of red-tape economy. He ought to have fought every Government Department in the country, and resigned in loud protest if they had not granted him this essential aid to the work of his chaplains.[150]

For reasons such as this, in March 1942, J.E.G. Quinn, a senior Territorial chaplain, wrote in his diary:

> We all feel that the men who now lead the RAChD are not the best men; that the regular chaplains are not capable of giving the spiritual lead we ought to have, and that at a time when the major part of the younger clergy are in the Army they should be led by their own bishops and church leaders and not by an almost entirely separate institution composed of mediocrities.[151]

Six months earlier (and after Symons had expressed some qualms about the B.B.C.'s 'Radio Padre' initiative) James Welch, an Anglican clergyman, chaplain to William Temple and the B.B.C.'s Director of Religious Broadcasting, had written to Ronald Selby Wright:

> What I shall say to the Chaplain-General, poor fish, when I see him is that he, as Chaplain, and in charge of the spiritual administrations to the Forces, must put his foot down with the War Office and not stand any silly nonsense. The whole thing makes me absolutely wild. No wonder people are trying to unhorse our Mr. Symons.[152]

Indicative of these efforts to unseat the Chaplain-General was a letter addressed to the Army Council in August 1942 by J.P. Stephenson, a chaplain attached to an artillery regiment. In this sulphuric missive, Stephenson complained of a 'preposterous lie put out by the Chaplain-General's office', namely 'that only Regular chaplains served with the units that actually fought in Flanders [in] 1940', while deploring the fact that:

> The Chaplain-General in war has more Anglican clergy – and has much more power over his clergy – than the Bishop of London; yet the present holder of this high office is a man of whom the Bishop of St. Albans has said that he would not make him rural dean of his most rural rural deanery. His incompetence is felt throughout the Chaplaincy service, in particular through the type of men now too often chosen for promotion: ordained flunkeys, out to win the commander's favour and quite unqualified to encourage and guide their juniors.[153]

True to his burgeoning reputation as 'the People's Archbishop',[154] William Temple proved receptive to this widespread unrest among wartime chaplains, pursuing their complaints over matters ranging from leave allowances to the difficulties posed by their military rank. He also branded the Department's 'administrative methods', which one former chaplain described as 'dreary officialdom, a filling of many forms, military etiquette, and the ugly perpetuation of an irrelevant sectarianism and formalism', as 'inappropriate in spiritual work'.[155] Determined to hold a 'thorough enquiry' into the Department once the war was over, in the meantime (and particularly after succeeding to Canterbury in 1942) Temple endeavoured to sideline the Chaplain-General. In 1943, he suggested to Sir James Grigg, the Secretary of State for War, that a bishop should be appointed Deputy Chaplain-General as in the summer of 1915. When Grigg rejected this proposal in the interests of departmental cohesion, Temple turned instead to the Roman Catholic model and appointed an Anglican Bishop to the Forces in December 1943. The bishop in question was Leslie Owen, formerly Bishop of Jarrow, who became 'a kind of Provincial Suffragan' and was dignified with the title of Bishop of Maidstone.[156] This welter of criticism and web of conspiracy no doubt took its toll on Symons and it no doubt contributed to his premature departure from the War Office in October 1944. Although Symons was ostensibly 'invalided from the Service', the real reasons for his retirement were much more embarrassing – among his difficulties being 'woman trouble' and a drink problem which required Arthur Naylor's presence at the War Office for days on end.[157]

While the rules, size and temper of the Department clearly differed between the two World Wars, chaplains were recruited and commissioned according to procedures that remained largely unchanged from the First World War. For Anglicans and Catholics, the supply of emergency chaplains was largely dependent on the readiness of the diocesan clergy to volunteer and, perhaps most of all, on the willingness of their bishops to release them from parochial duties for an indefinite period. However, and as in the First World War, this situation was fraught with problems. For the Church of England, an ongoing decline in the number of younger clergy limited the pool of potential volunteers.[158] Furthermore, the residual appeal of pre-war pacifism, especially in the early months of the war, prevented some of the younger clergy from coming forward. In October 1938, and as efforts were being made to boost the number of Anglican clergy in the reserve forces, E.H. Thorold told Archbishop Lang 'that of all his applications only about two per cent were from clergy under 30. He told me that Aubrey of the United Board had the same difficulty about younger clergy.'[159] A case in point was Edward Leigh Phillips, a future airborne chaplain who was a convinced pacifist when war broke out. Indeed, his pacifist convictions were so familiar to his Brighton parishioners that in the aftermath of Dunkirk he was 'actually reported to the police by somebody who said that I had told my flock that if the Germans landed on the Downs . . . it would be our Christian duty to go and help them'.[160] Besides the currency of pacifist ideology, the development of the long-range bomber served to place the towns and cities of Great Britain very much in the front line of the war against Germany. This problem was exacerbated by the fact that the ratio of Anglican clergy aged under sixty-five to the general, and largely Anglican, population of England had fallen to a historic low.[161] While Symons was assiduous in circulating bishops for lists of available clergy, his success fell short of his efforts.[162] In October 1940, he complained to the Bishop of London that bishops were failing to produce new nominees and that some were not even providing updated lists. Worse still, many of their nominees had been rejected on medical grounds, some had not filled in their application forms and there had been 'certain withdrawals owing to the change of circumstances in some Parishes', a veiled reference to the effects of German bombing on the civilian population.[163] In December, Archbishop Lang acknowledged the difficulties Symons was experiencing, remarking in a letter to the Bishop of Pretoria:

> I doubt very much whether the Chaplain-General here can help you about Chaplains. I know that he is making a very great effort to try to get more from the English dioceses, but it is difficult to see where they are to come from. You see this war differs entirely from the last particularly in the fact that the clergy everywhere are bound to be among their people suffering as they do from these incessant raids.[164]

The demands of the Home Front were compounded by those of the other armed services. Unfortunately for the R.A.Ch.D., the pay and allowances of the army's emergency chaplains were less than what was enjoyed by their equivalents in the Royal Navy and the Royal Air Force.[165] Not only this, but the outbreak of war precipitated yet another debate in *The Times* on the rank, uniform and titles of army chaplains.[166] As late as 1944, Archbishop Temple acknowledged that clergymen preferred the Royal Navy or the Royal Air Force to the army. Besides questions of pay, in the senior service chaplains were without the perceived encumbrance of officer's rank and, in the R.A.F., they were exempted from the hazards of combat flying.[167] It was also clear to some that the ordeal of the First World War had stripped bare the invidious nature of army chaplaincy. As one letter to the *Church Times* put it in September 1939, the army chaplain's job was 'a spiritually dangerous one in many ways'. The pressure to be 'a man's man' and the natural desire to be 'popular in the mess' was conducive to 'slack methods' and a careless demeanour; army chaplains were prone to be regarded as 'a sort of Government official' and spiritual work was liable to become secondary to 'running concerts or looking after army huts'.[168]

For all of these reasons, for most of the war the Church of England was unable to supply enough chaplains to the army. Despite a short-lived sufficiency during the 'Phoney War' period (there were 'no vacancies' for Anglican chaplains by October 1939)[169] the situation soon changed dramatically. Recurrent defeats in Europe, North Africa and the Far East, the impact of the war on the Home Front and the huge expansion of the army meant that the R.A.Ch.D. was well short of its official establishment of Anglican chaplains by 1942. In a circular letter to the Anglican bishops in October 1941, Symons stated:

> I am sorry to say that we have not been able to reach even the minimum authorised establishment of Church of England Chaplains and there is now a deficiency of over a hundred [and] I hear from all sides of the difficulties experienced in Commands as a result of the acute shortage of Church of England chaplains . . . In placing this statement before you I am fully aware that you too have your difficult problem of manpower in the dioceses but I am appealing for your help to ensure the maximum spiritual provision for our fellow men and women in the Army.[170]

This was despite the best efforts of the government and the War Office to alleviate the situation. In November 1939, the upper age limit for emergency commissions was increased from 40 to 50 and it even rose to 57 in 1943, although it was intended that more elderly chaplains would be retained for home service.[171] Despite Temple's impression that the I.A.C. was purely preoccupied with chaplains' pay, this further raising of the age limit seems to have been prompted by its meeting in July 1943 where:

> The Chairman drew attention to the grave shortage of Chaplains especially in the case of the Church of England, and asked the Committee to send to the Chaplain-General any suggestions which might help to solve this problem. There was some discussion about admitting men over 55 as Chaplains, and it was agreed that the shortage was so severe that it was desirable to send the names of such men to the Chaplain-General. They might often be found suitable to fill vacancies at home even if they could not, for medical reasons, be sent overseas.[172]

While age limits were raised, it was also thought expedient to adjust the working ratio of chaplains to soldiers, this ratio being lowered from 1:1,100 in 1939 to 1:1,250 in 1942.[173] Nevertheless, in July of the following year a report by the Bishop of London for the Bishops' War Committee revealed that the army was still short of 450 Anglican chaplains, news that stirred the Anglican hierarchy into efforts to send at least 10 per cent of all parish clergy from each diocese into the armed forces.[174] However, by the end of the year this push had produced only a hundred extra army chaplains and the Chaplain-General was complaining that he was still short of 411 Anglican chaplains.[175] Consequently, in February 1944 Symons wrote to the Bishops' War Committee complaining that he was very doubtful that the Church of England could meet its commitments to 'the Army

Group which is now preparing for the Second Front' and that he was still faced with 'very large deficiencies' in overseas commands. In the event of the cross-Channel invasion, he warned, the vast majority of Anglican chaplains left in Great Britain would be either still in training or physically unfit to serve overseas.[176]

The Roman Catholic church also faced a manpower problem which echoed that of the First World War. When war broke out, Bishop Dey was informed by the D.C.G., Joseph Lynn, that another twenty-five Roman Catholic chaplains would be needed for the new expeditionary force and a further ten would be required at home to replace those regulars who would accompany the B.E.F. to France. Furthermore, there was an acute shortage of chaplains for the Territorial Army, which had only 50 of its theoretical establishment of 120 Roman Catholic chaplains.[177] However, even supplying the B.E.F. proved difficult, a problem that was exacerbated by the neutrality of Eire and by the fact that the War Office had for decades allowed a relatively high ratio of Roman Catholic chaplains to soldiers. In May 1940, and on the very day that the Germans launched their *blitzkrieg* on Holland, France and Belgium, John Coghlan (who was then serving as the Principal Roman Catholic chaplain of the B.E.F.) wrote in a memorandum to Bishop Dey:

> Quite recently I asked the War Office for 13 chaplains, to complete authorised War Establishment. [The] War Office said they proposed to send ten, but only seven have arrived. It is very necessary and urgent that the B.E.F. should be kept up to strength. As a matter of fact I think that you should immediately budget for some seven hundred chaplains. I am not speaking wildly or extravagantly; in the last war there were 850 Catholic chaplains, and of these 549 were in France. This war will demand even greater numbers, and more especially in this theatre of operations. I realise the difficulty of the problem with which you are faced, but it is imperative that the B.E.F. is kept up to strength. Failure to do this will have serious repercussions in that:
> a). The spiritual welfare of the men will be endangered and serious complaints will reach England.
> b). Deficiencies in our War establishment allotment may possibly be filled by non-Catholic chaplains . . .[178]

As in the First World War, there was a discernible inclination among the Roman Catholic hierarchy to leave the responsibility for finding chaplains to the religious orders. According to Coghlan's memorandum of May 1940, forty-seven out of 108 Roman Catholic chaplains in France were regular priests and no fewer than ten English and Scottish dioceses were not represented.[179] Nor was it simply a question of numbers as Coghlan believed that the regular clergy were grievously deficient in pastoral experience. In October 1939 he had even written to Dey:

> May I suggest . . . that secular priests of missionary [i.e. parish] experience be preferred to those of the Orders who are straight from Ordination and from monasteries where they have had no experience of missionary

work and organisation. The areas I have to allot to individual Chaplains are so immense that organising ability is a necessity.[180]

In fact, certain bishops seemed positively unsympathetic to the whole enterprise and such was the dismal track record of the diocese of Southwark in sending priests to the armed forces that Dey even attacked his old foe Peter Amigo in the Catholic press in 1942. Significantly, by the end of that year only seven of Southwark's 435 diocesan priests were serving with the armed forces, a situation which Amigo defended by claiming that his south-eastern diocese was very much in the forefront of the war against Germany.[181]

Although Coghlan had pleaded with Dey to 'call upon Ireland' in 1940 (Coghlan had been ordained for the diocese of Meath in 1913 and clearly saw Eire's neutrality as a minor detail)[182] by 1943 the shortage of Roman Catholic chaplains was still severe. Hence, Cardinal Hinsley felt obliged to point out to the bishops of England and Wales the potential benefit of releasing 10 per cent of their priests to the services. By this time, of 680 Roman Catholic chaplains in the armed forces, only 281 were diocesan priests from England, Wales and Scotland; 238 were regulars from Great Britain whilst the remainder (nearly 25 per cent) were priests from Ireland and overseas.[183] Nevertheless, the shortage of Roman Catholic chaplains remained an enduring feature of the war, Coghlan writing in October 1945:

> One of my greatest difficulties . . . in all theatres of operations throughout the entire war, was the finding of priests to replace casualties among chaplains and the satisfying of demands for more and more chaplains to cover the ever increasing number of units and areas. At no time were we the number of chaplains allowed by War Office Establishment; we were always at least sixty below it. In such straitened circumstances the only thing to do was to ensure that the operational troops had their full complement. This meant depriving the troops in the Home Commands and on the lines of communication of the chaplains to whom, in all justice, they were entitled; it also meant an almost unbearable physical and mental strain on individual chaplains who had to do work normally covered by two or three.[184]

Though still hard pressed, the more centralised bureaucracies of the Church of Scotland, the Methodist church and the United Board coped better. Inevitably, the recruitment and co-ordination of Presbyterian chaplains was greatly assisted by the union of the Church of Scotland and the United Free Church in 1929, a union which brought all but a handful of Scottish Presbyterians into a new national church.[185] Furthermore, guidelines drawn up in 1939 by the Manpower Sub-Committee of the Committee on Church and National Service ensured that within the Church of Scotland the competing demands of the armed forces and the Home Front were reconciled at a local level. These guidelines left individual presbyteries free to determine their own pastoral needs and, in the light of these, to release ministers to the army.[186] Although this meant that certain presbyteries, such as Mull and Kintyre, were reluctant to release any of their ministers, others, such as Strathbogie and Elgin, released at least 20 per cent of theirs.[187] By such means, the Church of Scotland was able to maintain an adequate supply of chaplains to the army despite the competing demands of the Home Front, the R.A.F., the Royal Navy and the Church of Scotland's wide-ranging canteen work with the forces.[188] By January 1942, the Church of Scotland had 214 chaplains serving with the army, a figure that represented a denominational ratio of 1:1,028.[189] A further reflection of the Church of Scotland's relative success in this respect was that in May 1943 its General Assembly learnt that its Committee on Chaplains to H.M. Forces had been 'just able to supply immediate needs' although a reserve of fifty ministers had proved impossible to muster.[190]

If the Church of Scotland rose to the task before it, then so too did the Methodist church. After the union of the Wesleyan, United and Primitive Methodists in 1932, a new Royal Navy, Army and Royal Air Force Board was constituted. In the aftermath of the Munich Crisis of 1938, the Board approached the General Purposes Committee of the Methodist church for permission to raise the number of Methodist ministers in the regular army reserve of officers from twenty to fifty. As in the appointment of chaplains to the Territorial Army, this involved the secretary of the Board granting permission on behalf of the church for individual Methodist ministers to accept 'liability for service in a national emergency'.[191] The efforts of the Board increased in proportion to the threat of war, its secretary being directed in May 1939 to send a letter 'to every Methodist Minister in Great Britain asking for co-operation' and to arrange for a deputation to visit each Methodist theological college in order 'to explain the aims' of its work.[192] Despite an ageing body of ministers, declining recruitment to the Methodist ministry and the strength of pacifist sentiment in the Methodist church (the Methodist Peace Fellowship had more than twice as many members as the Anglican Pacifist Fellowship in September 1939)[193] these efforts did not go unrewarded. By January 1940, and with the door now open for emergency commissions, there were 103 Methodist chaplains serving with the army, a number that had climbed to 118 by the following year. By January 1943, there were 183 Methodist ministers in the R.A.Ch.D., their number peaking at 222 in September 1944.[194] However, this growth was far from painless and nor was it, from the Board's point of view, entirely satisfactory. Such were demands in September 1942 that the Board felt obliged to ask the Home Missionary Committee 'to call the attention of Chairmen of Districts to the urgent needs of the Chaplaincy Services'. At the same time, it also asked the Committee 'to request the Conference Executive to allow the Board to nominate Probationers'.[195] However, even these expedients failed to avert a perceived crisis in January 1943, when the Board learnt that requirements were outstripping nominations and that ten more army chaplains would be needed within weeks.[196] Nevertheless, it was symptomatic of its overall success that these additional chaplains were duly found and that, even in the nervous days of early 1943, the Methodists comfortably exceeded the revised wartime ratio of chaplains to soldiers. In January 1943, the 183 Methodist chaplains of the British army were serving 161,051 of their co-religionists, representing a very favourable 1:880; indeed, this situation actually improved over the next twelve months, the prevailing ratio of Methodist chaplains to Methodist soldiers being more in the order of 1:800 by 1944.[197]

Rather surprisingly, it was the United Board (which, since Methodist reunion, now comprised only the Baptists and Congregationalists) that achieved the most favourable balance of chaplains to soldiers. Despite the strength of pacifist sentiment in Free Church circles in the inter-war years, the ageing profile of Baptist and Congregational ministers[198] and its own infrequent meetings (the Board met only three times between September 1939 and December 1941)[199] the United Board had sent 152 ministers to the army by May 1945. By comparison, in 1939 there had been a combined total of only twenty-two Baptist and Congregationalist ministers in the regular army, the T.A. and their respective reserves of officers.[200] The Board's success can be measured by the fact that in 1942 it had achieved a ratio in the order of one chaplain to 700 Baptist and Congregationalist soldiers, a clear indication that, regardless of denominational quotas, the unified Department was quite prepared to recruit chaplains from wherever clergy were available.[201]

Jewish chaplaincy was another story of remarkable wartime expansion. Although the Jewish War Services Committee was denied representation on the I.A.C. by Sir Reginald Brade in 1916 (ostensibly because of the 'unique nature' of 'problems which arise in connection with ministration to the Jewish soldiers')[202] a Jewish representative was eventually admitted to the I.A.C. by Sir Herbert Creedy ten years later.[203] However, Dayan Gollop, the 'Senior Jewish Chaplain to H.M. Forces', took charge of a tiny jurisdiction in 1926. Mass demobilisation since November 1918, the extensive reorganisation of the R.A.Ch.D. in the early 1920s and the tiny number of Jewish regulars serving in the British army at that time meant that there were no regular Jewish chaplains to oversee. In fact, at the height of the 'Phoney War' the army still had only two commissioned Jewish chaplains, both of whom were Territorials, and the application of at least one rabbi was rejected on the grounds that 'there were insufficient Jewish soldiers etc. for [the Department] to engage another chaplain'.[204] However, a great deal changed after the fall of France and a key factor that seems to have driven the expansion of Jewish chaplaincy was the large number of Jewish refugees from Germany, Austria and Czechoslovakia who enlisted in the foreign companies of the army's Pioneer Corps.[205] A further eight Jewish chaplains had been recruited through the Senior Jewish Chaplain by April 1941 and the total of Jewish chaplains had risen to twenty-two by January of the following year. Although this expansion secured a ratio of one chaplain for every 1,273 Jewish soldiers, this comparatively favourable situation was partly offset by the scattered distribution of this small minority throughout the army.[206]

Organisation and Training

In addition to the means whereby chaplains were recruited, the R.A.Ch.D. also owed much to First World War precedent with respect to its organisation at home and overseas. Indeed, it is instructive to note that, in terms of its senior personnel, in 1939 all but three of the Department's First, Second and Third Class C.F.s (including Arthur Naylor, the future D.C.G. of the B.E.F.) were veterans of the

First World War.[207] With the coming of war, some higher offices were revived; the post of Deputy Assistant Chaplain-General was reintroduced, its holders being tasked with the oversight of corps troops and of departmental affairs in army districts. Senior Chaplains were also reintroduced for army areas and fighting divisions.[208] However, the advent of armoured and airborne divisions meant that the army's divisional organisation was much more varied in the Second World War than in the First, a situation that was complicated by repeated adjustments to divisional establishments and by experiments with 'Mixed' divisions.[209] However, broadly speaking most infantry divisions had an establishment of sixteen chaplains, comprising 'about ten C. of E., three R.C. and three Free Church [chaplains], who might be Methodist, Presbyterian or Baptist'. In effect, this meant that Roman Catholic and Free Church chaplains were allotted to brigades, while Anglicans were sent to individual battalions. However, and in continuing deference to national sensitivities, it was intended that Church of Scotland chaplains would predominate in the army's Scottish divisions. Outside the divisional structure, chaplains were allotted to medium and heavy artillery regiments as well as to bases, general hospitals and lines of communication according to the official ratio of chaplains to soldiers.[210] However, the uneven supply of chaplains meant that the unified Department was obliged to fill vacancies without too much regard for notional quotas and denominational niceties. For example, when William Humphreys, an Anglican, was posted to the 75th Field Regiment of the Royal Artillery in 1941, he felt compelled to take 'nothing but Presbyterian services' as most of its men were Scottish Territorials. Similarly, in North Africa in November 1942 the Church of Scotland chaplains of the much-vaunted 51st (Highland) Division were outnumbered by their Anglican colleagues by a margin of five to four.[211] However, and as a former S.C.F. of 10th Armoured Division insisted, 'In the last resort it was not the denomination of the chaplain that mattered but his character and personality.'[212]

Although this quickly dissipated under the strains of war, a fleeting illusion of greater inter-denominational harmony visited the Department in its early months. This was due to Bishop Keatinge's agreement that Roman Catholic chaplaincy should be integrated into the unified Department in the event of another European war. However unlikely this scenario may have appeared in the halcyon days of the 'Ten Year Rule', Keatinge's successors lived to regret this decision. When war broke out, and in accordance with this agreement, John Coghlan, the Principal Catholic Chaplain, became Assistant Deputy Chaplain-General of the unified Department and joined the new British Expeditionary Force in France.[213] However, these arrangements appear to have proved unworkable. Consequently, after the B.E.F. was evacuated from France in 1940, a successful bid was mounted by Coghlan and Dey to extricate Roman Catholic chaplains from the unified Department. Thereafter, Roman Catholic chaplains were administered by a Principal Catholic Chaplain at the War Office and by a hierarchy of senior Catholic chaplains attached to armies, corps and districts.[214] As Coghlan (who resumed the role of Principal Catholic Chaplain) later explained, the unified policy was 'not a success' because:

> [I]t was found quite impossible to separate the purely administrative from the ecclesiastical and spiritual. A non-Catholic Senior Chaplain obviously cannot deal with Catholic matters since they do not come within the scope of his training and experience. The converse is equally true. In civilian life, for example, one cannot visualise a Catholic parish priest being directed in his parochial activities by the local Protestant vicar or vice versa.[215]

Although the Department failed to survive as a unified entity, it nevertheless succeeded in taking chaplains' training to new levels. However, if a paucity of initial training had been a common and justifiable cause of complaint during the First World War, this problem persisted during the early stages of the Second. To be sure, in the latter case it was mitigated by the existence of a substantial core of regular and Territorial chaplains, who had at least some experience of military life, and by a significant cadre of older reserve chaplains who were veterans of the First World War. Such veterans also ensured that at least some unofficial guidance was available for the novice chaplain almost from the outbreak of hostilities. In *A War-Time Chaplaincy*, R.L. Barnes, an Anglo-Catholic priest of the Community of the Resurrection, candidly recounted his varied experiences in the First World War, stressing all too prematurely the particular problems of demobilisation.[216] At much the same time, a manual of practical advice entitled *Clergy in War-Time* was published by C. Salisbury Woodward and Harry Blackburne, the Bishop and Dean of Bristol respectively. In his foreword, Archbishop Lang commended Blackburne's advice on the role and ministry of the army chaplain (which was essentially an explanation of the chaplain's role as it had evolved in the First World War) as advice that was 'simple, sincere, human and practical'.[217]

Nevertheless, despite the greater availability of useful experience and advice, younger reserve and emergency chaplains still found themselves in a similar predicament to their poorly prepared forebears of 1914–18. Edward Mitchell ('Gus') Claxton, who had been a curate in Dartford when war broke out, became an army chaplain in response to a letter from the Chaplain-General. Subsequently, Claxton found himself at Aldershot with forty other chaplains under the care of its A.C.G. Here, and in accordance with the peacetime practice of senior chaplains training new members of the Department on the job, a short course of lectures was provided on subjects such as 'The Chaplain and his Spiritual Contribution to the Army', 'The Rudiments of 1st Aid under Active Service Conditions' and 'Sexual problems and Continental Conventions (with special reference to the Expeditionary Force)'.[218] From Aldershot, Claxton proceeded to St. Nazaire to join the B.E.F.'s pool of chaplains and was eventually posted to 5th Infantry Brigade on the Belgian border, his training having done nothing thus far to dispel his fears that he was still 'very green'.[219]

However, Claxton was relatively lucky. In October 1939, the Bishop of Coventry wrote to Lang's secretary, Alan Don, complaining that:

> I am really rather distressed at the way in which Chaplains are being sent straight off to their units on joining up without any kind of instruction in

> Army life and ways at all. Only this week I have two instances of men who after no more than a day or two at Salisbury have been posted to units entirely on their own. However good these young fellows are at their ordinary job, they surely ought to have some instruction about Army life in some school for Chaplains before they are thus sent off. I myself got at least six weeks at Woolwich, and, though I hated it, it certainly helped me later on.[220]

While the Church of England's newly formed Bishops' War Committee pushed for remedial action, and even contemplated the creation of a single, tri-service school 'retained in civilian hands' as 'the offering of the Church to its Chaplains',[221] the Chaplain-General seems not to have grasped the importance of adequate preliminary training. Although Symons told Lang in January 1940 that he was planning three departmental schools in France and England, it was clear that these were to be 'of a refresher rather than of a training character'.[222]

Chiefly as a result of pressure from Archbishop Lang, it was not until June 1940 that an R.A.Ch.D. 'Reception Centre and Depot' was finally opened at Chester, an Anglican teacher training college being commandeered for the purpose. Intended for all new members of the unified Department, the school taught a fortnight's course of military and pastoral subjects and placed a strong (and sometimes controversial) emphasis on common worship. In terms of its curriculum, the programme taught the novice chaplain 'gas mask drill, how to salute, map-reading, the conditions under which he will work as a chaplain, his functions in connection with welfare work, the history of the Chaplains' department, and the elementary principles of military law'. Furthermore, students were required to give 'specimen sermons', to participate in discussions on church matters and to get used to their 'Sam Browne [belts] and the ideas of army life'.[223] Though clearly an improvement on the earlier regime at Aldershot, the impact of the Chester programme should not be exaggerated. There was no equivalent school for the Roman Catholic branch of the Department and early and pre-war chaplains never passed through its induction course.[224] Furthermore, however congenial its curriculum may have been for clergymen fresh from 'civvy street', the induction course at Chester laid insufficient emphasis on physical and practical training, a problem that was only remedied after the school was relocated to Tidworth and a new commandant appointed in 1942.[225] Inevitably, there were mixed reactions to the Chester course. While Edward Leigh Phillips was impressed by what he considered 'a very good introduction' and by the 'two very excellent wardens [who] had been chaplains in the First World War',[226] Leslie Skinner was wholly dismissive of both course and instructors and would have found his days at Chester 'useless' had he not roomed with Frank Woods, the dynamic former vice-principal of Wells Theological College who replaced Astbury as principal in October 1942.[227]

Once relocated to Tidworth and placed under Woods, many of the early deficiencies of the induction course appear to have been rectified. J. Frazer McLuskey, a Church of Scotland chaplain, remembered this improved training regime in glowing terms: 'We had arrived wondering how on earth a minister of religion fitted into the fighting machine, and in these two weeks the answer was given.'[228] As McLuskey explained:

> I shall always be grateful for this course, and, especially, for the chance it gave of a mental and spiritual reorientation. Woods had a remarkable gift for leading worship, and a warm, spontaneous friendship which was extended to every student. It was a happy course. We ran our cross-country, we turned out for our daily P.T., we did our best to take the organisation of the Army and of the Chaplains' Department with the seriousness which we felt it must deserve, and we learned to love the little parish church . . .[229]

However, in addition to nurturing mind, body and spirit, the course also succeeded in transmitting vital pastoral knowledge and techniques:

> We learned of the opportunities the Army offers the padre, and the place it gives him in its trust and affection. We learned some at least of the pitfalls to avoid. We heard a little of how the various branches of the Service work . . . We heard some good advice on the subject of religion and the ordinary soldier. We took turns at addressing the course as if it were a congregation of Tommies, and took turns too of saying what we thought the reactions of those Tommies would be. We left Tidworth very much wiser and, most of us felt, very much better men.[230]

While the Tidworth regime was emblematic of the intense emphasis on training which developed in Home Forces between Dunkirk and D-Day,[231] chaplains' training was also supplemented throughout the war by a spate of departmental pamphlets and memoranda. Conscious of the inexperience of his chaplains, John Coghlan issued a basic, four-page memorandum to Roman Catholic chaplains of the B.E.F. in December 1939, its guidance ranging from the need to maintain military secrecy to how to obtain communion wafers.[232] Similarly, in 1943, and for the benefit of the unified Department, Percy Middleton Brumwell (now Deputy Chaplain-General) published *The Army Chaplain: The Royal Army Chaplains' Department, The Duties of Chaplains and Morale*. With a brief foreword supplied by Symons, the pamphlet gave an outline history of the Department and summarised its administration and organisation. It also elaborated on the duties of the chaplain, emphasised 'The Vital Place of the Department in the Army' and devoted its concluding section to the critical issue of 'The Army Chaplain and Morale'.[233] In April 1944, and in preparation for the imminent invasion of France, J.W. Steele (now A.C.G. of Second Army) published *Notes for Active-Service Chaplains*. Intended to act as a 'guide and help' for chaplains in the coming campaign, the pamphlet comprised a summary of regulations, particulars of how to compile monthly reports, practical 'Hints for the Chaplain in the Field' and an inventory of essential equipment.[234] An equivalent memorandum was circulated to Roman Catholic chaplains the following month by R. Lester Guilly, the Senior Catholic chaplain of Second Army, a document that was based on the proceedings of previous conferences of Roman Catholic chaplains.[235] A similar approach was also adopted in the Far East. In December 1944, and as the reconquest of Burma began, a memorandum was circulated to the chaplains of Fourteenth Army entitled 'Hints and Suggestions for Chaplains serving in the Burma theatre of war'. This specified items of kit to be carried, outlined transport arrangements and clarified the chaplain's position in battle as well as departmental policy on the carrying of arms.[236]

However, the most prolific author of training memoranda for chaplains was Frederick Llewelyn Hughes, whose preoccupation with thorough training methods mirrored that of his great patron, Lieutenant-General (later Field Marshal) Bernard Montgomery.[237] In 1943, and with the war in North Africa over, Hughes analysed the role of front-line chaplains in a pioneering paper entitled 'The Chaplain's Duty in Battle', which he based 'on the whole experience of Eighth Army Chaplains'.[238] This was published in *The Chaplains' Magazine Middle East*, an inter-service magazine that began publication in January 1943.[239] Although a joint venture between army and R.A.F. chaplains, the numerical preponderance of the former ensured that the magazine became an important means of disseminating ideas and information among the Eighth Army's 'Brotherhood of Chaplains', as Hughes was wont to denote them. Fully aware of the debilitating dangers of inactivity and boredom, after the Axis surrender in North Africa Hughes issued a further memorandum entitled 'Some Advice on the Chaplain in Camp', which offered ideas as to how chaplains could combat symptoms of apathy among their men.[240] The invasion of Sicily in July 1943 duly brought forth a lengthier pamphlet entitled *The Chaplain in Invasion*, in which Hughes tackled the challenging duties involved in amphibious operations, including the different phases of preparation, embarkation, landing, battle, consolidation and reorganisation.[241] Finally, before leaving the Mediterranean early in 1944, Hughes published a comprehensive distillation of the Eighth Army's policy and experience in a pamphlet entitled *The Chaplains of the Grand Assault: a Summary of the Experience in the Field of the Eighth Army Brotherhood of Chaplains*. Running to more than forty pages, Hughes saw the pamphlet as a precursor to a 'comprehensive Chaplains' Field Handbook' and explained that its primary purpose was 'to define the policy of the Brotherhood and lay down our method and technique. We shall work on these lines until we or others improve on them, all of us knowing what we are trying to do and how we propose to do it.'[242]

A key feature of Hughes' pamphlets and memoranda was that they were based on reports written and collated by chaplains themselves, a system that Hughes appears to have instigated early in 1943.[243] However, under the impact of the Tunisian, Sicilian and Italian campaigns, the process of gathering and disseminating useful information had been greatly refined by 1944. In *The Chaplains of the Grand Assault,* and for the benefit of what Hughes described as the Department's 'corporate wisdom and intelligence', he urged chaplains to make notes on their work for the attention of their senior chaplains. This sharing of information and experience was also encouraged by a system of monthly situation reports and by special reports devoted to 'Battle Experience'. The latter reports were to be written 'After every engagement with the enemy' and were intended 'to register how the Faith has worked in action, and how we can improve our service, equipment and arrangements'.[244] By the eve of D-Day, this system had also become official policy in Second Army. In his *Notes for Active-Service Chaplains*, Steele described how the gathering and sharing of information would be orchestrated in North-West Europe:

> Monthly Reports will be rendered by all Chaplains to the Second Army. They will be made to the S.C.F. who is responsible for their administration, and will be rendered so as to *reach* him by the 15th of each month. [Corps] Chaplains who come under the direct administration of the D.A.C.G. will make their reports direct to him.
> S.Cs.F. will render the consolidated report to the D.A.C.G. so as to *reach* him by the 20th of each month . . .
> D.A.Cs.G. will render the consolidated report of the S.C.s.F. to the A.C.G. so as to *reach* him by the 24th of each month . . .[245]

Another indication of the rapid diffusion of these methods was that a similar system of reports was functioning among Fourteenth Army chaplains in Burma by the end of 1944.[246]

In addition to better training, systematic reflection and the assiduous dissemination of experience and ideas, chaplains were also supported in their work by a steady routine of conferences, retreats and refresher courses, all of which afforded further opportunities for collective reflection and discussion. Although Hughes stressed their importance in *The Chaplains of the Grand Assault*,[247] these events were a regular feature of departmental life at home and overseas from the early months of the war. In time, they gave rise to a 'Chaplains' Club' in Cairo and to 'Church Houses', or 'Religious Centres', in Jerusalem, Assisi and Brussels.[248] Their perceived value to the army as a whole is clear from a 1944 pamphlet entitled *Some Notes on the Conduct of War and the Infantry Division in Battle*, in which Montgomery ordered commanding officers in 21st Army Group to facilitate access to these 'schools of instruction'. As Montgomery put it, 'The importance of good Senior Chaplains is immense; and under them the chaplains must be welded into a team, all singing the same song and to the proper tune.'[249] Always keen to further this end, as A.C.G. of Eighth Army Hughes was active in promoting conferences among his subordinates. In April 1943, for example, he called for divisional conferences to be held throughout Eighth Army, suggesting topics for discussion and requesting that senior chaplains forward details of their proceedings to him.[250] One such conference was held two months later by the chaplains of 1st Armoured Division. Over a period of four days, they discussed strategies for 'The Christianising of the Army', the contribution which chaplains stood to make to the wider church and common problems of transport, equipment, communication and uniform. Each day began with matins and Holy Communion and ended with evensong and a devotional address.[251] Significantly, even in captivity gatherings such as this could prove their worth. For example, in June 1944 a conference was held at Woodlands Hospital in Singapore, where the assembled chaplains made a collective decision to hold only one Protestant service each Sunday in order to ensure the 'cutting out of competition' among chaplains of the unified Department.[252]

Despite the strong emphasis that came to be placed on chaplains' training, one vital aspect remained largely neglected until the latter part of the war. A lack of realistic battle training was a chronic and general weakness of the British army's training regime for much of the Second World War[253] and the Department suffered in consequence. While certain divisions developed in-house training programmes for their chaplains (those of 43rd Division were, for example, required to observe medical operations, learn vehicle maintenance and participate in field exercises)[254] there was a general lack of combat training for chaplains until the autumn of 1943. Coming fresh from the rigours of the Tunisian campaign, where he had noted the debilitating effects of combat on First Army chaplains who had never heard shots fired in anger, one of J.W. Steele's first priorities on becoming A.C.G. of Second Army in August 1943 was to establish a chaplains' battle school. Opened that September at Church Stowe in Northamptonshire, the school was run by the Defence Company of Second Army Headquarters and it subjected successive batches of chaplains to a gruelling training regime. In fact, so demanding was their battle school that chaplains had to be medically certified as 'fit for strenuous training' before attending one of its seven-day courses.[255]

Eric Gethyn-Jones, an Anglican chaplain with the 43rd (Wessex) Division, was certainly very grateful for what he learned at Church Stowe:

> The battle school training not only acclimatised us to the noise and conditions of warfare, but served even more to instruct one in the methods of self-preparation, personal protection, and the evacuation of wounded under fire. A cartoon in the mess ante-room at Church Stowe warned chaplains that in battle 'there is no divine right of padres.' The basic principles of use of cover, camouflage and movement were taught. Its inestimable value was fully recognised and, short though the period was, it must have saved many lives. Furthermore, it gave confidence and prepared the chaplain, mentally as well as physically, for the ordeal by fire.[256]

As intended, the course was credited with saving many lives. While this was very much the theme of a souvenir booklet entitled *Memories of Church Stowe*,[257] from his experience of the Normandy campaign Gethyn-Jones bore testimony to the higher survival rate that obtained among chaplains who had attended its courses. Significantly, he ascribed the death of one colleague to the 'inadequate training' he had received, the chaplain in question failing to recognise the distinctive sound of an incoming mortar round.[258] Church Stowe also proved invaluable as a means of weeding out those chaplains who were unfit to face a battlefield situation. As a Roman Catholic chaplain observed:

> The course included training in camouflage, use of ground, movement, crossing obstacles, booby-traps, mine detection, use of the compass at night, 'battle inoculation' and [a] 15 minutes obstacle course which included jumping into a pool and moving through a stream in February. Besides what it taught, then, the course also provided a useful test which enabled an estimate to be formed of the character, physique and capacities of the Chaplains who attended.[259]

A Role Revived

While there was a quantum leap in standards of training during the Second World War, the general pattern of the chaplain's ministry resembled that of 1914–18. Despite the activities of E.N.S.A. and the N.A.A.F.I. (not to mention those of religious organisations such as the Y.M.C.A. and the Salvation Army),[260] chaplains were once again sucked into a recreational role. Significantly, Harry Blackburne (one of the pioneers and advocates of this kind of work during the First World War) was keen to encourage its resumption in the Second. As Blackburne maintained, it was part and parcel of the chaplain's job to promote 'the welfare and happiness of the men'. Clearly anticipating another static war with Germany, in 1939 he recommended that the chaplain should organise 'concerts, football matches [and] boxing contests' and that he should establish recreation rooms 'when out of the line and in rest billets'. As Blackburne insisted, 'Every opportunity that occurs of doing anything for the comfort of the men should be at once seized upon, not in order to win the approval of those in authority (which it very well may), but simply because it is the Christ-like thing to do.'[261] This advice did not go unheeded. One Anglican chaplain recalled that during the 'Phoney War' in France 'Chaplains were involved in much welfare work. Troops with all kinds of troubles and complaints would seek their help. Cinema shows and concerts, football matches and discussions of one sort and another were arranged.'[262] As in the First World War, much of this work was an extension of the churches' work in civilian life; consequently, Free Church chaplains in the B.E.F. busied themselves with running Pleasant Sunday Afternoons.[263] However, once again Roman and Anglo-Catholics were inclined to downplay this sort of work. As John Coghlan advised Roman Catholic chaplains, 'The social welfare of the troops is not the primary concern of a Catholic Chaplain and he should not allow that time to be taken up with welfare work which should otherwise be spent in his apostolic work.' Nevertheless, even he accepted that a Roman Catholic chaplain 'should be ready to give every assistance in this direction as far as the time at his disposal allows'.[264]

Besides serving to promote military efficiency and morale in general, there could be very specific and urgent reasons for this kind of work. When Geoffrey Woolley became S.C.F. in Algiers at the end of 1942 (shortly after its occupation by the Allies) he found that a local abundance of cheap alcohol was a source of great concern for Major-General George Clark, 'the G.O.C. Lines of Communications'. As Clark reminded him:

> All the shops in Algiers were practically without goods . . . The only shops open were wine shops; soldiers tended to congregate in these during the evenings – there was nowhere else for them to go, apart from their billets . . . the wine contained a considerable amount of alcohol; spirits were powerful and frequently drugged; and in consequence after a few innocent drinks a soldier might be dead drunk on the floor or fighting an Arab who drew a knife.

Given the strategic background of the Anglo-American invasion of French North Africa, it was imperative not to alienate the former Vichy authorities simply because of indiscipline induced by a lack of licit recreation. As Woolley recalled:

> The attitude of the official French was still uncertain; disorders had already been numerous; if they continued our efficiency as well as our reputation with the French might be seriously impaired. So [Clark] asked me to improvise clubs and get the soldiers off the streets and out of the wine-shops.[265]

Consequently, Woolley and his chaplains rapidly established twenty soldiers' clubs in and around Algiers, buying up pianos and board games and requisitioning disused premises and stocks of Red Cross foodstuffs. In the absence of the N.A.A.F.I., this remarkable effort seems to have achieved the desired results. After a round of frenetic activity, Clark toured the new clubs and pronounced that they had solved the 'problem of the troops and their leisure hours'.[266]

However, some chaplains were in any case firmly convinced of the pastoral and missionary value of this kind of work. A case in point was Kenneth Oliver, a Territorial chaplain who had been a prominent figure in the Toc H movement prior to the war. According to Oliver, his duties as *de facto* entertainments officer of the 11th Royal Horse Artillery were dictated by the imperative to 'make friends with all ranks and to establish myself as a useful member of the regimental team'.[267] Although aware of the reluctance of some army chaplains 'to get involved in any activities that were not specifically "religious" ',[268] Oliver revelled in these duties. While his regiment was based near London during the months of the 'Phoney War', Oliver served as its P.T. instructor and, because 'the local pub was the only form of entertainment in the evening', he recruited variety performers from the capital who were prepared to give concerts free of charge – although 'some of the shows were fairly vulgar, to say the least'. Months later, while serving in the wastes of the Western Desert, Oliver became manager of the regimental canteen and, 'although some poured scorn on the "Holy Grocer", I knew I was making a valuable contribution to the welfare of the troops and their morale, while relieving an officer for more warlike duties'.[269] In all of these endeavours, Oliver consoled himself with the advice of 'Tubby' Clayton, namely 'Don't worry too much if none of the soldiers appear to need your services as a parson. You will find that very few of them will not be prepared to regard you as a friend.'[270]

In contrast to the situation before 1916, the presence of chaplains in the front line was never a point of dispute during the Second World War. As Harry Blackburne had anticipated in the autumn of 1939,[271] in the context of battle brigade chaplains resumed the role which they had played between 1916 and 1918. In December 1944, instructions aimed at infantry chaplains of the Fourteenth Army advised that in battle:

> [The] R.A.P. forms the best position.
> It is seldom possible to stay with Companies during operations – a Chaplain would only be a hindrance.

> Immediately after a Company 'show' the presence of the Chaplain is much appreciated.
> Daily visits to Companies when operations permit are essential.[272]

The work of Norman Jones, an Anglican chaplain who served with the 7th Black Watch at El Alamein in October 1942, is illustrative of the continuities between battlefield ministry in the two World Wars. During the opening phase of this set-piece offensive battle, Jones accompanied the battalion's medical officer and helped to establish the regimental aid post before venturing out with its stretcher-bearers in order to bring in the wounded. After a night of heavy fighting, daybreak found Jones confronting the task of burying the battalion's eighty or so dead, along with 'plenty of Germans and Italians also'.[273]

Although not always appropriate (W.H. Humphreys, who was an artillery chaplain in Italy, was told that he was 'just a bloody nuisance' when he ventured into the gun lines during a barrage)[274] the presence of the chaplain as a non-combatant in the front line continued to serve as an important moral example to those around him. As J.W. Steele stressed in *Notes for Active-Service Chaplains* of 1944:

> *Example counts*. The example of Chaplains can act either way – for good or ill – and it is for the Chaplain to make sure that it is for good. He does not need to worry about whether a Chaplain should be armed or not, for the example of an unarmed Chaplain has proved of more value than a battery of guns, and under certain circumstances a good example is likely to prove of more value than a good sermon.[275]

Naturally, this 'good example' varied according to circumstances. Sometimes it could take the form of a simple conversation. Stuart Hills, who served as a young officer with an armoured regiment in Normandy, remembered how his regimental chaplain 'had a quiet word with me, because he could see that I was upset' after some costly fighting at Berjou.[276] Similarly, in Italy in December 1943, E.N. Downing was called upon to speak to an unnerved soldier of the 4th Parachute Regiment:

> While we were holding this position [near Casoli], a party had to go out every night and occupy forward trenches. There was a night when one of the men refused to go down into the trench, and I was told to talk to him next morning. I learned that he was a Londoner, who some time before, in one of the heavy London air-raids, had been buried, and now had an apparently insurmountable phobia . . . It was decided to give him another chance that night, and I attempted some advice, which proved totally unpractical, and next day I saw him being taken away under guard. He gave me a sad look, and I knew I had been a dismal failure.[277]

A more successful and very conspicuous case of 'a good example' was the conduct of Rudesind Brookes while attached to the 1st Irish Guards at Anzio in 1944. During a seven-week period, this battalion fought under conditions that bore comparison with the worst aspects of the Western Front a generation earlier.[278] A Benedictine monk and former infantry officer, during a very heavy German bombardment Brookes emerged from his dugout and paced the battalion's lines reading his breviary. Although later depicted, even by Brookes himself, as a fit of monkish eccentricity,[279] this incident seems to be an obvious case of an experienced officer and chaplain seeking to strengthen the nerves of his battalion through a contrived display of normality.

The advent of the parachute chaplain added a new dimension to this moral leadership role in the Second World War. When the 1st Parachute Brigade was in training in 1941, the War Office was very reluctant to allow parachute chaplains to jump with their men. However, this idea had the support of the Department and of Brigadier-General Gale. Eventually, parachute training for chaplains was authorised and the first training jumps were made in December 1941 by Robert Talbot Watkins, a Methodist, and Bernard Egan, a Roman Catholic.[280] The army's parachute chaplains were something of an elite; all were volunteers and had to be exceptionally fit and under the age of thirty-two. Like all paratroopers, they were given their 'wings' after seven training jumps and were then entitled to 'parachute pay' of an extra two shillings a day.[281] As Egan put it, the shared dangers of this training proved to be a pastoral boon:

> There was no doubt that the position of a parachute chaplain made all the difference to his relations with the men. He could truly say that he was one of them, and the men, for their part, liked to feel that the chaplain was undergoing the same trials as themselves, and their mutual feeling of discomfort, nervousness, and exhilaration, were equally shared.

In fact, Egan believed that difficulties in establishing 'personal relations with the men' were 'more than halved' by this kind of training.[282] The bonds that were forged between chaplains and soldiers in parachute units help to explain the heavy casualties suffered by the Department in airborne operations. Three chaplains of the 6th Airborne Division were killed on 6 June 1944 while another was badly wounded and three more taken prisoner.[283] Three months later, of the fifteen chaplains to land with the 1st Airborne Division at Arnhem, two were killed and ten were taken prisoner.[284]

If chaplains resumed their role of being encouraging examples for others to follow, then they also returned to the unenviable duty of burying the dead and clearing the battlefield. In terms of British dead, it remained the chaplain's task to perform burial services and to mark and record the location of graves for referral to graves registration units.[285] Although the British army suffered much fewer fatal casualties than it had in the First World War, these were still disproportionately concentrated among the infantry and the burial of the dead on the battlefield remained a common and daunting task for infantry chaplains. A.R.C. Leaney, an Anglican chaplain who served with the 43rd (Wessex) Division in North-West Europe, left a vivid description of one such burial on the Dutch-German border in the winter of 1944–5:

> [21 November 1944] A melancholy day on which I went forward a short distance to bury on the spot a considerable number of our 5th Dorsets . . . It was one of the most miserable burials which I can remember: it was cold, wet underfoot, darkened by trees, the field where they lay scattered being an open approach to the wood they had captured . . . It took a long

> time. I suppose it is not clear to those who have not witnessed or taken part in one of these field burials how much the padre has to do . . . The searching of pockets and the general preparation of the body, which was usually roughly string-sewn in an old blanket, fell most often to the padre, whose office made others feel, I believe, that what would otherwise seem desecration or intrusion on the privacy of an unfortunate, was thus a reverent and kindly office. . . .[286]

However, the coming of age of armoured warfare and the full-scale mechanisation of the British army since the First World War served to bring additional horrors to the battlefields of the Second. As chaplain to the Sherwood Rangers Yeomanry, Leslie Skinner's dedication to recovering and burying the mangled and incinerated bodies of its tank crews was greatly admired.[287] The nature of such work was described by Eric Gethyn-Jones, who was called upon to recover some bodies from a burnt-out halftrack of the 12th King's Royal Rifle Corps in February 1945:

> The K.R.R.C.'s [medical officer] and his staff met me at the vehicle at the set hour, and an orderly and I began the gruesome business (my diary records it as 'the worst sight and job of my life') while the rest remained at a distance. A mortar bomb had landed slap in the middle of the canvas roof . . . Mills grenades had added to the destruction. It was thought four or five men had been sitting in the back. We picked away the canvas tatters and then, slowly and with considerable care, we worked our way with hands and a small entrenching tool through the shambles. We established that there had been four men in the vehicle, and identified them by their discs. One of the damaged grenades exploded when we dumped them into a nearby bomb crater. We were profoundly thankful when the task was completed without further loss of life.[288]

No less than in the First World War, the burial of the dead had profound implications for morale. Reflecting on the situation in southern Italy, the S.C.F. of the 46th Division wrote in his monthly report for September – October 1943 that burials were 'still a big problem' because:

> [T]here is always a large number of isolated burials despite all our efforts. The fluctuating nature of the fighting in the hills often meant that burials could not be taken for days, and the men had to be buried near where they lay. Except in a few cases where bodies lie in uncleared minefields, nearly all have been accounted for by the Chaplains who utilised the brief rest we had to go over the old fighting areas thoroughly . . . The [graves registration units] should be forward from the outset, checking sites of small cemeteries and isolated graves with the Chaplains, for it is often impossible for units and Chaplains to do more than a very hurried burial and the opportunity of going back to do the work more thoroughly does not always occur. Within two months the situation of the graves alters its appearance, and after that time it is difficult to find the sites in this sort of country. The whole question is a very important one, as it definitely has a bearing on morale – the men are very critical of the temporary expedients which the conditions force upon us at times, and they at least expect that these should be rectified as speedily as possible . . .[289]

As A.C.G. of Eighth Army, Hughes was anxious to stress the importance of proper and sensitive burial procedures. In *The Chaplains of the Grand Assault*, he wrote that 'An efficient padre can do first-class service to honour the dead, help the minds of passing troops, and assist the future location and care of graves by seeing that lone graves are avoided and central cemeteries made and used.'[290]

This acute sensitivity to the soldier's state of mind was born of a genuine and profound concern for the morale of the British army in the Second World War. Many senior generals, civil servants and politicians (among them Winston Churchill) believed that the men who comprised it were inferior fighting material to their fathers' generation. Brought up in the shadow of three quarters of a million war dead, of mass unemployment and in the midst of a less deferential society where pacifism had taken hold in the 1930s, the defeats that marked the early years of the war were in part ascribed to the unmilitary qualities (and even 'pansydom') of Britain's citizen soldiers. Partly because it was no longer able to resort to the death penalty as a deterrent to cowardice and desertion, the army came to place a heavy emphasis on monitoring and promoting the morale of its soldiers. To this end, a special Morale Committee was established at the War Office in 1942 in order to review and, where possible, improve the morale of Home Forces through incremental reforms to service conditions.[291] Nevertheless, because of his multi-faceted ministry the chaplain continued to be seen as a key agent in supporting and enhancing morale. As Hughes emphasised in *The Chaplains of the Grand Assault*, 'The padre's way to an army's heart is through conviction that religion assists its fighting.'[292]

Amid the calamities of the 1940 campaign in France and Belgium, it was clear that even the raw and ill-prepared chaplains of the B.E.F. did not neglect their assigned role of moral leadership. As Archbishop Lang wrote in a contemporary memorandum:

> The Chaplain General reported to me on June 21st 1940 that he had heard from many of the Officers of the B.E.F. as to the value of the Chaplains and their work. The Chief Staff Officer of one Division said that when his Division was hard pressed he told all non-combatants to go but he said that he must have the Chaplains as their presence was essential to the morale of the troops. A Naval Commander had said that the name given to the Chaplains [at Dunkirk] was 'Last off the Beach'. One of them (named Bishop) stayed for four days in order to see all the others off. Forty out of the 430 Chaplains with the B.E.F. were missing, two were known to be killed, and two or three were prisoners of war, and from 12 to 15 were wounded at home.[293]

However, it was clear that more was required of the army's chaplains than a stoical and consoling presence in defeat. Thus, with the threat of invasion looming after the fall of France, a new emphasis emerged on propounding the wider significance of the war and on urging the need for greater sacrifices upon the nation's citizen army. This emphasis was reflected by the publication in March 1941 of *Front Line Religion: The Padre Preaches*. Edited by Ronald Selby Wright (who was later to find fame as 'the Radio Padre') this was a compilation of twenty talks on the spiritual dimensions of the war that had been given to soldiers by serving or retired chaplains. Typical of them was A.R. Grant's address on 'St. George of England', which took as its text 1 Corinthians 16:13 ('Watch ye, stand fast in the faith, quit you like men, be strong'). Here, Grant declared:

> [St. George's] cross appears on our national flag – a red cross on a white background. How fitting a symbol under which to fight to-day – the Red Cross of Sacrifice against a background of motives which are sincere and pure, for I believe that the present conflict is a just and righteous war, engaged as we are in a fight against the evil which is in the world through lust and false ambition.[294]

At the same time, the Principal Catholic Chaplain was also keen to stress the part that chaplains could play in promoting the right military virtues. In February 1941 Coghlan wrote in his *Memorandum for Catholic Army Chaplains and Officiating Chaplains to the Forces*:

> Chaplains are 'men apart' and much is expected of them. On them, to a large extent, depends the Morale of the Christian Soldier and because of this they themselves must be living examples of the moral qualities expressed by the word MORALE, viz: – DISCIPLINE, THE FIGHTING SPIRIT and THE WILL TO WIN, SELF-CONTROL, SELF-RESPECT, LOYALTY, OBEDIENCE, DEVOTION TO DUTY and a HIGH SENSE OF HONOUR.[295]

Under the impact of further defeats in Greece, North Africa and the Far East, this rhetoric became more strident still. In 1942, William Maxwell published *Life in the Army: A Padre Talks to the Troops*. A Senior Chaplain and Church of Scotland minister, Maxwell claimed that his pamphlet was the product of 'many talks with officers and men' and that almost 'every paragraph' was 'the result of some conversation or comment'. This, however, seems to have added to its trenchancy, for Maxwell averred that:

> In all our storied history never have we had, with all our imperfections, so much worth defending, preserving, achieving . . . it is simple truth that never before have the forces of evil been massed with such diabolical malignancy and might against the forces of good. . . . never before has the contrast between good and evil been so clear, and the alignment of forces so unmistakable. Without [a] shadow of doubt we know that not only are we fighting for our life, and the defence of our beloved ones from slaughter, rape, and slavery, but also if we are defeated freedom and goodness shall perish utterly from the earth. This war is a terribly serious matter, a gigantic grapple with evil. If we have not recognized evil as a real thing before, we do now, and we see that it must be fought to the death.[296]

Given the realities of the situation, it was vital that the army rose to the challenge before it:

> In such an hour are we going to prove ourselves effete, rebellious, slack, degenerate, incapable of ardent endeavour, as Hitler brazenly declares that we are – or shall we be men, standing in the glory of our free manhood, informed and sustained by the faith of our fathers, men-at-arms

> with the old virtues and fortitude reborn in us, strong, fine, resolute, true; our stubborn, sturdy breed unpolluted and undiminished? That is the question; and the answer is not in doubt.[297]

In 1942 Percy Middleton Brumwell, the Deputy Chaplain-General at the War Office, also wrote *The Army Chaplain: The Royal Army Chaplains' Department, The Duties of Chaplains and Morale*. Although dealing with the history and the organisation of the Department, its concluding sections on morale (which identified its bases as 'The Will to Win', 'Self-Respect', 'Self-Control' and a 'High Sense of Honour') reflected the close linkage between chaplains and this fundamental issue at this critical stage of the war.[298] Indeed, in his foreword the Chaplain-General wrote that 'The subject of Morale is at the present time one of such vital interest and far-reaching consequences that I am certain the chapters on Morale will be welcomed by a wide circle of readers.'[299]

While the use and currency of this rhetoric by chaplains may appear regressive in view of the cautionary lessons of the First World War, it was not simply a product of military necessity. Indeed, it derived some of its strength and legitimacy from the reaction against liberal theology and its underlying assumptions that had been growing in Britain since the early 1930s, a reaction that was greatly accelerated by the crisis of the Second World War.[300] In July 1937, at the second ecumenical Life and Work Conference held at Oxford on the theme of 'Church, Community and State', Charles Raven had sensed the resistance of various conservative delegates towards his characteristic brand of liberal, utopian pacifism.[301] However, while on this occasion every shade of theological opinion had deplored what Raven termed 'the sheer evil of war',[302] four years later a more belligerent note was sounded from Basle by Karl Barth, the standard bearer of theological counter-revolution throughout the Protestant world. Already well known as an anti-Nazi, in his *Letter to Great Britain from Switzerland* of April 1941 Barth declared that:

> When the British Government declared war on Adolf Hitler's Germany in the autumn of 1939, it acted as the Government of a righteous State according to Christian standards . . . The Christians who do not realise that they must take part unreservedly in this war must have slept over their Bibles as well as over their newspapers.[303]

In fact, Barth repudiated any notion of fighting in the name of 'Western civilization', 'the brotherhood of men' or any other conceptions 'which might also be those of a pious Hindu, Buddhist or Atheist' and urged instead that the war should be fought 'unequivocally in the name of Jesus Christ'.[304]

This unequivocal missive had, significantly, been written at the invitation of the editors of the influential *Christian News-Letter*, namely the Anglican theologian A.R. Vidler, himself a 'semi-Barthian', and J.H. Oldham, a Presbyterian layman who by dint of his stature in the ecumenical movement was very much 'the *éminence grise* of international Protestantism'.[305] The changing mood of British Christianity was also evidenced in Charles Raven's impotent protests at the wartime attitudes of the Church of England and at what he perceived as unscrupulous Barthian support for the war.[306] In 1940 Raven insisted that: 'There is no theology of pacifism or of any other ideology. There is Christian theology, the interpretation of God's revelation of Himself in Christ; and this to me as to my hearers carries with it inescapably the pacifist way of life.'[307] Two years later he was still pleading his cause, arguing that:

> [Christ] could have met [crucifixion] by resistance . . . If ever there was occasion for a crusade, if ever the existence of God's cause seemed dependent upon a holy war, then surely was the time for it. In defence of liberty, justice, the will of God, the honour of Christ, let the issue be fought out. He would not fight – not because it was useless but because it was evil.[308]

However, by this stage of the war it was doubtful that even Raven was fully convinced by his own arguments, as was illustrated by the prayers of thanksgiving he offered in the chapel of Christ's College, Cambridge, for the much-needed victory at El Alamein.[309]

No less remarkable were developments in the Congregational Union of England and Wales, a body that had once been chaired by the prominent pacifist F.W. Norwood. In 1940, Nathaniel Micklem, a former pacifist and now a well-placed critic of liberal theology,[310] pronounced that pacifism in present circumstances was not merely misguided but was tantamount to blasphemy:

> To disclaim responsibility for maintaining the liberties of our people, hardly won by our forefathers through centuries of struggle and sacrifice, and to be willing to submit to a ruthless and mind destroying alien domination in order to avoid suffering and even death – that is blasphemy, and it is the final treachery to the human race. It is blasphemy, for it is the denial of God.[311]

Whereas F.W. Norwood had been elected chairman of the Congregational Union in the pacifist atmosphere of 1930, it was emblematic of a radically different mood in Congregational circles that Micklem was elected to the same position in 1944.[312]

It is against this military and ecclesiastical background that we can best understand the high-profile partnership that arose between Bernard Montgomery and Frederick Llewelyn Hughes from the autumn of 1942. Long before he arrived in North Africa, Montgomery had fully understood the value of the chaplain's role as a morale-raiser, an understanding that was no doubt partly grounded in his experiences as a First Army staff officer in the First World War.[313] While G.O.C. of South-Eastern Command in 1941–2, Montgomery had given an 'immediate warm welcome' to Bishop Bell's suggestion that bishops should play a greater role in supporting army chaplains and he had famously declared at a briefing conference that: 'The most important people in the Army are the Nursing Sisters and the Padres – the Sisters because they tell the men they matter to us – and the Padres because they tell the men they matter to God. And it is the men who matter.'[314] When he took command of Eighth Army in Egypt in August 1942, Montgomery embarked on a systematic campaign to raise its battered morale and this process necessarily involved the appointment of a new and more vigorous A.C.G. Consequently, Douglas Alexander Duncan, a regular army chaplain who had been in post for only five months,[315] was dismissed and Montgomery set about finding a replacement who was more to his taste. In the event, he chose Hughes, a former infantry officer who had won the M.C. in 1916 and had later trained for the priesthood at Bishops' College, Cheshunt, a theological college with a strongly evangelical pedigree. Having served his first curacy at Holy Trinity, Brompton, Hughes became vicar of St. Stephen's, Paddington, in 1930 and vicar of St. Peter's, Mansfield, in 1938. A Territorial chaplain since 1935, Hughes had arrived in the Middle East in 1940 as chaplain to the Sherwood Rangers, his local Yeomanry regiment.[316] Following a successful period as S.C.F. of the 1st Cavalry Division, where he had nurtured a 'broad fellowship' and a sense of a 'United Church' among its Protestant chaplains,[317] Hughes was acting as a corps D.A.C.G. when he was summoned to Eighth Army headquarters and interviewed in the following manner:

> [Montgomery:] Everybody ought to know at all levels what is the thing in his job which matters most . . . Now Padre, in your job and at your level, what is the thing that matters most?
> [Hughes:] Spiritual power.
> [Montgomery:] Now Padre, it will be your business as the big shot, never to take your eye off that . . . If you do take your eye off it, even for half a second, you will make your big mistake. And you will never get a chance to make another – not in this Army![318]

Hughes took this commission very much to heart. One of his first steps as A.C.G. of Eighth Army was to address a letter to its Protestant chaplains, reminding them that 'men will do their stern and present duty better with [their] just Purpose set before them and the light of their high calling shining in and on them'.[319] In recognition of such early efforts, Montgomery was generous in his praise of the contribution made to his victory at Alamein by the chaplains of Eighth Army. When A.J. Wilcox, the D.C.G. in the Middle East, visited Montgomery's headquarters in mid-November 1942 he found nothing but praise for the Department. As Wilcox reported:

> General Montgomery . . . stressed to me how much he relied upon the Chaplains for a higher standard of morale and discipline in his Army. He spoke very highly of the work of the A.C.G. (Rev. F.L. Hughes). The General is out to help us in every possible way and I was greatly impressed by his knowledge of our work and his great interest in it.[320]

Furthermore, at a later thanksgiving service held in St. George's Cathedral, Cairo, Montgomery pronounced that 'I would as soon think of going fighting without my artillery as without my Chaplains.'[321] On the first anniversary of Alamein in October 1943, Hughes wrote a piece for *Eighth Army News* in which he explained the importance that Montgomery attached to religion. Entitled 'The Silent Power', his article remarked that 'The High Command gives Religion a primary place as decisive in war' because:

> We are led by faith in the inviolate Supremacy of Almighty God. His throne is established over all. He remains The King for ever. He makes

> the fateful decision of national continuance [and] bends wars to His will . . . Our men have known stern times, been all out, reached the end of themselves, and tried Religion . . . Their plain, direct, dead-straight appeal to God for the extra ounce has often worked. They have discovered unseen help, and thought about an Unseen Helper.[322]

In 1944, Hughes returned to this theme of 'spiritual power' in *The Chaplains of the Grand Assault*, where he pronounced that 'The Army Commander and those near him know the worth to an army of a deep and widespread faith that we are gathered to battle by God Himself. They know that men to whom God has imparted His own desire to liberate the world will be impossible to stop'. Consequently, he urged chaplains to maximise 'the moral drive of our men who serve a moral God, and fight under a Cross as aggressive as the Swastika'.[323]

Although Stephen Louden has dismissed Hughes' combative and high-flown rhetoric as an echo of that 'fanciful out-of-touch language of World War I chaplains',[324] it was actually just what the army required and it certainly met with Montgomery's warm and consistent approval. In a speech delivered at the Mansion House in March 1944, Montgomery insisted that, as a pre-condition of victory, soldiers 'must have faith in God and [that] they must think rightly on the moral issues involved'.[325] With the final defeat of the Axis, he became even more convinced of the truth of this precept. In 1951, Montgomery declared:

> [M]oral purpose is the most powerful single factor in war. You do not get the best from soldiers unless they have a clear conscience in what they do and are confident that it is right . . . The moral brief must come from the Church. The Church must tell the soldiers not what is, but what should be behind their going forth.[326]

Furthermore, and with reference to his own 'Doctrine of Command', Montgomery wrote in his memoirs seven years later:

> I do not believe that today a commander can inspire great armies, or single units, or even individual men, and lead them to achieve great victories, unless he has a proper sense of religious truth; he must be prepared to acknowledge it, and to lead his troops in the light of that truth. He must always keep his finger on the spiritual pulse of his armies; he must be sure that the spiritual purpose which inspires them is right and true, and is clearly expounded to one and all. Unless he does this, he can expect no lasting success.[327]

Given their evident meeting of minds, it is not surprising that Montgomery considered Hughes to be 'a first class senior chaplain . . . the ideal of what an Army padre should be'.[328] Consequently, and bolstered by Montgomery's enthusiastic patronage, Hughes' position in the Department went from strength to strength. Known for his eloquence and benefiting from his association with the country's most celebrated general, Hughes made radio broadcasts for the B.B.C. after Alamein.[329] Furthermore, and at Montgomery's insistence, he returned to England early in 1944 in order to become D.C.G. of 21st Army Group as it prepared for the invasion of France and its campaign in North-West Europe.[330]

That autumn, Montgomery lobbied hard for Hughes' promotion to Chaplain-General. In September, he wrote to the Secretary of State for War:

> You once spoke about the Chaplain-General. Hughes is a Territorial; he would take the job if you decided he was the right man . . . Inspiration and guidance must come from above, and at present nothing happens in that line as far as the Chaplain-General's Dept. is concerned; I would say it is completely out of touch with the practical realities of the battlefronts. The new Chaplain-General should have been through the mill in this war.[331]

Accordingly, Montgomery dismissed the Bishop of Maidstone, another candidate for the post, as 'quite useless' and sent Hughes back to England in order to confer with Archbishop Temple.[332] Although Temple died unexpectedly at the end of October, this did not affect Hughes' promotion and he duly assumed the mantle of Chaplain-General in November 1944, his place at 21st Army Group being taken by G.P. Druitt, a regular chaplain and formerly D.A.C.G. of XII Corps.[333]

While Hughes' stress on 'spiritual power' resonated very deeply with Montgomery, it also had an impact on the policy of the Department. Firstly, it helped to focus the chaplain's duties, easing the retreat from the peripheral and even frivolous aspects of the chaplain's role. In August 1943, *The Chaplains' Magazine Middle East* stressed that:

> A chaplain is responsible for the moral and spiritual welfare of the men and women of the unit or units committed to his care. This is his special charge. Though a good chaplain naturally takes a keen interest in all sides of Army life, he may not undertake the duties of Education or Welfare Officer; nor is he allowed to become [president of the mess committee] or Sports Officer.[334]

These prohibitions were reiterated in J.W. Steele's *Notes for Active-Service Chaplains* of April 1944.[335] Secondly, it heightened the importance of retreats and refresher courses for chaplains. In November 1942, refresher courses for Eighth Army chaplains commenced in Jerusalem, the idea for the Jerusalem scheme (which aimed to benefit 'every Chaplain in the desert') being Montgomery's own.[336] Thirdly, in the light of Alamein and of Eighth Army's subsequent advance across Libya, Hughes systematised the role of the chaplain before, during and after battle. In *Some Advice on the Chaplain's Duty in Battle*, which was written in the winter of 1942–3 and based on material 'collated from the experience of the Brethren from Alamein to Tripoli',[337] Hughes divided this role into seven distinct phases and discussed the part that chaplains should play in each. These phases ranged from 'Eve of Battle Services' through 'Voluntary Companionship at Zero Hour' and 'Practical Service in Battle' to 'The Epilogue. Thanksgiving and Memorial Services'.[338]

An apparent consequence of this advice, which was firmly restated in *The Chaplains of the Grand Assault*,[339] was to elevate a ministry of prayer in the front line to the status of a solemn duty, a duty that was very widely observed by the last year of the war. F.G. Sutton of the 2nd Bedfordshire and Hertfordshire Regiment recalled of an attack at Monte Cassino in May 1944 that the battalion's chaplain moved from company to company saying a short prayer with each: 'It was the most moving service to which I had ever been. We all thought it might be our last, but nobody showed it.'[340] Similarly, on the first day of Operation Market Garden in September 1944, W.R. Chignell, chaplain of the 2nd Wing of the Glider Pilot Regiment, spent the time before take-off moving from glider to glider blessing their crews and their cargoes of airborne infantry; on the flight to Arnhem, Chignell was observed kneeling in prayer in the cockpit of his own glider.[341] Significantly, such was the currency of this ministry that it was also practised in Burma at the crossing of the Irrawaddy in February 1945.[342] Remarkably, it was even captured in a sound recording now kept by the Imperial War Museum. This features an unknown chaplain praying with men of the Royal Welch Fusiliers prior to an attack near Roermond in late 1944. With the boom of guns providing an ominous accompaniment to his petitions, his prayer ran:

> O God, our Father, we put ourselves into Thy care and in Thy keeping today. Grant, we beseech thee, as we go forward into this battle, that we may have the sense of Thy presence with us. Give us, we beseech Thee, such success that, when we overcome the enemy, help us to set forward that final victory which will bring back peace and happiness, truth and justice, liberty and freedom, unto all mankind everywhere. We ask for Thy help and for Thy protection, not only for ourselves but for all our comrades. We know that we are in Thy keeping. Grant us, therefore, such courage that we may do our duty faithfully, we may not shrink from danger but feeling that Thou art beside us we may conquer weariness and overcome all perils. Have mercy, we beseech Thee, on those who shall be wounded. Bring Thy comfort unto all who, in this battle, will lay down their lives and hasten the time when war shall be no more through Jesus Christ our Lord Amen.[343]

New Departures

While the chaplain sought to reinforce morale in many (sometimes dramatic) ways, the promotion of morale based on religious conviction was necessarily hampered by widespread religious ignorance among the army's citizen soldiers and a partial antidote to this was found in the new institution of 'Padre's Hour'. Very much a product of the difficult circumstances of 1942, 'Padre's Hour' had its origins in the training programme of the 1st Airborne Division and its moving force was its divisional commander, Major-General F.A.M. ('Boy') Browning. Significantly, Browning had recognised the need for remedial religious instruction while commanding 24th Guards Brigade and, as commander of the 1st Airborne Division, he gave his full attention to it. When John Hodgins, a trained school teacher, was appointed S.C.F. to his division Browning ordered him to institute a compulsory scheme of religious 'instruction by discussion'. However, Hodgins was wary of an adverse reaction to anything that savoured of Sunday school so he dubbed these weekly gatherings 'Padre's Hour'. The men were divided into small denominational groups and meetings usually took the form of a short introductory talk by the chaplain on a given subject followed by questions;

the men were allowed to sit at ease, smoking was permitted and officers were excluded in order to encourage discussion. While topics could be based on available pamphlets or selected by the chaplain, it became common practice for the men to choose subjects of particular interest to themselves.[344] According to a report sent to Archbishop Temple, the range of chosen subjects was exceptionally broad and a list of eighty-three examples included such questions as 'Science or Religion – Which should I believe?', 'Can a Christian be a Nazi or a Communist?', 'What good has the Church done?' and 'Is this War a Crusade?'[345]

Although the implementation of this scheme required Browning's active oversight, it was soon judged to be a runaway success. As Hodgins' successor testified in 1943, 'as far as the Hour was concerned they were never dull – in one case the [company sergeant-major] had to come in and remind the Padre he had been going for 1½ hours'.[346] Its value was also obvious to outsiders. In July 1942, Ronald Selby Wright wrote of a visit to the division:

> [M]et S.C.F. Airborne Division, who took me first to meet the Divisional G.O.C. Major-General 'Boy' Browning – a really first-class man, a Grenadier Guard and incidentally the husband of Daphne du Maurier . . . General Browning has fixed a period a week in each Company for 'Padre's Hour' in the training programme – not as an extra. I went to one of these and because I was to be there they were all Jocks (who had, incidentally, been on a tough raid recently). They listened, asked questions and were most friendly . . . The 'Padre's Hour' is a grand opportunity . . . and should do real good . . . Many of the men are 'devil-may-care' chaps but with this good G.O.C. and a tighter and more sensible 'Guards' discipline, they should do better.[347]

A further indication of the success of 'Padre's Hour' was its adoption throughout Northern Command in November 1942 and its rapid assimilation by the army at large. By the end of the war, 'Padre's Hour' had become an established feature of army life and was being supported and resourced by a Churches' Committee for Education in His Majesty's Forces.[348] 'Padre's Hour' even spread to the Fourteenth Amy in Burma, it being stated by the S.C.F. of 5th Indian Division in December 1944 that 'there are certain lull periods for each particular unit and the Chaplain can prove useful by his talks with the men. It has been found that troops welcome such hours and take a keen interest in the discussion.'[349]

However, 'Padre's Hour' was only one of many innovations in the wartime work of the R.A.Ch.D. The creation of the B.B.C. in 1922 had given the churches access to a vital new medium in the form of radio broadcasting. With the active support of John Reith (the managing director of the Company from 1922 to 1926 and director-general of the Corporation from 1927 to 1938) religious broadcasting gained an increasing share of airtime as the number of licence holders soared from 36,000 in 1922 to over eight million by the late 1930s.[350] Significantly, some of the most prominent religious broadcasters of these early years were (or, in Dick Sheppard's case, claimed to be) former army chaplains, men whose wartime ministries appeared to equip them with an understanding of the common man.[351] With the outbreak of war, the B.B.C. launched a new Forces Programme, its broadcasts being dominated by light music. Initially, the

Corporation saw little need for religion in its schedules, part of its rationale being that the spiritual needs of the armed forces were already well catered for. However, this opinion was not shared by James Welch, the Director of Religious Broadcasting, who saw an opportunity for developing a more lively style of religious broadcasting on the Forces Programme, a style that would take into account the limited religious background of many servicemen, their widespread resentment of compulsory church parades and the more relaxed ethos of its programming. Eventually, after much lobbying at home and listener research among servicemen in France, from early 1940 a brief and informal Sunday evening service was included in the Forces Programme, the service being largely devoted to hymn-singing. Over the following months, a more substantial diet of religious broadcasting emerged, with a morning service, a lunchtime talk, an evening service and an epilogue finding their way onto its Sunday schedules and an epilogue being added on Wednesday evenings.[352] By 1943, when the Forces Programme was absorbed by the B.B.C.'s General Overseas Service, religious broadcasting occupied a prominent place in broadcasting to service personnel. As a soldier with the army in the Middle East noted for Mass-Observation that year:

> A very big help to all denominations is the BBC, which does seem to have realised fairly fully the particular needs of the situation . . . Every Sunday morning there is a special service for 'Isolated Units', while in the evenings Dr. Nathaniel Micklem devotes a considerable number of his 'Christian News and Commentaries' to matters of interest to the Forces. Recently a series of talks has been given by an Air Force padre under the general heading of 'The Corporal asks the Question'.[353]

If Harry Blackburne had the distinction of inaugurating Sunday morning worship on the Forces Programme,[354] the serving chaplain who was to find greatest fame over the airwaves during the Second World War was a Church of Scotland minister named Ronald Selby Wright. A Toc H activist and chaplain to a battalion of Edinburgh Territorials since 1938, Selby Wright's chief qualification for his role as the 'Radio Padre' was the success of an earlier series entitled *Asking Why*. Based on his long-running work at an Edinburgh boys' club, this series consisted of discussions between Selby Wright and a group of juvenile inquirers on basic questions of faith and morals.[355] However, the catalyst for Selby Wright's incarnation as the 'Radio Padre' was the moral and spiritual plight of thousands of soldiers based on scores of isolated anti-aircraft sites across the British Isles. In the summer of 1941, James Welch received a delegation consisting of the Press and Entertainments Officer of 8th Anti-Aircraft Division and Robert Silvey, a listener research officer for the B.B.C. In the course of their meeting, a plea was entered for some religious broadcasts aimed at anti-aircraft personnel. With the support of Anti-Aircraft Command and of the Chaplain-General (who very much feared for the morality of sites with a female, A.T.S. presence) Selby Wright was identified by Welch as the chaplain best placed to provide broadcasts of this kind.[356]

Although Selby Wright's broadcasts began 'rather before the Padres' Hours became common in the army',[357] as with padre's hour their tone was relatively informal. Inspired by *Asking Why*, the first 'Radio Padre' broadcasts were presented as discussions rather than addresses and they went out in late 1941 under the title *Let's Ask the Padre*.[358] Although some civilian critics gave a cold reception to this pilot series, Welch was of the opinion that a more ambitious initiative was needed and *Let's Ask the Padre* was thought successful enough to warrant Selby Wright's full-time secondment to the B.B.C. for six months from March 1942. In order to lend his work more credibility, an important aspect of this secondment was Selby Wright's extended tour of gun sites and army bases across the country, a tour that he made with great diligence.[359] During this secondment, Selby Wright also gave around seventy broadcast addresses, his presence on the airwaves being reinforced by two-minute talks given in the midst of *Ack-Ack, Beer-Beer*, a variety programme aimed at anti-aircraft personnel.[360] Although presented in a cosy fireside style, these broadcasts were predictably conformist in tenor, generally upholding the virtues of army discipline, Christian morality and the justice of the national cause. Significantly, although Selby Wright was unfailingly familiar in his treatment of discussants on *Let's Ask the Padre*, he was nevertheless addressed as 'Sir' throughout. Moreover, although the first programme of this series addressed the vital question 'What About After the War?' Selby Wright was not to be drawn on politics, his view being that:

> A better Britain is impossible without better Britons in it. That may be trite but it's none the less true. Unless we build on the change of heart in men we'll still go on hoping and quarrelling and cheating and mistrusting till Doomsday. In other words, all sensible men, and I dare say it, especially soldiers, realise this – we've got to get back to real Christianity.[361]

Despite these limitations, there can be no doubt that in 1942 the 'Radio Padre' became a national broadcasting phenomenon. Although aimed at service personnel, his broadcasts also drew a great many listeners from the civilian population, thus fulfilling Welch's hope that religious broadcasting to the armed forces would help to transform the culture of religious broadcasting as a whole.[362] In August 1942, Selby Wright even conducted a radio interview with the new Archbishop of Canterbury, William Temple, who answered questions 'about the Palaces, stipends, etc. of Bishops [and] about the Church's message to the world today'.[363] At one point, Selby Wright was second only to Tommy Handley in terms of popularity, his average audience being around seven million. In addition to the multitudes who tuned into his broadcasts on subjects ranging from 'What is all this about getting married?' to 'The Spirit that Wins', Selby Wright's success was reflected in the publication of his broadcast talks and by a flood of personal correspondence. As he later remembered, he required the help of the B.B.C. and of an army clerk to deal with a post bag that could amount to a thousand letters a day.[364] Crucially, he also came to enjoy cross-denominational support for his avowedly non-sectarian broadcasts; as Selby Wright put it, 'even the Roman Catholics were very good, they supported it tremendously'.[365] However, and most importantly of all, his broadcasts appear to have been well received by their intended audience. As a Mass-Observation report put it in 1943, his stock among serving soldiers was 'extremely high', a fact that stemmed from his exceptional talents as a communicator:

> [T]here is no doubt that his weekly message does get over to a very large number of men. A few are critical, alleging that he is over simple and consequently platitudinous, but on the whole men seem to pay far more attention to him than the majority of padres. His direct approach, his simple language that is *not* coupled with any patronising air (as so often) make people stop and listen, and he adds to this by doing slightly unorthodox things that show him to be a human being – a good example of this is the beginning of his Christmas broadcast with Vera Lynn's recording of 'I'm dreaming of a White Christmas' . . .[366]

Notwithstanding the success of his broadcasting work, it appears that Selby Wright was never wholly enamoured of it and he appears to have been positively relieved when his gruelling six-month secondment to the B.B.C. ended and he was offered the post of S.C.F. of his old division in September 1942. As he confided in his diary:

> The Chaplain-General told me this great news. He was very kind when I saw him today at the War Office. I only hope I'll do the job well. There is nothing I'd like more – Senior Chaplain of the [52nd] Lowland Division – whoever thought I'd ever become that? Certainly not I![367]

However, these celebrations proved premature and within a few weeks of writing this he had been persuaded by M.I. 9, a branch of British military intelligence dealing with escapees and evaders,[368] to recommence his regular broadcasts; those beginning with the phrase 'Good Evening, Forces'[369] were encoded messages for the benefit of British prisoners of war waiting to hear news of escapees via hidden wireless sets. Although Selby Wright combined this work with his duties as Senior Chaplain to the 52nd Division, he eventually requested that he might be relieved of it, his radio persona entailing an insupportable workload of travelling, correspondence, speaking at public meetings and writing addresses that were greatly complicated by the codes employed by M.I. 9. Nevertheless, after a comparatively quiet period in Egypt and Palestine, he was eventually recalled to Britain to resume his coded broadcasts prior to D-Day. After a further request for release, Selby Wright was eventually allowed to spend the last months of the war as Senior Chaplain to the 10th Indian Division in Italy. However, even here he proved unable to escape the demands of the microphone and he continued his broadcasts 'off and on until the end of the war'.[370]

If the work of the 'Radio Padre' represented a largely successful attempt to close the physical and cultural distance between soldiers and chaplains, a more specific problem was posed by the growth of the women's Auxiliary Territorial Service during the Second World War. Although a Women's Army Auxiliary Corps had enjoyed a brief existence during the First World War, its numbers had remained small in absolute and in relative terms. From its belated creation early in 1917, the W.A.A.C. reached a wartime peak of just under 41,000 in November 1918.[371] In contrast, the Auxiliary Territorial Service was created on the outbreak of war in September 1939 and had grown to its wartime peak of 212,000 four years later.[372] Given the idealised vision of Christian womanhood cherished and propagated by the churches, the entry of so many women into the corrupting milieu of service life was a natural cause for concern, especially given the salacious (if largely unfounded) rumours that had surrounded the W.A.A.C. during the First World War.[373] These worries were also compounded by the fact that, unlike the First World War, when W.A.A.C. camps had been out of bounds for most male personnel, the majority of A.T.S. personnel were allocated to Anti-Aircraft Command, where young women crewed mixed gun sites alongside their male counterparts.[374] Furthermore, although chaplains were expected to be effective in working with men, they were generally considered to be ill equipped to work with women. Indeed, in 1918 the Wesleyan Royal Navy and Army Board noted that 'the pastoral visitation' of the W.A.A.C. at home was 'being undertaken in Camps and towns by the wives of Chaplains, and other ladies'.[375] By 1940, little had changed. In 1940, *The Times* reported that: 'The A.T.S. are ministered to as an integral part of the Army, and in this the chaplains occasionally have the help of voluntary workers, some of them deaconesses, but most without any such special training.'[376]

However, in view of what were perceived to be the particular needs of servicewomen, an interdenominational Committee of the Churches' Work for Women in the Forces was established in December 1939. Three years later, and as a result of the success of meetings organised by its workers, Archbishop Lang and the unified branch of the Chaplains' Department joined the committee in lobbying the War Office for the creation of a new establishment of twelve female chaplains' assistants. With the agreement of David Margesson, the Secretary of State for War, the first chaplains' assistants were duly commissioned by Archbishop Temple in a ceremony at Lambeth parish church in June 1942.[377] After several months, the 'experiment' was judged to be successful and the establishment of chaplains' assistants (or 'salaried women lay church workers' as *The Times* preferred to describe them) was doubled in March 1943. As *The Times* reported of their work:

> The lay church workers live near but not in the camps to which they are attached. They wear a purple badge and armlet with a gold cross and the letters C.W.W.F. – Churches' Work for Women in the Forces. Each worker has a small office where she is readily accessible to all members of the A.T.S. at hours when they are free to visit her. The newly appointed lay church workers, like those originally chosen, include members of the Church of England, the Church of Scotland, Presbyterian Churches, and of denominations represented on the National Free Church Council. They are ready to help all women who wish to consult them, irrespective of creed. Candidates are nominated by the Churches' Committee and are approved by the Chaplain-General and the A.T.S. Directorate. Selected candidates will be posted by the Chaplain-General to A.T.S. training centres, camps, or convenient centres for work with scattered units, such as A.A. mixed batteries, A.T.S billets etc.[378]

Although these women represented a variety of Protestant denominations, strongly evangelical candidates were usually rejected by the C.C.W.W.F., a policy that was no doubt intended to reduce the potential for friction but which naturally proved objectionable to some; indeed, it even raised a strong protest from Lieutenant-General Sir William Dobbie, a member of the Plymouth Brethren and hero of the defence of Malta.[379] The committee's selection policy may well have proved something of a liability in other respects, as there were never enough mature and theologically acceptable candidates to fill an establishment of chaplains' assistants which eventually grew to thirty-six. Furthermore, Anglican assistants were in short supply, a situation that probably reflected the Church of England's more conservative position on female ministry, a position that rather contrasted with that of William Temple and the principal Free Churches.[380] Nevertheless, there can be no doubt as to the value of these new auxiliaries to chaplains themselves. As Eric Gethyn-Jones recalled of the situation at the end of the war in North-West Europe:

> With the approach of the end of hostilities, there was a rapid build-up of non-combatant and administrative personnel, and around about V.E. Day, the number of A.T.S. in Brussels, for example, had risen to nearly three thousand. None of my chaplains in the city were happy about the prospect. They were unit or ex-unit padres, and the thought of having to cope with the female of the species in large numbers frankly frightened them – and me! Fortunately, the War Office came to the rescue. They telephoned, saying that they had two chaplain's assistants skulling around England with next to nothing to do . . . A day or two later, these very able ladies arrived and, very largely, the pastoral side of work among the girls was handed over to them.[381]

Another major difference between the work of the Chaplains' Department in the First and the Second World Wars stemmed from the number of chaplains who fell into enemy hands as prisoners of war and their view of their role in captivity. In 1914–18, relatively few chaplains were taken prisoner and, under the terms of the Geneva Convention of 1864, they were eligible for repatriation owing to their status as ambulance personnel.[382] A case in point was that of Benjamin O'Rorke of the 4th Field Ambulance, an Anglican chaplain who was captured while ministering to British wounded at Landrecies in August 1914 and who was repatriated after less than a year.[383] As a result of this situation, even officers' prison camps could find themselves without a resident chaplain and subject to the intermittent ministrations of a civilian clergyman or captive layman.[384] Furthermore, while they were prisoners chaplains were separated from all but their fellow officers. While O'Rorke evinced no inclination to visit camps for British other ranks during his rather comfortable sojourn in Germany, following the capitulation of Kut-al-Amara in 1916 the three chaplains of the 6th Indian Division were actually prevented by their Turkish captors from ministering to the British rank and file, whose treatment at Turkish hands eventually resulted in a death rate of nearly 70 per cent.[385] Given prevailing conditions, the only British prisoners of war who really benefited from the organised ministry of the Chaplains' Department during the First World War were those sick and wounded prisoners who were released into Swiss custody as internees.[386] However, this was not a popular ministry and one chaplain who was sent to the internment camp at Murren in 1917 even wrote to the Chaplain-General complaining that he 'had not joined up for a Swiss holiday and asking for a re-transfer to France'.[387]

With the coming of the Second World War, the situation was very different. Firstly, the Geneva Convention of 1929 had given captive chaplains the right of access to their fellow prisoners regardless of rank. As Article 16 stated:

> Prisoners of war shall be permitted complete freedom in the performance of their religious duties, including attendance at the services of their faith, on the sole condition that they comply with the routine and police regulations prescribed by the military authorities. Ministers of religion, who are prisoners of war, whatever may be their denomination, shall be allowed freely to minister to their co-religionists.[388]

Secondly, there was a strong determination to ensure that the religious needs of British prisoners of war were adequately met. In November 1939, Basil Staunton Batty, the suffragan Bishop of Fulham and Bishop for North and Central Europe stated that:

> During the last war more than 7,000 soldiers died in prison camps in Germany and no adequate provision was made for any spiritual ministration. I am trying to arrange that [civilian] British chaplains should be sent to such camps in the event of any British soldiers being taken prisoner in this war. The chaplains would have to be chosen with great care. They must be men with very great devotion to their work and prepared to face considerable self-sacrifice, for they would have to stay in Germany for the duration of the war.[389]

Furthermore, there was a general expectation that army chaplains would even go voluntarily into captivity in order to minister to prisoners of war. In fact, even after the Badoglio armistice of September 1943, the Chaplains' Committee of the Church of Scotland preferred its chaplains to remain in Italian prison camps (which would soon be seized by the Germans) rather than take the opportunity to escape.[390]

The expectation that chaplains would go where they were most needed greatly reduced the chances of escaping wholesale disasters, calamities that all too frequently befell the British army between 1940 and 1942. By September 1942, no fewer than eighty-six chaplains were officially listed as prisoners of war while another thirty-eight were listed as missing, though the great majority of these had in fact been captured at Singapore that February.[391] Given the continuing practice of running separate camps for officers and other ranks, after the experience of the First World War it was a tragic irony that officers' camps often held an embarrassing surplus of chaplains.[392] After the fall of France in 1940, no fewer than thirty-one chaplains, more than three-quarters of those taken prisoner, were held in a single *oflag* in Germany, giving a local chaplain to prisoner ratio of 1:40. Eventually, twenty-three of these clergymen were transferred to another *oflag*, where they served an even smaller flock of 200 fellow officers. At the same time, many s*talags* (camps for other ranks) had several thousand British inmates and no British chaplains.[393] Despite some redistribution of clerical prisoners in subsequent months,[394] the situation in German camps did not necessarily improve as the war went on. Notwithstanding the repatriation of some sick and wounded chaplains in October 1943,[395] the transfer of British prisoners of war from Italy to Germany after the Badoglio armistice created another excess of chaplains in officers' camps. As a Roman Catholic chaplain noted of an *oflag* at Rottenburg towards the end of that year, there were 'over twenty chaplains' among its 450 inmates. Furthermore, it was not until the summer of 1944 that the Germans were persuaded to allow some of these chaplains 'to go to other camps where they were needed'.[396]

If a degree of under-employment was inevitably the lot of many chaplains in captivity, on the whole the Germans and Italians (who had ratified the Geneva Convention) respected its requirements that prisoners of war be allowed to practice their religion and that they should have access to ministers of their own faith. In fact, the German and Italian authorities seem to have allowed many chaplains a good deal of latitude in their spiritual and pastoral work among prisoners. Chaplains at *Stalag* XX A at Thorn, for example, were able to pay extended visits to working parties in the surrounding countryside and chaplains captured at Tobruk in June 1942 were slowly but purposefully distributed among soldiers' camps in southern Italy.[397] Naturally, and as foreseen by Article 16, gatherings of prisoners for religious services did require a measure of supervision on behalf of the captive power, this supervision usually taking the form of the censorship of sermons and addresses. As standing orders issued at *Oflag* VII B at Eichstatt in September 1942 stated:

> Church services, sermons, religious addresses, and other religious activities (e.g. bible classes, field services) may only be held with the permission of the Commandant. The S.B.O. [the senior officer among the prisoners] will ask for permission in good time. Processions are forbidden in the camp. In the case of services with [a] sermon a copy of the sermon will be handed in to the [commandant's office] three days in advance. (For burial sermons one day in advance). The approved text will in no way be altered . . . An interpreter from the [commandant's office] must be present at every religious service or gathering. If, during such a service or gathering the foregoing regulations are infringed, the interpreter must stop the service (sermon etc.)[398]

Although chaplains rarely used religious services for calculated shows of defiance, camp authorities could sometimes show an excess of zeal. In one *oflag*, a Protestant service was interrupted after the hymn *Glorious things of thee are spoken* was inadvertently sung to the tune of the Austrian national anthem.[399] Similarly, in 1943, a Methodist chaplain was exiled to a miserable sub-camp of *Stalag* IV B after preaching 'a series of sermons on social justice, based on Amos and Hosea' which were afterwards deemed subversive.[400]

However, in their treatment of chaplains the German and Italian authorities generally adhered to the terms and spirit of the Geneva Convention, a position that suggests that chaplains were not viewed as significant threats to camp discipline or as potential escapees.[401] Significantly, some chaplains seem to have capitalised on the opportunities that captivity afforded. Paul Guinness spent much of his captivity hatching grandiose schemes for a global 'Christian revolution' that would involve the formation of a new 'Christian World Council' (to work 'side by side with a World Council of Nations'), the creation of 'an international news service' and the establishment of an 'International City' (complete with a 'Cathedral of all Nations') to support these endeavours. These schemes were published shortly after the war in *We Pledge Our Lives: A Post-War Manifesto from a war-time prison*.[402] In more concrete terms, when George Forster, a Roman Catholic chaplain, was transferred to an Italian camp for other ranks near Ancona, he entered an almost idyllic quasi-parochial existence. For several months previously the Roman Catholic prisoners had been well looked after by an English-speaking Italian priest and the experience 'was like coming into a well-established parish . . . It was a pleasant place for a Catholic chaplain, and results were very encouraging.'[403] Similarly, Douglas Thompson, a Methodist chaplain captured in North Africa in the summer of 1942, discouraged hopes of escape in the belief that his overriding duty lay in preparing his fellow prisoners for the challenges of the post-war world. Indeed, with respect to the ill-fated 'Great Escape' from *Stalag Luft* III at Sagan in March 1944, Thompson even wrote that:

> [The] padre, strangely enough, could almost be glad that [the Germans] did win. He was in a position very like that of Jeremiah, the Old Testament hero who spent a lifetime preaching an apparently treacherous policy of letting the enemy win the round in order that the Jewish people might win the game . . . I became convinced that England would get the best dividend from her captives, over their whole lifetime, if the men could work through their individual problems and develop the qualities which battle had revealed to them within themselves. I was sure that the returning prisoner could make a unique contribution to society if his camp had been his university. So often escape meant plunging back into activity with a host of unsolved problems, bedded more deeply in the mind. To conquer the life within the wire and oneself while behind it – this was the big thing.[404]

Although the chaplain's accustomed role of entertainments officer was in retreat during the Second World War, it seems to have paid dividends behind barbed wire, where the recreational needs of prisoners were acute and morale was liable to be low. In view of the fact that Article 27 of the Geneva Convention meant that officers in German and Italian hands were not obliged to work, the problem of whiling away months and years of captivity was most severely felt in officers' camps. Partly because of this double-edged privilege, libraries, theatres and even *ad hoc* universities flourished in the closed environment of the *oflag*.[405] At *Oflag* VII C in 1940, an inflated cadre of chaplains was the moving force behind the creation of 'Oflag VII C University'. As G.F. Miller recalled, from a series of simple lectures on the Bible:

> [A] whole lecture programme developed. Language classes were started, a course on Christian Ethics, and finally, with the help of the Chaplains of Peterhouse and Eton, a series of lectures was arranged to cover the whole day from eight to eight, six days a week . . . At one time lectures and classes were offered on over eighty different subjects, from Arabic to

> Logic, from Pure Mathematics to How to Lay Down a Cellar – anything to distract the mind from present circumstances, which at first were grim enough.[406]

This phenomenon was repeated across much of the German and Italian camp system. Arthur Royall, an officer of the 1st Border Regiment who was captured at Arnhem in September 1944, remembered that among the organised recreations available at *Oflag* 79 was a Theological Society and that he began his own studies in divinity 'under the tutorship of one of the eight Anglican Chaplains' in the camp.[407] For Douglas Thompson (who was quite happy to view prison camps as faculties of the university of life) P.G. 70, an Italian other ranks' camp near San Giorgio, became the venue for scriptural study circles, public lectures and seminars on practical Christianity.[408] Even in the Far East in the immediate aftermath of the fall of Singapore, theological courses were inaugurated in the island's prisoner-of-war camps. As the captive A.C.G. Far East put it, 'University Schemes were started in Southern Area and 18th Div[ision]. In each a Theological Faculty was incorporated and a full course of instruction [was] given by chaplains.' Twenty-four prospective ordinands attended these courses and many other prisoners also 'attended the lectures for instructional purposes'.[409]

Nevertheless, in marked contrast to the situation that prevailed in German and Italian camps, freedom of worship and access to chaplains was not automatically granted to British prisoners in the Far East because Japan had not ratified the Geneva Convention. Indeed, the Japanese attitude towards chaplains was capricious to say the least. On the Burma-Thailand railway, the prevailing mood could be very uncooperative. Malcolm Cowin, a Roman Catholic chaplain, reported that:

> The Japanese policy regarding religion was much the same at Nong Pladuk [in Thailand] as at other Camps in which I have been stationed. There has never been any question of freedom of worship; that has been forbidden. Services for the most part have been restricted to once a week and Sunday was not allowed as a Camp holiday. For long periods and with no explanation Services were forbidden, and when, with the greatest difficulty, permission was obtained to recommence them, sermons were prohibited . . . Although I made application scores of times to be allowed to visit adjoining camps where there were no Roman Catholic ministers to minister to the men, such permission was always refused, with no explanation and often rudely. With the result that hundreds of Catholics died denied the Sacraments, the supreme consolation of their faith, and burial by the priest . . . At a time when morale was low and full freedom of worship would have been of incalculable value, the Japanese went out of their way to obstruct chaplains in their work. They were indifferent to every kind of pleading. Throughout their captivity the prisoners of war were starved – starved of food – starved of clothing – of medical supplies – of news – of letters from home and starved of spiritual consolation.[410]

However, Henry Babb, an Anglican, found that his services at Chungkai were only obstructed in 1944 as the war in South-East Asia began to turn against the Japanese.[411] While the Japanese authorities at Singapore routinely forbade public prayers for the King or for the Allies,[412] in contrast to the situation in the labour camps on the notorious 'railway of death', Lewis Victor Headley thought that their outlook was generally 'one of complete indifference':

> [T]hey didn't care what you did as long as there was no order against it. You could hold services at any time you liked provided that it hadn't been forbidden by the higher authorities . . . Only on one occasion did we have an interdict and that was at Christmas [1943] when we'd come down to Sime Road [Camp] . . . But then I had a service in the Sime Road Chapel and we had scouts placed around the camp and they would warn us if anybody approached but nobody did and so our services went on unhindered.[413]

Besides difficulties with their captors, captive chaplains also faced problems of an internal kind. Often thrown together in large numbers and without guidance from the army or their own churches, under-employed chaplains did not necessarily discover fellow feeling in misfortune. For G.F. Miller, a Baptist chaplain who found himself in charge of thirty other chaplains in *Oflag* VII C in 1940, the experience proved something of a trial:

> Individually they were mostly good fellows, but collectively they were the most awkward team imaginable. They illustrated the ancient jibe about the relative merits of the clergy when spread abroad over the land and when gathered together in a heap. We were certainly gathered in a heap, and I attribute my sudden access of grey hair in the early forties to this experience.[414]

Even in the much harder conditions of the Far East, mutual antagonisms could still thrive. In Changi prison camp at Singapore, G.J. Chambers helped to while away the months by sparring with his Anglo-Catholic and Low Church colleagues over the manner of public worship, a battle that he faithfully recorded in his diary of captivity.[415]

If peace between padres did not always obtain, there were also difficult moral challenges to confront. Lengthy and indefinite separation from wives and families had a debilitating effect upon prisoners and, although the army had developed its own system of welfare officers, this was not available to the other ranks in captivity. Consequently, chaplains were on hand to witness the disintegration of numerous marriages. As W.A. Lathaen wrote to his bishop in 1944, family bereavements were difficult enough but far worse was news of a wife's infidelity. As Lathaen saw it, 'the most difficult and fullest part' of his work at *Stalag* XX A lay in 'assisting and advising a man who has received news of the infidelity of his wife, or a request to end the marriage because his wife has fallen in love with another man, or a report that his wife is conducting herself in a way not befitting a married woman'. In the space of fifteen months he had dealt with seventy men who had come to him for help and advice, help that involved 'long and intimate talks' with individuals who varied greatly 'in their upbringing and mental and emotional outlook'. Given the relaxation of divorce laws in England and Scotland in 1937 and 1938,[416] Lathaen found himself dispensing legal advice and assisting in divorce litigation – hardly a congenial task for an Anglican clergyman.

Although he sought to save marriages by counselling forgiveness or delay he found that 'The average man brings the letter and on the spot demands a divorce . . . after you have explained the various points and suggested possible ways to deal with his trouble, he leaves it entirely in your hands. Their confidence in you is rather embarrassing at times.'[417] For many chaplains, the emotional torment of prisoners and its troubling consequences was compounded by worrying indicators of sexual frustration and sexual deviancy. Douglas Thompson observed that 'Men were troubled by sexual fantasy, their dreams and day-dreams nagged at them. In the camp entertainments a Rabellaisian impurity gave both the outward symbols of what was going on and some vehicle for draining away this pent-up emotion.'[418] At Colditz, the language and behaviour of fellow prisoners also proved disconcerting for another Methodist chaplain. In April 1941, Joseph Ellison Platt confided in his diary that:

> Since the beginning of March homosexualism has occupied an increasingly large place in contemporary prison humour, and jocular references to masturbation are freer than is usual among healthy-minded adults. The arrival of a quantity of Oscar Wilde and Frank Harris literature has given a certain piquancy and openness to the discussion of perverse sexualism.[419]

Problems Old and New

Although Second World War chaplains have not incurred the same level of criticism as their forbears of the First World War, this is not to say that their role was any less sensitive or problematic. One controversial issue that rumbled on throughout the years of the Second World War was the army's regime of compulsory religious worship. This regime, which had been upheld in the British army and its forbears since the seventeenth century,[420] was inextricably associated with the custom of church parades and it was still being enforced under King's Regulations of 1940.[421] Significantly, the church parade and all it represented (namely religious coercion, additional spit-and-polish and the loss of half of the Sabbath) had been the subject of criticism and complaint among regular soldiers since the Victorian era and their complaints were echoed by many of the volunteers and conscripts of the First World War – and in particular by those Nonconformist soldiers who wished to uphold a voluntary approach to religion.[422] Indeed, when C.J. Simmons mounted his abortive attempt to reform the Chaplains' Department in 1931 he claimed to be motivated by a twofold desire 'to register my protest against the linking up of religion and war, and against compulsory church parades'.[423]

Although the controversy over church parades seemed 'almost a hardy annual' by 1941,[424] by 1942 the overall situation had placed the very principle of compulsion under threat. Not only was there a new and acute sensitivity to the mood and morale of ordinary soldiers but chaplains themselves were deeply divided over the issue. Ironically, even the potential benefits to morale that could be derived from rousing parade services could be achieved through the more informal (but still compulsory) 'Padre's Hour'. The dilemmas of the time were reflected in the public and private opinions of Ronald Selby Wright. In one of his earliest radio discussions entitled 'Should Church Parades Be Compulsory?' he aligned himself firmly with the conservatives, invoking the sacredness of the national cause and claiming that church parades were a concrete expression of the Christian civilisation which the nation was fighting to preserve:

> [T]he Army is part of the Forces of the Crown; and the King is King of a country which holds (though we all wish it were more often practised) that the service of God IS the most important part of life – which is the big reason (incidentally) why we're at war with a Hitler who, given his own way, wouldn't allow you to be a Christian.[425]

However, away from the microphone Selby Wright's views were rather different. In July 1942, he wrote in his diary, 'I told [Padre] Murray that I had come to the conclusion that the best way for religion in the Army is to have compulsory Padres' Hours [and] voluntary services on Sundays, and he agreed.' Later that year, while serving as S.C.F. of the 52nd (Lowland) Division, he persuaded the divisional commander to dispense with church parades but to require its soldiers 'to go to the Church of their denomination'.[426]

Although the Army Council had issued a general order in 1941 upholding the principle of compulsion and declaring its 'profound conviction of the value of religious inspiration as a source of spiritual and moral strength in the present conflict',[427] at a local level there was already a drift towards more pragmatic solutions. This 'sensible compromise in accordance with local conditions', as the Chaplain-General chose to describe it,[428] was often dictated by practical considerations, namely the number of units or soldiers involved and the size of available churches. Even before the war, limited space in some garrison churches meant that units at larger stations could only send a proportion of their men to parade services on any given Sunday and thus soldiers could find themselves on church parade as rarely as one week in every three.[429] As the army expanded and reliance on civilian churches increased in the war years, more parade services had to be arranged around normal parish services – not always successfully.[430] Hence, and after thorough investigation, the Morale Committee concluded in April 1943 that religious compulsion per se was not a source of serious disgruntlement among soldiers in Great Britain. Still, at the same meeting Symons took the opportunity to argue that the most common routine (i.e. of a compulsory parade service once a month with the minimum of attendant rigmarole) should enjoy the status of official policy.[431] This hybrid solution was accepted and promulgated by the Army Council three months later, King's Regulations having nothing specific to say about the frequency of church attendance.[432] Although Symons may have seen this as the best means of preserving the principle of compulsion, it is significant that there was no consensus over this issue in the higher reaches of the Department, Percy Middleton Brumwell having insisted in 1942 that:

> With the great moral issue at stake in this present war and the emphasis which is laid at every turn on the righteousness of the cause, it is very questionable whether the present moment should be chosen to cancel

> church parades or even make them voluntary. The effect of such cancellation would undoubtedly mean to the men and women of this country and other countries that this land has loosened its determination and lost its desire to uphold the religious basis on which our greatness in the past has been based.[433]

While the First World War saw no precursor of this tortured and wide-ranging debate over parade services, there were other problems which the generation of 1914–18 would have been all too familiar with. As in the First World War, it proved a difficult task for chaplains to rise above the secularising influence of their milieu and the brutalising experience of war. On the former count, between 1939 and 1945 chaplains showed the same inclination to dispense with the uniform of their Department in favour of that of their host units. E.M. Claxton remembered that, during the 'Phoney War', the Church of Scotland chaplain attached to the 1st Cameron Highlanders sported a kilt – 'which was strictly forbidden by the Royal Army Chaplains' Department but nobody else worried about it'.[434] Similarly, in June 1943 the chaplains of the 1st Armoured Division even requested that they be allowed to wear the beret of the formation to which they were attached, citing this as a widespread practice in other divisions.[435] Moreover, and despite some concerns to ensure that the war in Europe and North Africa did not degenerate into a squalid campaign of revenge against the Germans,[436] many front-line chaplains fully identified themselves with the unforgiving outlook of the front-line soldier. For Bill Cook of the 1st Derbyshire Yeomanry, the surrender of Axis forces in Tunisia in 1943 prompted a flow of belligerent letters to his fiancé using captured Axis stationery. In a moment of hesitant self-reflection he then wrote: 'I seem to have written a lot of silly and bellicose letters in a very exultant strain lately. I hope you won't be cross at all those Jerry and Italian field post cards and things I've sent you. Please, I don't like war really . . .'[437] Although Cook's pilfering and posturing were relatively trivial matters, as Senior Chaplain of 6th Armoured Division Geoffrey Druitt admitted to sharing in the soldier's pervasive 'lust for booty' towards the end of the Tunisian campaign. He also shared a common, and exaggerated, disdain for the martial qualities of the Italians, noting of one soldier in his diary: 'The nerves of our crew are getting very strained. Sitting under shelling and giving nothing nor fighting back is not easy. The [corporal] is an Italian on [his] father's side and shows it.'[438]

If some chaplains sought the spoils of war, others were irresistibly drawn to the thrill of action. During the 'Phoney War', and in flagrant violation of the Geneva Convention, Eric Gethyn-Jones carried a pistol while out on patrol with the men of the 5th Gloucestershire Regiment.[439] Similarly, during the bitter and confused fighting in and around Arnhem in September 1944, at least two chaplains of the 1st Airborne Division assumed the role of combatant officers, issuing tactical orders to the men of their respective battalions.[440] In the still more unforgiving context of the Burma campaign, chaplains were effectively obliged to carry arms as a matter of policy as the Japanese seemed unconstrained by the accepted rules of war. In this case, a universal loathing of the Japanese meant that the phenomenon of the armed chaplain met with approval rather than censure. Nevertheless,

George MacDonald Fraser of the 9th Border Regiment felt that the practice came more naturally to some chaplains than to others:

> I wondered then, and I wonder now, what the Church of England's policy was about padres who put themselves in harm's way; giving comfort to the wounded and dying, fine, but ethical problems must surely arise if Jap came raging out of a bunker into his reverence's path; the purple pips on the chaplain's shoulder wouldn't mean a thing to the enemy . . . And if a padre shot a Jap, what would the harvest be – apart from three ringing cheers from the whole battalion? In my own Church, the highly practical Scottish one, it would doubtless be classed as a work of necessity and mercy, but I wasn't sure about the Anglicans.[441]

In fact, he need not have worried, for extant 'Hints and Suggestions for Chaplains serving in the Burma theatre of war' stated that:

> It is regretted that conditions of war should produce the necessity for Chaplains to carry arms. Many Chaplains doubted the wisdom of this until such time as they gained first hand experience of the Japanese. Carrying a revolver is hardly sufficient because few people place any reliance upon this weapon except for work of very close range. It is only in exceptional circumstances that a Chaplain needs the use of firearms and on these occasions a rifle would prove the best form of protection. Defence of casualties or one's own protection should be the only reasons for the carrying of arms . . . The enemy is certainly no respecter of persons.[442]

Under this dispensation, the role of chaplains in this theatre of war became very much that of the soldier-priest. While E.M. Claxton's weapons of choice were a revolver and a Sten gun, A.H. Rodgers (an I.E.E. chaplain attached to the 2nd Border Regiment in 1944) learnt to appreciate that hand grenades were 'good things in [an] emergency'. During the battle of Imphal later that year, the wisdom of the prevailing pragmatism was brought home to Rodgers when he shot and killed a Japanese soldier who attacked him during an ambush.[443]

In addition to the perennial question of the bearing of arms, the issue of transport also returned to haunt chaplains. Notwithstanding the much greater availability of motorcars and motorcycles on unit establishments, transport problems could be even worse than in the First World War. As Frederick Llewelyn Hughes acknowledged:

> For some strange reason the chaplains, alone amongst the Services of the army, have no proper [inventory of equipment]. A chaplain is entitled only to a field communion set of an unsatisfactory pattern, and to a vehicle, often unsuitable, on a unit or formation [establishment], which may or may not be obtained for him, and which some C.O.s regard as fair spoil when the unit is short of transport.[444]

Although the culture of Eighth Army ensured that its chaplains were well provided for by 1944 (many by this time having the use of trucks equipped with wireless sets, harmoniums and petrol cookers)[445] earlier in the war chaplains often had to fight for their rights. When chaplain to a machine-gun battalion on the south coast of England in 1940–1, Bill Phillips found that his car had been 'handed over to the medical officer' and the 'transport question' also proved a source of difficulty for the senior chaplain in Northern Ireland at this time.[446]

Besides the uncertain availability of transport, there was also thc qucstion of the ground to be covered. In 1914–18, static warfare on the Western Front had served to concentrate large numbers of troops into forward areas. However, the situation at home and overseas during the Second World War could be much less favourable. In Great Britain, anti-aircraft sites and other military installations were often very widely scattered; one Anglican chaplain of an anti-aircraft division, who travelled around 31,000 miles by motorcar in a span of eighteen months,[447] recalled that 'at one period I had an area to cover which took in the whole of two English dioceses and part of five others, with over one hundred and thirty detachments of troops for whom to provide material and spiritual necessities'.[448] While the geographical and pastoral isolation of these units helped to inspire the 'Radio Padre' initiative, they were also periodically visited by their allocated chaplains, men who could never hope to exert more than an occasional and passing influence upon them. As Fraser McLuskey, a Church of Scotland chaplain attached to Northern Command, remembered, 'Here I learned what a soulless business it is being a chaplain on a strictly denominational basis to about fifty different units of every type and description scattered throughout one's district; how very exacting it was, how exhausting and depressing and, at times, how rewarding.'[449] In North Africa and the Middle East, lengthy supply lines and the fluid nature of mobile warfare in the desert could prove an even greater problem. As D.C.G. of Middle East Command in January 1942, A.J. Wilcox was responsible for Libya, Egypt, Palestine, Iraq, Iran and Eritrea – with Malta being added to his jurisdiction that April.[450] Joseph Stapleton, the senior Roman Catholic chaplain in the Middle East from 1941 to 1944, wrote that, under desert conditions, even his brigade chaplains were seriously over-stretched and that 'meeting with a Catholic chaplain in the prevailing conditions in the desert was often a matter of pure luck'.[451]

As in earlier times, chaplains also had the thankless task of leading the perennial fight against promiscuity and venereal disease, a role that was not helped by the moral inconsistencies of military policy towards these related problems. During the months of the 'Phoney War', for example, the military authorities in France once again connived in a system of regulated brothels, an approach that was encouraged by a spectacular surge in hospital admissions for venereal disease after the arrival of the B.E.F. in France.[452] While the army was prepared to be pragmatic in order to combat the spread of V.D., it nevertheless expected its chaplains to encourage purity and restraint. The tensions inherent in this dual approach were obvious. In June 1940 the Bishops' War Committee learned that 'Under Army Council instructions, during the first four weeks' service of every recruit, 40 minutes of every week is allotted to the Chaplain's lectures on moral subjects', which were compulsory. However, while chaplains were also 'encouraged to attend the Medical Officer's lectures on sex subjects in order that they may know what instruction is being given' they were forbidden from making any public interventions, any reservations about the medical officer's lectures having to be aired 'in private'.[453]

Consequently, battle was joined through the preaching of sexual continence to the men and by the exertion of moral pressure upon the military authorities. In the autumn of 1939, Arthur Naylor, the D.C.G. of the B.E.F., protested against the campaign for sexual health that was taking place in the 3rd Division under the aegis of its commanding officer, who was none other than Major-General Bernard Montgomery. On this occasion, Naylor's objection resulted in a stern rebuke for Britain's future hero from Lord Gort, the Commander-in-Chief of the B.E.F., Montgomery's own divisional orders having urged the sale of contraceptives in the N.A.A.F.I. and the promotion of approved brothels among the men.[454] However, it may have been an indication of Montgomery's growing regard for the work of his chaplains that, in 1942, he appeared to endorse their stand against vice, ordering that brothels in Egypt be placed out of bounds. As ever, concern with combating vice was based on the convergent interests of Christian morality, military efficiency and political necessity, public opinion in Britain and Egypt having grown restive at the army's apparent moral laxity.[455] In 1943, A.J. Wilcox wrote to Frederick Llewelyn Hughes noting that 'the old British public' was concerned by the high incidence of venereal disease among troops in the Middle East and warning that in 1942 'the admissions to hospital for venereal diseases . . . were higher than the admissions for battle casualties!'[456] However, the wider implications of this problem were obvious to all. As Middleton Brumwell warned from the salutary experience of the First World War:

> The 'human' instincts of men may lead a man to a moment of forgetfulness of his high calling, and his duty to his country and to his comrades. The report of the medical services in the last war makes sad reading in this respect. In the day of crisis in 1918, when the enemy broke through the line and pushed on and on . . . at that critical moment there were many thousands of men in hospital with preventable diseases . . . They were absent in that critical hour through lack of self-control.[457]

However, not all chaplains were inclined to be as strident in their condemnation of sexual misconduct. While Naylor was publicly arraigning Montgomery for encouraging vice, E.M. Claxton chose to accompany fellow officers to a brothel in Lille where, minus his clerical collar, he would sit and play the piano while keeping watch over his companions. As Claxton put it, 'I was actually very good. I didn't do anything wrong in the brothel. I used to keep my eye on them and prevent them from going upstairs. So if I saw them going upstairs I'd call them down again.' It was in order to preserve his anonymity on these jaunts that he acquired his nickname 'Gus'.[458] Other, more junior chaplains were equally pragmatic. In Italy later in the war, where venereal disease had spiralled out of control and where brothels had been placed out of bounds at the end of 1943 in order to satisfy Italian public opinion,[459] one medical officer was shocked to discover that his battalion's chaplain was distributing pornography as a means of keeping the men out of local brothels and away from the risk of infection.[460] Other chaplains simply avoided the issue. This tendency was condemned in the pamphlet *Talks to VD Patients*, a publication aimed at chaplains in India Command, where the incidence of venereal disease was the highest of all and where in 1943 it was claiming ten times more casualties than enemy action.[461] As the pamphlet's anonymous author put it:

> Today there is more immorality and loose living than there has been for a whole generation. This is proved by the enormous increase in the amount of V.D. in the armed forces. This fact alone is, in my opinion, a serious indictment of the whole Department. Our preaching and teaching has apparently been quite ineffective in the moral sphere . . . It is no use telling men that it is wrong of them to go with prostitutes, unless we tell them why. And we must tell them why *before* they go. That is what we have failed to do, because most of us have funked the issue. A few Chaplains give occasional mild doses of instruction in Sermons or Confirmation talks, but in this way they fail only too frequently to influence those who most need their help – especially in these days when the compulsory Church Parade is seldom held. A small proportion of Chaplains have given systematic teaching to their men in the Padre's Hour, which is usually the best opportunity, as it is the only occasion when they have all the men present, and on Parade . . . But there are a surprising number of Chaplains who admit that they have never tackled the subject of Sex and Morals, some of them because they do not know how to approach the subject.[462]

To be fair, this diffidence was not helped by the position of many senior officers. Although Wilcox rejoiced in the closure of brothels in Egypt and believed that the Department had 'the support of all the "top" in the matter',[463] commanding officers were often disposed to treat V.D. as a medical problem first and foremost. If chaplains were banned from publicly challenging medical officers during lectures on sexual hygiene, soldiers often received free issues of contraceptives, much to the chagrin of civilian moralists at home and despite the protests of churchmen as eminent as Archbishop Temple.[464] The problems which could arise from this approach were brought home to E.M. Claxton during his voyage to India in 1942. Prior to arrival at Cape Town, his brigadier lectured all officers on board their troop ship about the dangers of V.D. and ordered that every man leaving the ship should carry three contraceptives 'whether he likes it or not'. Although relatively liberal in these matters, Claxton joined his fellow chaplains in protesting this order, his Roman Catholic colleague being 'adamant that he would take it up with the War Office'. Consequently, the brigadier rescinded his order and made the carrying of condoms voluntary. Still, there was a sting in the tail. When the men of Claxton's battalion were paraded to receive their contraceptives, their commanding officer explained that, to spare everyone's blushes, the condoms would be placed on tables behind screens and that each man would go behind a screen and take (or not take) their allotted share. However, he concluded by announcing that 'I shall be the first to go and the padre will be the second.'[465]

The low-key approach that was adopted by many chaplains towards questions of sexual morality may also have been dictated by an appreciation of the intense emotional stress suffered by soldiers of this generation. The length of the Second World War and its protracted disruption of family life, the sheer distance of the army's main theatres of war (especially in the mid-war period), the recent liberalisation of Britain's divorce laws and the relaxed sexual mores of the war years all contributed to acute sexual and emotional problems for Britain's citizen soldiers. During the Italian campaign a distinct correlation was established between high rates of V.D. and the length of time that soldiers had spent overseas.[466] Similarly, in 1946 a chaplains' survey of more than 8,000 soldiers who had been abroad for more than three years showed 'that 6–10 per cent of the married men had reason to know their wives had been unfaithful' and, in view of those cases that remained undetected, its compilers were 'driven to the appalling conclusion that, after three years' separation, one wife in five was unfaithful'.[467]

Despite the creation of the army's own Directorate of Welfare and the institution of a system of local welfare officers,[468] the wider circumstances of the war ensured that the chaplain's responsibility for 'the moral and spiritual welfare' of the soldier resulted in a massive burden of personal welfare work. In October 1941, Charles Potts wrote to his fiancé from Cyprus:

> Yesterday a man came to see me to ask me if I could help to get him home leave – to go back to England – on compassionate grounds. His reasons being that (a) he had been away nearly a year (b) he was only 30, and he and his wife had had so little time together (c) he had recently been reported missing and this had given great anxiety and sorrow to his wife. This last clause was the only thing that could carry any weight, but even then he hadn't a hope of getting back to England on the strength of it. I hated to have to tell him so. I had to explain that there were thousands who have better reasons than he. Amongst the men here there are some of the regular Army who have had a fortnight's home leave in 8 years, having come straight from foreign service elsewhere to the Middle East at the beginning of the war. There are lots who have children that they have never seen . . .[469]

As an artillery chaplain in Italy, W.H. Humphreys also had the task of recommending soldiers for compassionate leave and, though he warmed to his role of regimental counsellor, he remembered this sphere of his work as 'a very gruelling performance'. On one occasion, he drove a sergeant across the Italian peninsula so that he could board a plane for England. The sergeant's wife and mother were suffering from cancer and both died on his way home.[470] More typically, in March 1945 Bill Cook of the 1st Derbyshire Yeomanry wrote to his fiancé from the same theatre of war:

> Today I took a laddie 50 miles there and 50 miles back to file a petition for Divorce. His wife had a child by another man last summer. He forgave her although she continued to be unfaithful. Then an airman came along and started to terrify the two real children of the family, so they have gone to our own man's parents. Now the wife is pregnant again with another man's child, what a mess . . .[471]

While individual chaplains grappled with the problem of church parade, the legitimacy of bearing weapons, the logistics of their ministry and with questions of sexual morality and personal welfare, the Department also experienced significant internal tensions. These were both military and ecclesiastical in origin. Of particular concern to senior chaplains was the lax attitude towards military discipline that was evinced by many wartime chaplains. Although this attitude was common enough among British soldiers of 1939–45, insubordination was particularly worrying among men who were charged with promoting the morale and efficiency of the army. As early as the Phoney War, 'Gus' Claxton noted the unruliness of his fellow chaplains in the B.E.F.'s 'pool of padres'; although it was under the notional command of an artillery officer, 'none of us did what we were told and he looked terrified the whole time'.[472] This disdain for military authority could take a very public form. In a transit camp in Tunisia in 1943, Spike Milligan noted the scant respect shown towards his commanding officer by the chaplain of the 56th Heavy Regiment, Royal Artillery:

> Sept. 21st 1943. This evening we collected the Camp Rubbish and lit a bonfire. We gathered around and sang (to the tune of Alouette)
> Balls to Jumbo
> Balls to Jumbo Jenkins
> Among those singing loudest is Captain Bentley, the Regimental Chaplain.[473]

Such attitudes could even flare into open rebellion. One notable rebel was Joseph McCulloch, a restless and discontented soul who had developed strong socialist leanings and strident anti-establishment views in civilian life, being the author of *A Parson in Revolt*, which was published in 1936 and for which Dick Sheppard wrote an introduction. Joining the Department from his 'semi-deserted' parish in rural Essex in October 1939, McCulloch professed to be appalled by what he saw as the 'middleclassdom' of the Church of England in the army, a cultural and social malady which he saw reflected in the chaplain's rank and its attendant privileges.[474] Frustrated in his frequent and unsuccessful petitions to serve overseas, with the help of a few sympathetic officers and other ranks he proceeded to compose a remarkable memorandum on army chaplaincy while serving as an anti-aircraft chaplain in England in the winter of 1940–1. Entitled 'NOTES ON THE CHRISTIAN SITUATION WITH PARTICULAR REFERENCE TO THE ROYAL ARMY CHAPLAINS' DEPARTMENT', he sent this memorandum to the Chaplain-General 'in order to obtain from the head of the Army Chaplains' Department his view of the matter and to learn how he resolved the dilemma which the document expressed'.[475] While critical of the organisation of the Department, the memorandum was unequivocally pacifist in tone and in content and it commenced with the statement 'It seems to me incontrovertible that the Christian Gospel enjoins absolute pacifism', sentiments that led him to be invited to resign his commission that April, an invitation that McCulloch had little choice but to accept.[476] Clearly a lone voice, his later attempt to have his memorandum published in 'a most widely circulated Church newspaper' was rebuffed by its editor.[477]

While the Chaplain-General was naturally unwilling to regard the Department as a debating society, many commanding officers also felt compelled to take a firm stand when confronted by chaplains who were prepared to take their hallowed role of the soldier's friend to new extremes. In July 1944, the Methodist and Roman Catholic chaplains of 84th General Hospital rebelled against their commanding officer over his ban on the distribution of extra cigarettes to men suspected of having self-inflicted wounds – a common and worrying disciplinary problem during the prolonged and bloody fighting in the Normandy *bocage*. As J.H. Humphries, the Methodist chaplain concerned, complained in his diary:

> It seems that every man who has a wound in his limb is suspect unless the cause is definitely known to be enemy action . . . The result is that genuine accidents bear the same label as [a] deliberately self-inflicted wound, and [it] remains so until an enquiry has been held. Also there is no distinction made, at first, between 'negligence' and 'deliberation.' As days pass before enquiries are made, many men are looked upon as criminals and who do not deserve this stigma. The C.O. particularly is guilty of this unfairness. I am *not* a soldier and know little of military law, but I do believe in the elementary principle of British jurisprudence which assumes a man to be innocent until he is proved guilty.[478]

The culmination of this rebellion was a major and unseemly row between the parties concerned. As Humphries' C.O. put it: 'I'm not going to argue . . . they are my orders and you can report me to the Chaplains' Department if you want to. It's a lot of bloody nonsense to give these men extra cigarettes to smoke when other men are fighting up at the front!' Humphries and his ally then threatened to dissociate themselves from the distribution of cigarettes altogether, to which their C.O. replied: 'I don't care a b--- what you do.'[479]

This willingness to challenge military authority on behalf of the ordinary soldier was even expressed in the national press. In February 1945, an anonymous chaplain agitated against a new leave system in Second Army that had been sanctioned by Montgomery himself, the chaplain concerned stating in a letter to *The Times*:

> Sir, – I know of nothing which has so provoked our men as the matter of [British Liberation Army] leave. Personally I feel that Field-Marshal Montgomery made a profound mistake in permitting the element of chance through his approval of the ballot instead of the normal procedure of the leave roster . . . I would suggest to Field-Marshal Montgomery that not only is a gamble ethically unsound but it is also unsound practically. Let us have no more ballots, but a return to the leave roster.[480]

Such incidents were liable to enrage regular chaplains and their response, in turn, inflamed resentment of the Chaplain-General and his minions. As the war deepened and signs of insubordination became more marked, some senior chaplains took this heavy-handedness to extremes. One of the most striking complaints levelled against the Department by J.P. Stephenson in August 1942 was that:

> At a Conference of First Army chaplains last month the Assistant Chaplain-General, a Mr Steele, expressed his loathing of indiscipline and said that he would not hesitate to shoot a chaplain who disobeyed his orders in battle. (On this I would comment, with respect, that the wording of a chaplain's commission does not authorize him to give orders.)[481]

During the Tunisian campaign of 1942–3, the battle against clerical indiscipline was waged relentlessly in Steele's First Army. Geoffrey Druitt, the S.C.F. of 6th Armoured Division, knew of one chaplain who failed to join his regiment, another who pleaded that 'he was not ordained for such work' and a third who was found 'Living in a hovel near HIR DIAHAM. He is for court martial. A great disgrace to us chaplains.'[482] A fourth delinquent was also court-martialled and sent home in disgrace after carousing with two French officers in public, a punishment that some felt was unduly severe.[483] Nevertheless, Druitt was adamant that the smack of firm discipline was essential as:

> It is often said 'A chaplain is a law unto himself' . . . This subject of discipline is a difficult one for the clergy. They are not normally accustomed to it and resent the first experience! Furthermore, coming into the Army as experienced priests, they are inclined to think that, providing they are a 'man's man', there is little, if anything, to learn. Therefore, when a [senior chaplain] puts his nose into their 'parish' with suggestions, criticisms or orders, the feeling of resentment is inevitable.[484]

The mood of the Department as a whole was not helped by the very different prospects and pay of its members. As in the First World War, regular chaplains rose very rapidly to positions of authority within the enlarged Department. J.W. Steele, for example, began the war as a Fourth Class chaplain at Winchester. However, by the summer of 1943 he was A.C.G. of Second Army and was responsible for no fewer than 680 chaplains.[485] In contrast, in April of that year the House of Commons was informed that 'the hope of promotion for a temporary chaplain who has served already for three years is extremely remote. Promotion to third class chaplains, who rank as majors, is extremely rare, and appointments as divisional chaplain go as a rule to those who joined the Service before war broke out'.[486] This picture was confirmed in December 1944, when Lieutenant-Colonel Thornton-Kemsley, M.P. for Aberdeen and Kincardine, told the House that a glance at the Army List was sufficient to show that chances of promotion were heavily stacked against the emergency chaplain.[487]

To aggravate matters, emergency chaplains were also disadvantaged in terms of pay, receiving 15s 4d per day, or 20 per cent less than regular, Territorial and even reserve chaplains. Although 15s 4d a day compared quite favourably with the pre-war incomes of Catholic priests and Free Church ministers,[488] rising costs of living served to reduce its real value, especially for older men with family responsibilities.[489] While the Bishops' War Committee protested these pay differentials in November 1941,[490] one M.P. told the House of Commons in April 1943 that the War Office had 'originally averaged the pay of a certain number of curates and upon that average decided the rate of 15s. 4d. a day for a chaplain'.[491] Nevertheless, while this situation was roundly criticised inside and outside the Department, some regular chaplains had the temerity to defend it. As Percy Middleton Brumwell argued:

> The difference leads to a certain criticism on the part of the 'emergency' chaplain. They are all doing the same work, but receiving different remuneration. But the man who foresaw the crisis and gave his word to serve,

> has assisted the department to prepare for the immediate necessities of mobilisation.[492]

However, and in contrast to the tactless position adopted by the D.C.G. at home, Frederick Llewelyn Hughes was very sympathetic towards the claims of his emergency chaplains in Eighth Army. In fact, in a circular dated April 1943, he broke the news that their pay was to be raised to 18s 2d per day after three years service and declared that 'Our representations have at last borne fruit.'[493] Still, this did not satisfy the sending churches and the first meeting of the reconvened I.A.C. in July 1943 was largely devoted to the vexed matter of pay and promotions, its members endorsing a highly critical memorandum of War Office policy that had been drawn up by the Church of Scotland's Committee on Chaplains to H.M. Forces. Although Roman Catholics were peripheral to this agitation, even Bishop Dey supported the document, observing 'that married men should not be called upon to make excessive sacrifices' and suggesting that 'a distinction should be drawn in the matter of pay between married and unmarried Chaplains'.[494] However, despite the unanimity of feeling on the I.A.C., the memorandum was rejected by the Army Council. Hence, when the I.A.C. met once again in October 1944, the Church of Scotland resumed the attack on War Office parsimony, its representative fuming that:

> In connection with the Army Council's suggestion that Chaplains in need should apply for War Service Grants, he considered that the rates of pay of Fourth Class chaplains were such that almost all of them would need to apply. Moreover, as the War Service Grants were in the nature of charity, he doubted whether Chaplains were eligible. He contrasted the Army Council's attitude towards chaplains with the high opinion which [Montgomery] had expressed regarding their work. As the proposals which the memorandum contained had been rejected, the matter was now out of his hands. He would have to report the position to the General Assembly of his Church, who might decide to submit a resolution to the Prime Minister, as they were entitled to do.

In response, Sir Frederick Bovenschen, the committee's chairman and Permanent Under Secretary of State for War, soothingly explained the position of the Army Council in relation to the wider question of armed forces pay, giving details of 'the recent increase in pay for length of service in which Chaplains would share' and drawing attention to 'the increases in family allowances for the Army generally', allowances 'which also applied to chaplains'.[495]

While conflicting standards of discipline and differentials of rank and pay provoked controversy in the Department, a further (and perhaps inevitable) source of friction were differences within and between denominations. Clearly, Anglican chaplains could still find plenty to argue about, a particular irritant for High Churchmen being the ecumenical tendencies of the unified Department. In November 1943, W.W. Bell complained to Frederick Llewelyn Hughes about the 'United Evening Service and Holy Communion' that was being held each week in Bari and flaunted in the pages of *Eighth Army News*, complaining that 'If there is no difference between ourselves and the non-conformists, then one or the other should cease to exist.'[496] While Hughes was forced to investigate these services, intra-denominational wrangling was not an Anglican preserve and it was very much to the fore when a new Senior Jewish Chaplain was required in 1944. When Dayan Gollop was pronounced 'permanently unfit for service' by a medical board in January, tensions quickly emerged between Orthodox and Reform Judaism. As Hughes reported to the War Office:

> The Jewish Chaplain who at Dayan Gollop's suggestion and with our approval . . . is acting in [his] absence is the Reverend L.I. Edgar a man of pronounced ability and great personal charm who is probably one of the most effective of the Jewish chaplains. So far as we are concerned he has already shown that he is a most efficient deputy . . . Mr. Edgar is however a Liberal Jew and a Modernist which may account for the Chief Rabbi's objection .[497]

Leslie Hardman, an Orthodox chaplain who sympathised with Edgar, remembered that '[H]e was a Reform Jew [and] the Orthodox community was annoyed when he was appointed the interim senior padre because they thought Orthodox boys would suffer but they didn't – he was wonderful.'[498] However, such opinion counted for little with the powerful Orthodox establishment and 'with the approval of the Chief Rabbi and at the request of the Jewish War Services Committee', the R.A.F.'s Senior Jewish chaplain was selected to succeed Gollop in preference to any of the army's serving Jewish chaplains.[499]

However, the most serious cause of ecclesiastical friction was the alleged failure of the unified system in 1940. Notwithstanding John Coghlan's hopes for 'a happy system of collaboration based on goodwill and mutual respect',[500] the reassertion of Roman Catholic separatism proved galling to many. As J.W. Steele put it from the perspective of the unified Department, Roman Catholics 'would never join with us' and their position was annoying 'for the simple reason that I [as an A.C.G.] had to get all the stuff with which they were to fight the war . . . and they just sort of cashed in on it without really contributing very much to the general run'.[501] Although relations between Protestant and Roman Catholic chaplains were usually amicable, their differences were compounded by further experience of Roman intransigence. Burials were a highly sensitive matter and Eric Gethyn-Jones was reported by a Roman Catholic chaplain because he had inadvertently buried a Roman Catholic soldier – 'the correct procedure was to bury the body, and then report the map reference to the nearest R.C. chaplain'.[502] In time honoured tradition, Protestant chaplains were again forbidden from using Roman Catholic churches, a great inconvenience given that, after the Norwegian debacle of 1940, the army fought most of its major European campaigns in areas that were predominantly Roman Catholic. As Frederick Llewelyn Hughes warned in *The Chaplains of the Grand Assault*:

> No R.C. Church may be used for services by any chaplain other than R.C., even though the local clergy are willing. This is ground to keep off. The first chaplain into villages and towns should automatically obtain from Town Major or O.C. Troops a suitable room or hall, mark it up 'British Church,' and leave it so marked for those who follow on. Each

succeeding chaplain improves it a bit, and we soon have decent churches of our own.[503]

While these restrictions required the construction and consecration of two 'motor-churches' for the campaign in North-West Europe,[504] they were exacerbated by the Roman Catholic position on mixed marriages. W.H. Humphreys, who served as chaplain to 17th Medium Regiment Royal Artillery in Italy, later admitted that 'there was a constant war going on' with his Roman Catholic counterpart over marriages between British soldiers and local women, with Humphreys greatly resenting the expectation that they should marry in a Roman Catholic church and bring their children up as Roman Catholics.[505]

And then there was the enduring (if mendacious) myth of Roman Catholic superiority in chaplaincy matters. One Anglican chaplain, A.R.C. Leaney, was stung when *Picture Post* published an issue entitled 'The Road to Victory' in September 1944. With its cover featuring a Roman Catholic chaplain and the caption 'FRONT LINE PADRE – Round the corner is the war; the Padre encourages the men who are going in'[506] Leaney felt that such coverage belittled the work of Anglican chaplains. As Leaney wrote to his wife the following month:

> That Picture Post padre was the RC one of this brigade. He was very annoyed – most of [the photographs] taken when he didn't know. He is a grand chap, but I was privately very vexed at the usual base implications that the C of E's are *not* 'front-line padres'. The photos were really taken well behind the line (I know exactly where) and the C of E padre is not on the photos because he was *in* the front line (C of E padre being someone you know very well!!) . . . Fr. Fisher has had plenty of front-line experience, but that was not it in those damn fool photos. Our SCF made a complaint about the stupidity of it all.[507]

The Reckoning

Despite their manifold problems, chaplains appear to have inspired much less criticism in the Second World War than in the First. In part, this was due to the fact that even front-line chaplains eschewed the visceral belligerence of many of their forbears. While this may have been a function of the less militaristic temper of this generation, it also appears to have been a lesson learnt from the First World War. Significantly, in the very first weeks of the war Harry Blackburne had warned chaplains against stoking 'feelings of hate'. Instead, he declared in *Clergy in War-Time*:

> As I write, my son starts out on active service at the Front as chaplain. May he and all his fellow chaplains be real pastors of their flocks, and may their ministrations give courage and comfort to those who are fighting in a cause which is manifestly just . . . A chaplain's task is to preach the gospel, and an integral part of that gospel is the message of love – love for what is just and true, love for freedom and honour, and love even for those against whom we are fighting, and with whom some day we hope to be friends.[508]

While these sentiments were not necessarily applied to the Japanese, they do appear to have set the tone of the Department's approach to the war against Germany and Italy. Despite the position of A.J. Wilcox (viz. 'Up with the Empire and sock the Boche!')[509] and the exalted and even florid rhetoric of Frederick Llewelyn Hughes, it is notable that even Hughes stressed the themes of righteousness, strength, unity and sacrifice above the iniquities of Nazi Germany and the depravity of the enemy. Similarly, although accused of threatening to shoot his own chaplains, J.W. Steele took a much softer approach to the Germans. Indeed, his fears that the campaign in North-West Europe might degenerate into a squalid campaign of revenge prompted him to request a Second Army service of dedication prior to the cross-Channel invasion, a service that was duly held just before D-Day.[510] This determination to limit the brutalisation of war proved less invidious for the Department and, in combination with the other functions of the chaplain, it proved more consoling for soldiers themselves. While serving with the 12th King's Royal Rifle Corps in Normandy in August 1944, Bill Deedes wrote to his wife:

> This evening our padre, a fine example of living Christianity, who spends his time under fire collecting wounded, came round. We had a short memorial service for some of B company, whom we couldn't recover the other day, and I'm pleased to say every man in the company turned up voluntarily . . . We sang *Abide With Me* and the padre preached a short sermon on 'though I walk through the shadow . . .' Like all simple things, it was impressive and did us good. He begged us again not to allow close contact with the dead and death breed familiarity or cease to be shocked – an appropriate request. In an effort to prevent oneself from getting unduly emotional, I fear, one treats these things as a matter of course. It's horrid but inevitable.[511]

As this letter indicates, the ministry of front-line chaplains was widely and sincerely admired and not least because of its evident risks. One hundred commissioned chaplains died at home or in active theatres of war between September 1939 and August 1945. Of these fatalities, sixty-nine were due to enemy action. While this figure includes six chaplains who died in captivity and one (R.H. Whitrow, the D.A.C.G. of London District, who was killed when a V-1 flying bomb fell on the Guards' Chapel in June 1944) the majority of these were killed in action or died of wounds received in the field.[512] Significantly, overall losses were proportionate to the number of fatalities suffered by the British army during the Second World War.[513] This convergence was very clearly marked during the campaign in North-West Europe in 1944–5, where twenty-four chaplains were killed as a result of enemy action and 30,276 British soldiers were killed or died of wounds.[514] During the fighting in Normandy, where the daily rate of Allied losses exceeded those of the British army at Passchendaele in 1917,[515] the 43rd Division alone lost three chaplains killed.[516]

Nevertheless, it was symptomatic of a rather different relationship between chaplains and military authority that the shower of awards received by chaplains in the First World War was not repeated in the Second. Only 101 Military Crosses and bars were awarded to members of the R.A.Ch.D. between July 1940 and

February 1946, less than half the number of M.C.s given to Anglican chaplains alone during the First World War.[517] Despite at least one recommendation,[518] no V.C. was awarded to a serving chaplain and the most generous acknowledgments of distinguished service in the field appear to have been two immediate D.S.O.s awarded to chaplains in Burma and North-West Europe.[519] This apparent lack of recognition perplexed and even embarrassed some senior chaplains. Ivan Neill, who served as S.C.F. of 43rd Division in Normandy, wrote:

> In Normandy [a staff officer] asked me if there were any chaplains I wished to recommend for decoration or award whose work had been outstanding. I replied that all had given of their best. Had any carried in wounded under fire? I asked how many times a day did he mean?[520]

Although Neill discovered 'that every chaplain had been recommended for decoration by his commanding officer and their brigadiers', he then learnt that:

> Awards were given to Brigades for allocation and they were normally divided between regiments, so the chaplains did not 'fit' into the scheme [and] brigadiers, all of whom spoke to me of their chaplains, did not feel entitled themselves to reduce an allocation to regiments in favour of chaplains . . . By the end of hostilities it was decided that Commander in Chief's Certificates should be given to outstanding personnel who had not been recognised by decoration or award, and this and Mentions in Despatches became the only other 'recognitions' which the chaplains received.[521]

Still, recognition could come in other ways. Besides front-line troops, prisoners of war were also liable to hold their chaplains in high regard and this was particularly true of British soldiers in Japanese hands, especially during the building of the Burma–Thailand railway. In this instance, by assuming their role of moral leadership and their mantle of the soldier's friend, many chaplains earned great respect in an invidious context where officers could be resented for the policy of 'limited co-operation' that was widely adopted and for the better pay they received for their labour, pay that increased their own prospects of survival.[522] One private of the 2nd Argyll and Sutherland Highlanders said of Henry Babb: 'He was an exceptionally good Padre . . . He tried to stop a lot of beatings going on and took a lot of punishment.'[523] Similarly, Lieutenant-Colonel Philip Toosey of the 135th Field Regiment, Royal Artillery, said of Malcolm Cowin:

> The man who inspired us all at the camps I was in was a Roman Catholic Jesuit priest called Father Cowin . . . He always wore his robes, he got badly beaten up, he wasn't in any way dogmatic but he was there all the time, to help us when we were in distress. He was really quite wonderful.[524]

Likewise, John Franks, a sergeant in the Royal Army Service Corps, remembered two chaplains who also sought to protect their fellow prisoners. E.W.B. Cordingly 'fought unceasingly for better treatment for the men' and was often beaten for his pains. In fact, such was Cordingly's standing that 'when one of us decided that Padre Cordingly deserved recognition . . . we went through a mock ceremony and elevated him to "Bishop" – after this he was always known as the "Bish" '. The other was J.N. Duckworth, whose example proved inspirational during the long trek through Thailand to the base camp at Songkurai:

> The physical stamina and strength of us all was taxed to the limit, therefore it was all the more remarkable that our 'pint sized' Padre was able to cover far more ground than any of us . . . He was always at hand to help where help was needed and his encouragement went a long way to ensure that the weaker ones in the column kept up with the party and in fact completed the journey.

Later, following an outbreak of cholera at the camp, Duckworth was kept in a pit for several days without food after protesting the failure of the Japanese to take effective precautions against the disease. Duckworth was, in Franks' view:

> [T]he finest example of a minister of the church that I have met in my lifetime. He also showed extreme courage when confronted by the brutality of the Japanese and was completely without fear, his only thought was the interest of the men and many owe their lives to him.[525]

However, chaplains also evoked a positive response from troops in much easier circumstances. In June 1943, a Mass-Observation report was prepared which explored the attitudes of troops towards 'The Chaplain to the Forces'. Based largely on the findings of a questionnaire circulated to male and female personnel who were 'not as yet on active service', the report acknowledged that chaplains faced considerable problems in their ministry to home camps. Not only were they plagued by a lack of resources and by incessant postings and re-postings, they were also dealing with a complete cross-section of British society; furthermore, their rank was an added encumbrance, constraining their 'off-duty work' of mixing with the men in their huts and canteens 'where informal advice and information plays so much part'. However, while it was recognised that chaplains were set apart by their 'different attitude of thought' and often by their 'strange language', it was stressed that they were 'almost universally respected as sincere' and that there was a general consensus that they were 'clean-living men who are genuinely trying to do a good job of work'. Furthermore, it was acknowledged that 'the men who criticise the chaplains have no idea of exactly what they expect from them' and that 'Active Service conditions' were liable to 'show considerable variation' on the evidence from home.[526]

While Montgomery declared himself to be very pleased with his chaplains' 'magnificent work' in July 1945,[527] other plaudits came from very different quarters. Army chaplaincy was paid the flattery of imitation when it served as the inspiration for industrial chaplaincy in post-war Britain and for the pioneering work of the Sheffield Industrial Mission, which was inaugurated in 1944 with the appointment of the first industrial chaplain by the Bishop of Sheffield, Leslie Hunter.[528] Furthermore, it was with the professed desire to finally 'liberate the chaplains as well as their congregations' that Labour M.P.s moved for the abolition of church parades in the House of Commons in March 1946. In this case, its advocates were careful to emphasise that this in no way reflected upon the work of chaplains themselves. As Tom Driberg put it:

> I should like to pay tribute in passing to the courage and good work of the chaplains. They have served splendidly during the war, they have been in action on land, on sea, and in the air, and for the first time, in this late war, we have had the remarkable example of chaplains flying with airborne troops and being dropped by parachute . . . They have undoubtedly shown a terrific example of courage and devotion, and I should be the last to subscribe to any suggestion for abolishing the institution of the Service chaplain as such.[529]

Labour's Secretary of State for War, Jack Lawson, concurred:

> It is quite true . . . that the padre has reached a very high standard . . . He has, for instance, shown great courage . . . The padre has also done good work in welfare, and I have heard some striking stories of how padres, when they have been in prisoner-of war camps, have helped to keep up the morale of the men and to inspire them under the most difficult circumstances [and] we shall try to maintain as far as we can the high standard attained during the war.[530]

Summary

The Royal Army Chaplains' Department seems to have emerged very creditably from the Second World War. With the basis of its wartime expansion already laid down, the Department was able to meet the army's immediate requirements for chaplains on the outbreak of war. Thereafter, and although the Anglicans and the Roman Catholics had chronic difficulty in meeting their recruitment targets, the terms of its emergency commissions enabled the Department to grow while avoiding the indiscriminate haemorrhaging of experience that was so characteristic of 1914–18. Furthermore, the unified Department developed an effective system of initial training, one that was reinforced by an ongoing routine of conferences and retreats and which even embraced battle schools by 1944. Besides their perennial obligation to conduct religious services for the troops, chaplains inherited a wide variety of non-regulation functions from earlier times. Thus, they sought to accommodate the army's recreational needs, they took their positions in the front line and they took their stand against immorality and vice – albeit with different approaches and with varying degrees of enthusiasm. Furthermore, from 1940 their accepted role as morale raisers was heightened by the experience of repeated defeats and by the need to foster among the nation's citizen soldiers the fighting spirit that victory required, an imperative that eventually told against their more frivolous recreational functions. However, there were other new developments during the war years. The need to enhance morale and motivation fuelled the meteoric rise of the informal 'Padre's Hour' while also, rather ironically, dictating a retreat from the army's hallowed tradition of formal church parades. New forms of chaplaincy work also arose out of legal, technological and military advances since 1918. Because of early defeats, the Geneva Convention of 1929 necessitated an extensive and challenging ministry to prisoners of war, a ministry that was often greatly valued in the context of lengthy, demoralising and even brutal captivity. Furthermore, the rise of radio broadcasting in the inter-war period gave the Department an important new platform in the form of the wireless and the 'Radio Padre'. Similarly, the growing potential of airpower required a peripatetic ministry to the scattered units of Anti-Aircraft Command and, more glamorously for a privileged few, to the army's new parachute units. Finally, the growing number of female soldiers in the British army led to the creation of new female auxiliaries for chaplains in the form of chaplains' assistants, women who eventually assumed prime responsibility for the care of the A.T.S.

However, the Department encountered formidable problems in rising to the challenge of the Second World War. Firstly, in combination with the Divorce Act of 1937, its duration conspired to place an enormous burden of welfare work on the chaplain's shoulders, a burden which could be awkward in view of the litigation that often resulted. Secondly, inter-denominational tensions endured, with Roman Catholic particularism fracturing the unity of the Department in 1940 and posing problems for chaplaincy work in Roman Catholic countries throughout the war. These internal tensions were compounded by a third problem, namely a common resentment of the regular chaplains who ran the Department and also of the way in which emergency chaplains were treated by army officialdom. This widespread resentment helped to bring down the Chaplain-General, C.D. Symons, in 1944 while recommending the popular and dynamic Frederick Llewelyn Hughes, a Territorial, as his successor. While Hughes also enjoyed the vital and unqualified support of Montgomery, their celebrated partnership belies an important difference between the two World Wars with respect to chaplains and their relations with military authority. Whereas chaplains in the First World War were perhaps too prone to submit to the demands and perspectives of the military hierarchy, the mood of the Department was much less deferential and far more critical in the Second. This change of heart was reflected in issues ranging from chaplains' pay to leave entitlements and even manifested itself in cases of sheer insubordination. Nevertheless, it was a fitting reflection of their part in the 'People's War' that the army's chaplains should have emerged from the Second World War with a greater standing in the army and, it would seem, in British society than they had enjoyed since the Crimean War.

Epilogue

From Victory in Europe to the Korean War

The surrender of Germany and Japan in May and September 1945 did not lead to a slackening of chaplains' efforts or to the solution of many of their problems. In organisational terms, the most pressing issues were demobilisation and the future size and composition of the R.A.Ch.D. With the end of the war in Europe and the Far East, most chaplains shared the urge of other service personnel 'to get out of uniform and back home as soon as possible'.[1] Given that demobilisation schemes favoured age and length of service as criteria for release, 'a very large proportion' of chaplains were among those eligible for an early return to civilian life. This point did not go unnoticed by the churches or by the War Office. As early as October 1944, Sir Frederick Bovenschen, the Permanent Under Secretary of State for War, raised the possibility of short service commissions for chaplains at a meeting of the I.A.C. and proposed 'that at an appropriate time all serving chaplains should be asked if they would care to volunteer for further service when the War was over'.[2] For Anglican chaplains, the 'appropriate time' came in March 1945 when a circular letter was issued by the Bishop of Maidstone with the authority of the archbishops of Canterbury, York and Wales. While acknowledging chaplains' concerns about their families and future careers, it reminded them that it was 'essential to maintain the Ministry of the Church in the Services and in the Forces of occupation'. Hence, while pledging the Church 'to do its utmost for them' upon their release, it called for volunteers to remain in post so that demobilisation would not 'denude the Services of their Chaplains'.[3] In stark contrast, the demobilisation of the A.T.S. meant that chaplains' assistants were in no great demand and, while the formation of the Women's Royal Army Corps in 1949 served to place them on a slightly better footing, their temporary status and the drastic post-war reduction of the army's female personnel meant that only one chaplain's assistant was still serving by 1952.[4]

With regard to chaplains themselves, it was clearly understood that more than an appeal to altruism was needed to prevent an exodus from the Department at the end of the war – especially given the longstanding grievances of those holding 'emergency' commissions. In October 1944, Frederick Llewelyn Hughes wrote to Bovenschen arguing that a system of short-service commissions offered the only solution:

> I have had the opportunity of discussing with the A.C.G. of the 2nd Army the general attitude among chaplains now serving to the question of their staying on in the Army, even though they might be entitled to leave it with their individual groups. I gather from the A.C.G. that in his opinion the number of chaplains who would freely elect to stay on (under the conditions now obtaining – i.e. an emergency commission of problematic duration) is very small indeed. He thought that there were possibilities in short service commissions, provided the conditions of service were made attractive enough.[5]

However, conscious that older, beneficed clergymen were likely to return to their own livings, Hughes went on:

> If short service commissions are to be granted I think that in the main they will have to go to the chaplains who in civilian life were curates, and the length of time which they would wish to serve would, I think, depend on whether the [gratuity] was sufficient at the end of their service to enable them to face the future, at any rate for a time, without the fear of financial embarrassment.[6]

The terms for short-service commissions in the R.A.Ch.D. were promulgated in 1946. These commissions could be granted for three, four or five years 'to selected clergymen or serving chaplains' not holding regular commissions; they were granted 'for service as chaplain, 4th class' and candidates had to be under the age of forty-five.[7] By this stage, more than 2,200 chaplains had been demobilised since the end of the war while 492 chaplains, excluding the Chaplain-General, were still in the Department. Of these, 166 were regulars (an increase having been authorised in July 1945 to compensate for the demise of the pre-war system of temporary chaplains), 150 were 'emergency' chaplains still awaiting their release while the remainder were chaplains holding the new short-service commissions.[8]

While the introduction of short-service commissions helped to avert a manpower crisis, the Department still struggled to meet its post-war commitments. The end of British rule in India in 1947 added to the Department's burdens as it was accompanied by the demise of the Indian Ecclesiastical Establishment, a body of government-maintained clergymen who had been responsible for a substantial proportion of the British regular army since the Indian Mutiny.[9] On the dissolution of the I.E.E. (and of the short-lived Indian Army Chaplains' Department, which had been inaugurated in June 1945) Hughes endeavoured to recruit former Indian chaplains for the Department. However, this initiative was complicated by financial considerations arising from the fact that members of the I.E.E. were civil servants rather than military officers. As Hughes wrote in frustration:

> 1. I need as many C/E Chaplains on Short Service Commissions as can be got.
> 2. These Indian 'windfalls' should not be just thrown away.
> 3. They will not come into my basket until they know –
> (a) Do they lose their compensation if they take a Short Service

> Commission? This is a good lump sum for the younger men and they see no sense in losing it.
> (b) Do they get increment of pay for their I.A.Ch.D. service? If not, they think they can do better elsewhere. I think the R.A.F. has agreed to grant increment of pay.
> (c) If they eventually obtain a Permanent Regular Commission, will their past service count for pension?
> 4. If these points can be cleared up the doubters will decide, and I may get some. Otherwise, this source of supply will vanish.[10]

As British troops were withdrawn for service elsewhere, the independence and partition of British India put further pressure on an over-stretched Department. Although the size of the army was greatly reduced in the late 1940s, in 1949 the working ratio of chaplains was raised to 1:1,000, an adjustment that reflected the perceived needs of the army's new National Servicemen and heightened fears of war with the Soviet Union.[11] In 1953, and given the additional responsibilities accrued since the end of the Second World War, the Department's regular establishment was raised from 166 to 200 at the instigation of Victor Pike, Hughes's successor as Chaplain-General.[12] However, this was a mixed blessing as the Department was already having problems of recruitment. With the number of curates in the Church of England having fallen by more than 50 per cent between 1938 and 1948, the pool of potential recruits was severely limited and, as the Korean War drew to a close in May 1953, the Department was short of fifty-five Anglican chaplains.[13] However, the Church of Scotland was also failing to provide enough chaplains. In May 1947, its Committee on Chaplains to H.M. Forces had warned that 'There is a widespread feeling in the Church that, because the war is over, the need for Chaplains has largely disappeared.'[14] This warning evidently went unheeded for Scotland's national church was seven chaplains short of its allotment six years later[15] and was even failing to produce a sufficient number of reservists. These developments did not go unnoticed as the Cold War deepened. In his address to the General Assembly of the Church of Scotland in 1951, Field-Marshal Sir William Slim, then Chief of the Imperial General Staff, admonished:

> [I]n your Short-Service Commissioned Regular Chaplains, your full-time establishment is 12 and you have given me only 6. That is the first time, I am told, that the Church of Scotland in the whole of its history has ever fallen short of its establishment. Believe me, this is not the time to fall short. Similarly, the Regular Army Reserve and the Emergency Reserve are much below what we should have . . . I know that you pray to God that there won't be a war, but if war does come those reserve chaplains will be a vital necessity and neither you nor I ought to face not being prepared.[16]

As Slim warned, growing tension between the Soviet Union and the West, the advent of N.A.T.O. with the Washington Treaty of April 1949 and Britain's commitment to deploy more troops to Europe in the event of war required a high state of readiness. Consequently, plans for mobilisation were being discussed on the I.A.C. from as early as July 1949. The model adopted was based on a system proposed by the Chaplain-General. As Hughes explained, in order to keep friction to a minimum 'it was for the Army to decide the number of chaplains required and for the churches to select the individuals required'.[17] By February of the following year, the nomination of clergy was well advanced and the committee professed itself pleased with 'the Chaplain-General's arrangements for the provision of chaplains in the event of mobilization'.[18] In April 1951, Hughes reported that he now had complete lists 'of clergy who have a liability to recall or who are eligible for a commission in the R.A.R.O.'[19] Conscious of the problems of 1914 and 1939, these lists were carefully tended and updated at the Chaplain-General's office. At the I.A.C. meeting of June 1952, Hughes' successor explained that they 'were constantly under review', with 'annual revision lists' being sent out to the churches which 'ensured that no changes were overlooked'. With nearly 1,800 reservists of all denominations now on the books, Victor Pike even declared that 'He was satisfied that planning had now reached the point where mobilization could be effected with the minimum amount of disturbance to the churches'.[20]

As the Department adjusted to the post-war situation and readied itself for World War Three, there were nevertheless periods in which its name and even its future were in doubt. The changes wrought in defence administration by Clement Attlee's Labour government meant that a permanent Minister of Defence was appointed to co-ordinate the armed services in 1946. Subsequently, a report was prepared by the Committee on the Organisation of the Common Services concerning a united chaplaincy service for the army, the Royal Navy and the R.A.F. However, after some debate on the Army Council, in which the Department was deemed to be neither 'inefficient or extravagant' in its existing form, the matter was deferred.[21] With the Prime Minister content 'to wait until the Ministry of Defence had settled down', the government refrained from taking any further action and the threat receded.[22] However, in 1949 the I.A.C. responded positively to a suggestion that the Department's title be changed to the 'Royal Army Chaplains' Corps', a designation which would have brought it into line with the other supporting branches of the army and which Hughes felt to be 'more suited to the Chaplaincy Services than that of Department'. The committee was warned that this initiative, which probably originated in the Chaplain-General's perennial desire to enhance departmental prestige and *esprit de corps*, was confidential and that 'certain steps had to be taken before the proposed change could become effective'. In the event, it made no further progress.[23]

Although victory over Germany and Japan had been won in 1945, the army's commitments in the post-war world ensured that peace proved more elusive. In the immediate aftermath of the war in Europe, British troops fought Communist partisans in Greece and around Trieste and the occupation of Germany was soon subsumed by preparations for a possible war with the Soviet Union. The army also rapidly resumed its time-honoured role as an imperial gendarmerie, now having the thankless task of policing Britain's 'slow retreat from empire'. While it acted on behalf of its French and Dutch allies in Indochina and Indonesia immediately after the war, the army's main responsibilities from 1945 to 1953 lay in India, Egypt, Palestine, Malaya, Kenya and Hong Kong.[24] Furthermore, and if its European and imperial commitments were not sufficient, Britain's role as a permanent member of its Security Council added another dimension to the army's responsibilities when the U.N. came into being in October 1945. In fulfilment of its U.N. obligations, in 1950 the British army sent the best part of two brigade groups to Korea as part of the U.N. bid to support the Republic of Korea against North Korean aggression. By the end of the Korean War in 1953, more than 60,000 British soldiers had seen service in the Korean peninsula.[25]

The army's extensive global commitments were fully reflected in the deployment of chaplains by 1952, when the I.A.C. heard reports of visits by the Chaplain-General and other committee members to Japan (a forward base for the war in Korea), Hong Kong, Malaya, Germany and Korea itself. Significantly, the greatest need for chaplains was felt in Malaya, where the army was engaged in a prolonged counter-insurgency campaign against the Communist, and predominantly Chinese, Malayan Races Liberation Army. As the new Chaplain-General, Victor Pike, put it:

> On the whole, conditions in Malaya (other than Singapore and the large cities) were much harder for troops than in Korea. Usually one chaplain was attached to two infantry battalions, and when it was realized that each of these battalions was responsible for covering 80 sq. miles of jungle by means of platoon patrols which stayed in the jungle for about five days at a time, it would be appreciated that there was a very great strain on the chaplains, who could only get to know the men by accompanying patrol after patrol into the jungle. Even so, many weeks elapsed before a chaplain completed a tour of his units in this manner. The provision of more chaplains for Malaya was a matter of the utmost urgency.[26]

However, the situation was very different in post-war Germany, the European cockpit of the Cold War and the army's greatest overseas commitment. Here, the work of chaplains could go far beyond their military responsibilities. Jewish and other chaplains had already been drawn into civilian relief work with the liberation of the concentration camps at Belsen in April 1945;[27] indeed, so preoccupied were Jewish chaplains with their religious and humanitarian work among the 'last relics of European Jewry' that in June 1945 Isaac Levy (the senior Jewish chaplain in the army of occupation) had felt obliged to issue a circular 'To all ranks of the Jewish Faith' addressing the complaint 'that the chaplains have not "been doing their stuff" lately'.[28] Chaplains subsequently extended their humanitarian efforts to the German population and in August 1947 Douglas Lister, a Church of Scotland chaplain, made a national appeal for clothing parcels to help German civilians through the coming winter, warning that 'Germany now stands in a very dangerous position physically, morally, and spiritually'.[29] Nor were the needs of the German churches overlooked. In August 1945, chaplains were involved in the 'religious screening' of dozens of German clergymen held in a P.O.W. camp near Mulheim. Although deemed to be 'politically innocent' by the Intelligence Corps, their task, as A.R.C. Leaney explained it, was 'to try to judge, with as much humility as we could, whether they would, on their release, preach the gospel, and that nothing – such as resentment – finally detrimental to all of us was likely to result from their teaching'.[30]

While the screening of German clergy occupied the energies of some, a much greater challenge to chaplains in Germany lay in keeping British soldiers in check and in thus helping to rebuild civil society in the British zone of occupation. But, as Ivan Neill remembered, post-war Germany proved to be a hard battleground for the Department:

> These were terrible days for the German people and there was a spirit of forlorn despair in many devastated places . . . The general public naturally looked on us with envy and if our behaviour lacked discipline then we lost their respect. There was a sad breakdown on our part in regard to alcohol . . . especially as officers were recalled home for demobilisation . . . Each stop spelt another occasion for release celebration and the shameful result was seen in the defeated German soldiery having to carry drunken British officers onto the boats bound for the United Kingdom.[31]

The climate of moral turpitude even affected chaplains themselves. In December 1945, a chaplain and four officers attached to the Control Commission in the British zone were court-martialled at Münster for 'taking part in a raid on a German spirit store'.[32] In accordance with Montgomery's determination to crack down on looters 'whatever the rank of the individual concerned',[33] John Birnie Allan, 'chaplain and welfare officer at the commission's headquarters at Bunde, was sentenced to be dismissed the service for conduct prejudicial to good order and discipline by seizing and taking away 3,900 bottles of gin, brandy, and Kümmel from a German store'.[34] While Neill, now a D.A.C.G., persuaded Lieutenant-General G.I. Thomas to clamp down on large, drink-sodden farewell parties in I Corps District,[35] in August 1946 Geoffrey Druitt, now A.C.G. of the British Army of the Rhine, gave a searing denunciation of its general moral state. As *The Times* reported:

> A condemnation of the morals of members of the British forces in Germany and a call for Christian discipline to save Germany from becoming 'the cesspool of Europe' have been pronounced by the assistant chaplain-general, the Rev. Geoffrey Druitt.
>
> Declaring that nothing was being done for Germany's soul, and appealing for a more active Christian spirit in the Treasury and the Foreign Office, he accused a 'sad proportion' of the armies of occupation of financial exploitation and of the corruption of German women. Unless it pulled itself together the Rhine Army and members of the other British forces would leave a shameful heritage in Germany. Referring to the 'spineless indifference' to obvious opportunities and 'horrid examples of carnal lust,' the message called for a halt to low living. 'The sin of Germany is our sin; and the future of Germany is our future.'[36]

Given its experience in tackling moral degeneracy and its manifold corollaries during the war years, the Department had anticipated problems of this kind, though possibly not on this scale. In the summer of 1945 Geoffrey Druitt issued a pamphlet entitled *Occupation of Germany: plans and policy affecting the Brotherhood of Chaplains*. Based on a scheme drafted during the closing months of the war, this pamphlet sought 'to promote a vision' of the Department's post-war work. As Druitt perceived it, this work should primarily consist of an ambitious scheme of religious education in the army of occupation, a scheme that would operate through local 'Church Centres' ('consisting of a Garrison Church and Chaplain's House') and through a larger 'Church House' in each corps district.[37] While garrison churches could be shared with the local population, requisitioned 'for the exclusive use of British military personnel' or adapted from 'other suitable premises',[38] the chaplain's house was to have a 'homely aspect' and was to be equipped with 'a small library, a writing room, games room and chapel'. Thus provided for, it could serve as a 'workshop' for the chaplain and would prove an 'invaluable' venue 'for making personal contacts, holding discussion groups, evening prayers, instruction classes and padre's hours etc.'[39] 'Church Houses', on the other hand, would be much larger facilities – 'requisitioned hotels (or similar premises)' – capable of accommodating residential courses of several dozen people. Thanks to Montgomery's patronage, each was to have an establishment of twelve staff, its own transport and a Third Class chaplain who would act as its Warden.[40] As Druitt hoped, they would host Christian theatre companies and film-shows and their residential courses would be addressed by 'Christian leaders' and by 'eminent Christian writers and speakers' such as Dorothy Sayers and C.S. Lewis. Each Church House would have a large library and, with James Welch having pledged the active support of the B.B.C., each would be equipped with 'a good wireless set'.[41] Through the combined efforts of local Church Centres and district Church Houses, Druitt hoped that his 'Religious Education Plan' would have 'a tonic effect' upon the army of occupation and that it would prove 'a source of inspiration and power to all concerned'. Clearly, Druitt was at the same time very much aware of the wider implications of this initiative for the de-Nazification of Germany, being careful to emphasise 'the need to re-educate the German people' and stressing the sobering fact that 'The [British Army of the Rhine] is the first band of British missionaries – by their life and conversation they are bound to influence the German people for good or evil, to the benefit or detriment of the whole human race.'[42]

Significantly, every effort seems to have been made to put this scheme into effect. In June 1945, the chaplains of 43rd Division were informed that the creation of garrison churches was now 'a priority'. Consequently, the 4th Dorsets established a church in the camp which they had occupied at Oerrel, its pioneer platoon converting 'an Entertainment Hut in a very sad state of disrepair'. 'Dorset Church', as it was known, was completed within a month and it was provided with all the fittings of a civilian church as well as with a 'Quiet Room-cum-Library'. As its incumbent, A.R.C. Leaney, wrote: 'The object of this Church is to be a visible sign of our faith, its power, its beauty and its truth, and a means of constant worship.'[43] In July, a former hotel at Iserlohn was converted into a 'Church House' for I Corps District, covering Westphalia.[44] Similar energy was evident in VIII Corps District, which covered Schleswig-Holstein, and later that year Mark Green, the warden of its Church House, published a booklet on *The Padre's Hour, 8 Corps District – B.A.O.R. Winter 1945*. Designed to ensure a 'continuity of teaching and discussion' across VIII Corps District (despite the disruptive effects of chaplains' 'demobilization, changes of location, etc.') the booklet outlined an extensive programme of talks which divided into six series, among them 'Raising the Moral Standard' and 'Marriage and the Home'.[45]

While these efforts were being made by the chaplains of the unified Department, the Roman Catholic chaplains of the B.A.O.R. were pursuing an identical strategy. Full use was made of any intact churches and various 'Mass centres' were established in heavily damaged areas of the British zone of occupation. With the cooperation of the Archbishop of Paderborn, a 'Retreat House' was also opened in its diocesan seminary in July 1945 as 'an answer to the problems of instruction both for converts and for Catholics whose religious instructions had been either forgotten or insufficient'. This facility could accommodate groups of up to fifty men for three-day retreats in which soldiers were strongly 'reminded of their duties and responsibilities to build up a virile Catholic family life'. As its incumbent, Cyril Crean, saw the retreats: 'By these periods of prayer and instruction the hard work devoted by the chaplains in the field to the spiritual care of their troops [was] completed and rounded off.'[46]

A major new asset in supporting the post-war work of the unified Department was the 'R.A.Ch.D. Training Centre and Depot' which was opened at Bagshot Park in 1947.[47] The need for a permanent post-war base for the Department had become apparent during the war; besides helping to sustain a sense of identity among 'the Brotherhood', it would ensure the future of chaplains' training after the closure of Tidworth. Hughes began agitating for this concession shortly after the end of the war in Europe and, when Montgomery was appointed Chief of the Imperial General Staff in 1946, a post which carried responsibility 'for the organisation of the Army and the welfare of everyone in it',[48] a depot was soon made available. As Hughes had argued, there could be no return to the *status quo ante bellum*, where the Department's 'central H.Q. was two rooms in the War Office' and its main 'corporate activity' had been its annual dinner. The 'Religious Centres' in Jerusalem, Assisi and Brussels had shown what could be done to inspire and co-ordinate the work of the army's chaplains and the victorious outcome of the war had clearly demonstrated 'That a healthy Chaplains' Department had much to do with battle-morale'. With the army of occupation in Germany now endowed with a 'spiritual Power House' in each Corps District, the contrast between the Department's 'systematic and effective religious team-work overseas' and its 'rare, clumsy catch-as-catch-can Conferences' at home was all too apparent and this imbalance could only be redressed with the creation of 'a permanent Depot, Training Centre and Home' in England.[49] Described as a 'parent of all Church Houses',[50] Hughes saw this facility as a base that would help the Department in three key respects. As Hughes claimed, it would:

1. Enable the R.A.Ch.D. to develop personal and corporate religious quality and build up the special technique of their calling in the Army . . .
2. Enable the R.A.Ch.D., through Courses for Officers and other ranks to undertake the religious training of the Army and feed-in the best thought of the Churches in a systematic way . . .
3. Enable the R.A.Ch.D. to organise a regular link-up with the Churches and so provide

a) a reserve of clergy informed on Religion in the Army.
b) a constant flow of militant Religion into the civil Church to counter pacifist propaganda damaging to morale for war.
c) a centre where ex-chaplains could keep in touch with us and be encouraged to uphold our Cause in Dioceses and Districts.[51]

As Hughes had foreseen, much of Bagshot's work was devoted to chaplains' training. A memorandum prepared for the I.A.C. in October 1947 stated that 'Certain courses and conferences have already been held there, and final arrangements are now being made for starting regular courses. These will include entrants' courses for incoming chaplains, refresher courses for serving chaplains and various courses for serving officers and other ranks.'[52] Much of this work comprehended the moral education of the army for, while five-day courses in 'Christian Leadership' had been a feature of Tidworth's curriculum towards the end of the war, the question of the religious and moral welfare of the army had acquired even greater significance with the passage of the National Service Act in May 1947. Highly controversial in political terms,[53] the principle and duration of National Service (or peacetime conscription) also caused great anxiety for the churches. In an age of 'moral austerity' after the upheavals of the Second World War, National Service guaranteed the army an annual infusion of corruptible young conscripts who might find themselves in the morally dangerous surroundings of post-war Germany, Egypt or the Far East.[54]

In February 1947, Geoffrey Fisher, the Archbishop of Canterbury, led a deputation of concerned parties to the War Office in order to discuss the moral implications of National Service. There it met the Secretary of State for War, Frederick Bellenger, the Chaplain-General, the Director of Army Education and other senior soldiers and civil servants. At their meeting, Fisher and his associates, who represented bodies ranging from the Head Masters' Conference to the Y.M.C.A., called for 'a positive moral attitude' in the training of National Servicemen and for sex education to take place only in conjunction with 'positive moral teaching'. The deputation also voiced its concern about 'the special conditions in Germany and Austria and the special temptations there incurred' and urged the case for training 'Officers, N.C.O.s and Chaplains' in the vital area of 'moral responsibility'. It concluded by asking whether 'any help from outside' was required in order to 'enable the Army to discharge this grave responsibility towards young conscripts'. As a result of this meeting, Hughes was prompted to make some inquiries into current teaching strategies among his chaplains and was alarmed to discover 'a great variety of doctrines in the methods adopted by chaplains in relating their ethical teaching, including that on sexual conduct, to their religious beliefs'. Consequently, Hughes drew up a new 'syllabus for the instruction of chaplains' and sought Fisher's approval for it.[55]

It was indicative of how seriously the question of National Service and morality was treated by the War Office that a circular was sent to home and overseas commands in July 1947 stressing the urgent need for 'systematic and sustained efforts directed towards the maintenance of a high standard of moral welfare in the Army . . . particularly in that large part of it which is required to serve overseas'. Significantly, it portrayed National Servicemen as:

> [Y]oung men who are immature in knowledge and experience [who] are not prepared for temptations which are intensified as a result of their separation from steadying home influences and are not fully aware of the great importance of maintaining a code of behaviour which will secure for them and the British nation whom they represent the high regard of the peoples among whom they are stationed.[56]

The circular also addressed the responsibilities of chaplains in this regard, which were summarised as being to 'stress the moral purpose of service in each theatre and the necessity for a high code of moral behaviour as Christians and Britons'. Among their specific duties were listed the leading of church services ('which induce reverence for God and personal and corporate responsibility for living up to Christian standards'); religious instruction; special services and briefings 'for men proceeding overseas' and the provision of 'Christian leadership courses at Bagshot Park, and Church Houses overseas, which train leaders to take a hand in the battle of ideas'.[57] It was a measure of the importance which Hughes attached to this growing dimension of the chaplain's work that he even told the I.A.C. in October 1947 that 'The main purpose of [Bagshot Park] was to provide guidance for chaplains on the lines to be followed in giving religious instruction to troops.'[58]

Under the zealous leadership of the Chaplain-General, the unified Department rose with determination to the needs of the times. In December 1947, or twelve months before the first National Servicemen were actually called up, a War Office memorandum noted that Hughes had already organised 'a number of marriage Schools' and that chaplains were 'constantly engaged in counselling men about marriage and devising means to take men's minds off women'.[59] Nor were the Roman Catholics to be outdone. That October, the I.A.C. learnt how 'some Roman Catholic chaplains had arranged for soldiers suffering from venereal disease to go into retreat for three days on discharge from hospital before resuming normal duties with their units'.[60]

However, these efforts to improve the moral character of army life were complicated by the continuing retreat from compulsory attendance at church services. Early in 1946, the Secretary of State for War, Jack Lawson, moved to revoke paragraph 1605 of King's Regulations which required soldiers' attendance at divine service 'unless granted special leave or prevented by military duty'.[61] As a socialist, a Methodist lay preacher and a veteran of the First World War, this cause was no doubt close to Lawson's heart but it was significant that the only support he received on the I.A.C. came from its Methodist member, Joseph Firth.[62] However, there was considerable support for Lawson's initiative among the massive Labour majority in the House of Commons, a point that Lawson duly made when the Army Council met to consider the question in March 1946.[63] Although military opinion on the Army Council was deeply divided, Lawson had already decided that change must come.[64] A fortnight later, and in order to avert a motion that would insert a clause abolishing compulsion into the Army and Air Force (Annual) Bill, Lawson promised that 'in due time steps will be taken to cancel or modify those paragraphs of King's Regulations which provide for compulsory church attendance in the Army'.[65] With the Prime

Minister, Clement Attlee, having given his blessing to this course of action, it also seemed to appease the vocal element of abolitionists in the House. As the mover of the clause, Tom Driberg (a Fleet Street journalist and the Labour M.P. for Maldon)[66] put it:

> I am most grateful to my right hon. Friend for what he has said. In view of the assurance he has given, that despite the technical difficulties, he is accepting the principle and intention of the new Clause, and on the understanding that 'due time' means as soon as possible, and that the Regulations will be drafted very carefully . . . I have great pleasure in asking leave to withdraw the Motion.[67]

Four months later, an amendment to King's Regulations was duly presented to the Army Council which allowed compulsion only in the case of boy soldiers aged under seventeen-and-a-half and on ceremonial occasions that involved religious services. The amended paragraph came into force that October.[68] However, although the dissidents on the Army Council had capitulated, they had done so only under very severe pressure from the House of Commons. In fact, it was symptomatic of the political coercion driving the whole process that John Freeman (an advertising consultant by profession and the Labour M.P. for Watford)[69] had declared that March:

> I have often noticed that on the whole professional soldiers who show great bravery in everything else, seem to be frightened out of their lives by Members of Parliament. I think [the Secretary of State] should tell his advisers that there will be an almighty row between the Army Council and the House of Commons if this point is not conceded to us.[70]

Although evidently a crowd-pleaser for Labour's under-employed backbenchers, the abolition of compulsory attendance in 1946 had been widely opposed by informed opinion in the churches and in the army. Furthermore, a number of M.P.s had spoken from the opposition benches against the call for abolition. Brigadier A.R.W. Low (a veteran of the campaigns in Greece, North Africa and Italy)[71] stated that although he was 'generally sympathetic with the sentiments that lay behind the proposal', it ignored the fundamental fact that the army was much more than a collection of private individuals and that compulsory church services had often helped to raise morale in the war years, 'a fact which will not be familiar to some hon. Members opposite who did not have the experience'.[72] Sir William Darling (who had 'taken part in many hundreds of church parades as a private soldier, a non-commissioned officer and an officer')[73] also argued that the Secretary of State's decision to amend King's Regulations was fundamentally wrong as it flew in the face of military wisdom and experience:

> It is not consideration of the feelings of individual soldiers or the preconceptions of politicians who may have served in the Army, with which [the Secretary] is concerned. He is concerned with the Army . . . The religion of an Army is the greatest and soundest prop of its morale . . . If he takes the advice of [Tom Driberg], he will believe that Cromwell knew nothing about the inspiration of men to battle . . . that great commanders like Nelson, Drake, Wellington and Haig, like Montgomery and Alexander

> knew, and know, nothing of the value of disciplined religion. If he is to take from the Army this support to the morale of the people of this country he, in my humble submission, is not discharging the duties of a Secretary of State for War.[74]

At the conclusion of the debate, the case against abolition was pithily summarised by Michael Astor, who had seen 'much fighting in Europe' during the recent war:[75]

> The Army is a society in itself, living its own life within the wider life of civilian population. It is training for particular functions in times of peace and a very vital function in times of war. I suggest that hon. Members who support the new Clause – I think, with very little experience of the matter – are in a poor position to judge the psychological effect on morale of a commander ordering a compulsory church parade. We have heard hon. Members who have been in uniform only a short time, or not at all, talking so blandly on this matter against the extremely strong evidence of well reputed commanders in the past. The main point is that the principle involved is the extent to which we shall allow a commander in the field to determine how he can influence morale and discipline.[76]

Misgivings about the voluntary system introduced in 1946 were deepened with the implementation of the National Service Act and the onset of the Cold War. Given his personal convictions and what he understood to be the lessons of the Second World War, Montgomery had always resisted the incremental abandonment of compulsion. As early as March 1945 he had written to Hughes: 'At the Camberley Conference I put the cat among the canaries over the matter of soldiers going to church. The A.G. [Sir Ronald Adam] had a terrific gruelling!!'[77] Hostile to the compromise of 1943, Montgomery was fiercely opposed to abolition in 1946, warning the War Office that 'The new order will affect adversely the morale of the Army in peace and war . . . The political chiefs are skating on very dangerous ground.'[78] These views were championed on the I.A.C. by Frederick Llewelyn Hughes. At its meeting in February 1950, Hughes reported that abolition had caused church attendance to slump and that 'military commanders were disturbed as to the possible effect of this on the morale of the Army should war break out'.[79] In April 1951 he was even more explicit, asserting that 'He was personally in favour of a compulsory church parade because communal worship was the greatest single factor in strengthening the soldier's conscience and thereby enhancing his morale'.[80] By this time, there can be little doubt that Hughes spoke for 'military commanders at all levels'.[81] Ironically, General Sir James Steele, Adam's successor as Adjutant-General and a supporter of abolition in 1946, had seen the error of his ways by 1949. That November he wrote a chastened memorandum for the Army Council in favour of restoration. Based on recent discussions with commanding officers, he argued that compulsory church attendance would benefit the morals and morale of the army to an extent that unaccompanied religious instruction never could. He also confessed that his earlier opinions had been unduly swayed by opinion in parliament and the press and asserted that it was the army's responsibility to 'safeguard the youth of the nation' while it served in its ranks.[82] Like Steele, eminent soldiers such as Field-Marshal Sir William Slim and Lieutenant-General Sir Gerald Templer also supported a return to compulsion, as did Lieutenant-Colonel M.C.A. Henniker, who wrote in the *Journal of the Royal United Service Institution* in 1950:

> Everyone who has ever taken part in a battle will agree that large numbers of men find solace in religion. It comforts them and makes them more staunch and brave. The effect is the same as confidence in their weapons. We go to great pains to give them good weapons and to train them in their use; so that when battle comes the soldiers may be confident in their weapons and use them to good effect. But, as we see, religion in battle is a good weapon, too. Surely then it is only prudent to train the soldiers in its use?[83]

A consensus among the churches also supported a return to a system of compulsion. While the Archbishop of Canterbury had opposed abolition and favoured 'a return to church parades in some form' in 1950,[84] opinion was particularly trenchant in the Church of Scotland. Significantly, it had accepted the end of compulsion with a cautious optimism, its Committee on Chaplains to H.M. Forces hoping that:

> [G]iven a sufficiency of good Chaplains, and the sympathetic co-operation of Commanding Officers, there is no reason why the new arrangement should not prove even more genuinely effective than the old . . . the Chaplain has an opportunity he never had before, and it is an opportunity which constitutes a challenge to the Church.[85]

However, by 1950 this sanguine mood had evaporated completely. Instead, the committee reported to the General Assembly:

> When [church parade] was abolished in 1946 the Chaplains loyally and honestly tried to do their best with the Voluntary Service, and in some cases, especially overseas, with a partial measure of success. But with the experience of these last few years to go on, the feeling has steadily grown that one of the finest features of the life in the Services has been lost, and the Committee consider that the time has now come to press for the restitution of the Church Parade to a recognised place in the life of a Unit.[86]

The views of Scotland's national church were put to the I.A.C. very forcefully in February of that year by Dr. John MacLagan, the convenor of its Committee on Chaplains to H.M. Forces. As MacLagan argued, there was no element of actual 'compulsion' to church parades 'since any man who had a valid reason for non-attendance could be excused'. In fact, 'The real issue was whether in a Christian country the armed forces of the Crown should or should not make the worship of God a part of regimental life.' Deploring the fact that in Scottish regiments 'the traditional association of corporate worship with regimental life was being lost' MacLagan argued that there was 'a strong feeling in the Scottish regiments in favour of church parades'. Even the United Board's representative, Osborn Wiles, thought that his Baptist and Congregationalist constituency 'would be mainly in favour of a return to some form of corporate worship in the Army', padre's hour being no effective substitute. While the Roman Catholic representative struck a more cautious note, as in 1946 only Joseph Firth (for the Methodists) was actually in favour of thc voluntary system. As Firth maintained, prior to 1946 'the element of real religion had been very small' in the army's compulsory system, adding that 'he had been sorry at the time that the initiative in abolishing [parade] services had not come from the churches'.[87]

However, there can be no doubt that Firth's was very much a minority position both among the churches and among senior army officers. Indeed, the Army Council was even standing by with an alternative to the existing voluntary system. As Sir George Turner, the chairman of the I.A.C., explained:

> This was that the existing regulations should be modified so as to allow commanding officers to order compulsory church parades, both at certain fixed intervals and on special occasions. Those at fixed intervals might well be ordered to coincide with the regimental week-ends when all ranks would necessarily be present with the unit and when the attendance of a band could most conveniently be arranged.[88]

Even though the current regulations may have allowed such a pattern without the need for specific amendments, the politicians concerned were unreceptive and even hostile. According to Michael Stewart, a former officer in the Intelligence Corps,[89] a return to the compulsory system might inflame public feeling against National Service and it would certainly antagonise members of the House of Commons, a decisive consideration after Labour's majority was slashed in the general election of February 1950. Thus, 'Manny' Shinwell, the Secretary of State for War and Minister of Defence from February 1950, declined to take any further action, a decision that Fisher at least understood and which the Army Council grudgingly accepted in May 1950.[90] Still, the issue remained a point of heated discussion on the I.A.C., with Hughes, MacLagan and M.E. Aubrey of the United Board joining forces in 1951 to task the hapless Turner on the restoration of some form of mandatory corporate worship.[91] However, Turner escaped another roasting at the next meeting of the I.A.C. because of the simultaneous and fortuitous retirement of all these protagonists, departures which allowed the subject to be quietly dropped from the committee's agenda.[92]

While the slow and controversial demise of compulsory attendance at routine religious services arguably weakened the historic links between the British army and the British churches,[93] its secularising significance should not be exaggerated. In addition to the heavy resistance it aroused, the move provoked a strong campaign for the restoration of compulsion in the army and in the churches over subsequent years, a campaign that drew strength from the growing prospect of another war in Europe. In any event, the army did not entirely renounce its right to require its soldiers' attendance at religious services in 1946. Furthermore, of the politicians and senior officers who condoned the abolition of compulsion at that time, many acted under the enduring and widely held conviction that compulsion was actually detrimental to the cause and interests of real religion. The abandonment of compulsion, moreover, had only a minimal impact on the chaplain's role. In view of the Department's record in the Second World War, it was significant that even the most strident parliamentary critics of compulsion did not question the need for army chaplains *per se*. By the middle of the twentieth century (and, indeed, as early as the middle of the nineteenth century) the chaplain's functions went far beyond presiding at parade services once a week. In fact, and as the context of the Cold War went on to show, chaplains remained key figures in the corporate life of the army. While they may have faced smaller congregations on any given Sunday, as in the First and Second World Wars they continued to play their acknowledged role as moral educators, morale-raisers and soldiers' friends in the citizen army of an avowedly Christian nation, their importance being underlined in the dreary context of post-war Germany, in the police actions which marked the end of empire and in the battlefields and prison camps of the Korean War.

Retrospect

By the mid-twentieth century the Royal Army Chaplains' Department had clearly established a secure place for itself in the life and affections of the British army. Nevertheless, its early history had been erratic. Forged from the wreckage of the army's previous system of regimental chaplaincy as one of the reforms of the Duke of York, the fledgling Department was subject to extensive reorganisation in 1809 and reduced to a small cadre of commissioned chaplains in the years after Waterloo. Moreover, its record during the Peninsular War, the greatest test of British army chaplaincy during the Napoleonic Wars, had been undistinguished; the Department's concentration on hospital work entailed high levels of sickness and absenteeism among its chaplains, failings that were seized upon by veterans of the campaign in the unsettled and anticlerical atmosphere of the post-Waterloo period.

However, after his appointment as Principal Chaplain in 1844, the driving ambition of George Gleig and his identification with the cause of army reform allowed a modest revival of the Department to take place in the years prior to the Crimean War, the ministry of the chaplain being linked to army education, to the moral improvement of the soldier and to the benefits these promised in terms of the army's overall discipline and efficiency. Nevertheless, the Department remained an Anglican preserve and it was still woefully short of commissioned chaplains upon the outbreak of the Crimean War in 1854. For the subsequent campaign in the East, the Department was forced to rely on the services of a large body of non-commissioned acting chaplains (many of whom were Presbyterians, Nonconformists or Roman Catholics) and it was mainly by virtue of their efforts that an adequate ministry was eventually provided to the army's camps and hospitals in Turkey and the Crimea. With the coming of peace in 1856, the Army Chaplains' Department benefited from a surge of public interest in the religious welfare of the soldier (a surge that was partly caused by the loss of a dozen chaplains in the East) and from a further round of army reforms necessitated by the hard lessons of the Crimean War. Hence, by the early 1860s the Department had been increased in terms of its size and diversified in terms of its religious composition, with its commissioned Anglican, Presbyterian and Roman Catholic chaplains being more closely integrated into the officer corps.

Although the geography and logistics of the colonial wars of the late Victorian period meant that their experience of active service was distinctly limited, the Anglican members of the Army Chaplains' Department worked hard to raise the moral standards of the British soldier in the home and colonial garrisons of the

British Empire. While this work was varied (ranging from leading temperance outings to managing clothing contracts for soldiers' wives) it also gave rise to an informal style of ministry that downplayed the chaplain's rank and stressed his identity as the 'soldier's friend'. Meanwhile, the Department's Presbyterian and Roman Catholic chaplains largely devoted their energies to a regimental ministry that was centred upon the army's Scottish and Irish regiments. At the same time, a growing number of Wesleyan ministers became involved in army work, whether on a part-time basis or as full-time, albeit non-commissioned, acting chaplains. However, the Boer War confirmed the Department's ultimate reliance on acting chaplains in times of emergency and its prolonged guerrilla phase served to put chaplains on the defensive. Once more the subject of strong suspicion among influential sections of the British public, the character of the British soldier (and, by implication, the work of the Department in recent decades) had to be defended against its detractors, a duty that revealed the extent of many chaplains' identification with the army and which invited strong censure from those critical of the war.

Despite the creation of the Territorial Force and the appointment of Territorial chaplains from 1908, during the First World War the Army Chaplains' Department once again reacted to the challenge of a major war by recruiting civilian clergymen for temporary service. Such was the scale of the army's expansion that the 5,053 chaplains who were commissioned between August 1914 and November 1918 exceeded the number of pre-war commissioned chaplains by a ratio of more than 40:1, and still there were chronic shortages which the churches were hard pressed to meet. Furthermore, the Department experienced remarkable diversification in religious terms. Whereas only three denominations had commissioned chaplains in August 1914, by November 1918 this had increased to eleven, a telling reflection of the national nature of the war effort. If the war saw several Nonconformist churches reconsider their historic misgivings concerning state aid in order to accept commissions for their chaplains, the Christian monopoly of the Department was also conclusively broken in the First World War as Jewish chaplains were commissioned and sent overseas on equal terms with their Christian counterparts. With the army reliant on wartime volunteers and, for the first time in its history, on conscripts from 1916, the role of the chaplain also changed dramatically during the First World War. While still expected to uphold the related interests of morality and military efficiency, chaplains were increasingly drawn into the vital and onerous task of raising and sustaining morale. Although this was rapidly translated into the provision of canteens in camps, billets and forward areas of the British army on the Western Front and elsewhere, from the winter of 1915–16 it increasingly involved providing an authoritative source of religious and moral justification for the war and (from brigade chaplains in particular) it demanded a conspicuous and hazardous presence in the front line. These changes were encouraged by Sir Douglas Haig and his army commanders on the Western Front and the victorious outcome of the war appeared to vindicate the recasting of the chaplain's role. However, while its new features were endorsed and applauded by senior officers, they were viewed with considerable suspicion in other quarters. For contemporary and inter-war commentators who were critical of the high command, disturbed by the human cost of the war and hostile towards the British establishment, the chaplain's wartime role was very much open to question, particularly given lingering doubts as to the legitimacy of war in the Christian tradition and the contrasts which this role presented with the professional values associated with the clerical renaissance of the nineteenth century. Thus, British army chaplains emerged with a mixed reputation from the maelstrom of the First World War. On the one hand, they had shown courage, compassion and solidarity with a whole generation of British men; this gave them an important and often high profile role in veterans' associations, in the commemoration of the war and, as the post-war careers of 'Tubby' Clayton and Studdert Kennedy serve to illustrate, in the public and political life of the nation. However, at the same time chaplains had also legitimised the bloodiest war in British history, a war whose conduct and purpose was increasingly questioned in the inter-war period.

With the coming of peace, the Department was reduced and extensively reorganised, with a premium being placed on administrative unity in reaction to the inter-denominational friction and centrifugal tendencies unleashed by the war. However, while internal concord was re-established in the inter-war Department, during the 1920s external criticism of the Department's record in the First World War began to accumulate. This was largely aimed at Anglican chaplains, it resonated with perennial undercurrents of anticlerical feeling in British society and it benefited from the lack of any official history of the Department's part in the war, from the absence of Bishop Gwynne and from the public self-recrimination of Studdert Kennedy in particular. While often mendacious and, in the case of Robert Graves, even downright dishonest, this criticism also thrived on a growing anti-war reaction in the churches and in British society, a reaction that eventually fuelled the growth of a mass peace movement whose practical and moral leadership was largely supplied by the churches. Significantly, contemporary pacifists identified the abolition, or at least the radical reform, of the Royal Army Chaplains' Department as one of their primary objectives. Although it was never seriously threatened with extinction from this quarter, pacifist sentiment does appear to have influenced attitudes to the Department among its sending churches, affecting in particular its ability to recruit departmental reservists.

Despite the power of the pacifist lobby, the Department's position actually became more, rather than less, secure as the international outlook worsened in Europe towards the end of the 1930s. However, during the course of the Second World War the Department still found it difficult to meet the requirements that were made upon it. Competing with the unprecedented demands of the Home Front as well as with those of the Royal Navy and the R.A.F., the residual currency of inter-war pacifism posed additional problems of recruitment for the Department, particularly as the younger clergy were a declining asset in many of the mainstream Protestant churches. Still, thanks to long-term planning dating back to the 1920s, the Department was in a higher state of readiness for the Second World War than it had been for any major conflict hitherto. It was, moreover, an illustration of the effectiveness of chaplaincy work a generation earlier that the model of army chaplaincy that had been forged in the crucible of the First

World War was substantially revived in the Second. In fact, recurrent defeats from the spring of 1940 to the summer of 1942 placed an even greater emphasis on the chaplain's role as a morale-raiser. This role was eventually taken to new and vaunted heights in Montgomery's Eighth Army and, on the basis of its success in North Africa and Italy, Eighth Army chaplaincy became a model for the rest of the British army.

However, while all of this demonstrates strong continuities in the Department's work between the two World Wars, the Second World War also saw a number of major innovations. The advent of radio broadcasting, the development of airborne warfare, the fragile morale of Britain's citizen soldiers, the army's greater use of female personnel and the terms of the Geneva Convention of 1929 gave rise, in turn, to the 'Radio Padre', the parachute chaplain, the 'padre's hour', the female chaplain's assistant and to an extensive ministry among British prisoners of war in Europe and the Far East. Furthermore, and in contrast to their forbears of 1914–18, army chaplains emerged with considerable credit from the Second World War. Despite their continuing and often thankless tasks of presiding at compulsory worship and preaching against immorality and vice, their continuing and hazardous work on the battlefield, their ministry in P.O.W. camps and a more critical approach to military authority served to enhance their reputation, a development that was encouraged by the manifest justice of the cause which they championed and the greatly reduced casualties incurred by the British army in the Second World War as compared to the First. While compulsory worship as a matter of routine was abolished in 1946, the significance of the chaplain did not necessarily diminish in the immediate post-war years. Indeed, the army still relied on its chaplains to provide moral support and guidance for its soldiers, a highly significant role in a period of moral austerity and peacetime conscription at home and in view of the political and military challenges thrown up by occupation duties in Europe and by colonial insurgencies in Africa and Asia. Furthermore, and as the case of Sam Davies clearly illustrates, between 1950 and 1953 chaplains still played a distinguished part on the battlefields and in the prison camps of the Korean War.

While it is plain that the Department played a major role in the British army from the late eighteenth to the mid twentieth century, other considerations also serve to illustrate that its history has a much greater significance for British religious history than is usually appreciated. As the Department was primarily responsible for the religious care of a national institution of the first importance, the widening of its denominational profile over the course of the nineteenth century was emblematic of the growing religious inclusiveness of the British state and even of changing conceptions of British national identity. In the course of a hundred years, the Department's commissioned chaplains developed from being an all-Anglican body in 1815 to one that included Presbyterians, Nonconformists, Roman Catholics and even Jews. This process was a natural corollary of the political emancipation of Britain's minority religious groups. For example, after Catholic Emancipation in 1829 and the consequent creation of an Irish Catholic bloc in the House of Commons, it proved impossible for the War Office to resist pressure for the regular payment of Roman Catholic priests as officiating clergymen. Furthermore, this political influence helped to ensure their appointment as acting chaplains in the Crimean War and their full admission to the Department as commissioned chaplains in its aftermath. Similarly, by 1862 Wesleyan Methodists had accrued enough political leverage to force their recognition from the War Office under the broad category of 'Other Protestants'. This recognition went on to facilitate the remarkable expansion of Wesleyan work in the army, much of which was funded by government from 1881, and it was mainly due to their own qualms regarding state aid that Wesleyan and other Nonconformist chaplains were not commissioned until the First World War.

In this process, the Department mirrored contemporary developments in the relationship between religion and national identity. In the early years of the nineteenth century, Protestantism, especially in its established forms, was integral to a sense of being British; however, by the beginning of the twentieth century, the key religious ingredient of British national identity was a non-specific form of Christianity.[1] On its creation in 1796, it was significant that no formal chaplaincy role was recognised in the British army for clergymen who were not of the Church of England or the Church of Scotland. However, this dispensation was challenged and gradually dismantled in the decades after Waterloo. Whereas only Anglican chaplains accompanied Wellington's army in the Peninsula and in the Waterloo campaign, a wide variety of recognised chaplains served the British army in the Crimea forty years later. Although their mutual relations on active service were usually amicable, in the wake of the recapture of Khartoum in 1898 an Anglican, a Presbyterian, a Wesleyan and a Roman Catholic chaplain could be *required* by their commanding officer, in this case the formidable Horatio Kitchener, to lead a joint service of commemoration for General Charles Gordon, one of the greatest heroes of Victorian Christianity.[2]

While many chaplains made a patriotic virtue of their willingness to work with each other from as early as the Crimean War, their functions also indicate the status of the Army Chaplains' Department as a reflection of an ideologically conservative national self-consciousness. On its formation in 1796, the Department was intended to serve as a bulwark against Jacobin extremism. Later, during the Napoleonic Wars, the chaplains of the new Department were used to counteract the spread of religious and, it was feared, political radicalism among the army's rank and file. In the later nineteenth century, commissioned Roman Catholic chaplains, who were usually trained in English seminaries and recruited from English dioceses, helped to insulate regiments of Irish Roman Catholics against Nationalist and Republican sedition. In the major wars of the twentieth century, this ideological aspect of British army chaplaincy became even more pronounced as chaplains of all denominations were called upon to support the nation's citizen soldiers in their successive struggles against Teutonic *kultur*, Nazi paganism and atheistic Communism.

While the existence of the Army Chaplains' Department says much about the religious component of British national identity in our period, it also reflects the enduring importance that was attached to religion in British society in the period *c.*1800–1950. The nineteenth and early twentieth centuries have been traditionally viewed by historians and sociologists of religion in Britain as an age of long-term secularisation, a process that has been linked to the emergence of an industrial, class-based society and whose progress has been tracked through statistics of individual churchgoing.[3] However, and in contrast to this picture, the history of the Department serves to underline the enduring cultural vitality of Christianity in nineteenth and early twentieth-century British society. This is a theme that has been developed by Callum Brown in particular, who has rightly emphasised that the true measure of religiosity in British society is not to be found in highly ambiguous statistics of regular religious practice but in the extent to which Christianity and Christian values permeated public and private life before the religious crisis of the 1960s.[4] Clearly, the birth and development of the Army Chaplains' Department over the previous 150 years illustrates the extent to which the need for publicly funded religious provision for the British army was taken for granted by successive generations of soldiers, parliamentarians and ordinary Britons. In this respect, the history of the Department reflects the enduring and self-conscious character of Britain as part of 'Christendom'; in other words, whether they were regular churchgoers or not, British men and women 'lived in a society where there were close ties between the leaders of the church and those in positions of secular power, where the laws purported to be based on Christian principles, and where, apart from certain clearly defined outsider communities, every member of the society was assumed to be a Christian'.[5] Crucially, in ultimate terms the Army Chaplains' Department was sustained not by the army but by a cost-conscious House of Commons whose elected members continued to vote public funds on an annual basis in order to guarantee religious provision for the officers and men of the British army. Ironically, this provision actually grew in the latter half of the nineteenth century and reached an unprecedented scale in the two World Wars. This support for the Department survived the penny-pinching of Randolph Churchill and the pacifism of Dick Sheppard and it was sustained despite radical shifts in the terms of British politics, regular changes in government, the widening of the popular franchise and declining levels of churchgoing in British society. While unpopular or unrepresentative national religious institutions (such as the Church of Ireland and the Church of England in Wales) fell prey to some of these factors, the Army Chaplains' Department, reflecting a truly national religious profile, positively thrived. Although the end of compulsory religious worship in the British army in 1946 was driven by pressure from the House of Commons, this move had been urged by many army chaplains during the Second World War, it was carried out in order to strengthen rather than undermine the position of the army chaplain and it made no difference to his privileged position in the army or to his other, numerous, points of contact with its soldiers. Clearly, like the survival of a semi-sacral monarchy and established, or national, churches in England and Scotland, the maintenance of the Department into the early years of the Cold War stands as a striking facet of the cultural vitality of British Christianity and of the survival of a British 'Christendom' until well into the twentieth century.

While shedding a good deal of light on the religious character of British society in the period of our study and on the limited impact of secularisation, the history of the Department also merits fuller recognition in the ecclesiastical history of modern Britain. Evidently, the Department has both reflected and driven ecclesiastical, theological and pastoral trends in the British churches. In the latter stages of the Napoleonic Wars, and through the good offices of Britain's only evangelical Prime Minister, it was dominated by the evangelical agenda of John Owen, who attained an unparalleled degree of religious influence in the British army and the Royal Navy. However, after years of retrenchment and atrophy between Waterloo and the Crimean War, during the mid-Victorian period a revitalised Department became a bastion of Ritualism and a rather unlikely forum in which a new and decidedly populist pastoral style could be modelled by younger chaplains, as it was by an emerging generation of clergymen in the critical urban parishes of the Church of England. During the First World War, when the Department very much reflected the nineteenth-century fragmentation of British religious and theological life, it became a testing ground for various theologies, forms of worship and styles of ministry and, for its Anglican majority, it served as an engine for institutional and liturgical change in the post-war Church of England. In turn, the Department in the Second World War reflected the growing strength of neo-orthodox theology and helped to inspire the institution of industrial chaplaincy in the post-war churches. Furthermore, in the form of the chaplain's assistant, it widened the field of female ministry in the church. However, and especially as a result of the two World Wars, perhaps the most significant contribution made by the Department to British church life lay in its promotion of practical ecumenism. While there were always sources of jealousy and division between chaplains of different denominations, from the 1850s through to the 1950s the Department threw together scores and eventually thousands of British clergymen who, though strongly and even bitterly divided on questions of doctrine and church order, were required to live and work together in the interests of a higher cause. The long-term ecumenical dividend that accrued from this scale of practical co-operation may well be incalculable but it was no doubt very considerable.

The history of the Department also illuminates trends in the history of its sending churches. With regard to the Church of England, the creation and consolidation of the Army Chaplains' Department can be seen as an early and decisive instance of nineteenth-century ecclesiastical reform. Furthermore, the origins and fate of the Army Chaplains Act of 1868 can only be understood in the context of the contemporary reform and reinvigoration of diocesan and parochial life. Similarly, far from being hermetically sealed from the affairs of the civilian church, the Anglican branch of the Chaplains' Department was profoundly affected by the Ritualist controversy of the 1860s and 1870s and it was still vulnerable to the smouldering rivalries of different church parties until well into the twentieth century. Similarly, the whole issue of army chaplaincy represented in microcosm the Nonconformist dilemma over the question of state-sponsored religion. However, the departmental dynamic towards greater religious inclusion also had divisive tendencies beyond the tender consciences of English and Welsh Nonconformists. While the funding and even the concept of army chaplaincy precipitated fierce and protracted debate among Wesleyan Methodists, moves towards a more inclusive Department after the Crimean War also exposed underlying national tensions between and within denominations. The issue of military chaplaincy sowed a certain rivalry between Britain's Presbyterian churches and promoted discord between the Roman Catholic hierarchies of England and Ireland. While tensions between the latter reached new heights in the First World War, at the same time military chaplaincy stoked historic animosities and tensions between the Church of England and the Church of Scotland. As a national institution that transcended their particular jurisdictions, the evolving organisation of the wartime Chaplains' Department proved to be a significant source of jealousy and rancour between these very different, albeit constitutionally comparable, churches.

The history of British army chaplains and of the Royal Army Chaplains' Department is clearly rich, multi-faceted and highly significant for a number of reasons. However, its real importance has been obscured by a mass of narrow and partisan writing on the subject. Although denominational, biographical and national studies of British army chaplains have proliferated in recent decades, very little attention has been paid to the experience of chaplains in general or to the wider history of the Royal Army Chaplains' Department. The uneven history of British army chaplaincy which has emerged from these endeavours has been further complicated by an influential pacifist critique that questions the legitimacy of military chaplaincy in general and the role and reputation of British army chaplains in particular. Very much a function of the strength of inter-war and Cold War pacifism on both sides of the Atlantic, this critique has been inspired by a particular, though far from consensual, understanding of Christian ethics and it has drawn quite freely on a number of disciplines, including psychology, sociology, literary studies and pastoral theology. However, historical claims and criticisms have also been made that are too often based on a disparate and highly selective body of historical evidence. Furthermore, in their British context, these claims and criticisms derive much of their moral force from an entrenched and highly misleading popular mythology of the First World War. However, this critique is thrown into question by much of the evidence produced in this study, a fact that can be demonstrated with respect to the eight paradoxes in the role of the British military chaplain that Alan Wilkinson posited.

Most of the historical evidence that Wilkinson cited to support his influential case dated from the two World Wars and, largely informed by a wider body of evidence from these conflicts, we can now turn to consider these alleged paradoxes in turn. Firstly, and perhaps most fundamentally, in ethical terms there is no necessary conflict 'between Christianity and the military profession'; this conviction stems from a specific moral tradition within Christianity and represents one side of a debate over the legitimacy of organised violence that is inherently inconclusive. Secondly, evidence from the two World Wars shows that British army chaplains have not widely succumbed to 'feelings of marginality and helplessness' due to their non-combatant status. Indeed, while some may have chafed under this restriction, it was through the chaplain's work as a non-combatant that the Department earned hundreds of battlefield awards, including three Victoria Crosses. Thirdly, the so-called 'tribal religion' of army chaplains was not necessarily knee-jerk jingoism but was very much rooted in just war precepts and in a broader sense of the justice of the national cause. Fourthly, the 'tension of being both a priest and an officer' and the 'class bias of the Church and its ministers' were symptoms rather than causes of the cultural distance that lay between the Anglican chaplain and the army's preponderance of nominal Anglicans. This distance was all too apparent in civilian life but the problem was far from insurmountable. Indeed, and in common with the civilian clergy, chaplains of ability and charisma could bridge this gap whereas ill-adjusted members of the Chaplains' Department were tempted to invoke their officer status as a blanket explanation for more personal failings and frustrations. Fifthly, the vaunted 'tension between the priestly and the social' role of the chaplain has also been exaggerated and this too was a problem that was largely inherited from civilian society, it being the fate of the churches nationally to run a huge array of social and recreational activities that generated few adult members. Sixthly, as a largely self-selecting body of volunteers, most chaplains were quite prepared to 'reinforce morale' and, as the right to conscientious objection was enshrined in British law, this duty was by no means in conflict with the rights of the conscientious objector. Seventhly, the 'prophetic role' of chaplains was largely exercised in their preaching on behalf of a national cause in which they believed and nor were they cravenly passive or mute in the face of controversial military procedures. While they commonly acted as prisoners' friends in courts martial during the First World War, the attitude of many chaplains towards military authority during the Second verged on the obstreperous. Finally, if the 'military and religious establishments' widely employed 'Religious and chivalric imagery' in order to 'romanticise war', this by no means incurred the opprobrium that Wilkinson claimed. Though controversial in view of the casualties and frustrated hopes of the First World War, such themes and motifs were even more integral to the British army's self-image in the Second. However, in this case there is no evidence to suggest that their use was widely regarded as inappropriate in a war that resulted in far fewer British casualties and which was widely understood to be a struggle on behalf of 'Christian civilisation'.

In conclusion, it is clear from this history of the Royal Army Chaplains' Department from 1796 to 1953 that the chaplains of the British army have too often been the subjects of strident, partisan and ill-informed criticism, a discourse that has not been affected by narrower, if more favourable, historical studies of British army chaplains and chaplaincy. While the origins and nature of this criticism are very much open to question, it is clear that the history of the Royal Army Chaplains' Department needs to be placed in a much wider historical context, with due recognition being given to its broader military, religious, political and cultural significance. From this standpoint, it is evident that there is still much more to be said about the history of the Department and of British army chaplaincy more generally and this study should at least serve as a new platform for future research. In the meantime, and notwithstanding all that has been alleged to the contrary, when one begins to take a more comprehensive view of the history of the Royal Army Chaplains' Department during the first 150 years of its existence it soon becomes apparent that the Department has good reason to take pride in its pastoral and military achievements.

Notes

Introduction

1 Davies, 1954, 19; Farrar-Hockley, 1995, II, 113.
2 Farrar-Hockley, 1995, II, 66–7.
3 Farrar-Hockley, 1995, II, 114–32.
4 Davies, 1954, 19–25; I.W.M. Sound, S. Davies.
5 Davies, 1954, n.p.
6 Farrar-Hockley, 1995, II, 266.
7 Davies, 1954, 31–3, 38–9.
8 Davies, 1954, 40–1, 52–3, 56, 67.
9 Davies, 1954, 68.
10 Davies, 1954, 69.
11 Davies, 1954, 80–3, 90–1, 97–8.
12 Davies, 1954, 87; Farrar-Hockley, 1993, 239.
13 Davies, 1954, 82.
14 Davies, 1954, 98–103.
15 Davies, 1954, 110–12.
16 Davies, 1954, 112, 115.
17 Davies, 1954, 127–8.
18 Davies, 1954, 124–5; Farrar-Hockley, 1993, 240.
19 Davies, 1954, 138–40.
20 Davies, 1954, 148–9.
21 Davies, 1954, 134–5, 154–5, Hastings, 2000, 330; Farrar-Hockley, 1993, 249.
22 Farrar-Hockley, 1995, II, 269–73.
23 Davies, 1954, 86, 143–4 ; R.A.Ch.D. Archive (R.C.), John Ryan monthly report, 30 April 1953.
24 Barnett, 1970, 483–4.
25 Hastings, 2000, 330, 345; Brown, 2006, 179–80.
26 Farrar-Hockley, 1994, 334; Hickman, 2005, 87–9, 100–1.
27 Hastings, 2000, 330, 347–8.
28 Herspring, 2001, 44.
29 Hastings, 2000, 341.
30 I.W.M. documents, E.C. Crosse; R.P.D.A., Rawlinson Papers, 'War History'.
31 Purcell, 1983; Lever, 1971; Raw, 1988.
32 Brown, 1996; Hagerty and Johnstone, 1996; Coulter, 1997; Thompson, 1990.
33 Dow, 1962; R.A.Ch.D. Archive, Dow.
34 Morgan, 1999, 48–55; Morgan, 2001, 1–27; Leonard, 1986; Dungan, 1997, 61–73.
35 *O.D.N.B.*; Purcell, 1983, 29, 160
36 Fitzgerald-Lombard, 1993, 136; Johnstone and Hagerty, 1996, 115–16.
37 Burchard, 1954, 535, n. 9; Loveland, 2004, 233–5.
38 Burchard, 1954, 529–30.
39 Burchard, 1954, 528.
40 Burchard, 1954, 534.

41 Burchard, 1954, 532–3.
42 Burchard, 1954, 533.
43 Burchard, 1954, 535.
44 Zahn, 1969, 28.
45 Zahn, 1969, passim.
46 Wilkinson, 1981, 249.
47 Wilkinson, 1981, passim.
48 Wilkinson, 1981, passim.
49 Louden, 1996, 123–4.
50 Louden, 2006, 15.
51 Louden, 2006, passim.
52 Bergen, 2001, 233; Dear and Foot, 1995, 468.
53 Peers, 1979, 129–31, 207, 215; Loveland, 2004, 238–9; Olson and Roberts, 1998, 10–20.
54 Maclear, 1981, 378.
55 Carver, 1998, 310.
56 Baxter, 2004, 267.
57 Temple, 1940, 31.
58 www.augsburgfortress.org/store/itemcontributor.jsp?contributorcode=4988; www.armchairinterviews.com/reviews/categories/christian_nonfiction/the_christian_handbook.php; www.amazon.co.uk/Christian-Handbook-Kristofer-Skrade/dp/0806652594. Viewed 4 March 2007.
59 Skrade, 2006, 515–18.
60 See, for example, Sheffield, 2001, passim; Bond, 2002, passim; Holmes, 2004, passim; Corrigan, 2004, passim; Todman, 2005, passim; Sheffield and Bourne, 2005, passim.
61 Snape and Skrade, 2007, 159–61.
62 Strachan, 2003, 331.
63 Bourke, 1999, 268–305.
64 Bourke, 1999, 270, 282, 296.
65 Louden, 1996, 120–1; Wilkinson, 1981, 251–2.
66 Graves, 1929, 242–3; 1960, 158–9 ; Montague, 1922, 71–2.
67 Graves, 1929, 243; 1960, 158–9; Montague, 1922, 82.
68 Wilkinson, 1978, 134; Moynihan, 1983, 144–5; Holmes, 2004, 506.
69 Graves, 1929, 242–3, 276; 1960, 158–9, 183; Bellenger, 1999, passim.
70 Wilkinson, 1978, 134; Holmes, 2004, 506; O'Rahilly, 1932, 1, 7.
71 Towler and Coxon, 1979, 23.
72 Montague, 1922, 70.
73 Raw, 1988, 2; Lever, 1971, 43–4; *O.D.N.B.*
74 Williams, 1999, 98–9, 159–60.
75 Snape, 2005 (a), 143.
76 Ballhatchet, 1993, 280–1.
77 P.R.O. WO 95/5308.
78 New College, CHU 5.1.8.
79 Polehampton, 1858, 227–8.
80 Shepherd, 1827, 75–6 footnote.

Origins and early years

1 McCormick, 2004, 45–6.
2 Bachrach, 2004, passim.
3 Laurence, 2004, passim; Griffin, 2002, passim; Furgol, 2002, 46–8; Herspring, 2001, 55–77.
4 Furgol, 2002, 66.
5 Childs, 2003, 47–8; Laurence, 1990, 9–12.

6 Furgol, 2002, 46; Barratt, 2000, 21, 61, 95–6; Griffin, 2002, passim; Laurence, 1990, 9–12.
7 Clode, 1869, II, 366–8; Cottesloe, 1930, 160; Childs, 1987, 39.
8 *Seventh Report*, 1809, 24; Western, 1965, 397.
9 Langford, 1991, 19–20.
10 Dow, 1962, 229.
11 Johnstone and Hagerty, 1996, 1.
12 Ward, 1765, 21.
13 Anon., 1786, 32.
14 Clode, 1869, II, 369; B.L., B.P. 8/5. (5.); Army List, 1776, 135–40.
15 B.L., B.P. 8/5. (5.)
16 *Army Lists*, 1776 and 1796.
17 Clode, 1869, II, 370. See, for example, Broughton, 1738, passim.
18 *Army Lists*, 1776 and 1796; Hughes, 1991, 11.
19 Ward, 1953, 35.
20 Cuthbertson, 1768, 156–7.
21 Cuthbertson, 1768, 157.
22 Simes, 1777, 242; Kopperman, 1987, 391; Frey, 1981, 62.
23 Worcestershire Record Office, CRO BA 2289/3/ii. I am grateful to Mrs Susan Jones for this reference.
24 Johnstone, 1959, passim.
25 Agar, 1758, passim.
26 Steppler, 1990, 13.
27 Cuthbertson, 1768, 155–6.
28 Mather, 1985, 278.
29 Cuthbertson, 1768, 156.
30 Graham, 1953, 333–34.
31 Harris, 1982, passim.
32 Dow, 1962, 185; *Historical Manuscripts Commission*, 1895, 200–34.
33 Dow, 1962, 184–5; Scouller, 1966, 278.
34 Snape, 2005 (b), 45; Anon., 1757, 11.
35 Dow, 1962, 23; *O.D.N.B.*
36 Cormack and Jones, 2001, 214.
37 Brumwell, 2002, 13, 20.
38 Kopperman, 1987, 392; Hamilton, 1959, 55.
39 Doughty and Parmelee, 1901, II, 28 footnote.
40 Frey, 1981, 115–17.
41 Lamb, 1809, 185–9; Holmes, 2001, 115; Bicheno, 2004, opposite 150.
42 Dow, 1962, 229.
43 *United Service Journal and Naval and Military Magazine*, 1837 (I), 474.
44 Kopperman, 1987, 395.
45 Kopperman, 1996, passim.
46 Telford, 1909–14, II, 33.
47 Ward, 1765, 60.
48 Clode, 1869, II, 368.
49 Ward, 1765, 63.
50 Williamson, 1783, 65–7.
51 Dow, 1962, 184.
52 Holmes and Szechi, 1993, M.1, 393.
53 Cottesloe, 1930, 150–7; Childs, 1976, Appendix H, 257–9.
54 Scouller, 1966, 376–84.
55 Guy, 1985, 93.
56 Williamson, 1782, 12, 19.
57 Guy, 1985, 94–9.
58 Brown, 1997, 68–9.
59 Houlding, 1981, 8–12.

60 Langford, 1991, 20.
61 Scouller, 1966, 278.
62 P.R.O., WO 4/3, 104.
63 N.A.M., 7405–25
64 Clode, 1869, II, 368.
65 Lewis, 1937–83, XL, 90–1.
66 Lewis, 1937–83, XL, 91.
67 Langford, 1991, 20.
68 Young, 1925, 28.
69 Brumwell, 2002, 117–18.
70 P.R.O., WO 34/13, 128.
71 Hayter, 1994, 120–1.
72 Carter, 1933, XII (1), 378.
73 Carter, 1933, XII (1), 358.
74 Frey, 1981, 116–17
75 Simes, 1777, 230.
76 *Seventh Report*, 1809, 24.
77 Simes, 1777, 229.
78 P.R.O., WO 4/69, 490. See also 489, 500, 501.
79 *Seventh Report*, 1809, 25.
80 Dow, 1962, 226–7.
81 Haythornthwaite, 2001, 123.
82 P.R.O., WO 3/11, 158.
83 *Seventh Report*, 1809, 24–5.
84 Duffy, 1990, 25.
85 Gates, 1994, 137.
86 *Seventh Report*, 1809, 25.
87 Jarvis, January 1930, 292; Holmes, 2001 (a), 110, 120.
88 Jarvis, January 1930, 292.
89 Jarvis, January 1930, 293; *Seventh Report*, 1809, 26.
90 Holmes, 2001 (a), 106–7.
91 *Gentleman's Magazine*, November 1796, 918.
92 Anon., 1800, 51–2.
93 Anon., 1800, 54–5.
94 Anon., 1800, 53–4.
95 *Seventh Report*, 1809, 26.
96 *Seventh Report*, 1809, 26; Haythornthwaite, 1989, 14.
97 Jarvis, January 1930, 292–3.
98 Holmes, 2001 (a), 88–9; Barnett, 1970, 238–9.
99 *Seventh Report*, 1809, 99.
100 Gamble, 1795, dedication.
101 *Seventh Report*, 1809, 27.
102 Jarvis, January 1930, 294.
103 James, 1800, I, 26.
104 *Seventh Report*, 1809, 27.
105 *Seventh Report*, 1809, 27–8.
106 Gleig 1845, 411.
107 *Seventh Report*, 1809, 109–10.
108 *Seventh Report*, 1809, 107–8.
109 *Seventh Report*, 1809, 30–1.
110 *Seventh Report*, 1809, 107.
111 *Seventh Report*, 1809, 31.
112 R.A.Ch.D. Archive, Cosserat, 19 July 1801.
113 R.A.Ch.D. Archive, Cosserat, 24 July 1801.
114 R.A.Ch.D. Archive, Cosserat, 31 July 1801.

115 R.A.Ch.D. Archive, Cosserat, 2 August 1801.
116 R.A.Ch.D. Archive, Cosserat, 5 August 1801.
117 R.A.Ch.D. Archive, Cosserat, 30 August 1801.
118 R.A.Ch.D. Archive, Cosserat, 20 September 1801.
119 *Seventh Report*, 1809, 119–20.
120 Fortescue, 1899–1930, X, 197.
121 Ormsby, 1809, I, 128.
122 *Seventh Report*, 1809, 120.
123 *Seventh Report*, 1809, 119.
124 *United Service Journal and Naval and Military Magazine*, 1837 (I), 474.
125 *Seventh Report*, 1809, 111.
126 *Seventh Report*, 1809, 112.
127 *Seventh Report*, 1809, 113–14.
128 *Seventh Report*, 1809, 121.
129 P.R.O., WO 7/66, 1; Esdaile, 2003, 87–9.
130 P.R.O., WO 7/66, 1, 65.
131 P.R.O., WO 7/66, 31.
132 P.R.O., WO 7/66, 83.
133 Jarvis, July 1930, 361–3; B.L., OIR 283.54.
134 Burns, 1999, 42.
135 P.R.O., WO 7/66, 3–4.
136 Jarvis, July 1930, 366.
137 P.R.O., WO 43/578, 195.
138 P.R.O., WO 43/578, 189–90.
139 P.R.O., WO 43/578, 190.
140 P.R.O., WO 43/578, 190–1.
141 P.R.O., WO 43/578, 193.
142 P.R.O., WO 43/578, 199–200.
143 P.R.O., WO 4/345, 258.
144 P.R.O., WO 7/60, 180; Jarvis, July 1930, 367.
145 Hill, 1920, 12; *India Register, 1857*, xxxvi.
146 P.R.O., WO 7/61, 307.
147 P.R.O., WO 7/63, 69–70.
148 P.R.O., WO 7/62, 108.
149 Jarvis, July, 1930, 371–2.
150 P.R.O., WO 7/60, 127–30.
151 P.R.O., WO 7/60, 96.
152 P.R.O., WO 7/62, 69.
153 Fontana, 2002, 122–45.
154 *Seventh Report*, 1809, 102.
155 Fontana, 2002, 255.
156 P.R.O., WO 7/61, 13.
157 P.R.O., WO 7/61, 214.
158 P.R.O., WO 7/61, 215–16.
159 P.R.O., WO 7/61, 349.
160 P.R.O., WO 7/61, 421.
161 Howard, 2002, 110.
162 P.R.O., WO 43/578, 197.
163 Muir, 1998, 9.
164 Duffy, 1990, 29–31.
165 P.R.O., WO 7/60, 38–41.
166 Stevenson, 1841, 172.
167 P.R.O., WO 7/60, 38–41.
168 P.R.O., WO 7/60, 256–7.
169 P.R.O., WO 7/60, 38–41.

170 P.R.O., WO 7/60, 38–41.
171 P.R.O., WO 7/60, 38–41.
172 P.R.O., WO 7/60, 104–6.
173 P.R.O., WO 7/60, 258.
174 Brett-James, 1961, 214.
175 Brett-James, 1961, 212.
176 Brett-James, 1961, 212–13.
177 P.R.O., WO 7/60, 229–32.
178 P.R.O., WO 7/60, 229–32.
179 Stevenson, 1841, 184.
180 Brett-James, 1961, 213.
181 P.R.O., WO 7/60, 229–32.
182 P.R.O., WO 7/60, 229–32.
183 P.R.O., WO 7/60, 255.
184 Gray, 1963, 422–3.
185 R.A.Ch.D. Archive, Gleig – Letters, 1845–6; *Times*, 30 November 1811, 3.
186 Gurwood, 1837, 62–3.
187 Jarvis, July 1930, 372.
188 P.R.O., WO 4/345, 230–1.
189 Glover, 1968, 583; Glover, 2001, Appendix 4, 368–9.
190 Taylor, 1978, 128, 237.
191 Taylor, 1978, 233–5.
192 Taylor, 1978, 233–6.
193 Taylor, 1978, 93–5, 238.
194 Taylor, 1978, 233, 240.
195 Taylor, 1978, 238.
196 P.R.O., WO 7/66, 124.
197 P.R.O., WO 7/61, 433–5.
198 Jarvis, July 1930, 374.
199 Fortescue, 1899–1930, X, 201; Oman, 1912, 327.
200 Foster, 1891, passim; Venn, 1954, passim.
201 Glover, 1968, 578.
202 Glover, 1968, 583; N.A.M., 2002–05–3, 7–19.
203 Glover, 1968, 583–4.
204 Rickwood, 1961, 53.
205 Uffindell, 2005, 61.
206 Howard, 2002, 101–4.
207 R.A.Ch.D. Archive, Journal of the Rev. George Watson, 18 April 1814, 26 April 1814, 8 May 1814, 16 May 1814.
208 Hibbert, 1975, 16–17.
209 Donaldson, 2000, 98.
210 Buckley, 1987, 256–7.
211 Oman, 1912, 205, 287; Uffindell, 2005, 152.
212 N.A.M., 2002–05–3, 3.
213 Holmes, 2001 (a), 249.
214 Moyle Sherer, 1825, 100–1.
215 Howard, 2002, 96–7.
216 Howard, 2002, 101.
217 P.R.O., WO 7/66, 65; Venn, 1954.
218 P.R.O., WO 7/62, 59.
219 P.R.O., WO 7/62, 68–9.
220 Ormsby, 1809, I, 127.
221 Ormsby, 1809, I, 129–30.
222 Glover, 1968, 582.
223 Oman, 1912, 327.

224 N.A.M., 2002–05–3, 4.
225 Uffindell, 2005, 175.
226 N.A.M., 2002–05–3, 4.
227 R.A.Ch.D. Archive, Journal of the Rev. George Watson, 1 May 1814.
228 Oman, 1912, 327.
229 Stevenson, 1841, 186; P.R.O., WO 7/62, 110.
230 Surtees, 1833, 177–9.
231 Evans, 1983, 203, 207–8.
232 Kincaid, 1981, 43–4.
233 Kincaid, 1981, 46–7.
234 Bell, 1867, I, 99.
235 Hathaway, 1993, 11; Evans, 1983, 211–14.
236 Nugent Bankes, 1886, 146.
237 Liddell Hart, 1999, 153–4.
238 Gleig, 1915, 4–5.
239 Gleig, 1904, 130.
240 Gleig, 1904, 129.
241 Gleig, 1904, 130.
242 Gleig, 1904, 130–1.

From Waterloo to the Crimea

1 Burroughs, 1994, 164.
2 Jarvis, January 1931, 448.
3 Gleig, 1845, 410.
4 Jarvis, January 1931 (a), 479–80.
5 Jarvis, January 1931 (b), 519.
6 *Army List*, 1830, 396.
7 P.R.O., WO 7/64, 18–19.
8 Foster, 1890, 46, 167; Curtois, 1826, title page.
9 Curtois, 1833, 5.
10 Tucker, 1886, 35.
11 *Hansard*, 3 March 1854, 319.
12 *United Service Journal and Naval and Military Magazine*, 1843 (I), 619.
13 P.R.O., WO 43/285, 46.
14 Jarvis, January 1931 (a), 448.
15 *Times*, 17 August 1887, 4.
16 *Times*, 7 March 1849, 6.
17 Hannam, 1830, 3.
18 Ferrar, 1922, 190.
19 Fortescue, 1899–1930, XI, 42–3.
20 P.R.O., WO 4/347, 125–6; WO 4/349, 138.
21 P.R.O., WO 4/349, 308.
22 Jarvis, January 1931 (b), 488.
23 P.R.O., WO 4/348, 14.
24 P.R.O., WO 4/349, 390.
25 P.R.O., WO 7/66, 65.
26 Dow, 1962, 266.
27 *Methodist Magazine*, 1812, 878.
28 *Methodist Magazine*, 1812, 878.
29 *Methodist Magazine*, 1812, 77–9.
30 *Methodist Magazine*, 1814, 559–60.
31 Jarvis, January 1931 (a), 450.
32 P.R.O., WO 7/60, 180; WO 4/348, 31.

33 Jarvis, January 1931 (a), 450.
34 Jarvis, January 1931 (a), 451,
35 Jarvis, January 1931 (a), 452–3.
36 *Report of the Proceedings of the [N.M.B.S.]*, 1824, 3.
37 Jarvis, January 1931 (a), 452–3.
38 Dow, 1962, 260.
39 *Acts of the General Assembly of the Church of Scotland*, 1812, Abridgment, 25 May 1812.
40 Jarvis, January 1931 (a), 445.
41 Jarvis, January 1931 (a), 456–7.
42 P.R.O., WO 7/68, Hodgson to Merry, 30 September 1826; Dow, 1962, 269.
43 P.R.O., WO 7/68, Hodgson to Merry, 30 September 1826.
44 Dow, 1962, 269–70.
45 P.R.O., WO 7/68, Hodgson to Merry, 30 September 1826.
46 P.R.O., WO 43/636, 181.
47 P.R.O., WO 43/636, 181.
48 P.R.O., WO 43/599, 11.
49 Jarvis, January 1931 (b), 491.
50 P.R.O., WO 43/659, 312.
51 *Acts of the General Assembly of the Church of Scotland*, 1839, Abridgment, 25 May 1839.
52 *Acts of the General Assembly of the Church of Scotland*, 1844, Abridgment, 21 May 1844.
53 P.R.O., WO 43/599, 7; WO 43/616, 21; Fontana, 2002, 260–2.
54 P.R.O., WO 43/616, 19.
55 P.R.O., WO 43/616, 182–5; Jarvis, January 1931 (b), 491–2; Fontana, 2002, 265–8.
56 P.R.O., WO 43/659, 300–1, 307–10.
57 Hagerty, 2004, 21.
58 *Hansard*, 3 March 1854, 314–25.
59 Jarvis, January 1931 (b), 518.
60 Jarvis, January 1931 (b), 519.
61 Jones, 1983, 55.
62 Jarvis, July 1931, 28–9.
63 Jarvis, January 1931 (b), 503.
64 Jarvis, July 1931, 29–30.
65 Jarvis, July 1931, 30–1.
66 Jarvis, July 1933, 323, Jarvis, July 1931, 44; Hendrickson, 1998, 52.
67 Jones, 1983, 1–2; Hendrickson, 1998, 52.
68 B.L., Add MS 28510, 94.
69 N.L.S., MS 3872, 79–80, 107.
70 N.L.S., MS 3872, 134, 136.
71 N.L.S., MS 3872, 169.
72 N.L.S., MS 3872, 181.
73 N.L.S., MS 3872, 215–19.
74 N.L.S., MS 3872, 253–4.
75 N.L.S., MS 3872, 86, 223.
76 B.L., Add MS 28510, 94; N.L.S., MS 3872, 257, 266.
77 N.L.S., MS 3872, 244–8.
78 N.L.S., MS 3872, 268.
79 N.L.S., MS 3872, 268.
80 N.L.S., MS 3872, 248–9.
81 N.L.S., MS 3872, 267.
82 N.L.S., MS 3872, 268.
83 B.L., Add MS 28510, 94.
84 N.L.S., MS 3872, 270.
85 Gleig, 1904, 23–5.
86 Gleig, 1904, 27–28.
87 B.L., Add MS 40398, 229.

88 Gleig, 1904, 33–8.
89 Gleig, 1904, 55.
90 Gleig, 1904, 56–8.
91 Gleig, 1904, 61.
92 Gleig, 1904, 71, 74–92.
93 *O.D.N.B.*
94 N.L.S., MS 3869, 162.
95 Jarvis, July 1931, 21.
96 N.L.S., MS 3869, 165–6.
97 B.L., Add MS 28510, 94.
98 N.L.S., MS 3870, 88.
99 Gleig, 1904, 111. My italics.
100 N.L.S., MS 3870, 91.
101 N.L.S., MS 3870, 94–5.
102 Gleig, 1904, 112–15.
103 Jarvis, July 1931, 26.
104 B.L., Add MS 28510, 94–5.
105 Knight, 1995, 119–22.
106 B.L., Add MS 29240, 334; Add MS 28510, 95.
107 Gleig, 1835, n.p.
108 Gleig, 1835, vii.
109 *United Service Journal and Naval and Military Magazine*, 1839 (III), 474.
110 Hichberger, 1989, 52.
111 *United Service Journal and Naval and Military Magazine*, 1839 (III), 473.
112 B.L., Add MS 40422, 308–12, 313–17.
113 B.L., Add MS 29240, 334.
114 Jarvis, July 1931, 31–4; Singh, 1986, 2–3.
115 Gleig, 1904, 27; *O.D.N.B.*; Peers, 1997, 118, 124.
116 N.L.S., MS 3870, 145.
117 Singh, 1986, 186.
118 Singh, 1986, 191.
119 Singh, 1986, 203.
120 B.L., Add MS 40559, 50.
121 B.L., Add MS 40559, 50.
122 B.L., Add MS 40559, 50–1.
123 B.L., Add MS 40559, 51–52.
124 B.L., Add MS 40559, 52.
125 B.L., Add MS 40559, 52.
126 B.L., Add MS 40559, 54–5.
127 Jarvis, July 1931, 32–3.
128 P.R.O., WO 4/348. Dakins' correspondence for the period 10 August 1842–26 March 1844 amounted to a mere sixty-five pages. Gleig's correspondence for his first twelve months as Principal Chaplain amounted to 236.
129 Jarvis, July 1931, 37–41.
130 Jarvis, July 1931, 37–9.
131 Jarvis, July 1931, 37–8.
132 Jarvis, July 1931, 38.
133 Jarvis, July 1931, 38.
134 *United Service Journal and Naval and Military Magazine*, 1839 (I), 70.
135 Burroughs, 1994, 171.
136 Gleig, 1846, 553.
137 *O.D.N.B.*; O'Day, 1988, 191–2.
138 Strachan, 1980, 785.
139 Gleig, 1845, 402.
140 Gleig, 1845, 404.

141 Gleig, 1845, 410–11.
142 Gleig, 1845, 411.
143 Gleig, 1845, 414.
144 Gleig, 1845, 415.
145 Gleig, 1845, 416.
146 Gleig, 1845, 416–18.
147 Gleig, 1845, 418.
148 Gleig, 1845, 419–20.
149 Gleig, 1845, 421.
150 Strachan, 1984, 87.
151 Jarvis, July 1931, 45–7.
152 Jarvis, July 1931, 45–8.
153 Strachan, 1984, 87; Jarvis, July 1931, 42.
154 *O.D.N.B.*
155 Strachan, 1984, 67; Gleig, 1846, 557.
156 Jarvis, July 1931, 49.
157 B.L., Add MS 28510, 95.
158 Gleig, 1845, 403.
159 Jones, 1983, 38, 52, 86–7.
160 Gleig, 1846, 542–3; *O.D.N.B.*
161 Strachan, 1984, 89–91.
162 Strachan, 1984, 94.
163 Gleig, 1846, 545.
164 Gleig, 1846, 548–50.
165 Strachan, 1984, 94.
166 Jarvis, July 1931, 49.
167 Jones, 1983, 71.
168 Jones, 1983, 96.
169 B.L., Add MS 28510, 95.
170 Jones, 1983, 197.
171 Jarvis, July 1931, 59–60.
172 R.A.Ch.D. Archive, Policy Letters, Ordnance Office Memorandum, 17 March 1847, Gleig to Herbert, 10 November 1845.
173 R.A.Ch.D. Archive, Policy Letters, 'Memorandum', 10 May 1848.
174 *Hansard*, 3 March 1854, 326–7.
175 Jarvis, July 1931, 59–60.
176 Jarvis, July 1931, 64.
177 Jarvis, July 1931, 65; *Army List*, April 1855, 504; Hagerty, 2004, 23–4; Hagerty and Johnstone, 2005, 420–1.
178 *Times*, 3 March 1854, 9.
179 Mawson, 2002 (b), 37.
180 Wright, 1857, 6.
181 Viz. Henry Egan to the Light Division; Robert Halpin to the 1st Division; Robert Hamilton to the Cavalry Division; George Lawless to the 2nd Division; George Mockler to the 3rd Division and Henry Press Wright to Headquarters, from whence he was transferred to the 4th Division when the army landed in the Crimea. Mawson, 2002 (a) and (b) passim; Wright, 1857, 27.
182 Shepherd, 1991, I, 79–89, 117–19.
183 Howard, 2002, Appendix VI, 237.
184 N.A.M., 7405–84–1.
185 Royle, 2000, 133.
186 N.A.M., 7405–84–1.
187 Small, 1897, 141.
188 Wright, 1857, 48–9.
189 Marsh, 1857, 219–20.

190 Gleig, 1857, 52–3.
191 *Times*, 2 November 1854, 9.
192 *Times*, 3 March, 1854, 9.
193 Jarvis, July 1931, 65.
194 Jarvis, July 1931, 66.
195 R.A.Ch.D. Archive, Policy Letters, Hawes to Hawkins, 30 October 1854.
196 *Times*, 27 November 1854, 8.
197 Jarvis, July 1931, 66.
198 *Times*, 28 October 1854, 4.
199 *Times*, 31 October 1854, 9.
200 R.A.Ch.D. Archive, Policy Letters, 'Appointment of Assistant Chaplains', October 1854.
201 *Times*, 2 November 1854, 9.
202 Jarvis, July 1931, 66.
203 Jarvis, July 1931, 67.
204 *Army List*, 1856–7, 606; Jarvis, July 1931, 69.
205 Jarvis, July 1931, 69; Shepherd, 1991, I, 188–90.
206 Mawson, 2002 (a) and (b) passim.
207 N.A.S., CH/1/2/8 [19].
208 *O.D.N.B.*; Roper, 1998, 96; Hendrickson, 1999, 6.
209 R.A.Ch.D. Archive, Rev. Alexander Fraser in the Crimea.
210 Mawson, 2004 (b), 41; Candlish, 1854, passim.
211 Mawson, 2004 (b), 40–1.
212 Hagerty and Johnstone, 2005, 419–20.
213 Johnstone and Hagerty, 1996, 6; Mawson, 2001 (b), 38–40; Hagerty and Johnstone, 2005, 425.
214 *Wesleyan Missionary Notices*, Third Series, II, January 1856, 11–12.
215 *Wesleyan Missionary Notices*, Third Series, III, March 1856, 34.
216 *Wesleyan Missionary Notices*, Third Series, III, April 1856, 63–4; Mawson, 2002 (b), 41.
217 Gleig, 1857, 61.
218 R.A.Ch.D. Archive, Policy Letters, Hawkins to Lefroy, 28 September 1855.
219 Wright, 1857, 6.
220 Smyth, 1968, 85.
221 Wright, 1857, 83 footnote.
222 *Hansard*, 11 April 1856, 881.
223 Mawson, 2002 (a), 34.
224 Candlish, 1854, 34–5.
225 Wright, 1857, 25–6.
226 Wright, 1857, 35.
227 Gleig, 1857, 9–10, 55, 60.
228 Paget, 1956, 66.
229 Wright, 1857, 14–15.
230 Pearse, 1897, 117.
231 Baumgart, 1999, 143.
232 Holmes, 2001 (a), 249.
233 Mawson, 2002 (b), 35.
234 *Select Committee on Army before Sebastopol*, 1854–5, 171–82.
235 *Select Committee on Army before Sebastopol*, 1854–5, 171–2; Shepherd, 1991, II, 390–1.
236 Stewart, January 1932 (a), 142.
237 R.A.Ch.D. Archive, Letters of L.J. Parsons, 18 May 1855.
238 Stewart, January 1932 (a), 142.
239 Shepherd, 1991, II, 391.
240 *Select Committee on Army before Sebastopol*, 1854–5, 174.
241 *Select Committee on Army before Sebastopol*, 1854–5, 179.
242 R.A.Ch.D. Archive, Rev. Alexander Fraser in the Crimea.
243 R.A.Ch.D. Archive, Rev. Alexander Fraser in the Crimea; Mawson, 2002 (b), 40–1.

244 Mawson, 2002 (a) and (b), passim.
245 Hagerty and Johnstone, 2005, 430–1.
246 Paget, 1956, 159.
247 Hagerty, 2004, 25.
248 *Times*, 29 November 1854, 10.
249 R.A.Ch.D. Archive, Rev. Alexander Fraser in the Crimea.
250 R.A.Ch.D. Archive, Rev. Alexander Fraser in the Crimea.
251 *Army List*, April 1855, 504.
252 *Select Committee on Army before Sebastopol*, 1854–5, 173.
253 *Select Committee on Army before Sebastopol*, 1854–5, 179.
254 R.A.Ch.D. Archive, Policy Letters, insert.
255 *Times*, 9 October 1855, 10.
256 *Times*, 12 October 1855, 8.
257 *Times*, 9 November 1855, 5.
258 Mawson, 2002 (a), 32.
259 *Times*, 26 December 1855, 9.
260 Mawson, 2002 (b), 33.
261 R.A.Ch.D. Archive, Rev. Alexander Fraser in the Crimea.
262 R.A.Ch.D. Archive, Rev. Alexander Fraser in the Crimea.
263 N.A.M., 7405–84–1.
264 *Times*, 1 January 1855, 10.
265 Hagerty and Johnstone, 2005, 435–7; Murphy, 1961–2, 255–6.
266 Paget, 1956, 159–60.
267 Hagerty and Johnstone, 2005, 436.
268 Gleig, 1857, passim.
269 Paget, 1956, 160; Hagerty and Johnstone, 2005, 426.

From the Crimea to South Africa

1 Anderson, 1958, 165; Roper, 1998, 95.
2 Anderson, 1971, 61.
3 Mawson, 2002 (a) and (b) passim; Anderson, 1971, 53–4; R.A.Ch.D. Archive, Rev. Alexander Fraser in the Crimea.
4 Jarvis, July 1931, 76–7; Jarvis, July 1933, 325.
5 Jarvis, July 1931, 74–5; Costello, 1996, 115.
6 *O.D.N.B.*
7 *Hansard*, 11 April 1856, 878–80.
8 *Hansard*, 11 April 1856, 880.
9 *Hansard*, 11 April 1856, 880–1.
10 P.R.O., WO 3/577; Carshore, 1857, 14.
11 P.R.O., WO 3/577; *Army List*, April 1855, 505; Mawson, 2002 (a) and (b), passim; Jarvis, July 1933, 321.
12 Jarvis, July 1933, 327–8.
13 Haig, 1984, 223.
14 Haig, 1984, 298–300.
15 Knight, 1995, 135–41; Haig, 1984, 303–4.
16 Farwell, 1981, 58–67.
17 Jarvis, July 1933, 327–8.
18 Jarvis, July 1933, 326–7.
19 Jarvis, July 1933, 329–30.
20 Jarvis, July 1933, 330.
21 Jones, 1983, 155.
22 Jarvis, July 1933, 322–3; Jones, 1983, 165.
23 Jarvis, July 1933, 322.

24 Jones, 1983, 170.
25 R.A.Ch.D. Archive, Circular Memoranda, no. 1 *Hints and Instructions to Military Chaplains*, March 1857, 4.
26 R.A.Ch.D. Archive, Circular Memoranda, no. 1 *Hints and Instructions to Military Chaplains*, March 1857, 5.
27 R.A.Ch.D. Archive, Circular Memoranda, no. 1 *Hints and Instructions to Military Chaplains*, March 1857, 5.
28 R.A.Ch.D. Archive, Circular Memoranda, no. 1 *Hints and Instructions to Military Chaplains*, March 1857, 8.
29 Jarvis, July 1933, 324–5.
30 *Report of General Eyre's Commission*, 1862, XXXII, 736.
31 *Report of General Eyre's Commission*, 1862, XXXII, 770–1.
32 *Report of General Eyre's Commission*, 1862, XXXII, 772–3.
33 *Colburn's United Service Magazine*, 1867 (II), 216–17.
34 Spiers, 1992, 74.
35 *Colburn's United Service Magazine*, 1872 (I), 348.
36 Clarke, 1938, 9.
37 Clarke, 1938, 9–10.
38 Clarke, 1938, 10, 12.
39 N.L.S., MS 3871, 205.
40 *First Report from the Select Committee on Army Estimates*, 1888, VIII, 458.
41 Monro, 1922, 135.
42 Monro, 1922, 136.
43 Farwell, 1981, 202–4; McLeod, 1996, 150–1.
44 *R.C.C.*, 1875, 294.
45 Thompson, 1990, 269.
46 Blackburne, 1955, 19, 23.
47 Bristow, 1912, 49–50.
48 *United Service Magazine*, 16, 1897–8, 250.
49 *United Service Magazine*, 16, 1897–8, 251.
50 *United Service Magazine*, 16, 1897–8, 251.
51 Trustram, 1984, 109.
52 Trustram, 1984, 113.
53 Clarke, 1938, 8.
54 Blackburne, 1955, 20–1; Findlay, 1941, 103.
55 Thompson, 1990, 264–6.
56 *R.S.C.S.*, 1909, 846.
57 M.A.R.C., Minutes of the Royal Navy and Army Board, November 1911 – January 1918, 35.
58 Thompson, 1990, 260.
59 Brown, 1914, 75.
60 Thompson, 1990, 267.
61 *First Report from the Select Committee on Army Estimates*, 1888, VIII, 461.
62 Skelley, 1977, Table III A-1, 313.
63 Spiers, 1992, 143–4; Trustram, 1984, 116–26.
64 Wilkinson, 1981, 255.
65 Burns, 1999, passim.
66 Gleig, 1868, 265; Jarvis, July 1933, 333.
67 R.A.Ch.D. Archive, Circular Memoranda, no. 19, 'Personal interviews freed for last Friday of the month', 1 November 1872.
68 R.A.Ch.D. Archive, Circular Memoranda, no. 2 'Military Chaplains Dress at Levees', 30 May 1863; no. 5 *Chaplains not to take Houses on Lease*, 7 February 1867; no. 7 *Religious Instruction generally Unsatisfactory*, 25 January 1867.
69 Burns, 1999, 31.
70 O'Day, 1988, 193–4; Jarvis, July 1933, 335.

71 R.A.Ch.D., Circular Memoranda, no. 25 *G.R. Gleig's farewell address*, 9 April 1875.
72 Jarvis, 1935, 22–3.
73 *Times*, 19 April 1875, 7.
74 Jarvis, January 1931 (b), 497.
75 Jarvis, January 1931 (b), 498–9.
76 Jarvis, January 1931 (b), 500–1.
77 R.A.Ch.D., Gleig – Letters 1845–6, Gleig to Blomfield, 17 March 1846.
78 Jarvis, July 1933, 351–2.
79 Jarvis, July 1933, 352.
80 Jarvis, July 1933, 353–4; Hendrickson, 1998, 65–6.
81 N.L.S., MS 3871, 72.
82 Burns, 1999, 192–203.
83 Gleig, 1868, 273.
84 Gleig, 1868, 251.
85 Gleig, 1868, 251.
86 Gleig, 1868, 252.
87 *Colburn's United Service Magazine*, 1879 (III), 160.
88 *Colburn's United Service Magazine*, 1879 (III), 160–1.
89 P.R.O., WO 32/6429.
90 Gleig, 1868, 273; L.P.L., Tait Papers, CLXI, 90–8.
91 *R.C.C.*, 1875, 288.
92 *Hansard*, 9 June 1868, 1298–1301; 11 June 1868, 1385–93; 12 June 1868, 1465–8.
93 *Bill Intituled*, 1867–8, 13–19; Jarvis, July 1933, 353–8.
94 L.P.L., Tait Papers, CCVI, 389.
95 P.R.O., 32/4017.
96 *Hansard*, 9 June 1868, 1300.
97 Jarvis, July 1933, 357–8.
98 Jarvis, July 1933, 358; N.L.S., MS 3871, 180–3.
99 Kelly, 1910, 111.
100 *D.E.B*; *O.D.N.B.*
101 Jackson, 2000, 30–8, 42–3, 62, 69–70.
102 Rule, 1883, 25.
103 Rule, 1883, 25.
104 Rule, 1883, 24–5.
105 Rule, 1883, 26–7; Watkins, 1981, 65.
106 Watkins, 1981, 66–7.
107 Watkins, 1981, 68.
108 Rule, 1883, 34.
109 Watkins, 1981, 71–2.
110 Watkins, 1981, 72–3.
111 Watkins, 1981, 73.
112 Watkins, 1981, 73.
113 Watkins, 1981, 77; Hendrickson, 1999, 8–9.
114 Rule, 1883, 67.
115 Rule, 1883, 69.
116 Watkins, 1981, 76.
117 Watkins, 1981, 85–6; Kelly, 1910, 125.
118 Watkins, 1981, 90.
119 Kelly, 1910, 122.
120 Watkins, 1981, 76–7.
121 Kelly, 1910, 146–51; Hendrickson, 1999, 21.
122 Watkins, 1981, 88–90.
123 Watkins, 1981, 90.
124 Hendrickson, 1999, 9.
125 Rule, 1883, 61–5.

126 Hendrickson, 1999, 18–20.
127 Watkins, 1981, 93.
128 *O.D.N.B.*
129 Rule, 1883, 116.
130 Parsons, 1988, 53–6.
131 See, for example, Yates, 1999, passim.
132 Watkins, 1981, 76, 83; Knollys, 1894, II, 316.
133 Knollys, 1894, II, 317.
134 Farwell, 1981, 222.
135 Wood, 1906, I, 245.
136 Knollys, 1894, II, 317.
137 Knollys, 1894, II, 251–2.
138 Knollys, 1894, II, 253.
139 Jarvis, July 1933, 331.
140 Knollys, 1894, II, 253.
141 Knollys, 1894, II, 252–3.
142 Mews, 1973, 204.
143 Yates, 1999, 124–37.
144 Mews, 1973, 204.
145 Knollys, 1894, II, 254.
146 Knollys, 1894, II, 255.
147 Knollys, 1894, II, 257.
148 Jarvis, July 1933, 335.
149 Jarvis, July 1933, 335–6.
150 Jarvis, July 1933, 336.
151 Jarvis, July 1933, 336.
152 Jarvis, July 1933, 336.
153 Jarvis, July 1933, 336–8.
154 Jarvis, July 1933, 338–9.
155 Jarvis, July 1933, 335–41.
156 Jarvis, July 1933, 342.
157 Jarvis, July 1933, 343.
158 Jarvis, July 1933, 345–6.
159 Jarvis, July 1933, 350.
160 Jarvis, July 1933, 343.
161 Knollys, 1894, II, 315; *Queen's Regulations*, 1873, par. 164.
162 Lawson, 1929, passim.
163 Knollys, 1894, II, 318–20.
164 Knollys, 1894, II, 321–2.
165 Yates, 1999, 389.
166 Knollys, 1894, II, 322.
167 Knollys, 1894, II, 324.
168 Knollys, 1894, II, 324–5; *O.D.N.B.*
169 Knollys, 1894, II, 327–9.
170 Yates, 1999, 238.
171 Knollys, 1894, II, 329.
172 Knollys, 1894, II, 329–30.
173 *United Service Magazine*, 9, 1894, 401.
174 Anon., 1856, 17–20.
175 Dobbie, 1988, 29.
176 Dobbie, 1988, 12.
177 Dobbie, 1988, 29.
178 Edghill, 2002, 53–4.
179 Rule, 1883, 108–9.
180 Rule, 1883, 109.

181 Anon., 1864, 15–16.
182 Anon., 1864, 13.
183 R.A.Ch.D. Archive, Circular Memoranda, no. 15 *Army Scripture Readers: how to be used by chaplains*, 28 September 1871.
184 Anon., 1879, 9.
185 Rule, 1883, 108.
186 Robinson, 1898, 118–19.
187 Farwell, 1981, 199.
188 *R.C.C.*, 1900, 195.
189 Jarvis, 1937, 428.
190 N.L.S., MS 3871, 72.
191 *Times*, 19 April 1875, 7.
192 Jarvis, 1937, 425.
193 *Crockford's*, 1865.
194 N.L.S., MS 3871, 74.
195 Jarvis, 1937, 421.
196 N.L.S., MS 3871, 73.
197 R.A.Ch.D. Archive, Circular Memoranda, no. 27 *Report of Address delivered by Bishop Claughton to the Chaplains*, 10 June 1875.
198 R.A.Ch.D. Archive, Circular Memoranda, no. 27 *Report of Address delivered by Bishop Claughton to the Chaplains*, 10 June 1875.
199 R.A.Ch.D. Archive, Circular Memoranda, no. 27 *Report of Address delivered by Bishop Claughton to the Chaplains*, 10 June 1875.
200 R.A.Ch.D. Archive, Circular Memoranda, no. 27 *Report of Address delivered by Bishop Claughton to the Chaplains*, 10 June 1875.
201 R.A.Ch.D. Archive, Circular Memoranda, no. 27 *Report of Address delivered by Bishop Claughton to the Chaplains*, 10 June 1875.
202 O'Day, 1988, 194.
203 *R.C.C.*, 1875, 290.
204 *R.C.C.*, 1875, 291.
205 *R.C.C.*, 1885, 77.
206 *First Report from the Select Committee on Army Estimates*, 1888, VIII, 455–6.
207 *R.C.C.*, 1885, 85.
208 Parsons, 1988, 28.
209 *Times*, 15 October 1885, 3.
210 *R.C.C.*, 1885, 78.
211 *R.C.C.*, 1875, 292.
212 *R.C.C.*, 1885, 78.
213 *United Service Journal and Naval and Military Magazine*, 1843 (I), 619–20.
214 Wright, 1858, 99.
215 Wright, 1858, 100.
216 R.A.Ch.D. Archive, Circular Memoranda, no. 36 'Address to Chaplains, and instructions', 1 February 1878.
217 R.A.Ch.D. Archive, Circular Memoranda, Unnumbered 'Letter regarding confirmations', 14 December 1875; no. 34, 'Confirmations 1878', 14 January 1878.
218 Jarvis, 1937, 434.
219 Jarvis, 1937, 428.
220 N.L.S., MS 3871, 144–5.
221 P.R.O., WO 32/6217.
222 *Crockford's*, 1899.
223 *Army List*, 1901, 1409.
224 *First Report from the Select Committee on Army Estimates*, 1888, VIII, 458.
225 Pascoe, 1901, I, 107–24.
226 Edghill, 1887, 2–4.

227 *First Report from the Select Committee on Army Estimates*, 1888, VIII, 459.
228 P.R.O., WO 32/6217.
229 Spiers, 1992, 33.
230 *Second Report from the Select Committee on Army Estimates*, 1888, VIII, 552.
231 Spiers, 1992, 168; *O.D.N.B.*
232 *Times*, 5 August 1887, 6.
233 *Times*, 5 August 1887, 6.
234 N.L.S., MS 3871, 195.
235 N.L.S., MS 3871, 195–6.
236 N.L.S., MS 3871, 200–1.
237 *Fifth Report from the Select Committee on Army Estimates*, 1888, IX, 372.
238 Yates, 1999, 140–3.
239 R.A.Ch.D. Archive, Policy Letters, Debate on Army Estimates, 1890.
240 Wolseley, 1903, I, 3–4; Findlay, 1941, 141; Thompson, 1990, 198–9.
241 R.A.Ch.D. Archive, Policy Letters, Debate on Army Estimates, 1890.
242 Costello, 1996, 118.
243 Compton, 1893, 105.
244 R.A.Ch.D. Archive, Policy Letters, Edghill to Stanhope, 14 April 1890.
245 R.A.Ch.D. Archive, Policy Letters, Edghill to Stanhope, 14 April 1890.
246 R.A.Ch.D. Archive, Policy Letters, Edghill to Stanhope, 14 April 1890.
247 R.A.Ch.D. Archive, Policy Letters, Edghill to Stanhope, 14 April 1890.
248 R.A.Ch.D. Archive, Policy Letters, Memorandum, 18 April 1890.
249 P.R.O., WO 32/6217.
250 *First Report from the Select Committee on Army Estimates*, 1888, VIII, 463.
251 *Church Times*, 26 April 1901, 488.
252 *Church Times*, 19 April 1901, 459.
253 Winnington Ingram, 1940, 23.
254 Winnington Ingram, 1940, 24.
255 P.R.O., WO 32/6217.
256 *R.C.C.*, 1885, 78–9.
257 N.L.S., MS 3871, 74.
258 *Times*, 15 December 1876, 3.
259 *First Report from the Select Committee on Army Estimates*, 1888, VIII, 462.
260 *Times*, 30 December 1902, 2.
261 *First Report from the Select Committee on Army Estimates*, 1888, VIII, 455.
262 *First Report from the Select Committee on Army Estimates*, 1888, VIII, 461–2.
263 Acland-Troyte, 1881, 64.
264 Farwell, 1981, 219.
265 Wyndham, 1899, 66–7.
266 Wyndham, 1899, 67.
267 Gordon, 1929, 180.
268 *R.C.C.*, 1875, 309.
269 Jarvis, 1937, 443; *R.C.C.*, 1885, 88; Findlay, 139–41; R.A.Ch.D. Archive, Beach Papers, no. 15 Soldiers' Institute at Aldershot; *First Report from the Select Committee on Army Estimates*, 1888, VIII, 459.
270 *Church Times*, 23 March 1900, 351.
271 *R.C.C.*, 1900, 195.
272 *Church Times*, 2 December 1898, 673.
273 *R.C.C.*, 1900, 195.
274 Yates, 1999, 70–1.
275 Pollock, 1998, 36–7; *Church Times*, 20 May 1898, 567.
276 *R.C.C.*, 1900, 195; Findlay, 139.
277 R.A.Ch.D. Archive, Beach Papers, no. 17 'Papers on the Guild of the Holy Standard'.
278 *Church Times*, 20 May 1898, 567.
279 Costello, 1996, 116–17.

280 *First Report from the Select Committee on Army Estimates*, 1888, VIII, 457.
281 Bull, 1904, 11, 33–4.
282 Bull, 1904, 11.
283 Welch, 1998, passim.
284 *R.C.C.*, 1900, 193–4.
285 *R.C.C.*, 1900, 194.
286 *United Service Magazine*, 15, 1897, 619–23; 16, 1897–8, 249–53, 646–50.
287 Hardy, 1902, 51.
288 *Church Times*, 16 February 1900, 189.
289 *Church Times*, 16 February 1900, 189.
290 *Times*, 15 December 1899, 9.
291 Taylor, 1978, 291, 344–5.
292 P.R.O., WO 32/6624.
293 *Times*, 5 July 1858, 6.
294 Brown, 1997, 21.
295 *Army List*, 1863–4, 702.
296 Jarvis, July 1933, 322.
297 Thompson, 1990, 204; Costello, 1996, 115.
298 P.R.O., WO 43/357, 30, 84.
299 *Correspondence between Moderator of General Assembly of Presbyterian Church in Ireland and Secretary of State for War*, 1859, XVII, 137.
300 *Times*, 21 October 1858, 4.
301 *Correspondence between Moderator of General Assembly of Presbyterian Church in Ireland and Secretary of State for War*, 1859, XVII, 137.
302 *Times*, 25 November 1858, 7.
303 *Times*, 4 October 1858, 4.
304 Hanham, 1973, Appendix II, 179–81.
305 *Army List*, January 1879, 593–4.
306 *First Report from the Select Committee on Army Estimates*, 1888, VIII, 451, 453.
307 *Army List*, April 1899, 1262–3.
308 Scott, 1915–50, VII, 448.
309 Coulter, 1997, 60–1; Howson, 2004, 254–5.
310 Thompson, 1990, 205–18.
311 R.A.Ch.D. Archive, Policy Letters, Under Secretary to Moderator, 13 March 1885.
312 R.A.Ch.D. Archive, Policy Letters, Brown to Hartington, 16 February 1885.
313 R.A.Ch.D. Archive, Policy Letters, Kinnear to Hartington, 17 February 1885.
314 R.A.Ch.D. Archive, Policy Letters, Under Secretary to Moderator, 13 March 1885; Under Secretary's memorandum, 3 March 1885.
315 R.A.Ch.D. Archive, Policy Letters, War Office memorandum, 16 February 1887.
316 R.A.Ch.D. Archive, Policy Letters, War Office memorandum, 16 February 1887.
317 *R.S.C.S.*, 1900, 436–7, 440–3; Scott, 1915–50, VII, 448.
318 *R.S.C.S.*, 1866, 3–7.
319 *First Report from the Select Committee on Army Estimates*, 1888, VIII, 451.
320 *R.S.C.S.*, 1879, 257.
321 *R.S.C.S.*, 1866, 3.
322 Jarvis, 1937, 442.
323 Kelly, 1910, 123–4.
324 *First Report from the Select Committee on Army Estimates*, 1888, VIII, 454; Thompson, 1990, 222.
325 *W.C.M.*, 1859, 323.
326 *W.C.M.*, 1859, 323, 325–6; 1860, 537.
327 *W.C.M.*, 1860, 556.
328 Watkins, 1981, 111.
329 *W.C.M.*, 1878, 110–11.
330 *Second Report from the Select Committee on Army Estimates*, 1888, VIII, 574.

331 Watkins, 1981, 83; *W.C.M.*, 1859, 297.
332 *W.C.M.*, 1878, 229–30.
333 Watkins, 1981, 99–100, 112; *W.C.M.*, 1878, 229–30; Thompson, 1990, 171.
334 *W.C.M.*, 1878, 230.
335 *W.C.M.*, 1900, 369–70.
336 M.A.R.C., Minutes of the Royal Navy and Army Sub-Committee, October 1896 – April 1904, 264.
337 Kelly, 1910, 146.
338 Kelly, 1910, 155.
339 Watkins, 1981, 145–7.
340 Watkins, 1981, 157–8.
341 *W.C.M.*, 1900, 368–9.
342 *W.C.M.*, 1900, 369.
343 Thompson, 1990, 196–7.
344 *W.C.M.*, 1900, 457.
345 Thompson, 1990, 197; *First Report from the Select Committee on Army Estimates*, 1888, VIII, 459.
346 Watkins, 1981, 102.
347 Watkins, 1981, 102–3.
348 Thompson, 1990, 170.
349 *Second Report from the Select Committee on Army Estimates*, 1888, VIII, 574; Thompson, 1990, 226.
350 M.A.R.C., Minutes of the Royal Navy and Army Sub-Committee, October 1896 – April 1904, 379–80; Watkins, 1981, 109.
351 *Times*, 31 January 1925, 14.
352 Watkins, 1981, 111.
353 M.A.R.C., Minutes of the Royal Navy and Army Sub-Committee, October 1896 – April 1904, 254; Watkins, 1981, 109–10.
354 M.A.R.C., Minutes of the Royal Navy and Army Sub-Committee, October 1896 – April 1904, 408; Watkins, 1981, 111.
355 Brown, 1988, 136–8.
356 Brown, 1988, 154.
357 Brown, 1988, 194–5.
358 Watkins, 1981, 197.
359 Watkins, 1981, 198.
360 Watkins, 1981, 173–4.
361 Watkins, 1981, 181.
362 Thompson, 1990, 188.
363 Thompson, 1990, 178; Watkins, 1981, 177–94; W.M.M.S., Box No. 53, 4.
364 Watkins, 1981, 197.
365 Johnstone and Hagerty, 1996, 9.
366 *Times*, 5 July 1858, 6.
367 S.D.A., Bishop Grant, Godley to Grant, 28 March 1859; Grant memorandum, 31 March 1859.
368 S.D.A., Bishop Grant, Godley to Grant, 28 March 1859; Hagerty and Johnstone, 2005, 441.
369 *Times*, 15 October, 1885, 3.
370 Hagerty and Johnstone, 2005, 441.
371 Johnstone and Hagerty, 1996, 9–10.
372 Costello, 1996, 116–17.
373 Spiers, 1996, 337.
374 *Times*, 21 February 1879, 6.
375 *Times*, 21 February 1879, 6.
376 Farwell, 1981, 242; *Times*, 4 September 1886, 6.
377 *Times*, 26 February 1879, 7.
378 *R.C.C.*, 1885, 91–2.

379 Hughes, 1950, 211.
380 Norman, 1984, 183.
381 O'Meara, 1886, 4–6.
382 Norman, 1984, 184; Madigan (ed.), 1995, 351–2.
383 Norman, 1986, 185.
384 Hagerty, 2004, 23.
385 R.A.Ch.D. Archive, Policy Letters, Draft letter from Hawes to Grant, January 1859; Johnstone and Hagerty, 1996, 8.
386 Samuel, 1989, 103, 110–11; MacRaild, 1999, 86–91; Connolly, 1982, passim.
387 Johnstone and Hagerty, 1996, 10.
388 S.D.A, Forces 1895–1899, Cruise to Butt, 13 December 1895.
389 *Army List*, April 1899, 1262–3; Fitzgerald-Lombard, 1993, passim.
390 Fitzgerald-Lombard, 1993, passim.
391 Pastoral letter by Bishop Ullathorne dated 23 April 1850. I am grateful to Dr. Judith Champ for this information.
392 Knight, 2004, 238; Morris, 1966, between 416 and 417.
393 Fitzgerald-Lombard, 1993, passim.
394 Johnstone and Hagerty, 1996, 12.
395 Heimann, 1995, 137–41; Gilley, 1995, 55.
396 O'Meara, 1886, 149.
397 Farwell, 1981, 219.
398 Pollock, 1998, 72.
399 Farwell, 1981, 219.
400 Wood, 1906, II, 174.
401 Churchill, 2002, 155.
402 Pollock, 1998, 250, note 5.
403 Watkins, 1899, 59–60.
404 *First Report from the Select Committee on Army Estimates*, 1888, VIII, 455.
405 R.A.Ch.D. Archive, Policy Letters, Edghill to War Office, 11 May 1888.
406 R.A.Ch.D. Archive, Policy Letters, Edghill to War Office, 24 February 1888.
407 *Army List*, April 1899, 1262–3; *Crockford's*, 1899.
408 P.R.O., WO 32/6217.
409 *First Report from the Select Committee on Army Estimates*, 1888, VIII, 453.
410 Smyth, 1968, 118–19.
411 Jarvis, 1937, 440–1; *Army List*, January 1879, 593–4.
412 L.P.L., Tait Papers, CCLV, 409–14.
413 L.P.L., Tait Papers, CCLV, 415, 417, 421; Morris, 1966, 588.
414 Jarvis, 1937, 442; Williams, 1967, 256–7.
415 *Times*, 18 August 1883, 5.
416 L.P.L., Benson Papers, IX, 151–3.
417 L.P.L., Benson Papers, IX, 155.
418 P.R.O., WO 32/6435.
419 P.R.O., WO 32/6435.
420 P.R.O., WO 32/6435.
421 P.R.O., WO 32/6436.
422 *First Report from the Select Committee on Army Estimates*, 1888, VIII, 462.
423 *Times*, 3 June 1865, 6.
424 Watkins, 1981, 177–9.
425 *Crockford's*, 1899.
426 Morris, 1966, 222; Greaves, 2006, 95.
427 Morris, 1966, 318; *Crockford's*, 1899; David, 2005, 172.
428 *Times*, 3 February 1900, 12.
429 S.D.A., Forces 1900–1904, Fleming to Butt, 5 February 1900.
430 *Times*, 14 July 1900, 12.

431 R.A.Ch.D. Archive, Dow, 101–3; Johnstone and Hagerty, 1996, 21–7; Blunden, 1980, 286; *Church Times*, 2 February 1900, 135; Kelly, 1900, 87–90.
432 Kelly, 1900, 59–61.
433 M'Clelland, 1902, 33.
434 Small, 1897, 204.
435 Kelly, 1900, 61.
436 Churchill, 2002, 155.
437 *Church Times*, 25 May 1900, 602.
438 *Church Times*, 11 May 1900, 556.
439 *Church Times*, 25 May 1900, 602.
440 Nasson, 1999, 279; Farwell, 1999, 319.
441 *R.S.C.S.*, 1902, 738–9.
442 *R.S.C.S.*, 1902, 746; *R.S.C.S.*, 1900, 438–9.
443 *R.S.C.S.*, 1900, 438–9; *R.S.C.S.*, 1901, 778–9.
444 Bull, 1904, 248–9.
445 Welch, 2005, 93–4.
446 *Church Times*, 16 August 1901, 187.
447 'Convention for the Amelioration of the Condition of the Wounded in Armies in the Field', August 1864, Articles 1–3.
448 Watkins, 1981, 182–3.
449 Watkins, 1899, 167.
450 Kelly, 1900, 73.
451 *Church Times*, 23 August 1901, 213.
452 Clode, 1869, II, 389.
453 Jarvis, 1937, 441–2; Johnstone and Hagerty, 1996, 28.
454 Gordon, 1929, 180.
455 Spiers, 1998, 66.
456 Judd and Surridge, 2002, 194.
457 Surridge, 1997, passim.
458 Marks, 1905, 20.
459 Bull, 1904, 81.
460 Bull, 1904, 97.
461 Bull, 1904, 263.
462 *Times*, 4 February 1905, 7; *O.D.N.B.*
463 *R.S.C.S.*, 1902, 742.
464 M'Clelland, 1902, n.p.
465 M'Clelland, 1902, 85.
466 Stearn, 1992, 144.
467 Watkins, 1899, 186–8.
468 Watkins, 1899, 201.
469 Cuthbertson, 2000, passim.
470 Cuthbertson, 2002, passim; Bebbington, 1982, 121–4.
471 Watkins, 1901, 245.
472 Snape, 2005 (b), 79; Judd and Surridge, 2002, 4–5, 248.
473 Swarbreck, 1902, 186.
474 Swarbreck, 1902, 182–3.

The First World War

1 *Times*, 1 November 1901, 7.
2 Wessels, 2000, 82.
3 *Church Times*, 26 April 1901, 491.
4 Winnington Ingram, 1940, 21.
5 *Times*, 1 November 1901, 7; *Times*, 29 March 1938, 18.

6 Whitlow, 1938, 48–51.
7 Whitlow, 1938, 76.
8 Whitlow, 1938, 48.
9 Whitlow, 1938, 72–4, 88; Thorold, 1938, 95; *Times*, 29 March 1938, 18.
10 R.A.Ch.D. Archive, 'Dean of Battle – the story of a fighting parson, the Very Rev. A.T.A. Naylor', 20.
11 Thorold, 1938, 95.
12 *Church Times*, 6 June 1902, 711.
13 P.R.O., WO 32/9322.
14 Spiers, 1994, 212.
15 R.A.Ch.D. Archive, Chaplains for Expeditionary Force.
16 Thorold, 1938, 94.
17 Thorold, 1938, 95.
18 L.P.L., Davidson Papers, CXXXVIII, 181.
19 Whitlow, 1938, 92.
20 Savile, 1924, 366; Whitlow, 1938, 92.
21 L.P.L., Davidson Papers, CXXIII, 178–80.
22 L.P.L., Davidson Papers, CXXIII, 193.
23 L.P.L., Davidson Papers, CXXIII, 195.
24 L.P.L., Davidson Papers, CXXXVIII, 182–4.
25 P.R.O., WO 32/5632.
26 P.R.O., WO 32/5634.
27 R.A.Ch.D. Archive (R.C.), Box 28, Undated memorandum.
28 R.A.Ch.D. Archive (R.C.), Box 28, 'Short Service Commissions for Roman Catholic Chaplains (1909)'.
29 *Truth*, 3 November 1909, 1039–40.
30 R.A.Ch.D. Archive (R.C.), Box 28, 'Petition' (May 1909).
31 Brown, 1997, 27–8.
32 Thompson, 1990, 255–6.
33 P.R.O., WO 32/5635.
34 M.A.R.C., Minutes of the Royal Navy and Army Sub-Committee, October 1896 – April 1904, 363.
35 *General Annual Report of the British Army for the year ending 30 September 1913*, 94; Snape, 2005 (b), 174–5.
36 Thompson, 1990, 247–50; *Baptist Handbook*, 1914, 410–11.
37 Beckett, 1985, 128–9; Westlake and Chappell, 1991, 3–4.
38 *Times*, 29 March 1938, 18; M.A.R.C., Minutes of the Royal Navy and Army Sub-Committee, September 1904 – May 1911, 348.
39 *R.S.C.S.*, 1909, 862–3.
40 P.R.O., WO 32/6624.
41 P.R.O., WO 32/6624.
42 Johnstone and Hagerty, 1996, 43.
43 Thompson, 1990, 273; *Baptist Handbook*, 1915, 380.
44 Thompson, 1990, 274–5.
45 P.R.O., WO 32/4020; *Statistics of the Military Effort of the British Empire*, 1992, 30; Corrigan, 2004, 40.
46 *Statistics of the Military Effort of the British Empire*, 1992, 235.
47 Simkins, 1994, 241; *General Annual Report of the British Army for the year ending 30 September 1913*, 94; Marrin, 1974, 278, n. 90; Anon., 1916 (a), 315.
48 P.R.O., WO 32/4020.
49 Thompson, 1990, 385, 387; *Statistics of the Military Effort of the British Empire*, 1992, 190.
50 Marrin, 1974, 17–18.
51 Snape, 2005 (a), 150.
52 I.W.M. Documents, E.C. Crosse.
53 Digby, 1917, 7.

54 I.W.M. Documents, E.C. Crosse.
55 *Times*, 6 February 1918, 3.
56 P.R.O., WO 32/5636.
57 R.A.Ch.D. Archive, R/AChD Precedent Book.
58 L.P.L., Davidson Papers, CCCXLV, 4.
59 Madigan, 2006, 176–80.
60 Wilkinson, 1978, 128; L.P.L., Davidson Papers, CCCXLV, 115, 174.
61 *R.S.C.S.*, 1918, 293.
62 *Times*, 5 February 1919, 5.
63 L.P.L., Davidson Papers, CCCXLV, 218.
64 Bickersteth, 1996, 181.
65 L.P.L., Davidson Papers, CCCXLIII, 49.
66 Anon., 1916 (a), 315; Thorold, 1938, 96.
67 Digby, 1917, 2.
68 L.P.L., Davidson Papers, CCCXLIII, 49.
69 *Times*, 5 February 1919, 5.
70 Digby 1917, 3.
71 I.W.M. Documents, E.C. Crosse.
72 Digby, 1917, 2.
73 Raymond, 1968, 124–5.
74 Liddle Collection, M.S. Evers.
75 *Times*, 16 August 1911, 10; L.P.L., Davidson Papers, CCCXLIII, 51.
76 Pickering, 1989, 182–206; McLaren, 2005, 13.
77 Whitlow, 1938, 98.
78 Kennedy and Howell, 1917, passim.
79 Bickersteth, 1996, 81.
80 Thorold, 1938, 96.
81 Vernon Smith, 1915, passim; Winnington-Ingram, 1940, 113.
82 Bell, 1935, II, 761.
83 *Church Times*, 23 July 1915, 87.
84 *Times*, 8 July 1915, 6.
85 *Church Times*, 23 July 1915, 87.
86 L.P.L., Davidson Papers, CCCXLIII, 291.
87 L.P.L., Davidson Papers, CCCXLIII, 307; P.R.O., WO 32/5636.
88 L.P.L., Davidson Papers, CCCXLIII, 291.
89 *Church Times*, 23 July 1915, 87.
90 Thorold, 1938, 94; Dowland, 1997, 64–106; Jackson, 1960, 145.
91 C.M.S.A., XACC/18/F/1 Diaries of L.H. Gwynne, 22 February 1918.
92 *Times*, 21 July 1915, 9, *Times*, 4 December 1957, 13; Jackson, 1960, 5–6, 11.
93 Pollock, 1998, 163–4; Jackson, 1960, 21.
94 Jackson, 1960, 129–30, 144.
95 L.P.L., Davidson Papers, CCCXLV, 199.
96 Jackson, 1960, 144–6.
97 C.M.S.A., XACC/18/F/1 Diaries of L.H. Gwynne, August 1914 – May 1915.
98 Bell, 1935, II, 761.
99 Bickersteth, 1996, 67; Wilkinson, 1978, 127; Brown, 1996, 65–6.
100 C.M.S.A., XACC/18/F/1 Diaries of L.H. Gwynne, 22 May 1917.
101 Brown, 1996, 63–4.
102 I.W.M. Documents, E.C. Crosse; Blackburne, 1932, 169.
103 Barry, 1970, 58–60.
104 P.R.O., WO 32/5636.
105 Anon., 1916 (a), 320–1; Digby, 1917, 3.
106 P.R.O., WO 32/5636.
107 P.R.O., WO 32/5636; Blackburne, 1932, 88; R.P.D.A., Rawlinson, 1918, 5.
108 P.R.O., WO 32/5636.

109 *O.D.N.B.*
110 P.R.O., WO 32/5636; *Statistics of the Military Effort of the British Empire*, 1992, 191; Brown, 1996, 94; *Times*, 8 July 1915, 6.
111 *J.R.U.S.I.*, 1922, 422, 427.
112 *J.R.U.S.I.*, 1922, 422.
113 Drury, 1922, 46.
114 P.R.O., WO 32/4020.
115 L.P.L., Davidson Papers, CCCXLIII, 48.
116 L.P.L., Davidson Papers, CCCXLIII, 51.
117 *Times*, 28 March 1918, 9.
118 Middlebrook, 2000, 97–100.
119 Winnington Ingram, 1940, 108–9, 112.
120 L.P.L., Davidson Papers, CCCXLIII, 58.
121 L.P.L., Davidson Papers, CCCXLIII, 49.
122 Middlebrook, 2000, 110–12.
123 *R.S.C.S.*, 1915, 531–3.
124 *R.S.C.S.*, 1915, 536; 1900, 432; *Times*, 30 April 1934, 16.
125 *Times*, 30 April 1934, 16.
126 R.A.Ch.D. Archive, R/AChD Precedent Book.
127 Drury, 1922, 47.
128 Drury, 1922, 47; Smyth, 1968, 162–63.
129 Johnstone and Hagerty, 1996, 77.
130 *Times*, 13 March 1915, 2.
131 Edmonds, 1932, 137.
132 L.P.L, Davidson Papers, CCCXLIII, 207.
133 R.A.Ch.D. Archive (R.C.), Box 28, 'Military Chaplains during War 1914–18', French to the War Office, 31 July 1915.
134 *R.S.C.S.*, 1916, 369; R.A.Ch.D. Archive (R.C.), Box 28, Williamson to Simms, 25 August 1915; Magnus, 1958, 300.
135 *R.S.C.S.*, 1916, 369.
136 R.A.Ch.D. Archive, Blackburne papers, 'Conference of A.C.G.s of Armies', 6–7 June 1916, 6–7 November 1917.
137 R.A.Ch.D. Archive (R.C.), Box 28, Gosling to Bourne, 21 November 1917.
138 *Statistics of the Military Effort of the British Empire*, 1992, 190.
139 R.A.Ch.D. Archive, Chaplains for Expeditionary Force.
140 Johnstone and Hagerty, 1996, 73–4; Johnstone, 1992, 33.
141 Anon., 1916 (a), 338.
142 Johnstone and Hagerty, 1996, 76.
143 Anon., 1916, 338–9.
144 Dungan, 1997, 62; Johnstone and Hagerty, 1996, 86–8.
145 Aan de Wiel, 2003, 168–70.
146 Dungan, 1997, 62; Leonard, 1986, 6.
147 Miller, 1973, 313; Johnstone and Hagerty, 1996, 185.
148 Leonard, 1986, 6–7.
149 Leonard, 1986, 4; R.P.D.A.,'War History'.
150 Oldmeadow, 1944, II, 119.
151 Hagerty, 1998, passim; R.P.D.A., 'War History'.
152 R.A.Ch.D. Archive (R.C.), Box 28, Circular letter, 3 May 1915.
153 R.P.D.A., 'War History'.
154 Anon., 1916 (a), 339.
155 *Statistics of the Military Effort of the British Empire*, 1992, 190.
156 L.P.L., Davidson Papers, CCCXLIV, 23.
157 Bickersteth, 1996, 181.
158 R.A.Ch.D. Archive (R.C.), Box 28, Bourne to Ryan, 12 May 1917.
159 R.A.Ch.D. Archive (R.C.), Box 28, Morgan to Bourne, 13 January 1917.

160 R.A.Ch.D. Archive (R.C.), Box 28, Morgan to Bourne, 13 January 1917.
161 R.P.D.A., 3230.VII.A.3.F, Bourne to Simms, 6 November 1917.
162 Aan de Weil, 2003, 276; Taouk, 2003, 38–9.
163 P.R.O., WO 32/5634.
164 R.P.D.A., 3230.VII.A.3.F, Walsh to Gleeson, 30 April 1918.
165 Taouk, 2003, 39; Aan de Weil, 2003, 276.
166 Aan de Weil, 2003, 293.
167 Johnstone and Hagerty, 1996, 186–7; *Times*, 22 June 1918, 9; 4 October 1918, 3.
168 Anon., 1916 (a), 332.
169 *R.S.C.S.*, 1915, 535.
170 *R.S.C.S.*, 1915, 535–6.
171 R.A.Ch.D. Archive, Dow, 128–9.
172 *Statistics of the Military Effort of the British Empire*, 1992, 190; *R.S.C.S.*, 1917, 386.
173 *R.S.C.S.*, 1916, 384; MacLeod, 2001, 79–97.
174 *R.S.C.S.*, 1917, 368.
175 *R.S.C.S.*, 1917, 407, 411.
176 R.A.Ch.D. Archive, Dow, 128.
177 Anon., 1916 (a), 334; *R.S.C.S.*, 1916, 384.
178 *R.S.C.S.*, 1918, 298, 308.
179 *R.S.C.S.*, 1918, 317.
180 Thompson, 1990, 226–33, 243–4, 273–6.
181 Johnstone and Hagerty, 1996, 77.
182 *Statistics of the Military Effort of the British Empire*, 1992, 190.
183 Boullier, 1917, 9; Robinson and Hair, 2001, 6.
184 Boullier, 1917, 12, 43, 64–66; Robinson and Hair, 2001, 74.
185 *Army List*, July 1915, 1795–6; Thompson, 1990, 281.
186 Anon., 1929, passim.
187 *Army List*, July 1915, 1795–6.
188 Thompson, 1990, 293–6.
189 Lloyd George, 1938, I, 451.
190 Lloyd George, 1938, I, 451.
191 A.L.R.P.C., Baptist Union Minute Book, January 1914 – December 1915, 124.
192 *O.D.N.B.*
193 A.L.R.P.C., Baptist Union Minute Book, January 1914 – December 1915, 139, 318.
194 A.L.R.P.C., Baptist Union Minute Book, January 1914 – December 1915, 184–5.
195 A.L.R.P.C., Baptist Union Minute Book, January 1916 – December 1917, 249, 363.
196 Thompson, 1990, 387; *Statistics of the Military Effort of the British Empire*, 1992, 190.
197 M.A.R.C., Minutes of the Primitive Methodist Special Army Committee and Army Committee, 190.
198 M.A.R.C., Minutes of the Primitive Methodist Special Army Committee and Army Committee, 86, 92.
199 M.A.R.C., Minutes of the Primitive Methodist Special Army Committee and Army Committee, Shakespeare to Horton, 18 January 1918.
200 M.A.R.C., Minutes of the Primitive Methodist Special Army Committee and Army Committee, 103.
201 M.A.R.C., Minutes of the Primitive Methodist Special Army Committee and Army Committee, 108.
202 R.A.Ch.D. Archive, R/AChD Precedent Book.
203 Snape, 2005 (a), 210–11, 237.
204 *Times*, 6 October 1915, 9; *Army List*, November 1918, II, 1797; R.A.Ch.D. Archive, R/AChD Precedent Book.
205 R.A.Ch.D. Archive, R/AChD Precedent Book.
206 *Hansard*, 23 November 1916, 1626.
207 *Times*, 6 October 1915, 9.
208 Morgan, 1999, 43–4.

209 A.L.R.P.C., Baptist Union Minute Book, January 1914 – December 1915, 96–7, 124.
210 *Army List*, July 1915, 1795; *Statistics of the Military Effort of the British Empire*, 1992, 190.
211 Rabinowitz, 1936, 200; Englander, 1994, 343.
212 Englander, 1988, passim.
213 Rabinowitz, 1936, 200–2.
214 Anon., 1916 (a), 351; Adler, 1922, 16.
215 *Army List*, July 1915, 1796a.
216 *Times*, 13 March 1915, 11.
217 *Army List*, July 1915, 1795; *Statistics of the Military Effort of the British Empire*, 1992, 190.
218 *R.S.C.S.*, 1917, 369.
219 M.A.R.C., Minutes of the Royal Navy and Army Board, November 1911 – January 1918, 343–8.
220 *R.S.C.S.*, 1917, 270; M.A.R.C., Minutes of the Royal Navy and Army Board, November 1911 – January 1918, 346.
221 M.A.R.C., Minutes of the Royal Navy and Army Board, November 1911 – January 1918, 347–8.
222 M.A.R.C., Minutes of the Royal Navy and Army Board, November 1911 – January 1918, 348.
223 P.R.O., WO 32/14826.
224 *R.S.C.S.*, 1917, 270.
225 P.R.O., WO 32/14826.
226 A.L.R.P.C., Baptist Union Minute Book, January 1916 – December 1917, 141–3; Rawlinson, 1918, 4.
227 *R.S.C.S.*, 1917, 385–7.
228 Rawlinson, 1918, 4.
229 Middlebrook, 2000, 149.
230 *R.S.C.S.*, 1917, 370.
231 *R.S.C.S.*, 1918, 290; *J.R.U.S.I.*, 1922, 423.
232 *R.S.C.S.*, 1918, 291–3.
233 *R.S.C.S.*, 1918, 290–3.
234 I.W.M. Documents, E.C. Crosse.
235 Duncan, 1966, 18.
236 Johnstone and Hagerty, 1996, 75.
237 May, 1929, 139.
238 May, 1929, 139.
239 May, 1929, 139.
240 I.W.M. Documents, R. Bulstrode.
241 L.P.L., Davidson Papers, CCCXLV, 95.
242 Brown, 1996, 41–2; Barry, 1964, 43.
243 C.M.S.A., XACC/18/F/1 Diaries of L.H. Gwynne, 3 January 1918.
244 L.P.L., Davidson Papers, CCCXLV, 52.
245 May, 1929, 176.
246 May, 1929, 176.
247 May, 1929, 176, 178.
248 May, 1929, 178.
249 May, 1929, 177–8.
250 *R.S.C.S.*, 1918, 292–3; M.A.R.C., Minutes of the Royal Navy and Army Board (with Royal Air Force after 1918), January 1918 – January 1925, 30, 44, 54.
251 May, 1929, 180.
252 United Board, *Memoranda of Information for Chaplains to the Forces and Officiating Clergymen*, n.d., 4–5.
253 I.W.M. Documents, E.C. Crosse.
254 Digby, 1917, foreword.

255 Digby, 1917, 35–7.
256 Digby, 1917, 35.
257 R.A.Ch.D. Archive (R.C.), Box 28, *Instructions to Chaplains by the Reverend J.M. Simms, C.M.G., D.D., K.H.C., Principal Chaplain, British Army in the Field*, December 1915.
258 Griffiths, 1994, 183.
259 Rawlinson, 1917, preface.
260 Rawlinson, 1917, passim.
261 Rawlinson, 1918, passim.
262 *Notes on Service in the Army Chaplains Department*, 1917, passim.
263 R.A.Ch.D. Archive, *Practical Advice*, passim.
264 L.P.L., Davidson Papers, CCCXLV, 17.
265 *The Chaplains' Bulletin*, October 1917, 1.
266 *The Chaplains' Bulletin*, December 1917, passim.
267 *The Chaplains' Bulletin*, March 1918, 28.
268 Digby, 1917, 16.
269 Digby, 1917, 16.
270 Digby, 1917, 31.
271 McLaren, 2005, 47.
272 I.W.M. Documents, T.G. Rogers; Robinson and Hair, 2001, 91.
273 I.W.M. Documents, C.I.S. Hood. Hood was killed in action while serving as an artillery chaplain on the Western Front in April 1918.
274 Horne, 1995, 109–10.
275 Pym and Gordon, 1917, 111.
276 Pym and Gordon, 1917, 108.
277 Pym and Gordon, 1917, 108.
278 Snape (a), 2005, 208–16; Reznick, 2004, 17–41.
279 Messenger, 2005, 458; Anon., 1916 (b), 184.
280 *R.S.C.S.*, 1915, 549.
281 C.M.S.A, XACC/18/F/1 Diaries of L.H. Gwynne, 14 April 1915.
282 Winnifrith, 1915, 164.
283 Watkins, 1915, 181.
284 Creighton, 1916, 9, 11.
285 C.M.S.A., XACC18/F/1 Diaries of L.H. Gwynne, 3 March 1915.
286 I.W.M. Documents, J.B. Marshall.
287 P.R.O., WO 32/5636.
288 Lever, 1971, 43.
289 McLaren, 2005, 48.
290 Wearmouth, 1958, 57–8.
291 Wearmouth, 1958, 58.
292 Geare, 1918, 79.
293 Barry, 1970, 53.
294 C.M.S.A., XACC/18/Z/1 Army book.
295 I.W.M. Documents, E.C. Crosse.
296 Pym and Gordon, 1917, 109.
297 Liddle Collection, M.S. Evers.
298 Boullier, 1917, 75.
299 Adler, 1922, 12, 47; *Times*, 13 March 1915, 11.
300 I.W.M. Documents, E.C. Crosse.
301 Montell, 2002, 42–3.
302 Montell, 2002, 43.
303 Montell, 2002, 44.
304 Horne, 1995, 109.
305 McLaren, 2005, 58.
306 Moynihan, 1988, 69–70.
307 A.L.R.P.C., Baptist Union Minute Book, January 1916 – December 1917, 318.

308 L.P.L., Davidson Papers, CCCXLV, 53.
309 Montell, 2002, 99.
310 Liddle Collection, W.T. Croxford.
311 Liddle Collection, C.E. Raven.
312 Bickersteth, 1996, 234.
313 O'Rahilly, 1932, 433–4.
314 Creighton, 1916, 1.
315 Creighton, 1916, 4.
316 Creighton, 1916, 21.
317 Jackson, 1960, 146.
318 Johnstone and Hagerty, 1996, 86–90.
319 L.P.L., Davidson Papers, CCCXLIII, 111.
320 L.P.L., Davidson Papers, CCCXLIII, 154.
321 L.P.L., Davidson Papers, CCCXLIII, 184.
322 I.W.M. Documents, E.C. Crosse.
323 Johnstone, 1992, 64, 81–3.
324 Author's Collection, G.H. Ogden, 8 October 1915.
325 Kennedy, 1916, 163.
326 Kennedy, 1916, 163.
327 Kennedy, 1916, 148–9.
328 I.W.M. Documents, E.C. Crosse.
329 R.A.Ch.D. Archive, R/AChD Precedent Book.
330 *Statistics of the Military Effort of the British Empire*, 1992, 191; L.P.L., Davidson Papers, CCCXLIII, 211.
331 I.W.M. Documents, E.C. Crosse; Author's Collection, G.H. Ogden, 3 January 1916.
332 Horne, 1995, 172–5.
333 Cooper, 1993, 48.
334 Creighton, 1916, 32.
335 Jackson, 1960, 164.
336 Wilkinson, 1978, 127; Duncan, 1966, 21.
337 Haig, 1987, 15 January 1916.
338 Barry, 1970, 60.
339 Blackburne, 1955, 51.
340 L.P.L., Davidson Papers, DLXXXIII, 70–1.
341 *King's Regulations*, 1912, par. 1333.
342 L.P.L., Davidson Papers, CCCXLIV, 146.
343 R.A.Ch.D. Archive, Blackburne Papers, 'Conference of A.C.G.s of Armies held at D.C.G.'s office, Aug. 17, 1916'.
344 Bourne, 2001, 119.
345 Boullier, 1917, 78.
346 Boullier, 1917, 79.
347 Forbes, 1918, 44–5.
348 MacDonald, 1991, 200.
349 Studdert Kennedy, 1918 (b), 22–33.
350 C.M.S.A., XACC 18/F/4, 'Sermons from September 1916', 2 December 1917.
351 C.M.S.A., XACC 18/F/4, 'Sermons from September 1916', 2 December 1917.
352 Snape, 2005 (a), 109–11.
353 R.A.Ch.D. Archive, Blackburne Papers, Circular, 17 June 1916.
354 Liddle Collection, M.S. Evers.
355 R.P.D.A., 3231.VII.A.3.F, Oddie to Rawlinson, 2 July 1916.
356 *Times*, 27 July 1916, 7.
357 Edmonds, 1932, 138.
358 R.A.Ch.D., Blackburne Papers, D/3723, 30 April 1917.
359 Barnes, 1939, 55.
360 James, 1998, 136–7.

361 *Times*, 21 April 1916, 4; Montell, 2002, 71–2.
362 *Times*, 27 September 1916, 9; 12 July 1918, 5; Raw, 1988, 65–75.
363 *Times*, 5 February 1919, 5; Holmes, 2004, 583.
364 C.M.S.A., XACC/18/Z/1 Army book.
365 R.P.D.A., 3242.VII.A.3.F, 17 October 1917.
366 Liddle Collection, M.S. Evers.
367 Johnstone and Hagerty, 1996, 115.
368 Liddle Collection, M.S. Evers.
369 R.A.Ch.D. Archive (R.C.), Box 28, Rawlinson to Bourne, 5 June 1918.
370 Howson, 2005, Tables 1–2, 69–70.
371 C.M.S.A, XACC/18/Z/1 Army book.
372 Barry, 1970, 54.
373 Johnstone and Hagerty, 1996, 138.
374 Anon., 1999, 274.
375 R.P.D.A., 3231.VII.A.3.F, Prevost to Rawlinson, 3 March 1916.
376 R.A.Ch.D. Archive (R.C.), Box 28, Rawlinson to Bourne, 5 June 1918.
377 Barnes, 1939, 37.
378 Author's Collection, Baron, 62–3.
379 Corrigan, 2004, 88–91; Barnes, 1939, 52.
380 I.W.M. Documents, E.C. Crosse.
381 I.W.M. Documents, E.C. Crosse.
382 I.W.M. Documents, E.C. Crosse.
383 Blackburne, 1917, 39; Gray, 1986, 35–6.
384 I.W.M. Documents, E.C. Crosse.
385 I.W.M. Documents, E.C. Crosse.
386 Bickersteth, 1996, 274–5.
387 C.M.S.A, XACC/18/Z/1 Army book; Montell, 2002, 97.
388 Digby, 1917, 85–6.
389 I.W.M. Documents, E.C. Crosse.
390 McLaren, 2005, 25.
391 R.A.Ch.D. Archive, *Practical Advice*, 1917, 8.
392 R.A.Ch.D. Archive, Tanner, 'An Army Chaplain's Work in War-Time'.
393 Blackburne, 1932, 87.
394 Blackburne, 1932, 91.
395 Blackburne, 1932, 89.
396 Harington, 1935, 232.
397 Moorman, 1947, 83.
398 Moorman, 1947, 42–75; *Times*, 29 December 1914, 3.
399 Moorman, 1947, 84–5.
400 Bickersteth, 1996, 182.
401 Moorman, 1947, 91; *Statistics of the Military Effort of the British Empire*, 1992, 190.
402 L.P.L., MS 2077, 160–77.
403 L.P.L., MS 2077, 62–3.
404 Moorman, 1947, 88–90; L.P.L., MS 2077, 87–91.
405 Blackburne, 1955, 52; Blackburne, 1917, vii–viii.
406 C.M.S.A., XACC/18/F/1 Diaries of L.H. Gwynne, 10 October 1916.
407 Blackburne, 1917, vii–ix; C.M.S.A., XACC/18/F/1 Diaries of L.H. Gwynne, 10 October 1916.
408 Blackburne, 1917, x.
409 Blackburne, 1917, ix.
410 Blackburne, 1917, vii; R.A.Ch.D. Archive, Blackburne Papers, correspondence of November 1916.
411 Blackburne, 1955, 52.
412 Boullier, 1917, 86.
413 Blackburne, 1917, v.

414 R.A.Ch.D. Archive, Blackburne Papers, 'Souvenir. Conference of Chaplains, FIRST ARMY B.E.F. Aire – September 26–27 1917'.
415 R.A.Ch.D. Archive, Blackburne Papers, 'Chaplains' Conference. Preliminary Notice', August 1918.
416 A.B.A., FHD/A5, 15 August 1918.
417 R.A.Ch.D. Archive, Blackburne Papers, circular 7 March 1917.
418 C.M.S.A., XACC/18/F/1 Diaries of L.H. Gwynne, 18–20 October 1917, 22 December 1917.
419 C.M.S.A., XACC/18/F/1 Diaries of L.H. Gwynne, 15 February 1918.
420 Liddle Collection, M.S. Evers.
421 R.A.Ch.D. Archive (R.C.), Box 28, Keatinge to Bourne, 21 September 1915.
422 McLaren, 2005, 65–6, 71–2, 86–7, 90, 91.
423 Watkins, 1915, 13–14; Winnifrith, 1915, 9, 92–3.
424 A.B.A., FHD/A5, 30 September 1915.
425 *Times*, 6 June 1916, 4; Bell, 1935, I, 690–708; Marrin, 1974, 48–9; Bailey, 1984, 196–7.
426 Allison, 2005, 41.
427 Fisher, 1917, 62–3.
428 Thompson, 1990, 465 n. 37; Anon., 1929, 165.
429 *Hansard*, 18 October 1916, 538; Falls, 1922, 11; Johnstone, 1992, 256.
430 Liddle Collection, J. Esslemont Adams.
431 Williamson, 1921, 53–5, 73.
432 Maclean Watt, 1917, 91–2.
433 R.P.D.A., 3230.VII.A.3.F, Devas to Rawlinson, 23 March 1919.
434 M.A.R.C., Minutes of the Royal Navy and Army Board, November 1911 – January 1918, 286–9.
435 M.A.R.C., Minutes of the Royal Navy and Army Board, November 1911 – January 1918, 304.
436 L.P.L., Davidson Papers, DLXXXIII, 72; CCCXLIV, 127–8.
437 Horne, 1995, 155.
438 I.W.M. Documents, E.C. Crosse.
439 Forbes, 1918, 71.
440 I.W.M. Documents, E.C. Crosse.
441 R.A.Ch.D. Archive (R.C.), Box 28, Gosling to Bourne, 6 December 1917.
442 Liddle Collection, M.S. Evers.
443 I.W.M. Documents, E.C. Crosse.
444 O'Rahilly, 1932, 474.
445 I.W.M. Documents, W.M. Murray.
446 A.B.A., FHD/A5, 10 August 1915.
447 McLeod, 1996, 18.
448 *Times*, 7 September 1917, 7; 25 March 1918, 11.
449 Talbot, 1917, 3–4.
450 Digby, 1917, 20.
451 Sheffield, 1996, 414.
452 Beckett, 1985, 144.
453 Hughes, 1985, 111.
454 Sheffield, 1996, 413–24.
455 Sheffield, 1996, 421.
456 Montague, 1922, 72.
457 Digby, 1917, 4, 7.
458 Digby, 1917, 4.
459 Digby, 1917, 14–15.
460 R.A.Ch.D. Archive, Blackburne Papers, 'The Chaplain's Status', undated.
461 *Times*, 8 July 1915, 6.
462 Harrison, 1995, 133–43.
463 Harrison, 1995, 144–6; Wilkinson, 1978, 106.

464 Holmes, 2004, 483.
465 Harrison, 1995, 139.
466 C.M.S.A., XACC/18/F/1 Diaries of L.H. Gwynne, 20 August 1916.
467 Creighton, 1916, 7.
468 Arthur, 2002, 94.
469 Studdert Kennedy, 1918 (b), 114–15.
470 Studdert Kennedy, 1918 (b) 102.
471 Studdert Kennedy, 1918 (b), 100.
472 Studdert Kennedy, 1918 (b), 107–8.
473 Studdert Kennedy, 1918 (b), 110.
474 Snape, 2005 (a), 111–14.
475 Gibbs, 1920, 116–17.
476 Gibbs, 1920, 364.
477 Grieves, 1997, 36.
478 Montague, 1922, 71–72.
479 Montague, 1922, 81.
480 O'Day, 1988, passim.
481 Author's Collection, Baron, 63.
482 Graham, 1919, 257.
483 Digby, 1917, 21–2.
484 Blackburne, 1932, 104.
485 Corrigan, 2004, 229.
486 C.M.S.A., XACC/18/F/1 Diaries of L.H. Gwynne, 1 May 1917.
487 Putkowski and Sykes, 1989, 134; Snape, 2004, 361–2; May, 1929, 177; Barry, 1964, 49.
488 *The Guardian*, 17 May 2005, 4.
489 Snape, 2004, passim.
490 Montell, 2002, 80.
491 Montell, 2002, 80–1.
492 Corrigan, 2004, 229.
493 Snape, 2004, 360–1; C.M.S.A., XACC/18/Z/1 Army book.
494 Downham, 2004, 131.
495 Steuart, 1931, 94–5.
496 Crozier, 1969, 51.
497 Dunn, 1994, 470.
498 Montague, 1922, 70.
499 Montague, 1922, 71–2.
500 Liddle Collection, M.S. Evers.
501 Johnstone and Hagerty, 1996, 129.
502 Day, 1937, 172–3.
503 Crozier, 1969, 76–7.
504 Liddle Collection, C.E. Raven.
505 Montague, 1922, 73.
506 Day, 1937, 180.
507 Graham, 1919, 257.
508 Graham, 1919, 257.
509 Gibbs, 1920, 108–9.
510 R.P.D.A., Correspondence, Brown to Rawlinson, 4 August 1918.
511 McLeod, 2001, 199.
512 McLeod, 2001, passim.
513 Madigan, 2006, 152.
514 Montague, 1922, 72.
515 McLeod, 2001, 209.
516 Drury, 1968, 123; *Baptist Handbook*, 1916, 398–9.
517 *J.R.U.S.I.*, 1922, 430.
518 Bailey, 1984, passim; Chapman, 2000, passim.

519 Mews, 1977, 374–5.
520 Barry, 1970, 57.
521 Wilkinson, 1978, 179–82, MacLeod, 2002, 74–82.
522 Creighton, 1920, 130.
523 Studdert Kennedy, 1918 (b), 119–44.
524 Studdert Kennedy, 1918 (a), 189.
525 Studdert Kennedy, 1918 (a), 172–3.
526 McLeod, 2001, 202.
527 Lever, 1971, 49; Clayton, 1920, 38.
528 Barry, 1970, 64.
529 Bickersteth, 1996, 274.
530 Studdert-Kennedy, 1982, 51; Wilkinson, 1978, 86–8, 283; 1998, 63–64; Madigan, 2006, 257.
531 A.B.A., FHD/A3, letter to army bishop 14 December 1918.
532 Wilkinson, 1978, 86, 271.
533 Wilkinson, 1978, 307; *Times*, 7 December 1918, 5.
534 *O.D.N.B.*; Lockhart, 1949, 257; Barry, 1970, 63.
535 Grimley, 2004, 18–19; Brown, 1996, 208–10; Snape, 2005 (a), 71; Ellis Roberts, 1942, 78.
536 Barry, 1970, 66.
537 Mews, 2004, 444.
538 Barry, 1970, 66.
539 Mews, 2004, 444; Barry, 1970, 67.
540 Barry, 1970, 69.
541 Wilkinson, 1978, 277–9; Mews, 2004, 446.
542 Hastings, 1991, 194; Studdert-Kennedy, 1982, 51.
543 Barry, 1970, 62.
544 L.P.L., MS 2883, 170–1.
545 L.P.L., MS 2883, 171.
546 *Chaplains' Bulletin*, October 1917, 4.
547 *Chaplains' Bulletin*, October 1917, 4.
548 *Times*, 15 January 1919, 6.
549 Henson, 1943, I, 208.
550 Creighton, 1920, 199.
551 Moynihan, 1983, 110.
552 Snape, 2005 (a), 90, Table 2, 146.
553 Taylor, 1993, passim.
554 Of the first 100 chaplains featured in Gwynne's Army Book, twelve were parochial clergymen of the diocese of London and five were parochial clergymen of the diocese of Winchester. The dioceses of Liverpool and Manchester furnished only one parochial clergyman each. C.M.S.A., XACC/18/Z/1 Army book.
555 Snape, 2005 (a), 42
556 Snape, 2005 (a), 34–5, 42–7.
557 Bell, 1916, 4–5.
558 Bell, 1916, 40.
559 Bell, 1916, 40–1.
560 Mews, 1973, 199–203.
561 Gray, 1986, 46–9; Barry, 1970, 58.
562 Wilkinson, 1978, 82–4; Gray, 1986, 49.
563 Creighton, 1920, 127; I.W.M. Documents, W.M. Murray.
564 Morgan, 1999, 50–1.
565 McLaren, 2005, 20; Tiplady, 1939, 3.
566 Tiplady, 1939, 8, 44–5, 61–4, 72–8.
567 Robinson and Hair, 2001, 144.
568 Fisher, 1917, 70.
569 Westerdale, 1917, 81, 84.

570 Westerdale, 1917, 82–3.
571 *Times*, 7 January 1919, 11.
572 *Statistics of the Military Effort of the British Empire*, 1992, 190.
573 *Times*, 20 March 1919, 8.
574 R.P.D.A., 3230.VII.A.3.F, Rawlinson to MacMullan, 23 November 1918.
575 *Times*, 13 January, 1919, 9; 25 February 1919, 5.
576 *O.D.N.B.*
577 *R.S.C.S.*, 1919, 310–11; *Times*, 30 April 1934, 16.
578 *Times*, 4 December 1957, 13.
579 C.M.S.A., XACC/18/F/1 Diaries of L.H. Gwynne, 16 September 1916, 19–20 October 1916, 7 February 1917.
580 C.M.S.A., XACC/18/F/1 Diaries of L.H. Gwynne, 17 October 1916.
581 C.M.S.A., XACC/18/F/1 Diaries of L.H. Gwynne, 3 September 1916, 28 September 1916.
582 *O.D.N.B.*; C.M.S.A., XACC/18/F/1 Diaries of L.H. Gwynne, 22 February 1918.
583 *Statistics of the Military Effort of the British Empire*, 1992, 190; *R.S.C.S.*, 1919, 310.
584 *R.S.C.S.*, 1919, 310.
585 *R.S.C.S.*, 1919, 311.
586 DeGroot, 1996, 407.
587 Barry, 1970, 60.
588 Jackson, 1960, 169.
589 *J.R.U.S.I.*, 1922, 431.
590 I.W.M. Documents, E.C. Crosse.
591 Barnes, 1939, 79.
592 Wilkinson, 1978, 307–9; Lever, 1971, 164.
593 See, for example, Coop, 1919; Scott and Middleton Brumwell, 1923; *Times*, 15 August 1925, 6.
594 Bushaway, 1992, 156; Ellis Roberts, 1942, 145.
595 Moynihan, 1983, 50, 56.
596 Bushaway, 2001, 498; Moynihan, 1983, 76–80; Gregory, 1994, 24–5; Bushaway, 1992, 154.
597 Porter, 2005, passim.

The Second World War

1 Thompson, 1990, 439–42; M.A.R.C., Minutes of the Royal Navy, Army and Royal Air Force Board, November 1932 – January 1945, 264.
2 Thompson, 1990, 442–4.
3 A.L.R.P.C., Baptist Union Minute Book January 1918 to December 1919, 355–65.
4 M.A.R.C., Minutes of the Primitive Methodist Special Army Committee and Army Committee, 233.
5 Thompson, 1995, 20.
6 P.R.O., WO 32/10479; Thompson, 1990, 446.
7 Thompson, 1990, 448–9.
8 Thompson, 1990, 447–8.
9 Thompson, 1990, 450.
10 Thompson, 1990, 453.
11 R.A.Ch.D. Archive (R.C.), *Précis for the Army Council*, May 1920.
12 P.R.O., WO 32/5969.
13 Mews, 1994, 452; Hastings, 1991, 97.
14 M.A.R.C., Minutes of the Royal Navy, Army and Royal Air Force Board, November 1932 – January 1945, 432.
15 *R.S.C.S.*, 1920, 350–2.
16 P.R.O., WO 32/10479; WO 32/10482.
17 Wilson, 1988, 777.

18 *R.S.C.S.*, 1920, 339.
19 P.R.O., WO 32/4020; Thompson, 1990, 457–60.
20 Barnett, 1970, 411; Carver, 1998, 136.
21 Middleton Brumwell, 1943, 36.
22 R.A.Ch.D. Archive, *Report of Conference of Regular Chaplains*, passim.
23 Robinson, 1999, 54–7.
24 *Hansard*, 7 March 1918, 2124–5.
25 *Times*, 20 April 1925, 16.
26 Thompson, 1990, 449.
27 *Times*, 31 January 1925, 14; R.A.Ch.D. Archive, Report on ACD Mesopotamia; Robinson, 1999, 57–8.
28 R.A.Ch.D. Archive, *Report of Conference of Regular Chaplains*, 3.
29 P.R.O., 32/4017.
30 P.R.O., 32/4017.
31 P.R.O., 32/4017.
32 Gray, 1986, 58–61; Machin, 2000, passim.
33 P.R.O., 32/4010.
34 P.R.O., 32/4010.
35 Hayward, 2002, 152; British Film Institute Film and TV Database.
36 Grieves, 1997, passim.
37 Graves, 1929, 242.
38 Graves, 1929, 242.
39 Graves, 1929, 294.
40 Sassoon, 1960, 304.
41 Sassoon, 1965, 177.
42 *O.D.N.B.*; Sassoon, 1960, 303–4.
43 Sassoon, 1965, 169.
44 Sassoon, 1965, 118–19.
45 *Times*, 15 November 1965, 12; 16 November 1979, 4.
46 Brophy and Partridge, 1930, 148.
47 Hastings, 1991, 186–92; Barron, 2006, passim; Mews, 1976, passim.
48 *O.D.N.B.*
49 Richards, 1983, 86.
50 Richards, 1983, 85–6.
51 Richards, 1983, 301.
52 Richards, 1983, 288.
53 Richards, 1983, 301.
54 Richards, 1983, 302.
55 Chapman, 1985, 117.
56 Madigan, 2006, 18.
57 Benstead, 1930, 13.
58 Benstead, 1930, 8.
59 Benstead, 1930, 297.
60 Benstead, 1930, 310–18.
61 Madigan, 2006, 20; Brophy and Partridge, 1930, 148.
62 C.M.S.A., XACC/18/Z/1 Army book; Robinson, 1999, 70–2.
63 *O.D.N.B.*; Thompson, 1919, passim.
64 Thompson, 1927, passim.
65 Brophy and Partridge, 1930, 148.
66 Bond, 2002, 35–8; Strachan, 2003, 331.
67 Remarque, 1982, 5; Blackburne, 1932, passim; Blackburne, 1955, 75.
68 Ceadel, 1980, 317; Dillistone, 1975, 212.
69 Dillistone, 1975, 211.
70 R.A.Ch.D. Archive, Blackburne papers, 'Chaplains. C. of E. 1st Army'.
71 Liddle Collection, C.E. Raven.

72 C.M.S.A., XACC/18/Z/1, Army book; Liddle Collection, C.E. Raven.
73 *O.D.N.B.*; Dillistone, 1975, 215.
74 Raven, 1935, 155.
75 Raven, 1938, 24, 26.
76 Raven, 1938, 57–9.
77 Dillistone, 1975, 228.
78 *O.D.N.B.*; Madigan, 2006, 256.
79 Hastings, 1991, 332.
80 Ellis Roberts, 1942, 263.
81 Matthews, 1938, 72.
82 C.M.S.A., XACC/18/F/1, 4 October 1914; Ellis Roberts, 1942, 79; Scott, 1977, 62–6; Lockhart, 1949, 257.
83 *Crockford's*, 1937. Sheppard's name does not appear in *The London Gazette* or in the *Army Lists* for the war years; P.R.O., WO 372/18; Ellis Roberts, 1942, 116–18, 189, 196; Madigan, 2006, 227, 235, 249–50.
84 P.R.O., WO 372/18; Hastings, 1991, 333.
85 Porter, 2005, 280–3.
86 *O.D.N.B.*
87 Studdert-Kennedy, 1982, 58.
88 Todman, 2005, 130.
89 Studdert-Kennedy, 1982, 61; Todman, 2005, 132.
90 Ceadel, 1980, 68, 94–5; Ellis Roberts, 1942, 216–17.
91 Barry, 1970, 128.
92 Bedborough, 1934, passim.
93 Raven, 1935, 22–3.
94 Raven, 1935, 23.
95 Todman, 2005, 90.
96 Mews, 1994, 461.
97 Ceadel, 1980, 317.
98 Raven, 1938, 20–1; Ceadel, 1980, 173–4; Ceadel, 1983, 401.
99 Sheppard, 1938, 148.
100 Raven, 1935, 179.
101 Ceadel, 1983, 401.
102 Dillistone, 1975, 223; *Times*, 28 March 1936, 8.
103 Scott, 1977, 238.
104 Coulter, 1997, 42–3; *O.D.N.B.*
105 Dillistone, 1975, 220–2.
106 L.P.L., MS 2884, 214; Hastings, 1991, 334; Scott, 1977, 228; Ellis Roberts, 1942, 296.
107 Barry, 1970, 127–8.
108 *Hansard*, 10 March 1931, 1139, 1141.
109 *Hansard*, 10 March 1931, 1142–3.
110 *Hansard*, 10 March 1931, 1140.
111 *Hansard*, 10 March 1931, 1139; *Times*, 3 October 1953, 8.
112 Robinson, 1999, 70; Ceadel, 1980, passim.
113 Johnstone and Hagerty, 1996, 191.
114 Sheppard, 1938, 145.
115 Sheppard, 1938, 145.
116 Johnstone and Hagerty, 1996, 191.
117 Johnston and Hagerty, 1996, 193.
118 P.R.O., WO 32/4016.
119 R.A.Ch.D. Archive, Interdenominational Advisory Committee, 60th Meeting, 3 November 1927.
120 R.A.Ch.D. Archive, Interdenominational Advisory Committee, 61st Meeting, 14 November 1928.

121 R.A.Ch.D. Archive, Interdenominational Advisory Committee, 63rd Meeting, 5 November 1930.
122 P.R.O., WO 32/4016.
123 P.R.O., WO 32/4016.
124 P.R.O., WO 32/4016.
125 P.R.O., WO 32/4016.
126 P.R.O., WO 32/4016.
127 P.R.O., WO 32/4023.
128 P.R.O., WO 32/4023.
129 *Times*, 9 February 1932, 15.
130 Tuckey, 1932, 117–19.
131 *Times*, 15 February 1938, 20.
132 L.P.L., Lang Papers, LXXIX, 51–2.
133 Robinson, 1999, 104.
134 French, 2000, 53, 64; Calder, 1996, 51–3.
135 R.A.Ch.D. Archive, Interdenominational Advisory Committee Meetings, 28 July 1943.
136 Iremonger, 1948, 551.
137 Robinson, 1999, 104.
138 L.P.L., MS 2448, 32–3.
139 Smyth, 1968, 220; Robinson, 1999, 104.
140 French, 2000, 79, 126.
141 *Times*, 21 July 1939, 11; *Army List*, January 1939, 1186.
142 L.P.L., Lang Papers, LXXIX, 81.
143 L.P.L., Lang Papers, LXXIX, 81.
144 L.P.L., Lang Papers, LXXIX, 302.
145 L.P.L., Lang Papers, LXXIX, 214.
146 L.P.L., Lang Papers, LXXIX, 262.
147 L.P.L., Lang Papers, LXXIX, 311, 316.
148 L.P.L., William Temple papers, LI, 341.
149 L.P.L., Lang Papers, LXXIX, 317.
150 McCulloch, 1943, 175.
151 I.W.M. Documents, J.E.G. Quinn.
152 N.L.S., ACC 11296/21, Welch to Selby Wright, 15 September 1941.
153 I.W.M. Documents, J.P. Stephenson.
154 Calder, 1996, 485.
155 McCulloch, 1943, 174; Iremonger, 1948, 550.
156 Iremonger, 1948, 551; Robinson, 1999, 88–91.
157 R.A.Ch.D. Archive, Interdenominational Advisory Committee Meetings, 12 October 1944; Chaplain General 1796– , Mackenzie to Easey, 13 July 1990.
158 Towler and Coxon, 1979, 30.
159 L.P.L., Lang Papers, LXXIX, 14–15.
160 I.W.M. Sound, E.L. Phillips.
161 Towler and Coxon, 1979, 30.
162 L.P.L., Lang Papers, LXXIX, 266, 304.
163 L.P.L., MS 2448, 30.
164 L.P.L., MS 2884, 231.
165 L.P.L., MS 2448, 8.
166 *Times*, 7 October 1939, 7; 12 October 1939, 9; 14 October 1939, 6; 19 October 1939, 6; 4 November 1939, 4.
167 Robinson, 1999, 94; Johnstone and Hagerty, 1996, 230.
168 *Church Times*, 15 September 1939, 230.
169 *Times*, 25 October 1939, 6.
170 L.P.L., Lang Papers, LXXIX, 304.
171 *Times*, 3 November 1939, 6; Middleton Brumwell, 1943, 27–8.
172 R.A.Ch.D. Archive, Interdenominational Advisory Committee Meetings, 28 July 1943.

173 *Times*, 12 October 1939, 9; P.R.O., WO 169/3886.
174 L.P.L., MS 2448, 42–3.
175 L.P.L., MS 2448, 46.
176 L.P.L., MS 2448, 48.
177 R.A.Ch.D. Archive (R.C.), Box 33, Lynn to Dey, 4 September 1939.
178 R.A.Ch.D. Archive (R.C.), Box 33, Coghlan to Dey, 10 May 1940.
179 R.A.Ch.D. Archive (R.C.), Box 33, Coghlan to Dey, 10 May 1940.
180 R.A.Ch.D. Archive (R.C.), Box 33, Coghlan to Dey, 18 October 1939.
181 Johnstone and Hagerty, 1996, 194.
182 Dempsey, 1947, ix.
183 Johnstone and Hagerty, 1996, 194–5.
184 Dempsey, 1947, 2–3.
185 Brown, 1997, 22.
186 *R.G.A.C.S.*, 1939, 937–9.
187 N.C.L., CHU 5.1/4. Ministers on Service. Statistical Record by Presbyteries (undated).
188 N.C.L. CHU 5.1/4. Ministers on Service. Statistical Record by Presbyteries (undated); Coulter, 1997, 74–96.
189 Robinson, 1999, Table 4.1, 104.
190 *R.G.A.C.S.*, 1943, 503.
191 M.A.R.C., Minutes of the Royal Navy, Army and Royal Air Force Board, November 1932 – January 1945, 297.
192 M.A.R.C., Minutes of the Royal Navy, Army and Royal Air Force Board, November 1932 – January 1945, 312–13.
193 Brown, 1988, 225–9; Ceadel, 1980, 210.
194 M.A.R.C., Minutes of the Royal Navy, Army and Royal Air Force Board, November 1932 – January 1945, 327, 339, 388, 440.
195 M.A.R.C., Minutes of the Royal Navy, Army and Royal Air Force Board, November 1932 – January 1945, 376.
196 M.A.R.C., Minutes of the Royal Navy, Army and Royal Air Force Board, November 1932 – January 1945, 388–9.
197 M.A.R.C., Minutes of the Royal Navy, Army and Royal Air Force Board, November 1932 – January 1945, 388, 416; P.R.O., WO 365/39.
198 Brown, 1988, Table 7.1, 230.
199 A.L.R.P.C., Baptist Union Minute Books, April 1939 – December 1941.
200 *Baptist Handbook*, 1939, 307; A.L.R.P.C., Baptist Union Minute Book, October 1944 – March 1946, 306.
201 Robinson, 1999, 86–7, Table 4.1, 104.
202 P.R.O., WO 32/14826.
203 P.R.O., WO 32/14825.
204 *Army List*, January 1940, 1400–1; I.W.M. Sound, L. Hardman.
205 I.W.M. Sound, H. Levy; Forty, 2002, 135–7.
206 *Army List*, April 1941, 1406–7; Robinson, 1999, Table 4.1, 104; I.W.M. Sound, L. Hardman.
207 *Army List*, January 1939, 1186–9.
208 Middleton Brumwell, 1943, 29–30.
209 Forty, 2002, 146–60.
210 Oliver, 1986, 98; I.W.M. Sound, J.W. Steele; Middleton Brumwell, 1943, 30.
211 R.A.Ch.D. Archive, F.L. Hughes Papers, Folder 1, Nominal Roll of Chaplains in 8th Army 1942–44.
212 Oliver, 1986, 98.
213 Johnstone and Hagerty, 1996, 196–7.
214 Dempsey, 1947, 92–4.
215 Dempsey, 1947, 3–4.
216 Barnes, 1939, passim.
217 Salisbury Woodward and Blackburne, 1939, 30–48.

218 L.P.L., Lang Papers, LXXIX, 83.
219 I.W.M. Sound, E.M. Claxton.
220 L.P.L., Lang Papers, LXXIX, 88.
221 L.P.L., MS 2448, 14.
222 L.P.L., Lang Papers, LXXIX, 147.
223 *Picture Post*, 14 March 1942, 19.
224 Robinson, 1999, 123–5.
225 Robinson, 1999, 128.
226 I.W.M. Sound, E.L. Phillips.
227 Skinner, n.d, 5–6.
228 McLuskey, 1997, 18.
229 McLuskey, 1997, 18.
230 McLuskey, 1997, 18–19.
231 French, 2000, 199–210.
232 R.A.Ch.D. Archive (R.C.), Box 33, 'Memorandum for All Chaplains (RC)'.
233 Middleton Brumwell, 1943, passim.
234 R.A.Ch.D. Archive, 'Notes for Active-Service Chaplains'.
235 R.A.Ch.D. Archive (R.C.), Box 3, 'To All R.C. Chaplains, Second Army'.
236 I.W.M. Documents, A. Thompson.
237 Hamilton, 2002, 642–4.
238 R.A.Ch.D. Archive, F.L. Hughes Papers, 8th Army Papers, 'Some Advice on the Chaplains' Duty in Battle'; Robinson, 1999, 168.
239 R.A.Ch.D. Archive, *Chaplains' Magazine Middle East*, January 1943, 1, 36.
240 R.A.Ch.D. Archive, F.L. Hughes Papers, 8th Army Papers, 'Some Advice on the Chaplain in Camp'.
241 R.A.Ch.D. Archive, F.L. Hughes Papers, 8th Army Papers, *The Chaplain in Invasion*.
242 R.A.Ch.D. Archive, F.L. Hughes Papers, 8th Army Papers, *Chaplains of the Grand Assault*, Introduction.
243 R.A.Ch.D. Archive, F.L. Hughes Papers, Folder 26, Cowx to Hughes, 19 January 1943; Cook, 1988, 84.
244 R.A.Ch.D. Archive, F.L. Hughes Papers, 8th Army Papers, *Chaplains of the Grand Assault*, 17.
245 R.A.Ch.D. Archive, 'Notes for Active-Service Chaplains', 32.
246 I.W.M. Documents, A. Thompson.
247 R.A.Ch.D. Archive, F.L. Hughes Papers, 8th Army Papers, *Chaplains of the Grand Assault*, 28–9.
248 Bussby, 1967, 23–4; P.R.O., WO 32/12469; R.A.Ch.D. Archive, F.L. Hughes Papers, 8th Army Papers, 'Proposed Permanent Depot for the R.A.Ch.D.'.
249 Montgomery, 1944, 8.
250 R.A.Ch.D. Archive, F.L. Hughes Papers, 8th Army Papers, 'Future Programme'.
251 R.A.Ch.D. Archive, F.L. Hughes Papers, 8th Army Papers, 'First British Armoured Division Report of Chaplains' Conference'.
252 I.W.M. Documents, G.J. Chambers. Chambers was held in Changi gaol.
253 French, 2000, 199–206.
254 Gethyn-Jones, 1988, 78–9.
255 Gethyn-Jones, 1988, 79.
256 Gethyn-Jones, 1988, 79.
257 R.A.Ch.D. Archive, *Memories of Church Stowe*.
258 Gethyn-Jones, 1988, 109.
259 R.A.Ch.D. Archive (R.C.), Box 3, 'The Campaign in North West Europe R.C. Chaplaincy Services'.
260 Snape, 2005 (a), 221–6.
261 Salisbury Woodward and Blackburne, 1939, 33, 40–1.
262 I.W.M. Documents, F.J. Brabyn.
263 P.R.O., WO 217/19.

264 Coghlan, 1942, 11.
265 Woolley, 1963, 154–5.
266 Woolley, 1963, 155–7.
267 Oliver, 1986, 17.
268 Oliver, 1986, 18.
269 Oliver, 1986, 77–8.
270 Oliver, 1986, 18.
271 Salisbury Woodward and Blackburne, 1939, 42–3.
272 I.W.M. Documents, A. Thompson.
273 I.W.M. Documents, N.F. Jones.
274 I.W.M. Sound, W.H. Humphreys.
275 R.A.Ch.D. Archive, 'Notes for Active-Service Chaplains', 2.
276 Hills, 2002, 141.
277 I.W.M. Documents, E.N. Downing.
278 Wood, 1997, 87.
279 Wheatley, 1983, 150; Johnstone and Hagerty, 1996, 215–16.
280 Dempsey, 1947, 141; van Roekel, n.d., 25.
281 R.A.Ch.D. Archive, F.L. Hughes Papers, Folder 26, 'Notes on chaplaincy work in an airborne division'.
282 Dempsey, 1947, 143.
283 Chandler and Collins, 1994, 149.
284 Johnstone and Hagerty, 1996, 241; van Roekel, n.d., 84.
285 Coghlan, 1942, 26–7.
286 I.W.M. Documents, A.R.C. Leaney.
287 Hills, 2002, 89–90.
288 Gethyn-Jones, 1988, 155.
289 R.A.Ch.D., F.L. Hughes Papers, Folder 26, 'Monthly Report' 46th Division, September – October 1943.
290 R.A.Ch.D. Archive, F.L. Hughes Papers, 8th Army Papers, *Chaplains of the Grand Assault*, 18.
291 Snape, 2005 (a), 117–19.
292 R.A.Ch.D. Archive, F.L. Hughes Papers, 8th Army Papers, *Chaplains of the Grand Assault*, 2.
293 L.P.L., Lang Papers, LXXIX, 190.
294 Selby Wright, 1941, 133.
295 Coghlan, 1942, 5–6.
296 Maxwell, 1942, 3–4.
297 Maxwell, 1942, 4.
298 Middleton Brumwell, 1943, 55–71.
299 Middleton Brumwell, 1943, 6.
300 Hastings, 1991, 294–7.
301 Raven, 1938, 35–43; Vidler, 1987, 262–3.
302 Raven, 1938, 43.
303 Barth, 1941, 14.
304 Barth, 1941, 16–17.
305 Vidler, 1977, 119–21; Hastings, 1991, 296, 303; *O.D.N.B.*
306 Wilkinson, 1986, 224; Raven, 1942, viii.
307 Raven, 1940, 9.
308 Raven, 1942, 75.
309 *O.D.N.B.*
310 *O.D.N.B.*
311 Hoover, 1999, 30.
312 *Times*, 15 February 1958, 8; *O.D.N.B.*
313 L.P.L. Davidson papers, DLXXXIII, 56–7.
314 L.P.L., Lang Papers, LXXIX, 311; Hamilton, 1983, 175.

315 R.A.Ch.D. Archive, F.L. Hughes Papers, 8th Army Papers, *Chaplains of the Grand Assault*, i.
316 *Crockford's*, 1947; R.A.Ch.D. Archive, Nye, 1981, 8.
317 R.A.Ch.D. Archive, F.L. Hughes Papers, Folder 26, Fereday to Hughes, 20 October 1942.
318 Hamilton, 1983, 175.
319 Louden, 1996, 75.
320 P.R.O., WO 169/3886.
321 Hamilton, 1986, 804; *Eighth Army News*, 9 October 1943, 2.
322 *Eighth Army News*, 9 October 1943, 2.
323 R.A.Ch.D. Archive, F.L. Hughes Papers, 8th Army Papers, *Chaplains of the Grand Assault*, 1–2.
324 Louden, 1996, 75.
325 Montgomery, 1958, 227.
326 Hamilton, 1986, 803–4.
327 Montgomery, 1958, 90.
328 Montgomery, 1958, 114.
329 Snape, 2005 (a), 127.
330 Montgomery, 1958, 204.
331 Hamilton, 1986, 118.
332 Hamilton, 1986, 119.
333 R.A.Ch.D. Archive, F.L. Hughes Papers, Letters: Montgomery-Hughes, 1944–58, 19 November 1944.
334 *Chaplains' Magazine Middle East*, August 1943, 126.
335 R.A.Ch.D. Archive, 'Notes for Active-Service Chaplains', 20–1.
336 P.R.O., WO 169/3886.
337 R.A.Ch.D. Archive, F.L. Hughes Papers, 8th Army Papers, *Chaplains of the Grand Assault*, 5.
338 R.A.Ch.D. Archive, F.L. Hughes Papers, 8th Army Papers, 'Some Advice on the Chaplain's Duty in Battle'.
339 R.A.Ch.D. Archive, F.L. Hughes Papers, 8th Army Papers, *Chaplains of the Grand Assault*, 6–7.
340 Parker, 2003, 305–6.
341 van Roekel, n.d., 46; Middlebrook, 1995, 88.
342 Pennington, 2004, xxv–xxvi.
343 I.W.M. Sound, Anon., 7698.
344 R.A.Ch.D. Archive, 'Padres Hours'.
345 L.P.L., William Temple papers, LI, 365–6.
346 R.A.Ch.D. Archive, F.L. Hughes Papers, Folder 26, 'Notes on Chaplaincy Work in an Airborne Division'.
347 N.L.S., ACC 7427, 6 July 1942.
348 L.P.L., William Temple papers, LI, 365; R.A.Ch.D. Archive, 'Padres Hours'.
349 I.W.M. Documents, A. Thompson.
350 Machin, 1998, 82; Stevenson, 1984, 407–8.
351 Wolfe, 1984, 4–9.
352 Wolfe, 1984, 268–74.
353 M.O.A., FR 1870 A, 6–7.
354 Wolfe, 1984, 274–5.
355 N.L.S., ACC 7427, 16 April 1942; I.W.M. Sound, R. Selby Wright.
356 Wolfe, 1984, 278.
357 I.W.M. Sound, R. Selby Wright.
358 N.L.S., ACC 11296/21, Welch to Selby Wright, 25 November 1941; Selby Wright, 1943, iv.
359 N.L.S., ACC 11296/21, Undated memorandum: 'The Proposed Appointment of the Rev. Ronald Selby-Wright, C.F., as "Radio Padre" '; ACC 7427, passim.
360 N.L.S., ACC 7427, 25 March, 2 April 1942; Selby Wright, 1943, p. iv.

361 Selby Wright, 1943, 8.
362 Wolfe, 1984, 279.
363 N.L.S., ACC 7427, 24 July 1942.
364 I.W.M. Sound, R. Selby Wright.
365 I.W.M. Sound, R. Selby Wright; Wolfe, 1984, 279.
366 M.O.A., FR 1870 A, 16.
367 N.L.S., ACC 7427, 24 September 1942.
368 Foot and Langley, 1979, 34–5.
369 Foot and Langley, 1979, 115.
370 I.W.M. Sound, R. Selby Wright.
371 *Statistics of the Military Effort of the British Empire*, 1992, 206.
372 Danchev, 1994, 311; Carver, 1998, 310.
373 Costello, 1985, 40; Shaw, 1996, 370–3; Harrison, 1995, 146.
374 DeGroot, 1997, passim; Shaw, 1996, 372; Carver, 1998, 310.
375 M.A.R.C., Minutes of the Royal Navy and Army Board (with Royal Air Force after 1918), January 1918 – January 1925, 33.
376 *Times*, 12 August 1940, 6.
377 Robinson, 1999, 160.
378 *Times*, 25 March 1943, 7.
379 Robinson, 1999, 159.
380 Robinson, 1999, 160–5; Wilkinson, 1986, 284.
381 Gethyn-Jones, 1988, 164–5.
382 'Convention for the Amelioration of the Condition of the Wounded in Armies in the Field', August 1864, Article 3.
383 O'Rorke, 1915, passim.
384 Liddle and Mackenzie, 2000, 320; O'Rorke, 1915, 95.
385 Moynihan, 1983, 36–7, 40.
386 A.L.R.P.C., Baptist Union Minute Book, January 1916 – December 1917, 208.
387 I.W.M. Documents, R. Bulstrode.
388 University of Minnesota Human Rights Library, 'Convention relative to the Treatment of Prisoners of War', July 1929, Article 16.
389 *Times*, 20 November 1939, 9.
390 Coulter, 1997, 250.
391 L.P.L., William Temple papers, LI, 289.
392 Smyth, 1968, 227.
393 Miller, 1951, 92.
394 R.A.Ch.D. Archive, *Daily Telegraph Prisoners of War Exhibition*, 1944, n.p.; N.C.L., CHU 5.1/8 'Report on distribution of chaplains from Oflag VI B'.
395 R.A.Ch.D. Archive, *Daily Telegraph Prisoners of War Exhibition*, 1944, n.p.
396 Dempsey, 1947, 201.
397 Wild, 1992, passim; I.W.M. Documents, W.A. Lathaen; Thompson, 1955, 82–3.
398 I.W.M. Documents, A.D.M. Hilton.
399 Miller, 1951, 97.
400 Thompson, 1955, 142.
401 I.W.M. Documents, W.A. Lathaen.
402 Guinness, 1945, 12–13, 45–9, 55–61, 75, 151–2.
403 Dempsey, 1947, 199–200.
404 Thompson, 1955, 165–6.
405 'Convention relative to the Treatment of Prisoners of War', July 1929, Article 27; Liddle and Mackenzie, 2000, 315–17.
406 Miller, 1951, 96.
407 I.W.M. Documents, A. Royall.
408 Thompson, 1955, 92–122.
409 Lewis Bryan, 1946, 9.
410 Smyth, 1968, 290–1.

411 I.W.M. Sound, H.C. Babb.
412 Smyth, 1968, 289–90.
413 I.W.M. Sound, L.V. Headley.
414 A.L.R.P.C., Baptist Union Minute Book, October 1944 – March 1946, 306; Miller, 1951, 95.
415 I.W.M. Documents, G.J. Chambers.
416 Machin, 1998, 104–5.
417 I.W.M. Documents, W.A. Lathaen.
418 Thompson, 1955, 112.
419 Ellison Platt 1980, 103.
420 Clode, 1869, II, 366–9.
421 *King's Regulations*, 1940 (1945 reprint), par. 1605.
422 Snape, 2005 (a), 139–41; 2005 (b), 184–7.
423 *Hansard*, 10 March 1931, 1187–8.
424 Findlay, 1941, 137.
425 Selby Wright, 1943, 33.
426 N.L.S., ACC 7427, 7 July 1942.
427 Middleton Brumwell, 1943, 42.
428 P.R.O., WO 163/161.
429 *J.R.U.S.I.*, 95, 1950, 473.
430 I.W.M. Sound, E.L. Phillips.
431 P.R.O., WO 163/161.
432 P.R.O., WO 163/161; P.R.O., WO 32/14687; Robinson, 1999, 100–1; *King's Regulations*, 1940 (1945 reprint), par. 1605.
433 Middleton Brumwell, 1943, 41.
434 I.W.M. Sound, E.M. Claxton.
435 R.A.Ch.D. Archive, F.L. Hughes Papers, 8th Army Papers, 'First British Armoured Division Report of Chaplains' Conference', June 1943.
436 Snape, 2005 (a), 129–30.
437 Cook, 1988, 106.
438 I.W.M. Documents, G.P. Druitt.
439 Gethyn-Jones, 1988, 24.
440 van Roekel, n.d., 25, 35; Hastings, 2004, 58.
441 MacDonald Fraser, 2000, 162–3.
442 I.W.M. Documents, A. Thompson.
443 I.W.M. Sound, E.M. Claxton; I.W.M. Documents, A.H. Rodgers.
444 R.A.Ch.D. Archive, F.L. Hughes Papers, 8th Army Papers, *Chaplains of the Grand Assault*, 15.
445 R.A.Ch.D. Archive, F.L. Hughes Papers, 8th Army Papers, *Chaplains of the Grand Assault*, 15.
446 I.W.M. Sound, E.L. Phillips; P.R.O., WO 166/296.
447 McCulloch, 1943, 175.
448 McCulloch, 1943, 170.
449 McLuskey, 1997, 23.
450 P.R.O., WO 169/3886.
451 Dempsey, 1947, 32.
452 Harrison, 2004, 42–6.
453 L.P.L., MS 2448, 25.
454 Hamilton, 2002, 306–8; Todman and Danchev, 2002, 18–19.
455 Harrison, 2004, 104–8.
456 R.A.Ch.D. Archive, F.L. Hughes Papers, 'World War 2, 8th Army Letters (Copies)', Wilcox to Hughes, 31 August 1943; Ellis, 1990, Table 10, 307.
457 Middleton Brumwell, 1943, 69.
458 I.W.M. Sound, E.M. Claxton.
459 Harrison, 2004, 148–52.

460 Author's Collection, MacPherson Knowles.
461 Harrison, 2004, 198; Ellis, 1990, Table 10, 307.
462 'D.N.E.B.', n.d., 1.
463 R.A.Ch.D. Archive, F.L. Hughes Papers, 'World War 2, 8th Army Letters (Copies)', Wilcox to Hughes, 31 August 1943.
464 Ellis, 1990, 303–5; Harrison, 2004, 99.
465 I.W.M. Sound, E.M. Claxton.
466 Harrison, 2004, 151.
467 *Times*, 2 April 1946, 5.
468 Crang, 2000, 91–107.
469 I.W.M. Documents, C.W.K. Potts.
470 I.W.M. Sound, W.H. Humphreys.
471 Cook, 1988, 243.
472 I.W.M. Sound, E.M. Claxton.
473 Milligan, 1978, 123–4.
474 McCulloch, 1943, 170–1.
475 McCulloch, 1943, 176.
476 McCulloch, 1943, 176–81.
477 McCulloch, 1943, 181.
478 I.W.M. Documents, J.H. Humphries.
479 I.W.M. Documents, J.H. Humphries.
480 *Times*, 15 February 1945, 5.
481 I.W.M. Documents, J.P. Stephenson.
482 I.W.M. Documents, G.P. Druitt.
483 I.W.M. Documents, G.P. Druitt; Woolley, 1963, 155.
484 I.W.M. Documents, G.P. Druitt.
485 I.W.M. Sound, J.W. Steele.
486 *Hansard*, 22 April 1943, 1887.
487 *Hansard*, 7 December 1944, 893.
488 Brown, 1988, 227.
489 Dewey, 1997, 300, Table 16.1.
490 L.P.L., MS 2448, 35.
491 *Hansard*, 22 April 1943, 1887.
492 Middleton Brumwell, 1943, 26.
493 R.A.Ch.D. Archive, F.L. Hughes Papers, 8th Army Papers, Memorandum: 'Subject – Future Programme', April 1943.
494 R.A.Ch.D. Archive, Interdenominational Advisory Committee Meetings, 28 July 1943.
495 R.A.Ch.D. Archive, Interdenominational Advisory Committee Meetings, 12 October 1944.
496 R.A.Ch.D. Archive, F.L. Hughes Papers, Folder 26, Bell to Hughes, 22 November 1943.
497 P.R.O., WO 32/12467.
498 I.W.M. Sound, L. Hardman.
499 P.R.O., WO 32/12467.
500 Coghlan, 1942, 19.
501 I.W.M. Sound, J.W. Steele.
502 Gethyn-Jones, 1988, 153.
503 R.A.Ch.D. Archive, F.L. Hughes Papers, 8th Army Papers, *Chaplains of the Grand Assault*, 26.
504 Snape, 2005 (a), 227.
505 I.W.M. Sound, W.H. Humphreys.
506 *Picture Post*, 9 September 1944, 1, 12.
507 I.W.M. Documents, A.R.C. Leaney.
508 Salisbury Woodward and Blackburne, 1939, 47–8.
509 R.A.Ch.D. Archive, F.L. Hughes Papers, 'World War 2, 8th Army Letters (Copies)', Wilcox to Hughes, 31 August 1943.

510 Snape, 2005 (a), 129–30.
511 *Daily Telegraph*, 5 July 2005, 22.
512 Howson, 2006, 44–5.
513 Snape, 2005 (a), 137.
514 Howson, 2006, 44; Ellis, 1968, Table 3, 407.
515 French, 2000, 147.
516 Neill, 2000, 81–2.
517 Kamaryc, 1993, 213–15.
518 Neill, 2000, 76.
519 Latimer, 2005, 68–9; R.A.Ch.D. Archive, Druitt, *Occupation of Germany*, 9.
520 Neill, 2000, 76.
521 Neill, 2000, 76–7.
522 Flower, 1996, passim.
523 Moffatt and McCormick, 2003, 282.
524 Summers, 2005, 240.
525 I.W.M. Documents, J.W. Franks.
526 M.O.A., FR 1870 A, passim.
527 Snape, 2005 (a), 136–7.
528 Farish, 2002, 10–42.
529 *Hansard*, 29 March 1946, 707–8.
530 *Hansard*, 29 March 1946, 731.

Epilogue: From victory in Europe to the Korean War

1 Carver, 1998, 312.
2 R.A.Ch.D. Archive, Interdenominational Advisory Committee Meetings, 12 October 1944.
3 P.R.O., WO 32/11596.
4 P.R.O., WO 32/14820; M.A.R.C. Minutes of the Royal Navy, Army and Royal Air Force Board, May 1945–February 1955, 372–3.
5 P.R.O., WO 32/12038.
6 P.R.O., WO 32/12038.
7 R.A.Ch.D. Archive, Interdenominational Advisory Committee Meetings, 22 October 1947.
8 R.A.Ch.D. Archive, Interdenominational Advisory Committee Meetings, 22 October 1947; P.R.O., WO 32/12038; Hickman, 2005, xiv.
9 P.R.O., WO 32/14820.
10 P.R.O., WO 32/12315.
11 P.R.O., WO 32/14820; Farrar-Hockley, 1994, 332.
12 P.R.O., WO 32/12038.
13 Hastings, 1991, 437; P.R.O., WO 32/14820.
14 *R.G.A.C.S.*, 1947, 511.
15 P.R.O., WO 32/14820.
16 N.C.L., CHU 5.1/15, Address by Field Marshal Sir William Slim to the General Assembly, 1951.
17 P.R.O., WO 32/14820.
18 P.R.O., WO 32/14820.
19 P.R.O., WO 32/14820.
20 P.R.O., WO 32/14820.
21 P.R.O., WO 32/12037.
22 P.R.O., WO 32/12037; WO 32/14820.
23 P.R.O., WO 32/14820.
24 Barnett, 1970, 482; Carver, 1998, 312–44, 360–76.
25 Grey, 1988, 37–40, 42–3; Hickman, 2005, 100.
26 P.R.O., WO 32/14820.
27 Levy, 1995, passim; Dempsey, 1947, 188–94; I.W.M. Documents, E.J. Swift.
28 I.W.M. Documents, Misc. 180 (2719).

29 *Times*, 23 August 1947, 7.
30 I.W.M. Documents, A.R.C. Leaney.
31 Neill, 2000, 93.
32 *Times*, 15 December 1945, 3.
33 Montgomery, 1958, 357.
34 *Times*, 15 December 1945, 3.
35 Neill, 2000, 94.
36 *Times*, 9 August 1946, 3.
37 R.A.Ch.D. Archive, Druitt, *Occupation of Germany*, 12–14.
38 R.A.Ch.D. Archive, Druitt, *Occupation of Germany*, 18.
39 R.A.Ch.D. Archive, Druitt, *Occupation of Germany*, 14.
40 R.A.Ch.D. Archive, Druitt, *Occupation of Germany*, 14–15.
41 R.A.Ch.D. Archive, Druitt, *Occupation of Germany*, 15–17.
42 R.A.Ch.D. Archive, Druitt, *Occupation of Germany*, 24.
43 I.W.M. Documents, A.R.C. Leaney.
44 I.W.M. Documents, A.R.C. Leaney.
45 Green, 1945, passim.
46 Dempsey, 1947, 180–7.
47 Smyth, 1968, 315.
48 Montgomery, 1958, 417.
49 R.A.Ch.D. Archive, F.L. Hughes Papers, 8th Army Papers, 'Proposed Permanent Depot for the R.A.Ch.D.'
50 P.R.O., WO 32/12469.
51 R.A.Ch.D. Archive, F.L. Hughes Papers, 8th Army Papers, 'Proposed Permanent Depot for the R.A.Ch.D.'
52 R.A.Ch.D. Archive, Interdenominational Advisory Committee Meetings, 22 October 1947.
53 Hickman, 2005, xiv–xvi.
54 Brown, 2006, 177–87.
55 P.R.O., WO 32/12469.
56 P.R.O., WO 32/12469.
57 P.R.O., WO 32/12469.
58 P.R.O., WO 32/14820.
59 P.R.O., WO 32/12469.
60 P.R.O., WO 32/14820.
61 *King's Regulations*, 1940 (1945 reprint), par. 1605.
62 Crang, 2005, 92.
63 Crang, 2005, 99.
64 Crang, 2005, 99–100.
65 *Hansard*, 29 March 1946, 732.
66 *The Times House of Commons*, 1950, 181.
67 *Hansard*, 29 March 1946, 735.
68 Crang, 2005, 102.
69 *The Times House of Commons*, 1950, 155.
70 *Hansard*, 29 March 1946, 727.
71 *The Times House of Commons*, 1950, 89.
72 *Hansard*, 29 March 1946, 737.
73 *The Times House of Commons*, 1950, 246.
74 *Hansard*, 29 March 1946, 738–40.
75 *The Times House of Commons*, 1950, 215.
76 *Hansard*, 29 March, 1946, 740.
77 R.A.Ch.D. Archive, F.L. Hughes Papers, 'Letters, Montgomery-Hughes, 1944–58', Montgomery to Hughes, 26 March 1945.
78 Cited in Crang, 2005, 102.
79 P.R.O., WO 32/14820.
80 P.R.O., WO 32/14820.

81 P.R.O., WO 32/14820.
82 Crang, 2005, 103.
83 *J.R.U.S.I.*, 95, 1950, 476.
84 Crang, 2005, 97; P.R.O., WO 32/14820.
85 *R.G.A.C.S.*, 1947, 512.
86 *R.G.A.C.S.*, 1950, 559.
87 P.R.O., W.O. 32/14820.
88 P.R.O., W.O. 32/14820.
89 *The Times House of Commons*, 1950, 66.
90 Crang, 2005, 104–6.
91 P.R.O., WO 32/14820.
92 P.R.O., WO 32/14820.
93 Crang, 2005, 106.

Retrospect

1 Colley, 1992, 11–54; McLeod, 2000, 235–8; Wolffe, 1994, 260–1.
2 Snape, 2005 (b), 233–4.
3 Snape, 2005 (a), 1–3; Hempton, 2005, 191.
4 Brown, 2001, passim; Brown, 2003, passim; Brown, 2006, passim.
5 McLeod, 2003, 1.

Bibliography

Archival Sources

Angus Library, Regent's Park College, Oxford

Baptist Union Minute Book, January 1914 – December 1915
Baptist Union Minute Book, January 1916 – December 1917
Baptist Union Minute Book January 1918 – December 1919
Baptist Union Minute Book April 1939 – July 1940
Baptist Union Minute Book September 1940 – December 1941
Baptist Union Minute Book January 1942 – May 1943
Baptist Union Minute Book June 1943 – October 1944
Baptist Union Minute Book October 1944 – March 1946
United Board, n.d., *Memoranda of Information for Chaplains to the Forces and Officiating Clergymen*

Archdiocese of Birmingham Archives

FHD/A3 Francis H. Drinkwater – Chaplain to the Forces, 1915–1919
FHD/A5 Francis H. Drinkwater – War Diaries, 1915–18

Author's Collection

Barclay Baron, 'Unpublished Memoirs of YMCA Work'
Interview with Macpherson Knowles
The War Diary of the Rev. G.H. Ogden

British Library

Add. MS 28510 Contemporary Biography
Add. MS 29240 The Accounts of Ivychurch Co. Kent 1800–1840
Add. MS 40398 Peel Papers
Add. MS 40422 Peel Papers
Add. MS 40559 Peel Papers
B.P. 8/5. (5.) Regulations and Orders. II. Regulations and Treatises on Special Subjects. Pay and Allowances, *c.*1740
B.L. OIR 283.54 S.J. McNally, 'The Chaplains of the East India Company'

Church Missionary Society Archives, University of Birmingham

XACC/18/F/1 Diaries of L.H. Gwynne
XACC/18/F/4 Notebooks containing sermons and addresses delivered by L.H. Gwynne
XACC/18/Z/1 Army book

Imperial War Museum Department of Documents

87/59/1	F.J. Brabyn
87/10/1	R. Bulstrode
91/35/1	G.J. Chambers
80/22/1	E.C. Crosse
91/2/1	E.N. Downing
96/38/1	G.P. Druitt
86/67/1	J.W. Franks
88/59/1	A.D.M. Hilton
90/7/1	C.I.S. Hood
02/58/1	J.H. Humphries
96/38/1	N.F. Jones
95/30/1	W.A. Lathaen
PP/MCR/206	A.R.C. Leaney
67/180/1	J.B. Marshall
77/106/1	W.M. Murray
92/28/1	C.W.K. Potts
P 247	J.E.G. Quinn
96/38/1	A.H. Rodgers
77/107/1	T.G. Rogers
95/12/1	A. Royall
P 179	J.P. Stephenson
90/4/1	E.J. Swift
90/40/1	A. Thompson
Misc. 180 (2719)	

Imperial War Museum Sound Archive

7698	Anon.
7292	H.C. Babb
22572	Edward Mitchell ('Gus') Claxton
15475/6	Sam Davies
176365	Leslie Hardman
11543	Lewis Victor Headley
16481	William Haydn Humphreys
11572	Harry Levy
15439	Edward Leigh ('Bill') Phillips
8859/2	Ronald Selby Wright
10660/4	John William Steele

Lambeth Palace Library

Benson Papers
Davidson Papers
Lang Papers
Tait Papers
William Temple Papers
MS 2077 Diary of B.K. Cunningham, 21 March 1917–5 March 1919
MS 2448 Bishops' War Committee Minute Book, October 12th 1939 to June 17th 1944
MS 2883–4 Letters from Archbishop Lang

Liddle Collection, University of Leeds
GS 0404 W.T. Croxford
GS 0527 J. Esslemont Adams
GS 0531 M.S. Evers
GS 1329 C.E. Raven

Mass-Observation Archive, University of Sussex
FR 1870 A 'The Chaplain to the Forces', 1943

Methodist Archives and Research Centre, University of Manchester
Minutes of the Primitive Methodist Special Army Committee and Army Committee, October 1914-July 1924; Army and Navy Committee, June 1925; United Navy, Army and Royal Air Force Committee, July 1926 – April 1931
Minutes of the Royal Navy and Army Sub-Committee, October 1896 – April 1904
Minutes of the Royal Navy and Army Sub-Committee, September 1904 – May 1911
Minutes of the Royal Navy and Army Board, November 1911 – January 1918
Minutes of the Royal Navy and Army Board (with Royal Air Force after 1918), January 1918 – January 1925
Minutes of the Royal Navy, Army and Royal Air Force Board, November 1932 – January 1945
Minutes of the Royal Navy, Army and Royal Air Force Board, May 1945 – February 1955

National Archives of Scotland
CH1/2/8 Documents of Assembly, 1855

National Army Museum
2002–05–3 The Letters of Samuel Briscall
7405–25.1.A.I.1 Order of the Duke of Marlborough, 16 February 1704/5
7405–84–1 The Papers of the Rev. Henry Press Wright

National Library of Scotland
ACC 7427 Ronald Selby Wright Papers – Diary 1942
ACC 11296/21 [Ronald Selby Wright] Letters, May 1941 – September 1943
MS 3869–71 Gleig Papers: Correspondence
MS 3872 [G.R. Gleig] 'Memoirs of a long life of four score years'

New College Library, University of Edinburgh
Church of Scotland Chaplains to H.M. Forces, General Papers, CHU 5.1

Public Record Office (The National Archives)
Commander in Chief: Out-letters 1765 to 1868: WO 3/ 11, 577
Secretary at War: Out-letters 1684 to 1861: WO 4/ 3, 69, 345–9
Departmental Out-letters 1715 to 1862: WO 7/ 60–3, 66–8
Registered Files, General Series 1845 to 1985: WO 32/ 4010, 4016–17, 4020, 4023, 5632, 5634–6, 5969, 6217, 6429, 6435–6, 6624, 9322, 10479, 10482, 11596, 12037–8, 12315, 12467, 12469, 14687, 14820, 14825–6
Amherst Papers 1712 to 1786: WO 34/ 13
Secretary at War, Correspondence – Selected Very Old Series and Old Series Papers: WO 43/ 285, 357, 578, 599, 616, 636, 659

Public Record Office (The National Archives) (cont.)
War Office: Service Medal and Award Rolls Index, First World War: WO 372/ 18
War of 1914 to 1918 – War Diaries: WO 95/ 5308
War Office Council and Army Council Records: WO 163/ 161
War of 1939 to 1945 – War Diaries, Home Forces 1939 to 1946: WO 166/ 296
War of 1939 to 1945 – War Diaries, Middle East Forces 1939 to 1946: WO 169/ 3886
War of 1939 to 1945 – Private War Diaries 1939 to 1951: WO 217/ 19
Department of the Adjutant General, Statistics Branch – Published Statistical Reports 1939 to 1944: WO 365/ 39

Royal Army Chaplains' Department Archive, Amport House
Beach Papers
Blackburne Papers
Chaplain General 1796-
Circular Memoranda etc. addressed to the Church of England Chaplains by the Chaplain General
Chaplains for Expeditionary Force: allocation on mobilization
Chaplains' Magazine Middle East
Cosserat, D.P., 'Journal of a Voyage to Egypt'
Daily Telegraph Prisoners of War Exhibition, 1944
'Dean of Battle – the story of a fighting parson, the Very Rev. A.T.A. Naylor'
Dow, A., 'Ministers to the Soldiers of Scotland 1856–1945'
Druitt, G.P., 1945, *Occupation of Germany: Plans and Policy Affecting the Brotherhood of Chaplains*
Gleig – Letters, 1845–6
Green, M., 1945, *The Padre's Hour, 8 Corps District – B.A.O.R. Winter 1945*
F.L. Hughes Papers
Interdenominational Advisory Committee on Army Chaplaincy Services. Minutes of Meetings 50 to 65, 1922–1933
Interdenominational Advisory Committee Meetings, old copies of minutes, 1943–55
Journal of the Rev. George Watson (1787–1815) Chaplain to the Forces (25th March 1814 – 28th March, 1815)
Letters of L.J. Parsons
Memories of Church Stowe
'Notes for Active-Service Chaplains by the Assistant Chaplain-General Second Army'
Notes on Service in the Army Chaplains Department, 1917
Nye, R., 1981, *The Very Reverend F. Ll. Hughes*
'Padres Hours'
Policy Letters 1845 onwards
Practical Advice for the Guidance of Church of England Chaplains Attached to a Division in the Field, 1917
R/AChD Precedent Book (G.R. A.B. 401)
Report of Conference of Regular Chaplains held in the Royal United Service Institution Whitehall 24th and 25th June, 1925
Report on A.C.D. Mesopotamia
Rev. Alexander Fraser in the Crimea
Tanner, E.V., 'An Army Chaplain's Work in War-Time'

R.A.Ch.D. Archive (Roman Catholic), Bulford Camp
Box 3 The Campaign in N.W. Europe
Box 28 Correspondence prior to 1914; Military Chaplains during War 1914–18
Box 33 B.E.F. and B.L.A.

Reports of John Ryan, British Commonwealth Forces Korea
Précis for the Army Council, May 1920

Rawlinson Papers, Downside Abbey
3230.VII.A.3.F Correspondence of Dom Stephen Rawlinson as Principal Chaplain B.E.F. in France 1918–19
3231.VII.A.3.F Dom Stephen Rawlinson Correspondence with Bishops and Superiors 1916–1919
3242.VII.A.3.F Dom Stephen Rawlinson Military Awards and Honours First World War Recommendations etc.
Correspondence from Boer War 1900 through World War One to World War Two
'War History' Material 1925
Rawlinson, S., 1917 and 1918, *Roman Catholic Chaplains. Information and Hints*

Southwark Diocesan Archives
Bishop Grant. Chaplains. Military Correspondence re. Home Bases
Forces 1895–1899
Forces 1900–1904

Wesleyan Methodist Missionary Society, University of London, S.O.A.S.
Box No. 53, Correspondence: Egypt and Greece, 1882–1888

Parliamentary Papers

Select Committee on Army before Sebastopol, 1854–5, IX (Part 1)
Correspondence between Moderator of General Assembly of Presbyterian Church in Ireland and Secretary of State for War on Appointment of Ministers to Office of Chaplain or Assistant Chaplain of H.M. Forces, 1859, XVII
Report of General Eyre's Commission on libraries and reading-rooms for soldiers, 1862, XXXII
Bill Intituled An Act to afford greater Facilities for the Ministrations of Army Chaplains, 1867–8, I
First Report from the Select Committee on Army Estimates, 1888, VIII
Second Report from the Select Committee on Army Estimates, 1888, VIII
Fifth Report from the Select Committee on Army Estimates, 1888, IX
General Annual Report of the British Army for the year ending 30 September 1913, 1914

Newspapers and Periodicals
Acts of the General Assembly of the Church of Scotland
Army Lists
Baptist Handbook
The Chaplains' Bulletin
The Church Times
Colburn's United Service Magazine

Newspapers and Periodicals (cont.)
Crockford's Clerical Directory
The Daily Telegraph
Eighth Army News
Gentleman's Magazine
The Guardian
Hansard
India Register
Journal of the Royal United Service Institution
King's Regulations
The London Gazette
Methodist Magazine
Picture Post
Queen's Regulations
Reports of the Church Congress
Reports on the Schemes of the Church of Scotland
Reports to the General Assembly of the Church of Scotland
The Times
The Times House of Commons
Truth
United Service Journal and Naval and Military Magazine
United Service Magazine
Wesleyan Conference Minutes
Wesleyan Missionary Notices

Published Primary Sources

Acland-Troyte, J.E., 1881, *Through the Ranks to a Commission*, London
Adler, M. (ed.), 1922, *British Jewry Book of Honour*, London
Agar, W., 1758, *Military Devotion: or, the Soldier's Duty to God, His Prince and His Country*, London
Anon., 1757, *A System of Camp Discipline*, London
Anon., 1786, *Advice to the Lord Lieutenants of Counties, Commanding Regiments of Militia*, London
Anon., 1800, *Thoughts on Non-Residence, Tithes, Inclosures, Rare Landlords, Rich Tenants, Regimental Chaplains, &c.*, London
Anon., 1856, *A Letter to the Rev. Wm. Marsh D.D.*, London
Anon., 1864, *The Army Scripture Readers' and Soldiers' Friend Society*, London
Anon., 1879, *With the Troops in Zululand*, London
Anon., 1916 (a), 'The Churches and the Armies', *The Times History of the War*, 8, 313–52
Anon., 1916 (b), 'The Work of the Y.M.C.A.', *The Times History of the War*, 9, 179–200
Anon., 1999, 'A Padre's Story' in J.E. Lewis (ed.), *True World War I Stories*, London
Barnes, R.L., 1939, *A War-Time Chaplaincy*, London
Barry, F.R., 1970, *Period of My Life*, London
Barth, K., 1941, *A Letter to Great Britain from Switzerland*, London
Bedborough, G., 1934, *Arms and the Clergy (1914–1918)*, London
Bell, G., 1867, *Rough Notes of an Old Soldier*, London (2 vols)
Bell, G.K.A., 1916, *The National Mission of Repentance and Hope: A Report on the Chaplains' Replies to the Lord Bishop of Kensington*, London

Benstead, C., 1930, *Retreat: A Story of 1918*, London
Bickersteth, J. (ed.), 1996, *The Bickersteth Diaries, 1914–1918*, London
Blackburne, H., 1917, *Chaplains in Council*, London
——— 1932, *This Also Happened on the Western Front*, London
Boullier, J.A., 1917, *Jottings by a Gunner and Chaplain*, London
Brett-James, A (ed.), 1961, *Wellington at War 1794–1815*, London
Bristow, W.E., 1912, *In Khaki Clad: Reminiscences of the Barrack-Room*, London
Brophy, J. and Partridge, E. (eds), 1930, *Songs and Slang of the British Soldier: 1914–1918*, London
Broughton, T., 1738, *The Christian Soldier; or, the Duties of a Religious Life, Recommended to the Army: in a Sermon Preach'd before His Majesty's Second Regiment of Foot-Guards in the Tower-Chapel, on their leaving the Garrison, on Sunday, October 23rd, 1737*, London
Brown, A.D., 1914, *Manual of Information for Army and Navy Chaplains of the Wesleyan Methodist Church in India*, Simla
Buckley, R.N. (ed.), 1987, *The Napoleonic War Journal of Captain Thomas Henry Browne, 1807–1816*, Publications of the Army Records Society, 3
Bull, P.B., 1904, *God And Our Soldiers*, London
Bussby, F., 1967, 'The Chaplains' Club: from Cairo to Brussels', *J.R.A.Ch.D.*, 22–5
Cairns, D.S., 1919, *The Army and Religion*, London
Candlish, R.S., 1854, *Security in the Midst of Danger: the Ninety-First Psalm Applied, in a Sermon and Charge, delivered before the Free Presbytery of Edinburgh, met to ordain the Rev. Robert Boag Watson as Chaplain to the Forces*, Edinburgh
Carshore, J.J., 1857, *Bengal Chaplain's Vade-Mecum*, Lahore
Carter, C.E. (ed.), 1933, *The Correspondence of General Thomas Gage with the Secretaries of State, and with the War Office and the Treasury 1763–1775*, Yale Historical Publications Manuscripts and Edited Texts, 12
Chapman, G., 1985, *A Passionate Prodigality*, Southampton
Churchill, W.S., 2002, *The Boer War*, London
Clayton, P.B., 1920, *Tales of Talbot House: Everyman's Club in Poperinghe and Ypres 1915–1918*, London
Clode, C.M., 1869, *The Military Forces of the Crown*, London (2 vols)
Coghlan, J., 1942, *Memorandum for Catholic Army Chaplains and Officiating Chaplains to the Forces*, London
Compton, H. (ed.), 1893, *A King's Hussar*, London
Cook, H. and B., 1988, *Khaki Parish: Our War-Our Love*, Worthing
Cooper, B., 1993, *The Tenth (Irish) Division in Gallipoli*, Dublin
Cormack, A. and Jones, A. (eds), 2001, *The Journal of Corporal Todd*, Publications of the Army Records Society, 18
Creighton, L. (ed.), 1920, *Letters of Oswin Creighton, C.F. 1883–1918*, London
Creighton, O., 1916, *With the Twenty-Ninth Division in Gallipoli: a chaplain's experiences*, London
Crozier, F.P., 1969, *The Men I Killed*, Bath
Curtois, R.G., 1826, *The Ministerial Character considered in a sermon preached . . . in the Cathedral Church of Chichester*, London
——— 1833, *The Soldier's Manual: containing an instruction in some important doctrines and duties, and an exhortation against the besetting sins of his calling*, London
Cuthbertson, B., 1768, *A System for the Compleat Interior Management and Oeconomy of a Battalion of Infantry*, Dublin

Danchev, A. and Todman, D. (eds), 2002, *War Diaries 1939–1945: Field Marshal Lord Alanbrooke*, London
Davies, S., 1954, *In Spite of Dungeons*, London
Day, H.C., 1937, *An Army Chaplain's War Memories*, London
DeGroot, G.J. (ed.), 1996, 'The Reverend George S. Duncan at G.H.Q., 1916–1918' in A.J. Guy, R.N.W. Thomas and G.J. Degroot (eds), *Military Miscellany I*, Publications of the Army Records Society, 12
Digby, E., 1917, *Tips for Padres*, London
'D.N.E.B.', *Talks to V.D. Patients, By an Army Chaplain*, n.d.
Donaldson, J., 2000, *Recollections of the Eventful Life of a Soldier*, Staplehurst
Doughty, A. and Parmelee, G.W., 1901, *The Siege of Quebec and the Battle of the Plains of Abraham*, Quebec (6 vols)
Downham, P. (ed.), *Diary of an Old Contemptible*, Barnsley
Drury, W., 1922, 'The Initial Organization of the Army Chaplains' Department in the British Expeditionary Force', *J.R.A.Ch.D.*, 45–9
Drury, W.E., 1968, *Camp Follower: A Padre's Recollections of Nile, Somme and Tigris during the First World War*, Dublin
Duncan, G.S., 1966, *Douglas Haig as I Knew Him*, London
Dunn, J.C., 1994, *The War the Infantry Knew 1914–1919*, London
Edghill, J.C., 1887, *Letter from Rev. J.C. Edghill, D.D., Chaplain-General, to the Synod of Nova Scotia*, Halifax
Ellison Platt, J., 1980, *Padre in Colditz*, London
Englander, D. (ed.), 1994, *A Documentary History of Jewish Immigrants in Britain, 1840–1920*, Leicester
Farrar-Hockley, A., 1993, *The Edge of the Sword*, Stroud
Ferrar, M.L. (ed.), 1922, *The Diary of Colour-Serjeant George Calladine, 19th Foot*, London
Findlay, J.L., 1941, *Fighting Padre*, London
Fisher, P.J., 1917, *Khaki Vignettes*, London
Forbes, E.A., 1918, *Vermelles: Notes on the Western Front*, Edinburgh
Gamble, J., 1795, *Observations on Telegraphic Experiments. Or the different modes which have been, or may be adopted for the purpose of distant communication*, London
Geare, W.D., 1918, *Letters of an Army Chaplain*, London
Gethyn-Jones, E., 1988, *A Territorial Army Chaplain in Peace and War*, East Wittering
Gibbs, P., 1920, *Realities of War*, London
Gleig, G.R., 1835, *The Soldier's Help to the Knowledge of Divine Truth*, London
——— 1845, 'The Moral Discipline of the Army', *Quarterly Review*, 76, 387–424
——— 1846, 'Education and Lodging of the Soldier', *Quarterly Review*, 77, 526–63
——— 1857, *Religion in the Ranks*, London
——— 1868, 'The Church in the Army and Navy', *Blackwood's Edinburgh Magazine*, 103, 251–74
——— 1904, *Personal Reminiscences of the first Duke of Wellington with sketches of some of his guests and contemporaries*, Edinburgh
——— 1915, *The Subaltern*, London
Gordon, J., 1929, *My Six Years in the Black Watch 1881–1887*, Boston
Graham, G.S. (ed.), 1953, *The Walker Expedition to Quebec, 1711*, Publications of the Navy Record Society, 94
Graham, S., 1919, *A Private in the Guards*, London
Graves, R., 1929 and 1960, *Good-Bye To All That*, London

Guinness, P., 1945, *We Pledge Our Lives: a Post-War Manifesto from a War-time Prison*, London

Gurwood, J. (ed.), 1837, *The General Orders of Field Marshal the Duke of Wellington in the campaigns of 1809 to 1818*, London

Haig, D., 1987, *Haig's Autograph Great War Diary* [microfilm], Brighton

Hamilton, C. (ed.), 1959, *Braddock's Defeat: the journal of Captain Robert Cholmley's Batman, the journal of a British officer, Halkett's orderly book*, Norman

Hannam, E.P., 1830, *The Hospital Manual, or Soldier's Guide in the Hour of Sickess*, London

Hardy, E.J., 1902, *Pen Portraits of the British Soldier*, London

Hathaway, E. (ed.), 1993, *A Dorset Soldier: the autobiography of Sergeant William Lawrence*, Tunbridge Wells

Henson, H.H., 1943, *Retrospect of an Unimportant Life*, Oxford (2 vols)

Hibbert, C. (ed.), 1975, *A Soldier of the 71st*, London

Hills, S., 2002, *By Tank Into Normandy: a memoir of the campaign in North-West Europe from D-Day to V.E. Day*, London

Historical Manuscripts Commission, 1895, Fourteenth Report, Appendix, Part IX

Horne, J. (ed.), 1995, *The Best of Good Fellows: The Diaries and Memoirs of the Rev. Charles Edmund Doudney*, London

Iremonger, F.A., 1948, *William Temple Archbishop of Canterbury: His Life and Letters*, Oxford

James, C., 1800, *The Regimental Companion; containing the relative duties of Every Officer in the British Army*, London (2 vols)

Johnstone, S.H.F. (ed.), 1959, 'Letters of Samuel Noyes, Chaplain of the Royal Scots, 1703–4', *J.S.A.H.R.*, 37, 33–40, 67–71, 128–35, 145–52

Kelly, C.H., 1900, *Chaplains in Khaki: Methodist soldiers in camp, on the field, and on the march*, London

——— 1910, *Memories*, London

Kennedy, E.J., 1916, *With the Immortal Seventh Division*, London

Kincaid, J., 1981, *Adventures in the Rifle Brigade and Random Shots from a Rifleman*, Glasgow

Knollys, H. (ed.), 1894, *Life of General Sir Hope Grant with selections from his correspondence*, Edinburgh (2 vols)

Lamb, R., 1809, *An Original and Authentic Journal of Occurrences during the late American War*, Dublin

Levy, I. [Harry], 1995, *Witness to Evil: Bergen-Belsen*, London

Lewis, W.S., 1937–83, *Horace Walpole's Correspondence*, Oxford (48 vols)

Lewis Bryan, J.N., 1946, *The Churches of the Captivity in Malaya*, London

Liddell Hart, B. (ed.), 1999, *The Letters of Private Wheeler 1809–1828*, Moreton-in-Marsh

Lloyd George, David, 1938, *War Memoirs of David Lloyd George*, London (2 vols)

McCulloch, J., 1943, *We Have Our Orders*, London

MacDonald Fraser, G., 2000, *Quartered Safe Out Here*, London

McLaren, S.J. (ed.), 2005, *Somewhere in Flanders: Letters of a Norfolk Padre in the Great War*, Dereham

Maclean Watt, L., 1917, *In France and Flanders with the Fighting Men*, London

M'Clelland, R., 1902, *Heroes and Gentlemen: an army chaplain's experiences in South Africa*, Paisley

McLuskey, F., 1997, *Parachute Padre: Behind German Lines with the SAS France 1944*, Stevenage

Madigan, L. (ed.), 1995, *The Devil is a Jackass*, Stratton-on-the-Fosse
Marks, A., 1905, *The Churches and the South African War. 'Lest we Forget'*, London
Marsh. C.M., 1857, *Memorials of Captain Hedley Vicars, Ninety-seventh Regiment*, New York
Maxwell, W.D., 1942, *Life in the Army: A Padre Talks to the Troops*, Oxford
May, H.A.R., *Memories of the Artists Rifles*, London, 1929
Middleton Brumwell, P., 1943, *The Army Chaplain*, London
Miller, G.F., 1951, 'Prisoner of War', *J.R.A.Ch.D.*, 6, 91–100
Milligan, S., 1978, *Monty: His Part in My Victory*, London
Montague, C.E., 1922, *Disenchantment*, London
Montell, H. (ed), 2002, *A Chaplain's War: the story of Noel Mellish VC, MC*, London
Montgomery, B.L., 1944, *21 Army Group: Some Notes on the Conduct of War and the Infantry Division in Battle*, Belgium
——— 1958, *The Memoirs of Field-Marshal the Viscount Montgomery of Alamein*, London
Moyle Sherer, J., 1825, *Recollections of the Peninsula*, London
Moynihan, M. (ed.), 1983, *God On Our Side*, London
——— 1988, *People at War 1914–1918*, Newton Abbot
Neill, I., 2000, *Far From Tipperary*, Uckfield
Nugent Bankes, G. (ed.), 1886, *The Autobiography of Sergeant William Lawrence*, London
Oliver, K., 1986, *Chaplain at War*, Chichester
Olson, J.S. and Roberts, R. (eds), 1998, *My Lai: a brief history with documents*, Boston
O'Rahilly, A. (ed.), 1932, *Father William Doyle S.J.*, London
Ormsby, J.W., 1809, *An Account of the Operations of the British Army and of the state and sentiments of the people of Portugal and Spain*, London (2 vols)
O'Rorke, B.G., 1915, *In the Hands of the Enemy: being the experiences of a prisoner of war*, 1915
Paget, B. (ed.), 1956, *Henry Clifford V.C. his letters and sketches from the Crimea*, London
Peers, W.R., 1979, *The My Lai Inquiry*, New York
Plater, C., 1919, *Catholic Soldiers*, London
Pearse, H. (ed.), 1897, *The Crimean Diary and Letters of Lieutenant-General Sir Charles Ash Windham*, London
Pennington, W., 2004, *Pick Up Your Parrots and Monkeys: the life of a boy soldier in India*, London
Polehampton, E. and Polehampton, T.S. (eds), 1858, *A Memoir, Letters and Diary of the Rev. Henry S. Polehampton*, London
Pym, T.W. and Gordon, G., 1917, *Papers from Picardy*, London
Raven, C.E., 1935, *Is War Obsolete? A Study of the Conflicting Claims of Religion and Citizenship*, London
——— 1938, *War and the Christian*, London
——— 1940, *The Cross and the Crisis*, London
——— 1942, *Lessons of the Prince of Peace*, London
Raymond, E., 1968, *The Story of My Days: an autobiography 1888–1922*, London
Remarque, E.M., 1982, *All Quiet on the Western Front*, London
Report of the Proceedings of the Naval and Military Bible Society, 1824, London
Richards, F., 1983, *Old Soldiers Never Die*, London
Robinson, A.C. and Hair, P.E.H. (eds), 2001, *Reflections on the Battlefield: from infantryman to chaplain, 1914–1919*, Liverpool

Robinson, S., 1898, *A Life Record*, London
Rule, W.H., 1883, *An Account of the Establishment of Wesleyan Methodism in the British Army*, London
Salisbury Woodward, C. and Blackburne, H., 1939, *Clergy in War-Time*, London
Sassoon, S., 1960, *Memoirs of a Fox-hunting Man*, London
——— 1965, *Memoirs of an Infantry Officer*, London
Selby Wright, R., 1941, *Front Line Religion: The Padre Preaches*, London
——— 1943, *Let's Ask the Padre: Some Broadcast Talks*, Edinburgh
Seventh Report of the Commissioners of Military Enquiry, 1809, London
Sheffield, G. and Bourne, J., 2005, *Douglas Haig: war diaries and letters 1914–1918*, London
Shepherd, H., 1827, *Cursory Remarks on the Inefficiency of the Ecclesiastical Establishment of India*, London
Sheppard, H.R.L., 1938, *We Say 'No': The Plain Man's Guide to Pacifism*, London
Simes, T., 1777, *A Military Course for the Government and Conduct of a Battalion*, London
Singh, B.S. (ed.), 1986, *The Letters of the first Viscount Hardinge of Lahore*, Camden Society, Fourth Series, 32
Skinner, L., n.d., *The Man Who Worked on Sundays: the personal war diary June 2nd 1944 to May 17th 1945 of Revd. Leslie Skinner*, Stoneleigh
Small, E.M. (ed.), 1897, *Told From the Ranks: recollections of service during the Queen's reign by privates and non-commissioned officers of the British army*, London
Steuart, R.H.J., 1931, *March, Kind Comrade*, London
Stevenson, J., 1841, *A Soldier in Time of War*, London
Studdert Kennedy, 1918 (a), *The Hardest Part*, London
——— 1918 (b), *Rough Talks by a Padre*, London
Swarbreck, C., 1902, 'Notes from an Army Chaplain's Diary', *Ushaw Magazine*, 12, 176–92, 345–57
Surtees, W., 1833, *Twenty-five Years in the Rifle Brigade*, Edinburgh
Talbot, N., 1917, *Thoughts on Religion at the Front*, London
Telford, J. (ed.), 1909–14, *Wesley's Veterans*, London (7 vols)
Temple, W., 1940, *Thoughts in War-Time*, London
Thompson, D., 1955, *Captives to Freedom*, London
Thompson, E., 1919, *The Leicestershires Beyond Baghdad*, London
——— 1927, *These Men Thy Friends*, London
Tiplady, T., 1939, *The Cross at the Front*, London
Tucker, W.G., 1886, *Recollections of a Chaplain in the Royal Navy*, London
Tuckey, J.G., 1932, 'The Chaplain-General', *J.R.A.Ch.D.*, 117–19
Vernon Smith, G., 1915, *The Bishop of London's Visit to the Front*, London
Vidler, A.R., 1977, *Scenes from a Clerical Life*, London
Ward, E., 1765, *Mars Stript of his Armour: or the Army Displayed in all its True Colours*, London
Watkins, O.S., 1899, *With Kitchener's Army*, London
——— 1901, *Chaplains at the Front*, London
——— 1915, *With French in France and Flanders*, London
——— 1981, *Soldiers and Preachers Too*, Methodist Royal Navy, Army and Air Force Board
Wearmouth, R.F., 1958, *Pages from a Padre's Diary*, Cullercoats
Welch, J.C. (ed.), 1998, 'The Klip River Manoeuvres of 1903', *J.S.A.H.R.*, 76, 111–25
——— 2005, 'The Blockhouse Line', *J.S.A.H.R.*, 83, 93–109

Wessels, A. (ed.), 2000, *Lord Roberts and the War in South Africa 1899–1902*, Publications of the Army Records Society, 17
Westerdale, T.L.B., 1917, *Messages from Mars*, London
Wild, D., 1992, *Prisoner of Hope*, Lewes
Williamson, B., 1921, *'Happy Days' in France and Flanders*, London
Williamson, J., 1782, *A Treatise of Military Finance; containing the pay, subsistence, deductions and arrears of the Forces on the British and Irish Establishments*, London
——— 1783, *Advice to the Officers of the British Army*, London
Winnifrith, D.P., 1915, *The Church in the Firing Line*, London
Winnington Ingram, A.F., 1940, *Fifty Years' Work in London*, London
Wolseley, G., 1903, *The Story of a Soldier's Life*, London (2 vols)
Wood, E., 1906, *From Midshipman to Field Marshal*, London (2 vols)
Woolley, G.H., 1963, *Sometimes a Soldier*, London
Wright, H.P., 1857, *Recollections of a Crimean Chaplain*, London
——— 1858 [reprinted 1935], 'England's Duty to England's Army', *J.R.A.Ch.D.*, July 1935, 95–109
Wyndham, H., 1899, *The Queen's Service: being the experiences of a private soldier in the British infantry at home and abroad*, London
Young, A.H. (ed.), 1925, *The Revd. John Ogilvie, D.D. An army chaplain at Fort Niagra and Montreal 1759–1760*, Ontario Historical Society Papers and Records, 22

Electronic primary sources

'Convention for the Amelioration of the Condition of the Wounded in Armies in the Field', August 1864. University of Minnesota Human Rights Library, www1.umn.edu/humanrts/instree/1864
Consulted 7 March 2003.
'Convention relative to the Treatment of Prisoners of War', July 1929. University of Minnesota Human Rights Library, www1.umn.edu/humanrts/instree/1929
Consulted 13 February 2003.

Secondary Sources

Aan de Weil, J., 2003, *The Catholic Church in Ireland 1914–18*, Dublin
Allison, N., 2005, 'Shakespeare's man at the Front: the Great War ministry of the Revd William Cramb Charteris', *J.R.A.Ch.D.*, 40–5
Anderson, O., 1958, 'The Constitutional Position of the Secretary at War, 1642–1855', *J.S.A.H.R.*, 36, 165–9
——— 1971, 'The growth of Christian Militarism in mid-Victorian Britain', *English Historical Review*, 86, 46–72
Anon., 1929, 'Rev. Owen Spencer Watkins', *J.R.A.Ch.D.*, 165–8
Arthur, M., 2002, *Forgotten Voices of the Great War*, St. Helens
Bachrach, D.S., 2004, 'The Medieval Military Chaplain and His Duties' in D. Bergen (ed.), *The Sword of the Lord*, Notre Dame
Bailey, C.E., 1984, 'The British Protestant Theologians in the First World War: Germanophobia unleashed', *Harvard Theological Review*, 77, 195–221
Ballhatchet, K., 1993, 'The East India Company and Roman Catholic Missionaries', *Journal of Ecclesiastical History*, 44, 273–88
Barnes, J., 1979, *Ahead of His Age: Bishop Barnes of Birmingham*, London

Barnett, C., 1970, *Britain and Her Army*, London

Barratt, J., 2000, *Cavaliers: the Royalist Army at War 1642–1646*, Stroud

Barron, H., 2006, " 'Tis Very Embarrassing, Say What You Like, To be a Good Vicar in a Valley on Strike": The Church of England and its Relationship with the Durham Miners at the time of the 1926 Lockout', *Twentieth Century British History*, 17, 350–72

Barry, F.R., 1964, *Mervyn Haigh*, London

Baumgart, W., 1999, *The Crimean War 1853–1856*, London

Baxter, M., 2004, 'In Place of an Afterword' in D. Bergen (ed.), *The Sword of the Lord*, Notre Dame

Bebbington, D.W., 1982, *The Nonconformist Conscience*, London

Beckett, I., 1985, 'The Territorial Force' in I.F.W. Beckett and K. Simpson (eds), *A Nation in Arms: a social study of the British army in the First World War*, Manchester

Bell, G.K.A., 1935, *Randall Davidson*, Oxford (2 vols)

Bellenger, D.A., 1999, 'Religious Life for Men' in V.A. McClelland and M. Hodgetts (eds), *From Without the Flaminian Gate*, London

Bergen, D., 2001, 'German Military Chaplains in World War II and the Dilemmas of Legitimacy', *Church History*, 70, 232–47

Bicheno, H., 2003, *Rebels and Redcoats: the American Revolutionary War*, London

Blackburne, H., 1955, *Trooper to Dean*, Bristol

Blunden, M., 1980, 'The Anglican Church during the War' in P. Warwick and S.B. Spies (eds), *The South African War: the Anglo-Boer War 1899–1902*, London

Bond, B., 2002, *The Unquiet Western Front: Britain's Role in Literature and History*, Cambridge

Bourke, J., 1999, *An Intimate History of Killing*, London

Brown, C.G., 1997, *Religion and Society in Scotland since 1707*, Edinburgh

——— 2001, *The Death of Christian Britain: understanding secularisation*, London

——— 2003, 'The secularisation decade: what the 1960s have done to the study of religious history' in H. McLeod and W. Ustorf (eds), *The Decline of Christendom in Western Europe, 1750–2000*, Cambridge

——— 2006, *Religion and Society in Twentieth-Century Britain*, Harlow

Brown, K.D., 1988, *A Social History of the Nonconformist Ministry in England and Wales, 1800–1930*, Oxford

Brumwell, S., 2002, *Redcoats*, Cambridge

Burchard, W.W., 1954, 'Role Conflicts of Military Chaplains', *American Sociological Review*, 19, 528–35

Burleigh, M., 2001, *The Third Reich: a new history*, London

Burns, A., 1999, *The Diocesan Revival in the Church of England, c.1800–1870*, Oxford

Burroughs, P., 1994, 'An Unreformed Army? 1815–1868' in D. Chandler and I. Beckett (eds), *The Oxford Illustrated History of the British Army*, Oxford

Bushaway, B., 1992, 'Name Upon Name: the Great War and Remembrance' in R. Porter (ed.), *Myths of the English*, Cambridge

——— 2001, 'The Obligation of Remembrance or the Remembrance of Obligation: society and the memory of World War' in J. Bourne, P. Liddle and I. Whitehead (eds.), *The Great World War 1914–45 2. The People's Experience*, London

Calder, A., 1996, *The People's War: Britain 1939–1945*, London

Carver, M., 1998, *Britain's Army in the Twentieth Century*, London

Ceadel, M., 1980, *Pacifism in Britain 1914–1945: the Defining of a Faith*, Oxford

——— 1983, 'Christian Pacifism in the Era of Two World Wars' in W.J. Sheils (ed.), *The Church and War*, Studies in Church History, 20, 391–408

Chandler, A., 1994, 'Munich and Morality: the Bishops of the Church of England and Appeasement', *Twentieth Century British History*, 5, 77–99
Chapman, M.D., 2000, 'Anglo-German Theological Relations during the First World War', *Journal for the History of Modern Theology*, 7, 109–26
Childs, J., 1976, *The Army of Charles II*, London
——— 1987, *The British Army of William III, 1689–1702*, Manchester
——— 2003, *Warfare in the Seventeenth Century*, London
Clarke, H.J. St. J., 1938, 'The Rev. William Sykes M.A., Q.H.C.', *J.R.A.Ch.D.*, 8–15
Colley, L., 1992, *Britons: Forging the Nation, 1707–1837*, London
Connolly, G.P., 1982, 'Little Brother Be At Peace: the Priest as Holy Man in the Nineteenth-Century Ghetto' in W.J. Sheils (ed.), *The Church and Healing*, Studies in Church History, 19, 191–206
Coop, J.O., 1919, *The Story of the 55th (West Lancashire) Division*, Liverpool
Corrigan, G., 2004, *Mud, Blood and Poppycock: Britain and the First World War*, London
Costello, C., 1996, *A Most Delightful Station: The British Army on the Curragh of Kildare, Ireland, 1855–1922*, Cork
Costello, J., 1985, *Love Sex and War*, London
Cottesloe, Lord, 1930, 'The Earliest Establishment – 1661 of the British Standing Army', *J.S.A.H.R.*, 9, 147–62
Crang, J.A., 2000, *The British Army and the People's War 1939–45*, Manchester
——— 2005, 'The Abolition of Compulsory Church Parades in the British Army', *Journal of Ecclesiastical History*, 56, 92–106
Cuthbertson, G., 2000, 'Pricking the "nonconformist conscience": religion against the South African War' in D. Lowry (ed.), *The South African War Reappraised*, Manchester
——— 2002, 'Preaching Imperialism: Wesleyan Methodism and the War' in D. Omissi and A.S. Thompson (eds), *The Impact of the South African War*, Basingstoke
Danchev, A., 1994, 'The Army and the Home Front 1939–1945' in D. Chandler and I. Beckett (eds), *The Oxford Illustrated History of the British Army*, Oxford
David, S., 2005, *Zulu: the heroism and tragedy of the Zulu War of 1879*, London
DeGroot, G.J., 1997, 'Whose Finger on the Trigger? Mixed Anti-Aircraft Batteries and the Female Combat Taboo', *War in History*, 4, 434–53
Dewey, P., 1997, *War and Progress: Britain 1914–1945*, Harlow
Dillistone, F.W., 1975, *Charles Raven: Naturalist, Historian, Theologian*, London
Dobbie, I, 1988, *Sovereign Service: the story of SASRA 1838–1988*, Aldershot
Dow, A.C., 1962, *Ministers to the Soldiers of Scotland*, Edinburgh
Dowland, D., 1997, *Nineteenth-Century Anglican Theological Training: The Redbrick Challenge*, Oxford
Duffy, M., 1990, 'The Caribbean campaigns of the British army 1793–1801' in A.J. Guy (ed.), *The Road to Waterloo*, London
Dungan, M., 1997, *They Shall Grow Not Old: Irish Soldiers and the Great War*, Dublin
Edghill, K., 2002, 'Dangerous Doctrines! The battle for Anglican supremacy in the British army, 1810–65', *J.S.A.H.R.*, 80, 36–57
Edmonds, J.E., 1932, *History of the Great War Based on Official Documents. Military Operations France and Belgium, 1916: Sir Douglas Haig's command to the 1st July: battle of the Somme*, London
Ellis, J., 1990, *The Sharp End: The Fighting Man in World War II*, London
Ellis, L.F., 1968, *History of the Second World War. Victory in the West II: The Defeat of Germany*, London
Ellis Roberts, R., 1942, *H.R.L. Sheppard: Life and Letters*, London

Englander, D., 1988, 'Anglicized not Anglican: Jews and Judaism in Victorian Britain' in G. Parsons (ed.), *Religion in Victorian Britain Volume I Traditions*, Manchester
Esdaile, C., 2003, *The Peninsular War*, London,
Evans, E., 1983, 'The Church in Danger? Anticlericalism in Nineteenth-Century England', *European Studies Review*, 13, 201–23
Falls, C., 1922, *The History of the 36th (Ulster) Division*, Belfast
Farrar-Hockley, A., 1990 and 1995, *The British Part in the Korean War*, London (2 vols)
——— 1994, 'The Post-War Army' in D. Chandler and I. Beckett (eds), *The Oxford Illustrated History of the British Army*, Oxford
Farwell, B., 1981, *For Queen and Country*, London
——— 1999, *The Great Boer War*, Ware
Flower, S.J., 1996, 'Captors and captives on the Burma-Thailand Railway' in B. Moore and K. Federowich (eds), *Prisoners of War and their Captors in World War II*, Oxford
Foot, M.R.D., and Langley, J.M., 1979, *MI 9*, London
Fortescue, J.W., 1899–1930, *A History of the British Army*, London (13 vols)
Forty, G., 2002, *British Army Handbook 1939–1945*, Stroud
French, D., 2000, *Raising Churchill's Army: the British army and the war against Germany 1919–1945*, Oxford
Frey, S.R., 1981, *The British Soldier in America*, Austin
Furgol, E., 2002, 'The Civil Wars in Scotland' in J. Kenyon and J. Ohlmeyer (eds), *The Civil Wars*, Oxford
Gardiner, J., 2004, *Wartime Britain 1939–1945*, London
Gates, D., 1994, 'The Transformation of the Army 1783–1815' in D. Chandler and I. Beckett (eds), *The Oxford Illustrated History of the British Army*, Oxford
Gilbert, M., 1989, *Second World War*, London
Gilley, S., 1995, 'Roman Catholicism' in D.G. Paz (ed.), *Nineteenth-Century English Religious Traditions*, Westport
Glover, M., 1968, 'An Excellent Young Man: the Rev. Samuel Briscall', *History Today*, 18, 578–84
——— 1977, *Wellington's Army in the Peninsula*, Newton Abbot
——— 2001, *The Peninsular War 1807–1814*, London
Gray, D., 1963, *Spencer Perceval 1762–1812: the Evangelical Prime Minister*, Manchester
Gray, D., 1986, *Earth and Altar: The Evolution of the Parish Communion in the Church of England to 1945*, Alcuin Club Collections, 68
Greaves, A., 2006, *Crossing the Buffalo: the Zulu War of 1879*, London
Gregory, A., 1994, *The Silence of Memory: Armistice Day 1919–1946*, Oxford
Grey, J., 1988, *The Commonwealth armies and the Korean War*, Manchester
Grieves, K., 1997, 'C.E. Montague and the Making of *Disenchantment*, 1914–1921', *War in History*, 4, 35–59
Griffin, M., 2002, 'The Foundation of the Chaplaincy Corps', *J.S.A.H.R.*, 80, 287–95
Griffiths, P., 1994, *Battle Tactics of the Western Front*, London
Grimley, M., 2004, *Citizenship, Community, and the Church of England: liberal Anglican theories of the state between the wars*, Oxford
Guy, A.J., 1985, *Oeconomy and Discipline: officership and administration in the British army 1714–63*, Manchester
Hagerty, J., 1998, 'Benedictine Military Chaplains During the First World War', *E.B.C. History Symposium*, 134–51
——— 2004, 'A Catholic Chaplain in the Crimean War', *J.S.A.H.R.*, 82, 21–31

Hagerty, J. and Johnstone, T., 2005, 'Catholic Military Chaplains in the Crimean War', *Recusant History*, 27, 415–46
Haig, A., 1984, *The Victorian Clergy*, London
Hamilton, N., 1983, *Monty: master of the battlefield 1942–1944*, London
——— 1986, *Monty: the Field Marshal 1944–1976*, London
——— 2002, *The Full Monty Volume 1: Montgomery of Alamein 1887–1942*, London
Hanham, H.J., 1973, 'Religion and Nationality in the Mid-Victorian Army' in M.R.D. Foot (ed.), *War and Society: historical essays in honour and memory of J.R. Western 1928–1971*, London
Harington, C., 1935, *Plumer of Messines*, London
Harris, F., 1982, 'The Authorship of the Manuscript Blenheim Journal', *Bulletin of the Institute of Historical Research*, 55, 203–6
Harrison, M., 1995, 'The British Army and the Problem of Venereal Disease in France and Egypt during the First World War', *Medical History*, 39, 133–58
——— 2004, *Medicine and Victory: British military medicine in the Second World War*, Oxford
Hastings, A., 1991, *A History of English Christianity 1920–1990*, London
Hastings, M., 2000, *The Korean War*, London
——— 2004, *Armageddon: the battle for Germany 1944–45*, London
Hayter, T., 1994, 'The Army and the First British Empire 1714–1783' in D. Chandler and I. Beckett (eds), *The Oxford Illustrated History of the British Army*, Oxford
Haythornthwaite, P., 1989, *Wellington's Military Machine*, London
——— 2001, *The Armies of Wellington*, London
Hayward, J., 2002, *Myths and Legends of the First World War*, Stroud
Heimann, M., 1995, *Catholic Devotion in Victorian England*, Oxford
Hempton, D., 2005, *Methodism: empire of the spirit*, New Haven
Hendrickson, K., 1998, *Making Saints: religion and the public image of the British army, 1809–1885*, Cranbury
——— 1999, 'Victorian Military Politics of Establishment and Religious Liberty: William H. Rule and the Introduction of Wesleyan Methodism into the British Army, 1856–1882', *War and Society*, 17, 1–23
Herspring, D., 2001, *Soldiers, Commissars and Chaplains*, Lanham
Hichberger, J., 1989 'Old Soldiers' in R. Samuel (ed.), *Patriotism: the making and unmaking of British national identity volume III: National Fictions*, London
Hickman, T., 2005, *The Call-Up*, London
Hill, E.E., 1920, *History of the Chaplains' Department in Western India*, London
Hinchliff, P., 1993, 'Africa' in J. McManners (ed.), *The Oxford History of Christianity*, Oxford
Holmes, G. and Szechi, D., 1993, *The Age of Oligarchy: Pre-industrial Britain*, Harlow
Holmes, R., 2001 (a), *Redcoat: the British soldier in the age of horse and musket*, London
——— 2004, *Tommy: the British soldier on the Western Front 1914–1918*, London
Hoover, A.J., 1999, *God, Britain, and Hitler in World War II: the view of the British clergy, 1939–1945*, Westport
Houlding, J.A., 1981, *Fit for Service: the training of the British Army, 1715–1795*, Oxford
Howard, M., 2002, *Wellington's Doctors: the British army medical services in the Napoleonic Wars*, Staplehurst
Howson, P., 2005, 'Deaths Among Army Chaplains, 1914–20', *J.S.A.H.R.*, 83, 63–77
——— 2006, 'Deaths Among Army Chaplains 1939–1946', *J.R.A.Ch.D.*, 45, 42–7
Hughes, C., 1985, 'The New Armies' in I.F.W. Beckett and K. Simpson (eds), *A Nation in Arms: a social study of the British army in the First World War*, Manchester

Hughes, D., 1991, *The Mutiny Chaplains*, Salisbury
Hughes, P., 1950, 'The Bishops of the Century' in G.A. Beck (ed.), *The English Catholics 1850–1950*, London
Jackson, H.C., 1960, *Pastor on the Nile*, London
James, L., 2001, *Warrior Race: a history of the British at war*, London
Jarvis, A.C.E., January 1930, 'My Predecessors in Office. I: the Reverend John Gamble', *J.R.A.Ch.D.*, 289–302
——— July 1930, 'My Predecessors in Office. II: the Venerable Archdeacon John Owen', *J.R.A.Ch.D.*, 360–80
——— January 1931 (a), 'My Predecessors in Office. III: the Very Reverend Robert Hodgson', *J.R.A.Ch.D*, 444–80
——— January 1931 (b), 'My Predecessors in Office. IV: the Reverend William Whitfield Dakins', *J.R.A.Ch.D.*, 481–520
——— July 1931, 'My Predecessors in Office. V: the Rev. Prebendary George Robert Gleig', *J.R.A.Ch.D.*, 15–77
——— July 1933, 'My Predecessors in Office. V: the Rev. Prebendary George Robert Gleig', *J.R.A.Ch.D.*, 320–58
——— 1935, 'My Predecessors in Office. V: the Rev. Prebendary George Robert Gleig', *J.R.A.Ch.D.*, 9–29
——— 1937, 'My Predecessors in Office. VI: the Right Reverend Piers Calveley Claughton', *J.R.A.Ch.D.*, 420–45
Johnstone, T., 1992, *Orange, Green and Khaki*, Dublin
Johnstone, T. and Hagerty, J., 1996, *The Cross on the Sword*, London
Judd, D. and Surridge, K., 2002, *The Boer War*, London
Kennedy, E. and Howell, A., 1917, *Some Records of the Life of Edmund John Kennedy*, London
Knight, F., 1995, *The Nineteenth-Century Church and English Society*, Cambridge
Knight, I., 2004, *The National Army Museum Book of the Zulu War*, London
Kopperman, P., 1987, 'Religion and religious policy in the British army, c.1700–96', *Journal of Religious History*, 14, 390–405
——— 1996, ' "The Cheapest Pay": alcohol abuse in the eighteenth-century British army', *Journal of Military History*, 60, 445–70
Langford, P., 1991, *Public Life and the Propertied Englishman*, Oxford
Latimer, J., 2005, *Burma: the Forgotten War*, London
Laurence, A., 1990, *Parliamentary Army Chaplains, 1642–1651*, Woodbridge
——— 2004, 'Did the Nature of the Enemy Make a Difference? Chaplains in the Wars of the Three Kingdoms, 1642–49' in D. Bergen (ed.), *The Sword of the Lord*, Notre Dame
Lawson, H.M. 1929, 'The Royal Engineers and the Iron Church', *J.R.A.Ch.D.*, 252–3
Leonard, J., 1986, 'The Catholic Chaplaincy' in D. Fitzpatrick (ed.), *Ireland and the First World War*, Dublin
Lever, T., 1971, *Clayton of Toc H*, London
Liddle, P. and Mackenzie, S.P., 2000, 'The experience of captivity: British and Commonwealth prisoners in Germany' in J. Bourne, P. Liddle and I. Whitehead (eds), *The Great World War 1914–45 1. Lightning Strikes Twice*, London
Lipner, J., 1994, *Hindus: their religious beliefs and practices*, London
Lockhart, J.G., 1949, *Cosmo Gordon Lang*, London
Louden, S.H., 1996, *Chaplains in Conflict*, London
——— 2006, 'Chaplains as whistle-blowers? You're having a laugh!', *J.R.A.Ch.D.*, 12–16
Loveland, A.C., 2004, 'From Morale Builders to Moral Advocates: U.S. Army Chaplains

in the Second Half of the Twentieth Century' in D. Bergen (ed.), *The Sword of the Lord*, Notre Dame

Machin, G.I.T., 1998, *Churches and Social Issues in Twentieth-Century Britain*, Oxford

——— 2000, 'Parliament, the Church of England, and the Prayer Book Crisis, 1927–1928', *Parliamentary History*, 19, 131–47

McCormick, M., 2004, 'The Liturgy of War from Antiquity to the Crusades' in D. Bergen (ed.), *The Sword of the Lord*, Notre Dame

MacDonald, L., 1991, *1914–1918: Voices and Images of the Great War*, London

Maclear, M., 1981, *Vietnam: The Ten Thousand Day War*, London

McLeod, D.H., 1996, *Religion and Society in England, 1850–1914*, Basingstoke

——— 2000, *Secularisation in Western Europe, 1848–1914*, Basingstoke

——— 2001, 'Varieties of Anticlericalism in Later Victorian and Edwardian England' in N. Aston and M. Cragoe (eds), *Anticlericalism in Britain c.1500–1914*, Stroud

——— 2003, 'Introduction' in H. McLeod and W. Ustorf (eds), *The Decline of Christendom in Western Europe, 1750–2000*, Cambridge

MacLeod, J.L., 2001, ' "It's own little share of service to the national cause": the Free Presbyterian Church of Scotland's chaplains in the First World War', *Northern Scotland*, 21, 79–97

——— 2002, ' "Greater Love Hath No Man Than This": Scotland's conflicting religious responses to death in the Great War', *Scottish Historical Review*, 81, 70–96

McLeod, W.H., 1999, 'Who is a Sikh?' in *Sikhs and Sikhism* (omnibus edition), New Delhi

Macquarrie, J., 1990, *The Concept of Peace*, London

MacRaild, D.M., 1999, *Irish Migrants in Modern Britain, 1750–1922*, Basingstoke

Magnus, P.M., 1958, *Kitchener: Portrait of an Imperialist*, London

Marrin, A., 1974, *The Last Crusade: The Church of England in the First World War*, Durham

Mather, F., 1985, 'Georgian Churchmanship Reconsidered: some variations in Anglican public worship', *Journal of Ecclesiastical History*, 36, 255–83

Matthews, C.H.S., 1938, *Dick Sheppard: Man of Peace*, London

Mawson, M.H., 2002 (a), 'Chaplains of the Crimean War, Part 1', *The War Correspondent*, 20

——— 2002 (b), 'Chaplains of the Crimean War, Part 2', *The War Correspondent*, 20

Messenger, C., 2005, *Call-To-Arms: the British Army 1914–18*, London

Mews, S., 1976, 'The Churches' in M. Morris (ed.), *The General Strike*, London

——— 1977, 'Neo-Orthodoxy, Liberalism and War: Karl Barth, P.T. Forsyth and John Oman 1914–18' in D. Baker (ed.), *Renaissance and Renewal in Christian History*, Studies in Church History, 14

——— 1994, 'Religious Life between the Wars, 1920–1940' in S. Gilley and W.J. Sheils (eds), *A History of Religion in Britain: Practice and Belief from Pre-Roman Times to the Present*, Oxford

——— 2004, 'Clergymen, Gentlemen and Men: World War I and the Requirements, Recruitment, and Training of the Anglican Ministry', *Nederlandsch Archief Voor Kerkgeschieden*, 83, 435–47

Middlebrook, M., 1995, *Arnhem 1944*, London

——— 2000, *Your Country Needs You: Expansion of the British Army Infantry Divisions 1914–18*, Barnsley

Miller, D.W., 1973, *Church, State and Nation in Ireland 1898–1921*, Dublin

Moffatt, J. and McCormick, A.H., 2003, *Moon Over Malaya: a tale of Argylls and Marines*, Stroud

Monro, C.C., 1922, 'The Royal Army Temperance Association', *J.R.A.Ch.D.*, 135–8
Moorman, J.R., 1947, *B.K. Cunningham*, London
Morgan, D.D., 1999, *The Span of the Cross: Christian Religion and Society in Wales 1914–2000*, Cardiff
——— 2001, *Cedryn Canrif: Crefydd a Chymdeithas yng Nghymru'r Ugeinfed Ganrif*, Cardiff
Morris, D.R., 1966, *The Washing of the Spears*, London
Muir, R., 1998, *Tactics and the Experience of Battle in the Age of Napoleon*, New Haven
Murphy, J.J.W., 1961–2, 'An Irish Sister of Mercy in the Crimean War', *Irish Sword*, 5, 251–61
Nasson, W., 1999, *The South African War, 1899–1902*, London
Norman, E., 1984, *The English Catholic Church in the Nineteenth Century*, Oxford
O'Day, R., 1988, 'The Clerical Renaissance in Victorian England and Wales' in G. Parsons (ed.), *Religion in Victorian Britain, Volume I: Traditions*, Manchester
Oldmeadow, E., 1944, *Francis Cardinal Bourne*, London (2 vols)
Oman, C., 1912, *Wellington's Army*, London
O'Meara, K., 1886, *Thomas Grant first Bishop of Southwark*, London
Parker, M., 2003, *Monte Cassino*, London
Parsons, G., 1988, 'Reform, Revival and Realignment: The Experience of Victorian Anglicanism' in G. Parsons (ed.), *Religion in Victorian Britain, Volume I: Traditions*, Manchester
Pascoe, C.F., 1901, *Two Hundred Years of the S.P.G.*, London (2 vols)
Peers, D.M., 1997, 'The Indian Army in the Mid-Victorian Press', *Modern Asian Studies*, 31, 109–42
Pickering, W.S.F., 1989, *Anglo-Catholicism: a study in religious ambiguity*, London
Pollock, J.C., 1998, *Kitchener: the road to Omdurman*, London
Porter, P., 2005, 'Beyond Comfort: German and English Military Chaplains and the Memory of the Great War, 1919–1929', *Journal of Religious History*, 29, 258–89
Purcell, W.E., 1983, *Woodbine Willie*, London
Putkowski, J. and Sykes, J., 1989, *Shot at Dawn: Executions in World War One by Authority of the British Army Act*, London
Rabinowitz, L., 1936, 'The First Jewish "Chaplain to the Forces" ', *J.R.A.Ch.D.*, 199–202
Rae, J., 1970, *Conscience and Politics: the British government and the conscientious objector to military service*, London
Raw, D., 1988, *'It's Only Me': a life of the Reverend Theodore Bayley Hardy*, Gatebeck
Reznick, J.S., 2004, *Healing the Nation: soldiers and the culture of caregiving in Britain during the Great War*, Manchester
Rickwood, G.O., 1961, 'Consecration of Standards, Guidons and Colours', *J.S.A.H.R.*, 39, 53
Royle, T., 2000, *Crimea: the great Crimean War, 1854–1856*, London
Samuel, R., 1989, 'An Irish Religion' in R. Samuel (ed.), *Patriotism: the making and unmaking of British national identity, volume II: minorities and outsiders*, London
Savile, G., 1924, 'The Army Fellowship of the C.E.M.S.', *J.R.A.Ch.D.*, 366
Scott, A.B. and Middleton Brumwell, P., 1923, *History of the 12th (Eastern) Division in the Great War*, London
Scott, C., 1977, *Dick Sheppard*, London
Scouller, R.E., 1966, *The Armies of Queen Anne*, Oxford
Shattuck, G.H., 1987, *A Shield and Hiding Place: the religious life of the Civil War armies*, Macon
Shaw, D., 1996, 'The Forgotten Army of Women: Queen Mary's Army Auxiliary Corps'

in H. Cecil and P. Liddle (eds), *Facing Armageddon: The First World War Experienced*, London
Sheffield, G.D., 1996, 'Officer-Man Relations, Discipline and Morale in the British Army of the Great War' in H. Cecil and P. Liddle (eds), *Facing Armageddon: The First World War Experienced*, London
——— 2000, *Leadership in the Trenches: officer-man relations, morale and discipline in the British Army in the era of the First World War*, Basingstoke
——— 2001, *Forgotten Victory*, London
Shepherd, J., 1991, *The Crimean Doctors: a history of the British medical services in the Crimean War*, Liverpool (2 vols)
Simkins, P., 1994, 'The Four Armies 1914–1918' in D. Chandler and I. Beckett (eds), *The Oxford Illustrated History of the British Army*, Oxford
Skelley, A.R., 1977, *The Victorian Army at Home*, London
Skrade, K., 2006, 'God and the British Soldier: Religion and the British Army in the First and Second World Wars', *Reviews in Religion and Theology*, 13, 515–18
Smyth, J., 1968, *In this Sign Conquer*, London
Snape, M., 2004, 'British Army Chaplains and Capital Courts-Martial in the First World War' in K. Cooper and J. Gregory (eds), *Retribution, Repentance and Reconciliation*, Studies in Church History, 40, 357–68
——— 2005 (a) *God and the British Soldier*, London
——— 2005 (b), *The Redcoat and Religion*, London
Snape, M., and Skrade, K., 2007, 'Letters to the Editor', *Reviews in Religion and Theology*, 14, 158–61
Spiers, E., 1992, *The Late Victorian Army, 1868–1902*, Manchester
——— 1994, 'The Late Victorian Army 1868–1914' in D. Chandler and I. Beckett (eds), *The Oxford Illustrated History of the British Army*, Oxford
——— 1996, 'Army organisation and society in the nineteenth century' in T. Bartlett and K. Jeffery (eds), *A Military History of Ireland*, Cambridge
——— 1998, 'Campaigning under Kitchener' in E. Spiers (ed.), *Sudan: the reconquest reappraised*, London
Stearn, R.T., 1992, 'War correspondents and colonial war, c. 1870–1900' in J.M. MacKenzie (ed.), *Popular Imperialism and the Military 1850–1950*, Manchester
Steppler, G.A., 1990, 'The British Army on the Eve of War' in A.J. Guy (ed.), *The Road to Waterloo*, London
Stevenson, J., 1984, *British Society 1914–45*, London
Stewart, C., January 1932, 'Parson Eade in the Crimea [Part I]', *J.R.A.Ch.D.*, 138–46
——— July 1932, 'Parson Eade in the Crimea [Part II]', *J.R.A.Ch.D.*, 189–97
Strachan, H., 1980, 'The Early Victorian Army and the Nineteenth-Century Revolution in Government', *English Historical Review*, 95, 782–809
——— 1984, *The Reform of the British Army 1830–54*, Manchester
——— 2003, *The First World War*, London
Studdert-Kennedy, G., 1982, *Dog-Collar Democracy: the Industrial Christian Fellowship, 1919–1929*, Basingstoke
Summers, J., 2005, *The Colonel of Tamarkan: Philip Toosey and the Bridge on the River Kwai*, London
Surridge, K., 1997, ' "All you soldiers are what we call pro-Boer": the military critique of the South African War, 1899–1902', *History*, 82, 582–600
Taylor, B., 1993, 'The Cowley Fathers and the First World War' in W.J. Sheils (ed.), *The Church and War*, Studies in Church History, 1993, 383–90
Taylor, G., 1978, *The Sea Chaplains: a history of the chaplains of the Royal Navy*, Oxford

Thomas, N., 2002, *The German Army in World War II*, Oxford
Thompson, J.H., 1995, 'R.F. Wearmouth, Army Chaplain', *Proceedings of the Wesley Historical Society*, 50, 19–20
Thorold, E.H., 1938, 'The Right Rev. Bishop John Taylor Smith', *J.R.A.Ch.D.*, 94–7
Todman, D., 2005, *The Great War: Myth and Memory*, London
Towler, R. and Coxon, A.P.M., 1979, *The Fate of the Anglican Clergy*, London
Trustram, M., 1984, *Women of the Regiment: marriage and the Victorian army*, Cambridge
Uffindell, A., 2005, *The National Army Museum Book of Wellington's Armies*, London
van Roekel, C., n.d., *The Torn Horizon: the Airborne chaplains at Arnhem*, Oosterbeek
Vidler, A., 1987, *The Church in an Age of Revolution*, London
Ward, S.H., 1953, 'Army Chaplains', *J.S.A.H.R.*, 31, 35
Western, J.R., 1965, *The English Militia in the Eighteenth Century*, London
Westlake, R. and Chappell, M., 1991, *British Territorial Units 1914–18*, London
Wheatley, A (ed.), 1983, *Father Dolly The Guardsman Monk*, London
Whitlow, M., 1938, *Everybody's Bishop*, London
Wilkinson, A., 1978, *The Church of England and the First World War*, London
——— 1981, 'The Paradox of the Military Chaplain', *Theology*, 84, 249–57
——— 1986, *Dissent or Conform? War, Peace and the English Churches 1900–1945*, London
——— 1998, *Christian Socialism: Scott Holland to Tony Blair*, London, 1998
Williams, M.J., 1967, 'The Egyptian Campaign of 1882' in B. Bond (ed.), *Victorian Military Campaigns*, London
Williams, S.C., 1999, *Religious Belief and Popular Culture in Southwark, c.1880–1939*, Oxford
Wilson, T., 1988, *The Myriad Faces of War*, Cambridge
Winter, J.M., 2006, *The Experience of World War I*, London
Wolfe, K.M., 1984, *The Churches and the British Broadcasting Corporation 1922–1956: the Politics of Broadcast Religion*, London
Wolffe, J., 1994, *God and Greater Britain: religion and national life in Britain and Ireland 1843–1945*, London
Wood, I.S., 1997, ' " 'Twas England Bade Our Wild Geese Go": soldiers of Ireland in the Second World War' in P. Addison and A. Calder (eds), *Time to Kill: The Soldier's Experience of War in the West 1939–1945*, London
Woodworth, S.E., 2001, *While God is Marching On*, Lawrence
Yates, N., 1999, *Anglican Ritualism in Victorian Britain 1830–1910*, Oxford
Zahn, G.C., 1969, *Chaplains in the R.A.F.*, Manchester

Reference Works

Bourne, J.M. (ed.), 2001, *Who's Who in World War One*, London
British Film Institute Film and T.V. Database, http://ftvdb.bfi.org.uk
Chandler, D.G. and Collins, J.L. (eds), 1994, *The D-Day Encyclopaedia*, Oxford
Dear, I.C.B. and Foot, M.R.D. (eds), 1995, *The Oxford Companion to the Second World War*, Oxford
Eliade, M. (ed.), 1987, *The Encyclopaedia of Religion*, New York (16 vols)
Esposito, J.L. (ed.), 1995, *The Oxford Encyclopaedia of the Modern Islamic World*, Oxford (4 vols)

Fitzgerald-Lombard, C., 1993, *English and Welsh Priests 1801–1914*, Stratton-on-the-Fosse

Foster, J., 1890, *Index Ecclesiasticus*, Oxford

——— 1891, *Alumni Oxonienses 1715–1886*, Oxford (4 vols)

Holmes, R. (ed.), 2001 (b), *The Oxford Companion to Military History*, Oxford

James, E.A., 1998, *British Regiments 1914–18*, Heathfield

Kamaryc, R.M., 1993, *The Military Cross Awarded to Officers and Warrant Officers from 1937 to 1993*, Harlow

Lewis, D.M. (ed.), 1995, *The Blackwell Dictionary of Evangelical Biography 1730–1860*, Oxford (2 vols)

Oxford Dictionary of National Biography

Roper, M., 1998, *The Records of the War Office and related departments 1660–1964*, London

Scott, H., 1915–1950, *Fasti Ecclesiae Scoticanae*, Edinburgh (8 vols)

Statistics of the Military Effort of the British Empire during the Great War, 1914–1920, 1992, London

Venn, J.A., 1954, *Alumni Cantabrigienses Part II from 1752 to 1900*, Cambridge (6 vols)

Unpublished Dissertations

Brown, A.M, 1996, 'Army Chaplains in the First World War', St. Andrews University Ph.D.

Coulter, D.G., 1997, 'The Church of Scotland Army Chaplains in the Second World War', Edinburgh University Ph.D.

Farish, R., 2002, 'An Investigation into the Practical Application of Industrial Mission and Industrial Chaplaincy', Birmingham University M. Phil.

Fontana, V.J.L., 2002, 'Some Aspects of Roman Catholic Service in the Land Forces of the British Crown', Portsmouth University Ph.D.

Jackson, S.I., 2000, 'Methodism in Gibraltar and its Mission in Spain, 1759–1842', Durham University Ph.D.

Jones, D., 1983, 'The Rev. G.R. Gleig and Early Victorian Army Education', Queen's, Belfast M.A.

Madigan, E.T.M., 2006, 'Anglican Army Chaplains on the Western Front, 1914–1918', Trinity College Dublin Ph.D.

Mews, S.P., 1973, 'Religion and English Society in the First World War', Cambridge University Ph.D.

Robinson, A., 1999, 'The Role of British Army Chaplains during World War Two', Liverpool University Ph.D.

Taouk, Y., 2003, 'The Roman Catholic Church in Britain during the First World War: a study in political leadership', University of Western Sydney Ph.D.

Thompson, J.H., 1990, 'The Free Church Army Chaplain 1830–1930', Sheffield University Ph.D.

Index

STUDIES IN MODERN BRITISH RELIGIOUS HISTORY

Previously published volumes in this series

XI
Rural Society and the Anglican Clergy, 1815–1914
Encountering and Managing the Poor
Robert Lee

XII
The Church of England and the Holocaust
Christianity, Memory and Nazism
Tom Lawson

XIII
Religious Politics in Post-Reformation England
edited by Kenneth Fincham and Peter Lake

XIV
The Church of England and the Bangorian Controversy, 1716–1721
Andrew Starkie

XV
Martyrs and Martyrdom in England, c.1400–1700
edited by Thomas S. Freeman and Thomas F. Mayer

XVI
John Henry Williams (1747–1829): 'Political Clergyman':
War, the French Revolution, and the Church of England
Colin Haydon

XVII
Religion, Reform and Modernity in the Eighteenth Century:
Thomas Secker and the Church of England
Robert G. Ingram